BUDDHIST DYNAMICS

in Premodern and Early Modern Southeast Asia

The **Nalanda-Sriwijaya Centre (NSC)** at the Institute of Southeast Asian Studies, Singapore, pursues research on historical interactions among Asian societies and civilizations. It serves as a forum for comprehensive study of the ways in which Asian polities and societies have interacted over time through religious, cultural, and economic exchanges and diasporic networks. The Research Series provides scholars with an avenue to present the outcome of their research and allows an opportunity to develop new or innovative approaches in the sphere of intra-Asian interactions.

The **Institute of Southeast Asian Studies (ISEAS)** was established as an autonomous organization in 1968. It is a regional centre dedicated to the study of socio-political, security and economic trends and developments in Southeast Asia and its wider geostrategic and economic environment. The Institute's research programmes are the Regional Economic Studies (RES, including ASEAN and APEC), Regional Strategic and Political Studies (RSPS), and Regional Social and Cultural Studies (RSCS).

ISEAS Publishing, an established academic press, has issued more than 2,000 books and journals. It is the largest scholarly publisher of research about Southeast Asia from within the region. ISEAS Publishing works with many other academic and trade publishers and distributors to disseminate important research and analyses from and about Southeast Asia to the rest of the world.

BUDDHIST DYNAMICS

in Premodern and Early Modern Southeast Asia

EDITED BY

D. Christian Lammerts

INSTITUTE OF SOUTHEAST ASIAN STUDIES
Singapore

Published in Singapore in 2015 by
ISEAS Publishing
Institute of Southeast Asian Studies
30 Heng Mui Keng Terrace
Pasir Panjang
Singapore 119614
E-mail: publish@iseas.edu.sg
Website: <http://bookshop.iseas.edu.sg>

ISEAS Library Cataloguing-in-Publication Data

Buddhist dynamics in premodern and early modern Southeast Asia / edited by D. Christian Lammerts.
Papers originally presented to a Conference on Buddhist Dynamics in Premodern Southeast Asia, organized by the Institute of Southeast Asian Studies on 10–11 March 2011.
1. Buddhism—Southeast Asia—History.
2. Southeast Asia—Civilization—Buddhist influences.
I. Lammerts, Dietrich Christian.
II. Conference on Buddhist Dyanmics in Premodern Southeast Asia (2011 : Singapore).
BQ406 B92 2015

ISBN 978-981-4519-06-9 (soft cover)
ISBN 978-981-4519-07-6 (e-book, PDF)

Cover image: "Janaka receives the instruction of Nārada." Glazed terracotta Jātaka plaque with Mon caption. From the Ānanda Temple in Pagan, Myanmar. Eleventh Century C.E. Image.
Courtesy of Lilian Handlin.

Typeset by Superskill Graphics Pte Ltd
Printed in Singapore by Mainland Press Pte Ltd

CONTENTS

Acknowledgements vii

The Contributors ix

1. Introduction 1
D. Christian Lammerts

2. An Untraced Buddhist Verse Inscription from (Pen)insular Southeast Asia 18
Peter Skilling

3. How Many Monks? Quantitative and Demographic Archaeological Approaches to Buddhism in Northeast Thailand and Central Laos, Sixth to Eleventh Centuries CE 80
Stephen A. Murphy

4. Miniature Stūpas and a Buddhist Sealing from Candi Gentong, Trowulan, Mojokerto, East Java 120
Titi Surti Nastiti

5. A Bronze Hoard from Muara Kaman, Kutei 138
E. Edwards McKinnon

6. Re-exploring the Buddhist "Foundation Deposits" at Chedi Chula Prathon, Nakhon Pathom 172
Nicolas Revire

7. Aspects of Buddhism in Tenth-Century Cambodia 218
Hiram Woodward

8. Revisiting the Cult of "Śiva-Buddha" in Java and Bali 261
Andrea Acri

9. Building a Buddhist Monarchy in Đại Việt:
Temples and Texts under Lý Nhân-tông (r.1072–1127) 283
John K. Whitmore

10. Sīhaḷa Saṅgha and Laṅkā in Later Premodern Southeast Asia 307
Anne M. Blackburn

11. Dynamics of Monastic Mobility and Networking in
Seventeenth- and Eighteenth-century Upper Burma 333
Alexey Kirichenko

12. Buddhist Diplomacy: Confrontation and Political Rhetoric
in the Exchange of Letters between King Alaungmintaya
and King Banya Dala of Pegu (1755–56) 373
Jacques P. Leider

13. Court Buddhism in Thai-Khmer Relations during the Reign
of King Rama IV (King Mongkut) 417
Santi Pakdeekham

Index 429

ACKNOWLEDGEMENTS

I am most grateful to the Nalanda-Sriwijaya Centre and especially to Tansen Sen and Geoff Wade for their enthusiastic support of this volume and the 2011 conference that formed its basis. Too few academic institutions recognize the importance of the comparative study of religion and history in precontemporary Southeast Asia and place it at the center of their mission. For this the Nalanda-Sriwijaya Centre has my deepest appreciation. Lucy Liu and Betty Tan deserve mention for their skillful handling of administrative complexities. Although unfortunately their work is not represented in the pages that follow, I thank Arthid Sheravanichkul, Steve Collins, Goh Geok Yian, Arlo Griffiths, Pamela Gutman, U Htun Yee, Nasha bin Rodziadi Khaw, John Miksic, and Rod Orlina for their participation in the conference.

The production of this volume has been aided by several individuals. I am indebted to Arlo Griffiths, Alexey Kirichenko, Tom Borchert, Joyce Iris Zaide, Andrea Acri, Derek Heng, and Rommel Curaming for assistance with various aspects of the editorial process. At ISEAS Publishing I offer sincere thanks to Triena Ong, Ng Kok Kiong, and Rahilah Yusuf.

THE CONTRIBUTORS

Andrea Acri is Visiting Research Fellow, Nalanda Sriwijaya Centre, Institute of Southeast Asian Studies, Singapore. He was formerly post doctoral Fellow, Asia Research Institute, National University of Singapore.

Anne M. Blackburn is Professor of South Asia Studies and Buddhist Studies, Department of Asian Studies, Cornell University.

Alexey Kirichenko is Assistant Professor, Institute of Asian and African Studies, Moscow State University.

D. Christian Lammerts is Assistant Professor of Buddhist and Southeast Asian Studies, Department of Religion, Rutgers University.

Jacques Leider is with the French School of Asian Studies (École française d'Extrême-Orient), Chiang Mai.

E. Edwards McKinnon is Honorary Research Associate, Archaeology Unit in the Nalanda-Srivijaya Centre, Institute of Southeast Asian Studies, Singapore.

Stephen A. Murphy is Curator (Southeast Asia), Asian Civilisations Museum, Singapore.

Titi Surti Nastiti is Researcher at the National Research and Development Centre of Archaeology, Jakarta.

Santi Pakdeekham is Lecturer in Thai and Khmer, Department of Thai and Oriental Languages, Faculty of Humanities, Srinakharinwirot University, Bangkok.

Nicolas Revire is Visiting Lecturer, Faculty of Liberal Arts, Thammasat University, Bangkok.

Peter Skilling is with the French School of Asian Studies (École française d'Extrême-Orient), Bangkok.

John K. Whitmore is Research Associate, Center for Southeast Asian Studies, University of Michigan, Ann Arbor, Michigan.

Hiram Woodward is Curator Emeritus, Asian Art, Walters Art Museum, Baltimore.

1

INTRODUCTION

D. Christian Lammerts

The papers collected in this volume were presented at a conference held in March 2011 at the Nalanda-Sriwijaya Centre, Institute of Southeast Asian Studies. The conference aimed to bring together scholars from diverse disciplinary backgrounds and different geographical, linguistic, and temporal specializations and encourage historical criticism on Buddhism in premodern and early modern Southeast Asia. As such it was one of the first and only conferences devoted to this broad, necessarily comparative, and deceptively straightforward topic. In a simplistic sense Buddhism as a general intellectual, institutional, devotional, literary, and social phenomenon was a dominant force throughout much of Southeast Asia during the precontemporary period, attested through its early traces at Dvāravatī, Śrīkṣetra, Śrīvijaya, Haripuñjaya, and Campā, across the medieval terrains of Đại Việt, Pagan, Angkor, Majapahit, and Sukhothai, and in the later polities of Mrauk U, Ava, Lan Xang, Sipsongpanna, and elsewhere. Regional Buddhists, regardless of how we define the ascription, were responsible for an array of innovations and cultural products that cut across diverse fields of learning and ritual, ranging from medicine, law, alchemy, political economy, and grammar to scriptural hermeneutics, apotropaic technologies, and art and architecture. However, as the papers in this volume suggest, the Buddhist cultures of historical Southeast Asia are best understood as multivocal, marked by a dynamism and difference that varies across geography and time. It is therefore more appropriate to speak of Southeast Asian Buddhism in the plural — of Buddhisms rather than a Buddhism — and it is to this plurality that one sense of the "dynamics" of the volume's title seeks to draw our attention.

Today the study of historical Buddhisms in premodern and early modern Southeast Asia stands at an encouraging juncture. In many ways the field — or rather the constellation of multi- and inter-disciplinary scholarly projects seeking to understand different facets of regional Buddhist pasts — is in the process of being re-envisioned. Comparison and macrohistory are becoming increasingly desirable frameworks of analysis although critical of their past prejudices. Scholarship is marked by a turn towards careful examination of local and vernacular expressions of Buddhist culture as well as a return to long-standing questions concerning the transregional diffusion and networked interrelationships among varied texts, aesthetic forms, and religious ideas and practices. Following several decades that produced many important works focused on recuperating the distinctive micronarratives of local Buddhisms, a trend that was a more or less self-conscious corrective to what were perceived as colonialist or orientalist onslaughts against autonomy, regionalism or globalism has once again become a key agendum for research. This possibility has resulted from increased distance from the colonial and nationalist contexts that gave rise to early "Indianization" and subsequent "localization" or indigenist theory, as well as a growing recognition of the historical importance of transculturation and networks of exchange within Southeast Asia and the Buddhist world more generally that had been neglected in studies of local meaning-making.[1] Much current comparative work continues to focus on historical relations between Southeast Asia and Laṅkā or the Indian subcontinent across the Bay of Bengal,[2] although intra-Southeast Asian networks and forms of exchange are beginning to receive due attention,[3] as are broad Eurasian parallels.[4]

This increased attention to processes of regional exchange and to questions of transculturation has not diminished the central importance of a parallel commitment to microhistorical studies of Buddhist texts, practices, and lives focused determinately on the locale.[5] Such projects untangle local intricacies and question individual motives, laying the foundation upon which broader historical-comparative projects on the meaning and effects of macroprocesses can be built. The goal of such work is not the construction and defence of some chimerical national, sub-national, or regional identity ("Thai Buddhism", "Arakanese Buddhism", "Southeast Asian Buddhism"), but rather an attempt to grasp how the ideas, products, and practices of Buddhists in historical Southeast Asia are inexorably grounded in the "particular times and terrains where they dwelled and in the material and cultural exchanges available in those times and terrains".[6] The "dynamics" of our title is meant to suggest this additional sense of the constant interplay between these local and global forces in history as well as the variable angles of analytical view available to scholarship.

We may celebrate that our archive of primary textual, art historical, and archaeological sources, and resources for their study, continue to expand through intensified institutional support and individual initiatives. New research on regional manuscript libraries has recently brought to light hitherto unknown vernacular, Pali, and Sanskrit texts, alongside ever proliferating variant recensions of known texts.[7] New inscriptions and art historical and archaeological finds continue to be uncovered, documented, and published.[8] In certain quarters there are redoubled efforts to make these materials available for study and increasing interest in them among young scholars. Doubtless a great deal of work remains to be done in this area, however, and it is hoped that within the coming years scholars, local and global educational institutions, Buddhist organizations, and government and non-governmental bodies will contribute to much-needed efforts of preserving primary manuscript, epigraphic, archaeological, and art historical materials and making them widely available through reasonably priced publications or open access digital repositories.

Methodologies have been made more self-reflexive and enlarged to embrace interdisciplinary perspectives. Some of the most pronounced recent shifts have been those that ask us to reassess previously axiomatic paradigms. Scholars have begun to interrogate the implications of basic vocabularies inherited from earlier generations. Foremost among these efforts has been the intensive criticism of the rubric "Theravāda", a classification which still provides much to think about, though which can no longer be defended as meaningfully descriptive of historically emic understandings or identities.[9] Similarly, the range of productive oppositions that enframed earlier developmental, ethnographic, and sociological accounts of Southeast Asian Buddhism — Indic/vernacular, orthodox/heterodox, authentic/syncretic, esoteric/exoteric, canonical/non-canonical, etc. — have been subjected to ongoing scrutiny.[10] Although it is still possible to argue that certain of these oppositions or elements within them may appear or have analytic value in specific instances of historical discourse (whose particular meanings in such contexts require careful explication), they are misleading and limiting when taken as strict ontological or epistemological categories structuring regional Buddhisms in general.

Boundaries between "Buddhism" and other areas of culture have become increasingly permeable. Precontemporary regional Buddhisms are no longer viewed as rarefied theologies of relevance only to religionists, philologists, and archaeologists, but as integrated constellations of effective discourse and practice that require attention in any meaningful attempt to understand cultural or social history before the present. It is now not unreasonable to expect that new scholars — regardless of the period, languages, and Buddhisms of specialization — are aware of, and engaged with, work emanating from anthropology, religious studies, literary studies, history, philology, epigraphy, archaeology, and art history. Also, they must work in one or several vernacular languages as well as one or several cosmopolitan languages such as Pali, Sanskrit, or Chinese.[11] This new emphasis placed on both local and transregional languages (and with them their historical, territorial, and literary frames of reference) marks a considerable departure from earlier approaches to scholarly training, in which it was more common for specialization to focus intensively on one or the other side of this shifting divide.

There are still vast unexplored frontiers. There has been disproportionately more interest in certain topics rather than others; for example, in institutional monastic histories and state-saṅgha relations. Certain scholars continue to use the prejudicial language of "Buddhist" and "secular" domains in describing the region's past. Among other things, such presuppositions have held back the study of Buddhist social and intellectual history beyond the monastery and royal court as well as of the actual variety of Buddhist literature in the region, which has yet to receive full consideration. Although approaches to Buddhist literature have become more pluralistic, and no longer privilege narrowly conceived "canonical" Indic texts over vernacular, bilingual, or local Pali or Chinese compositions, many genres have not received due attention.[12] Among these especially are the Buddhist disciplinary or scientific genres — e.g., medicine, alchemy, poetics, law, astrology, husbandry — for which there are thousands upon thousands of surviving manuscripts, though virtually no scholarship.[13] Vernacular poetry remains *terra incognita* in Western scholarship, despite the fact that it was one of the most popular forms of Buddhist textual production between the fifteenth and nineteenth centuries.[14] I do not mean to overdraw this picture of neglect, for the fact remains that there has been little work that focuses on even more conventionally "mainstream" literatures such as *vinaya* or *abhidhamma* in premodern and early modern Southeast Asian historical contexts.[15] Finally, although there has been a great deal of careful philological or interpretive work on manuscripts, epigraphy, and iconography, there have been far fewer studies that have utilized such approaches to inform broader theoretical or comparative arguments in Buddhist social or intellectual history.[16]

The papers included in this volume represent some of these current opportunities and challenges in the study of Southeast Asian Buddhisms. Peter Skilling's opening contribution presents a fascinating study of the life of a little known Buddhist verse in Sanskrit that represents what appears to be a distinctively (pen)insular Southeast Asian textual tradition, equal in authority to that of the much better known and more widely disseminated *ye dharmā* stanza. Transmitted in only this region, the verse is attested by fourteen inscriptions dated between the sixth and seventh centuries CE ranging from the west coast of the central Malay Peninsula to as far east as Northeastern Borneo (modern Brunei). Skilling shows that certain contexts of the verse suggest connections farther afield to Karṇasuvarṇa (Bengal), indicating that it may have travelled along ancient maritime trade routes. After examining in detail each instance of the verse, he discusses its plausible school-affiliation, function, and scriptural status, while raising additional questions concerning patronage and production. Like a number of the papers included in the volume, his study constitutes an important contribution to ongoing scholarly efforts to describe with greater precision the Buddhist geography of early Southeast Asia while remaining critically sensitive to the genuine historical diversity of textual and ritual practices in the region.

The next essay by Stephen Murphy also takes a particular Southeast Asian terrain as its focus, advancing a provocative hypothesis concerning monastic demographics in the Khorat Plateau between the sixth through eleventh centuries CE. Combining an impressive archaeological survey of surviving Dvāravatī *sīmā* stones (monastic ritual boundary markers) and modern monastic population statistics with the methodology of demographic archaeology, Murphy proposes that we can provisionally calculate estimates for monastic numbers in the region during this period. In the course of this quantitative argument he presents a close reading of the distribution and narrative aesthetics of *sīmā* stones, allowing him to draw important insights concerning the riverine transmission of regional monasticism and its relationship to settled communities and lay patronage.

Titi Surti Nastiti's paper examines the palaeography of Sanskrit formulae inscribed on miniature stūpas and a Buddhist sealing found at the important archaeological site of Candi Gentong in Trowulan, Mojokerto, East Java. These epigraphical materials are distinctive in that they are earlier than the Candi Gentong temples themselves (which date to c.1470 CE), and also because they employ the Kawi script. With the exception of some Kawi examples from Borobudur, a form of Early Nāgarī was commonly used on miniature stūpas and sealings in the region. Through a close comparison with the Kawi script used in the Borobudur miniature stūpas and also in regional Kawi epigraphy (most importantly the tenth century Ālasantan copper-plate inscription, also from Trowulan), Nastiti concludes that these materials seem to have a local origin (i.e. were not "imports" from Borobudur or elsewhere) and in fact constitute evidence for the earliest phase of Buddhism in East Java.

E. Edwards McKinnon presents an important unpublished collection of bronze material, including Buddha figures and ritual implements, reportedly found near Muara Kaman, Kutei in East Kalimantan, a site which is noteworthy as the location of the famed Sanskrit epigraphs of Mūlavarman, dated by certain scholars as the earliest inscriptions from the archipelago.[17] Although their find-site and current whereabouts are uncertain, McKinnon examined these bronzes in 1994, and his photographs of twenty-three items may constitute the only surviving record of their existence. Following a useful introduction that discusses the importance of Kutei in the context of other early maritime Buddhist sites bordering the Makassar Strait, McKinnon offers an inventory of and commentary on each item of the collection.

The contribution by Nicolas Revire comprises a detailed consideration of "ritual deposits" dating to the eighth–ninth centuries CE excavated at the site of Chedi Chula Prathon in Nakhon Pathom, Thailand. Focusing in particular on the intriguing presence of a *khakkhara* ("staff"), the only material example of which that has been found in mainland Southeast Asia, Revire argues that these deposits functioned in rituals associated with the consecration or reconsecration of the site. Through a broad survey of textual and iconographic sources from across the Buddhist world, as well as especially suggestive proximate Burmese and Javanese parallels, he shows how the presence of the *khakkhara* connects Chedi Chula Prathon to a regional Buddhist ritual geography during the late first millennium CE.

Hiram Woodward's rich and probing paper discusses a number of important aspects of Buddhism in tenth-century Cambodia, a period when "patterns of life in Angkor were becoming established" 200 years before the expansion of Buddhism under Jayavarman VII, on which there has been comparatively little detailed scholarship despite the available epigraphic and iconographic testimony. Woodward's methodology, too rarely employed in the study of Southeast Asian Buddhism, brings epigraphy, literature, and art into conversation to reveal much about the otherwise inaccessible scriptural and ritual culture of Buddhism in the Angkorean realm during this period. Though a close study of a the maṇḍala-like iconographic structure of an important four-sided stele now in the National Museum, Bangkok, he discusses the implications of a unique integration of textual themes from the *Kāraṇḍavyūha-sūtra* and *Mahāvairocana-sūtra*, hinting, moreover, at the connections these two texts may suggest with Campā, Java, or lands still farther afield. Other images are read similarly in the broad context of textual and doctrinal history, such as the four *caitya* established around 989 CE at Kbal Sre Yeai Yin, which contain telling variations in iconographic structure, pointing towards knowledge of the *Guhyasamāja Tantra*.

Although Woodward's paper touches on the important issue of the relationship between Śaivism and Buddhism in early Angkor, Andrea Acri delivers a thorough-going critique of the long-standing problem of "Śiva-Buddha" in Java and Bali between the fifth through fifteenth centuries CE. Acri sets his remarks in the context of an adroit discussion of previous scholarly attempts by Kern, Gonda, Hunter, Seyfort Ruegg, Sanderson, and others to theorize the complex relationships between Śaivism and Buddhism in both Indonesia and on the Indian subcontinent. This broad vantage constitutes an important intervention — one which is particularly germane to the comparative study of Indonesian Śaiva and Buddhist literature — as most scholars of Southeast Asia do not frequently enough place their analyses in the context of both the proximate locale and parallel situations elsewhere in the wider Southern Asian world. Building on this discussion, as well as his own research in an impressive archive of Javanese and Sanskrit *tutur* texts and *kakawin*s, Acri argues that earlier ahistorical accounts of the unity, coalition, or syncretism of the two systems must be recalibrated, that what is needed is an approach that is sensitive to the context-specific ways in which different genres express historically variable relationships. While what Acri terms the Balinese "*status quo*" may indeed have entailed the more or less explicit separation of the two systems, other sources suggest motivations, perhaps especially among Buddhist authors during the Singhasari-Majapahit period, to assert commonality or appropriate certain features of Śaiva discourse in the service of certain arguments.

John Whitmore's far-ranging and valuable essay describes the efforts of the monarch Lý Nhân-tông and his three royal predecessors who established Đại Việt to officially propagate Buddhism in the eleventh and early twelfth centuries CE. His contribution is especially welcome since there is comparatively little in the way of scholarship on the history of precontemporary Vietnamese Buddhism. Usefully supplementing Woodward's and Acri's focus on the interaction of Buddhism with Brāhmaṇical forms, Whitmore's paper begins with an account of the remarkable complexity and diversity of Vietnamese Buddhism in relation to the power of local cults up to the eleventh century. Drawing on a careful reading of Chinese histories, inscriptions, chronicle testimonies, biographies, and spirit tales, he shows how king Lý Nhân-tông moved closer to the more explicit adoption of Thiền (Chan) Buddhism as espoused by his close monastic advisors. Although monks like Thông Biện acknowledged the existence in the realm of earlier and alternative forms of Buddhism transmitted from India (Tianzhu), such as that of the so-called Vinītaruci lineage, and inscriptions from Nhân-tông's reign consistently link Đại Việt with the subcontinent as the potent source of Buddhism, the new Thiền orientation arriving from Song China brought with it the circulation of Chinese Chan transmission texts. Importantly, the royal promotion of this transmission history "brought a conceptual unity to Vietnamese Buddhism focused on the court and establishing the Thiền school over the multiplicity of monks and temples" throughout the realm. Nhân-tông's extensive patronage of Buddhism was, Whitmore argues, in part an attempt to encompass the local powers and diverse practices of the realm. He concludes with a useful reflection on the comparative significance of these events in the context of policies towards Buddhism among the later kings of the Trần dynasty and the interaction of Buddhism and kingship elsewhere at Śrīvijaya, Campā, Bagan, and Angkor.

Narratives of transregional contact between local and Lankan monastics in Pali and vernacular Southeast Asian monastic histories (*vaṃsa*) have been quarried by generations of scholars to erect putatively empirical accounts of the dissemination of "orthodox" Sīhaḷa, "Theravāda", or Mahāvihārin monastic lineages in the region. Anne M. Blackburn argues in her contribution that such narratives may not, however, be well suited to such a purpose; at least not until they are properly assessed in light of additional textual and especially epigraphic sources. Through an innovative reading of the c. sixteenth century *Jinakālamālī* and versions of the *Tamnān (Mūlasāsanā) Wat Pa Däng*, Blackburn suggests that references to "Laṅkā" (or sites and teachers thus affiliated) are less documentary than performative or workly. Her analysis shows that narratives of exchange with the Lankan saṅgha (including reordination), and representations of Laṅkā as a locus of power and authority, are not concerned with the establishment or defense of a "Theravāda" or Mahāvihāravāsin monastic pedigree or identity, or with religious exchange as the work of kings, points frequently stressed in earlier scholarship. Rather, invocations of Sīhaḷa must be read as symptomatic of more local concerns — e.g., with grammar, disciplinary acumen, and ritual efficacy — that have less to do with the Island as an actually existing geographical realm than with Laṅkā as a rhetorical image and ideal that is mobilized at crucial moments in *vaṃsa* argument.

The papers by Alexey Kirichenko, Jacques P. Leider and Santi Pakdeekham also focus on intra-Southeast Asian interactions, although in the context of the later early modern mainland. Drawing on an impressive array of unpublished manuscript sources from a number of genres — monastic biographies, chronicles, royal orders — Kirichenko's paper provides a detailed account of the rise and significance of regional Buddhist monastic centres in eighteenth–nineteenth Century Burma. Importantly, he shows how and why during this period "non-central" monastic networks began to emerge and compete with the earlier court-based networks of the seventeenth–eighteenth centuries. Following a fascinating depiction of the "semi-closed" structure of the court saṅgha in the seventeenth century, Kirichenko argues that subsequently Buddhist education and textual production begins to take place for the first time beyond the walls of royal cities such as Prome, Ava, or Chiang Mai. From the eighteenth century, then, villages and secondary cities like Pakhan, Hsalingyi, Amyint, and Talot emerge as alternative locations that provided desirable monastic career opportunities and were to an important degree autonomous from the royal court saṅgha of the capital city.

Scholars do not often conceptualize early modern Buddhist exchange in terms of royal diplomatics. Part of the reason for this is that we lack a certain record of the actual practice of diplomacy or royal communication for many areas of the precontemporary Buddhist world. Drawing on a rich archive of epistles sent between the Burmese king Alaungmintaya and the Mon king Banna Dala during their military campaigns against each other in the 1750s, Jacques Leider's paper examines the distinctive motivations and local meanings that inform their use of Buddhist diplomatic rhetoric. To a degree paralleling Blackburn's attention to the productive capacity of invocations of "Laṅkā", Leider argues that the use of value-laden Buddhist rhetorics — ideals of the *dhammarāja* and *cakkavatti*, displays of merit and petitions for omniscience, references to *Jātaka* or other prestige or protctive texts — was a strategy employed by these rulers to conjure status and authority in the context of diplomatic communication.

Buddhist diplomacy is also the theme of Santi's concluding paper, which explores aspects of Buddhist textual, ritual, and institutional monastic exchange between the Cambodian and Siamese courts in the nineteenth and early twentieth centuries. Particularly interesting about his account is the emphasis it places on the translation of Thai vernacular Buddhist literature (specifically versions of the *Paṭhamasambodhikathā* and *Traibhūmikathā*-related cosmological treatises) into Khmer, in certain cases for the purposes of serving the sermon-making or curricular needs of the newly emergent Dhammayutika Nikāya in Cambodia. Santi also considers the important role monks played as couriers of diplomatic messages, couched in allegorical references to scriptural texts, and as agents of the Siamese and Cambodian courts.

Notes

1. Pollock, *The Language of the Gods*, pp. 525–65.
2. Compare Manguin, Mani, and Wade, *Early Interactions*.
3. See, for example, Khin, *Le Cambodge*; Hansen, *How to Behave*; Munier, "17th to 19th Century Burmese Murals".
4. Lieberman, *Strange Parallels*, Vols. 1 and 2. We however lack a historical survey that closely examines the development of Southeast Asian Buddhism in the context of parallel transformations elsewhere in the Buddhist world.
5. As Anne Blackburn has recently argued, an emphasis on the local is required to do justice to the range of issues at stake in Buddhist history, even when scholars are concerned with understanding global processes such as colonialism. See Blackburn, *Locations of Buddhism*.
6. Taylor, "Surface Orientations", p. 949.
7. There are a number of major manuscript-related initiatives either underway or recently completed, including (by area):
   Laos and Thailand: The Preservation of Lao Manuscripts Program and the Digital Library of Lao Manuscripts <http://www.laomanuscripts.net>; Hundius, "Preservation"; Kongdeuane et al., *Literary Heritage of Laos*; Skilling and Santi, *Pāli Literature Transmitted in Central Siam*; Skilling and Santi, *Pāli and Vernacular Literature Transmitted in Central and Northern Siam*; Santi, *Piṭakamālā*; Unebe, *Wat Ratchasittharam*; Lagirarde, "Les manuscrits". For a good overview of major recent projects in Tai manuscript preservation and research, see Grabowsky, "Thai Manuscripts", parts 1 and 3; and Hundius, "Thai Manuscripts", part 2. It is worth mentioning that François Lagirarde has been working on a substantial project on Northern Thai *tamnān* related manuscripts, which will include a digital archive to appear in the near future. **Vietnam:** The Digital Library of Hán Nôm <http://www.nomfoundation.org>. **Burma:** Anne Peters' continued work with Burmese Manuscripts in German collections, now past its seventh volume (see most

recently Peters, *Birmanische Handshriften, Teil 7*); Pruitt and Bischoff, *Catalogue*; Maung Maung Nyunt, *Mran mā nuiṅ ṅaṃ pāḷi*; Thu Nandar, *The Catalogue of Materials*; Thaw Kaung, Nyunt Maung, et al., *Palm-leaf Manuscript Catalogue*; Htun Yee, Ito, et al., *Documents*; Win Tint, *Database*; Peter Nyunt et al., *The Database of the Fragile Palm Leaves Collection* <fpl.tusita.org>. **Yunnan:** 中国贝叶经全集 [Zhongguo bei ye jing quan ji] / *The Complete Chinese Pattra Buddhist Scriptures*; Yin, Daniels, Kuai and Yue, eds., *A Synopsis of Tay (Chinese Shan) Old Manuscripts*; Yin and Daniels, eds., *A Synopsis of Old Manuscripts in Gengma County*. **Cambodia:** de Bernon, Kun, and Leng, *Inventaire provisoire*; de Bernon, "Preservation".

8. For some recent major projects related to regional epigraphy see the following (by area): **Vietnam**: Papin, "Aperçu"; Trịnh and Vũ, *Thư mục thác bản văn khắc Hán Nôm Việt Nam*; Trịnh, Nguyễn, and Papin, *Tổng tập thác bản văn khắc Hán Nôm*. **Indonesia**: Perret, Suhadi, and Kartakusuma, "Le programme franco-indonésien"; Griffiths, "Inscriptions of Sumatra". **Laos**: Michel Lorillard, "Les recherches épigraphiques". **Cambodia**: Gerschheimer, "Le Corpus des inscriptions khmères"; Estève and Vincent, "L'about inscrit". **Campā**: Griffiths, Lepoutre, Southworth, and Thành, "Études du corpus des inscriptions du Campā III"; Griffiths and Southworth, "La stèle d'installation de Śrī Satyadeveśvara"; Griffiths and Southworth, "La stèle d'installation de Śrī Ādideveśvara". **Arakan**: Jacques Leider has been working on an inventory of Arakan inscriptions. From 2005 until 2009 Kyaw Minn Htin collaborated on this project which among other things resulted in his paper "Early Buddhism in Myanmar: *Ye Dhammā* Inscriptions from Arakan" in Manguin, Mani, and Wade, *Early Interactions*, pp. 385–406. **Burma**: Munier, *Burmese Buddhist Murals*; Than Tun, ed., *Nhoṅḥ tve. kyok cā myāḥ*; Sein Win et al., *Thūpāruṃ kyok cā*. **Lan Na**: Penth, Phanphen, Silao, et al., *Corpus of Lān Nā Inscriptions*; Buchmann, *Northern Thai Stone Inscriptions*. **Thailand (Siam and Lan Na)**: *Thankhomun charuk nai prathet Thai / Database of Thai Inscriptions* <http://www.sac.or.th/databases/inscriptions/th/main.php>.
9. Skilling, "Theravāda in History"; Skilling, Carbine, Cicuzza, and Santi, *How Theravāda*.
10. Compare McDaniel, *The Lovelorn Ghost*, pp. 100–20, 222–30.
11. It is crucial not to overstress such distinctions, and neglect the ways in which vernacular languages might take on cosmopolitan characteristics and functions, and vice versa. Of course, there are not a few contexts in which languages such as Burmese (e.g., among the Khamti Shan in Northeast India) fulfil cosmopolitan roles, or are still further layered in complex linguistic hierarchies involving third or even fourth languages.
12. Very recently there have been important philological contributions towards our understanding of regional Buddhist composition in Pali, including: Cicuzza, *A Mirror Reflecting the Entire World*; Kieffer-Pülz, *Sīmāvicāraṇa*;

Kieffer-Pülz, "Die *Paṭhamasambodhi*"; Toshiya Unebe, *Southeast Asian Buddhist Literature*; Santi, *Jambūpati-sūtra*; Yamanaka, *Die Vessantaradīpanī*; Ñāṇindena, *Uppātasanti*. A major advance in our understanding of Buddhist composition in Vietnam is Nguyen, *Zen in Medieval Vietnam*. A provisional list of recent publications of premodern vernacular or *nissaya* Buddhist texts would run to many pages. Representative of some important contributions include Nyunt Maung, *Rhve ti guṃ*; Than Htaik, *Sāsanavaṃsa*; Dhammananda-thera, *Tathāgatuppatti*; Bampen, Udom, Hundius, et al., *Panyasachadok*; Ratchabandittayasathan, *Thammasat Pakon*.

13. See Reynolds, "Thai Manual Knowledge"; Pattaratorn, *Divination*. On medicine in Vietnam, see Thompson, "Scripts and Medical Scripture" and "Signification as Limitation". On Burmese medical manuscripts, see Mya Nyunt, *Mran mā. cheḥ kyamḥ*; on manuscripts concerning poetics and grammar, see Maung Maung Nyunt, *Rheḥ khet mran mā cā pe chuiṅ rā kyamḥ myāḥ le. lā mhu*. In Burma important grammatical works have been edited for publication or republished recently; for example, several important nineteenth century works, including Visuddhācāra's Pali recension and nissaya of Gaṅgādāsa's *Chandomañjarī* and Sayadaw U Budh's nissaya on the *Vuttodaya*, have been republished together in Visuddhācāra et al., *Chanḥ kyamḥ 6 coṅ tvai* [Six treatises on prosody].
14. This is more the case on the mainland. There are long-standing traditions of scholarship on Buddhist verse texts in Old Javanese, on which see the paper by Andrea Acri below. For areas of the mainland there have been notable exceptions, especially for certain Khmer and Tai/Lao language materials, although such work has been typically less explicitly focussed on Buddhism. See, for example, Saveros, *Guirlande*; Koret, "*Leup Phasun*"; Hudak, *Indigenization*; Compton, *Courting Poetry*. There is also comparatively more work on Buddhist poetry by scholars writing in mainland vernaculars.
15. Although on *vinaya,* see Kieffer-Pülz and Peters, "*Die Pātimokkhapadattha-anuvaṇṇanā*"; Keiffer-Pülz and Peters, "The *Vinayasaṅkhepaṭṭhakathā*".
16. Some important exceptions include Veidlinger, *Spreading the Dhamma* and Mikaelian, *La royauté*. Steven Collins' momentous *Nirvana and other Buddhist Felicities*, although not centrally concerned with locally-produced Southeast Asian texts, is also a recent example.
17. de Casparis, "Some Notes on the Oldest Inscriptions of Indonesia".

References

Bampen Rawin, Udom Roongruangsri, Harald Hundius, et al. *Kansuksa choeng wikhro Panyasachadok chbap Lanna Thai / A Critical Study of Northern Thai Version of Panyasa Jataka*. Chiang Mai: Chiang Mai University, 1998.

de Bernon, Olivier, Kun Sopheap, and Leng Kok-An. *Inventaire provisoire des manuscrits du Cambodge, Première partie*. Paris: École française d'Extrême-Orient, 2004.

de Bernon, Olivier. "Preservation of Manuscripts in Cambodia: A long standing effort". In *The Literary Heritage of Laos: Preservation, Dissemination and Research Perspectives*, edited by Kongdeuane Nettavong et al., pp. 310–24. Vientiane: National Library of Laos, 2005.

Blackburn, Anne M. *Locations of Buddhism: Colonialism & Modernity in Sri Lanka*. Chicago: University of Chicago Press, 2010.

Buchmann, Marek. *Northern Thai Stone Inscriptions (14th–17th Centuries): Glossary*. Wiesbaden: Harrassowitz, 2011.

de Casparis, J.G. "Some Notes on the Oldest Inscriptions of Indonesia". In *A Man of Indonesian Letters: Essays in Honour of Professor A. Teeuw*, edited by C.M.S. Hellwig and S.O. Robson, pp. 242–56. Dordrecht: Foris, 1986.

Cicuzza, Claudio, ed. and trans. *A Mirror Reflecting the Entire World: The Pāli Buddhapādamaṅgala or "Auspicious Signs of the Buddha's Feet*. Bangkok and Lumbini: Fragile Palm Leaves Foundation and Lumbini International Research Institute, 2011.

Collins, Steven. *Nirvana and other Buddhist felicities*. New York: Cambridge University Press, 1996.

Compton, Carol J. *Courting Poetry in Laos: A Textual and Linguistic Analysis*. Dekalb: Northern Illinois University, 1979.

Dhammananda-thera. *Tathāgatuppatti kyamḥ* [Treatise on the Arising of the Tathāgata]. Yangon: Pan shwe, 2010.

Estève, Julia and Brice Vincent. "L'about inscrit du musée national du Cambodge (K.943): nouveaux éléments sur le bouddhisme tantrique à l'époque angkorienne". *Arts Asiatiques* 65 (2010): 133–58.

Gerschheimer, Gerdi. "Le Corpus des inscriptions khmères". *BEFEO* 90–91 (2003): 478–82.

Grabowsky, Volker. "Tai Manuscripts in the Dhamma Script Domain: Surveying, Preservation and Documentation", Part 1. *Manuscript Cultures* 1 (2008): 16–23.

——. "Tai Manuscripts in the Dhamma Script Domain: Surveying, Preservation and Documentation", Part 3. *Manuscript Cultures* 3 (2010): 25–33.

Griffiths, Arlo. "Inscriptions of Sumatra: Further Data on the Epigraphy of the Musi and Batang Hari River Basins". *Archipel* 81 (2011): 139–75.

—— and William Southworth. "La stèle d'installation de Śrī Satyadeveśvara: une nouvelle inscription du Campā trouvée à Phước Thiện". *Journal Asiatique* 295 (2007): 349–81.

—— and William Southworth. "La stèle d'installation de Śrī Ādideveśvara: une nouvelle inscription de Satyavarman trouvée dans le temple de Hoà Lai et son importance pour l'histoire du Pāṇḍuraṅga". *Journal Asiatique* 299, no. 1 (2011): 271–317.

——, Amandine Lepoutre, William A. Southworth, and Thành Phần. "Études du corpus des inscriptions du Campā III: Épigraphie du Campā 2009–2010: prospection sur le terrain, production d'estampages, supplément à l'inventaire". *BEFEO* 96-96 (2008–2009): 435–97.

Hansen, Anne. *How to Behave: Buddhism and Modernity in Colonial Cambodia 1860–1930*. Honolulu: University of Hawaii Press, 2007.

Htun Yee, Toshikatsu Ito, et al. *Documents of Myanmar Socio-Economic History*, 15 vols. Toyohashi: Aichi University, 2002–2011 <http://taweb.aichi-u.ac.jp/DMSEH/>.

Hudak, Thomas John. *The Indigenization of Pali Meters in Thai Poetry*. Athens: Ohio University Press, 1990.

Hundius, Harald. "Tai Manuscripts in the Dhamma Script Domain: Surveying, Preservation and Documentation", Part 2. *Manuscript Cultures* 2 (2009): 21–25.

——. "The Preservation of Lao Manuscripts". In *New Research on Laos / Recherches nouvelles sur le Laos*, edited by Yves Goudineau and Michel Lorrillard, pp. 361–68. Paris: EFEO, 2008.

Khin Sok. *Le Cambodge entre le Siam et le Vietnam (de 1775 à 1860)*. Paris: EFEO, 1991.

Kieffer-Pülz, Petra, ed. and trans. *Sīmāvicāraṇa: A Pāli letter on monastic boundaries by King Rāma IV of Siam*. Bangkok and Lumbini: Fragile Palm Leaves Foundation and Lumbini International Research Institute, 2011.

——. "Die *Paṭhamasambodhi*: Eine 'indochinesische' Buddhabiographie?". *Zeitschrift der Deutschen Morgenländischen Gesellschaft* 160, no. 2 (2010): 415–30.

Kieffer-Pülz, Petra and Anne Peters. "*Die Pātimokkhapadattha-anuvaṇṇanā* des Vicittālaṅkāra aus Ca-laṅḥ". In *Pāsādikadānaṁ: Festschrift für Bhikkhu Pāsādika*, edited by M. Straube, R. Steiner, J. Soni, M. Hahn, and M. Demoto, pp. 275–92. Marburg: Indica et Tibetica, 2009.

——. "The *Vinayasaṅkhepaṭṭhakathā:* an Unknown Vinaya Handbook?". In *Buddhist Studies in Honour of Professor Sodo Mori*, pp. 117–27. Tokyo: Kokusai Bukkyoto Kyokai, 2002.

Kongdeuane Nettavong et al., eds. *The Literary Heritage of Laos: Preservation, Dissemination and Research Perspectives*. Vientiane: National Library of Laos, 2005.

Koret, Peter. "*Leup Phasun* (Extinguishing the Light of the Sun): Romance, Religion, and Politics in the Interpretation of a Traditional Lao Poem". In *Contesting Visions of the Lao Past: Lao Historiography at the Crossroads*, edited by Christopher E. Goscha and Soren Ivarsson, pp. 181–208. Cophenhagen: NIAS Press, 2003.

Lagirarde, François. "Les manuscrits en Thaï du nord de la Siam Society". *Journal of the Siam Society* 84, no. 1 (1996): 91–115.

Lieberman, Victor. *Strange Parallels: Southeast Asia in Global Context, c.800–1830. Volume 1: Integration on the Mainland*. New York: Cambridge University Press, 2003.

——. *Strange Parallels: Southeast Asia in Global Context, c.800–1830. Volume 2: Mainland Mirrors: Europe, Japan, China, South Asia, and the Islands*. New York: Cambridge University Press, 2009.

Lorillard, Michel. "Les recherches épigraphiques au Laos". *BEFEO* 90–91 (2003): 475–78.

Manguin, Pierre-Yves, A. Mani, and Geoff Wade, eds. *Early Interactions between South and Southeast Asia: Reflections on Cross-Cultural Exchange*. Singapore: Institute of Southeast Asian Studies, 2011.

Maung Maung Nyunt. *Mran mā nuiṅ ṅaṃ pāḷi nhaṅ. piṭakat cā pe samuiṅḥ sac* [A new catalog of Pali and Buddhist literature in Burma]. Yangon: Cā pe bimān, 2003.

——. *Rheḥ khet mran mā cā pe chuiṅ rā kyamḥ myāḥ le. lā mhu* [Textual Studies in Premodern Buddhist Literature]. Yangon: Sabei Beikman, 2008.

McDaniel, Justin Thomas. *The Lovelorn Ghost & the Magical Monk: Practicing Buddhism in Modern Thailand*. New York: Columbia University Press, 2011.

Mikaelian, Grégory. *La royauté d'Oudong: Réformes des institutions et crise du pouvoir dans le royaume khmer du XVIIe siècle*. Paris: Presses de l'Université Paris-Sorbonne, 2009.

Munier, Christophe. *Burmese Buddhist Murals: Epigraphic Corpus of the Powin Taung Caves*. Bangkok: White Lotus, 2007.

——. "17th to 19th Century Burmese Murals in the Context of Thai and Lanna Murals". Unpublished paper presented at the International Buddhist Studies Conference, Marseille, 2010.

Mya Nyunt. *Mran mā. cheḥ kyamḥ mya cā cu ca raṅḥ* [A Catalogue of Burmese Medical Manuscripts]. Unpublished diploma thesis, Universities Central Library, Yangon, 1974.

Ñāṇindena, Bhaddanta. *Uppātasanti-paritta-vaṇṇanā*. Unpublished PhD dissertation, State Pariyatti Sāsana University, Mandalay 2009 [in Pali].

Nguyen, Cuong Tu. *Zen in Medieval Vietnam: A Study and Translation of the Thiền Uyển Tập Anh*. Honolulu: University of Hawaii Press, 1997.

Nyunt Maung, ed. *Rhve ti guṃ samuiṅḥ pyui*. [Verses on the History of Shwegadon Pagoda]. Yangon, 2003.

Papin, Philippe. "Aperçu sur le programme 'Publication de l'inventaire et du corpus complet des inscriptions sur stèles du Viêt-Nam". *BEFEO* 90–91 (2003): 465–72.

Pattaratorn Chirapravati. *Divination au Royaume de Siam: Le Corps, La Guerre, Le Destin*. Paris: Presses Universitaires de France, 2011.

Penth, Hans, Phanphen Khruathai, Silao Ketphrom, et al. *Corpus of Lān Nā Inscriptions*, 11 vols. Chiang Mai: Archive of Lan Na Inscriptions, Chiang Mai University, 1997–2005.

Perret, Daniel, Machi Suhadi, and Richadiana Kartakusuma. "Le programme franco-indonésien d'inventaire des inscriptions 'classiques' du monde malais". *BEFEO* 90–91 (2003): 473–74.

Peters, Anne. *Birmanische Handshriften, Teil 7: Die Katalognummern 1201–1375*. Stuttgart: Franz Steiner, 2010.

Pollock, Sheldon. *The Language of the Gods in the World of Men: Sanskrit, Culture, and Power in Premodern India*. Berkeley: University of California Press, 2006.

Pruitt, William and Roger Bischoff. *Catalogue of the Burmese-Pali and Burmese Manuscripts in the Library of the Wellcome Institute for the History of Medicine*. London: The Wellcome Institute for the History of Medicine, 1998.

Ratchabandittayasathan, ed. *Thammasat Pakon*. Bangkok: Royal Institute, 2008.

Reynolds, Craig. "Thai Manual Knowledge". In *Seditious Histories: Contesting Thai and Southeast Asian Pasts*, by Craig Reynolds, pp. 214–42. Seattle: University of Washington Press, 2006.

Santi Pakdeekham. *Piṭakamālā, "The Garland of the Piṭaka"*. Bangkok: Fragile Palm Leaves Foundation and Lumbini International Research Institute, 2011.

——, ed. *Jambūpati-sūtra: A Synoptic Romanized Edition*. Bangkok and Lumbini: Fragile Palm Leaves Foundation and Lumbini International Research Institute, 2009.

Saveros Pou. *Guirlande de cpāp'*. Paris: Cedorek, 1988.

Sein Win et al., ed. *Thūpāruṃ kyok cā*, 2 vols. [Htupayon Inscriptions]. Yangon: Ministry of Culture, 2009–10.

Skilling, Peter. "Theravāda in History". *Pacific World* 11 (Third Series, Fall 2009): 61–93.

—— and Santi Pakdeekham. *Pāli Literature Transmitted in Central Siam*. Bangkok: Fragile Palm Leaves Foundation and Lumbini International Research Institute, 2002.

—— and Santi Pakdeekham. *Pāli and Vernacular Literature Transmitted in Central and Northern Siam*. Bangkok: Fragile Palm Leaves Foundation and Lumbini International Research Institute, 2004.

——, Jason A. Carbine, Claudio Cicuzza, and Santi Pakdeekham. *How Theravāda is Theravāda? Exploring Buddhist Identities*. Chiang Mai: Silkworm Books, 2012.

Taylor, Keith. "Surface Orientations in Vietnam: Beyond Histories of Nation and Region". *Journal of Asian Studies* 57, no. 4 (1998): 949–78.

Than Htaik, ed. *Sāsanavaṃsa cā tamḥ* [Treatise on the History of the *Sāsana*]. Yangon: She yat, 2010.

Than Tun, ed. *Nhoṅḥ tve. kyok cā myāḥ* [Recently discovered inscriptions]. Yangon: Myanmar Historical Commission, 2005.

Thaw Kaung, Nyunt Maung, et al. *Palm-leaf Manuscript Catalogue of Thar-lay (South) Monastery*. Yangon: Myanmar Book Centre, 2006.

Thompson, C. Michele. "Scripts and Medical Scripture in Vietnam: Nôm and Classical Chinese in the Historic Transmission of Medical Knowledge in Pre-Twentieth Century Vietnam". *Thời Đại Mới* 5 (July 2005): 1–12.

———. "Signification as Limitation: Minh Mạng's Prohibition on Use of Nôm and the Resulting Marginalization of Nôm Medical Texts". In *Looking at It from Asia: The Processes that Shaped the Sources of History of Science*, edited by F. Bretelle-Establet, pp. 393–411. Dordrecht: Springer, 2010.

Thu Nandar. *The Catalogue of Materials on Myanmar History in Microfilms*, 2 vols. Tokyo: Tokyo University of Foreign Studies, 2004.

Trịnh Khắc Mạnh and Vũ Lan Anh. *Thư mục thác bản văn khắc Hán Nôm Việt Nam / Catalogue des inscriptions du Việt-Nam,* 4 vols. Hanoi: Nhà xuất bản Văn hóa, 2007.

Trịnh Khắc Mạnh, Nguyễn Văn Nguyên, and Philippe Papin. *Tổng tập thác bản văn khắc Hán Nôm / Corpus des inscriptions anciennes du Việt-Nam*, 22 vols. Hanoi: Nhà xuất bản Văn hóa-thông tin, 2005–2009.

Unebe, Toshiya, ed., タイ国ワット・ラジャシッダラム寺院他所蔵写本に基づく蔵外仏典の研究 [Thai koku Wat Ratchasittharam jiin hoka shozō shahon ni moto zoku zō gai butten no kenkyū] / *A Study of Non-Canonical Buddhist Literature Based on Manuscripts Preserved in Wat Ratchasittharam etc*. Nagoya: Nagoya University, 2012.

———. パーリ語およびタイ語写本による東南アジア撰述仏典の研究 [Pali go oyobi Thai go shahon ni yoru tōnan ajia senjutsu butten no kenkyū] / *A Study of Southeast Asian Buddhist Literature Based on Pāli and Thai Manuscripts*. Nagoya: Nagoya University, 2008.

Visuddhācāra, et al. *Chanḥ kyamḥ 6 coṅ tvai* [Six treatises on prosody]. Yangon: Buddhist Literature Group, 2011.

Win Tint. *Database of Myanmar Studies Source Materials in Parabaik Manuscripts*, 7 vols. Meiktila: Meiktila University Library, 2002–2007.

Yamanaka, Yukio. *Die Vessantaradīpanī: Ein Pāli-Kommentar aus Nordthailand*. Unpublished PhD dissertation, Albert-Ludwigs-Universität, 2009.

Yin Shaoting, Christian Daniels, Kuai Yongsheng and Yue Xiabao, eds. *A Synopsis of Tay (Chinese Shan) Old Manuscripts in the Dehong Autonomous Region of Yunnan, China*. Kunming: Nationalities Publishing House, 2002.

Yin Shaoting and Christian Daniels, eds. *A Synopsis of Old Manuscripts in Gengma County of Yunnan, China*. Kunming: Nationalities Publishing House, 2005.

中国贝叶经全集 [Zhongguo bei ye jing quan ji] / *The Complete Chinese Pattra Buddhist Scriptures*, 100 vols. Beijing: Renmin chubanshe, 2006–2010.

2

AN UNTRACED BUDDHIST VERSE INSCRIPTION FROM (PEN)INSULAR SOUTHEAST ASIA

Peter Skilling

INTRODUCTION

ajñānāc cīyate karma, janmanaḥ karma kāraṇaṃ |
jñānān na cīyate karma, karmābhāvān na jāyate ||

Through ignorance, karma is accumulated;
Karma is the cause of rebirth.
Through wisdom, karma is not accumulated;
In the absence of karma, one is not reborn.

This verse is not known from any Indian inscription, and it is yet to be traced in any Indian Buddhist text, whether in the original Indic language or in Tibetan or Chinese translation.

Southeast Asia is rich in epigraphic material: historical, secular records (royal *praśasti* with their lineages and accounts of temporal deeds); historical, religious records (the foundation and dedication of buildings or images); and non-historical religious records containing praises of brahmanical or Buddhist deities, scriptural citations, *dhāraṇī*, or mantra. As in India, several or all of these elements can be combined in a single record.

MAP 2.1

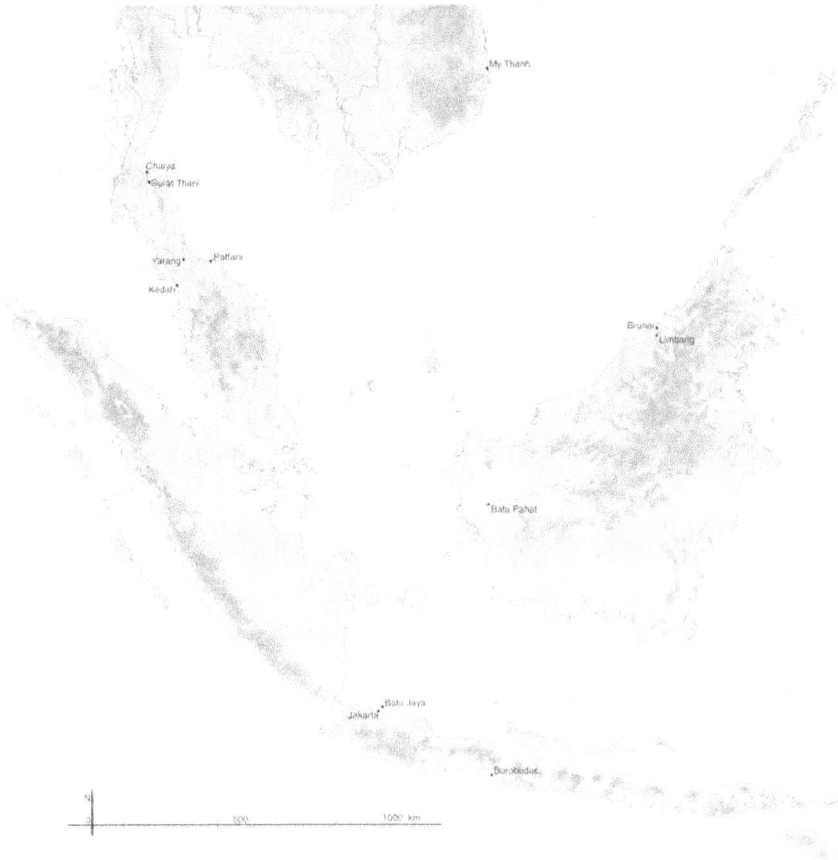

Religious records can be read for the information they contain about the diffusion of Buddhist practices or ideas in the region. In this chapter, I trace the travels of a single Sanskrit verse, which is known from lithic inscriptions from three neighbouring sites in north peninsular Malaysia, from three sites on the island of Borneo (one each from Brunei, Sarawak, and Kalimantan), as well as from a terracotta tablet and gold plates from Java. At the end, I briefly examine the relationship of the verse to the texts and stūpa images with which it is associated.

The documentation of some of the artefacts discussed here goes back to the first half of the nineteenth century, a period of expansion and consolidation of the horizons of orientalist knowledge; their modern history reflects the shifting boundaries and fortunes of the region that we know today as "Southeast Asia". The first notices of some of the inscriptions were published in Calcutta, then capital of British India, known today as Kolkata, the capital of Paschim Banga (former West Bengal). One of the artefacts was in fact removed to Calcutta, where it remains today. Early studies were published by scholars or colonial officers associated with the Asiatic Society of Bengal, then the leading organization for Asian studies, in the pages of the *Proceedings* or *Journal* of the Society. Other artefacts, from the Dutch East Indies, were published by Dutch scholars. The prevailing framework was antiquarian; at the time, field archaeology was in its infancy. Only the Batu Jaya artefacts come from scientific excavation. The inscriptions have been studied and discussed by some of the giants of Indology and epigraphy — James Prinsep, H. Kern, B.Ch. Chhabra, D.C. Sircar, and J. de Casparis, followed in the post-colonial period by scholars of Malaysia, Indonesia, and Thailand. The Borneo sites have not received the attention that they deserve as significant evidence for the history of the great island, about which so little is known, and for the history of insular Southeast Asia. In this chapter, I discuss the objects from the point of view of contemporary Buddhist studies. I hope this survey will inspire further research, as well as concerted action to protect and preserve the monuments.

1. STONE SLAB FROM BUKIT MIRIAM, KEDAH, MALAYSIA

A stone slab inscribed with two Sanskrit verses from Bukit Miriam in Kedah, northwestern Malaya, was reported by Colonel Low in 1849 (Figure 2.1). Low noted that the stone "was lying under the centre of the foundation of a ruin of an ancient brick building in Keddah, near Buket Murriam. This building had been very small, not more than 10 or 12 feet square." The slab was subsequently lost, and today the text is known only from Low's eye-copy and reading.[1] The first verse is the familiar *ye dharmā hetuprabhavā* stanza, which is well known from numerous examples across Asia:[2]

ye dharmā hetuprabhavā teṣā[ṃ] hetū[ṃ] tathāgato (?)
yeṣā[ṃ] ca yo nirodha eva[ṃ] vādī mahāśramaṇo.

The second verse is the stanza cited at the beginning of this article (for a translation, see above):

FIGURE 2.1
Stone slab from Bukit Miriam, Kedah, Malaysia

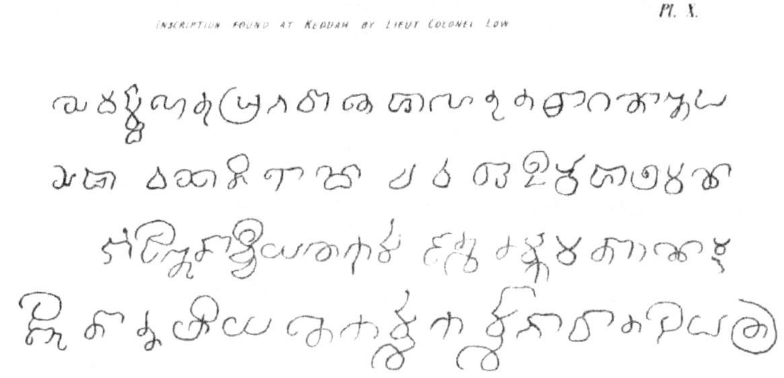

ajñānāc cīyate karma janmanaḥ karma kāraṇam
jñānān na kriyate[3] *karmma karmmābhāvān na jāyate*

Our knowledge of the script depends on Low's eye-copy. According to his copy, the stanzas were written in a somewhat cursive form of the early script of the region, which I shall here call Southeast Asian Brāhmī.[4] Chhabra notes that "on the strength of what little can be made out of the eye-copy, it possibly stands, as Kern has pointed out, in relation with the sea-captain Buddhagupta's inscription" (No. 2 following), and describes it as "a little earlier" than the latter, which he dates to the fifth century CE.[5] According to Allen's Table 3, scholars have dated the inscription from the fourth to the fifth centuries.[6] Now that we have a corpus of affiliated inscriptions, new palaeographic studies are a desideratum.

2. MAHĀNĀVIKA BUDDHAGUPTA INSCRIPTION FROM SEBERANG PERAI (FORMER PROVINCE WELLESLEY) MALAYSIA

A "Copy of an Inscription on a Stone found near the ruins of a Buddhist Temple in Province Wellesley, Malayan Pen[insula]" was published in the *Journal of the Asiatic Society of Bengal* in 1835.[7] See Figures 2.2 to 2.4.

In 1848, Low gave an account of the discovery in the pages of the same journal: "I discovered this inscription while engaged in excavating some old ruins on a sandy side in the northern district of this Province. It has been engraved on a sort of slate and seems to form part only of a much larger inscription…."[8] His remarks, which included a very preliminary reading

FIGURE 2.2
Mahānāvika Buddhagupta Inscription from Seberang Perai (former Province Wellesley), Malaysia

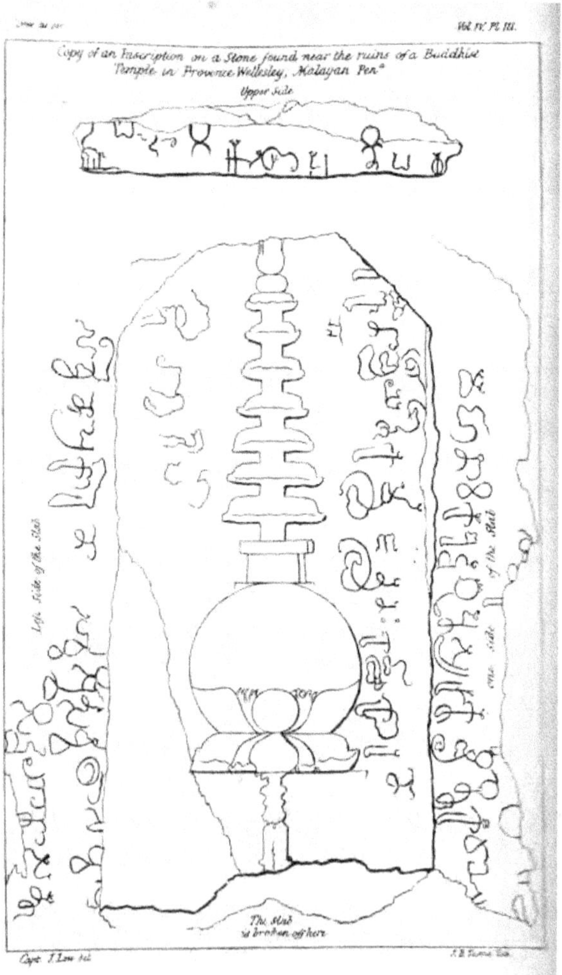

FIGURE 2.3
Mahānāvika Buddhagupta Inscription, Kolkata, Indian Museum (photo by Peter Skilling)

FIGURE 2.4
Mahānāvika Buddhagupta Inscription (rubbing)

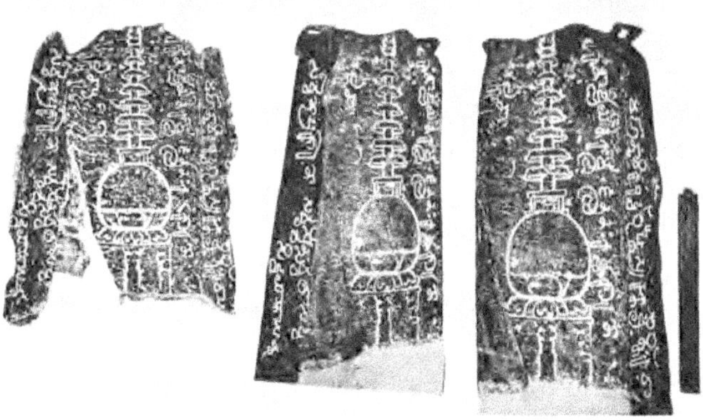

supplied by James Prinsep, were followed by a somewhat improved but still unsatisfactory reading by Laidlay.[9] In 1935, Chhabra offered a much better reading.[10] Low presented the slab to the Asiatic Society of Bengal in Calcutta on 14 January 1835. When the Indian Museum was established in 1866, the slab was transferred to the new museum with the bulk of the Asiatic Society collections. It remains there till this day.[11]

The stone contains three elements:

(1) a stūpa with seven superposed parasols, carved in low relief on the main face;
(2) a verse inscribed vertically on the main face, flanking the stūpa, of which the following can be clearly read:
[Right hand side, reading downwards]
ajñānāc cīyate karmma janmanaḥ karmma kāraṇam
[Left hand side, also downwards]
jñānā x *ī....*[12]
(3) a prose text inscribed vertically on either flank of the slab. Chhabra treats this as a single textual unit to be read downwards starting on the left side, as follows:

[line to outermost right]
mahānāvikabuddhaguptasya raktamṛittika[13]*-vās[tavyasya?]*[14]
[lines to outermost left]
sarvveṇa prakāreṇa sarvvasmin sarvvathā sa[r]vva...|
siddhayāt[r]ā[ḥ] santu.

This may be rendered as "Of Buddhagupta the great sea-captain, resident (?) of Raktamṛttikā ... in every manner, in all cases, absolutely, ... all ..., may the voyages be successful!"

The preserved letters are neatly engraved examples of calligraphic Southeast Asian Brāhmī. Chhabra and Sircar both assign the epigraph to the fifth century CE. De Casparis relates the script to that of the Tārumā inscriptions of West Java, which he dates to the latter half of the fifth century; Kongkaew dates the inscription to the seventh century.[15]

On the one hand, Chhabra accepted Kern's earlier identification of Raktamṛttikā, "Red Earth", with the Chinese toponym Chitu 赤土, "Red Earth", placed by Chinese sources from the early seventh century onwards somewhere on the Malay peninsula.[16] On the other hand, in 1961–62, monastic sealings bearing the name "Raktamṛttikā-mahāvihāra" in letters of the seventh to eighth centuries were discovered at Rājbāḍīdāṅgā, District Murshidabad, West Bengal (now Paschim Banga).[17] This inspired a new identification of Buddhagupta's place of residence, and placed it within a wider geographical perspective.[18] Xuanzang reported on his visit in the first half of the seventh century to a monastery in the Bengal region whose name he transliterated as Lao-duo-wei-zhi 絡多未知, which seemingly corresponds to *Raktamṛttikā,[19] located near Karṇasuvarṇa, the capital of Gauḍa.[20] The sanctity of this site was enhanced by the fact that nearby were several stūpas held to have been erected by King Aśoka at places visited by the Buddha himself, and a temple with traces where the four past Buddhas had sat and walked up and down.[21] According to Xuanzang, Karṇasuvarṇa boasted ten monasteries and over two thousand monks, who belonged to the Sāṃmitīya school. The flourishing state had riverine connections to the ancient port of Tāmralipti (modern Tamluk, Dist. Purba Medinapur, Paschim Banga [West Bengal]), which Indian literature consistently presents as one of the points of departure for Southeast Asia.[22]

It is certainly possible that Buddhagupta came from Raktamṛttikā in Bengal, but Raktamṛttikā seems to have been only the name of a *vihāra*, not of a town. Would a "great sea-captain" be described as a resident of a *vihāra* (if the reconstruction *vāstavya* is correct)? Or could the rare term *mahānāvika* simply mean "great sea-farer", and Buddhagupta, whose name means "protected by the Buddha", simply have been a sea-faring monk? The possibility that Buddhagupta was a monk from Raktamṛttikā remains, although one might then expect a title like *bhikṣu* or *sthavira*. The term *mahānāvika* is known from Prakrit legends from Ghantasala in Andhra Pradesh, and more recently from a gold seal from Bang Kluay, south Thailand.[23] In Pali, the term *nāvika* occurs in a variety of narrative contexts in the *Jātaka* and other texts.[24]

The exact import of *siddhayātrā*, which occurs in several Southeast Asian inscriptions, is uncertain, and its meaning has been the object of considerable discussion, particularly in the context of the old Malay (seventh century) Śrīvijaya inscriptions.[25]

3. STONE INSCRIPTION FROM KAMPUNG SUNGAI MAS, KEDAH, MALAYSIA

In 1980, a stone slab, inscribed on one side and depicting a stūpa in bas-relief, was recovered in Kampung Sungai Mas, Kedah.[26] Today it is displayed in the Muzium Lembah Bujang, Merbok, Kedah. The top portion of the slab is broken off and lost; in its present condition it measures 41 × 22-25 × 5 cm (Figure 2.5). To the left of the stūpa, the first half of the *ajñānāc cīyate karma* verse is inscribed vertically, to be read upwards:

ajñānāc cīya[t]e [ka]rmma janmanaḥ karmma kāra[ṇaṃ].

To the right of the stūpa, the rest of the verse is inscribed vertically downwards:

[jñanān na cī]yate ka[rmma] karmābhāv[ān na jāya]te.

The script is similar to that of the Buddhagupta inscription. Dates between the fifth to the seventh centuries have been suggested.

FIGURE 2.5
Stone inscription from Kampung Sungai Mas, Kedah, Malaysia (photo by Tharaphong Sisuchat)

4. TERRACOTTA TABLET AND GOLD FOIL PLATE FROM BATUJAYA, WEST JAVA, INDONESIA[27]

Batujaya is a complex of monuments in Kabupaten Krawang, West Java, near or within the ancient state of Tarumanagara, known from fifth-century inscriptions at Bogor and Tugu. The complex "is situated on a broad track of alluvial land east of the Jakarta Bay, at the mean altitude of 2.5 m to 3.0 m above sea level ... approximately 15 km upstream from the modern mouth of the Tarum River (the Citarum, one of the largest streams of West Java) ... [It] appears to have been located at the former confluence between the present day Citarum and an ancient branch of its delta flowing north into the Java Sea, some eight km away."[28] See Map 2.2. Among the thirty sites, thirteen have been identified as brick temples. The Segaran V temple (Unur Blandogan), the largest of the complex, has a platform that supported what was originally a stūpa. Moulded clay tablets were recovered there in 1995, 1997,[29] and 2001. The tablets (Figure 2.6) are a variation of one of the most widely distributed Southeast Asian iconographic models: a Buddha seated on a throne, legs pendant, flanked by a pair of lissome bodhisatvas, with three Buddhas seated in a row above, and flanked, along the edges, by tall stūpas topped by superimposed parasols.[30] A unique feature of the Batujaya tablets is an inscription along the base of the tablets in spindly letters, which has not yet been successfully read.

4.1. Terracotta tablet inscription

A broken inscribed terracotta tablet was found in 1999. In its present state, it is 6.5 cm long, 5.0 cm wide, 1.1 cm thick (Figure 2.7). On each side there is a broken-off three-line inscription in Southeast Asian Brāhmī. The recto (so-described) carries the latter part of lines *a-c* of the *ajñānāc cīyate karma* verse:[31]

1. *[ajñānāc c](ī)yate karmma* ||
2. *[janmanaḥ karma] kāraṇam* ||
3. *[jñānān na cīyate] karm[m]a* ||.

The verso seems to cite a different text, too fragmentary to make sense of:

1. ... *ma*
2. ... *thāya* ||
3. ... *bhadraḥ* ||.

MAP 2.2
West Java: Tarumanagara, Batujaya and Buni Culture Complex sites

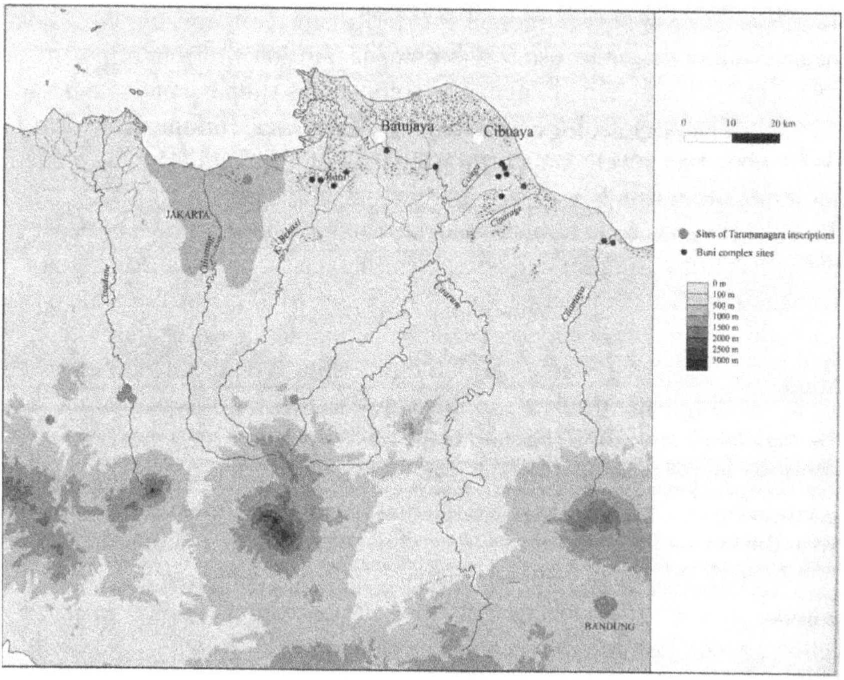

4.2. Golden inscription I

Four fragments of an inscription on gold foil discovered in 2002 carry our inscription (Figure 2.8):[32]

1. *ajñānā[c=]cīyate kar[m]ma [jñā]naḥ kar[m]ma [….] jñāna cīyate kar[m]ma*
2. *kar[m]mābhāva[n=na ja]yate*

4.3. Golden inscription II

Another inscription measuring 5 × 2.5 cm was discovered in 2004 (Figure 2.9). It carries the verse in 3 lines:[33]

1. *°ajñānāc=cīyate karmma janmanaḥ*
2. *karmma kāraṇam jñānaṇṇah kramaṇaḥ*
3. *karmma karmmābhāvān=na jāyate.*

FIGURE 2.6
Terracotta tablet from Batu Jaya (photo by Hasan Djafar, 2004)

FIGURE 2.7
Terracotta tablet inscription from Batu Jaya (photo by Hasan Djafar, 2000)

FIGURE 2.8
Gold foil inscription I from Batu Jaya (photo by Hasan Djafar, 2002)

FIGURE 2.9
Gold foil plate inscription II from Batu Jaya
(photo by Hasan Djafar, 2004)

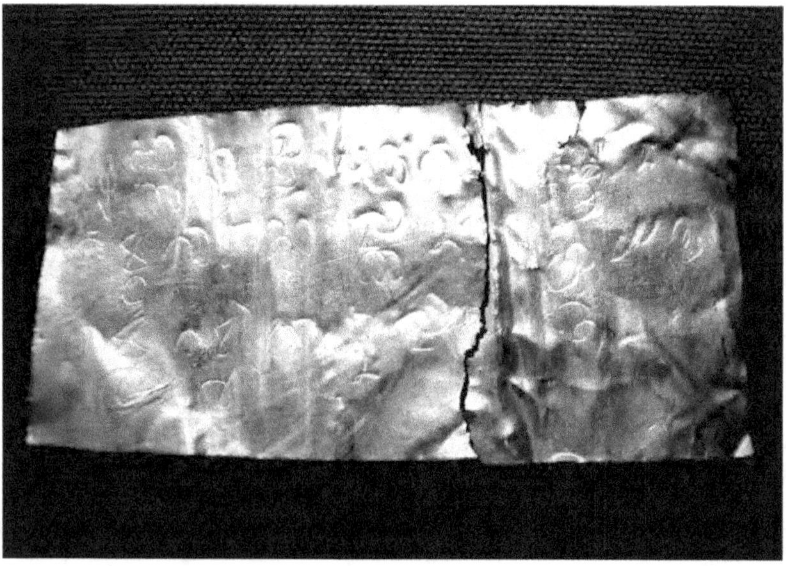

Another small gold foil inscription from the site has apparently not yet been read.[34]

5. GOLD PLATES FROM THE NATIONAL MUSEUM, JAKARTA, INDONESIA

Eleven gold plates, inscribed on both sides in Sanskrit, were "discovered" in the Jakarta Museum in 1946 (Figure 2.10). How they got there and where they came from remains a mystery. In 1956, J.G. de Casparis published a detailed study, transcription, and translation of the inscribed texts. He concluded that the plates probably came from Indonesia itself, and noted that, like the *pratītyasamutpāda* inscriptions of India, the plates most probably "served as relics", that is, "were inscribed to constitute a deposit in a religious foundation such as a stūpa", or "one of the large Buddhist temples in Indonesia".[35] The practice of depositing sacred texts is well attested from Buddhist sites across Asia.[36]

De Casparis described the script as "a transitional phase between the Pallava script and the Old Javanese script of the oldest period",[37] and assigned the broad dates "between about 650 and 800 A.C.".[38] The study of this unique record is hampered by the fact that no photographs of the plates have been published to date.[39]

The plates can be divided into two groups on the basis of size and contents. Eight plates (*a* to *h*) are larger (25.5 × 9.5 cm), while three (*i* to *k*) are considerably smaller (21 × 6.5 cm).[40] The contents are as follows:

FIGURE 2.10
Gold plates from the National Museum, Jakarta, Indonesia (photo by Peter Skilling)

(1) *a*, *b*, *h*: prose *sūtra* on *pratītyasamutpāda*;
(2) *c-g*: prose commentary on the preceding;
(3) *i*, *j*: verses;
(4) *k*: symbols.

(1) The *sūtra* broadly parallels the *Ādi-sutra* of the *Nidānasaṃyukta* and related texts.[41] It lists the twelve factors (*aṅga*) of conditioned arising (*pratītyasamutpāda*) (= *ādi*) and then defines them (= *vibhaṅga*), in progressive order (*anuloma*) only. De Casparis gives a detailed analysis, comparing the text to parallels in Pali, Sanskrit (Nalanda brick inscription, *Abhidharmakośa-bhāṣya* and *Abhidharmakośa-vyākhyā* citations, etc.), and Chinese (Xuanzang's translation). He concludes that it is a Sarvāstivādin version brought to Java in about the sixth century CE.[42] There are, however, numerous differences between the inscribed text and the *Ādi-sutra*. We know much more about *pratītyasamutpāda* than we did fifty years ago, and more versions of the *pratītyasamutpāda sūtra* have become available.[43] I prefer to leave the school affiliation of the gold plate recension open.[44]

(2) Plate *c* opens with three verses. These are followed by a hitherto unknown commentary on *pratītyasamutpāda*, for which it does not include any title or any information about authorship. De Casparis examines the commentary in detail and concludes that it belongs to the Mahāyāna, specifically the Madhyamaka.[45] However, in fact, the commentary does not contain a single identifiable "Mahāyānistic" element. It has many unique features, and I prefer to let the text rest as a commentary of an undetermined author and tradition.[46]

De Casparis reads the three verses that open plate *c* as follows:[47]

1. *rūpinas sarvvasattvā hi sarvve santu nirāmanāḥ*
   sarvve bhadrāni paśyanti mā kaścit pāpam āgamat ||
2. *ajñānāc cīyate karma janmanaḥ karma kāraṇaḥ* (*sic*: read *kāraṇaṃ*)
   jñānān na cīyate karma karmābhāvāt na jāyante (*sic*: read *jāyate*) ||
3. *ye dharmmā hetuprabhavā hetun teṣān tathāgata uvāca*
   teṣāñ ca yo nirodhaḥ evamvādī mahāśramaṇaḥ ||

(3) Plate *i* contains two and a half verses. De Casparis notes that "the whole strophe was very carelessly written."[48]

1. *ajñānāc cīyate karma janmanaḥ karma kāraṇaṃ*
   jñānān na cīyate karma karmmābhāvān na jāyate

2. *ye dharmmā hetuprabhavāḥ hetun teṣāṃ tathāgato avadat*
teṣāñ ca yo nirodha evamvādī mahāśramaṇaḥ kuśalam
3. *sarvapāpasya [a]kāraṇaṃ kuśalasyopasaṃpadā* ||

Plate *j* contains three verses:[49]

1. *ajñānāc cīyate karmma janmanaḥ karma kāranaḥ* (*sic*: read *kāraṇaṃ*)
jñānān na [c]cīyate karmma karmmābhāvān na jāya[n]te (*sic*: read *jāyate*)
2. *ye dharmā hetuprabhavā hetun teṣāṃ tathāgata uvāca*
teṣāñ ca yo nirodha evamvādī mahāśramaṇaḥ ||
3. *rūpiṇas sarvvasattvā hi sarvva santi nirātmikāḥ*
sarvve bhadraṃ vipaśyanti mā kaścit pāpam āgaman ||

(4) Plate *k* bears symbols, including "a beautifully engraved lotus flower ... beneath a *cakra* [wheel] with eight rims, a moon (?), and two weapons, which may be identified as a *triśūla* [trident] and an *aṅkuśa* [goad]."[50]

Thus the larger plate *c* and the smaller plates *i* and *j* give us three examples of the *ajñānāc cīyate karma* and *ye dharmā* verses in combination with other verses.

kuśalaṃ at the end of plate *i*, verse 2, may be an interpolation, or an invocation or blessing like *śubhaṃ* or *maṅgalaṃ*. Plate *i*, verse 3, seems to be incomplete, since it gives only the first two lines of a celebrated verse. I cite a complete version from the anthology *Udānavarga* as edited by Bernhard from Central Asian manuscripts:[51]

sarvapāpasyākāraṇaṃ kuśalasyopasampadaḥ |
svacittaparyavadanam etad buddhasya śāsanam || 61

This verse summary of the (or of *a* or *any*) Buddha's teaching is known (with variants) from an inscription engraved in early Kuṣāṇa Brāhmī script on a natural rock face in Swat (present Pakistan)[52] and an ink inscription on a wooden slab written in Northwestern Kharoṣṭhī script from Niya, present-day Xinjiang, China.[53] The stanza occurs in texts of the Mahāsāṃghika-Lokottaravādins (*Mahāvastu*,[54] *Prātimokṣa-sūtra*,[55] *Bhikṣunī-vinaya*[56]), the Sarvāstivādins (*Prātimokṣa-sūtra*),[57] the Mūlasarvāstivādins (*Prātimokṣa-sūtra*),[58] and the Mahāvihāravāsin Theravādins (*Dhammapada, Mahāpadāna-sutta*),[59] as well as in texts of uncertain school affiliation like the Patna *Dhammapada*[60] and (in Chinese translation) the *Ekottarikāgama*.[61] The verse is sometimes placed at the end of manuscripts, along with the *ye dharmā* stanza,[62] or at the end of volumes in Tibetan Kanjurs.[63] It is, I believe, the only verse apart from the *ye dharmā* that is so employed.

De Casparis cites the *Mahāmāyūrī-vidyārājñī* as a parallel to plate *c*, verse 1 and plate *j*:[64]

sarve sattvāḥ sarve prāṇāḥ sarve bhūtāś ca kevalāḥ |
sarve vai sukhinaḥ santu sarve santu nirāmayāḥ |
sarve bhadrāṇi paśyantu mā kaścit pāpam āgamat ||

In the Sanskrit *Upasena-sūtra* in a manuscript from Turfan dated to the seventh century, the Buddha bestows the verses as a *mantrapada* against snake-bite:[65]

sukhinaḥ sarvve satvā hi sarvve satvā nirāmayāḥ |
sarvve bhadrāṇi paśyaṃtu mā caiṣāṃ pāpam āgamat ||

The verse also occurs in the *Vaiśalīpraveśa-mahāsūtra* and its parallel embedded in the *Bhaiṣajyavastu* of the Mūlasarvāstivādin *Vinaya*, both preserved in Tibetan translation. It is found in the Sanskrit counterpart of the *Vaiśalīpraveśa*, the *Mahāmantrānusāriṇī*, which, like the *Mahāmāyūrī* mentioned above, belongs to the *Pañcarakṣā* collection, and in the Tibetan translation of another *rakṣā*, the *Bhadrakarātrī-sūtra*.[66]

The verse is lacking in the Pāli counterpart of the *Upasena-sūtra*, the *Upasena-āsīvisa-sutta*.[67] But there are parallels elsewhere in Pāli: in the *Cullavagga* of the *Vinaya*, in the *Ahīrāja-sutta*, and in the *Khandhavattajātaka*:[68]

sabbe sattā sabbe pāṇā sabbe bhūtā ca kevalā
sabbe bhadrāni passantu mā kiñci (var. *kañci*) *pāpam āgamā* ||

In all of the Pali versions, it comes last in a set of four verses which are described as a *rakkhā* or *paritta* against snake-bite. In this capacity, the Pali verses are known as *Khandhaparitta*, No. 10 in the Lankan "Book of Protections," *Pirit-pota*.[69] Two of the set of four verses have parallels in the Sanskrit *Upasena-sūtra*; the first line of the *Mahāmāyūrī* citation is parallel to that of the Pāli verse cited here, but does not occur in the *Upasena-sūtra*.

As transcribed by de Casparis, the verse presents numerous difficulties, some of which he discusses in his notes. It is beyond the scope of this paper to deal with them, but I can conclude that the verse of the Jakarta gold plates is a popular stanza for protection and blessing that found its way into many texts, including the ((Mūla)Sarvāstivādin) *Upasena-sūtra* and the *Mahāmāyūrī*, a popular *rakṣā* which was translated into Chinese by the first half of the fourth century, and which was eventually included in the "Five Protections" (*Pañcarakṣā*) of Northern India, Nepal, and Tibet.[70]

6. INSCRIBED ROCK FROM BATU PAHAT, KALIMANTAN, INDONESIA[71]

A massive rock in the vicinity of the Kapuas River, West Kalimantan, Indonesia, is engraved with a set of inscriptions that include both the *ye dharmā* and *ajñānāc cīyate karma* stanzas (Figures 2.11 and 2.12). An early sketch of the rock appeared in *Tijdschrift voor Indische Taal-, Land-, en Volkenkunde*, Batavia, 1911, p. 325 (Figure 2.13). Chhabra, who described and transcribed the verses, wrote that "the rock in question, which is described as pyramidal in shape, is situated close to the springs of Soengei Tekarek at Batoe Pahat. To judge from the photograph, the face of the stone is almost completely covered with at least eight upright figures carved in low relief. The top-ornament, consisting of a series of superposed parasols, clearly indicates that seven of them are meant for effigies of stūpas ... the space on the body of each of the stūpas has been utilized for shorter inscriptions."[72] The photographs show that the rock is massive, and that the monument is quite unique. I have no further information about the context, or habitational or otherwise related sites.[73]

Chhabra makes no reference to script or date, except to say that the inscriptions are "somewhat later in date" than the *yūpa* inscriptions of East Kalimantan; since he dates the latter to *circa* 400 CE,[74] one may suppose he means to place the Batu Pahat inscription somewhere in the mid- or later fifth century. He notes that "the carvings are partly damaged and the inscriptions, too, have suffered a good deal", but he was able to give a rough transcription that identified the inscriptions as the *ajñānāc cīyate karma* and *ye dharmā* verses, repeated alternately, the former as numbers 1, 3, 6, and 8, and the latter as numbers 2, 5, and 7.

The central inscription, number 4, is described as "the longest and probably the most important of the group". Chhabra was not able to read much of it, and all that can be said is that it contains a date and a personal

FIGURE 2.11
Inscribed rock from Batu Pahat, Kalimantan, Indonesia (photo by Machi Suhadi)

FIGURE 2.12
Inscribed rock from Batu Pahat (back view, photo by Machi Suhadi: detail)

FIGURE 2.13
Inscribed rock from Batu Pahat

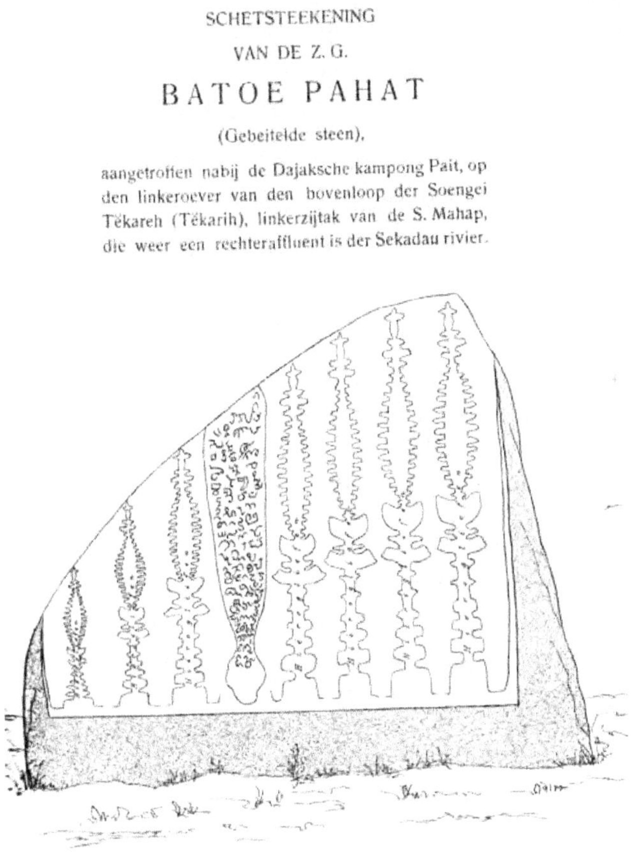

name, and refers to a dedication. One of the decipherable words is *caitya*. If this inscription can be read further, it should tell us more about the history of the rock and of Buddhism in the region.

Chhabra notes "that each of the seven shorter epigraphs contains also a few words in addition to the stanza."[75] He suggests that these may be "nothing but the names of some devotees", but from his transcription it is possible to suggest that they are the names of the seven Buddhas, as follows:[76]

Main Verse	*Additional Inscribed Words*	*Seven Buddhas*
(1) *ajñānāc cīyate*	*śa(?) ga(?) -e(?) ga(?)*	Śākyamuni
(2) *ye dharmā*	*– ā — - nya(?) — - kya(?)*	Kāśyapa
(3) *ajñānāc cīyate*	*nā(?) ka ma(?) ne(?)*	Kanakamuni
(4) –	—	—
(5) *ye dharmā*	*kra ka pu(?) nu sa(?) sya*	Krakutsunda
(6) *ajñānāc cīyate*	*vi(?) su(?) bhu(?) na(?)*	Viśvabhu
(7) *ye dharmā*	—	[Śikhin]
(8) *ajñānāc cīyate*	*vi(?) pu (?) vi (?)*	Vipaśyin

Chhabra's readings are incomplete and tentative, but the identification seems certain because of the number seven — seven verses associated with seven stūpas — and because the discernable elements of the names fit the traditional order, going back in time, from Śākyamuni to Vipaśyin. Furthermore, the stūpas decrease in height from right to left, which conforms to the tradition that the height of the Buddhas from Vipaśyin to Śākyamuni decreased progressively.[77]

If Chhabra's transcriptions are accurate, some of the names might be in Prakrit or in hybrid Sanskrit, since he reads *sa* in numbers 1 and 6 where standard Sanskrit would have *śa*. The available endings suggest that the names were in the genitive case: the stūpa and the *gāthā* of Śākyamuni, the stūpa and the *gāthā* of Kāśyapa, etc. For the association of verses with the Buddhas of the past, one may compare the concluding verses of the *Prātimokṣa-sūtra*s of the Mahāsāṃghikas, Sarvāstivādins, and Mūlasarvāstivādins, which assign verses to each of the seven Buddhas.[78]

7. INSCRIBED STONE STŪPA FROM MAKAM DAGANG, BANDAR SERI BEGAWAN, BRUNEI

A monolithic stone stūpa bearing the *ajñānāc cīyate karma* stanza on its base from Bandar Seri Begawan, the capital of Brunei, was published with photographs by Kongkaew Weeraprajak in *The Silpakorn Journal* in 1985.[79] The stūpa is in Makam Dagang Cemetery, an old Muslim burial ground on a hilltop overlooking the Brunei River in Jalan Residency; it remains there today, without any protection or special attention.[80] The tall, tapering stūpa is four-sided (Figure 2.14). Each side has the same design: a square base supports three circular rings and a round drum, above which rise at least eleven superposed parasols. The original number may have been thirteen. Kongkaew gives the height as about 4 feet. At least three

FIGURE 2.14
Inscribed stone stūpa, Dagang Cemetery, Bandar Seri Begawan, Brunei

faces of the base are inscribed, but two of them are too effaced to interpret. The one line that can be read (Figure 2.15) gives the opening line:

[*a*]*jñānāc cīyate ka*[81]

8. INSCRIBED STONE STŪPA FROM KAMPUNG BUANG ABAI, LIMBANG, SARAWAK, MALAYSIA

Another inscribed stūpa was found in the Muslim cemetery at Kampung Buang Abai on a hillside on a bank of the Limbang River, in Limbang District, Sarawak, Malaysia (Figures 2.16 to 2.20). The site, about 20 minutes from Limbang town by river, is about ten miles due southwest of Bandar Seri Begawan. The basic design resembles that of the Brunei stūpa, with deeper definition, but it appears that the Buang Abai stūpa was not carved fully in the round, but has a flat back. At present the stūpa

FIGURE 2.15
Inscription, stone stūpa, Dagang Cemetery, Bandar Seri Begawan, Brunei

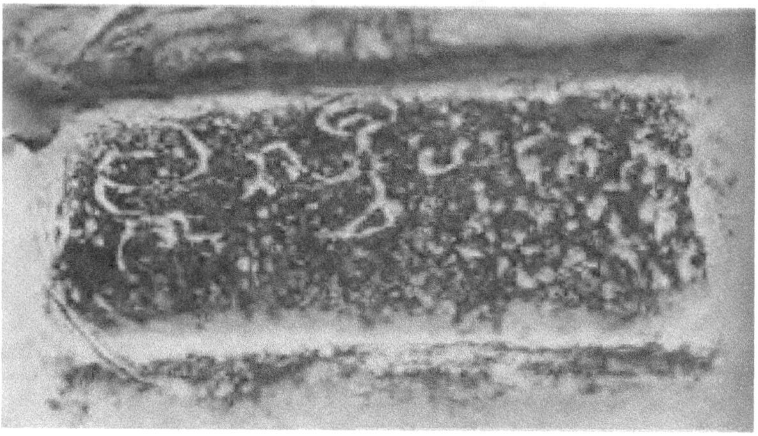

FIGURE 2.16
Stone stupa in its present position, Kampung Buang Abai, Limbang, Sarawak, Malaysia (photo Rod Orlina, May 2012)

FIGURE 2.17
Close-up of Kampung Buang Abai stone stupa, showing inscription (photo Rod Orlina, May 2012)

FIGURE 2.18
Close-up of Kampung Buang Abai stone stupa, showing relief stupa (photo Rod Orlina, May 2012)

FIGURE 2.19
Close-up of Kampung Buang Abai stone stupa, showing relief stupa (photo Rod Orlina, May 2012)

FIGURE 2.20
Inscribed stone stūpa, Kampung Buang Abai, Limbang, Sarawak

measures 42 × 70 × 33 cm.[82] Two lines of inscription can be made out on the rectangular base (Figure 2.21):[83]

aj[ñ]ānāc cīyate karmma
[ja]n[ma]na[ḥ] karmma kāraṇa[ṃ].

The base at the back also bears an inscription, but it is too effaced to read.

Both the Makam Dagang and Buang Abai stūpas carry the *ajñānāc cīyate verse*, probably originally in full. In both cases, Kongkaew dates the script, a variety of Southeast Asian Brāhmī classed as "Pallava" in Thai, to the twelfth century B.E., that is, *circa* 650–750 CE.[84] The inscriptions share features or palaeographic fashions like the rectangular double *ra*,[85] and a seventh century date seems reasonable. According to Haji Matussin Bin Omar,[86] these are the only stūpas discovered in the area to date; he suggests that they may have been removed from an unknown Buddhist site or sites to be reused as gravestones. He notes that stone blocks from the old site of Kota Baru have been reused in this manner at several old Muslim cemeteries in Brunei. At both the Makam Dagan cemetery and the Royal cemetery nearby, there are mounds, red baked bricks, and stone architectural elements. There is an urgent need for protection and scientific

FIGURE 2.21
Inscription, stone stūpa from Buang Abai, Limbang, Sarawak

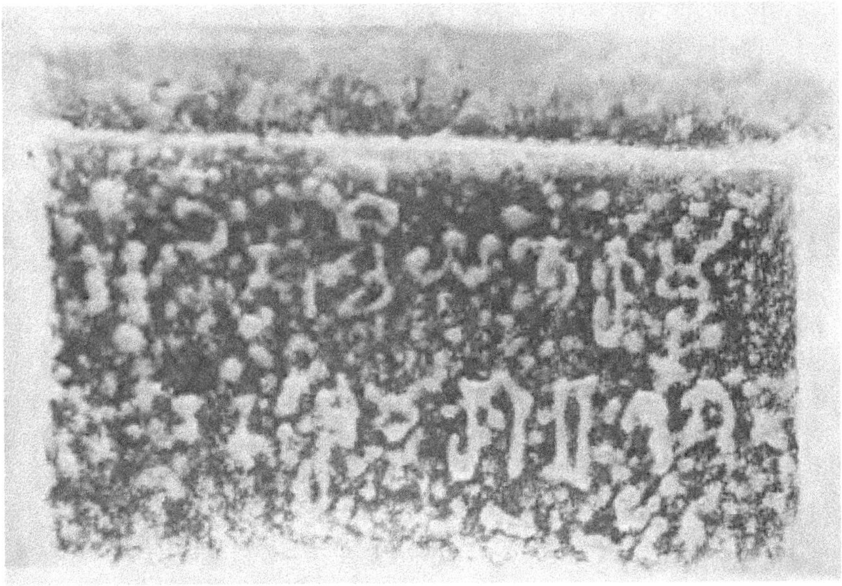

excavation of both sites, which are important to the history of Brunei and of the region.

DISTRIBUTION OF THE *AJÑĀNĀC CĪYATE KARMA* VERSE

With the exception of the Jakarta gold plates, of which the provenance is unknown, the inscriptions studied here were all found along the estuaries or river systems of Southeast Asia. Inscriptions 1, 2, and 3 are from the west coast of the central Malay Peninsula. The precise find-spots of Inscriptions 1 and 2 are not known. Inscription 1 was found near Bukit Miriam, a hill or outcrop (*bukit*) to the north of the Muda River; Inscription 2 was found at an unidentified site in the Northern District of Province Wellesley,[87] which lies south of the Muda River. Inscription 3 was found at Kampung Sungai Mas, near the mouth of the Muda in Kedah. Allen notes that Bukit Miriam is 2.4 kilometres north of Kampung Sungai Mas, on the same (west) side of the Sungai Terus.[88] The region in general, defined by the Muda and Merbok Rivers and their tributaries, is rich in archaeological remains: during his survey of the area in the late 1930s, Quaritch Wales identified thirty sites, at least five of which may have been Buddhist, the remainder Brahmanical.[89] Quaritch Wales discovered, *inter alia*, a clay tablet inscribed with three Sanskrit verses from the "Questions of Sāgaramati" (*Sāgaramati-paripṛcchā*), a Mahāyāna sūtra (Figure 2.22).[90] A second tablet with the same verses, this time from Kampung Sungai Mas, has recently been found.[91] The verses enumerate the qualities of the Tathāgata and describe *pratītyasamutpāda* from the viewpoint of insubstantiality, and can possibly represent the *dharmakāya*.

It appears that the stone used for the three slabs was extracted and carved locally, although scientific testing remains to be conducted. Allen and Christie differ on the whether the inscriptions were found *in situ*. Allen asserts that they remain in their primary contexts: "there is no convincing evidence that any of the objects have been removed to a secondary location since their initial placement in or on the ground."[92] For Christie, on the other hand, that the three stones "may have been removed from an early shrine or group of shrines in the Musa valley seems very likely".[93]

Inscription 4 is from West Java. The provenance of Inscription 5 is not known, although, as de Casparis suggests, it is likely that it is from Java itself. Inscriptions 6, 7, and 8 are from the island of Borneo. While Inscription 6 was found upriver in western Borneo, Inscriptions 7 and 8 come from Brunei and Limbang in the northeast of the island. Brunei was

FIGURE 2.22
Verses from *Sāgaramati-paripṛcchā*

an ancient entrepôt of considerable importance, and remains from the area include large quantities of ceramics from the Tang and Sung periods.[94] Little is known of the political geography of the huge island of Borneo during the period in question, so we cannot even surmise whether there was a single political or cultural entity, or a series of discrete deltaic trading states. Given the fact that overland routes were obstructed by jungle, rivers, and mountains, and that communication must have been restricted to the coasts, the latter seems more likely.[95] O'Connor holds that "evidence suggests that there was a Hindu-Buddhist settlement in the Kapuas basin area".[96]

The possibility that the grand mariner Buddhagupta of Inscription 2 might have been connected with Karṇasuvarṇa in Bengal has been discussed above. Kedah — the Kaṭāha of Indian inscriptions and literature — stood at the head of the Straits of Malacca, and was one of the most important

FIGURE 2.23
Buddhagupta inscription, detail (photo Peter Skilling)

FIGURE 2.24
Stone stūpa finial from Nakhon Pathom, Bangkok National Museum

ports and entrepôts of the western Malay Peninsula, the western end of trans-peninsular routes to the Gulf of Siam. The Straits of Malacca led past Sumatra and on to Java, to Borneo, to the islands of today's Philippines, to Champā, to China, Korea, and Japan. The *ajñānāc cīyate karma* stanza appears at several nodal points along the ancient trade routes from India to China, with the proviso that routes are complex and multidirectional, and there is no reason to suggest that the verse moved in any single direction.

STATUS OF THE *AJÑĀNĀC CĪYATE KARMA* VERSE

The *ajñānāc cīyate karma* verse was inscribed at eight different sites in (pen)insular Southeast Asia, between the latter half of the fifth and the eighth centuries CE, or, more realistically, during the sixth and the seventh centuries. More inscriptions may once have existed, and have since been destroyed or lost, or await discovery — inscriptions on precious metals only survive by miracle.[97]

What was the status of the *ajñānāc cīyate* verse? In most cases, it is associated with other verses or words attributed to the Buddha.[98] In the Jakarta Museum plates and the Kalimantan inscription,[99] the *ajñānāc cīyate karma* verse precedes the ubiquitous *ye dharmā* verse. The contexts leave no doubt that the stanza was revered as *Buddhavacana*, the word of the Awakened One — that it enjoyed full canonical authority.[100] If my interpretation of the Batu Pahat inscription is correct, the massive stone record there invoked not only Śākyamuni, but all of the seven Buddhas.

SCHOOL AFFILIATION OF THE *AJÑĀNĀC CĪYATE KARMA* VERSE

Where did the verse come from? Who spread it in the region? Laymen or monastics? If the latter, what school or order disseminated it over such a wide area? Here it is customary to turn to scholar-monk and Vinaya specialist Yijing, who travelled, lived, and studied in Southeast Asia from 671 to 672 and from 688 to 695 — which very possibly coincides with at least some of the inscriptions. Debate about the location of Śrīvijaya, where the formidable memorialist spent several years, continues without resolution, but it is in any case likely that he visited the important entrepôt of Kedah, the site of three of the inscriptions. Yijing states that the four main *nikāya*s or Buddhist monastic orders were represented "in the islands of the Southern Sea — consisting of more than ten countries".[101] This statement is routinely invoked in discussions on the Buddhism of

Southeast Asia, but it is too vague to offer much help in understanding the evolution of Buddhism across the vast area involved. Yijing and many of his contemporaries in North India saw Buddhism through the model of the four schools, and Yijing's statement does not amount to much more than saying that any of the schools could have been in the region.

Is it possible to trace the *ajñānāc cīyate karma* verse to any specific textual tradition? The *ajñānāc cīyate karma* verse and associated texts, including the *ye dharmā* stanzas on the Jakarta gold plates and the *ye dharmā* inscribed on a stone from Site 1, Kedah,[102] are all in Sanskrit. Like the *ye dharmā*, the *ajñānāc cīyate karma* verse should have been acceptable to all schools in terms of doctrinal content. It can be interpreted as a summary of dependent arising (*pratītyasamutpāda*), as follows:

In natural order (*anuloma*):

ajñānāc cīyate karma
= the formations are contingent upon ignorance (*avidyāpratyayāḥ saṃskārāḥ*);
janmanaḥ karma kāraṇaṃ
= the arising (*samudaya*) of the remaining factors (*aṅga*);

In reverse order (*pratiloma*):

jñānān na cīyate karma = with the cessation of ignorance, the formations cease (*avidyānirodhāt saṃskāranirodhaḥ*);
karmābhāvān na jāyate = the cessation (*nirodha*) of the remaining factors (*aṅga*).

The *ye dharmā* verse was interpreted in similar fashion:

ye dharmā hetuprabhavāḥ = *pratītyasamutpannāḥ dharmāḥ*
(*anuloma*): *teṣāṃ hetuṃ* = *avidyāpratyayāḥ saṃskārāḥ*
(*pratiloma*): *teṣāṃ nirodha* = *avidyānirodhāt saṃskāranirodhaḥ*.

That all instances of the verse and the related texts are in Sanskrit does not say anything about the school affiliation. While different schools did transmit their scriptures in different Indic languages, and linguistic identities are reflected in Indian inscriptions that cite canonical texts, this may not be the same where the local dialects were non-Indic, as in Southeast Asia.[103] The same may be said of the script: in order to be understood, any established school, or any school seeking to gain a foothold in the region, would have adopted the already prevalent Southeast Asian Brāhmī script (while instances of early Nāgarī do occur, for example, in the Ratubaka inscription and on numerous moulded tablets, the Northern scripts never caught on). Nor do the accompanying texts help us at this stage of research. The *ye dharmā* and *sarvapāpasya* verses and the *pratītyasamutpāda-sūtra* were universally accepted. The *sukhinaḥ sarvve satvā hi* verse can be traced to (Mūla)Sarvāstivādin texts, but it also occurs in the *Mahāmāyūrī*, a popular *rakṣā* text, belonging to an early group of verses used as a charm against snake-bite. Even beyond that, a similar set of verses is well known in the modern Hindu tradition, in which for many they are part of the daily recitations.[104] In the Jakarta gold plates, the *sūtra* and commentary should presumably belong to the same school as the *ajñānāc cīyate karma* verse, but the school affiliation of the Jakarta texts, if any, remains undetermined.

No parallels to the *ajñānāc cīyate karma* stanza occur in the "Pali canon" transmitted by the Mahāvihāravāsin Theravādins of Ceylon.[105] I have been unable to trace the verse in the (Mūla)Sarvāstivādin texts that survive in Sanskrit and in translation.[106] It therefore seems unlikely that (Mūla)Sarvāstivādins were responsible for the inscriptions, despite Yijing's statement that they were predominant in the region. Although a number of texts of the Lokottaravādin branch of the Mahāsāṃghika school have been preserved, and do not contain the verse, the Mahāsāṃghikas remain a possibility: no complete corpus of a Lokottaravādin canon survives, and we know next to nothing about the texts of other branches of the Mahāsāṃghikas, some of which had centres in the south of India, an area that played a significant role in the dissemination of Indian culture to Southeast Asia. This brings us to the Sāṃmitīyas, the least known of the major schools, for the simple fact that their canon has not come down to us, and only a few non-canonical texts have been preserved in Sanskrit and Prakrit, and in Chinese and Tibetan translation.[107] We have discussed the possibility that Buddhagupta was a resident of the Raktamṛttikā-vihāra at Karṇasuvarṇa, in present-day West Bengal, where the Sāṃmitīya school was well represented. The Sāmmitīya saṃgha was also well established in Sindh, another centre of the Indian seaborne trade. Yijing places the Sāmmitīyas in Southeast Asia before the Mahāsāṃghikas (though in small numbers) which accords with the proposed early dates for the inscriptions. The Sammitīyas remain a possible candidate, but there are other possibilities. The verses could belong to another of the remaining "eighteen schools", whose presence was not noticed or noted by the contemporary witness Yijing, even if he is generally considered reliable: de Casparis describes him as "not only perfectly honest, but also learned and well informed".[108] There is some resonance in terms of vocabulary in a prose passage on the *pratītyasamutpāda* in the immense Sanskrit *Saddharmasmṛtyupasthāna-sūtra*, again of uncertain school if any, which may merit further scrutiny.[109] Could the verse occur in the voluminous literature of the Mahāyāna? There is nothing indicatively Mahāyānistic about the verse, or the associated texts, and it is not prominent in any of the well-known Mahāyāna *sūtra*s.

What is the function of the verse? I doubt that there is, or that there can, or should be, a single or simple answer. The practice of installing texts, the Buddha's word, was widespread across Asia — the texts empower or consecrate an image or a stūpa. This may well be the case with the *ajñānāc cīyate karma* inscriptions. But are there other possibilities? Could the inscriptions have funerary or memorial functions as well? Was, for example, the Buddhagupta slab erected by Buddhagupta himself, during his lifetime — or can it be a posthumous memorial? The *ajñānac cīyate karma* verse is certainly associated with the stūpa, and more than just that: it is regularly associated with a *particular type* of stūpa, which "is widely distributed around mainland, peninsular, and insular Southeast Asia in the form of stone stūpas, relief carvings, small bronzes, and moulded images ... a widely distributed regional type that is not imported or based on any immediate Indian protoype."[110] This stūpa type, however, goes beyond the geographical range of our stanza — it is, for example, associated with the Pali *ye dhammā* stanza in Siam, rather than with Sanskrit texts as in the Southern Seas. Examples from Prachinburi in eastern Thailand (Figures 2.25A and 25B) and from Tuy Hoa in Vietnam (Figure 2.26), from Central Java (Figures 2.27 and 2.28) and Bali (Figures 2.29 and 2.30) are remarkably similar, and are close to the stūpas and stūpa reliefs of Java and elsewhere. The stūpa type seems to be a regional Southeast Asian development — a remarkable spread of similar forms across a wide region for a period of several centuries, which merits serious study and further precision.[111]

Returning to this verse inscription after many years — much of my research was done in the early 1980s — I reflect that the *ajñānāc cīyate karma* verse presents an extraordinary case. Here we have a verse that is found at eight sites. It is associated with other well-known verses. It is written for display on stone, and for installation on clay and gold. It is written on two of the most exceptional Buddhist documents of Buddhist Southeast Asia — the golden book of Jakarta and the Batu Pahat rock.

The *ajñānāc cīyate karma* stanza is a verse of power and benediction, but it is not known in any Indian or other Buddhist text. It is equal to the *ye dharmā* stanza, and it stands in its own right with the *pratītyasamutpāda*

FIGURE 2.25A AND B
Prachinburi, Prachinburi National Museum, Prachinburi, Thailand
(photo by Peter Skilling)

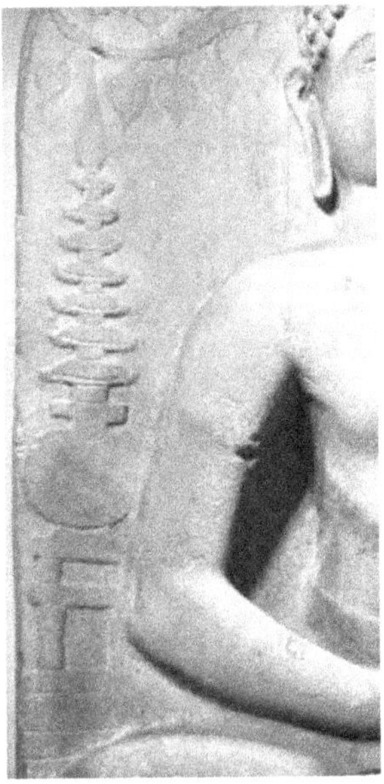

FIGURE 2.26
Inscribed stele from Phu Yen, Tuy Hoa, Vietnam
(photo Tran Ky Phuong)

FIGURE 2.27
Bronze stūpa. Central Java, 8th–9th c., 18.5 × 6 cm.
National Museum No. 5610

FIGURE 2.28
Bronze stūpa. Candi Ijo, Prambanan, Central Java, 8th–9th c., 28 × 5.8 cm. Sonobudoyo Museum No. 247 1C 139

FIGURE 2.29
Stone relief of stūpa from Bedoeloe, Bali

Figuur 3. Pajoeng-reeks van een relief-stūpa als op figuur 2. Bĕdoeloe (Bali). Zie figuur 5.

Foto O. D. 9331.

formula and with *rakṣā* verses. What is the source of its authority? Could the verse come from a text that was redacted in Southeast Asia, that is, a local text that circulated in the region? This possibility must be left open. In any case, there remains the question of *choice*, of *selection*. Who selected the *ajñānāc cīyate karma* verse, and who chose to associate it with stūpas, stūpa reliefs, and installations? Was the selection and sanction done by a local *saṃgha*, codified as one of their ritual practices, perhaps (and I stress, *perhaps*) connected with funerals? Who were the sponsors? Who sponsored the opulent Jakarta gold plates, and why?

The stone slabs and stūpas from the Malay Peninsula and Borneo were public documents. Who erected them? Were they set up by individuals, or by local *saṃgha*s or Buddhist communities? How were the slabs received? Were they objects of reverence or offerings? Were they loci for ceremonies? The lack of context gives us little if anything to go on, but these are

FIGURE 2.30
Stūpa from stone relief, Bedoeloe, Bali

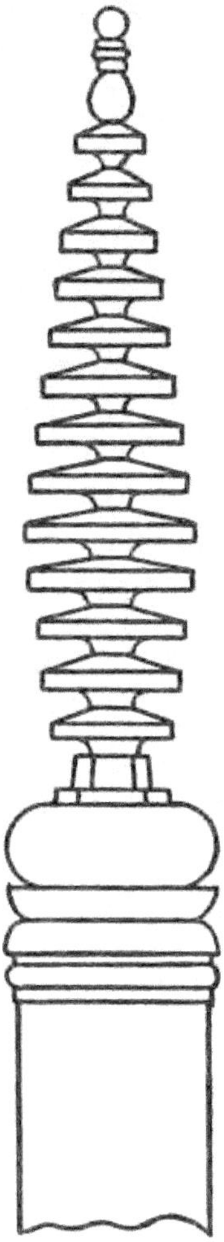

Figuur 7. Reconstructie-schets van een der relief-stūpa's bij Bĕdoeloe (Bali). Afmetingen geschat. Zie figuur 2 en 3.

questions that need to be asked, especially in light of the new material remains of Buddhist ritual and liturgical cultures that have recently come to light. Recent research and publication, for example by Rod Orlina and by Arlo Griffiths, has given a glimpse of a ritual presence of the goddess Mahāpratisarā in the archipelago from Mindanao to Sumatra — a deity who is present in Java in the form of bronze statues and a large stone relief on the walls of Candi Mendut in Central Java, and who travelled to China where she inspired some of the earliest printed documents in the world in the form of yantras.[112] Mahāpratisarā joins other female deities like Tārā and Cundā, for whom there is iconographic if not yet explicit local ritual evidence. The peninsular and insular worlds of the "Southern Seas" shared in a wide culture of ritual and ideas that stretched from Central Asia to East Asia.[113] Inscriptions from the region show the presence of some key Mahāyāna practices, aspirations like *praṇidhāna* and *pariṇāmana*, and of Tantric installations connected with Hevajra, who also has an iconographic presence in Sumatra, and who enjoyed a particular vogue in North India, Tibet, and the Khmer lands from the tenth to twelfth centuries.

The variety of the material realization of the inscribed texts and their wide distribution precludes any easy conclusions. The inscriptions reveal worlds in contact, in close conversation; the evidence for Buddhist activity is embedded in an organic and layered complexity. The sites have often been inhabited by much earlier pre- and proto-historic communities, which can be traced through grave and trade goods, technological accomplishments, and alterations of the landscape. A new picture of textual, ritual, and iconographic networks is tentatively beginning to emerge. There is a long way to go to assimilate and to understand them, but the research embodied in the present volume and other publications contributes to new perspectives that guide us further in our quest for understanding.

Acknowledgements

I thank Kanniṭhā Kasiṇa-Ubol and Pierre-Yves Manguin for supplying materials, Pierre Pichard for preparing the maps, and Rod Orlina, Oliver Lee, Arlo Griffiths and D. Christian Lammerts for their help with photographs and information about the sites. I am indebted to Santi Pakdeekham, Adeline Woon, Saerji, Dan Stuart, and Giuliana Martini for helping in many ways, and to Mattia Salvini for catching a grievous error at the eleventh hour. I am grateful to Ulrich Timme Kragh for his help in putting the text into final form.

Notes

1. Lieut.-Col. [James] Low, "On an Inscription from Keddah", *Journal of the Asiatic Society of Bengal* 18, no. 1 (March 1849): p. 247 and Pl. X. This is supplemented by J.W. L[aidlay], "Note on the Foregoing", which

includes a transcription of the verses in Nāgarī, reproduced as Chap. XXII in *Miscellaneous Papers relating to Indo-China*, Vol. I, edited by Reinhold Rost, pp. 233–34 (London: Trübner & Co, 1886) along with some further remarks, including those by Kern (p. 234). See also B. Ch. Chhabra, *Expansion of Indo-Aryan Culture during Pallava Rule (as evidenced by inscriptions)* (Delhi: Munshi Ram Manohar Lal, 1965), pp. 18–20 (first published in *Journal of the Asiatic Society of Bengal, Letters* Vol. I (1935): 1–64); Michel Jacq-Hergoualc'h, *La civilisation de ports-entrepôts du Sud Kedah (Malaysia) V^e^–XIVe siècle* (Paris: L'Harmattan, 1992), pp. 224–26; idem, *The Malay Peninsula: Crossroads of the Maritime Silk Road (100 BC–1300 AD)*, translated by Victoria Hobson (Leiden: Brill, 2002), pp. 219–21. See Jane Allen, "An Inscribed Tablet from Kedah, Malaysia: Comparison with Earlier Finds", *Asian Perspectives* XXVII, no. 1 (1986–1987): 35–57, Table 3, for a list of published reports and references with a summary of their contents. Low describes the material as "a sort of slate", but Allen (pp. 39–41) suggests that the material was more probably shale. For the archaeology of Kedah up to 1957, see Michael Sullivan, "Excavations in Kedah and Province Wellesley, 1957", *Journal of the Malayan Branch of the Royal Asiatic Society* XXXI, Pt. 1 (1958): 188–223. See also (in Malay) Nik Hassan Shuhaimi Nik Abdul Rahman and Othman Mohd. Yatim, *Warisan Lembah Bujang* (Kuala Lumpur, [1992] 2006).

J.W. Laidlay was appointed Co-secretary of the Asiatic Society of Bengal, Calcutta, in November 1846 and Secretary in 1847 during Sir Henry Hardinge's tenure as President (October 1844–47). He contributed a number of articles to the *Proceedings* and the *Journal of the Asiatic Society* — see Rajendralal Mitra, A.F.R. Hoernle, and Baboo P.N. Bose, *Centenary Review of the Asiatic Society 1784–1884* (Calcutta: The Asiatic Society, [1885] 1986), p. 152.

2. For the *ye dharmā* stanza, see P. Skilling, "A Buddhist inscription from Go Xoai, Southern Vietnam and notes towards a classification of *ye dharmā* inscriptions", in *80 pi Sattrachan Dr Prasert Na Nakhon: ruam botkhwam wichakan dan charuek lae ekasan boran* [80 Years: A collection of articles on epigraphy and ancient documents published on the occasion of the celebration of the eightieth birthday of Prof. Dr Prasert Na Nagara] (Bangkok: Phikhanet Printing Center, 1999 [2542]), pp. 171–87; idem, "Traces of the Dharma: Preliminary reports on some *ye dhammā* and *ye dharmā* inscriptions from Mainland South-East Asia", *Bulletin de l'École française d'Extrême-Orient* 90–91, pp. 273–87; idem, "Buddhist sealings and the *ye dharmā* stanza", in *Archaeology of Early Historic South Asia*, edited by Gautam Sengupta and Sharmi Chakraborty (New Delhi/Kolkata: Pragati Publications/Centre for Archaeological Studies and Training, Eastern India, 2008), pp. 503–25. For the *ye dhammā* inscriptions of Arakan, see Kyaw Minn Htin, "Early Buddhism in Myanmar: *Ye Dhammā* Inscriptions from Arakan", Chap. 19

in *Early Interactions between South and Southeast Asia: Reflections on Cross-Cultural Exchange*, edited by Pierre-Yves Manguin, A. Mani, and Geoff Wade (Singapore: Institute of Southeast Asian Studies; New Delhi: Manohar India, 2011), pp. 385–406.

3. Here all other complete versions read *na* ***cīyate***, "is not **accumulated**," instead of *na* ***kriyate***, "is not **created**."
4. No ancient, indigenous name of the script is known. Since the nineteenth century, modern scholars have assigned different names to what is in principle the same script: Pallava/Pallawa, pre-Angkorian, etc. It seems better to use a more neutral term like "Southeast Asian Brāhmī" until and unless better terminologies are found.
5. Chhabra, *Expansion of Indo-Aryan Culture*, p. 26.
6. Allen, "An Inscribed Tablet".
7. *Journal of the Asiatic Society of Bengal* IV (1835), Pl. III, reproduced in R. Rost, *Miscellaneous Papers relating to Indo-China*, facing p. 225. Province Wellesley, now officially named Seberang Perai, is a narrow coastal strip opposite the island of Penang, which was leased to the British East India Company in Penang by the Sultan of Kedah in 1800.
8. Lieut.-Col. James Low, "An Account of Several Inscriptions found in Province Wellesley, on the Peninsula of Malacca", *Journal of the Asiatic Society of Bengal* XVII, Part 2 (July 1848): 62–66; reprinted in Rost, *Miscellaneous Papers relating to Indo-China*, pp. 223–26.
9. J.W. Laidlay, "Note on the Inscriptions from Singapore and Province Wellesley. Forwarded by the Hon. Col. Butterworth, C.B. and Col. J. Low", *Journal of the Asiatic Society of Bengal* XVII, Part 2 (July 1848): 66–72; reprinted in Rost, *Miscellaneous Papers relating to Indo-China*, pp. 227–32.
10. Chhabra, *Expansion of Indo-Aryan Culture*, pp. 20–26; Jacq-Hergoualc'h, *The Malay Peninsula*, pp. 214–16. Jacq-Hergoualc'h, *La civilisation de ports-entrepôts*, pp. 219–22, gives the text of the Buddhagupta inscription twice, since he also includes it with the inscriptions on the large rock at Cherok Tokun (pp. 217–19). The mistake (which from his notes might go back to Lamb) stems from the fact that Low reports both inscriptions in the same article, the Tokun inscription as (A), the Buddhagupta epigraph as (B). See Allen, "An Inscribed Tablet", Table 2, for a summary of publications on the inscription. For further references, see Dinesh Chandra Sircar, *Select Inscriptions bearing on Indian History and Civilization from the Sixth Century B.C. to the Sixth Century A.D.*, Vol. I ([Calcutta 1965] 3rd edition, Delhi and Madras: Asian Humanities Press, 1986), No. 73 (p. 497). Sircar's reading is baffling: it opens with the *ye dharmā* verse, gives a full reading of the nearly effaced lines *c* and *d* of the *ajñānāc cīyate karma* verse, and omits the entire section beginning with *sarvveṇa*. It appears as if the eminent epigraphist conflated several eye-copies.
11. See John Anderson, *Catalogue and Hand-book of the Archaeological Collections in the Indian Museum*, Part II, *Gupta and Inscription Galleries*

([Calcutta: 1883] Patna: Indological Book Corporation, repr. 1977), pp. 189–90. The slab is M.P.1, under "Malay Peninsula". Originally it was displayed on the second-floor open-air Inscription Gallery — see Figure 2.3, where it is splashed with pigeon droppings — but now has disappeared into the storage. For other photos, see Chhabra, *Expansion of Indo-Aryan Culture*, Pl. 3 (good estampages, here reproduced as Figure 2.4), and Shyamalkanti Chakravarti, *A Descriptive Catalogue of the Prakrit and Sanskrit Inscriptions in the Epigraphy Gallery Indian Museum*, Indian Museum Catalogue No. 2 (Calcutta: Indian Museum, 1977) Pl. III, fig. 2. The inscription has been studied along with the Kampung Sungai Mas inscription (No. 3 following) by Kongkaew Weeraprajak, "Charuek runraek khong malaysia" [The Earliest Sanskrit Inscriptions Found in Malayasia], *The Silpakorn Journal* 33, no. 4 (1989): 30–37.

12. Only the first few *akṣaras* of the third and fourth lines can be read; the rest is defaced. However, as noted by Chhabra (*Expansion of Indo-Āryan Culture*, p. 22, n. 2), the *ī* is quite clear, suggesting that the inscription read *cīyate* along with the other versions, against the supposed *kriyate* of No. 1.
13. For the superfluous *i*, which is clear in the photograph, and for the earlier readings of Kern, cf. Chhabra, *Expansion of Indo-Aryan Culture*, p. 22, nn. 3, 4, and 5, and p. 23.
14. For *vāstavya* in Indian Buddhist inscriptions, see Keisho Tsukamoto, *A Comprehensive Study of the Indian Buddhist Inscriptions*, Part I, *Texts, Notes and Japanese Translation* (Kyoto: Heirakuji Shoten, 1996), I Bihār 2, Kurkihar 59, IV Sāñcī 95.5, Saheṭh-Maheṭh 7.20, III Nāsik 16.7, 8–9, Kaṇheri 14.2. For its use in the colophon of an eleventh century Nepalese *Aṣṭasāhasrikā Prajñāpāramitā* manuscript, see Luciano Petech, *Mediaeval History of Nepal (c. 750–1482)* (Serie Orientale Roma, LIV, Rome: Istituto per il Medio ed Estremo Oriente, 1984), p. 46, ult. *Śrī-Laṃjuguṅke vāstavya Gaṅgarāṇakena lekhitam-idaṃ*.
15. Kongkaew, "Charuek runraek", p. 30.
16. For the Red-Earth land, see Paul Wheatley, *The Golden Khersonese* (Kuala Lumpur: University of Malaya Press, [1961] 1980), Chap. III.
17. Sudhir Ranjan Das, *Rājbāḍīdāṅgā: 1962 (Chiruṭī: Jadupur), An Interim Report on Excavations at Rājbāḍīdāṅgā and Terracotta Seals and Sealings* (The Asiatic Society Monograph Series, Vol. XIV, Calcutta: Asiatic Society, 1968), pp. 56–59 and Pls. I.1, III. Later finds are reported, for example, in *Indian Archaeology 1968–69 — A Review*, edited by B.B. Lal (New Delhi: Archaeological Survey of India, 1971), p. 43 and *Indian Archaeology 1972–73 — A Review*, edited by M.N. Deshpande (New Delhi: Archaeological Survey of India, 1978), pp. 37–38. See also Debala Mitra, *Buddhist Monuments* (Calcutta: Sahitya Samsad, 1971), p. 236; Sircar, *Select Inscriptions*, p. 497, n. 3; Chakravarti, *A Descriptive Catalogue*, p. 6.

    Monastic seals, which give the name of a monastery (*vihāra*) or great monastery (*mahāvihāra*), are known from many sites in Northern India, but have not, so far as I know, been found in the Deccan, the South, or outside of India. For Buddhist seals and sealings, see Kiran Kumar Thaplyal, *Studies in Ancient Indian Seals: A Study of North Indian Seals and Sealings from circa Third Century B.C. to Mid-Seventh Century A.D.* (Lucknow: Akhila Bharatiya Sanskrit Parishad, 1972), pp. 206–22 (for monastic seals, especially pp. 206–16); J. Ph. Vogel, "Seals of Buddhist Monasteries in Ancient India", *Journal of the Ceylon Branch of the Royal Asiatic Society*, Centenary Volume (1845–1945), New Series, Vol. I (Colombo, 1950), pp. 27–32. Many more seals and sealings have come to light in excavations in recent decades.

18. The finds at Rājbāḍīḍāṅgā — such as one sealing in seventh–eighth century Pallava script and one in Roman letters — might suggest that the area had international connections, but that would be normal for an estuarine site. For a Greek seal, see Das, *Rājbāḍīḍāṅgā: 1962*, p. 60, Pl. I, 2 and 2A. *Indian Archaeology 1968–69 – A Review*, edited by B.B. Lal (New Delhi: Archaeological Survey of India, 1971), p. 43 mentions a sealing bearing "Roman letters". For a sealing in "seventh–eighth century Pallava script", see *Indian Archaeology 1968–69*, p. 43. A "South Indian Pallava" sealing discovered in 1970 is mentioned but not illustrated in *Indian Archaeology 1972–73 – A Review*, edited by M.N. Deshpande (New Delhi: Archaeological Survey of India, 1978), p. 37.

19. The first character 絡 *lao* or *luo* (*lok* in Cantonese), which is not listed in Karlgren's dictionary, is regularly used to transcribe Sanskrit *ra* or *rak*. The three remaining characters 多未知 are reconstructed by Karlgren as having had the following pronunciation in archaic Chinese: ˛tâ-mjʷẹi'-tạ, thus resembling °*tamṛttikā*. See Bernhard Karlgren, *Analytic Dictionary of Chinese and Sino-Japanese* (New York: Dover Publications, 1974 [first published Paris: Paul Geuthner, 1923]), s.v. nos. 1006, 1303, 1218.

20. Li Rongxi, *The Great Tang Dynasty Record of the Western Regions* (Berkeley: Numata Center for Buddhist Translation and Research (BDK English Tripiṭaka 79), 1996), pp. 303–305 (see also Li Rongxi, *A Biography of the Tripiṭaka Master of the Great Ci'en Monastery of the Great Tang Monastery* [Berkeley: Numata Center for Buddhist Translation and Research (BDK English Tripiṭaka 77), 1995], pp. 109–10), and the classical translations — Samuel Beal, *Si-Yu-Ki: Buddhist Records of the Western World*, Vol. II ([London: Routledge 1884] New Delhi: Motilal Banarsidass, 1981), pp. 201–204; Thomas Watters, *On Yuan Chwang's Travels in India (A.D. 629–645)*, 2nd Indian ed. ([London: Royal Asiatic Society, 1904–05] New Delhi: Munshiram Manoharlal, 1973), pp. 191–93; Prabodh Chandra Bagchi, *She-kia-fang-che* (Santiniketan: Visva-Bharati, 1959), p. 106; Samuel Beal, *The Life of Hiuen-Tsiang by the Shaman Hwui Li* ([London: K. Paul, Trench, Trübner, 1911] New Delhi: Munshiram Manoharlal, 1973), pp. 131–32.

21. Li, *The Great Tang Dynasty Record*, pp. 303–305. The Biography (Li, *A Biography of the Tripiṭaka Master*, p. 109; Beal, *The Life of Hiuen-Tsiang*,

p. 131) mentions only 300 monks, but agrees on their school and the number of monasteries.

22. The archaeological record from Tamluk — although systematic work remains to be undertaken — apparently does not reflect the supposed importance of Tāmralipti: see, e.g., Kaushik Gangopadhyay, "Archaeological Investigation at Tamluk: An Early Historic Settlement in Coastal West Bengal", *Pratna Samiksha: A Journal of Archaeology*, Kolkata: Centre of Archaeological Studies and Training, Eastern India, new series, vol. 1 (2010), pp. 53–63.
23. J. Ph. Vogel, "Prakrit Inscriptions from Ghantasala", in *Epigraphia Indica* XXVII, edited by B. Ch. Chhabra and N. Lakshminarayan Rao (Delhi: The Manager of Publications, 1956; repr. New Delhi 1985), no. 1, Inscription E, line 1: *mahānavika sivaka*. For *mahānāvika* and *mahānāikan*, a possible parallel occurs in early Tamil literature; ibid., p. 2, and p. 2, n. 3. Further, see Tsukamoto, *A Comprehensive Study*, II Ghaṇṭasāla 5, pp. 299–300. For the gold seal and Bang Kluay, see Bunchar Pongpanich, *Roi lukpat* [*Beyond Beads*] (Bangkok: Matichon Publishing House, 2552 B.E. [2009]) / **บัญชา พงษ์พานิช, รอยลูกปัด** (**กรุงเทพฯ: มติชน**, 2552), pp. 162–76.
24. For Pali references, see Margaret Cone, *A Dictionary of Pali*, Part II (Bristol: The Pali Text Society, 2010), p. 531; for Buddhist Sanskrit, see Franklin Edgerton, *Buddhist Hybrid Sanskrit Grammar and Dictionary*, Vol. II: Dictionary (New Haven: Yale University Press, 1953, repr. Delhi: Motilal Banarsidass, 1972), p. 355, s.v. *pauruṣeya*, where *nāvika* is one of the members of a ship's crew (described as five, with only four enumerated), at *Avadānaśataka* I p. 200.5, II p. 61.5. The late ninth-century Sanskrit-Tibetan lexicon *Mahāvyutpatti* §§3850–55 lists six, giving the Tibetan equivalent *gru pa* (boatman) for *nāvika* (§3850). Here *nāvika* seems to be a sailor, but the term can also be used for inland waterways and hence mean ferryman. According to the classical Sanskrit dictionary *Amarakośa*, the *nāvika* holds the rudder — *karṇadhāras tu nāvikaḥ*; see A.A. Ramanathan, ed., *Amarakośa with the unpublished South Indian commentaries Amarapadavivṛti of Liṅgayasūrin and the Amarapadapārijāta of Mallinātha*, Adyar: The Adyar Library and Research Centre, 1971, vol. I, pp. 162–63 (ad v. I, 12.12b).
25. See Chhabra, *Expansion of Indo-Aryan Culture*, p. 23, n. 2, and pp. 24–26. For *mahānāvika* in this context, see Suchandra Ghosh, "Coastal Andhra and the Bay of Bengal Trade Network", *South Asian Studies* 22 (2006) (London: The Society for South Asian Studies/The British Academy), pp. 65–68. For the Old Malay inscriptions, see e.g., Pierre-Yves Manguin and Tan Sri Dato' Dr. Mubin Sheppard, eds., *Sriwijaya: History, Religion and Language of an Early Malay Polity: Collected Studies by George Cœdès and Louis-Charles Damais* (Monograph of the Malaysian Branch, Royal Asiatic Society no. 20, Kuala Lumpur: 1992).
26. The Kampung Sungai Mas inscription was studied and read independently in Kongkaew, "Charuek runraek", published in 1989 in Thai with an English

summary. She dates the inscription to the seventh century (or, in Thai, to twelfth century, Buddhist Era). I intially read the inscription from the photographs of the chalked inscription that accompany Kongkaew's article, later consulting the colour photo by Tharapong Srisuchat in the Office of the National Culture Commission, *Ancient Trades and Cultural Contacts in Southeast Asia* (Bangkok: The Office of the National Culture Commission, 1996), p. 37. The difficulty lies not only in the reproduction, but in the fact that the letters seem incomplete or imperfect, and some forms — like the double *-mm-* are unusual. It is regrettable that none of the other publications listed below give clear reproductions of the inscription. The first publication of the inscription that I know of is that in Allen, "An Inscribed Tablet", (1986–87), which was followed by Jan Wisseman Christie, "The Sanskrit Inscription recently discovered in Kedah, Malayasia", in *Modern Quaternary Research in Southeast Asia*, edited by Gert-Jan Bartstra and Willem Arnold Casparie, vol. 11 (1988–89) (Rotterdam: A.A. Balkema, 1990), pp. 39–53. See also Jacq-Hergoualc'h, *La civilisation*, pp. 222–24 and doc. 243; idem, *The Malay Peninsula*, pp. 216–19 and fig. 89; and Machi Suhadi, "Mantra Buddha di Negara ASEAN", in *Proceedings/Pertemuan Ilmiah Arkeologi V, Yogyakarta 4–7 Juli 1989*, I. *Studi Regional/Regional Studies*, Ikatan Ahli Arkeologi Indonesia, 1989, pp. 108–109 (full article pp. 103–32). Allen and Wisseman Christie discuss the broader physical environment in some detail.

27. The inscription is read in Hasan Djafar, *Kompleks Percandian Batujaya: Rekonstruksi Sejarah Kebudayaan Daerah Pantai Utara Jawa Barat*, Pustaka hikmah Disertasi (PhD) Seri 5 (Bandung: Kiblat Buku Utama, École française d'Extrême-Orient, Pusat Penelitian dan Pengembangan Arkeologi Nasional, KITLV Jakarta dan Tot, 2010), pp. 89–93. For the Batujaya site, see Pierre-Yves Manguin and Agustijanto Indrajaya, "The Archaeology of Batujaya (West-Java, Indonesia): An Interim Report", Chap. 23 in *Uncovering Southeast Asia's Past: selected papers from the 10th International Conference of the European Association of Southeast Asian Archaeologists, the British Museum, London, 14th–17th September 2004*, edited by Elisabeth A. Bacus, Ian Glover, and Vincent C. Pigott (Singapore: NUS Press, 2006), pp. 245–57; and Pierre-Yves Manguin and Agustijanto Indradjaja, "The Batujaya Site: New Evidence of Early Indian Influence in West Java", Chap. 5 in *Early Interactions between South and Southeast Asia*, edited by Manguin, Mani and Wade. I am grateful to Pierre-Yves Manguin for sending me materials related to the site over the years.
28. Manguin and Indrajaya, "The Archaeology of Batujaya", p. 246.
29. Peter Ferdinandus, *Recent Archaeological Excavations in Blandongan Site, Batujaya, Karawang, West Java* (Jakarta: Badan Pengembangan Kebudayaan dan Pariwisata, Deputi Bidang Pelestarian dan Pengembangan Kebudayaan, Bagian Proyek Penelitian dan Pengembangan Arkeologi, 2002), pp. 11–12 and Pl. 8.

30. Manguin and Indrajaya, "The Archaeology of Batu Jaya", pp. 249–50 and Fig. 23.6; Manguin and Indrajaya, "The Batujaya Site", pp. 115–16; Djafar, *Kompleks Percandian Batujaya*, pp. 89–91 and Figs. 3.36, 3.38–39. A number of mistakes in interpretation (the report is, after all, preliminary) should be noted: the central figure is not a Bodhisatva but a Buddha, and the *ajñānāc cīyate karma* formula is not a *mantra*.
31. My reading is based on photos 3.43 and 3.44 in Djafar, *Kompleks Percandian Batujaya*, p. 92, Inskripsi Terakota (Fragmen). Djafar's reading (p. 92) is substantially the same.
32. Djafar, *Kompleks Percandian Batujaya*, pp. 92–93: Inskripsi Emas I, photos 3.45 and 3.46. The reproductions of the plates are not sufficiently clear to read, and I give Djafar's reading as it stands.
33. Djafar, *Kompleks Percandian Batujaya*, p. 93: Inskripsi Emas II, photo 3.47. The reproduction is not sufficiently clear to read, and I reproduce Djafar's reading as it stands.
34. Djafar, *Kompleks Percandian Batujaya*, p. 93: Inskripsi Emas III, photos 3.47 and 3.48.
35. J.G. de Casparis, *Prasasti Indonesia II: Diterbitkan oleh dinas purbakala Republik Indonesia/Selected Inscriptions from the 7th to the 9th century A.D.* (Bandung: Masa Baru, 1956), pp. 48, 52, 55–56.
36. De Casparis, *Prasasti Indonesia II*, p. 63, and n. 57; pp. 100, 105–107. The inscriptions are also transcribed in Drs. Boechari, *Prasasti Koleksi Museum Nasional: Jilid I* (Jakarta: Museum Nasional, 1985/86), pp. 225–37. For some examples, see Oskar von Hinüber, *Sieben Goldblätter einer Pañcaviṃśatisāhasrikā Prajñāpāramitā aus Anurādhapura* (Göttingen: Vandenhoeck & Ruprecht, 1983), esp. pp. 3–6; Roderick Whitfield et al., *Treasures from Korea: Art through 5000 years* (London: British Museum Publications, 1984), §§116–17; and Hwang, Su-yong, ed., *The Arts of Korea III: Buddhist Art* (Seoul: Dong Hwa Publishing Co., 1979), §§ 50–51.
37. De Casparis, *Prasasti Indonesia II*, p. 49.
38. Ibid., p. 52.
39. In 1993, through the good offices of the late E. Gene Smith, then head of the U.S. Library of Congress, Jakarta, I was able to examine the plates during a visit to the museum. The surface was so shiny and the letters were so lightly inscribed, that it was impossible to glimpse the letters for more than an instant, or to catch them with the camera.
40. De Casparis' numbering seems to be based on that of the Jakarta Museum catalogue. Plate *h* gives the conclusion of the *sūtra*, with line 1 following naturally after the last line of plate *b*. The conclusion of the *sūtra* is followed by "a very elaborate mark of punctuation". The remainder of plate *h* lists the component planes of the "realm of sense-pleasures" (*kāmadhātu*) — four Continents (*dvīpa*), eight Great Hells (*mahānaraka*), the *pretaloka*, and the animal realm (*tiryagjāti*) — plus various views (*dṛṣṭi*), and seems unrelated

to the following plate *c*. De Casparis notes this problem (*Prasasti Indonesia II*, pp. 102–103), but seems to accept the order as it stands. Furthermore, plate *g* should follow plate *e*. The correct order of the larger plates therefore seems to be *a*, *b*, *h*, *c*, *d*, *e*, *g*, *f*, with *a*, *b*, *h* making up one set containing the *sūtra*, and *c*, *d*, *e*, *g*, *f* making up a second part, containing the commentary. *i*, *j*, and *k* cannot be placed.

41. The *Nidānasaṃyukta*, a section of the *Saṃyuktāgama* of the Sarvāstivāda school dealing with causation, survives in Sanskrit manuscript fragments from Central Asia: see Chandrabhāl Tripāṭhī, *Fünfundzwanzig Sūtras des Nidānasaṃyukta*, Sanskrittexte aus den Turfanfunden, VIII, Sūtra 16 (Göttingen: Vandenhoeck & Ruprecht, 1962), pp. 157–64. This text had not been published at the time of de Casparis' study. For an English translation, see John M. Cooper, "Two Sūtras on Dependent Origination", in *Buddhist Studies Review* 1, no. 1 (1983–84): 31–33, to be read in conjunction with P. Skilling, "Comments on 'Two Sūtras on Dependent Origination'", *Buddhist Studies Review* 1, no. 2 (1983–84): 13–42. See de Casparis, *Prasasti Indonesia* II, p. 60 and nn. for references to further parallels.
42. De Casparis, *Prasasti Indonesia II*, pp. 60–75.
43. For a recent bibliography, see Gudrun Melzer, "A Copper Scroll Inscription from the Time of the Alchon Huns", in *Manuscripts in the Schøyen Collection: Buddhist Manuscripts*, Vol. III, edited by Jens Braarvig (Oslo: Hermes Publishing, 2006), pp. 251–78.
44. See here Prapod Assavavirulhakarn's remarks in *The Ascendancy of Theravāda Buddhism in Southeast Asia* (Chiang Mai: Silkworm Books, 2010), p. 76.
45. De Casparis, *Prasasti Indonesia II*, pp. 75–103.
46. The commentarial tradition need not be Śrāvaka or Mahāyāna: the notion that any text, monument, or icon must be classified according to formal scholastic categories of Śrāvakayāna, Mahāyāna, or Vajrayāna is in many cases historically misdirected, and seems driven by modern researchers' compulsion to fit Buddhism into manageable and comfortable categories by ignoring grey areas and complexity. In an addendum (pp. 339–411), de Casparis notes a relationship between the commentary and Ullaṅgha's *Pratītyasamutpādaśāstra*, a work known only from its Chinese translation, referring to Vasudev Gokhale, *Pratītyasamutpādaśāstra des Ullaṅgha kritisch behandelt und aus dem Chinesischen ins Deutsche übertragen* (PhD dissertation, Rheinische Friedrich-Wilhelms-Universität zu Bonn, 1930).
47. De Casparis, *Prasasti Indonesia II*, pp. 113–14; Boechari, *Prasasti Koleksi Museum Nasional*, p. 228.
48. De Casparis, *Prasasti Indonesia II*, p. 123; Boechari, *Prasasti Koleksi Museum Nasional*, pp. 235–36.
49. De Casparis, *Prasasti Indonesia II*, pp. 123–24; Boechari, *Prasasti Koleksi Museum Nasional*, p. 236. In verse 3, one expects *sukhinaḥ* instead of *rūpiṇaḥ*.

50. De Casparis, *Prasasti Indonesia II*, pp. 47–48.
51. Franz Bernhard, ed., *Udānavarga: Band I, Einleitung, Beschreibung der Handschriften, Textausgabe, Bibliographie* (Sanskrittexte aus den Turfanfunden, X, Göttingen: Vandenhoeck & Ruprecht, 1965), p. 353 (Chap. XXVIII,1).
52. G. Bühler, "Three Buddhist Inscriptions in Swat", *Epigraphia Indica* IV (1896–97), pp. 133–35; Bernhard, *Udānavarga*, p. 353.
53. Aurel Stein, *Kharoṣṭhī Inscriptions Discovered by Sir Aurel Stein in Chinese Turkestan* (Oxford: Clarendon Press, 1920), no. 510b1 (repr. New Delhi: Cosmo Publications, 1997, p. 185) (ref. noted in Bernhard, *Udānavarga*, p. 353, n. 4).
54. É. Senart, ed., *Le Mahāvastu*, Tome III (Paris: Imprimerie Nationale, 1907), p. 420.12.
55. W. Pachow and Ramakanta Mishra, eds., *The Prātimokṣa-Sūtra of the Mahāsāṅghikas* (Allahabad: Ganganatha Jha Research Institute, 1956), p. 43.5; and Nathmal Tatia, ed., *Prātimokṣasūtraṃ of the Lokottaravādimahāsāṅghika School* (Tibetan Sanskrit Works Series, 16, Patna: Kashi Prasad Jayaswal Research Institute, 1975), p. 36.22.
56. Gustav Roth, ed., *Bhikṣuṇī-Vinaya: [Manual of Discipline for Buddhist Nuns] including Bhikṣuṇī-prakīrṇaka and a summary of the Bhikṣu-prakīrṇaka of the Ārya-mahāsāṃghika-lokottaravādin* (Tibetan Sanskrit Works Series, XII, Patna: K.P. Jayaswal Research Institute, 1970), pp. 52, 67.
57. Klaus T. Schmidt, ed., *Der Schlussteil des Prātimokṣasūtra der Sarvāstivādins: Text in Sanskrit und Tocharisch A verglichen mit den Parallelversionen anderer Schulen* (Sanskrittexte aus den Turfanfunden, XIII, Göttingen: Vandenhoeck & Ruprecht, 1989), p. 73 (v. 7), p. 93.1.
58. Schmidt, *Der Schlussteil des Prātimokṣasūtra*, p. 33.1; Anukul Chandra Banerjee, *Two Buddhist Vinaya Texts in Sanskrit: Prātimokṣa Sūtra and Bhikṣukarmavākya* (Calcutta: The World Press Private Ltd, 1977), p. 55.7.
59. *Dhammapada*, v. 183; *Dīghanikāya* II 49.26 (refs. are to the Pali Text Society editions).
60. Gustav Roth, "Particular Features of the Language of the Ārya-Mahāsāṃghika-Lokottaravādins and their Importance for Early Buddhist Tradition", in *The Language of the Earliest Buddhist Tradition*, edited by Heinz Bechert (Göttingen: Vandenhoeck & Ruprecht, 1980), v. 358, p. 129; Margaret Cone, "Patna Dharmapada, Part I: Text", *Journal of the Pali Text Society* 13 (1989), p. 198, v. 357. For a possible Sāṃmitīya school-affiliation of this text, see Peter Skilling, "On the School-affiliation of the 'Patna Dhammapada'", *Journal of the Pali Text Society* XXIII (1997), pp. 83–122. For several more secondary Pali references, see Bernhard, *Udānavarga*, p. 353.
61. Russell Webb, ed., *Buddhist Studies Review* 2, No. 1-2 (1985), p. 39; Nathmal Tatia, ed., *Abhidharmasamuccaya-bhāṣyam* (Patna: Kashi Prasad Jayaswal Research Institute (Anantalal Thakur, ed., *Tibetan Sanskrit Works Series*,

No. 17)), p. 142. In Tibetan, it is preserved, for example, in Vasubandhu's *Gāthāsaṃgraha*, v. 14; Śamathadeva, *Abhidharmakośa-upāyikā-ṭīkā*, Peking Kanjur, Otani reprint, catalogue no. 5595, reprint vol. 118, *mṅon pa*, *tu*, folio 242a6. The author of the *Da zhidu lun* discusses this verse together with the *ye dharmā* stanza; see Étienne Lamotte, tr., *Le Traité de la Grande Vertu de Sagesse de Nāgārjuna (Mahāprajñāpāramitāśāstra)*, Tome II (Louvain: Institut Orientaliste, [1949] 1967), pp. 1075–76.

62. See the Tibetan version of the *Pratītyasamutpāda-sūtra*, in N. Aiyaswami Sastri, *Ārya Śālistamba Sūtra* (The Adyar Library Series, 76, Madras: Adyar Library, 1950), p. 72, bottom (transliterated Sanskrit, not in the Peking ed.).
63. See Peking Kanjur, Otani Reprint, vol. 7, *rgyud* vol. *ba*, folio 310a6; vol. 27, *mdo* vol. *i*, folio 376a5 (abbreviated); and vol. 39, *mdo* vol. *su*, folio 330a4.
64. De Casparis, *Prasasti Indonesia II*, pp. 338–39. Cf. Shūyo Takubo, ed., *Ārya-Mahā-Māyūrī Vidyā-rājñī* (Tokyo: Sankibo, 1972), p. 6.18–20. De Casparis, *Prasasti Indonesia II* (Addendum I., p. 338), gives "d'Oldenburg, p. 222, lines 16 sqq." as his source. This must refer to an article in the journal *Zapiski Vostochnago Otdelnija Imp. Russk. Archeol. Obschestva*, vol. 2, 1899 (title from Takubo, "Abbreviations"), which is not available to me.
65. Ernst Waldschmidt, *Das Upasenasūtra* (Göttingen: Vandenhoeck & Ruprecht, 1957), p. 40. On the use of the *Upasena-sūtra* stanzas as a *paritta*, see also Henrik H. Sørensen, "The Spell of the Great, Golden Peacock Queen: The Origin, Practices, and Lore of an Early Esoteric Buddhist Tradition in China", *Pacific World: Journal of the Insitute of Buddhist Studies*, 3rd Series, No. 8 (Fall 2006), pp. 89–123. A Sanskrit fragment of the *Upasena-sūtra* is also given in Ernst Waldschmidt, "Ein zweites Daśabalasūtra", *Mitteilungen des Instituts für Orientforschung* 6 (1958), pp. 382–405 (reprinted in Heinz Bechert, ed., Ernst Waldschmidt, *Von Ceylon bis Turfan, Schriften zur Geschichte, Literatur, Religion und Kunst des indischen Kulturraumes. Festgabe zum 70. Geburtstag am 15. Juli 1967* (Göttingen: Vandenhoeck & Ruprecht, 1967), pp. 347–70. There are further parallels in Chinese.
66. For these versions, see Peter Skilling, *Mahāsūtras: Great Discourses of the Buddha*, Vol. I: Texts (Sacred Books of the Buddhists, XLIV, Oxford: Pali Text Society, 1994), Mahāsūtra 10, §§ A.3.18, B.3.18, A.6.18, B.6.18, C.3.16. C.6.16.
67. *Saṃyutta-nikāya* IV, pp. 40–41.
68. *Vinaya* II, p. 110.14; *Aṅguttara-nikāya* II, p. 73.4; *Jātaka* 203, Vol. II, p. 146.15, respectively.
69. Lily de Silva, *Paritta: A historical and religious study of the Buddhist ceremony for peace and prosperity in Sri Lanka*, Spolia Zeylanica, Vol. 36, part 1 (Colombo, Sri Lanka: National Museums, 1981), pp. 5–6.
70. Louis Renou and Jean Filliozat, eds., *L'Inde Classique: manuel des études indiennes* II (Hanoi: École française d'Extrême-Orient, 1953), §2014.

71. I am grateful to Machi Suhadi for supplying the photographs, through the offices of the late E. Gene Smith.
72. Chhabra, *Expansion of Indo-Aryan Culture*, pp. 53–57.
73. For a brief note on "the archaeological remains of the Hindu period" along the Kapuas River, which "offered the same facilities for colonisation of western Borneo [as did the Mahakam River for eastern Borneo]", see R.C. Majumdar, *Suvarṇadvīpa: Ancient Indian Colonies in the Far East*, Vol. 1 ([Calcutta: Modern Pub. Syndicate, 1937–38] New Delhi: Gian Publishing House, 1986), p. 130. Majumdar's knowledge of the inscriptions depended on the first edition of Chhabra's *Expansion of Indo-Aryan Culture*, that is, the version published in the *Journal of the Asiatic Society of Bengal, Letters* Vol. I (1935). There is a brief mention in Pauline C. M. Lunsingh Scheurleer, Marijke J. Klokke, and Rijksmuseum (Netherlands), *Ancient Indonesian Bronzes: A catalogue of the exhibition in the Rijksmuseum Amsterdam with a general introduction* (Leiden; New York: E.J. Brill, 1988), p. 37.
74. De Casparis assigns a similar date to the *yūpa* inscriptions; see J.G. de Casparis, *Indonesian Paleography: A history of writing in Indonesia from the beginnings to c. A.D. 1500* (Leiden: Brill, 1975), pp. 14–18.
75. Chhabra, *Expansion of Indo-Aryan Culture*, p. 56.
76. Column 1 identifies the main verse inscription; Column 2 gives Chhabra's readings of the additional words without any emendation (including his question marks in parentheses); Column 3 gives "standard" Sanskrit names for the seven Buddhas (but in fact there are many variant forms across texts and time). The names are at the end of verses 1, 2, and 3, but are in verses 5, 6, and 8 placed in the middle. Chhabra does not read lines 5–8 of No. 7, which are presumably effaced.
77. See I.B. Horner, tr., *Chronicle of Buddhas (Buddhavaṃsa) and Basket of Conduct (Cariyāpiṭaka)* (The Minor Anthologies of the Pali Canon, Part III, London and Boston: Pali Text Society, 1975), p. xxxii, where the height of the seven Buddhas from Vipassin to Gotama, measured in *hattha*s or *ratana*s, is given as 80, 70, 60, 40, 30, 20, and 18, respectively. For the seven Buddhas in general, see Paul Demiéville, editor-in-chief, *Hôbôgirin: Dictionnaire encyclopédique du bouddhisme d'après les sources chinoises et japonaises*, troisième fascicule: Bussokuseki–Chi (Paris: Librairie d'Amérique et d'Orient Adrien Maisonneuve, 1974), pp. 195b–197a. The seven superposed umbrellas of the stūpa shown in relief on the Buddhagupta inscription *might* also refer to the seven Buddhas.
78. See Pachow and Mishra, *The Prātimokṣa Sūtra*, pp. 42–45; Nathmal Tatia, ed., *Prātimokṣasūtra of the Lokottaravādimahāsāṅghika School*, Tibetan Sanskrit Works Series 16 (Patna: Kashi Prasad Jayaswal Research Institute, 1975), pp. 36–37; Schmidt, *Der Schlussteil*, pp. 73–74 (Sarvāstivādin) and pp. 92–93 (Mūlasarvāstivādin); and Banerjee, *Two Buddhist Vinaya Texts*,

pp. 54–56. In the latter source, the association of the verses with the Buddhas is given in the commentaries.

79. Kongkaew Weeraprajak, "Charuek khong prathet brunai" [Inscriptions of Brunei, in Thai], *Silpakorn* 29, no. 5, Nov. 2528 [1985]), pp. 26–36 / **กองแก้ว วีระประจักษ์, จารึกของประเทศบรูไน**. See further Matassim bin Haji Jibah, "Notes on Tombstones recently found in Brunei", *Brunei Museum Journal* 5, no. 2 (1982): 23–25 and pl. 7a (full article pp. 19–36). It is not clear when the inscribed stūpa was discovered: Kongkaew received photographs in 1980, and Matassim bin Haji Jibah describes it as "discovered recently" in his 1982 publication. The Bandar Seri Begawan inscription is also reported (without photographs) in Christie, "The Sanskrit Inscription", pp. 49–50, and in Machi Suhadi, "Mantra Buddha", pp. 112–13. Christie learned about the inscription and received a photograph from Prof. Claude Jacques, Paris. Supplementary information on the location of the find sites is from a letter to the present writer from Haji Matussin Bin Omar, Director of Museums, Brunei Darussalam, dated 30 October 1986, and more recently from Rod Orlina and Arlo Griffiths (2011–12).

80. I am grateful to Rod Orlina and Oliver Lee for information about the present location and to Rod Orlina, Oliver Lee, Arlo Griffiths, and Christian Lammerts for supplying photographs during the course of this study.

81. I initially read the inscription from the photographs published in Kongkaew, "Charuek khong prathet brunai". Here Kongkaew reads *jānāc*...; however, the *ña*, subscribed to the *ja*, is clear.

82. Rod Orlina, email, 18 June 2012. It seems that the condition of the stūpa has apparently deteriorated since the time of Kongkaew's article, and the topmost part has gone missing.

83. Kongkaew reads *[jā]nāccīyate karmma / na karmma kāra*. The photograph is unclear; however, an *a* may be fairly discerned at the beginning of the first line, as can the *na* of *janma*, with a blurred subscript, the top of which is quite clearly a *ma*, and the final *ṇa* of *kāraṇam*, in the second line. As the stone is very pock-marked, it is impossible to distinguish the *visarga* of *janmanaḥ* or the *anusvāra* of *kāranaṃ* from the spots in the photograph.

84. Her dating is based on a perceived resemblance to the Khau Rang inscription from Prachin Buri, Thailand, which bears the date Śaka 561 = CE 639: see Anonymous, *Charuek nai prathet thai*, Vol. I (Bangkok: National Library of Thailand, 2529 [1986]), pp. 35–39 and Pl. p. 36; Anonymous, *Prachum silacharuek*, Pt. 4 (Bangkok: The Prime Minister's Office, 2513 [1970]), Inscription No. 119.

85. The *ma* and the *ra* agree with some early seventh century examples: see, for example, L.C. Damais, "Les écritures d'origine indienne en Indonésie et dans le Sud-Est Asiatique continental", *Bulletin de la Société des Études Indochinoises*, Nouvelle Série, Tome XXX, No. 1 (Saigon: B.S.E.I., 1955),

chart A, "type pallawa ancien". For general charts, see Anonymous, *Charuek nai prathet thai*, pp. 18–19 and 24.

86. See note 79.
87. If Province Wellesley/Seberang Perai (see note 7 above) belongs administratively to the modern Malaysian state of Penang, it geographically belongs to Kedah, along with Inscriptions 1 and 3.
88. Allen, "An Inscribed Tablet", p. 35.
89. H.G. Quaritch Wales, "Archaeological Researches on Ancient Indian Colonization in Malaya", *Journal of the Royal Asiatic Society, Malay Branch* XVIII, Part 1 (February 1940): 1–85; see more recently Nik Hassan Shuhaimi Nik Abdul Rahman, *The Encyclopedia of Malaysia*, Vol. 4, *Early History* (Singapore: Archipelago Press, 1998), pp. 80–81, 90–97, 104–109, et passim.
90. Quaritch Wales, "Archaeological Researches", pp. 8–10, and Pl. 8; Jacq-Hergoualc'h, *La civilisation*, pp. 228–29.
91. The new inscription will be published by Nasha Roziadi Khaw.
92. Allen, "An Inscribed Tablet", p. 51.
93. Christie, "The Sanskrit Inscription", p. 48.
94. See, inter alia, Robert Nicholl, "Brunei and Camphor", *Brunei Museum Journal* 4, no. 3 (1979): 52–81; Robert Nicholl, "Brunei Rediscovered: A Survey of Early Times", *Brunei Museum Journal* 4, no. 4 (1980): 219–37; Matussin bin Omar, *Archaeological Excavations in Protohistoric Brunei* (Bandar Seri Begawan: Muzium Brunei 1981), Part I, Chap. I: A Brief History of the Brunei Sultanate.
95. For a *mukhaliṅga* from the Kapuas River basin at the juncture of the Kapuas and Sepaoek Rivers, West Kalimantan, see S.J. O'Connor, "Note on a *mukhaliṅga* from Western Borneo", *Artibus Asiae* XXIX, no. 1 (1967): 93–96 and figs. 1–4.
96. O'Connor, "Note on a *mukhaliṅga*", pp. 95–96.
97. When I first wrote this sentence, in the early 1980s, the Batujaya inscriptions had not yet come to light.
98. Technically speaking, the *ye dharmā* verse as a whole was spoken by a disciple; however, the first three lines are a summary of the teaching of the Mahāśramaṇa, that is, the Buddha.
99. Whether read from the left or the right, the *ajñānāt* verse comes first.
100. See P. Skilling, "Scriptural Authenticity and the Śrāvaka Schools: An Essay towards an Indian Perspective", *The Eastern Buddhist* 41, no. 2 (2010): 1–47.
101. Li Rongxi, *Buddhist Monastic Traditions of Southern Asia: A Record of the Inner Law Sent Home from the South Seas by Śramaṇa Yijing*, translated from the Chinese (Taishō Vol. 54, No. 2125) (Berkeley, California: Numata Center for Buddhist Translation and Research [BDK English Tripiṭaka 93-I], 2000), p. 12; and J. Takakusu, *A Record of the Buddhist Religion as Practised in India and the Malay Archipelago (A.D. 671–695)* ([London, 1896] New Delhi: Munshiram Manoharlal, 1982), p. 10; see also pp. xxiii–xxv.

102. Quaritch Wales, "Archaeological Researches", p. 7 and Pl. 6. The gold plates use both *uvāca* and *avadat*, and the Kedah stone *avadat*. For a preliminary and increasingly outdated note on the different recensions of the *ye dharmā* stanza, see Peter Skilling, "A Buddhist inscription from Go Xoai".
103. For example, the Ratubaka inscription from central Java, written in Sanskrit verse, refers to the Abhayagiri branch of the Theravāda, whose scriptures most probably were in Pāli, as were those of the Mahāvihāra branch: see J.G. de Casparis, "New Evidence on Cultural Relations between Java and Ceylon in Ancient Times", *Artibus Asiae* 24 (1961), pp. 241–48. However, this is not relevant to our argument, since it is not a scriptural citation. For the four schools and their languages, see Peter Skilling, "Theravāda in History", *Pacific World: Journal of the Institute of Buddhist Studies*, Third Series, Number 11 (Fall 2009): 61–93.
104. On inquiry, many Hindus can immediately recite the verses, which I first heard intoned as a blessing by the bride's grandmother, Tripti Chakravarty, at the wedding reception of Stefan Baums and Rita Banerjee at the Oberoi Grand Hotel, Kolkata, 20 February 2011. Most informants give the source of the verses as "the Upaniṣads"; they are not found, however, in to the Upaniṣads proper, but perhaps in ancillary matter.
105. This statement is based on a search for several of the keywords in the *Pāli Tipiṭakaṃ Concordance* — *aññāṇa, cināti,* and *kārana*. *Cīyate* is rare in the Pali canon, and an equivalent of *janma* does not seem to be attested: on the whole, the vocabulary of the verse seems late and technical in relation to early Pali and early Sanskrit Buddhist literature.
106. It is true that not all of these have been edited, and that no comprehensive index exists. But one might expect a verse that was widely disseminated in (pen)insular Southeast Asia to have been prominent in literature, or that it would come from an important and well-known scripture, or have been associated with a popular narrative. This is the case with the *ye dharmā* stanza, which occurs only once in the story of Śāriputra and Mahāmaudgalyāyana, a seminal narrative of the early formation of the Buddha's monastic community.
107. In "On the School-affiliation of the Patna *Dhammapada*", I suggest that the Patna *Dhammapada* and several canonical inscriptions from District Monghyr, Bihar, should belong to the Sāṃmitīyas.
108. De Casparis, *Prasasti Indonesia II*, p. 70, n. 81.
109. See Daniel Stuart, *A Less Traveled Path: An Edition, Translation and Historical Study of the Second Chapter of the Saddharmasmṛtyupasthānasūtra*, PhD dissertation to be submitted to the Group in Buddhist Studies at the University of California at Berkeley, 2012.
110. Peter Skilling, William Southworth, and Tran Ky Phuong, "A Buddhist Stele from My Thanh in the Phu Yen Province of Central Vietnam", in *Abhinandanamala: Nandana Chutiwongs Felicitation Volume*, edited by Leelananda Prematilleke (Bangkok: SPAFA Regional Centre of Archaeology

and Fine Arts, in collaboration with the Abhinandanamala Committee, Colombo, 2010), pp. 487–513.

111. The one study that takes this type of stūpa into account is Johanna Engelberta van Louizen-de Leeuw, "The stūpa in Indonesia", in Anna Libera Dallapiccola in collaboration with Stephanie Zingel-Avé Lallement, *The Stūpa: Its Religious, Historical and Architectural Significance* (Wiesbaden: Franz Steiner Verlag, 1980) (Beiträge zur Südasienforschung Südasian-Institut Universität Heidelberg, Band 55), pp. 277–300.

112. See Arlo Griffiths, "Ein zehnarmige Mahāpratisarā aus Java im Museum für Asiatische Kunst", *Indo-Asiatische Zeitschrift* 15 (2011), pp. 2–9; Arlo Griffiths, "Inscriptions of Sumatra: Further Data on the Epigraphy of the Musi and Batang Hari River Basins", *Archipel* 81 (2011): 139–75. Six bronze images are identified by Gerd J.R. Mevissen, "Images of Mahāpratisarā in Bengal: Their Iconographic Links with Javanese, Central Asian and East Asian Images", *Journal of Bengal Art* 4, Gouriswar Bhattacharya Volume (1999), pp. 99–129, pls. 8.6–7. For Candi Mendut, see ibid., fig. 8.8. Griffith's research has recently uncovered the ritual use of a verse aspiration from the *Suvarṇabhāsottama-sūtra* at Pulau Sawah in Sumatra.

113. See Peter Skilling, "Buddhism and the Circulation of Ritual in Early Peninsular Southeast Asia", Chap. 18 in *Early Interactions between South and Southeast Asia: Reflections on Cross-Cultural Exchange*, edited by Manguin, Mani and Wade, chapter 18, pp. 371–84.

Bibliography

Allen, Jane. "An Inscribed Tablet from Kedah, Malaysia: Comparison with Earlier Finds." *Asian Perspectives* XXVII, no. 1 (1986–87): 35–57.

Anderson, John. *Catalogue and Hand-book of the Archaeological Collections in the Indian Museum*, part II, *Gupta and Inscription Galleries*. Patna: Indological Book Corporation, 1977 [first published, Calcutta 1883].

Anonymous. *Prachum silacharuek*, Pt. 4/. Bangkok: The Prime Minister's Office, 2513 B.E. [1970]. *ประชุมศิลาจารึกภาคที่ ๔*. กรุงเทพฯ: โรงพิมพ์สำนักทำเนียบนายกรัฐมนตรี, ๒๕๑๓.

Anonymous. *Charuek nai prathet thai*, Vol. I. Bangkok: National Library of Thailand, 2529 B.E. [1986]. *จารึกในประเทศไทย เล่ม ๑*. กรุงเทพฯ: หอสมุดแห่งชาติ กรมศิลปากร, ๒๕๒๙.

Bagchi, Prabodh Chandra. *She-kia-fang-che*. Santiniketan: Visva-Bharati, 1959.

Banerjee, Anukul Chandra. *Two Buddhist Vinaya Texts in Sanskrit: Prātimokṣa Sūtra and Bhikṣukarmavākya*. Calcutta: The World Press Private Ltd, 1977.

Beal, Samuel. *Si-Yu-Ki: Buddhist Records of the Western World*, vol. II. New Delhi: Motilal Banarsidass, 1981 (first published London, Routledge, 1884).

——. *The Life of Hiuen-Tsiang by the Shaman Hwui Li*. New Delhi: Munshiram Manoharlal, 1973 (first published London, K. Paul, Trench, Trübner, 1911).

Bernhard, Franz, ed. *Udānavarga: Band I, Einleitung, Beschreibung der Handschriften, Textausgabe, Bibliographie*. Sanskrittexte aus den Turfanfunden, vol. X. Göttingen: Vandenhoeck & Ruprecht, 1965.

Boechari, Drs. *Prasasti Koleksi Museum Nasional: Jilid I*. Jakarta: Museum Nasional, 1985/86.

Bühler, J. Georg. "Three Buddhist Inscriptions in Swat". In *Epigraphia Indica* vol. IV, pp. 133–35, edited by E. Hultzsch (1896-97). India: Archaeological Survey of India, Department of Archaeology.

Bunchar Pongpanich. *Roi lukpat* [*Beyond Beads*]. Bangkok: Matichon Publishing House, 2552 B.E. [2009] / บัญชา พงษ์พานิช, รอยลูกปัด. กรุงเทพฯ: มติชน, 2552.

Chakravarti, Shyamalkanti. *A Descriptive Catalogue of the Prakrit and Sanskrit Inscriptions in the Epigraphy Gallery Indian Museum*, Indian Museum Catalogue No. 2. Calcutta: Indian Museum, 1977.

Chhabra, B. Ch. *Expansion of Indo-Aryan Culture during Pallava Rule (as evidenced by inscriptions)*. Delhi: Munshi Ram Manohar Lal, 1965 (first published in *Journal of the Asiatic Society of Bengal*, vol. I (1935): 1–64).

Christie, Jan Wisseman. "The Sanskrit Inscription recently discovered in Kedah, Malayasia", In *Modern Quaternary Research in Southeast Asia* 11 (1988–1989), edited by Gert-Jan Bartstra and Willem Arnold Casparie, pp. 39–53. Rotterdam: A.A. Balkema, 1990.

Cone, Margaret. "Patna Dharmapada, Part I: Text". In *Journal of the Pali Text Society* 13 (1989): 101–217.

——. *A Dictionary of Pali*. Part II. Bristol: The Pali Text Society, 2010.

Cooper, John M. "Two Sūtras on Dependent Origination". In *Buddhist Studies Review* 1, no. 1 (1983–84): 31–33.

Damais, L.C. "Les écritures d'origine indienne en Indonésie et dans le Sud-Est Asiatique continental". In *Bulletin de la Société des Études Indochinoises*, Nouvelle Série, Tome XXX, No. 1, pp. 365–82. Saigon: B.S.E.I., 1955.

Das, Sudhir Ranjan. *Rājbāḍīdāṅgā: 1962 (Chiruṭī: Jadupur), An Interim Report on Excavations at Rājbāḍīdāṅgā and Terracotta Seals and Sealings*. The Asiatic Society Monograph Series, vol. XIV. Calcutta: Asiatic Society, 1968.

de Casparis, J.G. *Prasasti Indonesia II: Diterbitkan oleh dinas purbakala Republik Indonesia/Selected Inscriptions from the 7th to the 9th century A.D.* Bandung: Masa Baru, 1956.

——. "New Evidence on Cultural Relations between Java and Ceylon in Ancient Times". In *Artibus Asiae* 24 (1961): 241–48.

——. *Indonesian Paleography: A history of writing in Indonesia from the beginnings to c. A.D. 1500*. Leiden: Brill, 1975.

de Silva, Lily. *Paritta: A historical and religious study of the Buddhist ceremony for peace and prosperity in Sri Lanka*. Spolia Zeylanica, vol. 36, part 1. Colombo, Sri Lanka: National Museums, 1981.

Demiéville, Paul, ed. *Hôbôgirin: Dictionnaire encyclopédique du bouddhisme d'après les sources chinoises et japonaises*. Troisième fascicule: Bussokuseki–Chi. Paris: Librairie d'Amérique et d'Orient Adrien Maisonneuve, 1974.

Deshpande M.N., ed. *Indian Archaeology 1972–73 – A Review*. New Delhi: Archaeological Survey of India, 1978.

Djafar, Hasan. *Kompleks Percandian Batujaya: Rekonstruksi Sejarah Kebudayaan Daerah Pantai Utara Jawa Barat*. Pustaka hikmah Disertasi (PhD) Seri 5. Bandung: Kiblat Buku Utama, École française d'Extrême-Orient, Pusat Penelitian dan Pengembangan Arkeologi Nasional, KITLV Jakarta dan Tot, 2010.

Edgerton, Franklin. *Buddhist Hybrid Sanskrit Grammar and Dictionary*. vol. II: Dictionary. Delhi: Motilal Banarsidass, 1972 (first published, New Haven: Yale University Press, 1953).

Ferdinandus, Peter. *Recent Archaeological Excavations in Blandongan Site, Batujaya, Karawang, West Java*. Jakarta: Badan Pengembangan Kebudayaan dan Pariwisata, Deputi Bidang Pelestarian dan Pengembangan Kebudayaan, Bagian Proyek Penelitian dan Pengembangan Arkeologi, 2002.

Gangopadhyay, Kaushik. "Archaeological Investigation at Tamluk: An Early Historic Settlement in Coastal West Bengal". In *Pratna Samiksha: A Journal of Archaeology*, pp. 53–63. Kolkata: Centre of Archaeological Studies and Training, Eastern India, new series vol. 1, 2010.

Ghosh, Suchandra. "Coastal Andhra and the Bay of Bengal Trade Network". In *South Asian Studies* 22, pp. 65–68. London: The Society for South Asian Studies/The British Academy, 2006.

Gokhale, Vasudev. "Pratītyasamutpādaśāstra des Ullaṅgha kritisch behandelt und aus dem Chinesischen ins Deutsche übertragen". Ph.D. dissertation. Bonn: Rheinische Friedrich-Wilhelms-Universität zu Bonn, 1930.

Griffiths, Arlo. "Ein zehnarmige Mahāpratisarā aus Java im Museum für Asiatische Kunst". In *Indo-Asiatische Zeitschrift* 15 (2011), pp. 2–9.

———. "Inscriptions of Sumatra: Further Data on the Epigraphy of the Musi and Batang Hari Rivers Basins". In *Archipel* 81 (2011): 139–75.

Horner, I.B., tr. *Chronicle of Buddhas (Buddhavaṃsa) and Basket of Conduct (Cariyāpiṭaka)*. The Minor Anthologies of the Pali Canon, Part III. London and Boston: Pali Text Society, 1975.

Hwang, Su-yong, ed. *The Arts of Korea III: Buddhist Art*. Seoul: Dong Hwa Publishing Co., 1979.

Jacq-Hergoualc'h, Michel. *La civilisation de ports-entrepôts du Sud Kedah (Malaysia) Ve–XIVe siècle*. Paris: L'Harmattan, 1992.

———. *The Malay Peninsula: Crossroads of the Maritime Silk Road (100 BC–1300 AD)*, translated by Victoria Hobson. Leiden: Brill, 2002.

Karlgren, Bernhard. *Analytic Dictionary of Chinese and Sino-Japanese*. New York: Dover Publications, 1974 (first published Paris: Paul Geuthner, 1923).

Kongkaew Weeraprajak. "Charuek runraek khong malaysia" [The Earliest Sanskrit Inscriptions Found in Malayasia (with an English summary)]. In *The Silpakorn Journal* 33, no. 4 (1989): 30–37. / ก่องแก้ว วีระประจักษ์, "จารึกรุ่นแรกขอมาเลเซีย", *ศิลปากร*, ปีที่ ๓๓ เล่มที่ ๔ เดือนกันยายน - ตุลาคม ๒๕๓๒.

——. "Charuek khong prathet brunai" [Inscriptions of Brunei, in Thai], *Silpakorn* 29, no. 5, Nov. 2528 B.E. [1985]), pp. 26–36 / ก่องแก้ว วีระประจักษ์, "จารึกของประเทศบรูไน". *ศิลปากร*, ปีที่ ๒๙ เล่มที่ ๕ เดือนพฤศจิกายน ๒๕๒๘.

Kyaw Minn Htin. "Early Buddhism in Myanmar: *Ye Dhammā* Inscriptions from Arakan". In *Early Interactions between South and Southeast Asia: Reflections on Cross-Cultural Exchange*, edited by P.Y. Manguin, A. Mani, and G. Wade, pp. 385–406. Singapore: Institute of Southeast Asian Studies; New Delhi: Manohar India, 2011.

Laidlay, J.W. "Note on the Inscriptions from Singapore and Province Wellesley. Forwarded by the Hon. Col. Butterworth, C.B. and Col. J. Low". *Journal of the Asiatic Society of Bengal* XVII, pt. 2 (July 1848): 66–72. [reprinted in *Miscellaneous Papers relating to Indo-China*, vol. I, edited by R. Rost, London: Trübner & Co, 1886, pp. 227–32].

——. "Note on the Foregoing". In *Miscellaneous Papers relating to Indo-China*, vol. I, edited by R. Rost, pp. 233–34. London: Trübner & Co, 1886.

Lal, B.B., ed. *Indian Archaeology 1968–69: A Review*. New Delhi: Archaeological Survey of India, 1971.

Lamotte, Étienne, tr., *Le Traité de la Grande Vertu de Sagesse de Nāgārjuna (Mahāprajñāpāramitāśāstra)*, Tome II. Louvain: Institut Orientaliste, 1949 (repr. 1967).

Li Rongxi. *A Biography of the Tripiṭaka Master of the Great Ci'en Monastery of the Great Tang Monastery*. Berkeley: Numata Center for Buddhist Translation and Research (BDK English Tripiṭaka 77), 1995.

——. *The Great Tang Dynasty Record of the Western Regions*. Berkeley: Numata Center for Buddhist Translation and Research (BDK English Tripiṭaka 79), 1996.

——. *Buddhist Monastic Traditions of Southern Asia: A Record of the Inner Law Sent Home from the South Seas by Śramaṇa Yijing*, translated from the Chinese (Taishō Vol. 54, No. 2125). BDK English Tripiṭaka 93-I. Berkeley, California: Numata Center for Buddhist Translation and Research, 2000.

Low, James. "An Account of Several Inscriptions found in Province Wellesley, on the Peninsula of Malacca". *Journal of the Asiatic Society of Bengal* XVII, pt. 2 (July 1848): 62–66 (reprinted in Rost, R. *Miscellaneous Papers relating to Indo-China*. London: Trübner & Co, 1886, 223-26).

——. "On an Inscription from Keddah". In *Journal of the Asiatic Society of Bengal* 18, no. 1 (March 1849): 247.

Lunsingh Scheurleer, Pauline C. M., Marijke J. Klokke, and Rijksmuseum (Netherlands). *Ancient Indonesian Bronzes: a catalogue of the exhibition in the Rijksmuseum Amsterdam with a general introduction*. Leiden; New York: E.J. Brill, 1988.

Machi Suhadi. "Mantra Buddha di Negara ASEAN". In *Proceedings/Pertemuan Ilmiah Arkeologi V, Yogyakarta 4–7 Juli 1989*, I. *Studi Regional/Regional Studies*, pp. 103–32. Ikatan Ahli Arkeologi Indonesia, 1989.

Majumdar, R.C. *Suvarṇadvīpa: Ancient Indian Colonies in the Far East*, vol. 1. Calcutta: Modern Pub. Syndicate, 1937–38. Reprint New Delhi: Gian Publishing House, 1986.

Manguin, Pierre-Yves and Agustijanto Indrajaya. "The Archaeology of Batujaya (West-Java, Indonesia): An Interim Report". In *Uncovering Southeast Asia's Past: selected papers from the 10th International Conference of the European Association of Southeast Asian Archaeologists, the British Museum, London, 14th–17th September 2004,* chapter 23, pp. 245–57. Edited by Elisabeth A. Bacus, Ian Glover, and Vincent C. Pigott. Singapore: NUS Press, 2006.

—— and Agustijanto Indrajaya. "The Batujaya Site: New Evidence of Early Indian Influence in West Java". In *Early Interactions between South and Southeast Asia: Reflections on Cross-Cultural Exchange*, edited by Pierre-Yves Manguin, A. Mani, and Geoff Wade, chapter 5. Singapore: Institute of Southeast Asian Studies; New Delhi: Manohar India, 2011.

—— and Tan Sri Dato' Dr. Mubin Sheppard, eds. *Sriwijaya: History, Religion and Language of an Early Malay Polity: Collected Studies by George Cœdès and Louis-Charles Damais*. Monograph of the Malaysian Branch, Royal Asiatic Society no. 20. Kuala Lumpur, 1992.

Matassim bin Haji Jibah. "Notes on Tombstobes recently found in Brunei". In *Brunei Museum Journal* 5, no. 2 (1982): 19–36.

Matussin bin Omar. *Archaeological Excavations in Protohistoric Brunei*. Bandar Seri Begawan: Muzium Brunei, 1981.

Melzer, Gudrun (in collaboration with Lore Sander). "A Copper Scroll Inscription from the Time of the Alchon Huns". In *Manuscripts in the Schøyen Collection: Buddhist Manuscripts*, vol. III, edited by Jens Braarvig, pp. 251–78. Oslo: Hermes Publishing, 2006.

Mevissen, Gerd J.R. "Images of Mahāpratisarā in Bengal: Their Iconographic Links with Javanese, Central Asian and East Asian Images". In *Journal of Bengal Art* 4, Gouriswar Bhattacharya Volume (1999), pp. 99–129.

Mitra, Debala. *Buddhist Monuments*. Calcutta: Sahitya Samsad, 1971.

Mitra, Rajendralal, A.F.R. Hoernle, and Baboo P.N. Bose. *Centenary Review of the Asiatic Society 1784–1884*. Calcutta: The Asiatic Society, [1885] 1986.

Nicholl, Robert. "Brunei and Camphor". In *Brunei Museum Journal* 4, no. 3 (1979): 52–81.

——. "Brunei Rediscovered: A Survey of Early Times". *Brunei Museum Journal* 4, no. 4 (1980): 219–37.

Nik Hassan Shuhaimi Nik Abdul Rahman. *The Encyclopedia of Malaysia*, vol. 4, *Early History*. Singapore: Archipelago Press, 1998.

—— and Othman Mohd. Yatim. *Warisan Lembah Bujang*. Kuala Lumpur, [1992] 2006.

O'Connor, S.J. "Note on a *mukhaliṅga* from Western Borneo". In *Artibus Asiae* 29, no. 1 (1967): 93–98.

Pachow, W. and Ramakanta Mishra, eds. *The Prātimokṣa-Sūtra of the Mahāsāṅghikas*. Allahabad: Ganganatha Jha Research Institute, 1956.

Petech, Luciano. *Mediaeval History of Nepal (c. 750–1482)*. Serie Orientale Roma, LIV. Rome: Istituto per il Medio ed Estremo Oriente, 1984.

Prapod Assavavirulhakarn. *The Ascendancy of Theravāda Buddhism in Southeast Asia*. Chiang Mai: Silkworm Books, 2010.

Quaritch Wales, H.G. "Archaeological Researches on Ancient Indian Colonization in Malaya". In *Journal of the Royal Asiatic Society, Malay Branch* XVIII, Part 1 (February 1940): 1–85.

Ramanathan, A.A., ed. *Amarakośa with the unpublished South Indian commentaries Amarapadavivṛti of Liṅgayasūrin and the Amarapadapārijāta of Mallinātha*. Vol. I. Adyar: The Adyar Library and Research Centre, 1971.

Renou, Louis and Jean Filliozat, eds. *L'Inde Classique: manuel des études indiennes* II. Hanoi: École française d'Extrême-Orient, 1953.

Roth, Gustav, ed. *Bhikṣuṇī-Vinaya: [Manual of Discipline for Buddhist Nuns] including Bhikṣuṇī-prakīrṇaka and a summary of the Bhikṣu-prakīrṇaka of the Ārya-mahāsāṃghika-lokottaravādin*. Tibetan Sanskrit Works Series, vol. XII. Patna: K.P. Jayaswal Research Institute, 1970.

——. "Particular Features of the Language of the Ārya-Mahāsāṃghika-Lokottaravādins and their Importance for Early Buddhist Tradition". In *The Language of the Earliest Buddhist Tradition*, edited by Heinz Bechert, pp. 97–135. Göttingen: Vandenhoeck & Ruprecht, 1980.

Rost, R. *Miscellaneous Papers relating to Indo-China*. London: Trübner & Co, 1886.

Sastri, N. Aiyaswami. *Ārya Śālistamba Sūtra*. The Adyar Library Series 76. Madras: Adyar Library, 1950.

Schmidt, Klaus T., ed. *Der Schlussteil des Prātimokṣasūtra der Sarvāstivādins: Text in Sanskrit und Tocharisch A verglichen mit den Parallelversionen anderer Schulen*. Sanskrittexte aus den Turfanfunden, vol. XIII. Göttingen: Vandenhoeck & Ruprecht, 1989.

Senart, É., ed. *Le Mahāvastu*, tome III. Paris: Imprimerie Nationale, 1907.

Sircar, Dinesh Chandra. *Select Inscriptions bearing on Indian History and Civilization from the Sixth Century B.C. to the Sixth Century A.D.* vol. I, 3rd ed. Delhi and Madras: Asian Humanities Press, 1986 (first published, Calcutta 1965).

Skilling, Peter. "Comments on 'Two Sūtras on Dependent Origination'". In *Buddhist Studies Review* 1, no. 2 (1983–84): 136–42.

———. *Mahāsūtras: Great Discourses of the Buddha*. Vol. I: Texts. Sacred Books of the Buddhists, XLIV. Oxford: Pali Text Society, 1994.

———. "On the School-affiliation of the 'Patna Dhammapada'". In *Journal of the Pali Text Society* XXIII (1997): 83–122.

———. "A Buddhist inscription from Go Xoai, Southern Vietnam and notes towards a classification of *ye dharmā* inscriptions". In *80 pi Sattrachan Dr Prasert Na Nakhon: ruam botkhwam wichakan dan charuek lae ekasan boran –* [80 Years: A collection of articles on epigraphy and ancient documents published on the occasion of the celebration of the 80th birthday of Prof. Dr. Prasert Na Nagara], pp. 171–87. Bangkok: Phikhanet Printing Center, 1999. [B.E. 2542].

———. "Traces of the Dharma: Preliminary reports on some *ye dhammā* and *ye dharmā* inscriptions from Mainland South-East Asia". In *Bulletin de l'École française d'Extrême-Orient* 90–91 (2003-04): 273–87.

———. "Buddhist sealings and the *ye dharmā* stanza". In *Archaeology of Early Historic South Asia*, edited by G. Sengupta and S. Chakraborty, pp. 503–25. New Delhi/Kolkata: Pragati Publications/Centre for Archaeological Studies and Training, Eastern India, 2008.

———. "Theravāda in History". In *Pacific World: Journal of the Institute of Buddhist Studies*, 3rd Series, no. 11 (Fall 2009): 61–93.

———. "Scriptural Authenticity and the Śrāvaka Schools: An Essay towards an Indian Perspective". *The Eastern Buddhist* 41, no. 2 (2010): 1–47.

———. "Buddhism and the Circulation of Ritual in Early Peninsular Southeast Asia". In *Early Interactions between South and Southeast Asia: Reflections on Cross-Cultural Exchange*, edited by P.Y. Manguin, A. Mani, and G. Wade, chapter 18, pp. 371–84. Singapore: Institute of Southeast Asian Studies; New Delhi: Manohar India, 2011.

———, William Southworth, and Tran Ky Phuong. "A Buddhist Stele from My Thanh in the Phu Yen Province of Central Vietnam". In *Abhinandanamala: Nandana Chutiwongs Felicitation Volume*, edited by Leelananda Prematilleke, pp. 487–513. Bangkok: SPAFA Regional Centre of Archaeology and Fine Arts, in collaboration with the Abhinandanamala Committee, Colombo, 2010.

Stein, Aurel. *Kharoṣṭhī Inscriptions Discovered by Sir Aurel Stein in Chinese Turkestan*. Oxford: Clarendon Press, 1920 (reprint New Delhi: Cosmo Publications, 1997).

Stuart, Daniel. "A Less Traveled Path: An Edition, Translation and Historical Study of the Second Chapter of the Saddharmasmṛtyupasthānasūtra". PhD dissertation to be submitted to the Group in Buddhist Studies at the University of California at Berkeley, 2012.

Sullivan, Michael. "Excavations in Kedah and Province Wellesley, 1957". In *Journal of the Malayan Branch of the Royal Asiatic Society* XXXI, pt. 1 (1958): 188–223.

Sørensen, Henrik H. "The Spell of the Great, Golden Peacock Queen: The Origin,

Practices, and Lore of an Early Esoteric Buddhist Tradition in China". In *Pacific World: Journal of the Insitute of Buddhist Studies*, 3rd Series, No. 8 (Fall 2006): 89–123.

Takakusu, J. *A Record of the Buddhist Religion as Practised in India and the Malay Archipelago (A.D. 671–695)*. London, 1896 (Repr. New Delhi: Munshiram Manoharlal, 1982).

Takubo, Shūyo, ed. *Ārya-Mahā-Māyūrī Vidyā-rājñī*. Tokyo: Sankibo.

Tatia, Nathmal, ed. *Prātimokṣasūtraṃ of the Lokottaravādimahāsāṅghika School*. Tibetan Sanskrit Works Series, vol. 16. Patna: Kashi Prasad Jayaswal Research Institute, 1975.

——. *Prātimokṣasūtra of the Lokottaravādimahāsāṅghika School*. Tibetan Sanskrit Works Series 16. Patna: Kashi Prasad Jayaswal Research Institute, 1975.

——. *Abhidharmasamuccaya-bhāṣyam*. Tibetan Sanskrit Works Series no. 17, edited by Anantalal Thakur. Patna: Kashi Prasad Jayaswal Research Institute, 1976 (reprint, 2nd edition, 2005).

Thaplyal, Kiran Kumar. *Studies in Ancient Indian Seals: A Study of North Indian Seals and Sealings from circa Third Century B.C. to Mid-Seventh Century A.D.* Lucknow: Akhila Bharatiya Sanskrit Parishad, 1972.

Tharapong Srisuchat. *Ancient Trades and Cultural Contacts in Southeast Asia*. Bangkok: The Office of the National Culture Commission, 1996.

Tripāṭhī, Chandrabhāl. *Fünfundzwanzig Sūtras des Nidānasaṃyukta*. Sanskrittexte aus den Turfanfunden vol. VIII. Göttingen: Vandenhoeck & Ruprecht, 1962.

Tsukamoto, Keisho. *A Comprehensive Study of the Indian Buddhist Inscriptions*, Part I, *Texts, Notes and Japanese Translation*. Kyoto: Heirakuji Shoten, 1996.

van Louizen-de Leeuw, Johanna Engelberta. "The stūpa in Indonesia". In *The Stūpa: Its Religious, Historical and Architectural Significance*, pp. 277–300. Edited by Anna Libera Dallapiccola in collaboration with Stephanie Zingel-Avé Lallement. Beiträge zur Südasienforschung Südasian-Institut Universität Heidelberg, Band 55. Wiesbaden: Franz Steiner Verlag, 1980.

Vogel, J. Ph. "Seals of Buddhist Monasteries in Ancient India." *Journal of the Ceylon Branch of the Royal Asiatic Society*, Centenary Volume (1845–1945), new series, vol. I. Colombo, 1950.

——. "Prakrit Inscriptions from Ghantasala." In *Epigraphia Indica* XXVII, edited by B. Ch. Chhabra and N. Lakshminarayan Rao. Delhi: The Manager of Publications, 1956 (reprint, New Delhi, 1985).

von Hinüber, Oskar. *Sieben Goldblätter einer Pañcaviṃśatisāhasrikā Prajñāpāramitā aus Anurādhapura*. Göttingen: Vandenhoeck & Ruprecht, 1983.

Waldschmidt, Ernst. *Das Upasenasūtra*. Göttingen: Vandenhoeck & Ruprecht, 1957.

———. "Ein zweites Daśabalasūtra". In *Mitteilungen des Instituts für Orientforschung* 6 (1958): 382–405. Reprinted in Ernst Waldschmidt, *Von Ceylon bis Turfan, Schriften zur Geschichte, Literatur, Religion und Kunst des indischen Kulturraumes. Festgabe zum 70. Geburtstag am 15. Juli 1967*, pp. 347–70. Edited by Heinz Bechert. Göttingen: Vandenhoeck & Ruprecht, 1967.

Watters, Thomas. *On Yuan Chwang's Travels in India (A.D. 629–645)*. 2nd Indian ed. New Delhi: Munshiram Manoharlal, 1973 (first published, London: Royal Asiatic Society, 1904–05).

Webb, Russell, ed. *Buddhist Studies Review* 2, no. 1–2 (1985).

Wheatley, Paul. *The Golden Khersonese*. Kuala Lumpur: University of Malaya Press, 1980 (first published in 1961).

Whitfield, Roderick et al. *Treasures from Korea: Art through 5000 years*. London: British Museum Publications, 1984.

3

HOW MANY MONKS? Quantitative and Demographic Archaeological Approaches to Buddhism in Northeast Thailand and Central Laos, Sixth to Eleventh Centuries CE

Stephen A. Murphy

INTRODUCTION

This article explores a number of ways in which to reconstruct the possible extent of monastic Buddhism in the Khorat Plateau during the Dvāravatī period. In an attempt to so, it is consequently multidisciplinary in its conception, being primarily archaeological while also drawing on areas of anthropology, art history, demographics and Buddhist studies. In doing so, it attempts to move beyond the sole analysis of archaeological and art historic objects in order to investigate the social, demographic and geographical factors that lie behind the production of these artefacts. It proposes to do so by a number of quantitative means: first, by giving hypothetical population estimates of urban centres/moated sites during the Dvāravatī period and consequently the number of monks these settlements could have supported. These estimates are then used to consider how many monks may have been sustained according to these figures. Second, by carrying out a quantitative analysis of *sema* stone numbers and their distribution throughout the Khorat Plateau this also provides a method to calculate the number of possible consecrated spaces (viz., *sīma*) in the region and their geographic extent. The analysis shows that institutional, monastic Buddhism primarily spread and settled along the major river systems throughout the region. Third, by plotting the distribution, quantity and quality of Buddhist narrative artwork on *sema* to pinpoint the locations of possible workshops and centres. This also allows for a number of conclusions to be drawn in terms of the socio-economic support needed to develop and maintain workshops and craftsmen and relates directly to population densities.

It should, however, be stated at the outset that this paper proposes nothing more than a possible *scenario* to aid in explaining and understanding the extent and spread of Buddhism during this period. I am here using the term "scenario" in reference to Donn Bayard's cautionary remarks regarding archaeology and the use of models.[1] As Bayard explains, a model, strictly speaking should be based on reliable datasets which are testable and "ideally consists of a set of relationships between variables to which more or less precise numerical values may be assigned".[2] As will become clear in this paper, the assigning of such precise figures to the subject under investigation (viz. Buddhism) is unrealistic given the current incomplete state of the datasets from the region and time period in question. Therefore, I adopt the term "scenario" over "model" to emphasize the fact that what is being proposed here is an interpretive framework as opposed to a testable hypothesis in the strictly scientific sense.

The issue of population growth in archaeological studies has been linked to both cultural change and urbanization.[3] The origin of complex societies in Southeast Asia occurs in tandem with the arrival of universal religions such as Buddhism and Brahmanism. The Buddhism that appears in the Dvāravatī period seems to be closely tied to wet-rice growing, settled communities, albeit widely dispersed, which had adequate population densities to sustain it. Surprisingly however, in a Southeast Asian context, particularly in discussions regarding "Indianization",[4] analyses of this kind are unfortunately lacking. This absence of the prerequisite demographic data seems all the more problematic when we consider the leading demographic archaeologist, Fekri A. Hassan's comments on the subject who states, "We can no longer ignore the relationship between population and culture. Questions of human ecology and adaptation, which are central to many of the more recent discussions in archaeology, cannot be answered adequately without examining the role of demographic variables."[5]

This article, therefore, proposes some initial methods and approaches to this issue and uses early Buddhism in the Khorat Plateau during the Dvāravatī period as a case study. It is hoped that this will stimulate debate and possibly new ways of looking, investigating and consequently understanding the development of early urbanization and the origins of civilizations in the region.

DVĀRAVATĪ AND ITS GEOGRAPHICAL EXTENT

Defining exactly what is meant by the term "Dvāravatī" is a somewhat problematic exercise and much debate and disagreement still surround the use and application of this term. A full analysis of this issue is beyond the scope of this discussion. However the following description is provided to clarify how the term is applied in this paper.

Put simply, Dvāravatī simultaneously refers to the beginnings of history in Thailand and the arrival of religious and cultural influences primarily from the South Asian subcontinent, specifically Buddhism, and to a lesser extent Brahmanism, into the region. The term has been used to describe an art style, a kingdom, an early state, a material culture and a chronological period.[6] Early scholarship in the late nineteenth and early twentieth century envisioned Dvāravatī as a Buddhist kingdom holding sway over a geographical area that encompassed all of what is today modern Thailand.[7] A large degree of projecting modern political, national and religious practices back onto the past was present in this definition. This claim was largely arrived at by matching the boundaries of the hypothesized kingdom and the extent of Dvāravatī style art.

In the last two to three decades, however, this view has been largely refuted by continual research into the period, be it archaeological, epigraphic or art historic. Today, there is a general consensus that the Dvāravatī political entity was restricted to central Thailand and spanned the sixth to ninth centuries CE.[8] The question, however, of what this entity was is still open to debate. Most scholars have moved away from the idea that it was a centralized state and see it more as a loose confederation of urban centres, usually consisting of moated sites on the major river systems.

Dvāravatī art and material culture, however, had a larger geographical and chronological spread, being found throughout the Khorat Plateau and at sites such as ancient Haripunchaiya (modern day Lampun) in northern Thailand. Chronologically they span a period of the sixth to eleventh centuries, some 200 years longer than the evidence for their political counterpart. The presence of Buddhism is also a key indicator of what can be termed Dvāravatī culture and, therefore, sites possessing Dvāravatī style Buddhist art, religious architecture or other forms of material culture such as fingermarked bricks, pottery or stucco usually become classified as Dvāravatī.

In this paper the term Dvāravatī is used to describe a common art style, material culture and the presence of Buddhism during the sixth to eleventh centuries CE based primarily in central Thailand but also in the Khorat Plateau and to a lesser extent in northern Thailand. By using the term Dvāravatī, it should be emphasized, however, that this paper does not support the idea that there was a central Dvāravatī political entity that held sway over all of the Chao Phraya Basin or the Khorat Plateau. Instead, it sees the political situation somewhat differently. The evidence to date from settlement patterns and the archaeological record points more to the emergence of urban centres located at moated sites along the major river systems or close to the coast. These sites may have exerted varying degrees of control over their surrounding hinterlands and perhaps smaller sites in their direct vicinity. However, it is unlikely that at any stage they controlled large areas of the region. The view of largely independent urban centres also raises the possibility of local rulers actively engaged in the patronage of Buddhism in return for the legitimization of their positions by high-ranking Buddhist monks.

The Khorat Plateau as defined in this paper encompasses the regions of northeast Thailand and Central Laos, the latter location consisting mainly of the lowland areas of Vientiane, Khammoune and Savannakhet provinces (Figure 3.1). This definition is somewhat wider than the more conventional one, which usually refers only to northeast Thailand. It is argued, however, that the definition presented here is valid as the modern political divide centring on the Mekong River distorts the geographical homogeneity of the region.[9] Buddhism was free to spread along both sides of this river system since before the colonization of the region in the nineteenth and twentieth centuries the Mekong was a vital route of communication, transport and trade as opposed to a modern boundary between nation states.

The Khorat Plateau lies at an average height of about 170 metres above sea level and dominates the physical geography of the area. The Plateau is bordered by the Phetchabun and Dangrek Mountains ranges to the west and south respectively and to the north and east by the course of the Mekong River and the Truong Son Cordillera mountain range in central and southern Laos.

FIGURE 3.1
Map of the Khorat Plateau showing the major river systems and mountain ranges

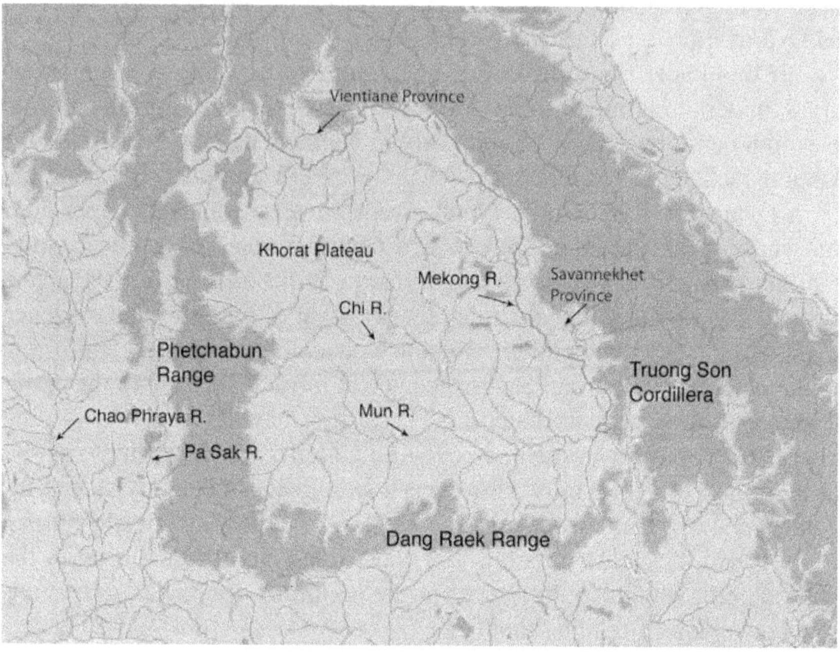

PATRONAGE AND DEMOGRAPHIC CONSIDERATIONS RELATING TO BUDDHIST MONASTICISM AND SOCIETY

A primary assumption of this paper is that Buddhism can usually only take hold in areas of sufficient socio-economic and urban development. This may initially seem at odds with certain perceptions of Buddhism which see it primarily as a religion based on the renunciation of society. However, as Greg Bailey and Ian Mabbett have shown, Buddhism as a phenomenon can be understood in at least three different ways: (1) as a religion that rejects the world; (2) as a religion engaged in public and political life; and (3) as a folk religion.[10] All three are plausible definitions and to a certain extent considered together, encompass the concept of Buddhism as a whole. However, for the purpose of this paper I shall focus more on analysing and attempting to reconstruct certain aspects of the second version, that is, Buddhism and its place in the societies it finds itself within.

Looking at the *sangha* as it exists today for instance, it can be observed that it is almost entirely dependent on the communities and societies it finds itself within in regard to not only its daily needs in terms of sustenance and basic necessities such as clothing and utensils, but also in regard to the construction of monasteries and religious monuments. The richer and more developed a society or urban centre it finds itself within, then in theory the more donations and support it can receive from both the local population and the ruling elites.

At times, however, economics are not always the prevailing factor. As Jane Bunnag has shown, sometimes the relative wealth and standing of a monastery can be due to the presence of a charismatic monk who is able to build up not only a large following of lay believers and therefore donations, but is also able to attract new monks to his temple, thus increasing its size and ability to serve the community.[11] In fact Bunnag argues that in modern Thai Buddhism (in Ayutthaya at least) pastoral activities and conferring merit on the lay community were seen as much more appropriate roles for a Buddhist monk than the pursuit of personal salvation through meditation which was perceived as "selfish" by the lay community.[12] Louis Gabaude also observed similar perceptions using data from a study carried out in 2008 by the Office of National Statistics.[13] The results show that of the 67,000 people surveyed over the age of thirteen, only 4 per cent of lay people practised meditation at least once a week, while 90 per cent thought that giving food to the monks was the most important activity.

Another major factor that goes a long way to determining the wealth and size of monasteries is whether or not they are recipients of royal or elite patronage. Tambiah points out that in a modern Thai context *wat luang* (royal temples) are usually famous, large, and also older than *wat raad* (commoner temples) and are under the patronage of aristocrats, top officials, and famous patrons.[14] *Wat raad* on the other hand, are usually more recently established, smaller and tend to be supported by ordinary people, although in some cases they too can have well-to-do patrons. However, if *wat raad* manage to reach a large enough size or gain sufficient enough prestige they can apply to be upgraded to royal wats.[15]

The importance of patronage and donation on the one hand and pastoral activities and facilitating the means to gain merit on the other are key aspects in regard to the ability of a monastery to exist, expand and grow. Monks in the Dvāravatī period would have most likely been keenly aware of this dynamic. Therefore, we can envisage a situation where they would have consciously sought to develop these types of social relationships as a means of propagating the religion. Evidence for donative practices and patronage during this period in the Khorat Plateau can be illustrated by two inscriptions in particular. The first, Inscription K404 from Baan Kaeng in Kaset Sombun district, Chaiyaphum province has been read and translated by Kaeokhlai.[16] In her reading she states that the donor's name was Cudamani, a high-ranking lady or queen, and was a person interested with making beneficial karma and was known for her moral integrity and "*dharma*-filled wisdom". The second inscription was found on a *sema* stone from Baan Panna in Sakhon Nakhon province.[17] It was discovered in the backyard of a local villager's house and given to the Ban Chiang Museum in 1997 for safe keeping. It is a two-line inscription in post-Pallava script, old Mon language dating to the ninth–tenth centuries and has been read by Weeraprajak.[18] His translation states that members of the Mipa Suraya Family had donated doors and windows to build a new temple.

The practice of patronage and donation is much better attested in an Indian context. As John Guy points out, at times it was not only the elite who were making donations to temples, but merchant guilds, thus highlighting the importance and to a certain extent the incentive for Buddhism to settle in areas linked in to pre-existing and profitable trade routes.[19] In the Khorat Plateau, these would have consisted of the major river systems, such as the Mun, Chi and Middle Mekong as discussed below.

Comparisons from Bharhut, Mathura and Sanchi in India are also informative in this regard. Gregory Schopen in a survey of inscriptions has shown that up to 40 per cent of donations at Bharhut were actually from monks, while at Mathura this figure is over 50 per cent, highlighting the fact that at certain times and locations in its history, the *sangha* possessed considerable wealth and resources.[20] Turning back to the Khorat Plateau, one inscription on a *sema* stone also casts light on this practice. The Hin Khon inscription (K388) has been interpreted by Woodward to represent a prince who had become a monk (*rājabhikṣu*). He not only dedicated four *sema* of high-quality stone but had also given large donations as well.[21] If Woodward's interpretation is correct then we here have a simultaneous example of a member of royalty and the monkhood giving a donation to a monastic community.

In an attempt to gain a greater level of understanding regarding Buddhism during the Dvāravatī period, particularly concerning its extent and density, it is proposed here that modern ethnographic data from Thailand concerning the number of monks in society, or more precisely, the ratio of monks to lay people can be employed as a possible approach to explore this question. For instance Tambiah, using figures from the Manpower Planning Division of the National Economic Development Board of Thailand for the year 1970, comes up with the following numbers; about 1.8 per cent of the male population were members of the *sangha*.[22] Of this figure about 25 per cent were temporary monks as the data was taken during Buddhist lent so the actual figure for permanent members was about 1.35 per cent of the male population or about 0.67 per cent of the entire population. Novices on the other hand represented about 0.3 per cent of the entire population, or about 0.6 per cent of the male population.

More recently Gabaude has looked at this question in more detail using statistical data spanning the years 1927–2008.[23] All in all, his figures roughly correspond with Tambiah's projections. For instance in 1966 he calculates that out of a population of 100,000 people, 0.57 per cent were monks. However, what comes through extremely clearly in his statistics is the sharp drop in the monks to lay person ratio over the ninety-year period. For example, in 1927 the figure was at 1.17 per cent while by 2008 it had dropped to only 0.39 per cent. Alternatively, this can also be expressed as one monk per 85 people in 1927 compared to one monk per 251 people in 2008. The reasons and factors for such a drop are too numerous to be discussed in this article. However, it should be noted that the population of Thailand increased over fivefold during this period.

Further demographic studies have been carried out by Volker Grabowsky who uses a number of censuses from the first quarter of the twentieth century.[24] The census of 1904 covered approximately three-fifths of the population since it did not cover north or northeast Thailand, Grabowsky collected provincial censuses from this region instead, dating from 1899 to 1908. From this Grabowsky calculates that in the twelve districts (*monthon*) surveyed there were 3,308,032 people. Of this 51,064 were monks, which means they represented 1.54 per cent of the overall population at this time.

For the purposes of this study, the pre-1950s figures are deemed to represent the most reliable ethnographic comparative data. Post-World War II Thailand experienced rapid economic development and this in turn would have had quite an effect on the *sangha* and society in general. The figures from 1904, 1927 and 1937 on the other hand reflect those of a society that is still more agrarian-based and premodern to a certain degree, which would be particularly true of areas such as the Khorat Plateau. Therefore as a rough rule of thumb, I suggest that the monk to lay person ratio in the nineteenth to early twentieth century could be calculated at 1 per cent of the total population. This estimate also closely matches evidence gathered by Landon between 1932 and 1937, which gives a figure of 150,213 monks for a population of 14.5 million, or just over 1 per cent.[25] Bearing the above factors and statistics in mind, it should be possible to analyse the archaeological record of given regions, sub-regions or specific urban sites in order to give hypothetical estimates for their population levels and consequently their potential to support the Buddhist *sangha*. For instance, an urban centre would need to be producing a sufficiently high surplus in terms of both agricultural produce and raw materials such as wood, brick, stone or even precious metals such as gold and silver. Furthermore, an urban centre would need a sufficiently large enough work force, so that there was the manpower available to commit to large-scale building projects such as stupas and monastery complexes. Another factor to consider is specialization of the work force. Societies and their urban centres need to reach a certain level of development before specialized professions emerge. The bronze casting ability exhibited by the sculpture from Baan Fai (Figures 3.2 and 3.3) and Baan Tanot, for example, both point to an extremely high level of technical and artistic ability. From this we can infer that a certain degree of specialization may have been reached and it is also possible to posit the existence of established workshops.

We now turn to a discussion of population estimates in the Dvāravatī period and in doing so propose approximate figures for numbers of monks present at certain settlements. In the following sections of this chapter I employ the 1 per cent monks to lay person figure proposed above as a guideline for calculating potential numbers of monks in the Dvāravatī period. I am effectively projecting modern statistical data back about ca.1,200 years to be used in conjunction with other plausible indicators for monastic numbers such as settlement size/population levels and quantitative analysis of *sema* stones. As stated at the outset, this methodology has its limitations and it should be noted that these are hypothetical estimates only and do not represent a "model" in the strictest sense of the word. It would therefore be best to understand the figures proposed below as representing possible scenarios for the period in question.

POPULATION LEVELS IN LATE PREHISTORY AND THE DVĀRAVATĪ PERIOD

In order to estimate the possible extent of Buddhist monasticism in regard to issues such as the number of monks present at sites during the Dvāravatī period, it is first necessary to propose population estimates for the regions and urban centres in question within the Khorat Plateau. Increase in population size during the formative stages of the development

FIGURE 3.2
A bronze Buddha image from the moated site of Baan Fai, Buriram province today housed at the National Museum Bangkok

of civilizations has been highlighted by a number of scholars as extremely influential and more often than not the "prime mover" in regard to urbanization.[26]

Firstly, a note of caution should be mentioned regarding archaeological methods of estimating populations as they are far from fail-safe and

FIGURE 3.3
A bronze bodhisattva image from the moated side of Baan Fai, Buriram province today housed at the National Museum Bangkok

represent approximations only. Bayard for instance states that these methods can be unreliable but does concede we should still undertake such estimates even with imprecise variables if only to highlight errors in our prior assumptions or the inadequacy of our present datasets.[27] Hassan on the other hand is somewhat more positive and points out that, even if accurate figures are not attainable, it is much more preferable to have rough estimates than nothing at all as these can still be informative.[28] Likewise, the works discussed below on this subject do not represent exact figures but are considered reliable enough in their calculations to make this study feasible in regard to drawing conclusions regarding early Buddhist monasticism in the region.

A number of overall estimates regarding population sizes can be drawn from comparative and ethnographic studies which allow for certain "ballpark" figures to be reached. For example, Hassan's review of the archaeological methods used to calculate site size based on numbers of households present and floor space required, arrives at a figure of 4.55m^2 of living space per person.[29] Another method is to use a formula to estimate the number of inhabitants of a village or town. This can be shown as follows:

$$\text{Number of inhabitants} = \text{constant} \times \text{site area}$$

The constant in this case is the number of persons per unit of a site area determined from modern village or town statistics. Colin Renfrew, using this method, for example, estimates that the population in the late Bronze Age Aegean was about 300 persons per hectare. As will be seen below this estimate is considerably higher than that given for Thailand.[30] Some of the best examples, however, of reconstructions of regional population sizes are those from Mexico and Mesopotamia.[31]

Turning our attention back to Southeast Asia, Charles Higham and Rachanie Thosarat have proposed a number of population estimates for areas and sites in the Khorat Plateau during the prehistoric period.[32] In discussing sites in the Chi river system they argue that with the coming of the Iron Age there is evidence for a rapid growth in population with settlements proliferating, some of which grew to be up to ten times larger than those in the Bronze Age. Citing the site of Baan Chiang Hian in Mahasarakam province as an example, they suggest that this 38.5 hectare site, with its area clearly defined by multiple moats, had a population of around 2,000 people. This figure is arrived at by assuming a population density of 50 people per hectare which is consistent with the estimates given above by Hassan. Furthermore, Chantaratiyakarn, having surveyed the surrounding landscape and settlement patterns argues that there would have been sufficient availability of rice land to sustain a population of 2,000 people at Baan Chiang Hian.[33]

Higham and Thosarat have also argued that the Iron Age site of Non Chai which had an area of over 38.5 hectares, stood 15 metres above the surrounding area and was excavated under the direction of Pisit

Charoenwongsa in 1977–78, may have had a population that "comfortably exceeded a thousand people, considerably larger than any known Bronze Age settlement".[34]

David Welch and Judith McNeil in their surveys of the Phimai area arrive at similar figures to Higham and Thosarat.[35] The authors looked at the relationship between three mutually dependent factors: population growth, the intensification of the agricultural system and centralization.[36] In order to investigate these issues they carried out two field surveys, KBAP1, a 300 square kilometre survey around Phimai in 1979–80 and KBAP2 a 700 square kilometre survey in 1989. They found five phases of occupation stretching from 1,000 BCE–1,300 CE.[37]

During the Prasat Phase (600–200 BCE) they argue that in the alluvial plains the population density "almost certainly reached 30 to 40 persons/km^2 and may have reached as high as 50". Furthermore, using modern yields as estimates, they project that flooded field farming could actually support a population of 75 to 125 persons/km^2.[38] By the classic Phimai phase (200 BCE–300 CE) population levels on the alluvial plain had reached 70 to 80 persons/km^2 and 30 person/km^2 on the terraces. The authors argue that the concentration of the population into large settlements of up to 2,000 people during this phase most likely encouraged further intensification of agriculture to produce sufficient yields.[39]

They further state that late prehistoric period farmers transformed the natural environment to a significant degree. Large sections of the floodplain and low terraces were transformed from wild grasslands to bunded fields for rice cultivation with the authors concluding that, "The pattern of settlement through all phases reflects the basic dependence of Phimai region settlements on wet rice agriculture".[40]

The authors estimate that approximately fifty people were living on each hectare of each habitation site.[41] They based this estimate upon village population densities during the period of their surveys (i.e. 1979–89) and assume that the needs of prehistoric villagers would have been similar to those today in terms of utilization of space. A detailed explanation of their population estimate technique is available in Welch's PhD thesis.[42]

Both Higham and Thosarat and Welch and McNeil are in agreement that by the late Iron Age/early Dvāravatī period, settlements could have possessed populations of around 2,000 people or more and that the intensification of farming, particularly in alluvial areas would have produced sufficient yield to support these habitations. As a rule of thumb, both also settle on a figure for the occupation of habitation sites at fifty people per hectare. Therefore, a 40 hectare site, the average size of a Dvāravatī moated settlement (see Figure 3.4) could support up to 2,000 people. Mudar, in her study of Dvāravatī settlements and site hierarchies in Central Thailand, has calculated that a 70 hectare site using transplanted wet rice agriculture would need a 2 kilometre radius catchment area to produce sufficient yield to sustain such a population.[43] Therefore a 40 hectare site would need just under a 1 kilometre catchment area to sustain its population. A site such as Muang Sema for example could initially have had a population of about 1,900 people (38 hectares) before it expanded in size probably

FIGURE 3.4
Map showing the major Dvāravatī moated sites in central and northeast Thailand and their size in hectares. Courtesy of Matthew D. Gallon.

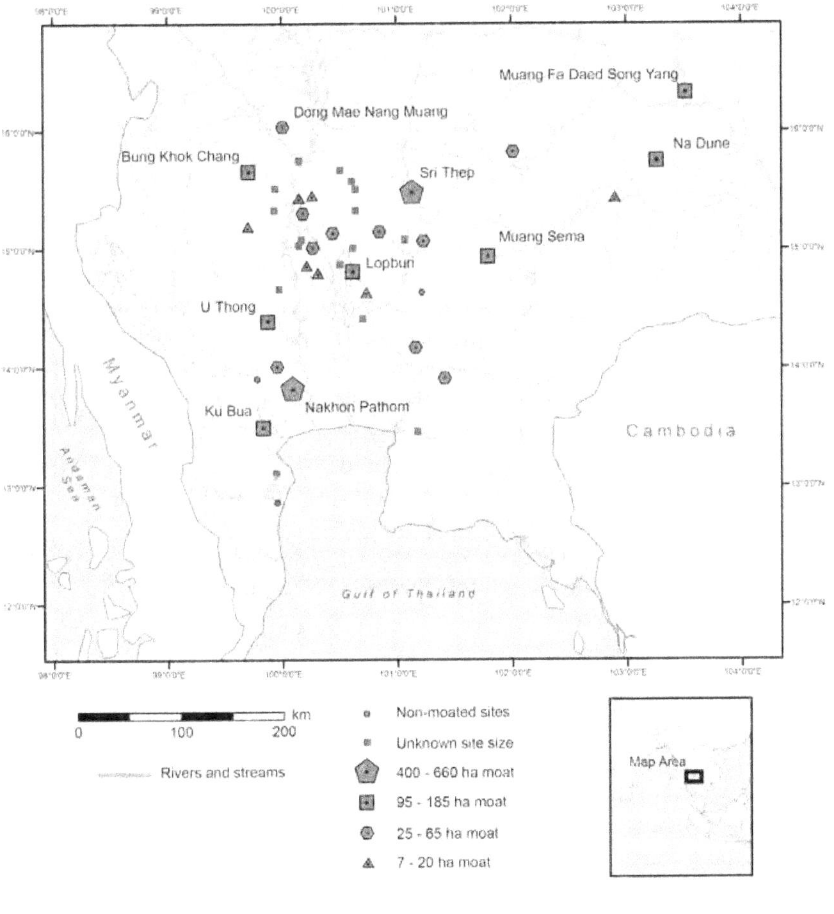

in the Khmer period to 150 hectares resulting in its population possibly growing to about 7,500 people.

Similarly Muang Fa Daed, at 170 hectares could have had a population of around 8,500. Sri Thep and Nakhon Pathom, the two largest Dvāravatī period sites both measure just over 600 hectares and would therefore give population estimates of about 30,000 people. However, perhaps only the inner moated area at these two latter sites functioned as the main urban settlement. If so the figures could be considerably less and perhaps more in line with Muang Sema or Muang Fa Daed.[44]

Interestingly in the one example where there is epigraphic evidence for population levels, the figures appear to fit very closely to that of the population estimates proposed above. A twelfth century inscription (K966) discovered at the site of Dong Mae Nang Muang in Nakorn Sawan province, mentions a local king named Sunat, who ruled at the city of Thanya Pura (modern day Dong Mae Nang Muang). Dated to 1167 CE, it states the population of the city was exactly 2,012 people and defines the geographical boundary of the city itself. It is written in Khmer on one face and Pali on the other, and its first translation was published in 1956.[45] Dong Mae Nang Muang is approximately 40 hectares in size; so using the fifty persons per hectare estimate, this would give a population of 2,000 people, matching almost exactly the number stated in the inscription.[46]

By combining population density figures from a sample of nine moated sites with the modern ethnographic and statistical data on monks to population ratios calculated above at 1 per cent, a number of proposed estimates can be arrived at as illustrated in Table 3.1.[47]

TABLE 3.1
The Size, Proposed Population Density and Estimated Number of Monks at Nine Dvāravatī Moated Sites in the Khorat Plateau

Site	*Hectares*	*Population density*	*No. of Monks*
Muang Sema	150	7,500	75
Muang Fa Daed	170	8,500	85
Roi Et	120	6,000	60
Baan Fai	38.5	1,925	20
Baan Korn Sawan	100	5,000	50
Baan Pa Khiap	70	3,500	35
Khantarawichai	100	5,000	50
Baan Nohn Muang	38	1,900	19
Baan Chiang Haeo	328	16,400	164

On the grounds of these estimates, Dvāravatī moated sites on the Khorat Plateau could hypothetically have a minimum population of around 1,900 people and a maximum of up to 16,400. Subsequently, even the smallest sites such as Baan Nohn Muang could have been able to support at least nineteen monks. Large-scale sites such as Muang Fa Daed or Baan Chiang Haeo could have supported anywhere up to 85–164 monks. Overall the figures illustrate that by the eighth to ninth centuries there could have been large numbers of monks present at the moated sites with the nine settlements discussed above alone potentially totaling 558 monks. Furthermore, I have recorded forty-five Dvāravatī moated sites in the region (Figure 3.5). Allowing for the possibility that monastic Buddhism was present at the majority of them, and taking the average monks per site at an amount averaged out from those in Table 3.1 we arrive at a figure of sixty monks per site or hypothetically approximately 2,700 monks spread out over these forty-five moated sites. This is to say, the region would have had the potential to support a figure in the region of 2,700 monks.

How do these figures compare to the archaeological record in terms of the quantity of artefacts attesting to the presence of Buddhist monasticism? In order to investigate this question, the discussion now turns to Dvāravatī *sema* stones from the Khorat Plateau.

SEMA STONES AND THE DISTRIBUTION OF BUDDHISM IN THE KHORAT PLATEAU

The figures given in Table 3.1 require as a prerequisite the ability to identify clearly defined settlements (in this case almost exclusively moated sites) which in turn allows for the size of the site to be measured. However, in some instances this is not always possible and as a result we need to turn to other forms of evidence in our attempts to calculate and correlate the density of Buddhism.[48] In the case of the Khorat Plateau this comes in the form of *sema* stones (Figure 3.6).

Sema are monumental stone objects which with 110 sites and over 1,200 of these objects documented to date, provide a unique means of tracking the spread and location of Buddhist monasticism in the Khorat Plataeu during the Dvāravatī Period.[49] Combined with the demographic archaeological approaches above, they provide an additional quantitative dataset with which to analyse the extent and location of monastic Buddhism during the period in question.

The function of *sema* stones are to demarcate Buddhist monastic ritual space, thus creating a boundary (in Pali referred to as a *sīmā*[50] which is also

FIGURE 3.5
Map showing the distribution of moated sites in the Khorat Plateau in blue and earthern mounds in yellow. Sites mentioned in this article; M1, Baan Korn Sawan; M5, Roi Et; M8, Baan Nohn Muang; M13, Muang Fa Daed; M14, Muang Sema; M19, Kantharawichai; M27, Baan Chiang Haeo; M28, Baan Pra Khiap; M41, Baan Muang Fai; E5 Baan Tat Tong

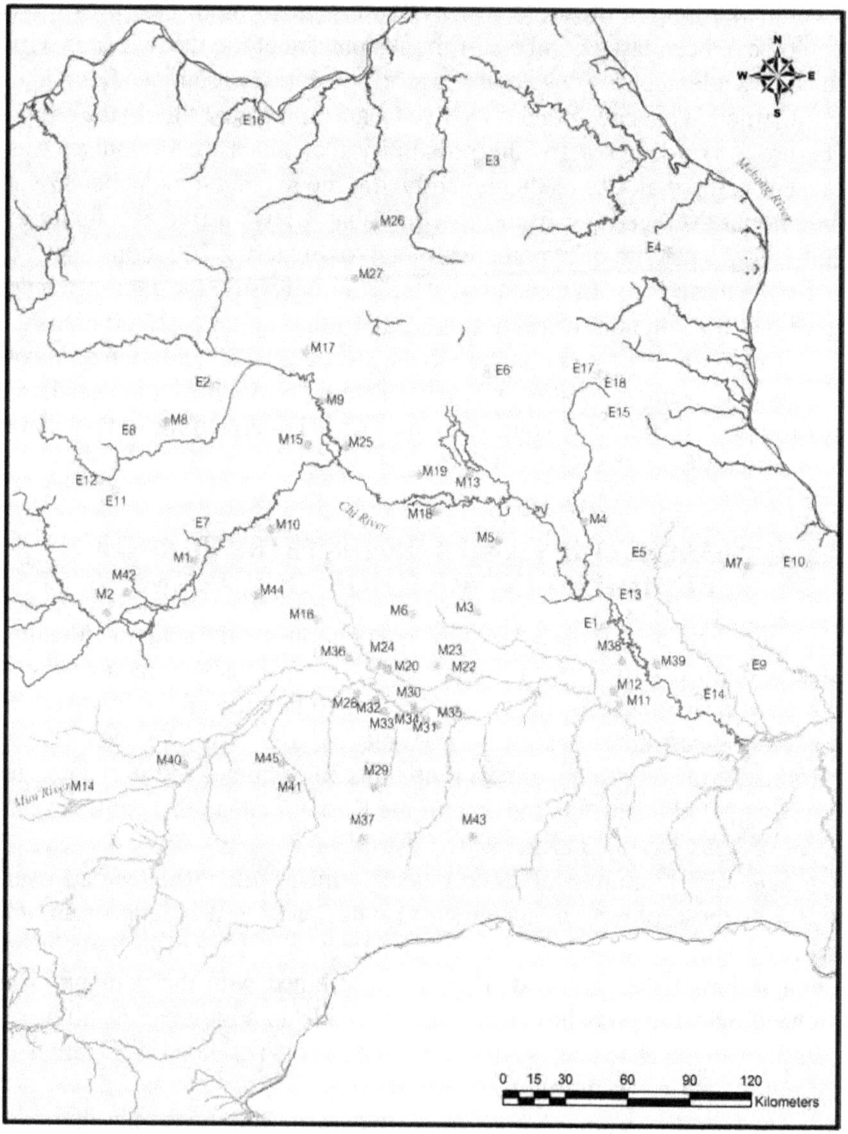

FIGURE 3.6
A slab type Dvāravatī *sema* stone with a stupa-*kumbha* motif from Yasothon province

the etymological origin of the Thai term *sema*). During the Dvāravatī period they were usually placed around *ubosots*, stupas and sometimes Buddha images.[51] Therefore, the existence of *sema* at a site is a clear indication that during a certain period of time a functioning Buddhist community was located there. Furthermore, in many cases, religious architecture such as *ubosots* and *vihāras* do not survive as they were usually made of perishable material such as bamboo and straw weave.[52] *Sema*, on the other hand, being made of a durable substance, survive to this day.

We can therefore use the amount of *sema* present to give an approximate indication of the size of a Buddhist community, or more accurately the number of possible consecrated boundaries present. There are a number of problematic variables with such an assumption, however. For example, the proposal that the amounts of *sema* surviving today reflect a close approximation to the amounts present during the Dvāravatī period is far from certain as it is difficult to estimate with any certainty the actual percentage of *sema* that may have existed at that time. This is due to the fact that *sema* can be made from a variety of materials, such as wood or natural features such as rivers, streams, trees or even anthills, all of which are perishable and are therefore undetectable in the archaeological record today. *Sema* can also be placed underground, again making them difficult to detect.[53]

Another problematic factor is that the numbers used to set up a consecrated boundary can vary from site to site and perhaps even within a site itself. Furthermore, it is probable that not all consecrated boundaries were functioning simultaneously, thus causing additional possible discrepancies when proposing approximate figures. However, despite these issues and when taken into consideration with the above discussion on population densities and monk to layperson ratios, the following proposed figures on possible sizes of Buddhist monastic communities should at least give an approximate indicator of how extensive monasticism could have been in the period in question (Table 3.2).

Firstly, at some sites which consist of only earthen mounds, between eight to fifteen *sema* can be present and can be taken to indicate the existence of a local monastery located within a small rural community. Extensive moated sites such as Muang Fa Daed on the other hand, have over 170 *sema*, indicating that there was a large-scale Buddhist community present (see Table 3.2). Furthermore, the presence or absence of artwork on *sema* may be seen as an important indicator as to the level of Buddhism present. *Sema* carved with high quality Buddhist art, usually *Jātaka* tales or Life of the Buddha stories (Figure 3.7) may represent well developed Buddhist communities receiving active patronage from lay-believers and local rulers. *Semas* lacking art or designs of any considerable artistic merit on the other hand, could be said to represent less well developed Buddhist communities, the theory being that in the Dvāravatī period at least, that they were not receiving patronage sufficient enough to support either an artistic workshop or employ the requisite skilled labour and provide the necessary resources.

FIGURE 3.7
Two fragmentary *sema* from Muang Fa Daed depicting an unidentified *jataka* kept at Wat Po Semaram temple (left) and an episode from the Life of the Buddha housed at Khon Kaen National Museum (right)

Distribution and Groups

Looking at the distribution of *sema* locations throughout the Khorat Plateau, the first clear pattern to emerge is that they can be grouped into three general geographic areas. They are; the Chi river system, the Mun river system and the Middle Mekong.[54] These river systems dominate the geographical landscape of the Khorat Plateau and it follows that the location of *sema* are closely tied to them (Figure 3.8).

In terms of distribution by amounts, the Chi and Middle Mekong river systems have almost identical proportions of sites. Out of the 110 sites surveyed, 48 are located along the Chi river system, 49 are in the Middle Mekong and 12 are located along the Mun river system.[55] In percentage terms, the Chi possesses 44 per cent of *sema* locations, the Middle Mekong possesses 45 per cent while the Mun possesses 11 per cent.

The Chi River System

The distribution of sites along the Chi river system spans the entire length of its course from Chaiyaphum in the west of the Khorat Plateau to its

FIGURE 3.8
Map showing the distribution of *sema* locations throughout the Khorat Plateau with the Chi river system shown in orange, the Mun river system in blue, the Middle Mekong in grey and Phnom Kulen in green

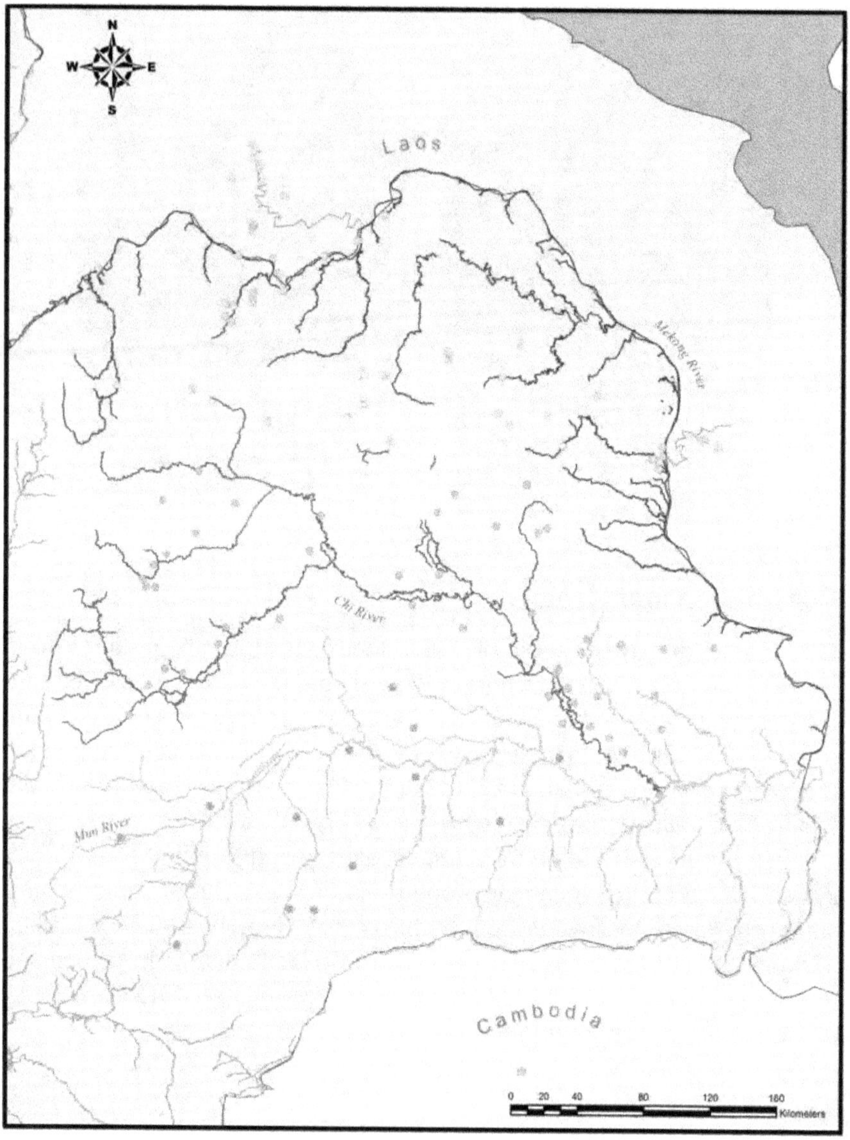

confluence with the Mun River in Ubon Ratchathani province in the east. The largest concentration of sites is located in the area surrounding the province of Yasothon, however significant amounts of sites are also found in Kalasin, Khon Kaen and Chaiyaphum provinces.

Looking at the distribution of sites along the Chi river system it is clear that the location of *sema* sites follow the course of this river and its tributaries. In Yasothon and Chaiyaphum in particular, sites are seen stretched out along the Chi River in close proximity to each other.

The Mun River System

This group exhibits much fewer sites. However, they are closely tied to and dependent on the Mun River and its tributaries. Apart from one site in Sri Saket province and another in Surin, the majority of sites are in either Buriram or Nakhon Ratchasima province. Sites in this region are located further apart than those found in the other two groups and *sema* are much less prevalent in this area than in the rest of the Khorat Plateau. This could be as a result of the much stronger Khmer or possibly Chenla influence in the region.[56]

The Middle Mekong

The Middle Mekong shows a less uniform distribution pattern. However, most sites are located either close to the Mekong River or on tributaries of it. For instance, the area around Vientiane province shows that sites cluster along the Nam Ngum River while on the southern side of the Mekong there is also a high concentration of sites around the area of Baan Phue district in Udon Thani Province. Sites in the Middle Mekong group stretch from Wang Sapung in the province of Loei in Thailand to three locations in Savannakhet province of Laos.[57]

As with the Chi and Mun Rivers, the majority of *sema* locations in the Middle Mekong closely follow the course of this river and a number of its tributaries, once again emphasizing the important role waterways and pre-existing trade routes played in the dissemination of this tradition.

Sema Clusters

By separating the locations of *sema* into three clear groups we can analyse their distribution patterns and characteristics. It is clear that the Chi river system in particular played a major role in the transmission and development of the *sema* tradition with many of the largest and most important sites, such as Muang Fa Daed, Baan Tat Tong and Baan Korn Sawan being located along its course.

Having divided *sema* locations into three distinct groupings, a closer analysis of distribution patterns allows for a subdivision into clusters (Figure 3.9). A total of eight clusters have been proposed with four of them being located along the Chi river system, three being located along the Middle Mekong and one along the Mun.[58] Certain sites, however, do not fit within the clusters and as a result are treated individually.

Sema Amounts and a Quantitative Analysis of Buddhist Monasticism

Analysing the amounts of *sema* present at individual sites and at clusters (Table 3.2, Figure 3.10) can allow for certain estimates of the extent and size of Buddhist monastic communities to be made. For example, *sema* were usually set up in pairs of eight or sixteen. It is therefore possible to propose that a site with thirty-two *sema* present may have had either four or two consecrated boundaries, depending on whether we consider *sema* being set up in sets of eight or sixteen.

If we take cluster 1 for example, the total amount of *sema* present is 369. Muang Fa Daed alone has 172, which would give twenty religious buildings or consecrated spaces if eight *sema* per boundary were used, or ten if in sets of sixteen. Taking the cluster as a whole would give a figure of forty-six (for eight) or twenty-five (for sixteen) consecrated spaces, be they stupas, *ubosots*, *vihāras* or open air ritual spaces. This therefore represents a significant Buddhist presence in the area defined by this cluster.

Using similar calculations, cluster 2 would have between eleven and nineteen consecrated spaces, cluster 3, between ten and fifteen, cluster 4 between seventeen to twenty-seven, cluster 5 between eleven and seventeen, cluster 6 between twenty-three and thirty-two, cluster 7 between two to three and cluster 8 about four. Taking *sema* stone numbers as a whole throughout the entire Khorat Plateau would give a figure of between 109 to170 consecrated spaces. Taking this postulation one step further by taking modern figures into consideration where in one instance it is stated that a consecrated space must be able to accommodate up to twenty-four monks,[59] then using the above figures we would arrive at between approximately 2,600 to 4,000 monks present in the Khorat Plateau during the Dvāravatī period. This figure, however, not only assumes that all sacred boundaries

FIGURE 3.9
Map showing the distribution of *sema* clusters in the Khorat Plateau

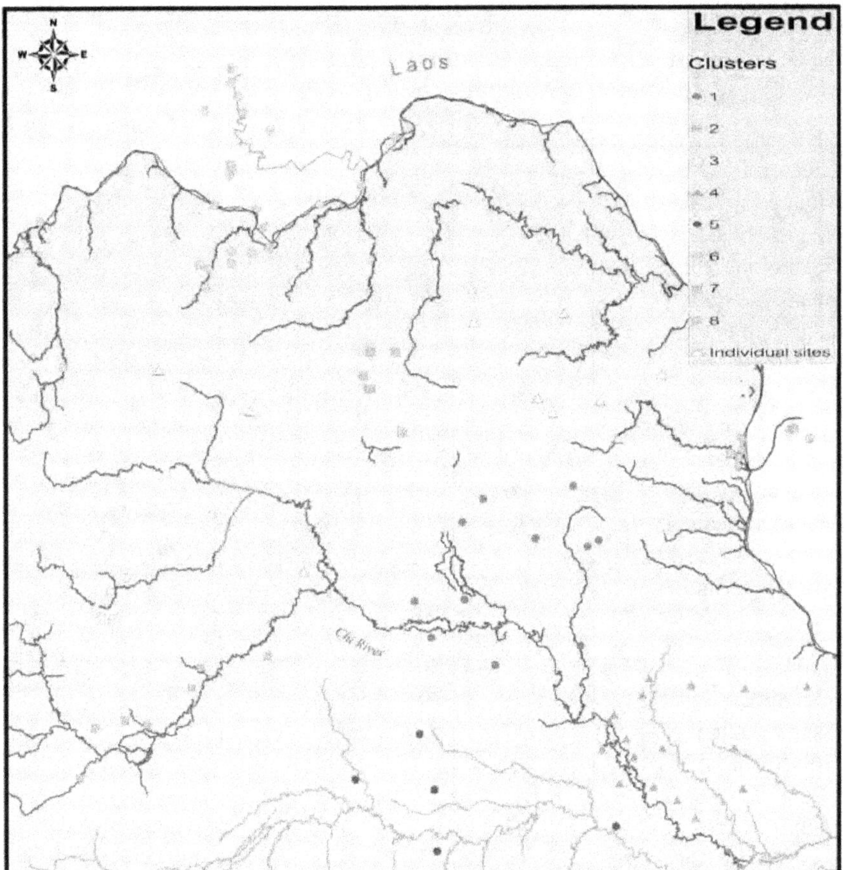

were functioning simultaneously which is most likely not the case but also that there was a set limit to the amount of monks that could be present with the consecrated area. There are too many variables present to take this figure as an accurate indication. However, when compared with the

TABLE 3.2
The Eight *Sema* Clusters in the Khorat Plateau Showing the Sites, Number of *Sema* Present and the Estimated Number of Consecrated Spaces

Site	*No. of sema*	*No. of boundaries if 8 sema are used*	*No. of boundaries if 16 sema are used*
Cluster 1			
Muang Fa Daed	172	20	10
Baan Sohksai	7	1	1
Baan Nong Hang	23	3	1
Baan Na Ngam	5	1	1
Baan Sangkhom Phathana	4	1	1
Nah Goh	30	4	2
Baan Muang Phrai	37	4	2
Roi Et Town	40	5	2
Khantarawichai	6	1	1
Mahasarakham Town	38	5	2
Baan Kud Namkin	1	1	1
Baan Non Sala	6	1	1
	Total: 369	47	25
Cluster 2			
Baan Po Chai	39	5	2
Non Sema Fa Rangeum	5	1	1
Baan Kut Ngong	27	3	2
Baan Nong Kai Non	15	2	1
Baan Nong Hin Tang	8	1	1
Muang Gao	6	1	1
Baan Korn Sawan	46	6	3
	Total: 146	19	11
Cluster 3			
Baan Non Muang	19	2	1
Baan Phai Hin	9	1	1
Baan Non Chat	14	2	1
Baan Bua Semaram	14	2	1
Baan Non Song	6	1	1
Baan Hua Kua	3	1	1
Baan Nong Hin Dtang	6	1	1

Baan Pao	2	1	1
Baan Phan Lam	21	3	1
Baan Kaeng	10	1	1
	Total: 104	15	10
Cluster 4			
Yasothon Town	13	1	1
Baan Tat Tong	26	3	1
Baan Song Beuoy	3	1	1
Baan Hua Muang	10	1	1
Baan Beung Gair	6	1	1
Baan Goo Jahn	1	1	1
Baan Nahm Kum Yai	1	1	1
Baan Koom Ngern	19	2	1
Phanom Phrai Town	4	1	1
Baan Puey Huadong	48	6	3
Mung Ngio	9	1	1
Baan Nah Mo Ma	16	2	1
Muang Samsip	23	3	1
Baan Phana	10	1	1
Baan Pai	u/d	0	0
Baan Si Bua	3	2	1
Baan Thung Yai	u/d	0	0
	Total: 192	27	17
Cluster 5			
Na Dun	5	1	1
Baan Salaeng Thon	0	0	0
Baan Brakum	3	1	1
Baan Muang Fai	1	1	1
Baan Pra Khiap	46	6	3
Phu Phra Angkhan	15	2	1
Muang Sema	17	2	1
Baan Nohn Sung	16	2	1
Baan Lopmohk	4	1	1
Baan Muang Dao	u/d	0	0
Baan Nong Pai	u/d	0	0
Baan Thung Wang	u/d	0	0
Baan Truem	8	1	1
	Total: 115	17	11

continued on next page

TABLE 3.2 – *cont'd*

Site	*No. of sema*	*No. of boundaries if 8 sema are used*	*No. of boundaries if 16 sema are used*
Cluster 6			
Baan Nong Kluem	22	3	1
Baan Hin Dtang	12	1	1
Wang Sapung	35	4	2
Phu Phra Baht	37	5	2
Baan Pailom	33	4	2
Baan Podhidtahk	10	1	1
Baan Daeng	u/d	0	0
Baan Na Sone	3	1	1
Baan Nong Khan Khu	2	1	1
Baan Hai	9	1	1
Baan Simano	4	1	1
Baan Thoun Loua	4	1	1
Baan Nong Khon	4	1	1
Baan Nam Pot	4	1	1
Baan Thalat	1	1	1
Baan Muang Kao	1	1	1
Baan Viengkham	4	1	1
Baan Sa Feu	4	1	1
Baan Somsanouk	4	1	1
Vientiane City	9	1	1
Muang Sanakham	1	1	1
Wiang Khuk	1	0	0
Baan Khok Khon	0	0	0
Baan Peng Chan	0	0	0
	Total: 204	32	23
Cluster 7			
Baan Don Kaeo	10	1	1
Baan Chiang	5	1	1
Nong Hahn Town	0	0	0
Phang Khon Sai	u/d	0	0
Baan Cham Pi	u/d	0	0
Baan Khon Sai	u/d	0	0
	Total: 15	2	2

Cluster 8			
That Panom Town	9	1	1
Baan Sikhai	7	1	1
Baan Kang	9	1	1
Baan Na Mouang	8	1	1
Baan Lak Sila	u/d	0	0
Baan Fang Daeng	u/d	0	0
Baan Saphang Thong	u/d	0	0
Baan Na Ngam	u/d	0	0
	Total: 33	4	4
Individual sites			
Baan Ma	16	2	1
Poo Noi	14	2	1
Baan Tah Wat	15	2	1
Baan Tah Krasoem	5	1	1
Baan Sri Than	1	0	0
Baan Na Oi	u/d	0	0
Baan Na-ang	u/d	0	0
Phon Phaeng	u/d	0	0
Baan Panna	u/d	0	0
Phnom Kulen	10	1	2
Baan That	u/d	0	0
Baan Choeng Doi	u/d	0	0
Baan Phu Phek	u/d	0	0
Baan Oop Mong	u/d	0	0
	Total: 51	8	6

Note: "u/d" stands for "undocumented" and represents sites where it was not possible to document exact *sema* numbers.

estimates given in Table 3.1 which outlines the demographics which gives a figure of a 2,700 strong *sangha* averaged out over the forty-five moated sites, the lower value of 2,600 may be plausible. It should, however, be noted once again that this figure reflects just one possible scenario and as has been stressed throughout, there are too many variables to consider this as a hard and fast number. Despite this, it seems fair to say that Buddhism had established a strong and widespread presence by the eighth to ninth centuries CE regardless of what the actual exact figure of monks may in fact have been.

FIGURE 3.10
Map showing the distribution of the amount of *sema* per site.

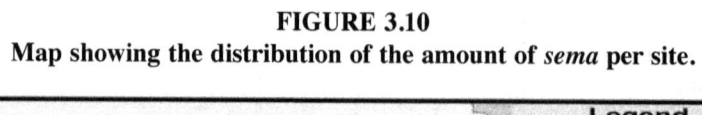

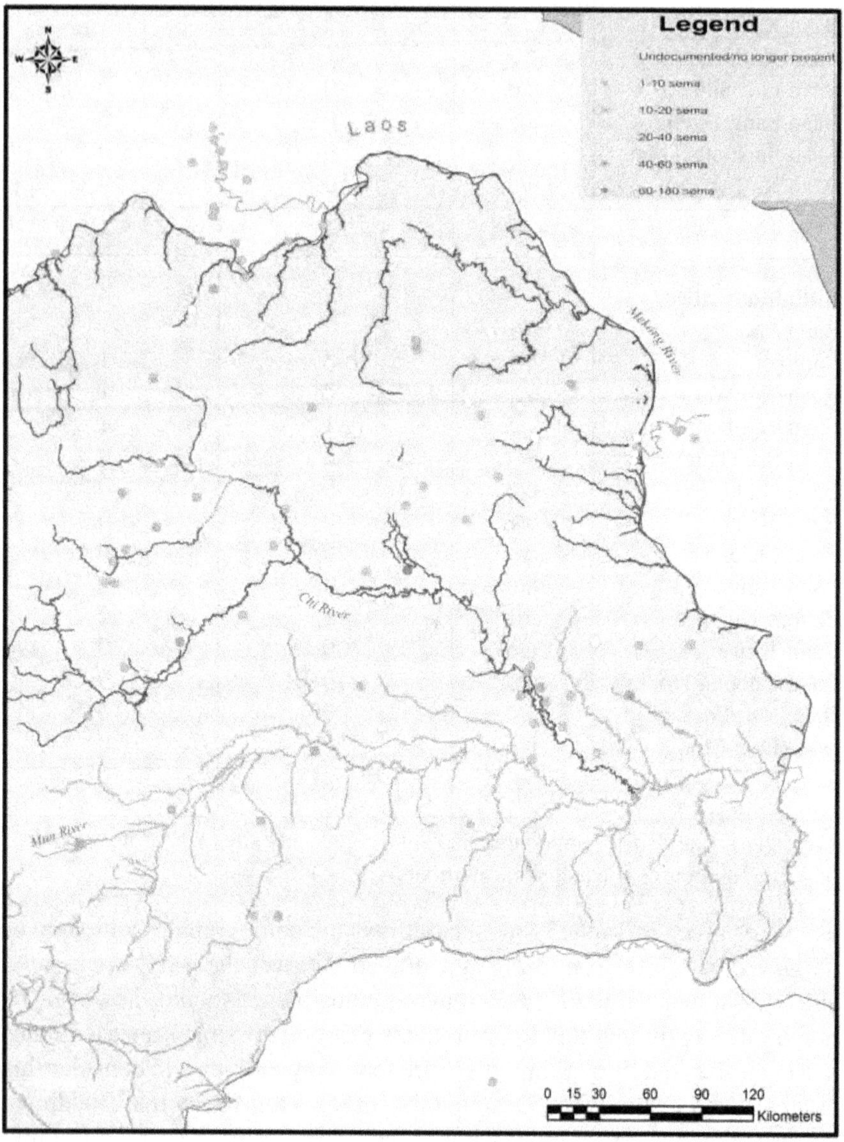

Looking at the distribution of Buddhist monasticism from this quantitative approach, it becomes clear that cluster 1 has the highest density and points to it being the most prominent centre of monastic activity in the Khorat Plateau. Cluster 6 also shows high numbers of potential consecrated spaces emphasizing that Buddhism had taken a strong hold along the Middle Mekong region. Also clusters 2, 3 and 4 show mid-range figures in comparison, illustrating that the religion had also settled in these areas, but perhaps not in as high a concentration as clusters 1 and 6.

Narrative Art and Its Distribution

The final aspect of material culture to be quantitatively analysed is the narrative art on *sema* stones. While the majority of previous studies on *sema* have focused on the narrative art carved on these objects from an aesthetic or iconographic point of view, little to no consideration has been given to the distribution of this art, the contexts within which it was produced or the actual number of *sema* that have narrative art in relation to those that do not.[60] However, upon plotting the locations of narrative art, it becomes immediately apparent that it has a very limited and restricted distribution, being confined to no more than nineteen sites in total. Of these nineteen sites, only six sites have more than ten *sema* with narrative art and only one site, Muang Fa Daed, has more than fifteen (Figure 3.11). Another factor to consider is that plain *sema* and *sema* carved with other motifs such as stupas and stupa-*kumbha* outnumber *sema* with narrative art at a ratio of approximately 10:1. Consequently, *sema* with narrative art should be viewed as the exception not the norm, a perspective that does not always come across in most literature on the subject.

The distribution of narrative art closely follows three clusters in particular. The sites of Muang Fa Daed and Baan Nong Hang in cluster 1 possess the highest number of *sema* of this kind. Muang Fa Daed has fifty-five *sema* with narrative art, Baan Nong Hang, has fourteen and Kunchinarai has one *sema* of this type. This cluster therefore has a total of seventy *sema* with narrative art, by far the highest concentration anywhere in the Khorat Plateau.

The second largest concentration is found in cluster 2. Baan Korn Sawan has twelve *sema* with narrative art while Baan Kut Ngong has ten, giving twenty-two in total. The vast majority of the narrative art on *sema* from clusters 1 and 2 date to the eighth to ninth centuries, with some examples from Muang Fa Daed and Baan Nong Hang also dating to the tenth to eleventh centuries.[61] Therefore, these two clusters, located along the course of the Chi River, clearly reflect the region in which the art of the *sema* tradition reached its apex.

The sites of Baan Nong Kluem and Baan Pailom in cluster 6 reflect a further significant grouping of narrative art. However, they are later in

FIGURE 3.11
Map showing the distribution of narrative art showing the amount of *sema* present at key sites

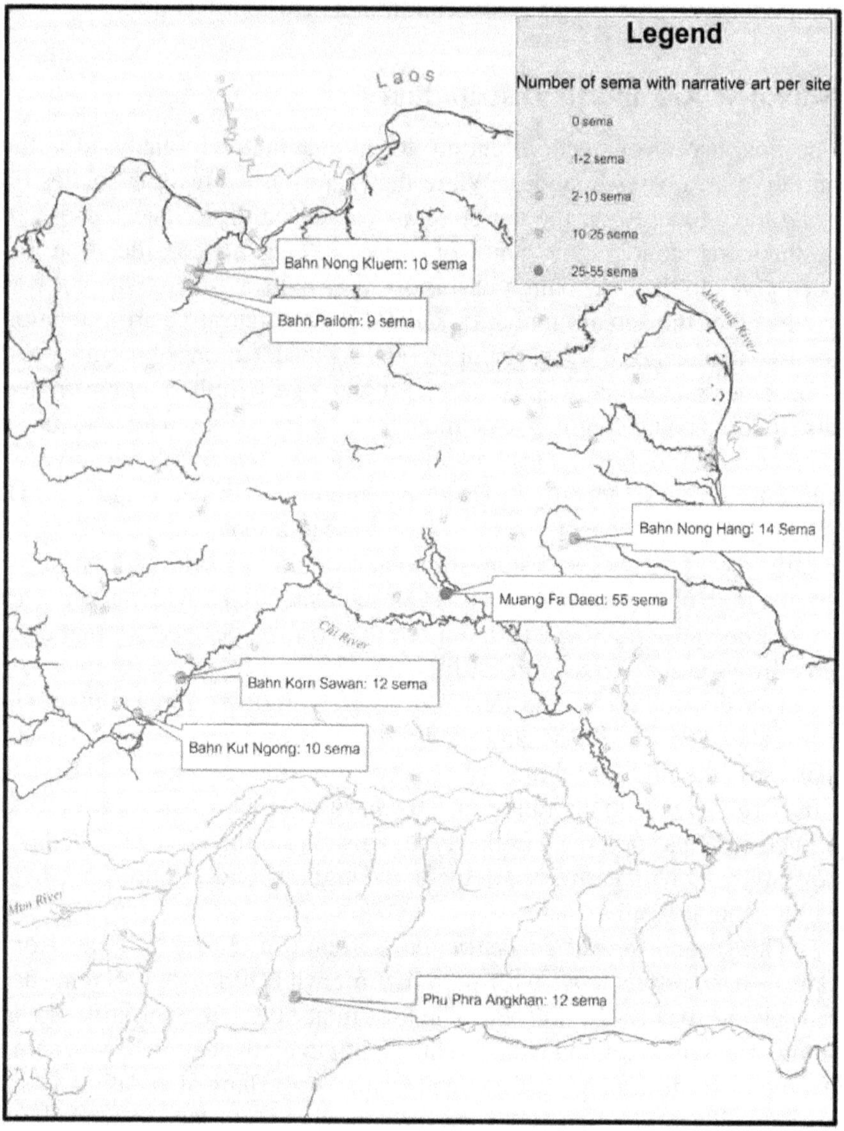

date, *circa* tenth to eleventh centuries and are stylistically different from the majority of other examples, being executed in a style similar to Khmer lintel art. The two sites combined have a total of nineteen narrative art *sema*. The narrative art, their close proximity to each other and artistic style strongly suggests that the same workshop or artists were responsible for the carving at both sites.

The site of Phu Phra Angkhan in cluster 5 is unusual from the point of view that no other sites in its proximity have narrative art. Also, the art depicted, mainly consisting of Buddha and bodhisattva images, is quite unique stylistically. It is therefore somewhat of an outlier in the distribution of narrative art. The remaining eleven sites possess either one or two *sema* with narrative art and therefore do not represent significant clustering of this tradition. However, their distribution is still informative in revealing how far the medium of narrative art spread throughout the Khorat Plateau. Sites such as Baan Podaak and Vientiane City reveal that narrative art had spread as far north as modern day Laos while the site of Baan Kum Ngoen in Yasothon shows that it was also present to a very limited extent in cluster 4.

From the analysis of the distribution of narrative art, it is most probable that this tradition originated in clusters 1 and 2, with perhaps Muang Fa Daed as the centre. It appears to have flourished here from the eighth century onwards and to a very limited extent spread out amongst other sites throughout the Khorat Plateau.

CONCLUSION: TOWARDS A DEMOGRAPHIC UNDERSTANDING OF BUDDHISM DURING THE DVARVATI PERIOD

This article has endeavoured to illustrate that the Khorat Plateau during the Dvāravatī period had the potential to support a comparatively large and well-developed Buddhist *sangha*. By using comparative statistical and ethnographic data on Buddhism in Thailand over the last century combined with techniques derived from demographic archaeology to calculate hypothetical population densities at settlements, it has proposed estimates of the possible size of the *sangha* during this period. The figure arrived at is that there could have been approximately 2,600 monks present during the Dvāravatī period or at the very least the Khorat Plateau had the potential to support this amount.

Approaching early Buddhism in this way also allows for a number of other conclusions to be drawn. In terms of density, it appears that the monks may have been settled primarily in the Chi river system around cluster 1 in particular, but also clusters 2, 3, and 4 to a lesser extent. This is also supported by the artwork on *sema* from these clusters as the majority of narrative art is once again from this region. It seems, therefore, that Buddhist monasticism flourished in the Chi river system during the

Dvāravatī period, based as it was, at large moated sites such as Muang Fa Daed. This site, having a possible population of over 7,000 people, would not only have had sufficient human resources to allow for specialization of crafts and skills, but also would have had a large enough pool of males, assuming there was no female ordination at the time, to allow a certain number of them to enter into the *sangha* without putting too much strain on the population and workforce of the settlement. Other large-scale sites such as Muang Sema in the Mun river system also had the potential to support a large monastic community but while Buddhism flourished at this site, there are only a handful of other sites in this river system that show evidence that the religion developed into more organized administrative units. It may well have been present at other sites to a lesser extent but if so, there is no clear archaeological evidence to illustrate this at present. Buddhism also spread along the Middle Mekong with *sema* being found as far north as Baan Talad in Vientiane province and as far south as Savannakhet province of Laos.

It appears that Buddhism had taken a firm hold in the Khorat Plateau during the Dvāravatī period with moated sites in particular having the potential human and material resources to allow for this religion to flourish. This in turn allowed for the creation of artistic masterpieces such as the *Jātaka* and Life of the Buddha scenes carved on *sema* stones, or the magnificent Buddha and Bodhisattva images cast in bronze. In doing so, they bequeathed us some of the finest Buddhist art to have ever been produced in a region that today makes up large areas of the modern states of Thailand and Lao PDR.[62]

This paper has explored the potential of approaching Buddhism from a demographic and quantitative angle. In doing so it is hoped that the results and estimates given will in some small way help to add to our understanding of the origins and spread of this religion, while at the same time highlighting a number of possible directions for future research on the subject.

Acknowledgements

I would like to thank the Nalanda-Sriwijaya Centre and D. Christian Lammerts in particular for the opportunity not only to publish in this volume but also to present at the Buddhist Dynamics in Premodern Southeast Asia Conference held in Singapore on 10–11 March 2011. Furthermore, to Leedom Lefferts, Louis Gabaude, and D. Christian Lammerts for providing comments and critical feedback on earlier drafts of this paper and Baas

Terwiel, Charles Higham and Angela Chiu for their help in finding source material. As always, however, the opinions, views and any possible errors present in this article are mine and mine alone.

Notes

1. Bayard, "Models, Scenarios, Variables and Supposition; Approaches to the rise of social complexity in Mainland Southeast Asia, 700 BC–AD 500", pp. 13–16, 30.
2. Ibid., p. 14.
3. Hassan, "Demographic Archaeology", p. 70.
4. For discussion and debates surrounding the Indianization concept see firstly Mabbett, "The 'Indianization' of Southeast Asia: reflections on historical sources", pp. 143–61, whose observations and conclusions have largely been proved correct by subsequent archaeological research over the past four decades. For further discussion on the subject, see Wolters, *History, Culture, and Region in Southeast Asian Perspectives*, Stark, "Early Mainland Southeast Asian Landscapes in the First Millennium A.D.", pp. 407–32, and O'Reilly, *Early Civilizations of Southeast Asia*.
5. Hassan, "Demographic Archaeology", p. 87.
6. For an up-to-date overview of the definitions and debates surrounding the term Dvāravatī, see Skilling, "Dvāravatī: Recent Revelations and Research", pp. 87–112; for a summary of the archaeological evidence, see Phasook Indrawooth, *Dvāravatī, A Critical Study Based on the Archaeological*; for definitions of the Dvāravatī art style, see Boisselier, *The Heritage of Thai Sculpture*, and Woodward, *The Sacred Sculpture of Thailand*; for issues regarding the dating of the Dvāravatī Period, see Barram and Glover, "Re-thinking Dvāravatī", pp. 175–82 and Glover, "The Dvāravatī Gap — Linking Prehistory and History in Early Thailand", pp. 79–86.
7. See in particular Damrong Rajanubhab, *Monuments of the Buddha in Siam*, and Coedès, *The Indianized States of Southeast Asia*.
8. Skilling, "Dvāravatī: Recent Revelations and Research", pp. 87–112.
9. Murphy, "The Buddhist Boundary Markers of Northeast Thailand and Central Laos, 7th–12th centuries CE: Towards an understanding of the archaeological, religious and artistic landscape of the Khorat Plateau", pp. 126–30.
10. Bailey and Mabbett, *The Sociology of Early Buddhism*, pp. 8–36.
11. Bunnag, *Buddhist monk, Buddhist layman: A study of urban monastic organization in central Thailand*, pp. 54–55.
12. Ibid., pp. 54–77.
13. Gabaude, "Approche du bouddhisme thaï", pp. 21–59.
14. Tambiah, *World Conqueror and World Renouncer: A study of Buddhism and polity in Thailand against a Historical Background*, p. 270.
15. Ibid.

16 Cha-em Kaeokhlai, "Phu Khio inscription, reading and translation/Sila charuek Phu Khio an lae plae mai", pp. 64–65.
17. Murphy, "The Buddhist Boundary Markers of Northeast Thailand and Central Laos, 7th–12th centuries CE: Towards an understanding of the archaeological, religious and artistic landscape of the Khorat Plateau", p. 93.
18. Kongkaew Weeraprajak, "Sema Inscription at Ban Panna/Charuek Baisema Baan Panna", pp. 53–57.
19. Guy, *Indian Temple Sculpture*, p. 44.
20. Schopen, *Bones, Stones and Buddhist Monks, Collected Papers on the Archaeology, Epigraphy, and Texts of Monastic Buddhism in India*, pp. 30–33; Schopen, *Buddhist Monks and Business Matters, Still More Papers on Monastic Buddhism in India*, pp. 382–94.
21. Woodward, *The Art and Architecture of Thailand, From Prehistoric Times through the Thirteenth Century*, p. 104; see also Filliozat, "Sur le Çivaisme et le Bouddhisme du Cambodge", p. 84.
22. Tambiah, *World Conqueror and World Renouncer: A study of Buddhism and polity in Thailand against a Historical Background*, p. 265.
23. Gabaude, "Approche du bouddhisme thaï", pp. 42–46.
24. Grabowsky, "The Thai Census of 1904: Translation and Analysis", pp. 49–85.
25. Cited in Tambiah, *World Conqueror and World Renouncer: A study of Buddhism and polity in Thailand against a Historical Background*, p. 268.
26. Hassan, "Demographic Archaeology", p. 84.
27. Bayard, "Models, Scenarios, Variables and Supposition; Approaches to the rise of social complexity in Mainland Southeast Asia, 700 BC–AD 500", p. 24.
28. Hassan, "Demographic Archaeology", p. 88.
29. Ibid., pp. 55–58.
30. Renfrew, *The emergence of civilization*.
31. See, for example, MacNeish, "Social implications of changes in population and settlement pattern of the 12,000 years of prehistory in the Tehuacan Valley of Mexico", pp. 215–50; Blanton, "Prehispanic adaptation in the Ixtapalapa region, Mexico", pp. 1317-1326, and McAdams and Nissen, *The Urak countryside: The natural setting of urban societies*.
32. Higham and Thosarat, *Early Thailand: From Prehistory to Sukhothai*, p. 169.
33. Chantaratiyakarn, "The research programme in the Upper Chi," pp. 565–643.
34. Higham and Thosarat, *Early Thailand: From Prehistory to Sukhothai*, pp. 213–15.
35. Welch and McNeill, "Settlement, agriculture and population changes in the Phimai region, Thailand", pp. 210–28.
36. Ibid., p. 222.
37. Ibid., p. 212.
38. Ibid., p. 223.

39. Ibid., p. 224.
40. Ibid. p. 226.
41. Ibid., note 1.
42. Welch, "Adaptation to Environmental Unpredictability: Intensive Agriculture and Regional Exchange at Late Prehistoric Centres in the Phimai Region, Thailand", pp. 322–25.
43. Mudar, "How Many Dvāravatī Kingdoms? Locational Analysis of the first Millennium A.D. Moated Settlements in Central Thailand", p. 14.
44. It has been argued, for example, that up to at least 15 per cent of the interior area of moated sites may have been taken up by public monuments; see Mudar, "How Many Dvāravatī Kingdoms? Locational Analysis of the first Millennium A.D. Moated Settlements in Central Thailand", p.14. Furthermore, survey and excavation work at the Dvāravatī moated site of Dong Mae Nang Muang has shown much higher levels of occupation within the interior moated area; see Murphy and Pimchanok Pongkasetkan, "Fifty Years of Archaeological Research at Dong Mae Nang Muang: An Ancient Gateway to the Upper Chao Phraya Basin", pp. 63–65.
45. Manit Vallibhotama, "Sri Dharmasokaraja".
46. Murphy and Pimchanok Pongkasetkan, "Fifty Years of Archaeological Research at Dong Mae Nang Muang: An Ancient Gateway to the Upper Chao Phraya Basin", p. 57.
47. The nine sites in Table 3.1 were selected on the basis that they have clear evidence of extant moats thus allowing for accurate approximations of their site size to be calculated.
48. Murphy, "The Buddhist Boundary Markers of Northeast Thailand and Central Laos, 7th–12th centuries CE: Towards an understanding of the archaeological, religious and artistic landscape of the Khorat Plateau", pp. 133–43.
49. Ibid., pp. 125, 202–204, 398–439.
50. Kieffer-Pülz, "Rules for the *sīmā* Regulation in the *Vinaya* and its Commentaries and their Application in Thailand", pp. 141–53.
51. Ibid., pp. 86–124; Arunsak Kingmanee, "Boundary Stones of the Dvāravatī Period: A preliminary overview", pp. 67–82.
52. Piriya Krairiksh, "Semas with Scenes from the Mahanipata-Jatakas in the National Museum at Khon Kaen", p. 42.
53. Kieffer-Pülz, "Rules for the *sīmā* Regulation in the *Vinaya* and its Commentaries and their Application in Thailand", pp. 145–46. At present, in neighbouring Burma there is little surviving archaeological evidence of *sīmā*s dated to the pre-Pagan and Pagan eras, despite numerous references to them in twelfth to fourteenth century inscriptions. The earliest tentative evidence comes from the city of Vesali in Rakhine State where excavators appear to have found fossilized wood *sīmā* markers around a brick structure which they identified as an ordination hall. The site itself has been dated between

the fifth and ninth centuries making it roughly contemporary with sites in the Khorat Plateau. At Thaton, carved sandstone *sīmā* markers perhaps dated to the eleventh to thirteenth centuries have been found around the site of the later Kalyani ordination hall. Thus in Burma markers may have been primarily, but not exclusively, constructed out of perishable materials. Regarding the Pagan era, Pierre Pichard identifies only eight monuments from this period, distinguished by a rectangular platform, that may have constituted ordination halls. See Murphy, "The Buddhist Boundary Markers of Northeast Thailand and Central Laos, 7th–12th centuries CE: Towards an understanding of the archaeological, religious and artistic landscape of the Khorat Plateau", pp. 101–102; Luce, *Old Burma: Early Pagan*, Vol. 1, p. 253; Pierre Pichard, *Inventory of Monuments at Pagan*.

54. This division was first proposed by Srisakra Vallibhotama in his article "Sema Isan", pp. 89–116, who grouped *sema* into the Chi River, the Mun River and Udon Thani-Sakon Nakon Basin. However, as *sema* have now come to light in Laos the last grouping has been re-evaluated in this paper and renamed "Middle Mekong" to reflect that fact that *sema* are located on both sides of this river system.
55. This gives a total of 109 sites. The remaining site giving a total of 110 is on Phnom Kulen, Cambodia and does not therefore fall in to one of the main three groups.
56. Srisakra Vallibhotama, *A Northeastern Site of Civilization: new archaeological evidence to change the face of Thai History/Aeng Arayatham Isan Chai lakthan borankadi plik chomna prawatisat Thai*, pp. 114–47.
57. Lorrillard, "Pour une Géographie Historique du Bouddhisme au Laos", p. 171.
58. For a more detailed discussion on what constitutes a cluster, see Murphy, "The Buddhist Boundary Markers of Northeast Thailand and Central Laos, 7th–12th centuries CE: Towards an understanding of the archaeological, religious and artistic landscape of the Khorat Plateau", pp. 155–84.
59. Giteau, *Le bornage rituel des temples bouddhiques au Cambodge*, p. 6. Giteau is here quoting from a booklet published by the Buddhist Institute of Phnom Penh, entitled the *Sima-vinicchaya-sankappa* (*Summary of the knowledge on sima*), in 1932 by Brah Visuddhivans Huot That.
60. For a summary of all literature published on *sema* to date, see Murphy "The Buddhist Boundary Markers of Northeast Thailand and Central Laos, 7th–12th centuries CE: Towards an understanding of the archaeological, religious and artistic landscape of the Khorat Plateau", pp. 108–22.
61. Ibid., pp. 213–14.
62. Buddhist narrative art executed in various mediums continues to thrive to this day in northeast Thailand. See, for example, the *Bun Phra Wet* painted scrolls as discussed by Leedom Lefferts "The *Bun Phra Wet* Painted Scrolls of Northeast Thailand in the Walters Art Museum", pp. 149–70.

References

Adams, R. McC. and H.J. Nissen. *The Urak countryside: The natural setting of urban societies*. Chicago: University of Chicago Press, 1972.

Bailey, Greg and Ian Mabbett. *The Sociology of Early Buddhism*. Cambridge: Cambridge University Press, 2003.

Barram, Andrew and Ian Glover. "Re-thinking Dvāravatī". In *From Homo Erectus to the living traditions; choice of papers from the 11th International Conference of the European Association of Southeast Asian Archaeologists*, edited by Jean Paul Pautreau et al., pp. 175–82, Chiang Mai: Siam Ratana Ltd., 2008.

Bayard, Donn. "Models, Scenarios, Variables and Suppositions: Approaches to the Rise of Social Complexity in Mainland Southeast Asia, 700BC–500AD". In *Early Metallurgy, Trade and Urban Centres in Thailand and Southeast Asia*, edited by Ian Glover, Pornchai Suchitta and John Villiers, pp. 13–38. Bangkok: White Lotus, 1992.

Blanton, R.E. "Prehispanic adaptation in the Ixtapalapa region, Mexico". *Science* 175 (1972): 1317–26.

Boisselier, Jean. *The Heritage of Thai Sculpture*. Bangkok: Asia Books, 1975.

Bunnag, Jane. *Buddhist monk, Buddhist layman: A study of urban monastic organization in central Thailand*. Cambridge: Cambridge University Press, 1973.

Chantaratiyakarn, P. "The research programme in the Upper Chi". In *Prehistoric Investigations in Northeast Thailand*, edited by C.F.W. Higham and A. Kijngam, pp. 565–643. Oxford: British Archaeological Reports (International Series), 231, 1984.

Coedès, George. *The Indianized States of Southeast Asia*. Honolulu: East-West Centre Press, 1968.

Filliozat, Jean. "Sur le Çivaisme et le Bouddhisme du Cambodge". *Bulletin de l'Ecole Française d' Extrême-Orient* 70 (1981): 59–99.

Gabaude, Louis. "Approche du bouddhisme thaï". In *Thaïland contemporaine*, edited by Stéphane Dovert and Jacques Ivonoff, pp. 21–59. Paris: Les Indes savantes; Bangkok: IRASEC, 2011.

Giteau, Madeleine. *Le bornage rituel des temples bouddhiques au Cambodge*. Paris: Ecole Française d'Extrême-Orient, 1969.

Glover, Ian. "The Dvāravatī Gap — Linking Prehistory and History in Early Thailand". *Bulletin of the Indo-Pacific Prehistory Association* 30 (2010): 79–86.

Grabowsky, Volker. "The Thai Census of 1904: Translation and Analysis". *Journal of the Siam Society* 84, no. 1 (1996): 49–85.

Guy, John. *Indian Temple Sculpture*. London: V & A Publications, 2007.

Hassan, Fekri A. "Demographic Archaeology". In *Advances in Archaeological Method and Theory,* Vol. 1, pp. 49–103. Academic Press, Inc., 1978.

Higham, Charles and Rachanie Thosarat. *Early Thailand: From Prehistory to Sukhothai*. Bangkok: River Books, 2012.

Indrawooth, Phasook. *Dvāravatī, A Critical Study Based on the Archaeological Evidence* (in Thai). Bangkok: Silpakorn University, 1999.

Kaeokhlai, Cha-em. "Sila charuek Phu Khio an lae plae mai". *Silpakorn* 33, no. 2 (1985): 64–65 (in Thai).

Kieffer-Pülz, Petra. "Rules for the *sīma* Regulation in the *Vinaya* and its Commentaries and their Application in Thailand". *Journal of the International Association of Buddhist Studies* 20, no. 2 (1997): 141–53.

Kingmanee, Arunsak. "Boundary Stones of the Dvāravatī Period: A preliminary overview". In *Abhinandanamala, Nandana Chutiwongs Felicitation Volume*, edited by Leelananda Prematilleke, pp. 67–82. Bangkok: SPAFA Regional Centre of Archaeology and Fine Arts in collaboration with the Abhinandanamala Committee, Colombo, 2010.

Krairiksh, Piriya. "Semas with Scenes from the Mahanipata-Jatakas in the National Museum at Khon Kaen". In *Art and Archaeology in Thailand*, pp. 35–100. Bangkok: FAD, 1974.

Landon, K.P. *Siam in Transition*. Shanghai: Kelly & Walsh, Ltd., 1939.

Lefferts, Leedom. "The *Bun Phra Wet* Painted Scrolls of Northeast Thailand in the Walters Art Museum". *Journal of the Walters Art Museum A Curator's choice: Essays in honor of Hiram W. Woodward, JR* 64/65 (2006–2007): 149–70.

Lorrillard, Michel. "Pour une Géographie Historique du Bouddhisme au Laos". In *Rercherches Nouvelles sur le Laos/New Research on Laos*, edited by Yves Goudineau and Michel Lorrilard, pp. 113–81. Vientiane-Paris: Ecole française d'Extreme-Orient, 2008.

Luce, G.H. *Old Burma: Early Pagan*. 3 vols. New York: Artibus Asiae, 1969.

Mabbett, Ian. W. "The 'Indianization' of Southeast Asia: reflections on historical sources". *Journal of Southeast Asian Studies* 8, no. 2 (1977): 143–61.

MacNeish, R.S. "Social implications of changes in population and settlement pattern of the 12,000 years of prehistory in the Tehuacan Valley of Mexico". In *Population and economics*, edited by P. Deprez, pp. 215–50. Winnipeg: University of Manitoba Press, 1970.

Mudar, Karen. "How Many Dvāravatī Kingdoms? Locational Analysis of First Millennium A.D. Moated Settlements in Central Thailand". *Journal of Anthropological Archaeology* 18, no. 1 (1999): 1–28.

Murphy, Stephen A. "The Buddhist Boundary Markers of Northeast Thailand and Central Laos, 7th–12th centuries CE: Towards an understanding of the archaeological, religious and artistic landscape of the Khorat Plateau". PhD dissertation, Department of Art and Archaeology, School of Oriental and African Studies, University of London. 2010; Ethesis <http://eprints.soas.ac.uk/12204/>.

—— and Pongkasetkan Pimchanok. "Fifty Years of Archaeological Research at Dong Mae Nang Muang: An Ancient Gateway to the Upper Chao Phraya Basin". *Journal of the Siam Society* 98 (2010): 49–74.

O'Reilly, Dougald J.W. *Early Civilizations of Southeast Asia*. New York: Alta Mira Press, 2007.

Pichard, Pierre. *Inventory of Monuments at Pagan*. 8 Volumes. Paris: Unesco; Gartmore: Kiscadale, 1992–2001.

Rajanubhab, Damrong. *Monuments of the Buddha in Siam*. Translated by Suluk Sivaraksa and A.B. Griswold, 2nd ed. Bangkok: The Siam Society, 1973 [1926].

Renfrew, Colin. *The emergence of civilization*. London: Methuen, 1972.

Schopen, Gregory. *Bones, Stones and Buddhist Monks, Collected Papers on the Archaeology, Epigraphy, and Texts of Monastic Buddhism in India*. Honolulu: University of Hawaii Press, 1997.

——. *Buddhist Monks and Business Matters, Still More Papers on Monastic Buddhism in India*. Honolulu: University of Hawaii Press, 2002.

Skilling, Peter. "Dvāravatī: Recent Revelations and Research". In *Dedications to Her Royal Highness Princess Galyani Vadhana Krom Luang Naradhiwas Rajanagarindra on her 80th birthday*, edited. C. Baker, pp. 87–112. Bangkok: The Siam Society, 2003.

Stark, Miriam T. "Early Mainland Southeast Asian Landscapes in the First Millennium A.D.". *Annual Review of Anthropology* 35 (2006): 407–32.

Tambiah, Stanley. J. *World Conqueror and World Renouncer: A study of Buddhism and polity in Thailand against a Historical Background*. Cambridge: Cambridge University Press, 1976.

Vallibhotama, Manit. "Sri Dharmasokaraja". In *Thalang kaan prawatisaat ekasaan Boranakadi,* Year 12, Vol. 1. 1978 (In Thai).

Vallibhotama, Srisakra. "Sema Isan". *Muang Boran* 1, no. 2 (1975): 89–116 (in Thai).

——. *A Northeastern Site of Civilization: New archaeological evidence to change the face of Thai History/Aeng Arayatham Isan Chai lakthan borankadi plik chomna prawatisat Thai*. Bangkok: Matichon, 1990 (in Thai).

Weeraprajak, Kongkaew. "Sema Inscription at Ban Panna/Charuek Baisema Baan Panna". *Silpakorn* 50, no. 2 (2007): 53–57 (in Thai).

Welch, D.J. "Adaptation to Environmental Unpredictability: Intensive Agriculture and Regional Exchange at Late Prehistoric Centres in the Phimai Region, Thailand". PhD Dissertation, University of Hawaii, Honolulu. Ann Arbor: University Microfilms. 1985.

—— and McNeill, J.R. "Settlement, agriculture and population changes in the Phimai region, Thailand". *Bulletin of the Indo-Pacific Prehistory Association* 11 (1991): 210–28.

Wolters, O.W. *History, Culture, and Region in Southeast Asian Perspectives*. Ithaca, New York: Cornell Southeast Asia Program Publications, 1999.

Woodward, Hiram. *The Sacred Sculpture of Thailand*. Bangkok: River Books, 1997.

——. *The Art and Architecture of Thailand, From Prehistoric Times through the Thirteenth Century*. Leiden, Boston: Brill. 2005.

4

MINIATURE STŪPAS AND A BUDDHIST SEALING FROM CANDI GENTONG, TROWULAN, MOJOKERTO, EAST JAVA

Titi Surti Nastiti

I. INTRODUCTION

Candi Gentong is located in Jambumente village, Trowulan district, Mojokerto, East Java. The structure is made of two parts, which are called Candi Gentong I and Candi Gentong II. The latter is located about 25 metres north of Candi Gentong I.

The existence of Candi Gentong was first announced by J.W.B Wardenaar. He included it in the report of his visit to Trowulan when he was reporting back to Stamford Raffles as Lieutenant Governor of Java (1811–16) on 7 October 1815. In the report Wardenaar wrote about the "plan van Madjapahit" (plan of Majapahit). In 1890, R.D.M Verbeek also wrote regarding the "plan van Madjaphit" which included the existence of archeological remains of the Majapahit Kingdom at Trowulan as follows: (A) a temple of bricks called Candi Muteran by the inhabitants, (B) a heap of bricks which probably came from the ruins of a temple, (C) a temple of bricks called Candi Brahu, (D) a temple called Candi Gentong which was entirely ruined, (E) a temple called Candi Gedong, (F) a temple called Candi Tengah, (G) a gate called Gapura Jati Pasar by the inhabitants (it is currently called Gapura Wringin Lawang), (H) a gate called Bajang Ratu,

(I) the Joko Dolok statue (currently placed at Taman Apsari, Surabaya), (K) a large statue of a giant (*rākṣasa*) called Menak Jinggo and a statue of woman, (L) Ratu Putri Campa's grave (1448 CE), (M) the Segaran Pool, (N) Siti Hinggil (*high land*), (O) an *umpak* (stone base/pedestal that formed part of a house), and (P) a place which the inhabitants called Kedaton.[1]

When Candi Gentong was rediscovered it was already in ruins. The only remaining original structure was its base. The ruins formed a huge pile that looked like a *gentong* (large earthenware bowl for water), and because of this the inhabitants called it Candi Gentong. The shape of Candi Gentong I is square with the entry point located at the west. It is comprised of a central brick structure surrounded by two other structures (see Figure 4.1). Of Candi Gentong II only the base of the *candi* and its pit remain. The shape of Candi Gentong II is also square. Its central brick structure is surrounded by eight smaller structures located at eight points of the compass, but the one to the north has already vanished.

Based on the shape of the structures, it can be assumed that Candi Gentong I and II were designed as a *maṇḍala*.[2] This tells us that Candi

FIGURE 4.1
Candi Gentong I, Trowulan, Mojokerto, East Java

Gentong I and II are Buddhist temples. This is supported by the discovery of miniature stūpas and a Buddhist sealing in the pit of Candi Gentong I and II. Candi Gentong is located only around 360 metres from Candi Brahu which is known to have a Buddhist background. According to Wardenaar's report, in Muteran which is located not far from Candi Gentong, metal objects were found, including a golden Vairocana statue, a Kuvera statue, and bronze pots.[3] These findings are strengthened in light of Ann R. Kinney's suggestion that it is possible that Candi Brahu was the centrepiece of a Buddhist complex located at the northwest of the Majapahit capital. Thus three sites, Candi Muteran to the north, Candi Tengah, and Candi Gentong, once surrounded Candi Brahu.[4]

Candi Gentong I and II date to the Majapahit period. This is suggested by the fact that they are made of bricks, thought to be one of the characteristics of *candis* from this era, especially those *candis* which are found around Trowulan, such as Candi Brahu, Candi Tikus, Gapura Bajang Ratu, and Gapura Wringin Lawang. In addition, when Candi Gentong I and II were being restored, many ceramic sherds dating from the Chinese Yuan (1279–1367 CE) and Ming (1368–1644 CE) dynasties were found.[5] These dates were supported by carbon dating, which shows that Candi Gentong was built around 1470 ±100 CE.[6]

Kinney also notes that during excavation a number of important artefacts were found. The most interesting finding was a number of small miniature stūpas measuring ten to twelve centimetres high. One of the miniature stūpas bore an inscription in Kawi.[7] This is significant because prior to this finding, the only miniature stūpas in the region written in Kawi were those from Candi Brorobudur.[8]

Generally the script that was used to write Buddhist mantras on miniature stūpas[9] and Buddhist sealings is a form of Early Nāgarī. Examples include the miniature stūpas and Buddhist sealings that were found in Palembang, South Sumatera;[10] Gumuk Klinting, Banyuwangi, East Java;[11] Bawean island, East Java;[12] and Bali.[13] There are also Buddhist sealings found in Batujaya, Karawang, West Java that were written in a script that cannot be read (see Figure 4.2).[14] De Casparis stated that Nagārī is associated with Sanskrit and with Mahāyāna Buddhism,[15] and the use of Early Nāgarī in Indonesia was generally related to Buddhism,[16] aside from its appearance on some non-Buddhist statues of Singosari.

The central problem raised by this evidence is whether the inscriptions on the miniature stūpas and the Buddhist sealing from Candi Gentong and the miniature stūpas from Borobudur were made in the same period. Both sets of material were written in Kawi script and contain the *ye dharmā*

FIGURE 4.2
Buddhist sealing from Batujaya, Karawang, West Java with unidentified inscription at the bottom (Doc. Agustijanto Indrajaya)

formula. If the inscriptions date to the same era, a further question concerns whether the miniature stūpas and Buddhist sealing from Candi Gentong were manufactured in situ or if they came from Borobudur or elsewhere. This paper, therefore, aims to provide a date for these artefacts and discuss their provenance through a comparative analysis of the Candi Gentong paleography in light of inscriptions from Borobudur and elsewhere in Trowulan.

II. MINIATURE STŪPAS AND A BUDDHIST SEALING

Miniature stūpas and a Buddhist sealing from Candi Gentong I and II were found in 1996 when the sites were being restored. Miniature stūpas from Candi Gentong I were found in the pit of the central chamber 3 metres deep, while miniature stūpas from Candi Gentong II were found 1 metre deep. Miniature stūpas and a Buddhist sealing that were found in Candi Gentong I and II are now part of the collection of the Pusat Informasi Majapahit (Majapahit Information Centre), Trowulan, Mojokerto, East Java. It is not certain which miniature stūpas came from Candi Gentong I or Candi Gentong II, or from which location the sealing originated. There is no explanation regarding the exact find site of any of these materials.

The miniature stūpas and sealing were made of unbaked clay. Given their fragility, much of this material is badly damaged. Only five miniature stūpas were found in good condition in Candi Gentong I and II. The remaining miniature stūpas are damaged in the top and bottom part (see Figure 4.3). There are several fragments that can be identified and there are also fragments that cannot be identified due to the small size. There are thirty-two half damaged miniature stūpas, fifty-eight identifiable fragments (twelve top fragments, thirty-eight body fragments, and eight bottom fragments), and sixty-four unidentified fragments. The undamaged miniature stūpas have a measurement of 9 cm in height, 3.5 cm in diameter at the bottom, and 6 cm diameter around the body.

The shape of the miniature stūpas basically follows the shape of a stūpa which is made of four-sided base, the body (*aṇḍa*) which is shaped like a dome, and at the top is a *chattra* (umbrella) and *yaṣṭi* (stick). The miniature stūpas from Candi Gentong I and II are similar to a bell (*ghaṇṭa*) because the base is round and the body is oval and contains eight replicas of smaller stūpas. According to Kandahjaya, the iconography of eight small stūpas commemorates the eight great events in the lifetime of Śākyamuni, and are especially praised in the text known as the *Aṣṭamahāsthāna-caitya-vandanā-stava*.[17] The miniature stūpas from Candi Gentong I and II have no opening or cavity, and there is no stamp at the base. In all examples a part of the top has broken off. The inscription at the base of miniature stūpas was written in Kawi script, and contains an abbreviated form of the *ye dharmā* formula: *oṃ ye te svāhā* (see Figure 4.4).

From the fact that the inscriptions are not uniform, it can be assumed that the miniature stūpas were inscribed by different individuals. It is interesting that there is one example which was written using Kawi script but in a style similar to Early Nāgarī script (see Figure 4.5). There are parts of the inscription which are clearly written in Kawi script although elongated towards the bottom, similar to Early Nāgarī.

There is only one Buddhist sealing that was found in Candi Gentong.[18] It is round, 5.5 cm in diameter and 2 cm thick. On the front is an image of a seated Buddha beside whom there are smaller seated figures which, as I will show below, represent two Bodhisattvas. The Buddha is seated in

FIGURE 4.3
Miniature stūpa and Buddhist sealing from Candi Gentong, Trowulan, Mojokerto, East Java

FIGURE 4.4
Miniature stūpa with *oṃ ye te svāhā* inscription

FIGURE 4.5
Miniature stūpa written in Kawi script similar to Early Nāgarī

the centre with both legs hanging down (*pralambapāda*), while both feet are resting on a footstool. His hands are held in the gesture of putting in motion the wheel of the Law (*dharmacakra-mudrā*). To his right sits one of the Bodhisattvas, his right hand makes the gesture of giving (*varada-mudrā*) and the lotus (*padma*) is in his left hand. On the Buddha's left sits the other Bodhisattva. His right hand shows his palm upwards before his breast and unfortunately his left hand cannot be identified (see Figure 4.6 left).

A Buddhist sealing with a similar image of a Buddha and two Bodhisattvas was found at the Lovina beach site in Kalibukbuk, Buleleng, Bali (see Figure 4.7). According to Astawa, the sealing from Kalibukbuk shows the Buddha and two Bodhisattvas standing up. Therefore, Astawa compared this Buddha image with a bronze statue found in Thailand, which also depicts the Buddha and two Bodhisattvas standing. In this image, the two Bodhisattvas can be identified by their attributes as Avalokiteśvara (on the right) and Maitreya (on the left).[19] However, from my examination of the Kalibukbuk sealing it appears that the Buddha is not standing, but in a posture similar to that represented in the sealing from Candi Gentong; that is, seated and flanked by two standing Bodhisattvas. The Buddha is clearly seated in the centre with both legs hanging down (*pralambapāda*), while both feet are resting on a footstool. His right hand gesture is the *varada-mudrā* and his left hand gesture is unidentified.

The representation of the Buddha on the Candi Gentong sealing is similar to that of a bronze statue in the collection of Rijksmuseum

FIGURE 4.6
Buddhist sealing front (left) and back (right)

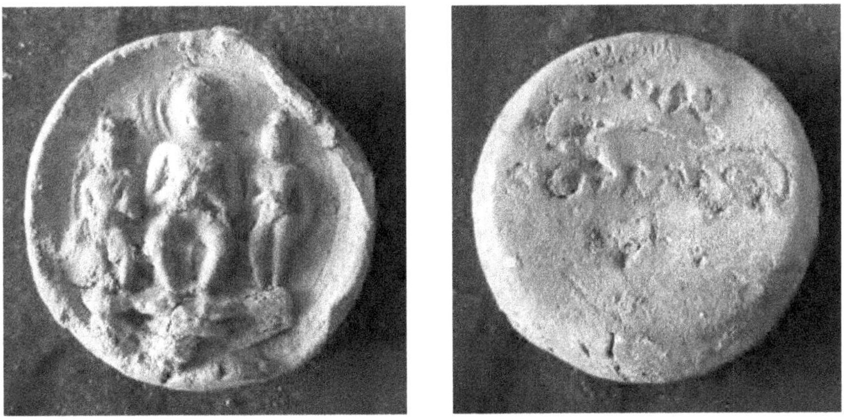

FIGURE 4.7
Buddhist sealing from Kalibukbuk, Bali (Doc. Balar Bali)

Amsterdam (MAK 388, 1940). In the bronze statue, which is thought to have originated from the first half of the ninth century CE, the Buddha is pictured sitting down on a slightly higher socle than his two companions. His right hand is held in the gesture of discussion (*vitarka-mudrā*), his left palm is facing upwards in his lap. To his right sits the Bodhisattva Avalokiteśvara, recognizable by the diminutive image of the Buddha Amitābha in his headdress and by his right hand which makes the gesture of giving (*varada-mudrā*) and the lotus (*padma*) in his left hand. On the Buddha's left the Bodhisattva likewise holds a lotus in his left hand. His right hand palm is facing upwards before his breast. This Bodhisattva could be identified as the Bodhisattva Vajrapāṇi because of the *vajra* standing on the lotus.[20]

These comparisons show that the hand gestures of the two Bodhisattvas in the Buddhist sealing from Candi Gentong are similar to the hand gestures in the bronze statue. Therefore, it can be proposed that the two Bodhisattvas in the sealing are Avalokiteśvara (Padmapāṇi) on the right and Vajrapāṇi on the left. Due to the damage, it cannot be known whether the headdress of Avalokiteśvara showed the Buddha Amitābha.

On the back of the Buddhist sealing there is an two-line inscription, similar to the miniature stūpas which contains the same mantra text (see Figure 4.6 right):

oṃ ye
te svāhā

III. DISCUSSION

I mentioned above that Candi Gentong is located in Trowulan, Mojokerto, which is thought to be the capital city of Majapahit kingdom, established in 1294 CE by Raden Wijaya who carried the title Śrī Mahārāja Narārya Saṅgrāmavijaya Śrī Kṛtarājasa Jayavardhana Anantavikrama Uttuṅgadeva. Majapahit was the last Hindu-Buddhist kingdom in Java before its fall in the late sixteenth century and the rise of the first Islamic kingdom in Demak.

In Trowulan area were found several inscriptions. Those inscriptions are Ālasantan (939 CE), Hara-Hara/Trowulan VI (966 CE), Mariboṅ/Trowulan II (1264 CE),[21] Wurare (1289 CE), Kubur Panjang (1291/2 CE), Balawi (1305 C.E.), Caṅgu/Trowulan I (1358 CE), Tirah/Karaṅ Bogĕm/Trowulan V (1387 CE), Trowulan III (fourteenth Century CE), and Śaka year inscriptions.[22] Each inscription represents every kingdom that had flourished in Central Java and East Java except Kaḍiri kingdom. The inscriptions from Old Matarām period were Ālasantan and Hara-hara/Trowulan VI; Siṅhāsari period were Mariboṅ/Trowulan II, Wurare, Kubur Panjang; and Majapahit period were Balawi, Caṅgu/Trowulan I, Trowulan III, Tirah/Karaṅ Bogĕm/Trowulan V, and Śaka year inscriptions.

The oldest inscription found in Trowulan is the Ālasantan inscription which was made during the period of King Siṇḍok (929–948 CE), who held the title Śrī Mahārāja Rakai Halu Dyah Pu Siṇḍok Śrī Īśānawikramadharmmotuṅgadeva. King Siṇḍok relocated the capital city of the kingdom from Central Java to East Java. Nevertheless the name of the kingdom was still Matarām as mentioned in the Turryān inscription (929 CE) (*kita tuwi sakweḥ ta hyaṅ prasiddha rumakṣa=ṅ kaḍatvan śrī mahārāja bhūmi matarām kita pinaka hurip=niṅ rāt kabaiḥ* = all of you celebrated gods who protect the palace of the Śrī Mahārāja of the state of Matarām, all of you will be alive in the world) and Ālasantan inscription (*kita prasiddha maṅrakṣa kaḍa[tvan śrī] mahārāja °i mḍaṅ °iṅ bhūmi matarām* = all of you celebrated [gods] who protect the palace of the Śrī Mahārāja at Mḍaṅ in the state of Matarām).

The relocation of the capital city is still being debated amongst scholars. Some argue that the relocation to East Java was due to economic factors, because the location of East Java was much more strategic than Central Java. Others have suggested that the move was made because of the threat posed by Śrīvijaya, or argued that the construction of the temples put pressure on the local habitants, or that there was imminent danger of a Mount Merapi eruption. I have suggested that the capital was relocated because there was already a plan to move to East Java in the beginning but the timing itself was moved forward due to the danger of natural disaster.[23]

As mentioned above the miniature stūpas in Candi Gentong I and II are inscribed in Kawi script with a Buddhist formula: *oṃ ye te svāhā*. Miniature stūpas with short Buddhist formulae inscribed in Kawi have also been found at Borobudur (see Figure 4.8). According to Boechari, these materials are not younger than the ninth century CE.[24] A total of 2,397 miniature stūpas and 252 Buddhist sealings were found at Borobudur.[25] Miniature stūpas and Buddhist sealings made of unbaked clay were found below two Bodhisattvas which cannot be identified since only the upper part of the body was found. Some of the miniature stūpas were stamped at the bottom. The Borobudur sealings have a variety of measurements: the largest has a diameter of 12 cm while the smallest is only 6 cm in diameter. These sealings were stamped with various representations, including the seated Buddha, Tārā, and rows of three to five stūpas. None of these sealings are inscribed.

FIGURE 4.8
Miniature stūpa from Borobudur, Magelang, Central Java
(Doc. Sugeng Riyanto)

Does the use of the Kawi script and the presence of similar short Buddhist inscriptions indicate that the miniature stūpas from Candi Gentong and Borobudur were produced in the same period? Unfortunately, given the fact that nearly all of the Borobudur miniature stūpas carry the same text, only three *akṣaras* are available for comparison with *akṣaras* from the Candi Gentong evidence. Nevertheless those *akṣaras* are clear enough to conclude that the script employed in the two locations is not identical. The fact that there are differences in the script from these two locations suggests that the miniature stūpas are unrelated.

Apart from being located in different geographical regions, there are three other facts that distinguish the Candi Gentong and Borobudur artefacts. First, the miniature stūpas found in Candi Gentong were all almost the same size while the miniature stūpas from Borobudur have a variety of measurements. Second, the miniature stūpas from Candi Gentong have no stamps while those from Borobudur are stamped at the bottom. Third, none of the Buddhist sealings from Borobudur are inscribed. Given these differences, it is likely that the miniature stūpas and Buddhist sealing from Candi Gentong did not come from Borobudur. It is possible that the artefacts were manufactured locally in the areas where the artefacts were found.

Analysis suggests that the type of Kawi script used on the miniature stūpas and Buddhist sealing from Candi Gentong is older than the script employed during the Majapahit period. To determine the age of this script I compared them with the Kawi epigraphy found around Trowulan (see Figure 4.9). After carefully examining the inscriptions, it appears that the script in Candi Gentong's miniature stūpas and Buddhist sealing are most similar to the script in the Ālasantan inscription[26] (see Table 4.1).

Although there are only a few Candi Gentong *akṣaras* that can be compared to the Ālasantan inscription, these have strong similarities. *Pa, ha,* and *ta* were written upright and are more angular in shape, while the ligature *sva* is slightly sloping, like the script from the ninth to tenth centuries CE. The use of serifs is very systematic, the *akṣaras ta* and *ha* have a single serif and the *akṣaras ya* and *sa* have double serifs. From this evidence, it can be assumed that the miniature stūpas and Buddhist sealing and Ālasantan letters share characteristics with the inscriptions from Siṇḍok, especially the fact of being upright, for *akṣaras* such as *pa, ma, va, ga, ṣa, sa,* and many others, with pronounced tendency towards squareness, but without the angularity.[27]

The Ālasantan inscription was found in Bejijong village, Trowulan, and it is the only copper-plate inscription found from the period of King Siṇḍok.[28] The Ālasantan inscription states that during the month of

FIGURE 4.9

Ālasantan inscription (Old Matarām)

Wurare inscription (Siŋhasāri)

Tirah/Trowulan V inscription (Majapahit)

TABLE 4.1
The Scripts from Borobudur, Candi Gentong, and Ālasantan

Script	Candi Borobudur Miniature stūpa	Candi Gentong		Ālasantan inscription
		Buddhist sealing	Miniature stūpa	
oṃ			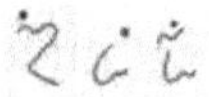	
ye				
te			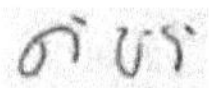	
sva				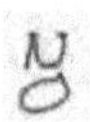
ha/hā				

Bhadravāda 861 Śaka (= 6 September 939 CE), the fifth day of the waxing moon, Śrī Mahārāja Rakai Halu Dyaḥ Siṇḍok Śrī Īśānavikrama gave an order to make land at Ālasantan a freehold belonging to Rakryān Kabayan, the mother of Rakryān Mapatih i Halu Dyah Sahasra.

Because there are similarities found between the akṣaras on the miniature stūpas and Buddhist sealing from Candi Gentong and those seen in the Ālasantan inscription, it can be assumed that the artefacts were manufactured around the period of King Siṇḍok. If these miniature stūpas were from the same period as the Ālasantan inscription, then the question becomes: did Candi Gentong experience several constructions before it became the Candi now known to date to the Majapahit period? If this is the case, then it might be that the first Candi Gentong was built around the time of King Siṇḍok. This is supported by the fact that Ālasantan inscription was found in Bejijong village, not far from Candi Gentong's location. Unfortunately, from the brick structure there are no indications that Candi Gentong was reconstructed several times.

IV. CONCLUSION

With reference to palaeography, the script found on the miniature stūpas and Buddhist sealing are older than the script from the Majapahit period and they are similar to the script used for the Ālasantan inscription. My tentative conclusion, which requires stronger evidence, is that the miniature stūpas and Buddhist sealing found in Candi Gentong I and Candi Gentong II do not date to the same period as the Candi Gentong monument itself, which was built during the Majapahit period. However the miniature stūpas and Buddhist sealing from Candi Gentong constitute evidence of the earliest phase of the Buddhist religion in East Java.

Notes

1. Verbeek, "De Oudheden van Majapahit", p. 6.
2. Kristinah, "Gapura dan Candi", p. 52.
3. Krom, "Inleiding tot de Hindoe-Javaansche Kunst", p. 184.
4. Kinney et al., "Worshiping Siva and Buddha", p. 173.
5. Ibid., p. 175.
6. Kristinah, "Gapura dan Candi", p. 51.
7. Kinney et al., "Worshiping Siva and Buddha", p. 174; Bronson and Jan Wisseman "Palembang as Śrīvijaya", p. 229.
8. Boechari, "Preliminary Report on some archaeological finds", pp. 90–95;

Santiko, "Some remarks on votive stupas", pp. 68–76; Miksic, Tranchim and Tranchim, "Borobudur: Golden Tales of Buddha", p. 34.

9. In Indonesia a miniature stūpa is more commonly called as *stūpika*. According to Liebert's (1976, p. 283) definition, a *stūpika* is a miniature stūpa, a small dome-like structure resembling a stūpa. It is also referred to as "votive stūpa".
10. Suhadi, "Inskripsi Stempel dari Palembang", pp. 49–61; Bronson and Jan Wisseman "Palembang as Śrīvijaya, pp. 229–30; Griffiths, "Inscriptions of Sumatra", pp. 142–46.
11. Issatriadi, "Miniature Stūpa Tanah Liat", 1996–1997.
12. Poesponegoro and Nugroho Notosusanto, "Sejarah Nasional Indonesia II", p. 308.
13. Miniature stūpas and Buddhist sealings that were found in Bali came from Pejeng, Tatiapi, Pura Pegulingan (Gianyar), Tampaksiring, and Kalibukbuk (Buleleng). Budiastra and Wayan Widi, "Miniatur Stūpa Tanah Liat Koleksi Museum Bali", 1980/1981; Astawa, "Miniature Stūpa Tanah Liat", pp. 17–18.
14. Djafar, "Kompleks Percandian Batujaya", pp. 89–90.
15. de Casparis, "Some Aspects of the Expansion of Nāgarī Script", p. 132.
16. In Indonesia there aren't many inscriptions that use Early Nāgarī or Nāgarī scripts. Early Nāgarī was used to write Buddhist mantra and about subjects that are related with Buddhist temples. For example, the Kalasan inscription (778 CE) was written regarding the construction of Candi Kalasan and the Kelurak inscription (782 CE) was written regarding the extension of Candi Sewu. The Early Nāgarī script also was used to inscribe Buddhist statues from Candi Jago from Siṅhasāri period (thirteenth century CE).
17. Kandahjaya, "The Lord of All Virtues", p. 3.
18. On the production of Buddhist sealings and related donative and ritual practices in Southeast Asia, see Skilling, "'Buddhist Sealings".
19. Astawa, "Miniature Stūpa Tanah Liat", p. 20; Diskul, "The Art of Śrīvijaya", fig. 11.
20. Scheurleer and Marijke J. Klokke, "Divine Bronze", p. 64.
21. The date written on the Mariboṅ/Trowulan II inscription is 1170 Śaka (1258 CE), but after further examination by Damais (1955, pp. 197–99) the inscription was actually written in 1186 Saka (1264 CE). The mistake is thought to have been caused because this inscription is a *tinulad,* a script which was not from the period to which the inscription is dated.
22. Śaka year inscriptions were written on tombstones (found at Tralaya and Putri Cempa Tombstones), *yoni* (Klinterejo), and on other stones that might be originated from temples at Trowulan area.
23. Nastiti, "Pasar di Jawa Masa Matarām Kuna", p. 24.
24. Boechari, "Preliminary Report on some archaeological finds", pp. 8–9.
25. Santiko, "Some remarks on Votive Stupas and Buddhist Sealings", p. 68.

26. The Ālasantan inscription consists of 4 copper plates with number 1, 2, 3, 4. The measurements are 44.50 cm × 19 cm, and only have inscription in one side with 12,18,19,20 lines. This inscription has been read by Wibowo in his article "Prasasti Alasantan tahun 861 Saka", *Majalah Arkeologi* II, no. 3 (1979): 3–51.
27. de Casparis, "Indonesian Paleography", p. 39.
28. In fact there are some copper inscriptions from King Siṇḍok period, but only the Ālasantan inscription was written in King Siṇḍok period; the other inscriptions were written in the Majapahit period.

Bibliography

Astawa, A.A. Gede Oka. "Miniature Stūpa Tanah Liat dari Situs Pantai Lovina Kalibukbuk, Buleleng, Bali". *Forum Arkeologi* no. II (2006): 11–24.

Boechari. "Preliminary Report on some archaeological finds around the Borobudur temple". *Pelita Borobudur. Reports and Documents of the Consultative Committee for the Safeguarding of Borobudur. 5th Meeting April 1976*, pp. 90–95. Jakarta: Departemen Pendidikan dan Kebudayaan Republik Indonesia, 1982.

Brandes J.L.A. "Oud-Javaansche Oorkonde, nagelaten transcripties van wijlen Dr. J.L.A. Brandes, uitgegeven door N.J. Krom". *VBG*, LX. Batavia: Albrecht & Co, 's Hage: M. Nijhoff, 1913.

Bronson, Bennet and Jan Wisseman Christie. "Palembang as Śrīvijaya. The Lateness of Early Cities in Southern Southeast Asia". *Asian Perspective* 2 XIX (2): 220–39.

Budiastra, Putu and Wayan Widia. *Miniatur Stūpa Tanah Liat Koleksi Museum Bali*. Bali: Proyek Pengembangan Permuseuman Bali, 1980/1981.

de Casparis, J.G. *Indonesian Paleography. A History of Writing in Indonesia from the Beginnings to C. C.E. 1500*. Leiden/Köln: E.J. Brill, 1975.

——. "Some Aspects of the Expansion of Nāgarī Script in South and South East Asia". In *South Asia 1*, edited by Graciela de la Lama, pp. 123–38. Mexico: El Colegio de Mexico, 1982.

——. "Where Was Pu Siṇḍok's Capital Situated". In *Studies in South and Southeast Asia Archaeology*, edited by H.I.R. Hinzler, vol. 2, pp 39–52. Leiden: Koentji Press, 1988.

Cohen Stuart, A.B. *Kawi Oorkonden in Facsimile, met Inleiding en Transcriptie*. Leiden: E.J. Brill, 1875.

Damais, Louis-Charles. "Études Javanaises: IV. Discussion de la date des Inscription". *BÉFEO* 17, no. 1 (1955): 7–290.

Diskul, M.C. Subhadradis. *The Art of Śrīvijaya*. Paris: Oxford University Press - UNESCO, 1980.

Djafar, Hasan. *Kompleks Percandian Batujaya. Rekonstruksi Sejarah Kebudayaan Daerah Pantai Utara Jawa Barat*. Jakarta, Bandung; Penerbit Kiblat Buku

Utama, École Française d'Extrême-Orient, Pusat Penelitian dan Pengembangan Arkeologi Nasional, KITLV-Jakarta, 2010.

Griffith, Arlo. "Inscriptions of Sumatra: Further Data on the Epigraphyof the Musi and Batang Hari Rivers Basins". *Archipel* 81 (2011): 139–75.

Issatriadi. *Miniature Stūpa Tanah Liat Bermaterai Gumuk Klinting*. Surabaya: Proyek Rehabilitasi dan Perluasan Museum Jawa Timur, 1976–77.

Kandahjaya, Hudaya. "The Lord of All Virtues". *Pasific World. Journal of the Institute of Buddhist Studies*, Third series no. 11 (2009): 1–24.

Kinney, Ann R., Marijke Klokke, and Lydia Kieven. *Worshiping Siva and Buddha. The Temple Art of East Java*. Honolulu: University of Hawai'i Press, 2003.

Kristinah, Endang. "Gapura dan Candi". In *Majapahit – Trowulan*, pp. 44–53. Jakarta: Direktorat Peninggalan Purbakala, 2006.

Krom, N.J. *Inleiding tot de Hindoe-Javaansche Kunst*, tweede deel. 's-Gravenhage Martinus Nijhoff, 1923.

Liebert, Gösta. "Iconographic Dictionary of the Indian Religions. Hinduism-Buddhism-Jainism". *Studies in South Asian Culture*, vol. V, edited by J.E. van Lohuizen-de Leeuw. Leiden: E.J. Brill, 1976.

Miksic, John, Marcello Tranchim, and Anita Tranchim. *Borobudur: Golden Tales of Buddha*. Singapore: Periplus Editions, 1990.

Nastiti, Titi Surti. *Pasar di Jawa Masa Matarām Kuna. Abad VIII-XI Masehi*. Jakarta: Pustaka Jaya, 2003.

Pigeaud, Th.G.Th. *Java in the Fourteenth Century: A Study in Cultural History. The Nagara-Kertagama by Rakawi Prapañca of Majapahit, 1365 C.E.*, vol. 1. The Hague: Martinus Nijhoff, 1960.

Poesponegoro, Marwati Djoened and Nugroho Notosusanto. *Sejarah Nasional Indonesia II*. Jakarta: Balai Pustaka, 2008.

Santiko, Hariani. "Some Remarks on Votive Stupas and Buddhist Sealings from Borobudur". *Majalah Arkeologi* I, no. 1 (1977): 68–76.

Scheurleer, Pauline Lunsingh and Marijke J. Kloke. *Divine Bronze. Ancient Indonesian Bronzes from AD 600 to 1600*. Leiden: E.J. Brill, 1988.

Skilling, Peter. "'Buddhist Sealing': Reflections on Terminology, Motivation, Donors' Status, School-Affiliation, and Print-Technology". In *South Asian Archaeology 2001. Proceeding of the Sixteenth International Conference of the European Association of South Asian Archaeologist, held in Collège de France, Paris, 2–6 July 2001*, vol. II *Historical Archaeology and Art History*, edited by Catherine Jarrige and Vincent Lefèvre, pp. 677–85. Paris: Editions Recherche sur les Civilisations, 2005.

——. "Buddhist Sealings in Thailand and Southeast Asia: Iconography, Function, and Ritual Context". In *Interpreting Southeast Asia's Past. Monument, Image and Text: Selected paper from the 10th International Conference of the European Association of Southeast Asia Archaeologist*, vol. 2, edited by Elisabeth A Bacus et al., pp. 248–62. Singapore: NUS Press, 2008.

Suhadi, M. "Inskripsi Stempel dari Palembang". *Bulletin Yaperna* III, no. 15 (1976): 49–61.

Wibowo, A.S. "Prasasti Alasantan Tahun 861 Saka". *Majalah Arkeologi* II, no. 3 (1979): 3–51.

Verbeek, R.D.M. "De Oudheden van Majapahit in 1815 en in 1887 (met een kaartje)". *TBG* 33 (1890): 1–15.

Yamin, Mohammad. *Tatanegara Majapahit*, vol. II. Jakarta: Prapantja, 1962.

Zoetmulder, P.J. *Kalangwan. A survey of Old Javanese Literature*. The Hague: Martinus Nijhoff, 1974.

5

A BRONZE HOARD FROM MUARA KAMAN, KUTEI

E. Edwards McKinnon

I. INTRODUCTION

In presenting my paper on the hoard of scrap bronze from Kutei at the conference on Buddhist Dynamics in Pre-modern Southeast Asia at ISEAS in Singapore in 2011, my intention was simply to make known the existence of the remnants of these mostly badly corroded and broken images. Although I was aware that these remains could be of some considerable art historical and archaeological significance, I did not feel that I had sufficient command of the subject of mediaeval bronze imagery to discuss the stylistic affinities or the dating of such materials in detail or to do more than introduce them to those who might have an interest in such artefacts. I am most grateful, therefore, to all those who have encouraged me to delve further into the subject of Buddhist bronze imagery and for the advice that I have been afforded. Any errors that remain in this essay are, of course, my own.

The hoard of bronze scrap was reputedly recovered at Muara Kaman, Kutei subdistrict, now in Kutei Kartanegara Regency, East Kalimantan province of Indonesia at some time during the late 1980s or early 1990s. During a visit to Samarinda, the provincial capital in 1994, I was kindly allowed to examine and to photograph some twenty-three objects then in the possession of an antique dealer, Haji Mohammad Bakri Udin. Whether or not these items are still to be seen in Samarinda at present time, or whether they had formed part of a larger hoard of Buddhist bronzes said to have been recovered from the Kutei area about the same time, or were found separately I do not know. The various fragments, although not seen *in situ* at the time of their recovery do, however, appear to be of sufficient importance to warrant a record being made of their existence.

I have also added notes on other bronze Buddhist images reputedly found in the Kutei area, including the magnificent bronze from Kuta Bangun, unfortunately damaged in a fire at the Colonial Exhibition in Paris in 1931; a small metal Buddha fragment from Sanggata further north on the coast of East Kalimantan and also the major bronze Buddha from Si Kendeng on the Karama river in neighbouring western Sulawesi (Celebes) to try to provide a broader setting for the finds.

II. THE REGIONAL SETTING

The island of Borneo, now divided into East Malaysia, Brunei and Indonesian Kalimantan, would appear to have been one of the earliest focuses of South Asian interest in Southeast Asia (Nilakanta Sastri 1949, p. 16). Indonesian links with northeastern and southern India were already well established by the beginning of the first millennium CE. Romano-Indian rouletted earthenware dating from the first century CE has been recovered in the coastal Buni region of west Java (Walker and Santoso 1977) and on the north coast of Bali (Ardika and Bellwood 1991).

The earliest known Sanskrit inscriptions in the archipelago, those of a ruler named Mūlawarman, dated on the basis of paleography to the late fourth or early fifth century CE were discovered at Muara Kaman and Kutei Lama in the Kutei region (de Casparis 1975, p. 18, 1986, p. 243). These inscriptions occurring at a strategic point on the Mahakam river in all probability reflect an early external interest in Kutei's rich alluvial gold-bearing hinterland. A second, slightly later group of Sanskrit inscriptions, again dated on the basis of palaeography and attributed to Pūrnavarman of Tārumā (Vogel 1925), is known from the area around Bogor and in Lebak of western Java, also reflecting interest in the gold bearing area to the south of Bogor (Edwards McKinnon, Djafar and Soeroso 1998).

The earliest appearance of Buddhist-related materials in Indonesia have occurred in southeastern Sumatra, in Melayu Jambi and Śrivijaya Palembang; in the Batujaya area of west Java (Manguin and Agustijanto Indrajaya 2006) and in central Java all about the same time in the seventh century CE, along what were the coasts of the maritime spice route between the eastern archipelago and south Asia. By the later first millennium, traces of Buddhism appear in the form of brick-built sanctuaries, imagery of both stone and metal, rock carvings and small sealings and votive tablets made of baked and unbaked clay. Brown (2011, p. 325) considers that the earliest bronze imagery of the Buddha in Southeast Asia must date to after the fifth century but is generally thought to have appeared in Indonesia by about the seventh century.

Relatively little is yet known of the development of Buddhism in eastern Kalimantan or the neighbouring western coast of Sulawesi (Celebes). It is this region, however, that has yielded some of the most important early bronze Buddhist imagery to be found in the Indonesian archipelago. Three sites in particular, Si Kendeng on the Karama river in western Sulawesi, plus Kuta Bangun and Muara Kaman in Kutei Regency, have all yielded traces of early Buddhist activity as witnessed by the bronze sculpture found there.

Though well known for its earlier neolithic phase, the recovery of a bronze image at Si Kendeng has proved difficult to place in a contemporary context. Muara Kaman on the other hand is an ancient though much-disturbed site on the Mahakam river that is of interest as the location of the earliest known Sanskrit inscriptions in the whole of Indonesia, as well as having yielded later finds. The inscriptions that are thought to date from the late fourth or early fifth century CE (Vogel 1918; de Casparis 1975, p. 18, 1986, p. 243), are possibly suggestive of active South Asian Brahmanical contact with the Mahakam region by this time. The recovery of numerous Buddhist images in the Kutei/Selat Makassar area, though somewhat off the beaten track as it were and the rock carvings at Batu Pait on the Kapuas river in western Kalimantan (Krom 1926, p. 72) suggest that this region and other parts of Borneo were also directly involved in the early stages of Buddhist activity in the archipelago. Important finds of Buddhist imagery have been made near Sambas, where a hoard of gold, silver and bronze imagery was discovered (Tan 1948; Nilakanta Sastri 1949) and a Buddha image is known to have been recovered from Desa Baringin B, near Candi Laras, Margasari, in South Kalimantan (Vida Verpaya Rusianti Kusmartono and Machi Suhadi 1998–99, pp. 113, 114).

III. THE SI KENDENG BUDDHA

The standing Buddha from Si Kendeng, on the right bank of the Karama river in western Sulawesi was recovered in 1921 (Van Heekeren 1972, p. 184) (see Figure 5.1). Initially dated to between the second and fifth

MAP 5.1
Kalimantan, the Selat Makassar and Sulawesi

Source: http://dmaps.com/carte.php?lib=indonesia_map&num_car=288&lang=en].

centuries (Bernet Kempers 1959, pp. 24, 31–32), it was long thought to be the earliest bronze image known in Indonesia and certainly the second largest (Fontein 1990, p. 180). More recent research by Western scholars suggests, however, that this late Amaravatī style image, in the open mode with the robe over the left shoulder, folds in the drapery that are treated as thin parallel grooves and with the right arm raised in front of the body, the hands are missing, may be more closely related to the Sri Lankan

FIGURE 5.1
The Si Kendeng Buddha

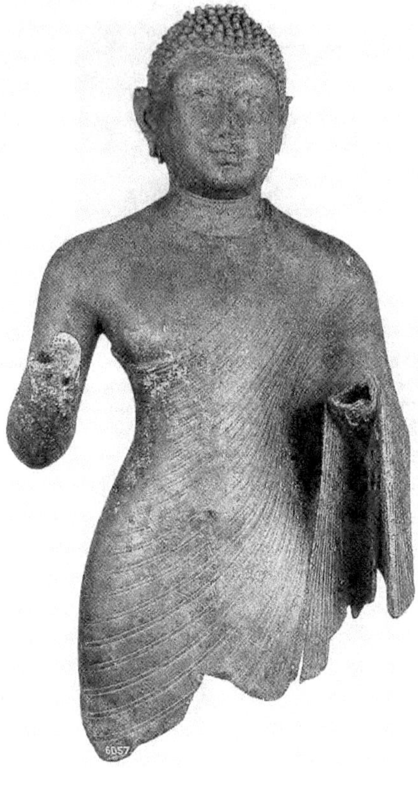

Source: Courtesy of the Museum Nasional, Jakarta.

Anuradhapura school of imagery of the eighth century (Schastok 1994, p. 47; Manguin 2010). It is, therefore, still one of the earliest larger bronzes known in the archipelago, though its presence in a relatively remote coastal part of western Sulawesi, without any as yet understood contemporary context, remains something of a mystery.

Nevertheless, it should be noted also that the Karama River valley has produced some of the earliest known settlement sites on Sulawesi and that it gives access to gold-bearing alluvia in its upper reaches. It is relatively close to and almost directly opposite the point where the delta of the great Mahakam River of eastern Kalimantan debouches into the Selat Makassar. The presence of an erstwhile Buddhist community on the lower course of the Karama in Sulawesi would thus appear to be linked to contemporary Buddhist communities on the east coast of Kalimantan also engaged in gold-winning activity and the early mediaeval inter-regional trade in gold. The bronze bell with a *vajra* top recovered from a neighbouring village Wulu (Fontein 1990, p. 180) may also be of some significance in this context.

No other Buddhist remains or signs of any permanent sacral site, such as the foundations of a brick-built structure have come to light in the immediate vicinity of where the Si Kendeng image was found (Van Heekeren 1972, p. 184). It should be remembered, however, that first millennium settlement sites — other than those with inscriptional evidence, have proved extremely difficult to identify or to date in Indonesia. Moreover, brick-built or stone temples did not evolve in southern India or Southeast Asia until about the sixth century, so that an early settlement or shrine in this relatively isolated region of western Sulawesi — other than the evidence of earlier lithic material and "prehistoric" pottery, may have been of an impermanent nature that has left little or no tangible evidence of its existence. Imagery would perhaps infer the presence of a community of Buddhist monks who may well have erected an image in no more than a small open-sided, brick-built platform roofed with thatch — as was the case in Kota Cina. If this was indeed the case, the organic remains which usually disappear rapidly without trace in the humid and often acid soils of the tropics would be almost impossible to identify. Domestic architecture was almost entirely of wooden structures and in such a situation, there would probably be no case for a shrine of more permanent construction other than just a simple construction of wood.

The Si Kendeng site is also said to have been damaged by flooding as the Karama River is occasionally subject to major spates. There are of course exceptional circumstances throughout the archipelago where artefacts and even human remains are preserved in peat swamps or shell deposits but in most cases lithic materials and earthenware are the sole survivors in such situations.

IV. KOTA BANGUN AND MUARA KAMAN

IV.1 The Kuta Bangun Buddha

An early bronze standing Buddha image was discovered in a house of a Muslim family on the bank of the Keham River that flows into the Uwu swamp on the right bank of the Mahakam River southwest of Muara Kaman, between Muara Muntai and Kuta Bangun in 1846/47 (Bosch 1927, p. 402) (see Figure 5.2). The image, from the top of the head down to the bottom of the robe, though the feet were missing, was 58 cm in height and it was originally considered to be dated to about the second to fifth centuries CE.

This bronze, usually known as the Kuta Bangun Buddha, is characterized by a graceful figure with a robe in the open mode and a low *uṣṇīṣa*. The robe, which clings to the body is virtually devoid of folds and is draped over the left arm. The right hand with the palm facing outwards is in *vitarka mudrā*. The left, with the index finger and thumb joined

FIGURE 5.2
The Kuta Bangun Buddha

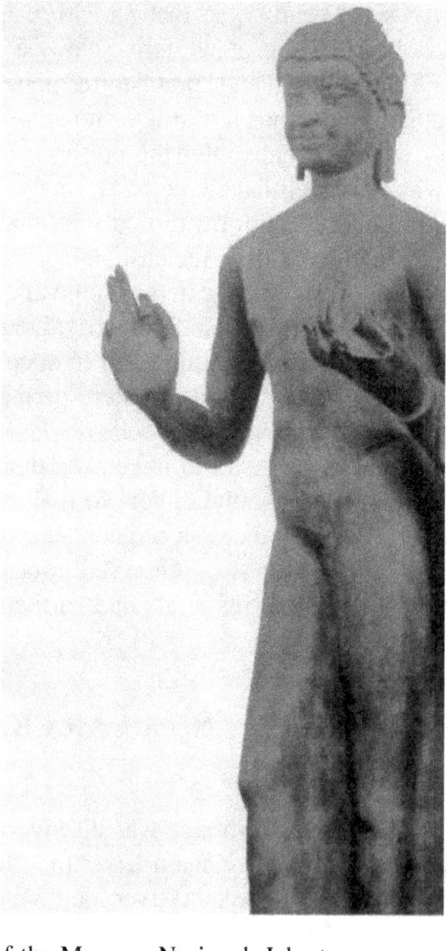

Source: Courtesy of the Museum Nasional, Jakarta.

in a ring, appears to be holding a small receptacle, no doubt a begging bowl, a symbol associated with Buddha defeating the fire snake which he then put in his begging bowl. Stylistically this is a post-Gupta image probably datable to the seventh or eighth centuries and has been related iconographically to a Buddha from Manyargading near Jepara in central Java. It was unfortunately very badly damaged in a fire at the Colonial Exhibition in Paris in 1931 with the damaged remnant reportedly kept, though no longer on display, in the Museum Nasional, Jakarta (Bernet Kempers 1959, p. 49).

The modern settlement of Kota Bangun itself is an important, but now badly disturbed archaeological site that has yielded masses of sherd material including large quantities of earthenware and imported Chinese stonewares dating from the Song (960–1279), Yuan (1279–1368) and Ming (1368–1644) periods (Boyce 1986). A magnificent gold *upavita*, now in the Kutei Museum, was recovered from a stoneware jar in an old burial ground at Kota Bangun in 1991 which may suggest the co-existence of both Buddhist and Hindu communities at this site. The earlier settlement was probably one of the last strongholds of Buddhism in the region during the onslaught of Islam in the seventeenth century. To date, only very limited archaeological research has been undertaken at Kota Bangun.

IV.2 Muara Kaman

The Muara Kaman site is located on a promontory of higher ground lying between the Kedang Rantau River and a former meander of the main stream at the confluence of the Kedang Rantau and the mighty Mahakam River (116° 43' E, 0° 09' S), upstream from the regency capital at Tenggarong. On its western side, the promontory rises some 10 to 15 metres above the normal level of the Kadang Rantau and then slopes down gradually to the edge of a broad morass, a former meander of the Mahakam River. The soil on this area of higher ground is predominantly a sandy loam overlying sand and an iron-rich deposit of laterite. The area at the edge of the former meander deserves further investigation as it would have provided an ideal landing place for boats arriving in Muara Kaman as well as affording an impressive view of the settlement on the higher ground.

Muara Kaman is a strategically located position as it commands riverine access to a rich hinterland, the broad alluvial gold-bearing region which was subject to the Bre-X stock market scandal of 1997. Seemingly there are no longer commercial gold-bearing deposits in this area, most having been worked out in antiquity. There is textual evidence for the existence of a small local pre-Islamic "Hindu" polity that persisted at Muara Kaman in Kutei until the seventeenth century (de Casparis 1986, p. 242). The inhabitants of this settlement, and those further upstream presumably succumbed eventually to the pressures of Islamisation from the Sultanate established at Kutei Lama.

As mentioned above, Muara Kaman is known for its association with the fifth century so-called *yūpa* inscriptions of Mūlawarman, the earliest known Sanskrit inscriptions in the Indonesian archipelago (de Casparis 1975, pp. 14–18, 1986, p. 243). Although there was some doubt about the original location of the first finds of these stones as three inscriptions found in 1940 were seemingly recovered at Kutei Lama (Chhabra 1949), the earliest Islamic settlement in the region, de Casparis was satisfied that the *yūpa* stones all came from Muara Kaman. My own observations

MAP 5.2
Muara Kaman : 1:50,000

would tend to confirm this, as when I visited Kutei Lama in early 1995 when a large new prefabricated steel-framed mosque was being erected on a bulldozed portion of the river bank, the recognizable exposed cultural material was mainly late Song and Yuan period imported stonewares.

Recoveries of Buddhist remains in the 1990s were not the first such finds from the Muara Kaman site. As long ago as 1840, a small gold seated Buddha, formerly in the regalia of the sultan of Kutei was also recovered here (Krom 1914, p. 151, Kern 1917, p. 57). One of the earliest reports on antiquities at Muara Kaman was that of H. von Dewall, who wrote

> On the 20 April [1847] I arrived at Muara Kaman, a kampong of thirty-nine houses and *lanang* (rafts) situated at the confluence of the river of the same name [i.e., the Kaman] and the Mahakam, on the left bank of both. Here I found a number of stone slabs piled up under the ground. It was on this spot also that the idol of massive gold, weighing 8 *tahil*, was discovered, which the sultan wears around his neck on state occasions. This is four-armed, well-proportioned and of good workmanship. The youthful prince, moreover wears beneath this idol another golden box-shaped object on which various mythical figure of the Hindu religion are shown in *alto-relievo*. The same appears to be of higher antiquity than the golden image, but like the idol, it was discovered beneath the stone slabs in the reign of Sultan Muhammad Salih-ud-din (quoted in translation by Vogel 1918, p. 208).

The massive "golden idol" is a Viṣṇu image, 12 cm in height that is probably local workmanship but displaying possible Mojopahit stylistic influence. The "golden box-shaped object" described by von Dewall is actually a cylindrical pendant known as the *uncal*, 9 cm in length and 3 cm in diameter that displays two scenes in relief from the Ramayana and is possibly of earlier late first millennium Javanese workmanship. The name *uncal* may derive from *uccaṇḍāstra*, a term meaning "a terrible arrow" (Liebert 1976, p. 308), and thus be a name relating to the scene of the shooting of the deer. One panel, probably the more important of the two and which is unfortunately somewhat damaged, illustrates Rāma slaying the deer, which depicts the moment of transformation of the deer into Marica, a *rākṣasa* or demon who was adept at casting spells. The deer had been sent by Rāvaṇa to lure Rāma from his hermitage in the forest. The second panel depicts Sītā seated in her garden in Laṅkāpura, the home of Rāvaṇa, together with servants, in which the deer is depicted concealed and surrounded by foliage in the bottom left of the panel.

In 1905, a visitor to Kutei, S.C. Knapper reported the presence of a gold Viṣṇu image and a gold tortoise then in the possession of the sultan, which were known to have come from Muara Kaman (Vogel 1918, pp. 207, 208). Coomaraswamy (1914, p. 26) quotes from the *Mahānirvāna Tantra* and notes that in Sri Lanka, metal tortoises were among small aquatic animal figures used in Buddhist rituals performed at the consecration of a *Tagāda* or reservoir.

The ground surface at Muara Kaman is greatly disturbed. Parts of the site were dug up by a Mr Tromp as early as 1885, the remains of whose treasure-seeking efforts were still to be seen by Witkamp in 1914. Witkamp remarked that the "early diggings were still visibly marked by deep depressions" (quoted in translation by Vogel 1918, p. 209). Several such deep depressions are still to be seen at the present time.

Despite the various important recoveries at Muara Kaman, very little scientific archaeological investigation has been undertaken at this site. The degree of disturbance is indeed considerable, but patience may be rewarded should carefully managed and intensive controlled excavation be undertaken. As far as I am aware, no Buddhist sealings or *stūpikas* have yet been recovered at Muara Kaman. In 1994, however, blocks and fragments of limestone masonry were still to be found scattered around on the surface when I visited the site. At the time, I did not notice any brick remains.

V. THE HOARD OF METAL REMNANTS

The following is a brief descriptive inventory of the items reputedly recovered as a hoard from Kutei in 1994. All images would appear to have been cast in bronze or a bronze alloy by the lost wax technique. An earthen core, confirming the use of a hollow-casting technique is directly visible within some of the fragments.

V.1 Standing Buddha Image

The height of this bronze with both the feet missing is approximately 9 cm. The Buddha is depicted as a standing figure with a close-fitting robe devoid of any folds and in the open mode, that is with the garment draped over the left shoulder, the right shoulder bare and a swag of cloth at the bottom of the lower hem. The *uṣnīṣa* is low, the curls of the hair formed in small, tight knots. The image has a lowered gaze with the head bent slightly forward. The right arm is held across the body with the upturned palm of the hand and extended fingers in what seems to be *vitarka mudrā*, though this mudrā is normally reserved for seated images; the left hand is missing. See Figure 5.3.

FIGURE 5.3
Standing Buddha (from the Muara Kaman hoard) (a) front, (b) rear

Source: Figures 5.3 to 5.15, 5.19 to 5.21 by the author.

A prominent swag of cloth is also apparent at the rear of the shoulders. This image would appear to reflect the south Indian later Amarāvatī or possibly Sri Lankan Anurādhapura style, datable to the seventh or eighth centuries CE.

V.2 Bodhisattva: Avalokiteśvara

Only the upper part of this badly corroded image remains. The torso is plain and virtually devoid of decoration, the right hand is in *abhaya mudrā*, the gesture of reassurance, the left arm missing from above the elbow. The distinctive, tall coiffure or *jaṭāmakuṭa* with the hair piled up elegantly over the head is reminiscent of south Indian seventh or eighth centuries Sri Lankan workmanship. See Figure 5.4.

This fragment appears to bear some similarity to south Indian or later Sri Lankan Anurādhapura images of Avalokiteśvara (Von Schroeder 1990, p. 253, Plate 61) and thus may date from as early as the seventh to eighth centuries.

FIGURE 5.4
Bodhisattva (from the Muara Kaman hoard) (a) front, (b) rear

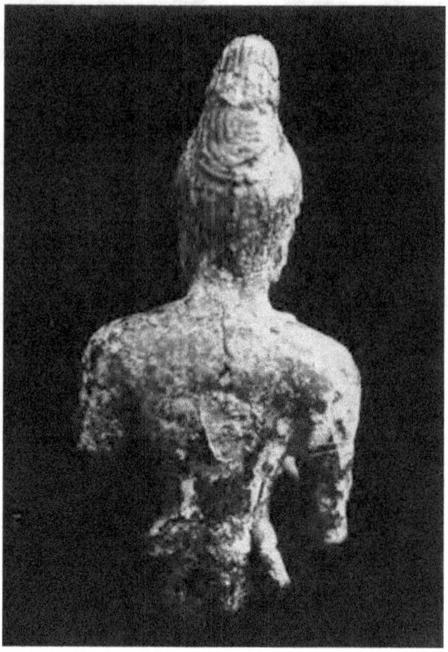

V.3 Bodhisattva

Again, a second badly corroded but also relatively plain, undecorated upper part of a boddhisatva image of which only the head, shoulders and upper part of the left arm remain with little or no trace of ornamentation other than a sash over the left shoulder. Vestiges of a badly corroded tall coiffure or *jaṭamakuṭa* is also reminiscent of early south Indian or Sri Lankan workmanship. See Figure 5.5.

Comparative images: This bronze also bears some similarity to south Indian or Sri Lankan *Maitreya* images in the Pallava style (von Schroeder 1990, p. 250, Plate. 60).

V.4 Lower Part of a Bodhisattva Figure

This lower body approximately 6 cm in height comprises a short, truncated robe or tunic with a bejewelled waistband, spindly legs and feet which may relate to either item 2 or 3 above. The short tunic may reflect either south Indian Pallava or Sri Lankan influence or possibly a local development

FIGURE 5.5
Bodhisattva with earthen core (from the Muara Kaman hoard)

in Bornean Buddhist iconography. Probably datable to the eighth or ninth centuries CE.

V.5 Torso with Left Arm, Bodhisattva Figure

This truncated torso, approximately 5 cm in height, with its left arm held forward at the side of the body, the hand holding what would appear to be the stem of a lotus reveals remains of the *trivali* at the neck and traces of what may be a necklace and a sash running from the left shoulder to the right hip. See Figure 5.7.

The image is bare-breasted with the top of the lower garment wrapped around the waist. Unfortunately, it is extremely difficult to determine what the remaining outlines actually mean.

FIGURE 5.6
Lower body, legs and feet of a Bodhisattva (from the Muara Kaman hoard)

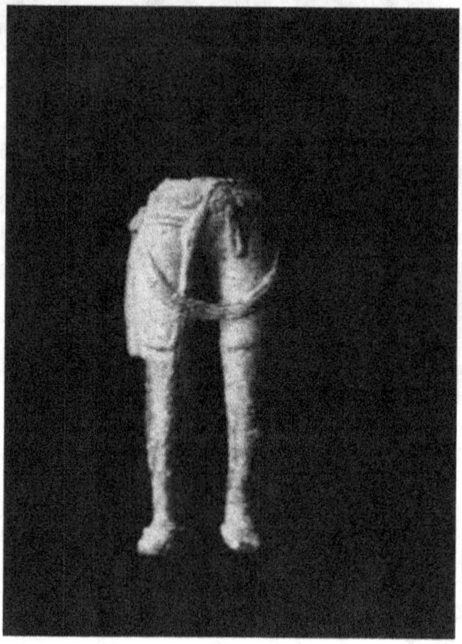

FIGURE 5.7
Bodhisattva torso with left arm and lotus (from the Muara Kaman hoard)

V.6 Waist and Legs of a Bodhisattva Image (Avalokiteśvara?)

Another, possibly locally produced, slimly cast fragment comprising only the waist and legs of a small image with the robe reaching to the ankles and with the feet slightly twisted in relation to the legs. This image has traces of an ornate belt and possibly a tiger mask on the right thigh which would determine it as an Avalokiteśvara. See Figure 5.8.

Comparable examples: An early image with somewhat similar treatment of the robe, datable to the seventh century was recovered from Bukit Seguntang, Palembang (Chutiwongs 2011, p. 4, fig. 2).

FIGURE 5.8
Two fragments of a Bodhisattva with distinct herring bone pattern on the robe (from the Muara Kaman hoard)

V.7 Fragmentary Standing Image: Right Shoulder, Torso and Lower Part of the Robe

Another fragmentary standing image comprising the right shoulder and upper part of the torso, the waist and part of the robe below the waist to the knees with a separate triangular portion of the lower part of the robe. The right hand is raised in what is seemingly *abhaya-mudrā*. A deep V-shaped cavity in the chest exposes the earthen core of the image. The robe which reaches to the ankles is marked with distinct pleats and a distinct vertical central pleat falls to the left foot. See Figure 5.9.

The treatment of the robe with its upswept folds and a pronounced vertical central part between the legs is similar to an early seventh century bronze from Bukit Seguntang, Palembang (Chutiwongs 2011, p. 19, plate 2).

FIGURE 5.9
Lower waist and leg portion of a Bodhisattva
(from the Muara Kaman hoard)

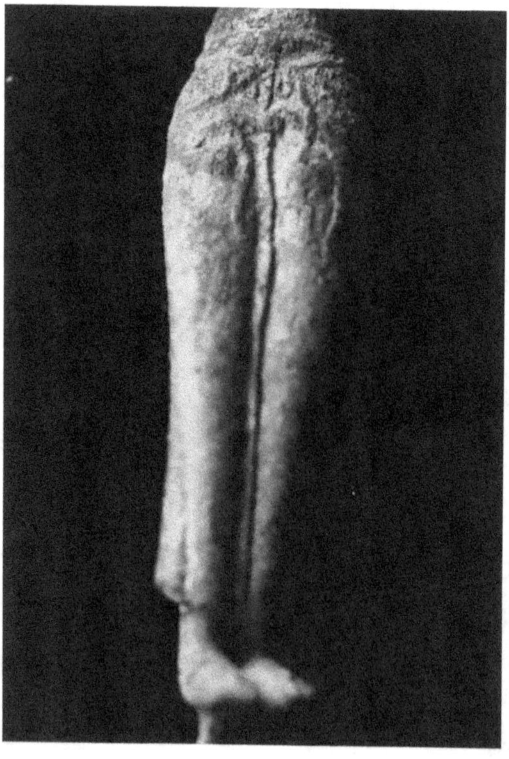

V.8 A Buddha Trinity with Provision for Bodhisattvas Flanking the Seated Buddha

This badly corroded seated Buddha with the robe in the closed mode, the right hand in *bhūmisparśa mudrā* and the left palm upward on the lap, seated on a lotus base, with part of an aurora to the left of the image and with two rectangular bases to the right and left of the central image. This is a relatively rare formula in bronzes found in Southeast Asia (Woodward 1988, p. 82).

The aurora displays traces of lobes or flame decoration around the outer edge. The lower base of the trinity is square cut and plain, seemingly devoid of any decoration, though the Buddha is seated on a lotus throne. The two accessory bases show traces of lotus decoration. Possibly dated to the first half of the ninth century to the early tenth century CE. This image seemingly displays influences from northeastern India — from Bengal or Bihar, or what is now modern Bangladesh. See Figure 5.10.

FIGURE 5.10
Badly corroded Buddha trinity with provision for bodhisattvas flanking the seated Buddha (from the Muara Kaman hoard)

Comparable examples: Similar seated Buddhas are known from Sambas, Palembang and in a mould for votive tables in Central Java (Woodward 1988, p. 82).

V.9 A Bodhisattva with Turban-like Crown

This is an unusual, somewhat stiffly portrayed figure with a high crown or *mukuṭa*, a necklace of large beads and crossed sashes over a bare breast with what appears to be a rectangular mantra case suspended in front of the lower chest. The robe reaches from the waist to just above the ankles. A belt or sash hangs diagonally from the right hip to the left thigh. The features of the face are relatively well preserved, the lobes of the ears pendent. Both arms are held away from the body, bent forwards at the elbows, a slightly longer portion of the right arm still extent compared with the left. Both hands are missing. See Figure 5.11.

FIGURE 5.11
Bodhisattva with a distinctive turban-like *muhkuta*
(from the Muara Kaman hoard)

Comparable examples: I have not been able to identify any similar images. A square-shaped gold mantra case, similar to the object suspended on the chest of the image, was recovered in the Wonoboyo hoard in Central Java.

V.10 A Detached Ornate Back Piece for the Throne of an Image

This base metal alloy fragment is some 8 cm in height and may have held a parasol or umbrella. The ornate design possibly represents a local stylistic development as the detail of the design elements are not clear. Three trefoil-like elements protrude from each side of the vertical rectangular portion of the back piece. See Figure 5.12.

FIGURE 5.12
A detached part of an ornate back piece of base metal for an image (from the Muara Kaman hoard)

The design of this back piece is possibly a later local development in the Kutei region datable to the eleventh century.

V.11 Miscellaneous Metal Scrap Fragments

Nine small items portrayed in Figure 5.13 were the final element photographed in the hoard from Kutei. These are, from top left to lower right as follows:

1. A small L-shaped fragment, round in cross-section, probably part of an arm.
2. The upper part of a torso in the open mode, possibly from a small standing Buddha image, with the right hand raised in *abhaya-mudrā*. The tips of the fingers are missing.
3. A lion with its left paw raised, most likely a fragment from an elaborate lion throne (*siṅhāsana*) of a seated image.
4. A right arm and hand, the fingers raised, pointing outwards in *abhya-mudrā*.

FIGURE 5.13
Miscellaneous scrap items (from the Muara Kaman hoard)

5. The lower part of a Buddha figurine, showing the bottom of the robe devoid of pleats and two feet, possibly the lower portion of (2) above.
6. A lion's paw (?).
7. A detached foot.
8. What appears to be a small foot with the lower part of the robe.
9. Part of a badly corroded arm.

Despite their small size, these fragments are of interest as they suggest the existence of possibly five additional images to those mentioned above. The lion with its left paw raised is a significant design element used in the support for a lotus throne — as seen on the base of the throne of a Sambas Buddha. Originally a Sassanian design, this motif also appears on a variety of textiles. The *Simhanādā Lokeśvara*, "the lion's roar" was interpreted as a recital of Buddhist doctrine (Liebert 1976, p. 270).

V.12 A Cylindrical Stūpa-like Bronze Lime Container

Cylindrical, stūpa-like two-part containers such as these which were seemingly used for lime, an element required for chewing *sirih* or betel nut, appear over much of insular and mainland Southeast Asia. Height approximately 10 cm. See Figure 5.14.

These bronze lime containers are common in Thailand. In Indonesia, small ceramic jars containing traces of lime have often been recovered in archaeological excavations. A somewhat similar vessel in bronze containing lime has been recovered from the Musi River in Palembang.

VI. EARLIER FINDS FROM MUARA KAMAN AND KUTEI

VI.1 A Standing Buddha from Muara Kaman

For the record, I include a photograph of a Buddha image reputedly standing about 10 cm in height which formerly belonged to a local farmer in Muara Kaman. The image was recovered while digging a roadside ditch near the school in Muara Kaman. This small, slim-waisted image in the *tribhaṅga* pose, with its small, tight curls, low *uṣnīṣa* and small visage, is in the open mode, the plain robe devoid of pleats draped over the left arm and the left hand holding the robe. The lower right arm and hand are missing. The feet are also lost. See Figure 5.15.

I have not been able to identify any similar or directly comparable images. The photograph of a photograph in the possession of the farmer was taken in early 1995.

FIGURE 5.14
A copper-bronze alloy lime container (from the Muara Kaman hoard)

FIGURE 5.15
A Standing Buddha found near the school at Muara Kaman

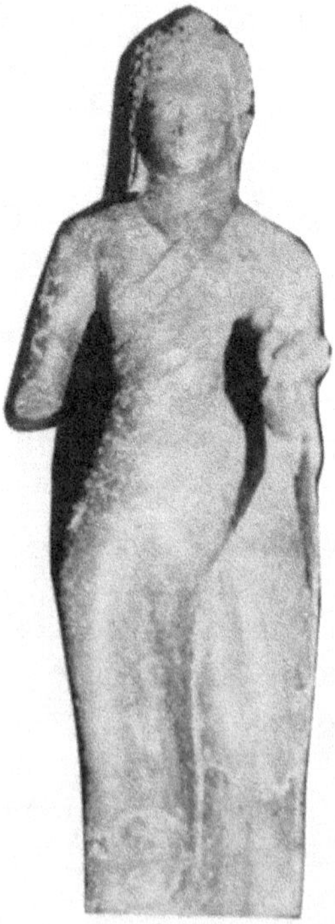

VI.2 A Standing Buddha from a Hoard from Kutei

This standing image, reputedly from Kutei has been illustrated by both Guy (2004, p. 15.13) and Sharma (2004, p. 22.7). See Figure 5.16. It is one of possibly as many as sixteen copper alloy bronzes said to have been recovered some ten years or more ago from a location in or near Muara Kaman. This figure, which is of south Indian inspiration stands an impressive 45.5 cm in height and may be dated to the eighth or ninth century CE. It has a low *uṣnīṣa*, a pronounced *trivali* at the neck, and distinctly

FIGURE 5.16
A standing Buddha from a hoard from Kutei

Source: From private collections made by the owners.

portrayed pleats in the robe. The right hand is held pointing downwards, palm outwards in *vyākhayana mudrā*, the mode of explanation. Sharma (2004) suggests that this image may date as early as the sixth century but in light of the ongoing discussion on dating, it is more likely to be an eighth century piece. Other images from this same hoard are said to be in Western collections.

VI.3 A Standing Buddha from Kutei

Also said to be from Kutei, this somewhat corroded standing image is 24.5 cm in height (Figure 5.17). It is now in a private collection. The features are somewhat corroded, the head displays a low *uṣnīṣa*. The robe is in the

FIGURE 5.17
A standing Buddha from Kutei

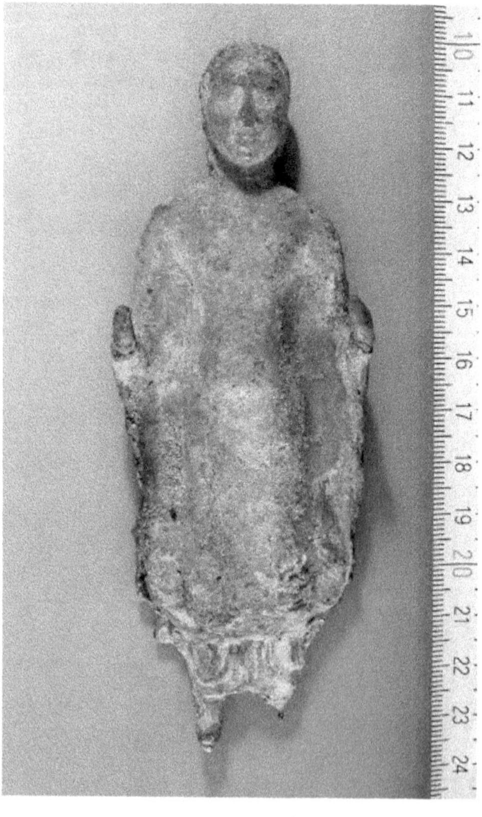

Source: From private collections made by the owners.

closed mode, covering both shoulders, with an absence of pleats. The lower hem displays what appears to be a similar arrangement as also appears in the following image, a feature that may be a Bornean localization and a product of the same workshop.

VI.4 A Standing Buddha from Kutei

Another smaller image, also somewhat corroded, 13.5 cm in height and in similar style to that illustrated in Figure 5.17, is also reputedly from Kutei. See Figure 5.18. The robe is in the closed mode, the robe over both shoulders and devoid of any pleats. The lower hem displays what appears

FIGURE 5.18
A standing Buddha from Kutei

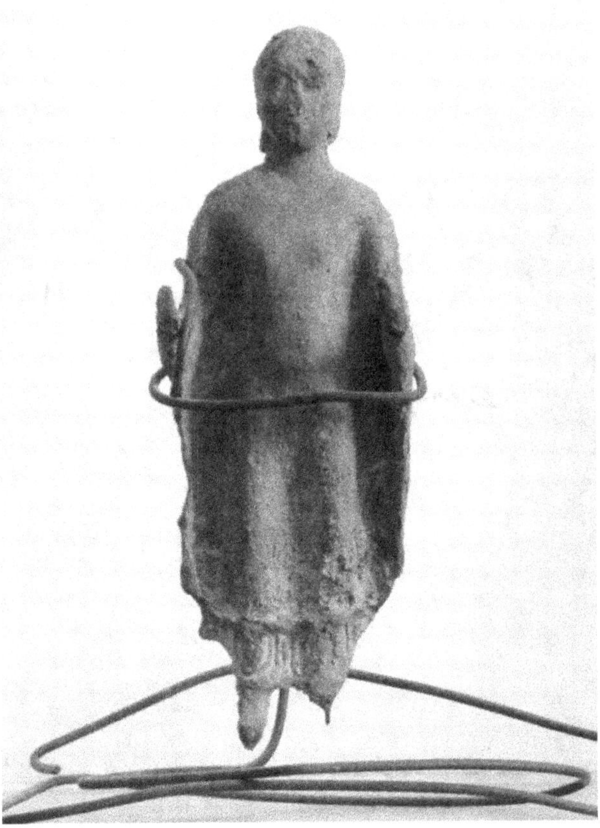

Source: From private collections made by the owners.

to be a similar design to the above, larger image. Traces of a bracket may be seen at the back of the head. It is also now in a private collection.

VI.5 A Seated Golden Buddha from Long Lalang on the Tabang River

Mention should also be made of a diminutive seated Buddha, 4.5 cm in height now in the Kutei Museum from Desa Long Lalang near Tabang on the Tabang river that flows into the Mahakam below Kota Bangun. This image, in the open mode with an aurora behind the head has small, tight curls and an insignificant *uṣnīṣa*. The right hand is in *bhūmisparśamudrā*, but with the hand somewhat unusually placed around the right knee. The left hand with the palm placed upwards is resting in the lap. It displays incisions in the robe on the left shoulder and on the lower legs. See Figure 5.19.

FIGURE 5.19
A gold seated Buddha from Long Lalang on the Tabang river, Kutei [Courtesy of the Musium Negeri Kutei].

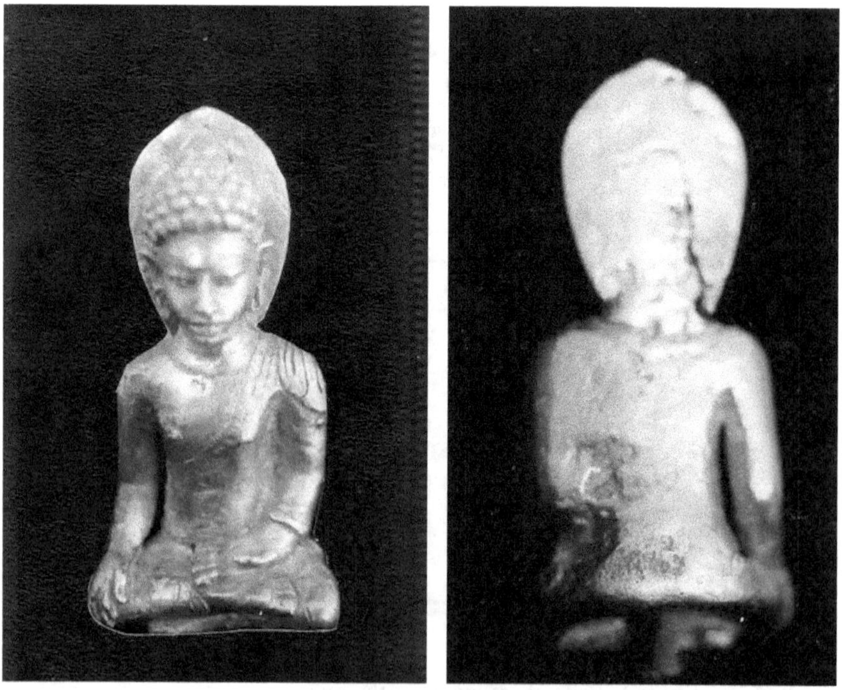

This image is, in all probability, of somewhat late, local workmanship with possible influence of Mojopahit period influence from eastern Java. It may date from as late as the fifteenth or sixteenth century and be one of the latest Buddha images known from this region.

VI.6 A Golden Tortoise Formerly in the Regalia of the Sultan of Kutei and Reputedly Recovered at Muara Kaman

This small solid gold tortoise (*kūrma*) was reputedly found at Muara Kaman (Figure 5.20). It is some 5 cm in length and weighs 340 grammes. Similar metal tortoises are known from votive deposits in Sri Lanka. There is mention of such creatures in the *Mahānirvana Tantra* (Coomaraswamy 1914, p. 26), though the tortoise would normally appear to be more closely associated with the second *avatāra* of Visnu.

I have included this item as it may possibly have served as sacral object in part of a Buddhist ritual.

VII. THE SANGGATA FINDS

The upper part of a base metal Buddha image and truncated portion of a *khakkhara* or monk's staff with a three armed bow and ornate sculpting

FIGURE 5.20
A miniature gold tortoise formerly in the regalia of the Sultan of Kutei, reputedly recovered at Muara Kaman [Courtesy of the Musium Negeri Kutei].

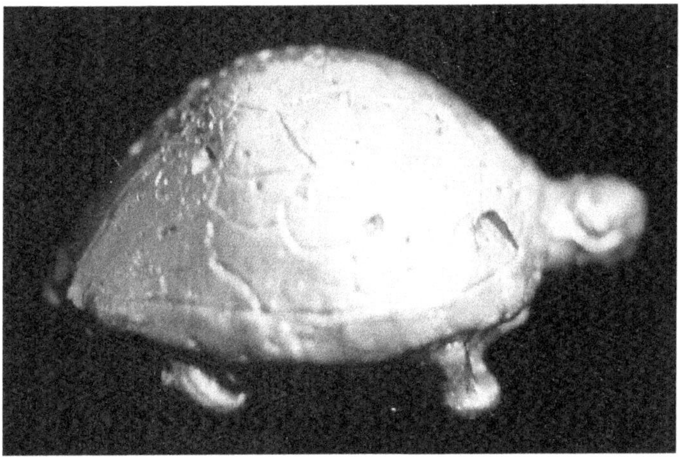

were recorded in Samarinda in 1995 (Edwards McKinnon 2000). The exact find spot of these fragments is not known but the information available suggested that they came from Sanggata on the coast further north of Samarinda. Their current whereabouts are unknown.

VII.1 The Sanggata Buddha

The Buddha cast in a base metal alloy, of which only the head, shoulders and right arm and hand remain is some 7 cm in height, displays a robe in the open mode, a low *uṣnīṣa*, small, tight curls over the head and a pronounced *trivali* at the neck. There is the remains of an oval-shaped bracket at the rear of the head. The remaining right hand is in *vitarka mudrā*. This suggests that it is in the late Amaravatī, Anurādhapura style and in all likelihood contemporary with the following remnant of a *khakkhara*, thus dating from the tenth or eleventh century. See Figure 5.21.

VII.2 The Khakkhara Fragment

The *khakkhara* fragment is of similar metal alloy to that of the Buddha, some 6 cm in height and approximately a similar shape to part of a filial illustrated by de Vries Robbé (1994, pl.6) in Central Javanese style that

FIGURE 5.21
The base metal Buddha fragment from Sanggata: (a) front; (b) rear

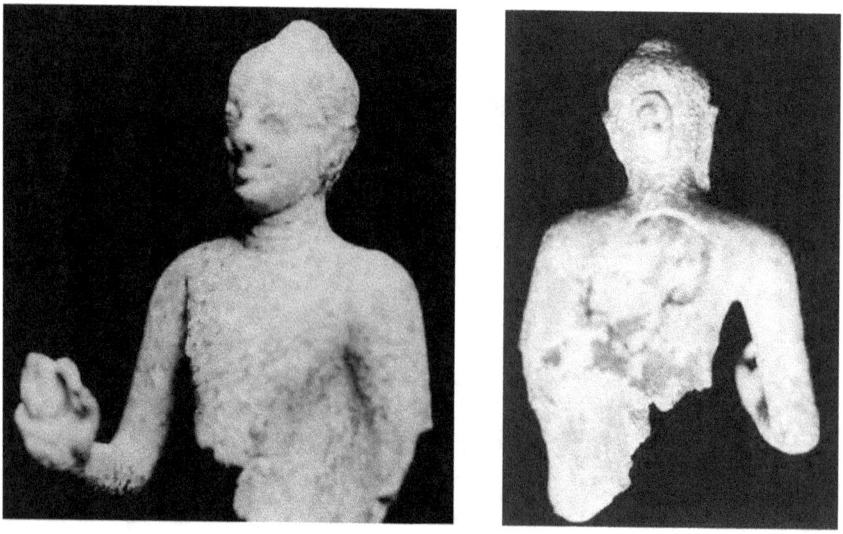

was found in the region of Magelang and initially reproduced by Van Erp (1943, p. 96). See Figure 5.22. Several such filials have been found in central and east Java. The treatment of the metal work of the remnant may suggest, however, that this is slightly later, and comparable to the sculpture visible on the rear plate of a late tenth to first half of the eleventh century Mahāvairocana from Nanjuk in East Java (Lunsingh Scheurleer 1994, plate 5). Interestingly, a more or less contemporary and almost complete *khakkhara* and additional fragments were recovered from the tenth century Intan shipwreck excavated in the Java Sea (Flecker 2002, p. 40).

No other fragments belonging to this artefact were seen. The metal alloy was covered in a whitish surface which may suggest that it has a high lead content.

FIGURE 5.22
A base metal *khakkhara* fragment from Sanggata

The *khakkhara* as used by mendicant monks comprised three parts, a wooden staff, a metal bow in the form of a circle (or oval) and fitted with up to six or eight rings (though numbers may vary to as few as two or three) fitted to the staff by a metal shaft and metal ferrule to protect the foot of the staff (de Vries Robbé 2004, p. 122). Portrayals of a variety of *khakkhara* appear in relief sculptures and in murals and on paintings (Revire 2009). The staff was seemingly used by monks whilst begging to keep cows and dogs at bay but was also used to alert the faithful that a monk was approaching so that merit could be earned by donating food. Such staffs also appear to have been used in rituals as specimens have been recovered in sacral deposits (Revire 2009).

Unfortunately nothing more is known of the find spot of these artefacts, nor, to my knowledge, have any further reports surfaced of finds in the Sanggata region. They do suggest, however, that Buddhist rituals were practised there and that further evidence for a Buddhist presence in the area may yet surface in the future.

Acknowledgements

I would like to thank Professor Robert L. Brown, Dr Andana Chutiwongs and Hiram W. Woodward who read earlier drafts of this paper and who all kindly offered advice and made several useful suggestions. I would also like to thank Christian Lammerts for his encouragement and patience in bringing this to a final publishable form. If there are any errors of any kind, they are of course, my own.

Bibliography

Ardika, I Wayan and Peter Bellwood. "Sembiran: The beginnings of Indian contact with Bali". *Antiquity* 65 (1991): 221–32.

Bellina, Bérénice, Elisabeth A. Bacus, Thomas Oliver Pryce and Jan Wisseman Christie, eds. *50 Years of Archaeology Essays in Honour of Ian Glover*. Bangkok: River Books, 2010.

Bernet Kempers, A.J. *Ancient Indonesian Art*. Amsterdam: van der Peet, 1959.

Bosch, F.D.K. "Oudheiden in Koetei". *Oudheidkundig Verslag*, (*O.V.*), Bijl. G. (1925): 132–46.

——. "Oudheden in Koetei". In *Midden-Oost-Borneo Expeditie 1925*, pp. 391–423. Weltevreden: Kolff. 1927.

Boyce, David J.S. *Kutai, East Kalimantan: A Journal of Past and Present Glory*. Kota Bangun (cycostyled) 1986.

Brown, Carrie C. "The Eastern Ocean in Yung-lo Ta-tien". *Brunei Museum Journal* 4, no. 2 (1978): 46–58.

Brown, Robert L. "The Importance of Gupta-period Sculpture in Southeast Asian Art History". In *Early Interactions between South and Southeast Asia: Reflections on Cross-Cultural Exchange*, edited by Pierre-Yves Manguin, A. Mani and Geoff Wade, pp. 316–31. Singapore: Institute of Southeast Asian Studies, 2011.

Chhabra, B.Ch. "Three more yupa inscriptions of King Mulavarman from Kutei (East Borneo)". *Bijdragen van het Kongingklijke Instituut* (BKI) 83 (1949): 370–74.

Chutiwongs, Nandana. "The Closing Chapter on Avalokitesdavara — Srivijaya and Maritime Southeast Asia". *Abhinandamala*. Colombo, 2011.

Coomaraswamy, Ananda K. *Bronzes from Ceylon, chiefly in the Colombo Museum. Memoirs of the Colombo Museum, Series A. No. 1*. Colombo: Colombo Museum, 1914.

de Casparis, J.G. *Indonesian Palaeography*. Leiden/Köln: Brill, 1975.

———. "Some notes on the Oldest Inscriptions of Indonesia". In *A Man of Indonesian Letters Essays in Honour of Professor A. Teeuw*, edited by C.M.S. Hellwig and S.O. Robson, pp. 242–56. Dordrecht: Foris, 1986.

Edwards McKinnon, Edmund. "A note on recent ceramic finds at Muara Kaman, Kabupaten Kutei, Kalimantan Timur". *Himpunan Keramik Indonesia Bimonthly Newsletter* 22, no. 5 (1995).

———. "Buddhism and the Pre-Islamic Archaeology of Kutei in the Mahakam Valley". In *Studies in Southeast Asian Art: Essays in Honor of Stanley J. O'Connor*, edited by Nora Taylor, pp. 217–40. Ithaca, N.Y.: Cornell University Southeast Asia Studies Program, 2000.

———, E., Hasan Djafar and Soeroso M.P. "Tarumanagara? A note on discoveries at Batujaya and Cibuaya, West Java". In *Southeast Asian Archaeology 1994. Proceedings of the 5th International Conference of the EurASEAA*, edited by P-Y Manguin, pp. 147–60. Hull: University of Hull, Centre for Southeast Asian Studies, 1998.

Flecker, Michael. *The Archaeological Excavation of the 10th Century Intan Shipwreck, Java Sea, Indonesia*. Oxford: BAR International Series, Archaeopress, 2002.

Fontein, Jan. *The Sculpture of Indonesia*. Washington: National Gallery of Art Exhibition Catalogue; New York: Abrams, 1990.

Guy, John. "South Indian Buddhism and Its Southeast Asian Legacy". In *Cultural Interface of India with Asia: Religion, Art and Architecture. National Museum Institute Monograph Series no. 1*, edited by Anupa Pande and Parul Pandya Dhar, pp. 155–17. New Delhi: National Museum Institute, 2004.

Kern, J. "Over de Sanskrit-opschriften van Moeara Kaman, in Kutei (Borneo). (ca. 400 A.D.)". In *Verspreide Gescriften VII*, pp. 55–76. S'Gravenhage: Nijhoff, 1917. (reprint of an article originally published in 1877).

Klokke, Marijke J. and Pauline Lunsingh Scheurleer, eds. *Ancient Indonesian Sculpture*. Leiden: KITLV, 1994.

Krom, N.J. "Inventaris der Oudeheden". In *Oudheidkundig Verslag.*, Bijl. T.

"Afdeeling Samarinda, Onder Afdeeling Tenggarong, Moeara Kaman." (1914), pp. 151, 152. *Hindoe-Javaansche Gescheidenis*. s'Gravenhage: Nijhoff, 1926.

Liebert, Gösta. *Iconographic Dictionary of the Indian Religions Hinduism – Buddhism–Jainism*. Leiden: Brill 1976.

Lunsingh Scheurleer, Pauline. "Bronze images and their place in ancient Indonesian culture". In *Ancient Indonesian Sculpture*, edited by P. Lunsingh Scheurleer and Marijke J. Klokke, pp. 76–97. Leiden: KITLV Press, 1994.

—— and Marijke J. Klokke, eds. *Ancient Indonesian Bronzes. A Catalogue of an Exhibition in the Rijksmuseum, Amsterdam*. Leiden: Brill, 1988.

Manguin, Pierre-Yves. "Pan-Regional Responses to south Asian Inputs in Early Southeast Asia". In *50 Years of Archaeology Essays in Honour of Ian Glover*, edited by Bellina, Bacus, Pryce and Christie, pp. 171–81. Bangkok: River Books, 2010.

—— and Agustijanto Indrajaya. "The Archaeology of Batujaya (West Java, Indonesia): An Interim Report". In *Uncovering Southeast Asia's Past Selected papers from the 10th International Conference of the European Association of Southeast Asian Archaeologists* edited by Elisabeth A. Bacus, Ian C. Glover and Vincent C. Pigott, pp. 245–57. Singapore: NUS Press, 2006.

——, A. Mani, Goeff Wade, eds. *Early Interactions between South and Southeast Asia Reflections on Cross-Cultural Exchange*. Singapore: Institute of Southeast Asian Studies. 2011.

Munoz, Paul Michel. *Early Kingdoms of the Indonesian Archipelago and the Malay Peninsula*. Singapore: Didier Millet, 2006.

Nilakanta Sastri, K.A. "A Note on the Sambas Finds". *Journal of the Malaysian Branch of the Royal Asiatic Society* 22, no. 4 (1949): 16–22.

Pande, Anupa and Parul Pandya Dhar, eds. *Cultural Interface of India with Asia Religion, Art and Architecture. National Museum Institute Monograph Series no. 1*. New Delhi: National Museum Institute (2004).

Revire, Nicolas. "À propose d'une 'tête' de khakkara conservée au Musée national de Bangkok". In *Aséanie en Asie du Sud-Est*, no. 24, December 2009, pp. 111–34.

Schastok, Sara. "Bronzes in the Amarāvatī style: Their role in the writing of Southeast Asian history". In *Ancient Indonesian Sculpture*, edited by Marijke J. Klokke and Pauline Lunsingh Scheurleer, pp. 33–56. Leiden: KITLV, 1994.

Sharma, D.P. "Early Buddhist Metal Images of South and Southeast Asia". *Cultural Interface*, 2004, pp. 248–95.

Skilling, Peter. "Buddhism and the Circulation of Ritual in Early Peninsular Southeast Asia". In In *Early Interactions between South and Southeast Asia: Reflections on Cross-Cultural Exchange*, edited by Pierre-Yves Manguin, A. Mani and Geoff Wade, pp. 371–84. Singapore: Institute of Southeast Asian Studies, 2011.

Tan, V.S. "Preliminary Report on the Discovery of the Hoard of Hindu Religious

Objects, near Sambas, West Borneo". *Journal of the South Seas Society* 5, no. 1 (1948): 31–42.

Van Erp, Th. "Een fraaie Hindoe-Javanaansche khakkara". *Maandblad voor Beeldende Kunsten* 20, no. 4 (1943): 95–96.

——. "Hindoe-Javanaansche khakkara's (vervolg)". *Maandblad voor Beeldende Kunsten* 20, no. 5 (1943): 120.

Van Heekeren, H.R. *The Stone Age of Indonesia*. Den Haag: Nijhoff, 1972.

Vida Verpaya Rusianti Kusmartono and Machi Suhadi. "Catatan Singkat tentang Candi laras, Provinsi Kalimantan Selatan". In *Pertemuan Ilmiah Arkeologi VII, Cipanas, 12–16 maret 1996. Jilid 5*, pp. 108–17. Jakarta: Proyek Penelitian Arkeologi Jakarta, 1998–99.

Vogel, J.Ph. "The Yupa Inscriptions of king Mulavarman, from Koetei (East Borneo). *Bijdragen v. h. Koningklijke Instituut* 74 (1918): 167–233.

Von Schroeder, Ulrich. *Buddhist Sculptures of Sri Lanka*. HongKong Visual Dharma Publications, 1990.

Walker, M.J. and Santoso Sugondho "Romano-Indian Rouletted Pottery in Indonesia". *Asian Perspectives* 20, no. 2 (1977): 228–35.

Wisseman Christie, Jan "State Formation in Early Maritime Southeast Asia". In *Bijdragen v. h. Koningklijke Instituut* 151, no. 2 (1995): 235–88.

Woodward, Hiram J. Jnr. "Southeast Asian Traces of the Buddhist Pilgrims". *Muse, Annual of the Museum of Art and Archaeology, University of Missouri – Colombia* 22 (1988): 75–91.

6

RE-EXPLORING THE BUDDHIST "FOUNDATION DEPOSITS" AT CHEDI CHULA PRATHON, NAKHON PATHOM

Nicolas Revire[1]

INTRODUCTION

The ruins of Chedi Chula Prathon[2] lie at the very heart of ancient Nakhon Pathom and date to approximately the second half of the first millennium, often labelled as the "Dvāravatī Period" (Figure 6.1). The monument was partially excavated for the first time by Pierre Dupont and his team in 1940[3] (Figures 6.2 to 6.4) and excavated again in 1968 by the Fine Arts Department of Thailand. The original appearance of the complete monument remains something of a mystery, since it was missing its superstructure and there seemed to be no comparable complete structures from this period with which to compare it. The question of the superstructure has, therefore, raised much speculation and discussion.[4]

Scholars subsequently focused much attention on the fine stucco and terracotta panels which were discovered at the foundation's base in 1968 (Figure 6.5). Various iconographic studies of the latter and disputes over their interpretation have divided the scholarly community with no consensus yet to be found. The panels were first studied by Jean Boisselier who saw illustrations of *jātakas*, revealing strong Indonesian or "Śrīvijaya influence", Mahāyāna in inclination.[5] Later on, Piriya Krairiksh, in the course of carrying out research for his PhD dissertation, interpreted these

FIGURE 6.1
Main archaeological sites in Nakhon Pathom

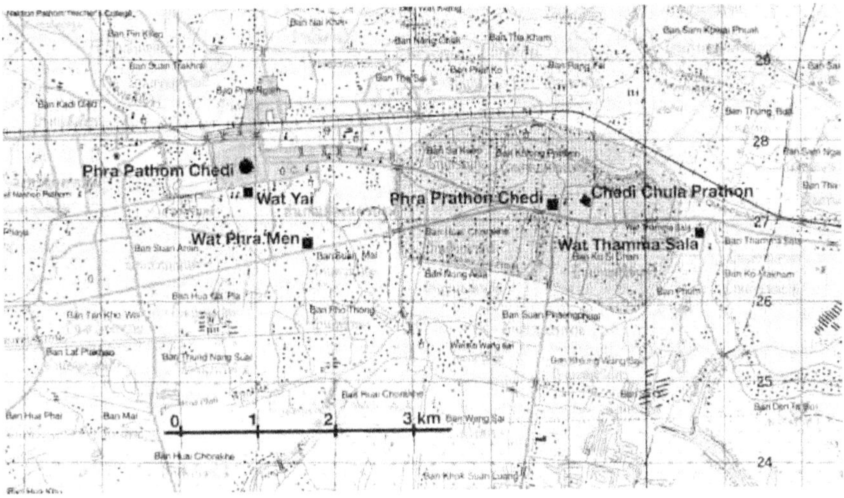

Source: Courtesy of Pierre Pichard.

FIGURE 6.2
Pierre Dupont with Thai officials and visitors in Chedi Chula Prathon, 1940

Source: Photographic archives of Thailand, EFEO, Paris, Inv.: 24932b.

FIGURE 6.3
Reconstitution of the ground plan of Chedi Chula Prathon, state III

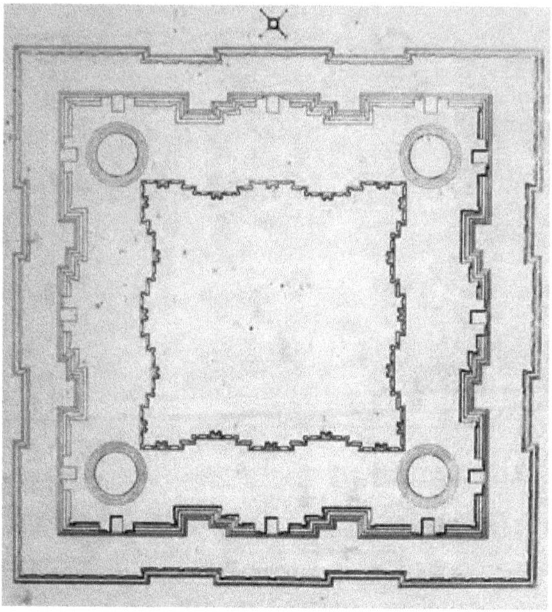

Source: After Dupont, *L'archéologie mône* I, pl. VI.

FIGURE 6.4
Cross sectional view, Chedi Chula Prathon, state III

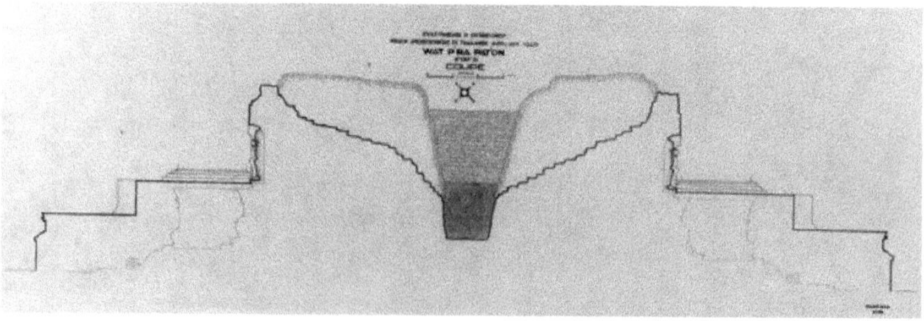

Source: After Dupont, *L'archéologie mône* I, pl. X.

FIGURE 6.5
***Jātaka* stucco relief from Chedi Chula Prathon**

Source: Phra Pathom Chedi National Museum, Inv.: 603/2519.

reliefs as Sanskrit *avadāna*s rather than Pāli *jātaka*s and saw evidence for a (Mūla)sarvāstivāda[6] presence in Chedi Chula Prathon.[7] Not long thereafter, Nandana Chutiwongs indicated that Piriya's deductions were somewhat inadequate.[8] All that can be safely concluded from these reliefs is that narrative traditions different from those transmitted in Pāli by the Mahāvihāra Theravādins of Sri Lanka may also be represented in the art of central Thailand. Some of these traditions may have been Mūlasarvāstivādin, but they might just as well have belonged to other schools or *nikāya*s using Sanskrit, Buddhist Hybrid Sanskrit, or different Prakrits such as, respectively, the Dharmaguptakas, the Mahāsāṃghikas, or the Mahīśāsakas, to name just a few.[9]

That is not all that can be said, however, about Chedi Chula Prathon. I have recently shown, for instance, the need to reconsider the material deposits from the site that were found in an archaeological context while paying particular attention to the well preserved *khakkhara* finial now displayed at the National Museum in Bangkok.[10] The present paper is a more focused study of the *khakkhara* finial along with the deposits at

Chedi Chula Prathon, based on the expectation that they may shed new light on some Buddhist practices and rituals in ancient Nakhon Pathom. It is important to consider these and other artefacts as a group, given the paucity of ritual objects that we have in general from the Dvāravatī culture. Thus, the first part of this paper explores the group of deposits collectively with some reflections on the relevant terminology, dating, and possible symbolic significance; the second part is a continuation of my earlier study on the *khakkhara*, offering now an improved description.

DEPOSITS: FUNCTION, DATE AND TERMINOLOGY

Some bronze objects, rather neglected in the scholarly literature, such as cymbals, a candelabrum with three side arms (Figure 6.6), a goblet, a *khakkhara* finial (Figure 6.7),[11] and several fragments of one mirror (Figure 6.8a) were deliberately placed beneath the structure of Chedi Chula Prathon

FIGURE 6.6
Excavated candelabrum from Chedi Chula Prathon

Source: Photographic archives of Thailand, EFEO, Paris, Inv.: 25163.

FIGURE 6.7
Excavated *khakkhara* finial from Chedi Chula Prathon

Source: Photographic archives of Thailand, EFEO, Paris, Inv.: 25164.

FIGURES 6.8
Left (6.8a), fragments of a mirror excavated at Chedi Chula Prathon; right (6.8b), rubbing of a mirror found in Prachin Buri

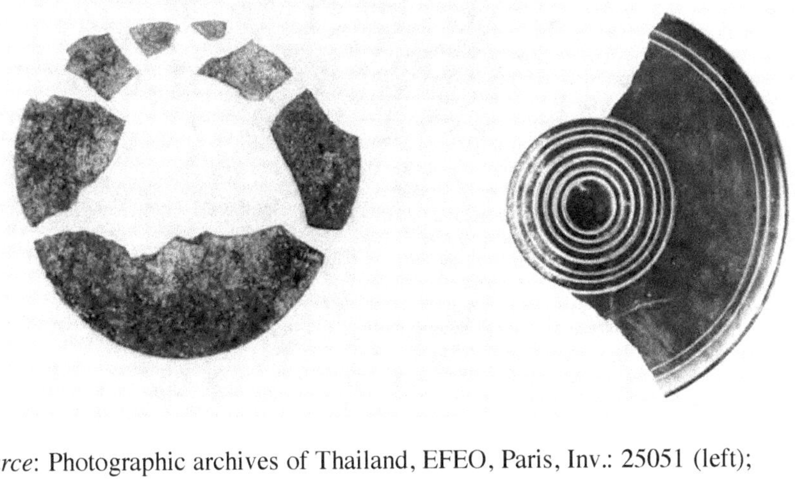

Source: Photographic archives of Thailand, EFEO, Paris, Inv.: 25051 (left); Inv.: 23556 (right).

and found in 1940. More accurately, these objects were found together in a pit under the pedestal of a seated stucco Buddha image, located in a niche, at the base of the central elevation which Dupont called the "massif central".[12] On three sides of the central part of the monument, other silver and bronze repoussé plaques (Figure 6.9) and bronze bells were also found in different pits or cavities which had been made by removing one or two bricks from the basement.[13] In addition to these finds, a bronze "rosette" (Figure 6.10a) as well as a gold cup, broken into two parts, were discovered in the rubble nearby.[14] This rubble also yielded two semi-precious zircons, one mounted on gold and the other unpolished.[15] Unfortunately, no photographs of the broken cup and zircons were provided, and it is not known at all where

FIGURE 6.9
Silver repoussé plaque with a gold Buddha from Chedi Chula Prathon

Source: Photographic archives of Thailand, EFEO, Paris, Inv.: 25055.

FIGURES 6.10
Left (6.10a), excavated "bronze rosette" from Chedi Chula Prathon; right (6.10b), golden lotus flower, unknown provenance

Source: Photographic archives of Thailand, EFEO, Paris, Inv.: 25154 (left); Musée Guimet, Paris, Inv.: MA 4647 (right).

these objects are located today. In any case, Dupont explicitly referred to all these artefacts as "votive objects" found in or nearby "foundation deposits". However, it is not clear what he meant by *dépôts de fondation*: consecration deposits, reliquaries, or both?[16]

Relics or Consecration Deposits?

We must bear in mind from the outset that no "corporal-relic" (*śarīradhātu*), "object-relic" (*paribhogadhātu*) or "textual-relic" (*dharmadhātu*) was ever found during the excavations at Chedi Chula Prathon, thus making it highly unlikely that the site was a *stūpa*.[17] Chedi Chula Prathon, as opposed to Wat Phra Men — another important site at Nakhon Pathom[18] — is, by its very name, perceived as a *caitya* (Skt.) or *cetiya* (Pāli), a *chedi* in Thai, that is a memorial to the Buddha or to an important dignitary, religious saint, or lay person. It could well then commemorate an important historical or religious event that has fallen into oblivion, rather than enshrine a physical "relic".[19] Recognizing these fine distinctions between *stūpa* and *chedi* as well as the construction process of the monument may help us understand the purpose of these "deposits".

In her study of temple consecration rituals in South and Southeast Asia, on the basis of the *Kāśyapaśilpa* (KŚ), Anna Ślączka observed that three rituals are at the core of the construction rituals of (generally Hindu) shrines: (1) the placing of the first bricks (*prathameṣṭakānyāsa*); (2) the placing of the main consecration deposit (*garbhanyāsa*) and (3), the placing of the crowning bricks (*mūrdheṣṭakānyāsa*). The *prathameṣṭakā* and *mūrdheṣṭakā* rituals consist of a ceremonial installation of (usually four, five or nine) bricks or stones in the prescribed location — either in the lower part of the temple or in the superstructure, while the placing of the "embryo" or *garbhanyāsa* can be more elaborate. The concrete difference between these ceremonies is in the number and variety of objects deposited. In practice, however, unless we have good archaeological context, it is often difficult to distinguish between these artefacts. A fourth ritual can also be included and that is the placing of objects below the pedestal of the main deity.[20]

According to Ślączka, however, there are very close similarities between Hindu and Buddhist consecration deposits and the ceremonies which accompany the placing of the deposited objects. In her view, Buddhist deposits showing closest correspondences to Indian texts originate from Sri Lanka, but they were also found in great numbers in all other areas of the "Sanskrit cosmopolis", including mainland Southeast Asia.[21] It might be appropriate, therefore, to bring her tentative conclusions, drawn as they are from South Asian and Sanskrit sources, to bear on the present context of first millennium monuments in Nakhon Pathom.[22] At least, her approach may well illustrate the possibility of hitherto unknown building rituals in Dvāravatī, even if an exact correspondence with the texts is often impossible to establish. We must also acknowledge the possibility of regional variations.

At Chedi Chula Prathon, while the superstructure is missing, traces of the ceremony of placing the first bricks are also lacking. Painted, carved and engraved bricks, belonging to state III of the monument, depicting a human figure or various motifs were found, however, beneath the miniature *caitya*s at the four corners, and could well have served a ritual function (Figures 6.11 and 6.12).[23] Admittedly, the main deposit (*garbha*)[24] of Chedi Chula Prathon has not been found and no stone or metal deposit box was ever exhumed. It is likely, however, that it was once located at the centre of the structure, but probably in a much lower stratum of the building itself.[25]

Interestingly, Boisselier mentioned bones and shell fragments of a very large tortoise carapace found at the deepest level of the monument in 1968. This may allude, Boisselier added, to the well-known legend of

FIGURE 6.11
Excavated bricks with motifs from Chedi Chula Prathon

Source: Phra Pathom Chedi National Museum, Inv.: 607, 610, 611, 613/2519.

FIGURE 6.12
Brick depicting a human face from Chedi Chula Prathon

Source: Phra Pathom Chedi National Museum, Inv.: 609/2519.

the tortoise supporting Mount Mandara as described by several Sanskrit texts although, in Southeast Asia, only artificial tortoises have thus far been found in archaeological contexts.[26] In addition to gold and silver tortoises, similar metal images of lotus flowers are also prescribed as parts of a "consecration deposit" for the foundation of a new building. The placing of a gold lotus flower together with the first bricks, for instance, is prescribed by the KŚ *prathameṣṭakānyāsa*.[27] A golden lotus flower somewhat reminiscent of the bronze "rosette" found in the rubble of Chedi Chula Prathon is on display at the Musée Guimet, Paris (Figure 6.10b). Unfortunately, the exact provenance is unknown, but it most certainly originated from a "consecration deposit" for another ancient monument in the region such as that found in Phong Tuek, Ratchaburi province.[28] Lastly, a stone tablet with five depressions, now kept in the Bangkok National Museum (Figure 6.13), is said to have been found near Chedi Chula Prathon in the early twentieth century; this is also generally thought to have been used for a ritual such as the foundation of a new monument or a "consecration" ceremony (*pratiṣṭhā*).[29]

FIGURE 6.13
Ritual stone tablet found in Nakhon Pathom

Source: National Museum Bangkok, Inv.: K 133/4.

In her study, Ślączka further distinguishes between the terms "relic" (*dhātu*) and "consecration deposit" (*garbha*). These terms, she writes, "are often confused in publications" despite the fact that the differences are numerous.[30] The most essential ones are listed in the table that she gives, reproduced as Figure 6.14. Because the aforementioned deposits at Chedi Chula Prathon were apparently "hidden" within the structure and because their presence or location seems to have been unknown to people (even treasure seekers) until the excavations took place, it seems reasonable to suppose that they were "consecration deposits" rather than relics. In other words, these artefacts were most likely inserted into the structure to serve a specific ritual function, but the building was not constructed for their sake. Moreover, the distribution of these deposits at the corners (northeast, southeast, southwest) and mid-points of the central elevation may further indicate their prescribed location for a consecration or more precisely, as we shall see later, a "reconsecration" ceremony of the monument.

FIGURE 6.14
Synoptic table

Relic	Consecration deposit
Can be divided	Are valid only when complete[13]
A building is constructed for the sake of the relics	A consecration deposit is inserted for the sake of the building
Has 'power' by itself	Has 'power' only when 'mantrified'
Should be venerated	Is venerated only during the installation
Installed on a visible, well-known place	Hidden within the building or in the ground.[14] the location is not marked
The believers are aware of the presence of relics and their location	The believers (or the visitors to the house or to a village) are usually unaware of the presence and location of a consecration deposit
In the *stūpas* of Sri Lanka: installed in the relic chamber	In the *stūpas* of Sri Lanka: installed under the floor of the relic chamber
No specific textual prescriptions for the location	Should be installed in a prescribed location
Not required for all temples and *stūpas*	Required for all types of buildings
Can function outside a building	Is connected with a specific building, image or settlement and has no function outside of it

Source: After Ślączka, *Temple Consecration Rituals*, p. 9.

Dating the Material

During the first excavations in 1940 at Chedi Chula Prathon, Dupont noticed three stages of modification for the basement and two different stages for the central elevation.[31] Given the location where the bronze and silver objects were uncovered on the terrace platform, they must have been deposited at a time when the monument was enlarged (Figure 6.4).[32] On the basis of stylistic analysis, Dupont assigned some of these objects (e.g. the repoussé plaques) to the very end of the "Dvāravatī period" but did not actually provide a date.[33] Later, Boisselier dated the third state of the basement, to which the deposits belong, to the late ninth or early tenth century,[34] while Piriya proposed the late seventh through early eighth century.[35] But for reasons to be discussed below, a compromise date of *circa* eighth to ninth century might be preferable.

My first argument is equally based on stylistic features of the repoussé plaques. For example, as Hiram Woodward has argued, the attendant figures wearing various sorts of conical headdresses can be closely linked to Bengal-style bronzes found in Thailand and dated to around the late eighth century.[36] Moreover, the gold Buddha in repoussé (Figure 6.9) has a circular looped halo which is also a feature found in eighth to ninth century Javanese images.[37] Finally, the motif that appears at the base of the same plaque, with a three blossomed lotus emanating from a single stalk,[38] can similarly be seen carved in high relief in central Java, at Caṇḍi Sewu (Figure 6.15), generally believed to date from the late eighth century.

My second argument is based on similar material that was allegedly found in central Java and dates from approximately the same period. Many mirrors, for instance, were found in Indonesia but often with unknown exact provenance (Figure 6.16). Yet, on rare occasions, bronze mirrors were discovered amongst the deposits in Caṇḍi Plaosan Lor (northern Main temple)[39] or near Caṇḍi Kalasan, in the Prambanan region,[40] and can thus be confidently dated to the foundation of these monuments, *circa* late eighth or mid-ninth century. Similarly, a *khakkhara* finial, nearly identical to the one from Nakhon Pathom, is equally said to come from the Prambanan region and is today kept in a private collection in the Netherlands. It can be roughly classified as belonging to the early "classical" period and stylistically dated to around the eighth or ninth century (Figure 6.17).[41]

Last but not least, a striking feature appearing at Chedi Chula Prathon in its third state, with strong "Śrīvijaya character" according to Woodward, again argues in favour of a date of the eighth or ninth century for the final

FIGURE 6.15
Niches on tripartite lotus-stalk from the interior of a chapel

Source: *In situ*, Caṇḍi Sewu, central Java.

FIGURE 6.16
Bronze mirror from central Java

Source: Musée Guimet, Paris, Inv.: MG 21108.

FIGURE 6.17
***Khakkhara* finial from central Java**

Source: Private collection, Amsterdam.

state of the monument. This new feature, also observed at sites 2 and 9 in U Thong and at Phra Borommathat in Chaiya, is the appearance of miniature *caityas* in brick built on the four corners of the upper terrace of the monument (Figure 6.3). Woodward has proposed the possibility that this "convention" spread over central Thailand and Java from Chaiya.[42]

Deconsecration and Reconsecration

As mentioned above, comparable objects in bronze (mirrors, *khakkhara* finials) are also found in great numbers in Java,[43] but, in most cases, we do not have the archaeological context that we have for Chedi Chula Prathon in Nakhon Pathom.[44] In this light, the bronze mirror reported to have been found among the so called "relics" of a deceased monk, buried in a *stūpa* near Caṇḍi Kalasan, is interesting.[45] Naturally, for reasons already stated above, the question arises whether this mirror may really have been considered as a "relic". This is unlikely because, firstly, Buddhist monks are usually not allowed to carry a mirror (Skt. *ādarśa*; Pāli: *ādāsa*) or even to look into one;[46] secondly, in addition to having a domestic function, mirrors also have significant symbolic and magical meanings.[47] This is particularly true for divination cults and consecration rituals.[48]

For example, Yael Bentor writes that, in Indo-Tibetan Buddhism, "when a receptacle [e.g. a *stūpa* or an image] requires considerable restoration, a ritual called *arga* is performed in which the deity that is invited to abide in the receptacle through the consecration ritual is requested to reside temporarily in a specially prepared mirror for the duration of the restoration".[49] More precisely, as Bentor stipulates in another instance, "a ritual of temporary *deconsecration* should be performed prior to the commencement of the repair work". This can only be achieved, she adds, "by requesting the *yi-dam* ["chosen Buddha" or simply often called "deity"] embodied in the receptacle to take residence in a ritual mirror for the duration of the repair work".[50] On the basis of these practices described by Bentor, one could reasonably infer, or at least conjecture, that the many mirrors found in Java as well as the fragments excavated at Chedi Chula Prathon may have played a similar ritual function.[51]

In the same vein, Bentor further notes that monks' requisites are normally offered to images portraying monastic figures or Buddha icons during the Indo-Tibetan consecration ceremony. Among the offerings is sometimes found a staff or *khakkhara* (*'khar-gsil* in Tibetan), which, no doubt, alludes to the "ordination" aspect of the consecration.[52] Interestingly, we can observe the same element of "ordination" today during Buddha image consecrations (*buddhābhiṣeka*) in Southeast Asia.[53] In Thailand, the rite of "ordination" and the consecration of a Buddha image are both referred to as *buat phra*, "ordaining the venerable one", and are seen by Donald Swearer as reenactments of the Buddha's life, precisely the story of Prince Siddhārtha's renunciation. Swearer also noticed a similar practice of offering an "iron walking stick", which could be a *khakkhara*, at the time of invoking Phra Upakut (Upagupta) before the actual consecration takes place in northern Thailand.[54] That a *khakkhara* finial was also deposited at the base of a niche containing a new Buddha image and at a subsequent stage during the enlargement of Chedi Chula Prathon, only reinforces the notion that the material may have served a significant ritual purpose during the reconsecration of the place.[55] In the section that follows, we shall see that, for centuries, the *khakkhara* widely took on various ritual or ceremonial functions across the Buddhist world.

THE *KHAKKHARA*: OMNIPRESENT AND MULTIVALENT

Among the objects found at Chedi Chula Prathon, as we have seen above, was a bronze finial for a *khakkhara* — a wooden staff topped by a metal finial in the form of a heart or a *bodhi*-leaf into which six smaller rings were originally inserted.[56] In the seventh century, such *khakkhara*-staffs[57] were used by many pilgrim monks during their travels to steady their way.[58] It might also have been used as a ritual implement, or even perhaps as a marker of monastic identities. Their exact purpose in the first millennium has yet to be determined.

Origins and Functions

Even before the formation of the Buddhist Saṃgha, many nomadic renunciants or *śramaṇa*s lived in India begging alms. Various kinds of staff were associated with these "holy men", hermits, or itinerant mendicants and the "staff" quickly became a central element of Brahmanical renunciation.[59] Chinese translations of the Mūlasarvāstivāda Vinaya, for example, record that Kāśyapa and his brothers were originally involved in "heterodox" practices like fire sacrifices. After he and his 500 disciples were converted by the Buddha, they were said to have abandoned their belongings such as "[clothing of] deer skin and tree bark, *khakkhara*, and ritual implements" by throwing them into the Nairañjanā River before following their teacher to take up the robes. This story confirms that non-Buddhist practitioners were already using the *khakkhara* even before the formation of the Buddhist community.[60]

According to later traditions, the Buddha himself used a staff of the *khakkhara* type.[61] The Chinese Dehui's fourteenth century *Baizhang Rules of Purity* (Ch. *Chixiubaizhangqinggui*),[62] for instance, refers to the *Khakkharasūtra* (Ch. *Dedaotichengxizhangjing*), where the Buddha is said to have told his disciples that they "should keep a staff topped by pewter because all the Buddhas of the past, present, and future have kept and will keep such a staff". This *sūtra* further reveals that "the pewter-topped staff equipped with two edges, each holding three rings, is said to have been produced by Kāśyapa Buddha, while a staff equipped with four edges holding twelve rings is said to have been innovated by Śākyamuni Buddha".[63]

In the first half of the seventh century, Xuanzang reported that the Buddha's *khakkhara*-staff was preserved along with other relics at Nagarahāra (modern Jalalabad, Afghanistan): "The staff of Tathâgata, of which the rings are white iron (*tin*?) and the stick of sandalwood, is contained in a precious case casket (*a case made of precious substance*)".[64] Thus, it is clear that the notion of the *khakkhara*-staff of the Buddha as an "object-relic" (*paribhogadhātu*) was well understood in some parts of the Buddhist world.[65]

In accordance with some *vinaya*s, the *khakkhara* is one of the eighteen possessions of wandering monks.[66] The extent of its use in daily routine, however, is uncertain. Writing on the basis of tradition and experience at the end of the seventh century, Yijing gives a detailed description of the *khakkhara*:

> As I myself saw, the staff used in the West (India) has an iron circle fixed on the top of it (...), the stick itself is made of wood, either rough or smooth, its length reaching to a man's eyebrows. (...) (T)he object of (using) such a staff is to keep off cows or dogs while collecting alms in the village.[67]

The function of the metal staff appears clear from this source. Yet, Yijing does not include the *khakkhara* among the thirteen necessities of a monk.[68] This is noteworthy since he was mostly interested in the *vinaya* scriptures. Perhaps by Yijing's time the *khakkhara* did not just fulfill the initial functions as described in the *vinaya*s. But had it already taken on a ritual significance?

Despite Yijing's statement, no actual *khakkhara* has yet been found, or at least identified, in India proper, although it is sometimes represented there in Buddhist narrative or iconic art. Nakhon Pathom aside, it is to Central Asia, China, Japan, and Java that we must also turn for significant comparative examples. In what follows, I briefly survey the textual and visual evidence of such *khakkhara*s along the path of Buddhist penetration, that is to say the land Silk Road, from India to Gandhāra, on to the deserts and oases of Central Asia with their cave-temples, and then to China and Japan before eventually reaching Southeast Asia by maritime routes.

The *Khakkhara* in South Asia

As we have seen above, the *khakkhara* may be indistinctly held by Buddhas, great disciples or arhats alike. Narrative Gandhāran sculpture depicting the Buddha's demise, for instance, often places Mahākāśyapa the elder holding a *khakkhara* at the foot of the Buddha's couch (Figure 6.18).[69] Pāla narrative steles show the monk Ānanda carrying a *khakkhara* beside the Buddha. This episode relates to the subduing of the elephant Dhanapāla (or Nālagiri) and may thus allude to the magical effects of the staff; he

FIGURE 6.18
Left, Buddha's final demise;
right, detail of Mahākāśyapa with a *khakkhara*

Source: Asian Art Museum, San Francisco, Inv.: B 60 S328.

who carries the *khakkhara* can destroy the powers of evil (Figure 6.19).[70] In another Bihar example from Site 3 at Nālandā, a stucco panel of the Buddha accepting alms with an attending monk carrying the rattling staff is very much in accordance with Yijing's visual observation as described above (Figure 6.20).[71]

By contrast, there are no visual or early textual examples of *khakkhara* or "rattling staffs" from southern India or Sri Lanka although there appears to be no lack of references to monastic walking sticks, staffs, etc. (*daṇḍa*, *kattaradaṇḍa* or *kattarayaṭṭhi*) throughout the Pāli Canon and commentaries. The *kattara*-staff or *kattaradaṇḍa*, for example, is found in many places in the Pāli Tipiṭaka, in pre-commentarial Pāli, and the earliest usages of *kattarayaṭṭhi* are in the commentaries (*c*. fifth century), where the term is used frequently.[72] In the *Buddhavaṃsa*'s account of the distribution of the relics of the Buddha, for example, it is noted that his "staff" was distributed with his bowl in Vajirā.[73] Monastic *daṇḍa*s are also discussed fairly extensively in the Pāli Vinaya as a form of monastic property allowable to monks. The Buddha explicitly allows the use of "staff" at Vin I, 188.[74] This provision seems to be somewhat contradicted by Vin II, 131,[75] which says only sick monks may use staffs, but such contradictions are not uncommon in the Pāli Vinaya.[76]

Reading some of the various treatments in the later Pāli commentaries and sub-commentaries, however, elicits interesting insights. Oskar von Hinüber, for instance, mentions that some Pāli sub-commentaries such

FIGURE 6.19
Left, taming the enraged elephant;
right, detail of Ānanda carrying a *khakkhara*

Source: Asian Art Museum, San Francisco, Inv.: B 6754.

FIGURE 6.20
Left, Buddha accepting alms;
right, detail of attending monk with a *khakkhara*

Source: *In situ*, Site 3, Nālandā.

as the *Sāratthadīpanī*,[77] composed by the learned Sri Lankan monk Sāriputta in the twelfth century,[78] refer to *kattaradaṇḍa*s or *kattarayaṭṭhi*s with ringed or rattling finials similar to *khakkhara*s. Von Hinüber is also of the opinion that the classical *khakkhara* was mostly prevailing in the Mūlasarvāstivāda Vinaya and that the sudden occurrence of a "rattling staff" in twelfth century Pāli texts might have been a consequence of the dispersal of Mūlasarvāstivādins in southern India and Sri Lanka, after the fall of their stronghold in Nālandā.[79] That said, we should be cautious not to simply assume that the *khakkhara* was exclusively used by monks affiliated to a unique Buddhist lineage (*nikāya*).[80]

The *Khakkhara* in Central and East Asia

In Central Asia, numerous mural paintings in the Kizil caves show monks holding *khakkhara*s (Figure 6.21).[81] These are usually said to date to the first half of the seventh century. At Dunhuang, a Buddha is sometimes shown standing with a bowl and a rattling staff. This iconography is frequently associated with Bhaiṣajyaguru, although the identification is not supported by inscriptions.[82]

In East Asia, the *khakkhara* was also a symbol of the wandering mendicant. When a monk stopped to stay somewhere, in classical Chinese, it was said that "he planted his *khakkhara*".[83] It is also an important leitmotif linked to the iconography of the descent to hell. This associates the roles of monks with the bodhisattva Kṣitigarbha (called Dizang in Chinese or Jizō in Japanese) and afterlife beliefs. Kṣitigarbha has enjoyed a cult of his own in China and Japan from at least the sixth century up to the present.[84] Early iconographic evidence of his depiction with a *khakkhara* is preserved in the Dunhuang caves, in illustrated manuscripts, in mural paintings, and on silk banners (Figure 6.22). In Vietnam, the *khakkhara*-staff is still used in ceremonies for the salvation of ancestors, during which a monk, who plays the role of Kṣitigarbha, carries the *khakkhara* and symbolically opens the doors of hells where the damned are caught.[85] The *khakkhara* is prominent too as an attribute held by the thousand-armed manifestation of another saviour bodhisattva, Avalokiteśvara (Ch. Guanyin; Jap. Kannon). Its clear sound is said to appease and delight beings.[86] The rattling staff is also one of the attributes held by Amoghapāśa (Jap. Fukūkenjaku), another form of Avalokiteśvara, in Japanese Tendai Buddhism.[87] From all of this, we can infer that the *khakkhara* was again perceived as a magical implement. Another example comes from a Korean story from the *Samguk Yusa* which mentions the monk Yangji, residing at the "Khakkhara temple"

FIGURE 6.21
Monk holding a *khakkhara* at Kizil

Source: After Le Coq, *Die Buddhistische Spätantike*, pl. 12; Berlin, Inv.: IB 8445.

("Seokjangsa") during the unified Sylla period (668–935), who was reported to move his *khakkhara* around the town of Gyeongju during alms rounds by magical means.[88]

In addition to these legends and stories, in 1987, archaeological *khakkhara*s from the Tang period (618–907) were found among the treasures of the Famen temple in a crypt, including one with twelve rings and made of gold.[89] Others have been found as intentional deposits in the underground chamber of the Qingshan pagoda, firmly dated to the eighth century.[90] Other fine depictions of monks holding a *khakkhara* are depicted in high-relief at the Dazu caves, Sichuan, and date from the Song dynasty (960–1279) (Figure 6.23). Some elaborate finials are also preserved in Japan from as early as the Nara period (710–794) where a few early examples survive

FIGURE 6.22
Silk banner from Dunhuang with Kṣitigarbha holding a *khakkhara*

Source: Musée Guimet, Paris, Inv.: MG 17664.

from Horyu-ji and Shoso-in.[91] Historical documents state that forty-one monks rattled *khakkharas* (Jap. *shakujō*) to accompany the chanting of the *Khakkharagāthā* at rites celebrating the *Kegon-e* or *Avataṃsaka* festival of Tōdai-ji in Nara.[92] Today in Japan, short-handled *khakkharas* are seen as ritual and musical objects in special Shingon and Tendai ceremonies, mostly esoteric in nature. Moreover, the *shakujō* is also used by some highly ranked monks or Buddhist ascetics called *yamabushi* (mountain ascetics) for magic or exorcism.[93] As regards Newar Buddhism, in Nepal, the *khakkhara* is there part of the "ordination ceremony" and is given to the young novice at the time of his initiation.[94]

The above references clearly show that, in Central and East Asia, the *khakkhara* is ubiquitous in the Buddhist cultural landscape. It became not only a symbol for wandering monks but also an attribute for saviour

FIGURE 6.23
A monk holding a *khakkhara*

Source: *In situ*, Beishan, cave 121, Dazu, Sichuan.

bodhisattvas. Furthermore, it was counted among the insignia of the abbot's authority and eventually took on a ritual or ceremonial function.

The *Khakkhara* in Southeast Asia

In ancient Java, the earliest evidences for the use of the *khakkhara* come from the famous stone reliefs of Borobudur and from first millennium archaeological finds. A relief from the "hidden base", possibly depicting a scene from the *Karmavibhaṅga*, shows a monk in the background holding a staff topped by a metal loop (Figure 6.24a). Another relief in the wall of the fourth gallery (IV-28) shows a monk standing to the proper right of Samantabhadra, holding a *khakkhara* in his right hand and an alms-bowl in his left (Figure 6.24b). The two *khakkhara*s represented at Borobudur

FIGURES 6.24
Scenes of monks holding a *khakkhara*; left (6.24a), from the "hidden base"; right (6.24b), from the fourth gallery

Source: *In situ*, Borobudur.

are of a slightly different type. Besides these iconographic depictions, a variety of other *khakkhara* finials have been discovered in central Java like the two on display at the Musée Guimet (Figure 6.25).[95] But as already noticed before, the most interesting *khakkhara* model for our purpose, which best compares with the Nakhon Pathom finial, is kept in a private collection in the Netherlands (Figure 6.17).

More complex *khakkhara* finials and other Buddhist paraphernalia, apparently loosely connected with esoteric practices, were also circulating in the area surrounding the Java Sea in the ninth to tenth centuries. These objects can be seen as part of the recently discovered cargo of the Cirebon and the Intan shipwrecks.[96] Interestingly, the *Saṅ Hyaṅ Kamahāyānikan*, a text probably composed around the same period (*c*. tenth century), mentions a staff, called a *kekari*, while discussing the monk's appearance.[97] *Kekari* almost certainly refers to a type of *khakkhara*.[98] Other archaeological finds seem to indicate that types of complex ritual *khakkhara* developed later. For instance, a unique and large bronze finial, today on display at

FIGURE 6.25
Bronze *khakkhara* finials from central Java

Source: Musée Guimet, Paris, Inv.: MG 3470 and MG 3473.

the Museum Sonobudoyo in Yogyakarta, is attached to a *vajra* at its base (Figure 6.26). Very elaborate four-pronged *khakkharas* with a *stūpa*-like finial and figures of divinities, wrathful and benevolent, have also been found in Java (Figure 6.27).[99] These various examples from museum or private collections are, unfortunately, often without exact provenance and the dates ascribed to them are frequently tentative.

In twelfth to thirteenth century Burma, sometimes a short-handled *khakkhara* is represented in Pagan mural paintings in scenes stylistically close to northern Indian art and iconography, such as the taming of Dhanapāla at the Loka-hteikpan and Kubyauk-gyi temples.[100] Further, the series of glazed plaques from the Ānanda temple show the *Mahājanaka-jātaka* in great detail with the bodhisatta, Janaka, depicted as a monk after his renunciation, holding a ringed finial staff (Figure 6.28).[101] Interestingly, one of the plaques bears the Old Mon caption "Janaka draws a line on the ground" (*janak crit ti*), that is with the *khakkhara* or rather a *kattaradaṇḍa* in hand. Where the Pāli of the *Jātaka*-commentary simply reads *kattaradaṇḍa*, the plaque shows what looks like a *khakkhara*. This is not so surprising since, as von Hinüber has pointed out, the term *kattaradaṇḍa* is described in some sub-commentaries precisely as a *khakkhara* (see *supra*).

FIGURE 6.26
A *khakkhara* finial with a *vajra*

Source: Museum Sonobudoyo, Yogyakarta, Inv.: 04.1040.

FIGURE 6.27
Four-pronged *khakkhara*

Source: Museum für Asiatische Kunst, Berlin, Inv.: MIK II 208.

FIGURE 6.28
Scenes of Janaka holding a ringed finial staff

Source: *In situ*, Ānanda temple, upper story; courtesy of Lilian Handlin.

A more recent Burmese reference to a "rattling hermit staff" is noticed in Sir James George Scott's *The Burman: His Life and Notions*, where we find the following account:

> Here and there throughout the country there are a few yatheit [*ṛṣi*], hermits who withdraw into solitude in forests and desert places. [...] There were a few such [hermit] cells cut in the rocks at the back of Mandalay Hill, and visitors to the sacred spot occasionally came across one of the hermits striding along, wrapped in thought, grasping *an iron staff hung with rings, the rattle of which warns the people* to get out of the way and not disturb the holy man's meditations.[102]

As regards examples of *khakkhara*s in Thailand from the first millennium, in addition to the Nakhon Pathom piece, I must mention the fragment of a *sema* stone (*sīmā* in Pāli), now kept in the Khon Kaen National Museum, which shows the upper body of a person with a shaved head, clearly a monk, bearing in his left hand a classical *khakkhara*, quite similar to the example from Chedi Chula Prathon. Above him is a seated figure (a woman?) in princely garb. Piriya identifies the scene as King Mahājanaka and Queen Sīvali from the *Mahājanakajātaka*.[103] His identification is based on a resemblance to an inscribed plaque from the Ānanda temple at Pagan mentioned above, but this is far from certain (Figure 6.29).[104] Furthermore, a recent discovery of ancient stucco reliefs from a cave locally called "Tham Yai Chung Lan" in Phetchaburi province, depicts a standing Buddha holding the staff. The scene has not been identified so far.[105]

Peter Skilling, in a recent personal communication, revealed that *khakkhara*s were used until recently in Siam by monks of the Annam *nikāya*, the Chinese Dharmaguptaka Vinaya lineage introduced from Vietnam in the nineteenth century. It was among the insignia presented by the King of Siam to monks of royal rank belonging to this *nikāya* and formerly presented to a new "ordinand" (Pāli, *upajjāya*) at the end of the "ordination ceremony" (P., *pabbajjā*), along with alms-bowl, sitting mat, and water-strainer, each with a specific chant.[106] In the same vein, it is possible that the ceremonial fan (P., *vījanī*) of the Theravāda order in Thailand may have a parallel genealogy, modelled after the *khakkhara*. Nineteenth century sculptures of "Phra Si Ariya", that is the future Buddha Metteyya, are often seen carrying an empty fan somewhat reminiscent in shape of the classical *khakkhara* (Figure 6.30).[107]

FIGURE 6.29
Left, *sema* stone depicting a monk with a *khakkhara*; right, detail

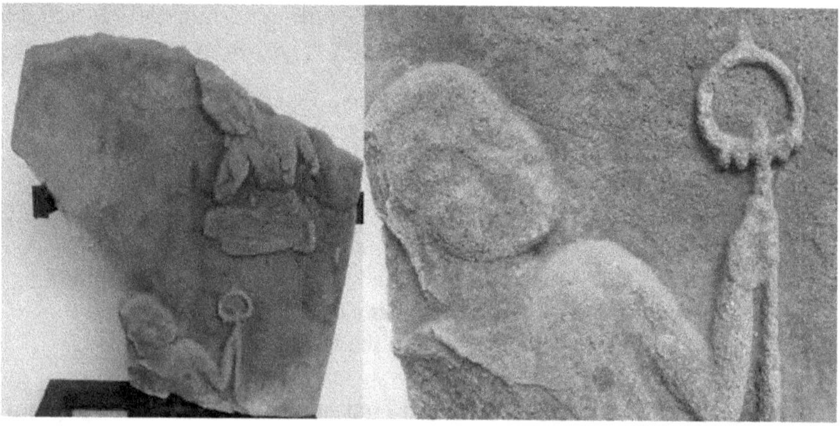

Source: Khon Kaen National Museum, Inv.: 504/2517.

FIGURE 6.30
Phra Si Ariya with a ceremonial fan

Source: In Buri National Museum, Inv.: 1/37 IB 2197.

CONCLUDING REMARKS

I may end this paper where I started by noting that it is not possible to call the deposited objects found on the upper terrace at Chedi Chula Prathon either "votive" or "relics" or to link them to the actual "foundation" of the monument. It only seems plausible to assert that these artefacts, including the *khakkhara*,[108] were once used during a consecration ceremony or, more accurately, to "reconsecrate" the monument and/or the Buddha images in the niches (Dupont's proposed state II for the central elevation or terrace state III), perhaps sometime around the late eighth or early ninth century. Modern observations in different Buddhist cultures further indicate that consecrations of a monument or Buddha images are often repeated on a periodic basis when restorations have taken place or a highly ranked monk or layperson has visited.[109] These modern practices thus seem to confirm the interpretation. Alternatively, a more neutral, but less specific, term to use for this material would be "ritual deposits".

Furthermore, some fruitful stylistic and iconographic comparisons have also been made between the archeological material found at Chedi Chula Prathon and, particularly, central Java. The exact vector for the contacts implied by these "commonalities", however, is not yet very clear. Could they be explained through the alleged Pāla and Mahāyāna stimuli of the Malay Peninsula bearing on "Dvāravatī" during the eighth or ninth century?[110] Adding to the evidence of a "shared vocabulary" between these two regions, striking similarities have also recently been shown between Wat Phra Men, in Nakhon Pathom, and the brick temple of Blandongan, an early Buddhist monument of the first millennium excavated at Batujaya in western Java.[111] The apparent relationship between the two regions, rather than the influence of one upon another, is far-reaching and certainly deserves further attention.

While the *khakkhara* apparently enjoyed great popularity in Central and East Asia since the advent of Buddhism, no actual models have survived in South Asia. In mainland Southeast Asia, the finial from Chedi Chula Prathon is the only object indicating former use of *khakkhara* that has been found and it is one of the earliest examples that we have for the first millennium, adding to the larger corpus found on Java. The attentive reader might have noticed that the few visual examples discussed for mainland Southeast Asia all seem to derive from early Mon cultures, that is, from first millennium central and northeast Thailand,[112] and the early Pagan period in Burma, but hasty conclusions should be avoided until further research is done. A great amount of literary and textual studies is still needed before we can fully understand the history of this implement.

What we know is that the *khakkhara* was a familiar object for most of the Buddhist world over a period that lasted centuries. It was an item permitted for use by monks in several *vinaya*s and, contrary to what has been argued by some scholars, no *nikāya*s had exclusive use of *khakkhara*s. Its common use went far beyond its original function as described in different *vinaya*s. As we have seen in various examples, the *khakkhara* also came to have clear ritual and iconographic significances. Although the *khakkhara* is found in many Mahāyāna scriptures and often used in the iconography of several Mahāyāna images in East Asia it does not in itself provide evidence for the presence of Mahāyāna Buddhism either in "Dvāravatī" or at Chedi Chula Prathon.[113] A detailed study of the later use of the *kattaradaṇḍa*, as found in at least one Pāli sub-commentary, would also be worth pursuing. The question thus remains to what degree the *kattaradaṇḍa* fulfilled the same functions as the *khakkhara*.

Notes

1. I am most grateful to Peter Skilling, one of my PhD advisors at Paris 3-Sorbonne nouvelle, for encouraging me in my research and sending me his extensive notes on the *khakkhara*. I have used these to some extent in the second part of this paper. I also wish to thank Arlo Griffiths, Laurent Hennequin, Christian Lammerts, and Anna Ślączka for their comments on an earlier draft, Hiram Woodward and Shi Zhiru for various assistance, Leedom Lefferts for editing the English and Pierre Pichard, Isabelle Poujol, Anna Ślączka, Jaap Polak, and Lilian Handlin for the authorizations to reproduce Figures 6.1–6.4, 6.6–6.10, 6.14, 6.17 and 6.28.
2. Which Dupont called Wat P'ra Pat'on. Different names and spellings have been used for this site, adding to the confusion. I employ here the name currently used by the Thai Fine Arts Department. This modern terminology, of uncertain age, implies that Chedi Chula Prathon is secondary (*chula*) to Phra Prathon Chedi and that the two are part of the same complex, but we do not know whether this was so originally.
3. Dupont, *L'archéologie mône*, I, pp. 65–98; see also the English translation (Dupont, *The Archaeology of the Mons*, I, pp. 49–74). The translation by Joyanto K. Sen, however, is misleading and cannot be completely relied upon. See Revire, "Review Article".
4. See, for instance, Dupont, *L'archéologie mône*, I, pp. 92–98; Piriya Krairiksh, "The Chula Pathon Cedi", pp. 84–88; also Dupont, *The Archaeology of the Mons*, I, pp. 66–74; and, most recently, Santi Leksukhum, "Conjectural reconstructions".
5. Boisselier, "Récentes recherches", pp. 61, 64.
6. The exact relationship between the Sarvāstivādins and the Mūlasarvāstivādins ["root Sarvāstivādins"] remains unclear. It is possible, however, that the latter group represented either the original congregation, a subsequent phase in the development of the Sarvāstivādins or simply reflected a regional variation centred around Mathurā, India, claiming superiority over the Sarvāstivādins of Kashmir and Gandhāra, already in decline by the seventh century. See Wynne, "On the Sarvāstivāda and Mūlasarvāstivāda".
7. Piriya Krairiksh, *Phutthasasana nithan*.
8. Nandana Chutiwongs, "Review Article", pp. 133–51; Woodward, *The Art and Architecture of Thailand*, pp. 76–77. In addition to Piriya, other scholars, largely basing their assumptions on Yijing's accounts, have argued for the large presence or influence of the (Mūla)sarvāstivādins in Southeast Asia during the first millennium. Such assertions, however, are often speculative

and somewhat tenuous. See Revire, "À propos d'une 'tête' de *khakkhara*", pp. 120–23.

9. In this vein, see Prapod Assavavirulhakarn, *The Ascendancy of Theravāda*, pp. 97–99. While admitting with Piriya that Hīnayāna "Sanskrit Buddhism" was probably present in Dvāravatī, Prapod confesses that "to identify this form of Sanskrit Hīnayāna as Sarvāstivādin goes beyond the evidence" (p. 98). Furthermore, the latter prevents us from hastily concluding that "*stūpas*" [or *caityas* for that matter] such as Chedi Chula Prathon may belong exclusively to one particular school of Buddhism, as he writes, "a *stūpa* is a public treasure, and any sect could participate in its decoration and veneration". (p. 104)
10. Revire, "À propos d'une 'tête' de *khakkhara*".
11. Dupont described the object as unidentifiable. It was first identified as a *khakkhara* finial by Piriya Krairiksh, "Semas with Scenes from the *Mahānipāta-Jātaka*", p. 47, n. 45. A decade earlier, it was vaguely referred to as a "couronnement de sceptre" by Subhadradis Diskul, "Pierre Dupont: *L'archéologie mône*", p. 167, n. 3.
12. Dupont, *L'archéologie mône*, I, p. 88; II: figs. 259–64. These objects were found precisely on the southwest side of the central structure, not on the "southeast side" as erroneously stated in the volume of plates (II, 67). To make the confusion even worse, the information given in the main text regarding the exact provenance of the mirror fragments conflicts with the inventory list of the excavated objects in the appendix, which states "northeast side" (I, 309, object-number 239).
13. Dupont, *L'archéologie mône*, I, pp. 87–90; II, figs. 255–57, 265–68.
14. Ibid., p. 87; for the "rosette", see fig. 258 (II).
15. Ibid., p. 87; object-numbers 351–53.
16. In Sri Lanka, for instance, relics housed in relic chambers and consecration deposit boxes (*yantragalas*) were employed simultaneously, often within one and the same building or *stūpa*; the main difference was that a deposit slab for consecration objects should be located on a much lower level, below the relic chamber. See Ślączka, *Temple Consecration Rituals*, pp. 251–52.
17. The term *stūpa* indicates any in-filled structure which is supposed to contain collected bodily remains, textual sacred sources, or objects believed to have been in physical contact with a hero, saint, or deity. See Bareau, "La construction et le culte des *stūpa*", p. 14.
18. For recent contributions on Wat Phra Men, see Revire, "Introduction à l'étude des bouddhas" and Revire, "Iconographical Issues".
19. In contrast, the neighbouring Phra Prathon Chedi (Phra Pradoṇa Cetiya) was thought, at least from about the thirteenth century onwards, to have contained the Brahmin Doṇa's measuring bowl (Pāli: *doṇa*; Skt: *droṇa*) used to divide the relics of the Buddha. See Woodward, "Studies in the Art of Central Siam", pp. 153–54 and Woodward, "Book Review: *The Archaeology of the Mons of Dvāravatī*", p. 80.

20. Ślączka, *Temple Consecration Rituals*, pp. 173ff and Ślączka, "The Depositing of the Embryo". This last ceremony is not dealt with in her publications.
21. See Ślączka, *Temple Consecration Rituals*, p. 251 and her appendix IV, pp. 344–86, for a list of the Buddhist consecration deposits excavated in South and Southeast Asia. For an incidental Buddhist account in the *Thūpavaṃsa* of the ritual concerned with building of a *stūpa* and enshrining its relics in Sri Lanka, see Jayawickrama, *The Chronicle of the Thūpa*, pp. 95–144; also Strong, *The Relics of the Buddha*, pp. 161–71. In modern Burma, many texts discuss different rituals associated with installing materials in *stūpa*s. For a published premodern treatise which reproduces the formulas (*gāthā*s) recited during consecration, see Khaṅ Khaṅ Cu, *Pisukā kyamḥ*. I thank Christian Lammerts for this reference. In Thailand, however, no written ritual manuals are found or seem to have survived, leading to the assumption that transmission has taken place only by example (Peter Skilling, personal communication).
22. While she admits that the *Kāśyapaśilpa* was probably too late a work, compiled in the eleventh to twelfth century, to have functioned as a model for many of the archaeological finds in the first millennium, Ślączka concludes that other similar Sanskrit treatises predate it by many centuries and can thus serve as guidelines (*Temple Consecration Rituals*, pp. 255–56); see also Ślączka, "The Depositing of the Embryo".
23. Boisselier, "Récentes recherches", p. 62; Piriya Krairiksh, "The Chula Pathon Cedi", chart IX. See also Fine Arts Departments, *Boranawatthu nai phiphithaphan*, pp. 175–77.
24. *Garbha* litteraly means "embryo", but is the term used in the majority of the texts. It is also called *yantragala* in Sri Lanka; see Ślączka, *Temple Consecration Rituals*, pp. 251–52, pls. 36–40.
25. Dupont reported a large pit in the central structure, probably dug at an unknown date by treasure seekers aiming at the main deposit (*L'archéologie mône*, I, p. 67); see Figure 6.4. A possible parallel would be the "casket" with five cavities in its upper surface discovered in monument no. 1 at Khu Bua, Ratchaburi province. See Quaritch Wales, "A stone casket from Satiñpra", p. 221. For other examples in Southeast Asia, see O'Connor, "Ritual Deposit Boxes", pp. 53–60.
26. Boisselier, "Récentes recherches", p. 63. Actually, the habit of placing a living tortoise in the foundation of a monument is an ancient Vedic tradition. It is mentioned in the *Śatapathabrāhmaṇa* VII, 5, 1, 1ff; VII, 4, 1, 15ff, etc., where the tortoise is identified as a form of Prajāpati who created all living beings; see Ślączka, *Temple Consecration Rituals*, pp. 3 n. 4, 17, 214 n. 47. For stone tortoises discovered in Angkor, see Pottier, "Embryons et tortues", p. 405 n. 95; also Ślączka, *Temple Consecration Rituals*, p. 352, pls. 21–22.
27. Ślączka, *Temple Consecration Rituals*, pp. 176, 222 n. 4.
28. Cœdès, "The excavations at P'ong Tük", pl. 7; also Ślączka, *Temple*

Consecration Rituals, p. 347. For gold and silver pieces found in Nakhon Si Thammarat province, see Jacq-Hergoualc'h, *The Malay Peninsula*, fig. 31.

29. Nandana Chutiwongs, "Le bouddhisme à Dvāravatī", p. 60; also Baptiste and Zéphir, *Dvāravatī,* p. 55, fig. 10. A similar ritual tablet was found in Nong Prong, Phetchaburi province (Baptiste and Zéphir, *Dvāravatī,* p. 189, fig. 3). For an "esoteric" interpretation of these stone tablets more in line with the specific initiation or *abhiṣeka* ritual of an individual, see Indorf and Reddy, "Distribution of the Ritual Trays".
30. Ślączka, *Temple Consecration Rituals*, pp. 7–10.
31. Dupont, *L'archéologie môn*e, I, pp. 66–72.
32. Dupont noted that the deposits were probably from the time when the facade of the central elevation was renovated, that is when the standing Buddha images in stucco (state I) were covered by the seated ones (state II). *L'archéologie môn*e, I, p. 87.
33. Dupont, *L'archéologie môn*e, I, pp. 88–90.
34. Boisselier, "Récentes recherches", pp. 61–63.
35. Piriya Krairiksh, "The Chula Pathon Cedi", p. 36.
36. Woodward, *The Art and Architecture of Thailand*, pp. 92–93, pl. 21.
37. Parimoo Krishnan, *On the Nalanda Trail*, pp. 92, 96; Miksic, *Old Javanese Gold*, pls. 80–81, 83, 84; Lerner and Kossak, *The Lotus Transcendent*, figs. 135–36, 139.
38. For a similar triple structure found in ancient Java, a three-armed candelabra in the shape of a lotus flower, see Fontein, *The Sculpture of Indonesia*, pp. 246, 248.
39. Ślączka, *Temple Consecration Rituals*, pp. 358–59.
40. Lunsingh Scheurleer and Klokke, *Divine Bronze*, p. 47.
41. De Vries Robbé, "A khakkhara fragment from Java", pp. 118–19, 130, fig. 3.
42. Woodward, *The Art and Architecture of Thailand*, pp. 93–94, fig. 15a; see also Piriya Krairiksh, "The Chula Pathon Cedi", plans 12, 26 and 35.
43. In addition to similar artefacts found in recently discovered shipwrecks, see discussion *infra*.
44. Another mirror fragment was found by Dupont in 1937 at Kok Wat, Prachin Buri province, but the exact provenance and the whereabouts are unknown; see Dupont, "Mission au Siam", p. 692 (Figure 6.8b).
45. Lunsingh Scheurleer and Klokke, *Divine Bronze*, p. 47.
46. Vin II, 106 (Horner, IV, pp. 144–45).
47. The Pāli Tipiṭaka is full of references to "metaphorical" and even to "magic" mirrors. See, for instance, the *Brahmajālasutta*, in D I, 11 (Rhys Davids, *Dialogues of the Buddha*, p. 24, n. 1).
48. For the significance of mirrors in Buddhism, see Naudou, "Symbolisme du miroir", pp. 59–82; Wayman, "The Mirror", pp. 251–69; Bentor, "On the Symbolism of the Mirror", pp. 57–71 and Bentor, *Consecration of Images*

and Stūpas, pp. 18, 83, 129–32, 167–68, 203, 267–69, 315, 331; Strickmann, *Mantras et mandarins*, pp. 206–11; Swearer, *Becoming the Buddha*, pp. 81–82, 220–22. For their significance in Taoism, see Wang Yucheng, "Les objets liturgiques du taoïsme", pp. 11–13. In Hinduism, mirrors are also prescribed in consecration rituals by the *Mayamata*, as part of a *maṅgala* sign for a Śiva temple deposit (MM 12.34) and for a shrine to Pārvatī as one of her attributes (MM 12.69). I thank Anna Ślączka for this latter information.

49. Bentor, *Consecration of Images and Stūpas*, p. xxi.
50. Bentor, "On the Symbolism of the Mirror", p. 64, my emphasis.
51. A similar practice of "transferring the deity" during repairs of images, *caityas*, etc., albeit in a "vase" rather than a mirror, is prescribed in a thirteenth century ritual treatise; see Skorupski, *Kriyāsaṃgraha*, pp. 171–72.
52. Bentor, *Consecration of Images and Stūpas*, p. 41. Louis Gabaude has recently exposed that the English term "ordination" used in Western scholarship, taken to be either the "lower" (Pāli, *pabbajjā*), or the "higher ordination" (P., *upasampadā*), is misleading in a Buddhist context and prefers to substitute for it "consecration". See Gabaude, "Note sur l'« ordination »". For the sake of clarity, however, I retain in this paper the distinction between "ordination" of persons and "consecration" of objects, images or monuments.
53. Bizot, "La consécration des statues", p. 109; Swearer, *Becoming the Buddha*, pp. 97–98, 122–23.
54. Swearer, *Becoming the Buddha*, p. 59. See also Strong, *The Legend and Cult of Upagupta*, p. 265, n. 20.
55. According to Ślączka, the presence of a *khakkhara* in a consecration deposit is unknown so far in South and Southeast Asia (personal communication). This would thus make the *khakkhara* finial found at Chedi Chula Prathon a unique piece of evidence. An "iron stick", however, is mentioned in Pura Pegulingan, Bali. See Ślączka, *Temple Consecration Rituals*, pp. 366–67.
56. Only five rings remain, but it is likely that there were originally six, as observed by de Vries Robbé, "A khakkhara fragment from Java", p. 118.
57. The objects may be varioulsy called and spelt *khakkharaka, khakkharika, khaṃkhkharika, khikkhirikā*, etc. in Sanskrit. These variations can be explained because the word is an onomatopoeia for the sound made when the rings clink together; thus, the basic definition of a *khakkhara* as a "jingling" or "rattling" staff.
58. Yijing's biographies of Chinese eminent monks, *circa* the second half of the seventh century, make several references to the "pewter-topped staff" or *khakkhara*. See Chavannes, *Mémoire composé à l'époque de la grande dynastie T'ang*, pp. 11, 60, 77, 100, 142.
59. Olivelle, "The Renouncer's Staff".
60. This is recounted in Gao Mingdao, "Mantan hanyi shengwen pini zhong de 'xizhang'". I wish to acknowledge Shi Zhiru's assistance for providing an English summary of the article written in Chinese.

61. Chinese textual materials discussed here make clear distinctions between a regular "walking staff" (Ch. *zhuzhang*) allowed to old and ailing monks and a *khakkhara* (Ch. *xizhang*); see Yifa, *The origins of Buddhist monastic codes in China*, pp. 115–17 and p. 249, n. 36. It is apparent in these sources that the *khakkhara* is a particular species of rattling staff with a round metal finial, distinct from the regular staff allowed to some monastics as in the Pāli Vinaya (see *infra*, the discussion on *daṇḍa*s).
62. These Chan monastic regulations are based on earlier Indian *vinaya*s and Chan regulations purportedly from the late first millennium. See Ichimura, *The Baizhang Zen Monastic Regulations*; also Yifa, *The origins of Buddhist monastic codes in China*.
63. See *T.* 785, vol. 17, p. 724a and *T.* 2025, vol. 48, p. 1139b quoted by Ichimura, *The Baizhang Zen Monastic Regulations*, pp. 223–24. For a slightly different interpretation of the numbers of rings, see Getty, *The Gods of Northern Buddhism*, p. 189; also Kieschnick, *The impact of Buddhism on Chinese material culture*, pp. 113, 115.
64. Beal, *Si-Yu-Ki*, p. 96, n. 51.
65. In the Shwedagon pagoda, Burma, several different narratives concerning the presence of the "object-relics" of the five Buddhas of this *kappa* exist. Among these, a "staff", not necessarily of the *khakkhara* type, is believed to be enshrined in the sacred site. See, for example, Halliday, "Slapat Rājāwan", p. 41; Pe Maung Tin, "The Shwe Dagon Pagoda", p. 41; also Stadtner, *Sacred Sites of Burma*, pp. 74, 80, 83–84.
66. The *khakkhara* is mostly mentioned in the Mūlasarvāstivāda Vinaya (e.g. *T.* 1470, vol. 24, pp. 375a21–28, 919b16) as well as the Four Part (Dharmaguptaka) Vinaya (e.g. *T.* 1428, vol. 22, pp. 956a6, 956a7). See Takakusu, *Taishō shinshū daizōkyō*. For further references from the Chinese Canon, see Gao Mingdao, "Mantan hanyi shengwen pini zhong de 'xizhang'".
67. Takakusu, *Record of the Buddhist Religion,* p. 191. For another reading in English of this passage by Yijing, see de Vries Robbé, "A khakkhara fragment from Java", pp. 123–24.
68. Takakusu, *Record of the Buddhist Religion,* pp. 54–55.
69. Ebert, *Parinirvāṇa*, pl. 10, 16; fig. 16 and 28.
70. For an earlier illustration of a seventh century stele from Sārnāth, see Jarrige, *L'âge d'or de l'Inde classique*, p. 197, fig. 34.
71. See also Paul, *The Art of Nālandā*, pl. 14.
72. Christian Lammerts (personal communication).
73. Horner, *Minor Anthology of the Pali Canon*, p. 98.
74. Horner, IV, p. 250.
75. Horner, V, pp. 181ff.
76. For other Pāli Vinaya references to (*kattara*)*daṇḍa*s, see Vin II, 76, 208, 210, 217 (Horner, V, pp. 100, 293, 296, 305); Vin III, 160 (Horner, I, p. 275). Incidentally, the *daṇḍa*-staff is often described as an instrument of forest-

dwellers. The dimension of a "staff" is given at Vin IV, 200 (Horner, III, p. 142). I am grateful to Christian Lammerts for these references.

77. Sp-ṭ II, 121, 128–29 (Be 1960).
78. Hinüber, *Handbook*, pp. 172–73.
79. Hinüber, "Ein Beitrag zur materiellen Kultur". For a similar opinion regarding the presumed early influence of the Mūlasarvāstivādins in mainland Southeast Asia, see Bizot, "La place des communautés du Nord-Laos", pp. 521–22.
80. I address this issue in details in Revire, "À propos d'une 'tête' de *khakkhara*", pp. 121–23.
81. Le Coq, *Die Buddhistische Spätantike*, pp. 19–20; also Grünwedel, *Altbuddhistische Kultstätten in Chinesisch-Turkistan*, fig. 239 and Museum für Indische Kunst, *Dokumentation der Verluste Band III*, pp. 146, 167. Unfortunately, most of these murals were kept in Berlin during the Second World War and did not survive the bombing.
82. Wong, *The Hōryūji Reconsidered*, p. 168, fig. 5. 34.
83. Wang-Toutain, *Le bodhisattva Kṣitigarbha*, pp. 276–77.
84. Wang-Toutain, *Le bodhisattva Kṣitigarbha*, pp. 8, 12. See also Zhiru, *The Making of a Savior Bodhisattva*.
85. Revire, "À propos d'une 'tête' de *khakkhara*", pp. 123–26.
86. Frank, *Le panthéon bouddhique au Japon*, p. 110.
87. Getty, *The Gods of Northern Buddhism*, p. 94.
88. Ha and Mintz, *Samguk Yusa*, pp. 291–92.
89. Yang, *The Golden Age of Chinese Archaeology*, pp. 465–67; fig. 160; also Kieschnick, *The impact of Buddhism on Chinese material culture*, p. 114, fig. 7.
90. Kyeongmi Joo thinks that this discovery is somehow related to the spread of esoteric Buddhism during that period in Tang China; see Joo, "On the Buddhist Reliquaries".
91. Mitsumori, *The Treasures of the Shōsōin*, pp. 27, 126–27. For some other examples, see Ohwaku, "The Form of Old-type Khakkhara".
92. De Visser, *Ancient Buddhism in Japan*, p. 583.
93. This application of exorcism has also been observed in Tibet, see Sanders, *Mudrā*, pp. 180–81.
94. Skorupski, *Kriyāsaṃgraha*, pp. 161–63.
95. Le Bonheur, *La sculpture indonésienne au musée Guimet*, pp. 235–37. There is also a series of similar *khakkhara*s kept in the Museum Radya Pustaka in Surakarta but these are unpublished.
96. Flecker, *Excavation of the 10th Century Intan Wreck*, pp. 40–41. The Cirebon cargo can be seen online at <http://cirebon.mariemont.museum/the-cargo/secondary-cargo/metalic-objects/buddhist-ritual-objects.htm?lng=en>. See also Nicolas, "Gongs, Bells, and Cymbals", pp. 63–64, 66, 78.
97. Schoterman and Teeuw, "A Monk's ABC", p. 204.

98. Kats, *Sang Hyang Kamahâyânikan*, p. 131. I wish to thank Arlo Griffiths for drawing my attention to this reference.
99. Moeller, *Javanische Bronzen*, pp. 47–51, pl. IV. For other published examples of this type, see Fontein, *The Sculpture of Indonesia,* pp. 270–71, cat. 98; Lunsingh Scheurleer and Klokke, *Divine Bronze,* p. 155, cat. 103.
100. Bautze-Picron, *The Buddhist Murals of Pagan*, p. 59, fig. 60; 191, fig. 240.
101. Duroiselle, "The Talaing Plaques on the Ananda Plates", pp. 32–37, pls. XVI–XVIII, figs. 71–82; see also Revire, "À propos d'une 'tête' de *khakkhara*", pp. 114–15, n. 9, fig. 3.
102. George Scott, *The Burman: His Life and Notions*, pp. 140–41, my emphasis. It is quite possible, however, that George Scott, in his account of the rings, got confused with some other ascetic or occult figure's staffs. There are staffs used by *yathe*s and *weikza*s (*vijjādhara*s) that have hollowed out adornments screwed on top and filled with *dat-lone* ("alchemy balls"). These make a rattling noise when the person walks (Tom Patton and Christian Lammerts, personal communications). On the Burmese *weikza*s's staff, see, for instance, Ferguson, "Masters of the Buddhist Occult", p. 72, figs. 1, 2 and 6.
103. Piriya Krairiksh, "Semas with Scenes from the *Mahānipāta-Jātaka*", pp. 47–48.
104. Revire, "À propos d'une 'tête' de *khakkhara*", p. 117, fig. 5. See also Murphy, "The Buddhist Boundary Markers of Northeast Thailand", p. 227, fig. 5.13. This *sema* stone is said to be originally from Ban Nong Hang, Kalasin province. The *khakkhara* is also depicted on a second *sema* stone whose location, according to Stephen Murphy, is today uncertain and may be in the hands of a private collector (Murphy, ibid., p. 273, fig. 5.74).
105. Revire, "À propos d'une 'tête' de *khakkhara*", pp. 118–19, fig. 6.
106. The occurrence of an "iron stick" (*mai lek* in Thai) is apparently also attested in Chiang Tung, Burma, and the Sipsong Panna, China, as a permanent requisite for the local monks. See Bizot, "La place des communautés du Nord-Laos", pp. 522–23. Leedom Lefferts (personal communication) recently saw in Ban Dong Phong, a village near Khon Kaen, Northeast Thailand, one similar "iron stick" used in procession by the head monk for the annual ceremony of *bun buak ban* during which, in essence, the village's houses, rice granaries, and boundaries are "cleansed" of ghosts, spirits, and other potentially harmful "things". The "staff" is reputed to have come from either Laos or Vietnam during the times of Rama V. Local villagers call it the "gold cane" (*mai thao thong*) and refer to the clicking metal discs as *king ling*, onomatopoetically repeating the sound.
107. Related to this is perhaps the visual representation of the monk Phra Malai referring to his descent to hell(s) with a magical fan. As we have seen, the *khakkhara* is also an important leitmotif in this respect that links the iconography and roles of the bodhisattva Kṣitigarbha with afterlife beliefs. A cross-cultural study of the descent to hell motif, literature, and rituals across Buddhist Asia remains to be done.

108. It occurs to me that this *khakkhara* was perhaps slightly damaged at the time of the "reconsecration" and thus "ritually" disposed of, rather than just discarded or later melted down which is likely to have been the normal procedure. The fact that bronze items were possibly melted down could explain the paucity of ritual objects that we have in general from the "Dvāravatī culture".
109. One can see almost daily, on Thai TV shows, members of the royal family and other high dignitaries participating in merit-making ceremonies and reconsecrations of such places. Following an earthquake that damaged the important *chedi* at Wat Phrathat Doi Suthep in 1988, for instance, Swearer observed a ceremony to reconsecrate the refurbished structure in November 1989. The event was apparently hosted by the governor of Chiang Mai province at the time (*Becoming the Buddha*, p. 44). Naturally, the same holds true with Buddha images following their restorations as they need to be reenacted and reconsecrated by monks, see Bizot, "La consécration des statues", p. 107, n. 12.
110. This was first asserted by Boisselier (1970), but somewhat contested by Quaritch Wales (1978).
111. Manguin and Agustijanto Indrajaya, "The Batujaya Site", p. 116; see also Revire, "Iconographical Issues", p. 79.
112. Because of a broad resemblance of the Khorat Plateau artefacts to those from Nakhon Pathom, the Khorat Plateau culture has often been called "Dvāravatī", but a close examination shows that the expressions of both cultures have their own distinct character. The large *sema* stones which mark the Khorat Plateau, for instance, are not found in the Chao Phraya valley. See Murphy, "The Buddhist Boundary Markers of Northeast Thailand".
113. Generally, the influence or presence of Mahāyāna in Dvāravatī is not contested by scholars, but the extent to which it may have reached Nakhon Pathom is not clear. For a short review of the proponents of "Mahāyāna influence" in Dvāravatī, see Brown, *The Dvāravatī Wheels*, p. 40, n. 115.

References

Baptiste, Pierre and Thierry Zéphir, eds. *Dvāravatī : aux sources du bouddhisme en Thaïlande*. Paris: Réunion des Musées nationaux, 2009.

Bareau, André. "La construction et le culte des *stūpa* d'après les *vinayapiṭaka*". In *Buddhism: Critical Concepts in Religious Studies, Vol. 1: Buddhist Origins and the Early History of Buddhism in South and Southeast Asia*, edited by Paul Williams, pp. 1–53. London and New York: Routledge, 2005. [Originally published in *Bulletin de l'École française d'Extrême-Orient* 50 (1960): 229–74]

Bautze-Picron, Claudine. *The Buddhist Murals of Pagan, Timeless vistas of the cosmos*. Bangkok: Orchid Press, 2003.

Beal, Samuel, tr. *Si-Yu-Ki. Buddhist Records of the Western World*. Delhi: Motilal Banarsidass, 1981. [1st ed. 1884]

Bentor, Yael. "On the Symbolism of the Mirror in Indo-Tibetan Consecration Rituals". *Journal of Indian Philosophy* 23 (1995): 57–71.

———. *Consecration of Images and Stūpas in Indo–Tibetan Tantric Buddhism*. Leiden: Brill, 1996.

Bizot, François. "La consécration des statues et le culte des morts". In *Recherches nouvelles sur le Cambodge*, edited by François Bizot, pp. 101–39. Paris: Publications de l'École française d'Extrême-Orient, 1994.

———. "La place des communautés du Nord-Laos dans l'histoire du bouddhisme d'Asie du Sud-Est". *Bulletin de l'École française d'Extrême-Orient* 87, no. 2 (2000): 521–22.

Boisselier, Jean. "Récentes recherches à Nakhon Pathom". *Journal of the Siam Society* 58, no. 2 (1970): 55–65.

Brown, Robert L. *The Dvāravatī Wheels of the Law and the Indianization of South East Asia*. Leiden: Brill, 1996.

Chavannes, Édouard, tr. *Mémoire composé à l'époque de la grande dynastie T'ang sur les religieux éminents qui allèrent chercher la Loi dans les pays d'Occident par I-Tsing*. Paris: Ernest Leroux, 1894.

Cœdès, George. "The excavations at P'ong Tük and their importance for the ancient history of Siam". *Journal of the Siam Society* 21 (1928): 195–210.

Dupont, Pierre. "Mission au Siam (23 juillet-22 août 1937) : recherches archéologiques à Nak'ôn Pathom et à Kok Wat". *Bulletin de l'École française d'Extrême-Orient* 37 (1937): 686–93.

———. *L'archéologie mône de Dvāravatī*. Paris: Publications de l'École française d'Extrême-Orient, 1959.

——— [trans. by Joyanto K. Sen with updates]. *The Archaeology of the Mons of Dvāravatī*. Bangkok: White Lotus Press, 2006.

Duroiselle, Charles. "The Talaing Plaques on the Ananda Plates". *Epigraphia Birmanica, being Lithic and other Inscriptions of Burma, II-2*. Rangoon: Government Printing and Stationary, 1962. [1st ed. 1921]

Ebert, Jorinde. *Parinirvāṇa; Untersuchungen zur ikonographischen Entwicklung von den indischen Anfängen bis nach China*. Stuttgart: Steiner, 1985.

Ferguson, John P. "Masters of the Buddhist Occult: The Burmese Weikzas". *Contributions to Asian Studies* 16 (1981): 62–88.

Fine Arts Department. *Boranawatthu nai phiphithaphan sathan haeng chat phra pathom chedi [Ancient artefacts from the Phra Pathom Chedi National Museum]*. Nonthaburi: Fine Arts Department, 2548 [2005].

Flecker, Michael. *The Archaeological Excavation of the 10th Century Intan Wreck, Java Sea, Indonesia*. Oxford: BAR International Series, Archaeopress, 2002.

Fontein, Jan with essays by R. Soekmono and E. Sedyawati. *The Sculpture of Indonesia*. New York: Abrams, 1990.

Frank, Bernard. *Le panthéon bouddhique au Japon. Collections d'Émile Guimet*. Paris: Réunion des musées nationaux, 1991.

Gabaude, Louis. "Note sur l'« ordination » sans ordre des arbres et des forêts". *Aséanie* 25 (juin 2010): 91–125.

Gao Mingdao [Friedrich Grohmann]. "Mantan hanyi shengwen pini zhong de 'xizhang'" ["Random chatter on the *khakkhara* as represented in Chinese Vinaya translations"]. In *Ruxue chanshi jinian lunwen ji [Festschrift in Memoriam of Meditation Master Ruxue]*, edited by the Committee for the Commemoration Volume in Honour of Meditation Master Ruxue, pp. 9–23. Taipei: Faguang wenjiao jijinhui, 1993. [In Chinese]

George Scott, James. *The Burman: His Life and Notions*. London: Macmillan and Co., 1882.

Getty, Alice. *The Gods of Northern Buddhism. Their History and Iconography*. New York: Dover Publications, 1988. [Reprint of the 2nd ed. 1928; 1st ed. 1914]

Grünwedel, Albert. *Altbuddhistische Kultstätten in Chinesisch-Turkistan*. Berlin: Reimer, 1912.

Ha, Tae-Hung and Grafton K. Mintz, tr. *Samguk Yusa — Legends and History of the Three Kingdoms of Ancient Korea*. Seoul: Yonsei University Press, 1997. [1st ed. 1972]

Halliday, Robert. "Slapat Rājāwan Datow Smin Ron". *Journal of the Burma Research Society* 13, no. 1 (1923): 1–67.

Hinüber, Oskar von. "Ein Beitrag zur materiellen Kultur des buddhistischen Klosterlebens". *Sprachentwicklung und Kulturgeschichte*. Stuttgart: Steiner, 1992.

——. *A Handbook of Pāli Literature*. Berlin: De Gruyter, 1996.

Horner, I.B., tr., *The Book of the Discipline (Vinaya-Piṭaka), Volume I (Suttavibhaṅga)*. Oxford: Pali Text Society, 1938.

——, *The Book of the Discipline (Vinaya-Piṭaka), Volume III (Suttavibhaṅga)*. Oxford: Pali Text Society, 1942.

——, tr., *The Book of the Discipline (Vinaya-Piṭaka), Volume IV (Mahāvagga)*. Oxford: Pali Text Society, 1951.

——, tr., *The Book of the Discipline (Vinaya-Piṭaka), Volume V (Cullavagga)*. Oxford: Pali Text Society, 1952.

——, *The Minor Anthology of the Pali Canon: Chronicles of Buddhas (Buddhavaṃsa) and Basket of Conduct (Cariyāpiṭaka)*. Oxford: Pali Text Society, 1975.

Ichimura, Shohei, tr. *The Baizhang Zen Monastic Regulations*. BDK English Tripiṭaka Series: Berkeley, Numata Center for Buddhist Translation and Research, 2006. (Also available from <www.bdkamerica.org/digital/dBET_T2025_Baizhang_2006.pdf>).

Indorf, Pinna and G. Swati Reddy. "Significance of the Distribution of the Ritual Trays with Symbolic Motifs Related to Sri or Lakshmi". Paper presented at the conference on "Buddhism across Asia: Networks of Material, Intellectual and cultural Exchange". Singapore, Institute of Southeast Asian Studies, 16–18 February 2009. [Unpublished]

Jacq-Hergoualc'h, Michel. *The Malay Peninsula: Crossroads of the Maritime Silk Road (100 b. c. – 1300 a. d.)*. Leiden: Brill, 2002.

Jarrige, Jean-François, ed. *L'âge d'or de l'Inde classique : l'empire des Gupta.* Paris: Réunion des musées nationaux, 2007.

Jayawickrama, N.A. *The Chronicle of the Thūpa and the Thūpavaṃsa*. London: Pali Text Society, 1971.

Joo, Kyeongmi. "On the Buddhist Reliquaries from the underground chamber of Qingshan temple (慶山寺) pagoda in T'ang dynasty". *Chungguksa Yongu [The Journal of Chinese Historical Research]* 29 (2004): 71–106. [In Korean]

Kats, J. *Sang Hyang Kamahâyânikan.*'s Gravenhage: Martinus Nijhoff, 1910.

Khaṅ Khaṅ Cu. *Pisukā kyamḥ*. Yangon: Burma Research Society, 1966. [In Burmese and Pali]

Kieschnick, John. *The impact of Buddhism on Chinese material culture*. Princeton: Princeton University Press, 2003.

Le Bonheur, Albert. *La sculpture indonésienne au musée Guimet*. Paris: Presses universitaires de France, 1971.

Le Coq, Albert von. *Die Buddhistische Spätantike in Mittelasien IV.* Berlin: Reimer, 1924.

Lerner, Martin and Steven Kossak. *The Lotus Transcendent: Indian and Southeast Asian Sculpture from the Samuel Eilenberg Collection*. New York: Metropolitan Museum of Art, 1991.

Lunsingh Scheurleer, Pauline and Marijke J. Klokke. *Divine Bronze: Ancient Indonesian Bronzes from A.D. 600 to 1600*. Leiden: Brill, 1988.

Manguin, Pierre-Yves and Agustijanto Indrajaya. "The Batujaya Site: New Evidence of Early Indian Influence in West Java". In *Early Interactions between South and Southeast Asia: Reflections on Cross-Cultural Exchange*, edited by Pierre-Yves Manguin, A. Mani and Geoff Wade, pp. 113–36. Singapore: Institute of Southeast Asian Studies, 2011.

Miksic, John. *Old Javanese Gold: The Hunter Thompson Collection at the Yale University Art Gallery*. Yale University Press, 2011. [Revised and expanded version of the 1st ed. 1990]

Mitsumori, Masashi, ed. *The Treasures of the Shōsōin. Buddhist and Ritual Implements*. Kyoto: Shikosha, 1993.

Moeller, Volker. *Javanische Bronzen*, Berlin: Museum für Indische Kunst, 1985.

Murphy, Stephen A. "The Buddhist Boundary Markers of Northeast Thailand and Central Laos, 7th–12th Centuries CE: Towards an understanding of the archaeological, artistic and religious landscapes of the Khorat Plateau". PhD dissertation, University of London, 2010.

Museum für Indische Kunst. *Dokumentation der Verluste Band III*. Berlin, 2002.

Nandana Chutiwongs. "Review Article on the Jātaka Reliefs at Cula Pathon Cetiya". *Journal of the Siam Society* 66, no. 1 (1978): 133–51.

——. "Le bouddhisme à Dvāravatī et à Hariphunchai". In *Dvāravatī : aux sources du bouddhisme en Thaïlande*, edited by Pierre Baptiste and Thierry Zéphir, pp. 59–73. Paris: Réunion des Musées nationaux, 2009.

Naudou, Jean. "Symbolisme du miroir dans l'Inde (Conférence prononcée au Musée Guimet le 31 janvier 1965)". *Arts asiatiques* 13 (1966): 59–82.

Nicolas, Arsenio. "Gongs, Bells, and Cymbals: The Archaeological Record in Maritime Asia from the ninth to the seventeenth centuries". In *2009 Yearbook for Traditional Music, Vol. 41*, edited by Don Niles et al., pp. 62–93. International Council for Traditional Music: Unesco, 2009.

O'Connor, Stanley J. "Ritual Deposit Boxes in Southeast Asian Sanctuaries". *Artibus Asiae* 28, no. 1 (1966): 53–60.

Ohwaku, Shinpei. "The Form of Old-type Khakkhara". *Bulletin of Teikyo Junior College* 8 (1991): 73–100. (Available from <http://ci.nii.ac.jp/naid/110004727890/en/>). [In Japanese]

Olivelle, Patrick. "The Renouncer's Staff: *triviṣṭabdha, tridaṇḍa,* and *ekadaṇḍa*". In *Collected Essays II: Ascetics and Brahmins*, pp. 231–48. Firenze: Firenze University Press, 2008.

Parimoo Krishnan, Gauri. *On the Nalanda Trail: Buddhism in India, China & Southeast Asia*. Singapore: Asian Civilisations Museum, 2007.

Paul, Debjani. *The Art of Nālandā. Development of Buddhist Sculpture AD 600–1200*. New Delhi: Munshiram Manoharlal Publishers, 1995.

Pe Maung Tin. "The Shwe Dagon Pagoda". *Journal of the Burma Research Society* 24, no. 1 (1934): 1–91.

Piriya Krairiksh. *Phutthasasana nithan thi chedi chula pathon/Buddhist Folk Tales Depicted at Chula Pathon Cedi*. Bangkok, 2517 [1974]). [In English and Thai]

———. "Semas with Scenes from the *Mahānipāta-Jātaka* in the National Museum at Khon Kaen". In *Art and Archeology in Thailand*, edited by the Fine Arts Department, pp. 35–65. Bangkok: Fine Arts Department, 1974.

———. "The Chula Pathon Cedi: Architecture and Sculpture of Dvāravatī". PhD dissertation, Harvard University, 1975.

Pottier, Christophe. "Embryons et tortues : les dépôts de fondation découverts au perron nord de la terrasse des Éléphants". *Bulletin de l'École française d'Extrême-Orient* 84 (1997): 402–407.

Prapod Assavavirulhakarn. *The Ascendancy of Theravāda Buddhism in Southeast Asia*. Chiang Mai: Silkworm Books, 2010.

Quaritch Wales, H.G. "A stone casket from Satiñpra". *Journal of the Siam Society* 52, no. 2 (1964): 217–21.

———. "The extent of Srivijaya's influence abroad". *Journal of the Malaysian Branch of the Royal Asiatic Society* 51, no. 1 (1978): 5–11.

Revire, Nicolas. "Introduction à l'étude des bouddhas en *pralambapādāsana* dans l'art de Dvāravatī : le cas du Wat Phra Men — Nakhon Pathom". M.A. thesis, University of Paris 3-Sorbonne nouvelle, 2008.

———. "À propos d'une 'tête' de *khakkhara* conservée au Musée national de Bangkok". *Aséanie* 29 (2009): 111–34.

———. "Iconographical Issues in the Archeology of Wat Phra Men, Nakhon Pathom". *Journal of the Siam Society* 98 (2010): 75–115.

Revire, Nicolas. "Review Article: Pierre Dupont's *L'archéologie mône de Dvāravatī* and its English translation by Joyanto K. Sen, in relation with continuing research". *Journal of the Siam Society* 99 (2011): 196–225.

Rhys Davids, T.W. tr. *Dialogues of the Buddha, Part I*. Oxford: Pali Text Society, 1899.

Sanders, Dale E. *Mudrā. A Study of Symbolic Gestures in Japanese Buddhist Sculpture*. New Jersey: Princeton University Press, 1985. [1st ed. 1960]

Santi Leksukhum. "Conjectural reconstructions of three ancient stupas at Nakon Pathom". In *Abhinandanamālā: Nandana Chutiwongs Felicitation Volume Supplementum*, edited by Leelananda Prematilleke, pp. 3–32. Bangkok and Colombo: The Abhinandanamala Committee, 2010. [In English and Thai]

Schoterman, J.A. and A. Teeuw. "Jinārthiprakṛti: A Monk's ABC". In *Bahasa-Sastra-Budaya: Ratna Manikam Untaian Persambahan Kepada Prof. Dr. P.J. Zoetmulder*, edited by Sulastin Sutrisno et al., pp. 202–39. Yogyakarta: Gadjah Mada University Press, 1985.

Skorupski, Tadeusz. *Kriyāsaṃgraha: Compendium of Buddhist Rituals. An Abridged Version*. Tring: The Institute of Buddhist Studies, 2002.

Ślączka, Anna A. *Temple Consecration Rituals in Ancient India: Text and Archaeology*. Leiden: Brill, 2007.

——. " 'The Depositing of the Embryo' — Temple Consecration Rituals in the Hindu Tradition of South and Southeast Asia: A Study of the Textual and Archaeological Evidence". In *Early Interactions between South and Southeast Asia: Reflections on Cross-Cultural Exchange*, edited by Pierre-Yves Manguin, A. Mani and Geoff Wade, pp. 433–42. Singapore: Institute of Southeast Asian Studies Publishing, 2011.

Stadtner, Donald M. *Sacred Sites of Burma, Myths and Folkore in an Evolving Spiritual Realm*. Bangkok: River Books, 2011.

Strickmann, Michel. *Mantras et mandarins : le bouddhisme tantrique en Chine*. Paris: Gallimard, 1996.

Strong, John S. *The Legend and Cult of Upagupta: Sanskrit Buddhism in North India and Southeast Asia*. Delhi: Motilal Banarsidass, 1994.

——. *The Relics of the Buddha*. Princeton and Oxford: Princeton University Press, 2004.

Subhadradis Diskul. "Pierre Dupont: *L'archéologie mône de Dvāravatī*. A review". In *Essays Offered to G.H. Luce by His Colleagues and Friends in Honour of His Seventy-Fifth Birthday. Volume 2: Papers on Asian Art and Archaeology*, edited by Ba Shin, Jean Boisselier and A.B. Griswold, pp. 166–74. Ascona: Artibus Asiae Supplementum 23, 1966.

Swearer, Donald K. *Becoming the Buddha: The Ritual of Image Consecration in Thailand*. Princeton and Oxford: Princeton University Press, 2004.

Takakusu, Junjirō, tr. *Taishō shinshū daizōkyō [Complete Tripitaka of the Taisho Period, 1912–26]*. Tokyo: Taishō issaikyō kankō-kai, 1924–32, 100 vols.

——, ed. *A Record of the Buddhist Religion as Practiced in India and the*

Malaya Archipelago. New Delhi: Munshiram Manoharlal Publishers, 1998. [1st ed. 1896]

Visser, M.W. de. *Ancient Buddhism in Japan: sūtras and ceremonies in use in the seventh and eighth centuries A.D. and their history in later times*. Leiden: Brill, 1935.

Vries Robbé, Arthur de. "A khakkhara fragment from Java". In *Ancient Indonesian sculpture*, edited by Pauline Lunsingh Scheurleer and Marijke J. Klokke, pp. 115–32. Leiden: KITLV Press, 1994.

Wang-Toutain, Françoise. *Le bodhisattva Kṣitigarbha en Chine du Ve au XIIIe siècle*. Paris: Publications de l'École française d'Extrême-Orient, 1998.

Wang Yucheng, "Les objets liturgiques du taoïsme à la lumière des récentes découvertes archéologiques". In *Histoire, archéologie et société : conférences académiques franco-chinoises*. Beijing: Cahier numéro 7 de l'École française d'Extrême-Orient, September 2004.

Wayman, Alex. "The Mirror as a Pan-Buddhist Metaphor-Simile". *History of Religions* 13, no. 4 (1974): 251–69.

Wong, Dorothy C., ed. *The Hōryūji Reconsidered*. Newcastle: Cambridge Scholars Publishing, 2008.

Woodward, Hiram W., Jr. "Studies in the Art of Central Siam, 950–1300 A.D.", PhD dissertation,Yale University, 1975.

——. *The Art and Architecture of Thailand from Prehistoric Times through the Thirteenth Century*. Leiden and Boston: Brill, 2003.

——. "Book Review: *The Archaeology of the Mons of Dvāravatī*, by Pierre Dupont; translated with updates, additional figures and plans by Joyanto K. Sen". *Marg* 60, no. 2 (2008): 79–81.

Wynne, Alexander. "On the Sarvāstivādins and the Mūlasarvāstivādins". *The Indian International Journal of Buddhist Studies* 9 (2008): 247–69.

Yang, Xiaoneng, ed. *The Golden Age of Chinese Archaeology*. New Haven: Yale University, 1999.

Yifa. *The origins of Buddhist monastic codes in China: an annotated translation and study of the* Chanyuan qinggui. Honolulu: University of Hawaii Press, 2002.

Zhiru. *The Making of a Savior Bodhisattva: Dizang in Medieval China*. Honolulu: University of Hawaii Press, 2007.

7

ASPECTS OF BUDDHISM IN TENTH-CENTURY CAMBODIA

Hiram Woodward

The importance of a key document for the history of Buddhism in Cambodia was recognized long ago.[1] This is the inscription of Vat Sithor (inventoried as K. 111), which recounts the career and accomplishments of a Buddhist teacher named Kīrtipaṇḍita and includes a royal proclamation (*ajñā*) in support of the practice of Buddhism. In an article published in 1883, Émile Sénart discussed this inscription, by way of background stating that the later Buddhism of northern India had been influenced heavily by Śaivism. "The *purohita* is the Brahmanic priest of the house of the king," he wrote, appropriating the voice of the Vat Sithor inscription. "Is it the intent to suppress this position? By no means, but his duties will be modified. He will become 'versed in the knowledge of letters and of Buddhist ceremonies', he will bathe the image of the Buddha on festival occasions, he will replace hymns with Buddhist teachings, the Vedas with Buddhist chants."[2]

Since 1883, the Vat Sithor inscription has been studied only intermittently, and there are surely many learned Buddhologists who have never heard of it.[3] The issues Sénart's comments raise are still alive today. How much of Kīrtipaṇḍita's outlook is due to the intrinsic nature of the Buddhism he espoused, how much to the constraints placed upon religious life in Cambodia in the 970s? Such matters will not be resolved in this paper, which merely concerns "Aspects of Buddhism" ("Some Minor Contributions" would be an equally valid title). A successful comprehensive study of the tenth century necessitates the careful weighing of evidence, both art historical and epigraphical, and will — eventually — depend on contributions from scholars with varied interests and training.

The tenth century is intrinsically important: this is when the patterns of life in Angkor were becoming established. The nature of the evidence, however, differs somewhat from that which survives from later centuries. The tenth-century inscriptions — like the Vat Sithor inscription — reveal a good deal about the nature of the Buddhism practised, but the art is not especially abundant, and there are no great surviving temple complexes. In later centuries, the situation was not the same. Great temple complexes stand out, like Phimai, in northeastern Thailand (*c*.1100), and the many temples of the Buddhist monarch Jayavarman VII (late twelfth century). But the inscriptions, especially in the case of Jayavarman, reveal frustratingly little about the Buddhism practised, especially its Tantric aspects.[4]

THE SETTING

The founder of the city of Angkor, King Yaśovarman (r. 889–*c*.910), established four hermitages (*āśrama*) in the city, two for followers of Śiva (the *brāhamaṇāśrama* and the *maheśvarāśrama*), one for followers of Viṣṇu (the *vaiṣṇavāśrama*), and one for Buddhists (the *saugatāśrama*).[5] At each an inscription was set up, with content that was almost entirely uniform (involving such matters, for instance, as participation in civic ceremonies) but made allowances for the different practices and beliefs of the different religious practitioners (K. 279, 290, 701, and 1228). All four inscriptions stated the main features of the social and cultural hierarchy, giving the top ranking to Brahmans (divided into *dvija* [the twice-born], *vipra* [learned ones], and Holders of the Three Vedas). The Buddhists who ranked below them were masters (*ācārya*) of either Buddhist knowledge (*Buddhajñāna*) or of grammar (*śābda*), preference being awarded to the *ācārya* versed in both. Incumbents of the Saugatāśrama included both monks (*bhikṣu*) and hermits (*yati*).

The emphasis on *śābda* in the four hermitages promoted a uniformity of rhetoric. No wonder we strain to hear a distinctively Buddhist voice. The values proclaimed in the Saugatāśrama inscription (K. 290) constituted a framework inside of which tenth-century Buddhism operated, and the Saugatāśrama itself appears to have remained active, for an addendum to the inscription dating from 1015 or 1025 records a donation to the monastery by Sūryavarman, the reigning monarch.[6] One indication of the degree of rhetorical uniformity is the used of the word "god" to describe the Buddha and other Buddhist beings. So we hear, for instance, about "two *deva*," one being Maitreya (Don Tri, 966 CE, K. 198), and an enumeration of *deva*, including the Buddha and various bodhisattvas (Thma Puok, 989 CE, K. 225, st. 11–12) — though, indeed, there may be no reason to think there were Buddhists in the community who had any objection.[7] In general, it is not clear whether the inscriptions have been written by Buddhists in accordance with the prevailing rules of speech or by Brahman pundits who have been asked by Buddhists to compose a text.

The fact that there were Brahmans who ranked above the sectarian practitioners at all four *āśrama* appears to accord with a view of them as ritual technicians, functionally distinct from believers seeking personal liberation. Many scholars have looked upon the situation in this manner, and Johannes Bronkhorst, in a far-ranging study, quoted approvingly the view of J.C. van Leur, who had written (in 1955) that "the 'Brahman mission' [in Southeast Asia] was not the preaching of any revealed doctrine of salvation, but the ritualistic and bureaucratic subjugation and organization of the newly entered regions".[8]

To what degree the situation in the Ayutthaya and Bangkok courts of later centuries, with their calendars of Brahmanical rituals within an overwhelmingly Buddhist society, resembled that of the early tenth century is another matter. In the preface to his treatise on Brahmanical rites, "Royal ceremonies of the twelve months", Siam's King Chulalongkorn (r. 1868–1910) described Brahmanism and Buddhism as functionally distinct, but in terms quite different from those of van Leur and Bronkhorst:

> Those who truly believed in Buddhism had no proper reason to hold the following of magical practices in respect. Later, however, those who followed Buddhism but had not attained the fruits of the path still experienced fear and terror on account of various dangers, and concern for their own well-being and fortitude, as the result of having previously worshipped and lived in fear of gods and divinities who had the power to punish both oneself and others for reasons that are not truly just — by bringing about sickness or pain of various sorts because of anger or hatred at not being paid homage or worshipped, or, as the result of merely feeling evil, harmfully causing people trouble in the form of sickness or food shortages, among other things. Therefore, people decided to pay homage and to make offerings, in order to prevent misunderstanding.[9]

The king, rightly or wrongly, believed that, structurally, his Theravāda Buddhism represented an entirely different paradigm. A stance such as this, pitting a normative Buddhism not only against Brahman ritualists but untold numbers of ordinary religious practitioners, would not, presumably, have been understood in tenth-century Cambodia.

A HERITAGE FROM CHAMPA: THE *KARAṆḌAVYŪHA SŪTRA* AND THE *MAHA-VAIROCANA-ABHISAṂBODHI TANTRA*

The period between the foundation of the Saugatāśrama and the accession of Rājendravarman in 944 is the most obscure. The key evidence is in the form of an inscribed stele (Figure 7.1), and there are few additional

FIGURE 7.1
Stele with Avalokiteśvara. Cambodia or Thailand, first half of the tenth century. Sandstone, H. 36 cm. Walters Art Museum, Baltimore, gift of Yoshie Shinomoto (25.194).

artefacts. Nevertheless, a small body of material makes it possible to conclude that two important scriptures were the *Kāraṇḍavyūha Sūtra* and the *Mahā-vairocana-abhisaṃbodhi Tantra* (the equivalent of its Tibetan title; henceforth it will be called the *Mahāvairocana Sūtra*, after its Chinese name).[10] The inscription at the Cham temple of Dong Duong, 875 CE, alludes to the *Kāraṇḍavyūha*, and, quite remarkably, the different gestures of guardian figures at the temple are enactments of passages in the text.[11] Another Cham inscription, meanwhile — that of An-thai (902 CE) — promulgates three Buddhist families and is based upon the *Mahāvairocana*, perhaps through some still-to-be-identified commentarial tradition.[12]

Something can be surmised about the prior history of these texts. Although it has been speculated that the *Kāraṇḍavyūha Sūtra* had been known in Java, the evidence is scanty.[13] The *Mahāvairocana Sūtra* did circulate in Java; Sanskrit verses from it have been preserved in a ritual Javanese text.[14] To what extent Buddhist monks travelled between Champa and Java is not known, but one likely meeting point was Chaiya, in peninsular Thailand. Chaiya's Wat Kaeo is a Cham-style temple, and the "Ligor" inscription, doubtless from Chaiya, provides evidence of a monarch belonging to Java's Śailendra dynasty.[15] The same inscription states that a triad of images was established in 775, an Avalokiteśvara (*Kajakara*, "lotus producer", a rare epithet), the Buddha (*Māranisūdana*, "destroyer of Māra"), and a Vajrapāṇi (*Vajrin*, "*vajra* holder", an epithet that will be discussed below). This is the triad that was the focus of the *Mahāvairocana Sūtra*.[16]

A role for the *Kāraṇḍavyūha Sūtra* in Cambodia was recognized by Boisselier and Nihom, but the Cambodian stele, dating from about the early tenth century, has added a new dimension, for two reasons.[17] One is that an inscription on the back includes the words of the mantra *oṃ maṇipadme hūṃ*, which first made its appearance in the sūtra. The other is that the lowermost arms of the Avalokiteśvara are lowered in a gesture, one that can be called *pretasantarpita*, "the satiated hungry ghosts". It can also be seen on the back of a stele in the Bangkok National Museum (Figures 7.2 and 7.4). This name refers to an event in the sūtra, when water flows from Avalokiteśvara's fingers in order to satisfy the thirst of the sufferers. *Pretasantarpita* appears as an iconic type in the Indian text the *Sādhanamālā*, but no contemporary Indian depictions have been identified, giving the Cambodian evidence exceptional interest.[18] (In this paper the name Avalokiteśvara, "the lord who looks down [upon the world with pity]", will be used rather than Lokeśvara, "the lord of the world",

FIGURE 7.2
Four-sided stele with nāga-protected Buddha, Avalokiteśvara, and other deities. Cambodia or Thailand, tenth century. Sandstone, H. 119 cm. National Museum, Bangkok, gift of the Prince of Nakhon Sawan, 1932. On Figure 7.3, the visible figures are 1A1, 1A2, 1B1, and 1B2.

Source: Photograph by Sanit Motsophong.

even though the latter is more frequently attested in epigraphy. The degree to which the names reflect distinct identities awaits future exploration.)

The Bangkok National Museum stele (Figures 7.2 to 7.4) attempts to integrate the *Kāraṇḍavyūha* Avalokiteśvara into a maṇḍala-like structure.

FIGURE 7.3
Stele in the National Museum, Bangkok (Figures 7.1 and 7.2).

(1C2) **Prajñāpāramitā**
five heads
ten arms
ur: elephant goad?

(1C1) **Avalokiteśvara**
eight arms
ur: lotus ul: lotus
(both lotus stems support Buddha images)
r2: rosary l2: goad
r3: book l3: flask
lr: lowered, *vara* ll: lowered, *vara*

(1B2) **Tārā (?)**
two arms
r: *abhaya* l: *vara*

(1B1) **Avalokiteśvara**
four arms
ur: rosary ul: book
lr: lotus ll: flask

(1D1) **Vajrapāṇi**
four arms
ur: club/sword ul: noose
ll: *vajra* ll: bell

(1D2) **Unidentified female**
four arms
ur: lotus ul: rosary
lr: *abhaya* ll: *abhaya*

(1A1) **Nāga-protected Buddha**

(1A2) Female figure (**Earth?**)
two arms

FIGURE 7.4
Back of the four sided-stele, Figure 7.2. On Figure 7.3, the visible figures are 1C1 and 1C2.

Source: Photograph by Sanit Motsophong.

The Buddha (1A1) and the bodhisattvas on the shorter flanking sides (1B1 and 1D1) represent the three families in the esoteric Buddhism of the *Mahāvairocana Sūtra*. Both Prajñāpāramitā (1C2, the goddess who stands for the Perfection of Wisdom texts) and the eight-armed Avalokiteśvara (1C1) are placed on the back side, one above the other. This object is not easy to date, but details of costume suggest it could well predate the expansion of support for Buddhism that occurred during the reigns of Rājendravarman (944–*c*.968) and Jayavarman V (*c*.968–1001/1002).[19] It was probably made in territories that are now part of Thailand, perhaps in the province of Prachinburi. At any rate, no indications of a comparable arrangement can be found in Cambodian epigraphy.

Nowhere else in the Buddhist world was the *Kāraṇḍavyūha* integrated with the *Mahāvairocana Sūtra*. The *Kāraṇḍavyūha* was composed in India around 400, but the extent to which it circulated is not clear; later it became a key text in Tibet. It was not translated into Chinese until the late tenth century. The *Mahāvairocana Sūtra*, on the other hand, achieved importance in China in the eighth century and, as stated above, was known in Java as well.[20]

The study of the Bangkok monument raises several issues that are not easily resolved. Among them is the relationship between the two Avalokiteśvara icons. There is no question that the eight-armed Avalokiteśvara (1C1) is to be associated with the *Kāraṇḍvyūha*. The four-armed Avalokiteśvara (1B1) evidently had a different identity. As Nandana Chutiwongs noted, his attributes are not attested in India, but there are earlier Cham examples.[21] Furthermore, the same attributes became a standard feature, defining the most common Avalokiteśvara for centuries. In addition to the *Mahāvairocana*, the texts of the older Mahāyāna tradition — the *Sukhāvatī-vyūha*, the *Amitāyurdhyāna Sūtra*, and the *Lotus Sūtra* — could well have played some role in how he was conceived.[22] Additional clues undoubtedly lie in both Khmer and Cham epigraphy.

The relationship among the female divinities is rather more complex and will be addressed again later in this paper. The placement of Prajñāpāramitā (here ten-armed) on the back is based upon her position in the eastern quarter of the maṇḍala outlined in the *Mahāvairocana Sūtra*. There, she is called the "Mother of all Protectors", indicating that the translator, Stephen Hodge, thought that the original Sanskrit term was *tāyin*, "protector."[23] Very probably Kīrtipaṇḍita's Vat Sithor inscription (after 968 CE, K. 111, st. 44) — one of the most important of the tenth-century Buddhist inscriptions — echoes this usage: *prajñāpāramitātārī jananī … tāyinām*, "Prajñāpāramitā-tārī [a compound discussed below], mother of the protector

Buddhas".[24] The maṇḍala described in the sūtra became the basis for the Womb Maṇḍala of the Shingon Buddhists of Japan, but it was elaborated, and Prajñāpāramitā herself was moved elsewhere.[25] Arguably the four-sided stele — in this minor respect — is a more faithful reflection of the text.

On each of the four sides, a male figure appears above, a female below. On the front face, where the female is very small, an identification as Earth has textual support.[26] That the two-armed figure at 1B2 is Tārā, an extension of Avalokiteśvara's compassion, can be surmised on the basis of the *Mahāvairocana Sūtra*, that is, through context, but there is little in the way of corroborating evidence. The Avalokiteśvara and the many-headed and many-armed Prajñāpāramitā on the back (figures 1C1 and 1C2) suggest that these two might be considered a couple. At the same time, there are reasons to pair Prajñāpāramitā with the nāga-protected Buddha of the opposite face. (The nāga-protected Buddha was the Khmer substitute for the supreme Buddha Mahāvairocana, as a result of a process not yet explained.)[27] There is evidence from Javanese sculpture of the tenth century that Mahāvairocana and Prajñāpāramitā were understood as a couple.[28]

The extent to which she was considered in sexual terms is not clear. A sexualized Prajñāpāramitā appears in a lost version of the *Guhyasamāja Tantra*, briefly summarized in Amoghavajra's *Eighteen Assemblies* (*T.* no. 869): "The Fifteenth Assembly is called *Yoga of the Secret Assembly*, and it was expounded in the *yoṣidbhaga* place, which is called the Prajñāpāramitā Palace."[29] (Amoghavajra, the great Tantric teacher, 705–774, arrived in China as a boy and travelled through Southeast Asia in the course of his visit to Sri Lanka, 741–746. The *Yoga of the Secret Assembly* was composed after his return to China.) For *palace*, Amoghavajra, here as elsewhere, used the character 宫 *gong*.[30] The concept of a location for the perfection of wisdom, if not the precise image, was an old one; in the *Perfection of Wisdom in 8,000 Lines* (*Aṣṭasāhasrikā Prajñāpāramitā*), the term *prajñāpāramitāvihāra* appears.[31] As far as later Tantric literature is concerned, Nairātmyā, partner of Hevajra in the *Hevajra Tantra*, is addressed as Prajñāpāramitā.[32]

RAJENDRAVARMAN, 944–*C.*968

One of the most important tenth-century Buddhist inscriptions is that of Prasat Beng Vien (K. 872), set up in 946 or after by King Rājendravarman, who came to the throne in 944. Rājendravarman's main temples were all Śaiva, yet his East Mebon inscription (952 CE) declares that he understood Buddhist doctrine (K. 528, st. 172).[33] In the Beng Vien inscription he is said to have conquered Rāmaṇya (Mon land, i.e., territories where Mon was spoken) and Champa (K. 872, st. 7), and it is possible that Buddhist monks or adepts were brought to the capital.[34] Beng Vien stands about 32 km southeast of Angkor, and other Buddhist temples were established nearby. One of the images recovered from the temple shows the Buddha in a pose borrowed from a late phase of Dvāravatī art, the left arm hanging at the side, the broken right surely originally performing *vitarka-mudrā* (Figure 7.5).[35] Key Dvāravatī examples have been found at U Thong and

FIGURE 7.5
Buddha image from Beng Vien. H. 46 cm. Cambodia, *c*.mid-tenth century. National Museum of Cambodia, on exhibition at the Angkor National Museum, Siem Reap.

Source: Photograph by Michael Vickery.

Chaiyaphum, but what brought about the adoption of the type in Dvāravatī, and at what date, have not been determined. Following Khmer conquests it continued as an important icon in northeastern Thailand, but depicted in Khmer style rather than Dvāravatī.[36]

There is a small niched monument, a *caitya* found in Angkor Thom, that suggests that in Cambodia both this iconic type and a related one, seen here, in which the palm of the left hand faces forward, were considered to represent Śākyamuni (Figures 7.6 and 7.7).[37] It appears below a nāga-protected Buddha. On the sides stand Avalokiteśvara (2B) and, probably, Vajrapāṇi (2D). On the back is a single-headed and four-armed female goddess (2C), presumably Prajñāpāramitā. Prajñāpāramitā's key attribute is the book, held here in the upper left hand. At the same time, the four attributes are identical to Avalokiteśvara's.[38] Too few freestanding images survive to resolve without question the identity of such four-armed female deities. Two published bronze images, one from around 900, the other probably first half of the tenth century, have a figure of a meditating Buddha in the chignon, and both have four arms, but they do not hold any attributes.[39] According to the iconographical prescriptions of the *Sādhanamālā*, an Indian text, both Prajñāpāramitā and Tārā bear images of the Buddha Akṣobhya in their crown.[40]

Seeing the two Buddhas juxtaposed raises the question of whether the Beng Vien inscription has language that permits distinguishing between them. If so, the term for Śākyamuni would have to have been *muni*. But even if some Buddhists made the distinction using this name, the inscription itself (in which the second term is *Jina*) appears not to. That the standing Buddha on the *caitya*, nevertheless, was a recognized icon is demonstrated by the existence of bronze images related in type, with incised diagonal lines on the robe and a segment of the robe covering the upper left arm (Figure 7.8). This bronze may be somewhat later in date and fall into the eleventh century. The existence of images similar in appearance could be understood to mean that the makers of the *caitya* recognized Theravāda Buddhists as fellow Buddhists, ones who worshipped Śākyamuni.

Although the *caitya* (which need not have had any connection with Beng Vien) suggests continuity with the beliefs embodied by the four-sided monument in Bangkok, the Beng Vien inscription itself attests to the presence of Buddhists with a different outlook. The inscription begins with invocations to the Buddha (st. 1), the Buddha's *cīvara*, like a sun destroying Māra's dark envy (st. 2), Lokeśvara (st. 3), and Prajñāpāramitā, the progenitor of the Buddhas (*jinasantānakāriṇī*, st. 4). The subject of dedication is an image of the Buddha called Muni (st. 18), and it is hoped

FIGURE 7.6
***Caitya* from Angkor Thom. Angkor National Museum, Siem Reap (Ka 049, N. 127, 5690). Photograph by Phillip Scott Ellis Green.**

FIGURE 7.7
***Caitya* in the Angkor National Museum, Siem Reap (Figure 7.6).**

(2C) Probably **Prajñāpāramitā**
Buddha in coiffure
four arms
ur: rosary ul: book
lr: lotus ll: flask

(2B) **Avalokiteśvara**
four arms
ur: rosary ul: book
lr: lotus ll: flask

(2D) Probably **Vajrapāṇi**
four arms
ur: sword ul: noose?
lr: *vajra*? ll: bell?

(2A1) **Nāga-protected Buddha**

(2A2) **Standing Buddha**
two arms
r: *abhaya* l: *vara*

FIGURE 7.8
Standing Buddha. Bronze, H. 11.6 cm. Cambodia or Thailand, tenth–eleventh century. National Museum, Bangkok (Sv 43).

Source: Photograph by Hiram Woodward.

(st. 23) that the fruit of the merit will lead all beings to a long stay in Sukhāvatī heaven. Lokeśvara (st. 3) is distinguished from the Avalokiteśvara of the *Kāraṇḍavyūha*: he has four arms and is like Viṣṇu and Śiva. The inscription appears rooted in Perfection Path Buddhism. Still, being the first known inscription to proclaim a Buddha-Avalokiteśvara-Prajñāpāramitā triad — the triad that, centuries later was to become the central element in Jayavarman VII's state religion — it invites questions.

A certain amount of speculation has arisen in an attempt to explain the development of the Buddha-Avalokiteśvara-Prajñāpāramitā triad, which has no clear textual source, but the issue cannot be easily resolved.[41] One complicating consideration is whether Tārā was a recognized deity, and if she was clearly differentiated from Prajñāpāramitā. Presumably there was some awareness of her. A two-armed figure on the Bangkok monument (at 1B2) was identified as a Tārā. The bronze female goddess discovered at Dong Duong, her two arms at her sides, was surely a kind of Tārā, a projection of the loving kindness that is a trait of the Avalokiteśvara of the *Kāraṇḍavyūha*.[42] Her single appearance in Khmer epigraphy is ambiguous — in the passage from the Vat Sithor inscription quoted above, where the name *prajñāpāramitātārī* appears. *Tārī* is presumably an unattested variant of *Tārā* or *Tāriṇī*; the compound could mean "the saviouress Prajñāpāramitā" or with somewhat less likelihood refer to a joint deity, Prajñāpāramitā-Tārā.[43] The ambiguous nomenclature opens the possibility that the two goddesses had something of a joint identity and that the Prajñāpāramitā of the inscriptions could have Tārā-like traits. In art, it is the five-headed, ten-armed goddess who is most clearly Prajñāpāramitā. The identity of the four-armed goddesses is less secure. At any rate, perhaps the Buddha triads, or some of them, were at least in part conceived as Buddha-Avalokiteśvara-Tārā triads. Maybe, given such issues, the goddesses should just be called Buddha Mothers — as in *jananī tāyinām*, "mother of the protector Buddhas" (Vat Sithor) or *jinasantānakāriṇī*, "progenitor of the Buddhas" (Beng Vien).

If originally the Avalokiteśvara-Buddha-Prajñāpāramitā triad was not at all Tantric, its Tantricization might have some connection with the degree of emphasis on the union of wisdom (*prajñā*) and means (*upāya*), and the understanding of the latter. The coupling was a prominent feature of the final stage of the Tantras, though the pairing of wisdom and skilful means occurs in much older texts as well, such as the *Aṣṭasāhasrikā Prajñāpāramitā* (as *prajñāpāramitām upāyakauśalyaṁ ca*).[44] David Snellgrove quoted a passage from the *Vimalakīrtinirdeśa*, "For pure Bodhisattvas their mother is the Perfection of Wisdom and their father is Skill in Means."[45] The meaning of *upāya* was not altogether consistent. Atiśa wrote that it was equivalent to the perfections that lead up to the perfection of wisdom.[46] Buddhaguhya's commentary on the *Mahāvairocana Sūtra* identified *upāya* with *karunā* (loving kindness), thus strengthening an association with Avalokiteśvara.[47] In the Mahāyāna, Avalokiteśvara demonstrates his compassion by projecting multiples of himself through meditation. So far, no passage saying that Avalokiteśvara and Prajñāpāramitā embody *upāya* and *prajñā* has been identified in a Cambodian inscription.

BAT CHUM

Bat Chum is a row of three brick sanctuaries at Angkor, where images were installed by the king's minister Kavīndrārimathana in 953. Long Sanskrit inscriptions were carved on the stone doorjambs of the three towers (K. 266, 267, 268, henceforth S, C, N), each the work of a different poet, and each having the same structure: invocations; praise of the reigning monarch; and an account of Kavīndrārimathana and his foundations, here and elsewhere. The installed images were the Buddha (or Jina, in st. S19), Prajñāpāramitā (Divyadevī at S19), and Śrīvajrapāṇi.[48] The invocations differ somewhat. In the invocation on the south tower, Prajñāpāramitā is not mentioned at all. Lokeśvara takes her place, and is described (st. S2) as four-armed (*caturbhuja*), as in the Beng Vien inscription. He also supports *dharma*.

In 1952, stone fragments with engraved alphabet diagrams were uncovered at Bat Chum, seven of them inside the central sanctuary. An eighth was found in the north tower, together with a fragment bearing an engraved *vajra*.[49] When fitted together, it seemed that the pieces with the letters originally came from at least two and more probably three complete diagrams.[50] It is not known whether they were originally hidden, as in a foundation deposit, or visible. What George Cœdès published in 1952 was a drawing of a reconstructed alphabet diagram (Figure 7.9; the numbers, giving the order in the Sanskrit alphabet, have been added).

Cœdès's analysis was amazingly far ranging. He recognized, for instance, that the diagram had a relationship to the system of interior *cakra* in *kuṇḍalinī-yoga*. He also made connections with mentions of a heart-lotus in each of the three inscriptions: *hṛtpadma* (st. C33); *svahṛd* (st. S19) and *hṛnnīraja* (st. N37). One stanza (C20), he thought, summed it up:

> *vuddhadivyasvabhāvena vaddhvā tādātmyalakṣaṇam*
> *saṃvandhaṃ yas svamanaso yogijñānam avāptavān* //
> Ayant réalisé l'union caractérisé pas l'identité de son proper esprit avec la nature divine du Buddha, il a acquis la science des yogin.[51]

Much more is now known about the alphabet diagram of Bat Chum than was the case when Cœdès wrote. Although Cœdès described it as a *yantra*, a magical diagram, François Bizot, with no specific knowledge, was able to

FIGURE 7.9
Reconstruction by George Cœdès of a lithic inscription found at Bat Chum, Angkor, showing a letter diagram (*prastāra*). The numbers (indicating the order of the letters in the Sanskrit alphabet) have been added.

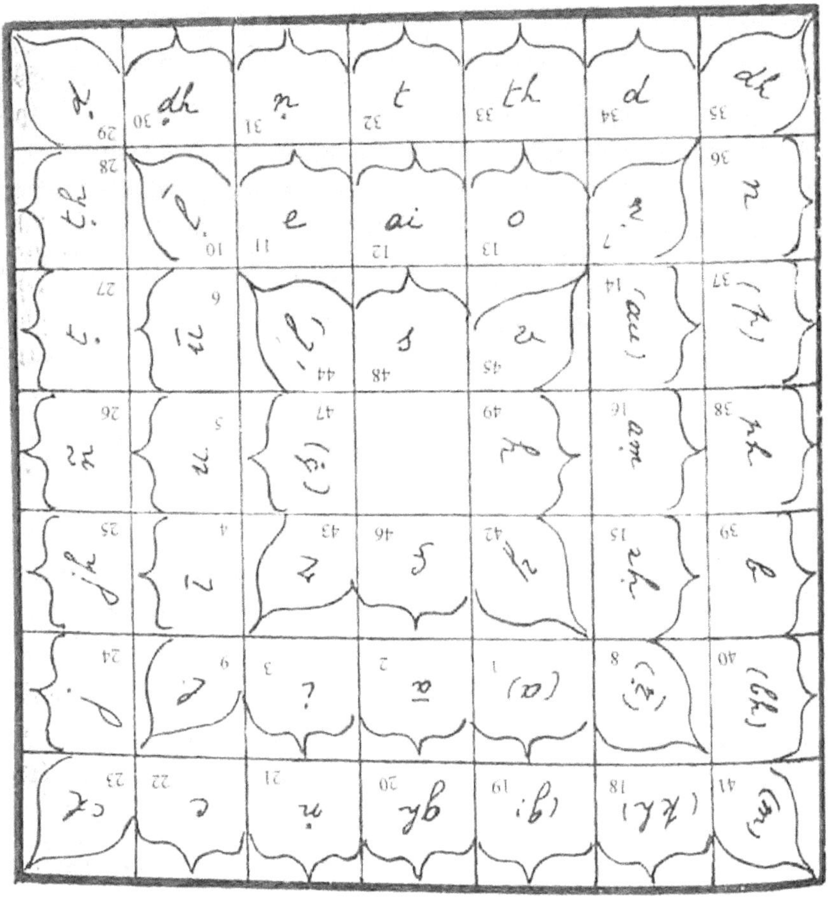

Source: After G. Cœdès, "Un *yantra* récemment découvert à Angkor."

correctly surmise that "its significance as a cosmogram and the fact that it is a literal depiction of the divine differentiates it from subsequent diagrams, which are instruments of magical coercion".[52] Diagrams displaying the alphabet were known as *prastāra* and they were like keyboards, of little use without instructions — instructions providing the specific location in the diagram of the phonemes constituting a mantra.[53] This was an elaborate way of keeping a mantra secret.

This particular *prastāra* is attached to two texts, one quite solidly, the other by inference. The first is the Hindu *Vīṇāśikhatantra*, which can be read in an English translation by Teun Goudriaan.[54] This tantra was claimed by a Cambodian inscription of 1052 (K. 235, Sdok Kak Thom) to have been used in a ceremony of 802, 250 years previously. The other is the lost *Sarvabuddhasamāyogaḍākinījālasaṃvara* (or *SBS*), briefly described by Amoghavajra as the ninth assembly of his *Introduction to the Yoga of the Eighteen Sections of the Vajraśekharatantra* (T 869).[55] On the basis of the Tibetan text of the *Uttarottaratantra* of the *SBS*, Toru Tomabechi reconstructed the *prastāra* described in the text.[56] Figure 7.10 is a re-drawing of Tomabechi's diagram, substituting Roman letters for Devanagari, and adding numbers that represent the order of the letters in the Sanskrit alphabet. (The last of the consonants, *m*, is the missing letter.)

The knowledge that the same alphabet diagram was attached to the *Vīṇāśikhatantra*, one of the Hindu texts purportedly used in a ritual in Cambodia in 802, opens another dimension. This text may not have reached Cambodia then, but it was surely known by 953. At Bat Chum, did familiarity with the letter diagram derive from its association with the *Vīṇāśikhatantra*, with a Buddhist text (perhaps even the *Sarvabuddhasamāyogaḍākinījālasaṃvara*), or with both texts simultaneously? This seems not to be an easy matter to resolve. In addition to the Hindu elements in the Buddhist tantras themselves, the environment in Cambodia was overwhelmingly Hindu, and, at Bat Chum, brahmans had a social position higher than Buddhist monks (*bhikṣu*; C37–38).

An additional element that seems to link the diagram to the Buddhist inscription might be pointed out, however. At one point in the *Vīṇāśikhatantra*, the diagram is compared to the cosmos:

> 248 *anenādhiṣṭhitaṃ devi cakravat parivartate /*
> *yathā tāragaṇaṃ sarvaṃ grahanakṣatramaṇḍalam //*
> 249 *dhruvādhiṣṭhitaṃ tat sarvam acalaṃ parivartate /*
> *tadvac charīraṃ devasya sarvabījagaṇaṃ hi yat //*
> 248. (this whole system) revolves like a wheel under His presidence, just like the complete host of stars [*tāra*], the orbit of planets [*graha*] and celestial bodies [*nakṣatra*],
> 249. the whole of which, presided by the Pole Star, revolves although being immovable. In the same way the body of the God which is identical with the complete host of Bījas ["seed syllables"].[57]

FIGURE 7.10
Letter diagram (*prastāra*) according to the *Sarvabuddhasamāyoga*, as reconstructed by Toru Tomabechi, redrawn with numbers indicating the order of the letters in the Sanskrit alphabet.

(17) k	(18) kh	(19) g	(20) gh	(21) ṅ	(22) c	(23) ch
(24) bh	(10) ḹ	(1) a	(2) ā	(3) i	(7) ṛ	(24) j
(39) b	(15) ḥ	(42) y	(46) ś	(43) r	(4) ī	(25) jh
(38) ph	(16) ṁ	(49) h	kṣaṃ	(47) ṣ	(5) u	(26) ñ
(37) p	(14) āu	(45) v	(48) s	(44) l	(6) ū	(27) ṭ
(36) n	(9) ḷ	(13) o	(12) āi	(11) e	(8) ṝ	(28) ṭh
(35) dh	(34) d	(33) th	(32) t	(31) ṇ	(30) ḍh	(29) ḍ

In the Bat Chum inscriptions, these celestial bodies do not appear, but the invocation to Prajñāpāramitā at the beginning of the central tower inscription (st. C3) says that "like the day of the full moon, she marks the fullness that is the all-knowingness of the Buddha (*vuddhasarvajña*)". In the north tower invocation (st. N3), "manifesting the charm (*līlā*) of her disk (*maṇḍala*), she is a sun (*ravi*) who lights the way to nirvana."[58] These mentions of the moon and sun could be taken as allusions to rings of the alphabet diagram, and to moon disks in which syllables are inscribed, thus strengthening Prajñāpāramitā's association with the diagram.

There is another way, somewhat more conjectural, that Prajñāpāramitā might be linked to the diagram. In the *Prajñāpāramitā* literature (and other texts, such as the *Mahāvairocana Sūtra*), there are circles of letters — of a different alphabet, the Arapacana syllabary — in which each letter stands for the correct apprehension of a different aspect of phenomena.[59] If the same practice is extended to the Sanskrit alphabet, then the alphabet as a whole could be understood as standing for the Perfection of Wisdom. Furthermore, there is the possibility that in each tower an alphabet diagram was originally paired with a stone slab with an engraved *vajra* — the diagram and *vajra* thus standing for the wisdom and means that engender enlightenment. At another site, a fragmentary inscription (K. 772, from Prasat Beng South, near Prasat Chikreng) appears to refer to the bell and *vajra* held in the hands of an adept as the two deities, Prajñāpāramitā and Vajrapāṇi.[60]

PHNOM TRAP

The triad that from the point of view of the *Mahāvairocana Sūtra* would be considered orthodox (Avalokiteśvara, the Buddha, Vajrapāṇi) hardly makes its way into epigraphy at all. Still, the greatest surviving tenth-century Buddhist sculptures, now in the Musée Guimet, constitute this very triad (Figure 7.11).[61] They were found in a mound not far from two groups of three sanctuary towers, one formerly called Phnom Trap (or Trop) A (IK 99), the other Phnom Trap D (IK 101), at a site in Kampong Cham province directly north of Phnom Penh.[62] Both temple groups appear to date from about the third quarter of the tenth century. A doorjamb inscription at Phnom Trap A (K. 94) provides names for the images installed there: Śrī Bhadrodayeśvara, the *ādideva*, established in 953; Aja, established in 960; and Upendra, established in 962.[63] The three may be identified as a *Śivalinga*, a Brahmā (*aja*, "unborn"), and a Viṣṇu (*Upendra*, "younger brother of Indra").

The carved-brick reliefs inside Phnom Trap D were formerly thought to have Vishnuite subject matter, but it has recently come to light that they are in fact Buddhist.[64] The Guimet sculptures, therefore, must have originally stood in the three sanctuaries of Phnom Trap D; they were the Buddhist counterparts of the images at Phnom Trap A. Avalokiteśvara would have been placed in the southern sanctuary, where the wall relief has an eight-armed depiction of the same bodhisattva, his lowermost two arms hanging down at the sides, palms forward. In the central sanctuary, there is another Avalokiteśvara, one with only four arms, but with the lower two

FIGURE 7.11
Triad of Avalokiteśvara, the Buddha, and Vajrapāṇi. Cambodia (Tuol Chi Tep, near Phnom Trap), third quarter of the tenth century. Sandstone, H. 119 cm, 97 cm, 111 cm. Musée des Arts-Asiatiques-Guimet, Paris (MG14912, MG14880, MG14892).

Source: Photos by Thierry Olivier. Photo credit: Réunion des Musées Nationaux / Art Resource, NY.

again hanging in the *vara* pose. In both sanctuaries the bodhisattvas are flanked by a pair of female divinities. Finally, in the northern sanctuary, Vajrapāṇi's, the carved bricks show a Vajrapāṇi with four raised arms, a *vajra* in his lower right hand, and his two knees bent and pointing outward (Figure 7.12).[65]

The structure echoes that of the Bangkok monument (Figure 7.2–7.4). It would replicate it more exactly if the eight-armed Avalokiteśvara had been placed in the central sanctuary instead of the southern one and if only he, rather than both he and the four-armed Avalokiteśvara, had displayed the *pretasantarpita* gesture associated with the *Kāraṇḍavyūha Sūtra*. If the female deities can be plausibly identified, Phnom Trap D will yield significant new insights into tenth-century Buddhism.

FIGURE 7.12
Vajrapāṇi inside the northern shrine at Phnom Trap D. Carved brick.

Source: Photograph by Phillip Scott Ellis Green.

JAYAVARMAN V (*C*.968–1000/01)

The Vat Sithor inscription (K. 111), from 968 CE or later, found in far eastern Cambodia, east of the Mekong in Kandal province, is explicitly Tantric.[66] It celebrates the accomplishments of an individual, namely Kīrtipaṇḍita, who, it is implied, travelled abroad in search of texts (with the boat of energy he crossed the oceans of all *śāstra*, st. 20). Kīrtipaṇḍita is described as wealthy (st. 24) and is said to have established images in 947 CE (st. 49). The inscription explicitly acknowledges both outer (*bāhya*) and secret (*guhya*) doctrine (st. 42).[67] It also mentions one of the best known Tantric texts, the *Sarvatathāgatattvasaṃgraha*. The words *tattvasaṅgrahaṭīkāditantram* (st. 29), translated by Sanderson as "the Tantra teachings of such texts as the *Tattvasaṃgraha* and its commentary", surely refer to the text scholars commonly refer to as the *STTS*.[68] It is interesting that he is said to have procured a text, rather than that having already been initiated into the *Mahāvairocana Sūtra* maṇḍala (as was quite possibly the case) he sought a teacher who would initiate him into the *STTS*. Kīrtipaṇḍita is credited (st. 37) with restoring an image of Muni — the Buddha — as well as more than ten images of Vajrin and Lokeśa, situated on a hill (st. 45).[69] Unfortunately, there is no single triad that is invoked. But a new image of Prajñāpāramitā was installed, as indicated in stanza 44, referred to above (the Prajñāpāramitātārī).

What is not clear is the extent to which Kīrtipaṇḍita was personally influential, in spreading Tantric doctrines elsewhere in Cambodia, and at what point in time. If he really did travel abroad, then connections with Java should be considered: the bronzes of the Surocolo maṇḍala, Lokesh Chandra has proposed, belong to the reign of Sindok (929–47).[70] Whether or not Kīrtipaṇḍita did have pupils, it seems probable that awareness of Trailokyavijaya, the key *krodha* (fierce one) in the *Sarvatathāgatattvasaṃgraha*, was his responsibility. Unlike Java, where bronzes representing Trailokyavijaya were made in the tenth century, Cambodia has bequeathed no tenth-century bronze images.[71] The inscription of Prasat Ta An (K. 240), about 47 km northwest of Angkor, records the foundation of a Śrī Trailokyavijaya and, in 979, material support offered to an image of Lokeśvara.[72]

Meanwhile, there is inscriptional evidence of the continuing importance of the *Kāraṇḍavyūha*. In 970, near Prasat Chikreng East, about 58 kms southeast of Angkor, a stele was found that records gifts to an image of Lokeśa (K. 417). This is the opening stanza:

> May Lokeśvara live, he of whom the best dust of his fingers aquified the enormous crackling fire which burns in the *avīci* hell! May my reverence to Him who takes away the pains of hell be a thousandfold![73]

The same inscription (st. 7) goes on to mention the eight perils (*aṣṭabhaya*), presumably referring to the eight dangers against which Avalokiteśvara offers protection, as had been depicted earlier at Buddhist cave temple sites in India.[74] Another inscription (K. 168), on the jamb of Prasat Chikreng East itself and dating from 972, records gifts to images of Ekādaśamukha, Lokeśvara, and Bhagavatī — that is, the Eleven-headed Avalokiteśvara, a second Avalokiteśvara, and Prajñāpāramitā.[75] A Cambodian tenth-century bronze depicting the Eleven-headed Avalokiteśvara has survived, and the *Kāraṇḍvyūha* mentions this form.[76] But there are also good reasons to think that the local Buddhists were familiar with the *Avalokiteśvara-ekādaśamukha Dhāraṇī*, an invocation of Avalokiteśvara in his eleven-headed form.[77]

A *caitya* with an attached inscription (Thma Puok, K. 225, 989 CE) was found at a spot south of the later temple of Banteay Chhmar.[78] This is a region that would have been in contact with the community responsible for the stele in the Bangkok National Museum (Figures 7.2 and 7.3). The inscription echoes chapter 3 of the *Kāraṇḍavyūha,* in referring to release (*mokṣa*) from existence and to the fires of sorrow (st. 12). The same stanza says that gods (*deva*) were placed in the directions (*dikṣu*). The gods were the Buddha-Mother (*Buddhamātṛ*), Indra, Maitreya, the Buddha, Lokeśvara, and Vajrin (st. 11). Finot surmised that the directions were those of four different monuments (though only one survives, or was ever carved), not of the faces of the single monument bearing the inscription.[79]

KBAL SRE YEAI YIN

Whereas there is only one *caitya* connected with the K. 225 inscription, at a site even further west, at Kbal Sre Yeai Yin in Banteay Meanchey province, four *caitya* were set up, probably around the same time (989 CE).[80] The source for the design of these *caitya* has not been established, nor has their exact historical relationship to the *caitya* of the Kathmandu Valley (the standing figures in niches and the diminished *stūpa*-bell element have roughly similar proportions).[81] There is no attached inscription, but the figures in niches make it possible to say a good deal about the local Buddhism. In addition to themes already noted — a structure provided by the *Mahāvairocana Sūtra*, the importance of the *Kāraṇḍavyūha Sūtra*, and the possible presence of Tārā — one additional text plays a role. Of the four stones, one is in the Musée Guimet (Figure 7.15), two are in the National Museum of Cambodia (Figure 7.13), and one, described as being in a ruinous state, may be in the archaeological depot in Siem Reap (Figure 7.14).

Only one of the three intact monuments has an image of the Buddha, the one in the Guimet, and that gives it pride of place. If the pattern already discerned holds, then Prajñāpāramitā occupies the back, the nāga-protected Buddha the front. In comparison with the Bangkok stele, the position on the lateral faces of the four-armed Lokeśvara and the bodhisattva with

FIGURE 7.13
Two faces of a *caitya* from Kbal Sre Yeai Yin. Ca. late tenth century. Sandstone, H. 147 cm. National Museum of Cambodia (Ga 1734). On Figure 7.14, the visible figures are 5C (left) and 5B (right).

Source: Photograph by Bertrand Porte.

FIGURE 7.14
Three *caitya* from Kbal Srei Yeai Yin. Top: Musée Guimet (no. 17487; Figure 7.15). Middle: National Museum of Cambodia, Phnom Penh (Ga 1735). Bottom: National Museum of Cambodia, Phnom Penh (Ga 1734; Figure 7.13).

(3C) **Prajñāpāramitā**
five heads
ten arms,
no attributes

(3B) **Vajradhara/Vajrasattva/Vajrin**
three heads,
supporting *pañcatathāgata*
six arms
ur: wheel ul: ___
mr: knife ml: ___
lr: *vajra* ll: bell

(3D) **Avalokiteśvara**
four arms
ur: rosary [ul: book]
lr: lotus [ll: flask]

(3A) **Nāga-protected Buddha**

* * *

(4C) **Prajñāpāramitā**
five heads
ten arms
no attributes

(4B) **Probably Avalokiteśvara**
two arms, at sides
palms forward, *vitarka*

(4D) **Vajrapāṇi**
four arms
ur: noose ul: water lily
lr: *vajra* ll: bell

(4A) **Bodhisattva**
two arms, at sides
palms inward, *vitarka*

* * *

(5C) **Prajñāpāramitā**
five heads
four arms
ur: ___ ul: book
ll & lr: arms at sides, palms outward

(5B) **Avalokiteśvara**
four arms
ur: rosary ul: book
lr: lotus [ll: flask]

(5D) **Avalokiteśvara**
two arms
arms at sides, *vara*

(5A) **Tārā** (?)
four arms
ur: lotus ul: rosary
ll & lr: arms at sides, probably *vara*

FIGURE 7.15
Vajradhara/Vajrasattva/Vajrin on one face of a *caitya* from Kbal Sre Yeai Yin. Sandstone, overall H. 230 cm. Musée des Arts-Asiatiques-Guimet, Paris (MG17487). On Figure 7.14, this figure is 3B.

Source: Photo by Michel Urtado. Photo credit: Réunion des Musées Nationaux / Art Resource, NY.

fierce demeanor is reversed (3B and 3D on Figure 7.14). The Bangkok Vajrapāṇi (Figure 7.3, 1D1) is replaced by another fierce bodhisattva at 3B (Figure 7.15) but reappears on the second *caitya* at 4D. There his feet again point outward, and his knees are bent, as at Phnom Trap (Figure 7.12), but his feet are placed upon the ground, symmetrically. A noose appears in the upper right hand and the upper left holds a blue water lily (*nīlotpala*). This is a reminiscence of older representations in which the *vajra* rests on a blue water lily held at shoulder height.[82] The pose and the presence of the noose suggest that there are some elements of Vajrapāṇi's manifestation as the *krodha* (fierce one) Trailokyavijaya.

Prajñāpāramitā appears on all three *caitya*, twice with five visible heads and ten arms and once with five heads and only four arms (3C). A single-headed female deity, at 5A, on the other hand, is more Tārā-like. The attributes in her upper hands, a lotus and a rosary, are those of Avalokiteśvara. Her lower arms hang at the sides, evoking Avalokiteśvara's *santarpita* gesture, as well as the Dong Duong bronze. Both aspects conform with Tārā's role as extension of Avalokiteśvara's powers.

Elements of Avalokiteśvara's *santarpita* identity seem to be present in two bodhisattvas, 4A and 4B, though the hands of both perform the gesture of instruction, which distinguish them from the lower hands in the Walters stele. The two bodhisattvas are differentiated from each other, in the orientation of the palms. It would be reasonable to maintain that 4B is the Avalokiteśvara of the *Kāraṇḍvyūha* and that 4A is some other bodhisattva, most likely Maitreya.

The unidentified fierce bodhisattva, 3B and Figure 7.13, has three heads and six arms.[83] That combination alone suggests a connection with the *Guhyasamāja Tantra*, a text more advanced than either the *Mahāvairocana Sūtra* or the *Sarvatathāgatattvasaṃgraha*. (An eighth-century reference to an early version was mentioned above, in connection with a sexualized Prajñāpāramitā.) Furthermore, one of the attributes of the bodhisattva, held in the upper right hand, is a wheel; this also has a connection with the *Guhyasamāja*. The *Guhyasamāja* is not an easy text to deal with. There are issues involving earlier and later versions; one complete translation into a Western language has received limited circulation; and extant partial translations do not make it easy to disentangle possible original meanings from the commentarial tradition.[84] At any rate, in the collection of descriptions of maṇḍalas known as the *Niṣpannayogāvalī* (*c*.1100), the deity at the centre of the *Guhyasamāja* maṇḍala is Akṣobhya, the *vajra*-family Jina, who has taken the place of the Vairocana who customarily occupies the central position. He is described as having three faces and six arms that hold, on the right, a lotus, discus, and *vajra*, and, on the left, a sword, jewel, and bell.[85] These attributes (minus the bell) are the ones that the text of the tantra attributes to the five Buddhas: Vairocana (wheel); Akṣobhya (*vajra*); Ratnavajra (*ratna*, gem); Amitābha (lotus); Amoghāgra (sword).[86] In other words, the directional Buddhas are imminent in the central one.

In the *Guhyasamāja* as well as in later tantras, a central role is taken by a figure variously called Vajrasattva, Vajradhara, or Vajrin. Vajrasattva first appeared in the *Sarvatathāgatattvasaṃgraha* and related texts as the first of sixteen protective beings. Then it became the practice for the adept to visualize his teacher in the form of Vajrasattva and to use Vajrasattva powers to assume the identity of the deity at the centre of a maṇḍala. This Vajrasattva had an established iconography, as a seated figure holding a *vajra* in his right hand in front of his chest and a bell in his left hand, placed upon his hip. Images of Vajrasattva were made throughout the lands that followed Tantric Buddhism. The Cambodian images were always small and made of bronze; some were probably made in tenth-century Cambodia, but none may have survived.[87]

In the *Guhyasamāja*, the Vajrasattva role is played by a figure generally called Vajradhara, who is considered the teacher and the selfhood of the body, speech, and mind of the five Tathāgatas (Buddhas, Jinas).[88] In chapter 1 of the tantra it is he who takes the central position.[89] A six-armed deity appears in the text in just one place, in a maṇḍala described in chapter 13. The adept contemplates a three-faced Vairocana, splendid like autumn; then a three-faced Vajrin, who is blazing; and finally a three-faced Rāgin. "He should meditate on the wheel, *vajra*, and great lotus in the right hand(s); he should reflect on the beautiful Vajras which have six arms wielding various weapons."[90]

On the basis of this passage, the figure on the *caitya* (3B and Figure 7.15) might be called Vajrin. He carries three of the six attributes (wheel, knife, and *vajra*) in his right hands — though they are not precisely in the right positions — and a fourth attribute, the bell, is in his lower left hand. The two missing objects would be a gem and a lotus. On the basis, however, of a later Cambodian Sanskrit inscription, that of Sab Bak (K. 1158, 1066 CE), it could be said that Vajrin's other names, Vajrasattva and Vajradhara, are equally valid.[91] This inscription mentions "Śrīśamāja" (st. 3, evidently referring to the *Guhyasamāja*). It also says (st. 2) that Vajrasattva is "the upholder of all the Buddhas" (*ādhāraḥ sarvavuddhānāṃ*). The Guimet monument could be said to contain a literal depiction of this upholding, with the five Jinas supported by the deity's three heads. Furthermore, implicit wordplay (Vajradhara, "*vajra* holder") suggests that Vajradhara is at least as legitimate a name as Vajrin and Vajrasattva.

The Guimet *caitya* would have to be considered the chief, as the only one of the three surviving *caitya* to display a nāga-protected Buddha. Another clue regarding the relationship among the monuments — one of unknown significance — is that it and Ga 1734 in the National Museum of Cambodia have square bases, while Ga 1735 has an octagonal base. The Guimet *caitya* is also the one with the most apparent traditional structure, with the Buddha on the front, Prajñāpāramitā on the back, and on the sides, an Avalokiteśvara opposed to a deity of the Vajrapāṇi family (here, Vajrasattva/Vajradhara/Vajrin). The conceptual framework of the *Mahāvairocana Sūtra* evidently had a degree of flexibility. In the case of the other two *caitya*, the orientation of the charts has been determined by the position of Prajñāpāramitā, considered to reside on the back. In fact, any of the four sides can be taken as the front. Nevertheless, it would seem that a generally related sense of structure is in effect. The positions are not entirely random.

One piece of epigraphical evidence might bear on this issue. It is the statement in the Thma Puok inscription that the gods are placed in the cardinal directions. There seems to be no suggestion that each has an assigned position in space. So even though there may be some structure, these are not maṇḍalas. Another piece of evidence is another, contemporary *caitya*, one in the Ashmolean Museum, Oxford.[92] On the front and back are female divinities, the raised arms holding a rosary and a book in the upper arms, and in at least one lowered right arm a lotus — that is, Avalokiteśvara's attributes. They are differentiated by the style of the coiffures (one tiered, the other cylindrical). On the sides stand a four-armed Avalokiteśvara, with his proper attributes, and another four-armed female deity, the surface too worn to be able to distinguish what is being held. Perhaps additional research will firm up the identity of a tenth-century Tārā, or distinguish among different aspects of Prajñāpāramitā. At present, it is tempting to suppose that the unusual combination of one male and three females has an entirely personal justification: the *caitya* honors a high-ranking personage, his two wives, and his mother.

IN RETROSPECT

Historians might read the foregoing and observe that crucial questions are not addressed: how many Buddhists were there? how many monks? did the monks follow *vinaya* rules? were they in contact with each other? across Cambodia? were their presumed disputes mild or virulent? was the discipline of secret mantras and initiations — all that was *guhya* —

adhered to, and did it bring about fissures? Most of these matters, indeed, may be ones about which we will remain forever ignorant. Then, there are issues that could perhaps be addressed with profit, but haven't, such as the extent to which Cambodian monks were in contact with Buddhists elsewhere, whether India, Sumatra, Java, or China. There, too, it may be hard to draw conclusions, the dates of texts being in dispute and the evidence of images spotty.

Another matter not explored is the art-historical aspect of the premises initially proposed — that the Buddhist value system was barely distinguishable from that of followers of Viṣṇu or Śiva. If that was the case, it should be expected that Buddhist images would not exhibit stylistic differences from the vast run of sculptures of the gods. Nor would it seem that Buddhist sculptors, perhaps by introducing foreign ideals of beauty, might have affected the development of sculpture as a whole. Still, there was a major stylistic shift in the second half of the tenth century — as seen at Banteay Srei, 967 CE — and it cannot be shown that sculptors of Buddhist images had no role at all in prompting or bringing about this change. It is a matter that may be worth exploring.

By and large, Buddhism appears to have persisted with a generally moderate level of activity in the tenth century, punctuated by a few striking endeavours, such as Kīrtipaṇḍita's commemoration by inscription and the establishment of the four Kbal Sre Yeai Yin *caitya*. Some of the concerns and iconic types of the tenth century set a pattern that endured. Other elements vanished. What has to be remembered is that it was not for another two centuries and the reign of Jayavarman VII that Buddhism became widely established across the kingdom. Therefore, when it can be shown that an iconic type of the late twelfth century had a forerunner in the tenth century, it means that a small number of monks maintained their practice decade after decade, leaving little in the way of material or inscriptional evidence.

The chief icon with lasting identity was the four-armed Avalokiteśvara, holding a rosary and a book in the upper arms, and a lotus and a flask in the lower. The eight-armed Avalokiteśvara associated with the *Kāraṇḍavyūha* did not survive the tenth century, nor did the *pretasantarpita* gesture (hands at sides, in *vara*), even when borrowed from the eight-armed bodhisattva by the four-armed or the two-armed. Still, the *Kāraṇḍavyūha Sūtra* must have continued to be studied and copied because at the temple of Banteay Chhmar, in northwest Cambodia, low-relief panels illustrating scenes from the sūtra were carved in the late twelfth century.[93]

The situation regarding female deities is less straightforward. In the Jayavarman VII period, Prajñāpāramitā appears in two different forms, one with eleven heads and twenty-two arms, the other with two arms, holding a lotus and a book. No images have been identified as Tārā. The multi-headed and ten-armed Prajñāpāramitās of the tenth century must be the predecessors of the twenty-armed goddesses of the Bayon period, despite the differences. The two-armed Prajñāpāramitā conforms to the description of the White Prajñāpāramitā in the Indian text the *Sādhanamālā*, a collection of visualizations (*c*.1100): two arms, holding a lotus and a book, and with an image of a Jina on the crown.[94] At some point the tenth-century presumed four-armed Prajñāpāramitā, as seen at 2C, was replaced, it would appear, by the two-armed form that accorded with the Indian textual prescription. The *caityas* discussed here provide no evidence of this change. A stele now in Honolulu and certain free-standing images, however, suggest that the shift did occur in the course of the tenth century.[95] The matter requires further study.

As for the *Guhyasamāja Tantra* (perhaps in a localized variant), it seems to have remained in circulation as a little-known but significant text. In one variant form or another, the principal six-armed deity at the centre of the maṇḍala (Akṣobhya, according to the *Niṣpannayogāvalī*) or the Vajrin/Vajradhara/Vajrasattva who takes his place appeared rarely but tellingly: on the northern interior lintel at Phimai (*c*.1100), and a hundred years later in a Bayon-period votive tablet, where he is seated between Saṃvara and Hevajra, seeming to indicate that the *Saṃvarodaya Tantra*, the *Guhyasamāja*, and the *Hevajra Tantra* each had its followers at the time.[96]

Notes

1. For assistance on various matters, I am grateful to Emma C. Bunker, Phillip Green, Arlo Griffiths, Hudaya Kandahjaya, Nandana Chutiwongs, Christian Lammerts, Christian Luczanits, Martin Polkinghorne, Bertrand Porte, Peter Sharrock, Jeffrey Sundberg, and Peter Szanto. They are not responsible for remaining errors. Studies of the tenth-century phase of Khmer Buddhism from recent decades include the following, in chronological order: Filliozat, "Sur le çivaïsme et le bouddhisme du Cambodge, à propos de deux livres récents", pp. 85–90; Nandana Chutiwongs, *The Iconography of Avalokiteśvara in Mainland Southeast Asia*, pp. 309–10; Sanderson, "The Śaiva Religion Among the Khmers (Part 1)", pp. 424–33; Snellgrove, *Angkor—Before and After*, pp. 74–77, 82–85; Harris, *Cambodian Buddhism: History and Practice*, pp. 3–17; Hiram Woodward, "The *Karandavyuha Sutra* and Buddhist Art in 10th Century Cambodia"; Sharrock, "Garuḍa, Vajrapāṇi, and Religious Change in Jayavarman VII's Angkor", pp. 114–15, 129–33; Estève, "Étude critique des phénomènes de syncrétisme religieux dans le Camboge angkorien", pp. 297–410; Sharrock, "Kīrtipaṇḍita and the Tantras"; Green, "The Many

Faces of Lokeśvara". The spelling of Khmer place and temple names is undergoing changes. In general, the spellings here conform with those on the valuable website Cisark <http://www.site-archeologique-khmer.org>. It is possible to search by inscription number on this site. Attention should also be drawn to the set of *Carte archéologique du Cambodge*, province by province, published by the Ministry of Culture and Fine Arts and the École française d'Extrême-Orient, 2006–07.

2. "Le purohita est le prètre brahmanique de la maison du roi. Va-t-on supprimer son office? En aucune façon; mai ses attributions seront modifiées. Il sera 'versé dans la connaissance des letters et des rites bouddhiques'; il en pratiquera les prescriptions, il baignera aux jours de fête la statue du Bouddha, et remplacera les hymnes par la predication bouddhisque, les védas par les stances bouddhiques." Aymonier, *Le Cambodge*, vol. 1, pp. 267–68, quoting from the article by Émile Sénart originally published in *Revue archéologique*, March–April 1883. Another early article was Hendrik Kern's study of the inscription of Banteay Nang (K. 214), published in Dutch in 1899. It appeared in French translation in Aymonier, *Le Cambodge*, vol. 2, pp. 308–18.
3. In addition to items listed in note 1, see Mertens, "Beobachtungen zur Herrschaftslegitimation im Ankor-Reich: Die buddhistisch orientierte Vat-Sithor-Inschrift von Jayavarman V".
4. Woodward, *The Art and Architecture of Thailand*, pp. 146–55, for Phimai; Clark, ed., *Bayon: New Perspectives* (Bangkok: River Books, 2007).
5. There is an analysis of the four inscriptions in Estève, "Étude critique", pp. 338–48, revising that in Cœdès, "Études cambodgiennes XXX: À la recherché du Yaçodharāçrama". The fourth inscription, K. 1228, was discovered in 1994. See Pottier, "About Yaçovarman's Buddhist āçrama in Angkor". For K. 290, Cœdès, "La stele de Tép Praṇaṃ (Cambodge)".
6. K. 290: Cœdès, *Inscriptions du Cambodge*, vol. 3, pp. 231–33.
7. K. 198: Cœdès, *Inscriptions du Cambodge*, vol. 6, p. 147. K. 225: Cœdès, *Inscriptions du Cambodge*, vol. 3, pp. 66–69. Hudaya Kandahjaya drew my attention to a passage in the *Lalitavistara* in which an epithet for the Buddha is *devātideva*, "lord of gods". Quoted in his article, "Notes on Buddhist Cosmology", with reference to P.L. Vaidya, *Lalita-Vistara* (Darbhanga: Mithila Institute, 1958), pp. 2, 219, and Bijoya Goswami, *Lalitavistara* (Kokata: Asiatic Society, 2001), pp. 5, 279.
8. Quoted (from *Indonesian Trade and Society*) in Johannes Bronkhorst, *Buddhism in the Shadow of Brahmanism*, p. 58.
9. Chulalongkorn, *Phra rātchaphitthī sipsǫng dūan*, pp. 2–3; for this passage and comparable statements by anthropologists, Woodward, "Art History", pp. 76–77.
10. Hodge, trans., *The Mahā-Vairocana-Abhisaṃbodhi Tantra*.
11. Woodward, "The Temple of Dong Duong and the *Kāraṇḍavyūha Sūtra*". For the text, Studholme, *The Origins of oṃ maṇipadme hūṃ*.
12. For the inscription (C. 138), Mabbett, "Buddhism in Champa"; Golzio,

ed., *Inscriptions of Campā*, pp. 89–91. For discussions of the inscription, Woodward, "Esoteric Buddhism in Southeast Asia", p. 345; Nandana, "Le bouddhisme du Champa"; Schweyer, "Buddhism in Čampā", pp. 313–16.

13. Nihom, *Studies in Indian and Indo-Indonesian Tantrism*, pp. 137–41.
14. Woodward, "Esoteric Buddhism", p. 339.
15. For the inscription, Cœdès, *Recueil des inscriptions du Siam Deuxième Partie*, pp. 20–24. For Wat Kaeo, Michel Jacq-Hergoualc'h, *The Malay Peninsula*, pp. 302–305. The re-dating of the Cham temple of Hoa Lai to an earlier period than previously thought strengthens the likelihood of a connection between Wat Kaeo in its present form and the 775 CE inscription. See Griffiths and. Southworth, "La stèle d'installation de Śrī Adideveśvara".
16. For early instances of the pairing of Avalokiteśvara with Vajrapāṇi, for example at Aurangabad, Linrothe, *Ruthless Compassion*, pp. 33–41, and Brancaccio, *The Buddhist Caves at Aurangabad*. These bodhisattvas are paired in the *Mañjuśrīmūlakalpa*: see Snellgrove, *Indo-Tibetan Buddhism*, p. 193.
17. Boisselier, "Précisions sur quelques images khmères d'Avalokiteśvara"; Nihom, *Studies in Indian and Indo-Indonesian Tantrism*, pp. 137–41; Woodward, "The *Karandavyuha Sutra*".
18. Questions are raised about how well-known the text was in India before the tenth century in Woodward, "The *Karandavyuha Sutra*", p. 77. Bautze-Picron, "The Universal Compassionate Bodhisattva", argues that it was well known. To the sources cited in Woodward, "The *Karandavyuha Sutra*", add Bühnemann, *Buddhist Deities of Nepal: Iconography in Two Sketchbooks*, pp. 33, 58, 87, and 104 ("Pretasaṃtarpita-Lokeśvara").
19. Nandana, "Iconography of Avalokiteśvara," pp. 380–81.
20. For Southeast Asia and China, Woodward, "Esoteric Buddhism", and Woodward, "Bianhong, Mastermind of Borobudur?".
21. Nandana, "Iconography of Avalokiteśvara", pp. 340–41.
22. These three texts are the ones outlined at the beginning of de Mallmann, *Introduction à l'étude d'Avalokiteçvara*.
23. Hodge, trans., *The Mahā-Vairocana-Abhisaṃbodhi Tantra*, p. 107. Nevertheless, the Chinese has here 導師 *daoshi* (spiritual guide) (*T*. 848, 18: 6c23) not 救世 *jiushi* (savior of the world), which translates *tāyin* in a passage in which the original Sanskrit has been preserved (*T*. 848, 18: 12a23; Hodge, *The Mahā-Vairocana-Abhisaṃbodhi Tantra*, pp. 143, 549).
24. Cœdès, *Inscriptions du Cambodge*, vol. 6, pp. 199, 206–207. For a further discussion of this passage, see below.
25. Tajima, *Les deux grands maṇḍalas*, pp. 80–86.
26. There is a figure of Earth in a maṇḍala in the *Mañjuśrīmūlakalpa*, "emerging from the earth", Marcelle Lalou, *Iconographie des étoffes peintes*, p. 64 and pl. VI, beneath Śākyamuni, with eight bodhisattvas.
27. For the question of the sources for the Khmer nāga-protected Buddha, two recent studies: Gaston-Aubert, "Nāga Buddhas in the Dvāravatī Period" and Sharrock, "The Nāga-enthroned Buddha of Angkor".

28. Lunsingh Scheurleer and Klokke, *Divine Bronze*, p. 99. On this topic, Sharrock, "Kīrtipandita and the Tantras".
29. Giebel, "The *Chin-kang-ting ching*", p. 193. The term *yoṣidbhaga* (a woman's vulva) appears in the sentence introducing both the *Guhyasamāja Tantra* and the *Hevajra Tantra*, but without a specific reference to Prajñāpāramitā.
30. *Jingongding jing*, *T.* 869, 18:287a29.
31. In the *Aṣṭasāhasrikā*, chap. 28, *prajñāpāramitāvihāreṇa* <http://www.uwest.edu/sanskritcanon>, "the dwelling of perfect wisdom". (Accessed 15 Feburary 2011.) See Conze, *The Perfection of Wisdom in Eight Thousand Lines*, p. 272. Also, in chap. 30 (p. 288), a pointed tower (*kūṭāgāra*) for the perfection of wisdom.
32. *Hevajra Tantra* 2.11.2: Farrow and Menon, *The Concealed Essence of the Hevajra Tantra*, p. 289.
33. Finot, "Inscriptions d'Aṅkor, IV, Mébôn", pp. 327, 348 ("ayant compris la doctrine bouddhique").
34. Cœdès, *Inscriptions du Cambodge*, vol. 5, pp. 97–105.
35. The image is illustrated in Boisselier, *La statuaire khmère et son evolution*, vol. 2, pl. 91. It is now on view in the Angkor National Museum, Siem Reap, numbered K. 1684, B. 790, B. 10.35.
36. Piriya Krairiksh, *The Roots of Thai Art*, pp. 264, 265, 275, 277; Woodward, *The Art and Architecture of Thailand*, pp. 137–38.
37. I thank Phillip Green for sharing a photograph.
38. It is believed that in Cambodia the goddess Devī is depicted with the attributes of Viṣṇu, presumably because she is considered Viṣṇu's sister. It is not clear what the implications are (if any). If Tārā is Avalokiteśvara's sister, maybe this image is Tārā. See Bhattacharya, *Les religions brahmaniques dans l'ancien Cambodge*, p. 91; Boisselier, *Le Cambodge*, p. 294.
39. Bunker and Latchford, *Khmer Bronzes*, pp. 149 and 168–69. The first, displaying stylistic connections with the Plai Bat Hill bronze tradition and now in the Muang Boran collection in Bangkok, was first published in Smitthi Siribhadra, "Notes sur un bronze d'époque angkorienne representant Prajñāpāramitā".
40. Bhattacharyya, *The Indian Buddhist Iconography*, pp. 197–98, 309.
41. Woodward "The Karandavyuha Sutra", pp. 78–80.
42. Woodward, "The Temple of Dong Duong"; Trian Nguyen, "Lakṣmīndralokeśvara, Main Deity of the Dong Duong Monastery".
43. Cœdès, *Inscriptions du Cambodge*, vol. 6, p. 207, n. 1. I thank Phillip Green for informing me that, based on a rubbing of the inscription, the reading *tārī* is correct.

    This is the stanza:

    XLIV. 37. tatsthāne sthāpitā sthityai sarvvavidvaṅśabhāsvataḥ
    38. prajñāpāramitātārī jananī yena tāyinām //

    And this is Phillip Green's translation (e-mail, 27 October 2011): "In that place the protectoress Prajñāpāramitā, Mother of Protectors, was established by him for the sake of continuing the luminous lineage of the Omniscient One." He considers *tārī* to be in a compound with *prajñāpāramitā* and treats it as a qualifying adjective.

44. Conze, *The Perfection of Wisdom in Eight Thousand Lines*, e.g., p. 295 (ch. 31), "hear about the perfection of wisdom and skill in means". Sanskrit text accessed (5 Feburary 2011) through <http://dsbc.uwest.edu/>.
45. Snellgrove, *Indo-Tibetan Buddhism*, p. 67.
46. Sherburne, *The Complete Works of Atīśa*, pp. 15, 225.
47. Hodge, trans., *The Mahā-Vairocana-Abhisaṃbodhi Tantra*, p. 77.
48. Cœdès, "Les inscriptions de Bàt Čuṃ". Elsewhere Cœdès pointed out that if Vajrapāṇi is subtracted from the invocations, the core triad is Buddha-Lokeśvara-Prajñāpāramitā: Cœdès, *Bronzes khmèrs*, pp. 37–38, n. 3.
49. Cœdès, "Un *yantra* récemment découvert à Angkor".
50. Cœdès, "Un *yantra*", pp. 467–68.
51. Cœdès, "Un *yantra*", p. 476: "Having realized the union characterized by the identity of his mind with the divine nature of the Buddha, he has acquired the awareness (*jñāna*) of the yogis".
52. "... sa significance de cosmogramme et le fait qu'il soit une figuration littérale de la divinité le differencie des diagrammes ultérieurs qui sont surtout des instruments de coercition magique." Bizot, "Notes sur les *yantra* bouddhiques d'Indochine", p. 156.
53. For a brief description, English, *Vajrayoginī*, pp. 52–54.
54. Goudriaan, *The Vīṇāśikhatantra*. On the name of the text, Sanderson, "Religion and the State", p. 235 n. 9.
55. English translation from the Chinese by Giebel, "The *Chin-kang-ting ching*", section 9, pp. 179–82.
56. Tomabechi, "The extraction of mantra".
57. Goudriaan, *The Vīṇāśikhatantra*, pp. 78, 123.
58. Cœdès, "Les inscriptions de Bàt Čuṃ", pp. 230, 233 (text), 242, 248 (translation).
59. For a discussion, Woodward, "Bianhong", pp. 36–38.
60. Cœdès, *Inscriptions du Cambodge*, vol. 7, pp. 104–105.
61. Baptiste and Zéphir, *L'Art khmer dans les collections du musée Guimet*, pp. 166–71.
62. IK numbers are the numbers to be found in Lunet de Lajonquière, *Inventaire descriptif des monuments du Cambodge*, where there is an illustration of one tower, vol. 1, p. LXXVII, fig. 33. See also Cisark (note 1 above).
63. Cœdès, *Inscriptions du Cambodge*, vol. 5, pp. 106–107.
64. This was first pointed out to me by Martin Polkinghorne. Since then, Phillip Green has visited the site, and he is undertaking a detailed analysis, as a section of his dissertation for the University of Florida. I thank both scholars for the pictures.
65. I am grateful for Phillip Green's pictures and for his identification of the attributes.

66. Cœdès, *Inscriptions du Cambodge*, vol. 6, pp. 195–211.
67. A Mantrayāna textual source is Skorupski, *The Sarvadurgatipariśodhana Tantra*, pp. 19 ("I will learn the Good Law in its open and hidden form") and 146 (text). I thank Peter Szanto for providing me with this reference. In Chinese Buddhism, the terms are 密教 *mijiao* esoteric Buddhism (*mi* = *guhya*) and 顯教 *xianjiao*, direct teaching, exoteric Buddhism. See Orzech, "The 'Great Teaching of Yoga'", pp. 42–43 and Orzech, "Esoteric Buddhism under the Tang", pp. 282–85.
68. Sanderson, "The Śaiva Religion", p. 427 n. 284. Sharrock, "Kīrtipaṇḍita and the Tantras", working with Skorupski, has made the same identification of this text. He suggests that the commentary in question is the one by Śākyamitra, formally the *Kośālāṅkāratattvasaṅgraha* (Tôh. no. 2503). For this text see Davidson, *Indian Esoteric Buddhism*, pp. 159–60. Another commentary, by Anandagarbha, the *Sarvatathāgatatattvasaṅgrahamahāyānābhisamaya-nāma-tantratattvālokarī-nāma-vyākhyā* (Tôh. no. 2510), may have been known both in Java and Ladakh: Woodward, "Esoteric Buddhism", p. 348 n. 55.
69. Phnom Trap?
70. Lokesh Chandra, "The Buddhist Bronzes of Surocolo", in Lokesh Chandra, *Cultural Horizons of India*, vol. 4, p. 124.
71. Lokesh Chandra, the entry "Trailokyavijaya", in Lokesh Chandra, *Dictionary of Buddhist Iconography*. For written evidence, Sundberg, "A Buddhist Mantra". For Trailokyavijaya in India, Linrothe, *Ruthless Compassion.*
72. Cœdès, *Inscriptions du Cambodge*, vol. 3, pp. 76–77.
73. Nihom, *Studies in Indian and Indo-Indonesian Tantrism,* p. 138; Cœdès, *Inscriptions du Cambodge*, vol. 2, pp. 48–50 (stanzas 1 and 4).
74. At Ajanta and Aurangabad. See Brancaccio, *The Buddhist Caves at Aurangabad,* pp. 160–61. Chapter 24 of the *Lotus Sūtra* lists twelve perils, but a list of eight became established in Tibet. There is a Tibetan icon whose Sanskrit name is Ekādaśamukha Aṣṭabhayatrāṇa (in the Narthang Pantheon). See Lokesh Chandra, *Buddhist Iconography*, vol. 1, p. 245, no. 631.
75. Cœdès, *Inscriptions du Cambodge*, vol. 6, pp. 168–69.
76. Discovered Songkhla, Thailand, illustrated in Piriya Krairiksh, *Art in Peninsular Thailand Prior to the Fourteenth Century A. D.* (Bangkok: Fine Arts Department, 1980), pl. 62, pp. 202–203. Studholme, *The Origins of oṃ maṇipadme hūṃ*, p. 138, *ekādaśaśīrṣa*. This term is also found earlier in the text, part 1, chap. 2 (= Studholme pp. 122–23). I thank Phillip Green for pinpointing these passages.
77. As argued by Green, "The Many Faces of Lokeśvara". There is a Sanskrit text of the seventh century or earlier and various Chinese versions, including ones by Xuanzang, 602–64 (*T.* 1071) and Amoghavajra (*T.* 1069). For the possible connection between the Eight Perils and the Eleven-headed Avalokiteśvara, see note 74.
78. Cœdès, *Inscriptions du Cambodge*, vol. 3, pp. 66–69.
79. Finot, "Lokeçvara en Indochine", p. 252.

80. Baptiste and Zéphir, *L'Art khmer dans les collections du musée Guimet*, pp. 183–85, for the number of *caitya* in the group and their present location. Illustrated also in Jessup and Zéphir, *Sculpture of Angkor*, pp. 242–44. For descriptions of the two *caitya* in the National Museum of Cambodia, Giteau, *Guide du Musée National* 2, pp. 11–12 (C. 12.5 = Ga 1734), 14–15 (C. 12.9 = Ga 1735). Also, for one of these two (Ga 1735), Lobo (ed.), *Angkor: Göttliches Erbe Kambodschas*, pp. 146–47. I thank Bertrand Porte for sending me the cataloguing sheets for Ga 1734 and Ga 1735. Although the *caitya* are sometimes referred to as boundary stones, how exactly they functioned cannot be determined. Miniature stūpas produced in substantial quantities in India in exactly this time period, at Bodhgaya, most likely served a memorial function. See Woodward, "The Life of the Buddha in the Pala Monastic Environment".
81. See Gutschow, *The Nepalese Caitya*. On early *caitya* (eighth century), Avalokiteśvara and Vajrapāṇi are placed on opposite faces (p. 113).
82. For this tradition, Bautze-Picron, "Le groupe des huit grands bodhisatva".
83. Sharrock, "Garuḍa, Vajrapāṇi, and Religious Change", pp. 131–32, called it "Vajrapāṇi-Trailokyavijaya". Lobo suggested this "deity should be considered as an early form of Hevajra": Jessup and Zéphir, *Sculpture of Angkor*, p. 244.
84. Fremantle, "A Study of the Guhyasamāja Tantra". There are various partial translations. Chap. 1: Tucci, *The Theory and Practice of the Mandala*, pp. 98–104. Chap. 6: Wayman, *Yoga of the Guhyasamāja Tantra*, pp. 25–28. Chap. 7: Snellgrove, "The Tantras", pp. 221–24. Chap. 12: Wayman, *Yoga of the Guhyasamāja Tantra*, pp. 28–35. For the historical position of the text, Sanderson, "The Śaiva Age", pp. 141–45 and Tanaka, "Nāgabodhi's *Śrī-guhyasamājamaṇḍalopāyikā-viṃśati-vidhi*".
85. Wayman, *Yoga of the Guhyasamāja Tantra*, pp. 126–27 (*Niṣpannayogāvalī* #2, the other *Guhyasamāja* maṇḍalas being #1 and #20, both Mañjuvajra).
86. Wayman, *Yoga of the Guhyasamāja Tantra*, pp. 30–31.
87. For studies of Vajrasattva in Cambodia, Sharrock, "Discussion of the Vajrasattva of Barong Lovéa Em, Kandāl" and Estève and Vincent, "L'about inscrit du musée national du Cambodge".
88. Wayman, *Yoga of the Guhyasamāja Tantra*, pp. 26, 28.
89. Tucci, *The Theory and Practice of the Mandala*, p. 100.
90. I thank Phillip Green for making a draft translation of the passage, stanzas 91–94 in chap. 13 (using the text in Fremantle, "Study", p. 282).
91. Chirapat Prapandvidya, "The Sab Bāk Inscription". Also, Estève, "Étude critique des phénomènes de syncrétisme religieux", pp. 541–46.
92. Bunker and Latchford, *Adoration and Glory*, pp. 184–85. All four faces are illustrated in Spink, *A Divine Art*, pp. 56–59.
93. One study is Nandana, *The Iconography of Avalokiteśvara*, pp. 320–26.
94. Bhattacharyya, *The Indian Buddhist Iconography*, pp. 197–98. The Buddha Akşobhya is on top of the head according to the text; in Cambodia the Buddha is shown in meditation, however, not in the earth-touching gesture.

95. The Honolulu stele is illustrated in Woodward, "The *Karandavyuha Sutra*", p. 79. Bronze: Bunker and Latchford, *Adoration and Glory*, no. 64, pp. 196–98 (private collection) and no. 67, pp. 204–205 (Museum of Fine Arts, Boston).
96. For illustrations, Sharrock, "The Mystery of the Face Towers", pp. 275 and 281. A related bronze now in the National Palace Museum, Taipei, is illustrated in Latchford and Bunker, *Khmer Bronzes*, p. 401. I thank Christian Luczanits for his observations concerning the votive tablet. For a Saṃvara-Guhyasamāja-Hevajra triad in a Pāla manuscript, Kim, *Receptacles of the Sacred: Illustrated Manuscripts and the Buddhist Book Cult in South Asia*, pp. 194–96.

References

Aymonier, Étienne. *Le Cambodge*. 3 vols. Paris: Ernest Leroux, 1900–04.

Baptiste, Pierre, and Thierry Zéphir. *L'Art khmer dans les collections du musée Guimet*. Paris: Éditions de la Réunion des musées nationaux, 2008.

Bautze-Picron, Claudine. "Le groupe des huit grands bodhisatva en Inde: genèse et développement". In *Living a Life in Accord with Dhamma: Papers in Honor of Professor Jean Boisselier on His Eightieth Birthday*, edited by Natasha Eilenberg, M. C. Subhadradis Diskul, and Robert L. Brown, pp. 1–55. Bangkok: Silpakorn University, 1997.

_____. "The Universal Compassionate Bodhisattva". *Silk Road Art and Archaeology* 10 (2004): 225–90.

Bhattacharya, Kamaleswar. *Les religions brahmaniques dans l'ancien Cambodge*. Paris: École française d'Extrême-Orient, 1961.

Bhattacharyya, Benoytosh. *The Indian Buddhist Iconography*. Calcutta: Firma K.L. Mukhopadhyay, 1968.

Bizot, F. "Notes sur les *yantra* bouddhiques d'Indochine". In *Tantric and Taoist Studies in Honour of R.A. Stein*, edited by Michel Strickmann, vol. 1, pp. 155–91. Bruxelles : Institut belge des hautes études chinoises, 1981.

Boisselier, Jean. *La statuaire khmère et son évolution*. 2 vols. Saigon: École française d'Extrême-Orient, 1955.

_____."Précisions sur quelques images khmères d'Avalokiteśvara: les bas-reliefs de Bantãy Čhmàr". *Arts Asiatiques* 11 (1964): 73–89. Translated as "Identification of Some Khmer Images of Avalokiteśvara: the Bantãy Chmàr Bas-reliefs". In *Studies on the Art of Ancient Cambodia: Ten Articles by Jean Boisselier*, translated and edited by Natasha Eilenberg and Robert L. Brown, pp. 305–40. Phnom Penh: Reyum, 2008.

_____. *Le Cambodge*. Paris: A. et J. Picard, 1966.

Brancaccio, Pia. *The Buddhist Caves at Aurangabad: Transformations in Art and Religion*. Leiden and Boston: Brill, 2011.

Bronkhorst, Johannes. *Buddhism in the Shadow of Brahmanism*. Leiden: Brill, 2011.

Bühnemann, Gudrun. *Buddhist Deities of Nepal: Iconography in Two Sketchbooks*. Lumbini: Lumbini International Research Institute, 2003.

Bunker, Emma C., and Douglas Latchford. *Adoration and Glory: The Golden Age of Khmer Art*. Chicago: Art Media Resources, 2004.

_____. *Khmer Bronzes: New Interpretations of the Past*. Chicago: Art Media Resources, 2011.

Chirapat Prapandvidya. "The Sab Bāk Inscription: Evidence of an Early Vajrayana Buddhist Presence in Thailand" *Journal of the Siam Society* 78, pt. 2 (1990): 11–14.

Chulalongkorn, King of Siam. *Phra rātchaphitthī sipsǭng dūan* [Royal Ceremonies of the Twelve Months]. Bangkok: Khlang Witthaya, 1964.

Clark, Joyce, ed. *Bayon: New Perspectives*. Bangkok: River Books, 2007.

Cœdès, George. "La stèle de Tép Praṇaṃ (Cambodge). *Journal Asiatique* 10th series, vol. 11 (1908): 203–28.

_____. "Les inscriptions de Bàt Čuṃ". *Journal Asiatique*, 10th series, 12 (1908): 213–54.

_____. *Bronzes khmèrs*. Ars Asiatica 5. Paris and Brussels: van Oest, 1923.

_____. "Études cambodgiennes XXX: À la recherche du Yaçodharāçrama". *Bulletin de l'École française d'Extrême-Orient* 32 (1932): 84–112.

_____. *Inscriptions du Cambodge*. 8 vols. Hanoi and Paris: École française d'Extrême-Orient, 1937–66.

_____. "Un *yantra* récemment découvert à Angkor". *Journal Asiatique* 240 (1952): 465–77.

_____. *Recueil des inscriptions du Siam Deuxième Partie: inscriptions de Dvāravatī, de Çrīvijaya et de Lavo*. Bangkok: Siam Society, 1961.

Conze, Edward. *The Perfection of Wisdom in Eight Thousand Lines & Its Verse Summary*. Bolinas CA: Four Seasons Foundation, 1973.

Davidson, Ronald M. *Indian Esoteric Buddhism: A Social History of the Tantric Buddhist Movement*. New York: Columbia University Press, 2002.

English, Elizabeth. *Vajrayoginī: her Visualizations, Rituals, and Forms*. Boston: Wisdom Publications, 2002.

Estève, Julia."Étude critique des phénomènes de syncrétisme religieux dans le Cambodge angkorien". Thèse de doctorat, École pratique des hautes études, Paris, July 2009, pp. 297–410.

_____ and Brice Vincent. "L'about inscrit du musée national du Cambodge (K. 943): nouveaux éléments sur le bouddhisme tantrique à l'époque angkorienne". *Arts Asiatiques* 65 (2510): 133–58.

Farrow, G.W. and I. Menon. *The Concealed Essence of the Hevajra Tantra*. Delhi: Motilal Banarsidass, 1992.

Filliozat, Jean. "Sur le çivaïsme et le bouddhisme du Cambodge, à propos de deux livres récents". *Bulletin de l'École française d'Extrême-Orient* 70 (1981): 59–99.

Finot, Louis. "Inscriptions d'Aṅkor, IV, Mébôn". *Bulletin de l'École française d'Extrême-Orient* 25 (1925): 309–52.

_____. "Lokeçvara en Indochine". In *Études asiatiques: publiées à l'occasion du vingt-cinquième anniversaire de l'École française d'Extrême-Orient*, 2 vols., vol. 2, pp. 227–56. Paris: G. Van-Oest, 1925.

Fremantle, Francesca. "A Study of the Guhyasamāja Tantra". Doctoral dissertation, University of London, 1971.

Gaston-Aubert, Jean-Pierre. "Nāga Buddhas in the Dvāravatī Period: A Possible Link between Dvāravatī and Angkor". *Journal of the Siam Society* 98 (2010): 116–50.

Giebel, Rolf W. "The *Chin-kang-ting ching yü-ch'ieh shih-pa-hui chih-kuei*: An Annotated Translation". *Journal of Naritisan Institute for Buddhist Studies* 18 (1995).

Giteau, Madeleine. *Guide du Musée National 2—Pièces d'architecture—Inscriptions*. Phnom Penh: Département du Tourisme [1966].

Golzio, Karl-Heinz, ed. *Inscriptions of Campā based on the editions and translations of Abel Bergaigne, Étienne Aymonier, Louis Finot, Édouard Huber and other French scholars and of the work of R. C. Majumdar: Newly presented, with minor corrections of texts and translations, together with calculations of given dates*. Aachen: Shaker Verlag, 2004.

Goudriaan, Teun. *The Vīṇāśikhatantra: A Śaiva Tantra of the Left Current*. Delhi: Motilal Banarsidass, 1985.

Green, Phillip Scott Ellis. "The Many Faces of Lokeśvara: Tantric Connections in Cambodia between the Tenth and Thirteenth Centuries". *History of Religions* 54, no. 1 (2014): 69–93.

Griffiths, A. and W.A. Southworth. "La stèle d'installation de Śrī Adideveśvara: une nouvelle inscription de Satyavarman trouvée dans le temple de Hoà Lai et son importance pour l'histoire du Pāṇḍuraṅga". *Journal Asiatique* 299 (2011): 271–317.

Gutschow, Niels. *The Nepalese Caitya: 1500 Years of Buddhist Votive Architecture in the Kathmandu Valley*. Stuttgart: Menges, 1997.

Harris, Ian. *Cambodian Buddhism: History and Practice*. Honolulu: University of Hawai'i Press, 2005.

Hodge, Stephen, trans. *The Mahā-Vairocana-Abhisaṃbodhi Tantra with Buddhaguhya's Commentary*. Abingdon, UK and New York: RoutledgeCurzon, 2005.

Jacq-Hergoualc'h, Michel. *The Malay Peninsula: Crossroads of the Maritime Silk Road*. Leiden: Brill, 2002.

Jessup, Helen Ibbitson and Thierry Zéphir. *Sculpture of Angkor and Ancient Cambodia: Millennium of Glory*. Washington: National Gallery of Art, 1997.

Kandahjaya, Hudaya. "Notes on Buddhist Cosmology". *Kristi* 2 (2009): 1–21.

Kim, Jinah. *Receptacles of the Sacred: Illustrated Manuscripts and the Buddhist Book Cult in South Asia*. Berkeley, Los Angeles and London: University of California Press, 2013.

Lalou, Marcelle. *Iconographie des étoffes peintes (paṭa) dans le Mañjuśrīmūlakalpa*. Paris: Geuthner, 1930.

Linrothe, Rob. *Ruthless Compassion: Wrathful Deities in Early Indo-Tibetan Esoteric Buddhist Art*. London: Serindia, 1999.

Lobo, Wibke, ed. *Angkor: Göttliches Erbe Kambodschas*. Bonn: Kunst- und Ausstellungshalle der Bundesrepublik Deutschland, 2007.

Lokesh Chandra. *Buddhist Iconography*. 2 vols. New Delhi: Aditya Prakashan, 1987.

_____. "The Buddhist Bronzes of Surocolo". In *Cultural Horizons of India*, by Lokesh Chandra, vol. 4, pp. 121–47. New Delhi: International Academy of Indian Culture and Aditya Prakashan, 1995.

_____. *Dictionary of Buddhist Iconography*, 15 vols. New Delhi: International Academy of Indian Culture and Aditya Prakashan, 1999–2005.

Lunet de Lajonquière, Étienne. *Inventaire descriptif des monuments du Cambodge*. 3 vols. Paris: Ernest Leroux, 1902–11.

Lunsingh Scheurleer, Pauline and Marijke J. Klokke. *Divine Bronze: Ancient Indonesian Bronzes from A. D. 600 to 1600*. Leiden: Brill, 1988.

Mabbett, Ian."Buddhism in Champa". In *Southeast Asia in the 9th to 14th Centuries*, edited by David G. Marr and A.C. Milner. Singapore: Institute of Southeast Asian Studies, 1986.

Mallmann, Marie-Thérèse de. *Introduction à l'étude d'Avalokiteçvara*. Paris: Presses universitaires de France, 1967.

Mertens, Annemarie. "Beobachtungen zur Herrschaftslegitimation im Ankor-Reich: Die buddhistisch orientierte Vat-Sithor-Inschrift von Jayavarman V". In *Vividharatnakaraṇḍaka: Festgabe für Adelheid Mette*, edited by C. Chojnacki, J.-U. Hartmann and V.M. Tschannerl, pp. 395–411. Indica et Tibetica no. 27. Swisstal-Odendorf, 2000.

Nandana Chutiwongs. *The Iconography of Avalokiteśvara in Mainland Southeast Asia*. Proefschrift, Rijksuniversiteit, Leiden, 1984.

_____. "Le bouddhisme du Champa". In Pierre Baptiste and Thierry Zéphir, *Trésors d'art du Vietnam: la sculpture du Champa*, pp. 65–87. Paris: Réunion des musées nationaux, 2005.

Nguyen, Trian. "Lakṣmīndralokeśvara, Main Deity of the Dong Duong Monastery: A Masterpiece of Cham Art and a New Interpretation". *Artibus Asiae*, 65 (2005): 5–38.

Nihom, Max. *Studies in Indian and Indo-Indonesian Tantrism: The Kuñjarakarṇadharmakathana and the Yogatantra*. Vienna: Sammlung De Nobili, 1994.

Orzech, Charles D. "The 'Great Teaching of Yoga', the Chinese Appropriation of the Tantras, and the Question of Esoteric Buddhism". *Journal of Chinese Religions* 34 (2006): 42–43.

_____. "Esoteric Buddhism under the Tang: From Atikūṭa to Amoghavajra (651–780)". In *Esoteric Buddhism and the Tantras in East Asia*, edited by Charles D. Orzech, Henrik H. Sørensen, and Richard K. Payne, pp. 263–85. Leiden and Boston: Brill, 2011.

Piriya Krairiksh [Phiriya Krairük]. *Art in Peninsular Thailand Prior to the Fourteenth Century A.D.* Bangkok: Fine Arts Department, 1980.

_____. *The Roots of Thai Art.* Translated by Narisa Chakrabongse. Bangkok: River Books, 2012.

Pottier, Christophe. "About Yaçovarman's Buddhist āçrama in Angkor". In *The Buddhist Monastery: A Cross-cultural Survey*, edited by P. Pichard and F. Lagirarde, pp. 199–208. Paris: École française d'Extrême-Orient, 2003.

Sanderson, Alexis. "The Śaiva Religion Among the Khmers (Part 1)". *Bulletin de l'École française d'Extrême-Orient* 90–91 (2003): 349–462.

_____. "Religion and the State: Śaiva Officiants in the Territory of the King's Brahmanical Chaplain". *Indo-Iranian Journal* 47 (2004): 229–300.

_____. "The Śaiva Age — the Rise and Dominance of Śaivism During the Early Medieval Period". In *Genesis and Development of Tantrism*, edited by Shingo Einoo, pp. 41–349. Tokyo: Institute of Oriental Culture, University of Tokyo, 2009.

Schweyer, Anne-Valérie. "Buddhism in Čampā". *Moussons* 13–14 (2009): 313–16.

Sharrock, Peter D. "The Mystery of the Face Towers". In *Bayon: New Perspectives*, ed. Joyce Clark, pp. 230–81. Bangkok: River Books, 2007.

_____. "Garuḍa, Vajrapāṇi, and Religious Change in Jayavarman VII's Angkor", *Journal of Southeast Asian Studies* 40 (2009): 111–51.

_____. "The Nāga-enthroned Buddha of Angkor". In *Khmer Bronzes: New Interpretations of the Past*, by Emma C. Bunker and Douglas Latchford, pp. 481–92. Chicago: Art Media Resources, 2011.

_____. "Discussion of the Vajrasattva of Barong Lovéa Em, Kandāl". In *Khmer Bronzes: New Interpretations of the Past*, by Emma C. Bunker and Douglas Latchford, pp. 493–96. *Chicago*: Art Media Resources, 2011.

_____. "Kīrtipaṇḍita and the Tantras". *Udaya* 10 (2009).

Sherburne, Richard. *The Complete Works of Atīśa*. New Delhi: Aditya Prakashan, 2000.

Skorupski, Tadeusz. *The Sarvadurgatipariśodhana Tantra: Elimination of All Evil Destinies*. Delhi: Motilal Banarsidass, 1983.

Smitthi Siribhadra. "Notes sur un bronze d'époque angkorienne représentant Prajñāpāramitā". In *Art and Archaeology in Thailand II*, pp. 117–19. Bangkok: Fine Arts Department, 1975.

Snellgrove, David, trans. "The Tantras: Supreme Englightenment". In *Buddhist Texts through the Ages*, edited by Edward Conze, pp. 221–24. New York: Harper Torchbooks, 1964.

Snellgrove, David. *Indo-Tibetan Buddhism: Indian Buddhists and Their Tibetan Successors*. Boston: Shambhala, 2002. [1st published 1987.]

_____. *Angkor—Before and After: a Cultural History of the Khmers*. Trumbull CT: Weatherhill, 2004.

Studholme, Alexander. *The Origins of* oṃ maṇipadme hūṃ*: A Study of the Kāraṇḍavyūha Sūtra*. Albany: State University of New York Press, 2002.

Spink. *A Divine Art: Sculpture of South East Asia*. London: Spink, 1997.
Sundberg, Jeffrey Roger. "A Buddhist Mantra Recovered from the Ratu Baka Plateau". *Bijdragen tot de Taal-, Land- en Volkenkunde* 159 (2003): 163–88.
Tajima, Ryujun. *Les deux grands maṇḍalas et la doctrine de l'ésotérisme shingon*. Tokyo: Maison Franco-japonaise; Paris: Presses universitaires de France, 1959.
Tanaka, Kimiaka. "Nāgabodhi's *Śrī-guhyasamājamaṇḍalopāyikā-viṃśati-vidhi—*The Sanskrit Text Restored from the *Vajrācāryanayottama*". In *Genesis and Development of Tantrism*, edited by Shingo Einoo, pp. 425–33. Tokyo: Institute of Oriental Culture, University of Tokyo, 2009.
Tomabechi, Toru. "The extraction of mantra (mantroddhāra) in the Sarvabuddhasamāyogatantra". In *Pramāṇakīrtiḥ: Papers Dedicated to Ernst Steinkellner on the Occasion of his 70th Birthday,* edited by B. Kellner, H. Krasser, H. Lasic, M.T. Much, and H. Tauscher, 2 parts, Wiener Studien zur Tibetologie und Buddhismuskunde 70, part 2, pp. 903–23. Vienna: Arbeitskreis für tibetische und buddhistische Studien, Universität Wien, 2007.
Tucci, Giuseppe. *The Theory and Practice of the Mandala*. New York: Samuel Weiser, 1971.
Wayman, Alex. *Yoga of the Guhyasamāja Tantra*. Delhi: Motilal Banarsidass, 1977.
Woodward, Hiram W., Jr. "Art History: Accomplishments and Opportunities, Hopes and Fears". In *The Study of Thailand*, edited by Eliezer Ayal, pp. 76–77. Athens, Ohio: Center for International Studies, University of Ohio, 1978.
_____. "The Life of the Buddha in the Pala Monastic Environment". *Journal of the Walters Gallery* 48 (1990): 13–27.
Woodward, Hiram. *The Art and Architecture of Thailand From Prehistoric Times through the Thirteenth Century*. Leiden and Boston: Brill, 2003.
_____. "Esoteric Buddhism in Southeast Asia in the Light of Recent Scholarship: a Review Article". *Journal of Southeast Asian Studies* 35 (2004): 329–54.
_____. "The *Karandavyuha Sutra* and Buddhist Art in 10th-Century Cambodia". In *Buddhist Art: Form & Meaning*, edited by Pratapaditya Pal, pp. 70–83. Mumbai: Marg Publications, 2007.
_____. "Bianhong, Mastermind of Borobudur?". *Pacific World: Journal of the Institute of Buddhist Studies*, 3rd series, vol. 11 (2009): 25–60.
_____. "The Temple of Dong Duong and the *Kāraṇḍavyūha Sūtra*". In *From Beyond the Eastern Horizon: Essays in Honour of Lokesh Chandra*, edited by Manjushree Gupta, pp. 43–52. New Delhi: Aditya Prakashan, 2011.

8

REVISITING THE CULT OF "ŚIVA-BUDDHA" IN JAVA AND BALI

Andrea Acri

INTRODUCTION

As testified to by the extant written sources and archaeological remains, Śivaism was the dominant religion in Java and Bali. However, Śivaism coexisted alongside Buddhism for more than a millennium, from *circa* the fifth century CE through the late fifteenth century in Java, and on Bali until today.[1] The coexistence of the two religions eventually gave rise to phenomena of confrontation, dialectic and integration that have attracted scholarly attention since the late nineteenth century. The most influential studies have sanctioned the view that the variety of "Hinduism" widespread in Java and Bali was fundamentally syncretic in character, forming a blend of Śaiva and Bauddha elements. What has been generally termed the "religion of Śiva-Buddha" or "Hindu-Buddhist religion" (in Indonesian *Agama Siwa-Buda* or *Agama Hindu-Buda*), and ascribed to the Hindu-Buddhist era (*jaman Hindu-Buda*) of Javanese history, has been characterized mostly in terms of "identity", "syncretism", "parallelism" or "coalition". Whether the emphasis be laid on equality, integration or symbiosis between the two systems, their respective deities or their paramount goals, the dynamics shaping the resulting "cult of Śiva-Buddha" have often been regarded as having been subjected to distinctive local features that set this tradition apart from the more rigidly sectarian South Asian traditions from which it originated.[2]

Even though our understanding of (Tantric) Śivaism and (Tantric) Buddhism in the Indian Subcontinent and Tibet has improved dramatically over the last two decades, the majority of the most recent studies touching upon these religious traditions in Indonesia appear to be insufficiently aware of these developments. It seems thus worthwhile to discuss once again the relationship between Śivaism and Buddhism in the Subcontinent and in the Archipelago from a comparative perspective, in the hope that this approach will stimulate a cross-fertilization between the disciplines of Indology and Indonesian studies.

The basic idea that my paper tries to convey is that the nature of the equation of the paramount principles of Śivaism and Buddhism as expressed by a number of Old Javanese sources from the Singhasari-Majapahit period has not always been correctly grasped, and that alleged instances of "Javanese syncretism" should now be challenged.

SURVEYING THE APPROACHES TO THE JAVANO-BALINESE "ŚIVA-BUDDHA RELIGION"

The 'identity' paradigm was at first formulated by Kern.[3] On account of his reading of the Old Javanese Kakawin *Sutasoma* by Mpu Tantular (*c*.fourteenth century CE), he suggested that in ancient Java there occurred a mixture or blending (*vermenging*) of Śiva and Buddha. As he based himself mostly on the comparison with Nepalese and Indian sources, he did not consider the Javanese local culture to have been an important factor in shaping this situation. This view was supported by Krom[4] on the basis of iconographical evidence, but adjusted by Rassers[5] who, although still endorsing the term "blending", explained it in terms of local background and ancestral myths of the Malayo-Polinesian tribe, especially as reflected by the popular Balinese tale of Bubhukṣa and Gagaṅ Akiṅ.[6] Both Krom[7] and Rassers[8] alongside the term "blending" also used "syncretism". Use of the term syncretism was endorsed by Zoetmulder,[9] but was opposed by Pigeaud,[10] who defined the relationship of Śivaism and Buddhism in Majapahit Java as "parallelism". According to him, that dichotomous religious structure developed as a result of the classificatory attitude and dualistic pattern of thought that were common features of the ancient Javanese culture.

Unsatisfied with the previous perspectives, Gonda[11] employed the term "coalition", which from the point of view of theology implies a search for the same ultimate goal using different and distinct methods. To corroborate his theory, Gonda[12] pointed at the occurrence of similar phenomena in Nepal and Cambodia, and showed that many Old Javanese sources equated not only Śiva with Buddha but also with the highest manifestation of truth belonging to several other schools as well. Gonda's view was endorsed by Soebadio,[13] according to whom this coalition involved no mixing of systems, but rather presupposed different ways to achieve the ultimate truth, just as two different paths lead towards the summit of a mountain. This idea was adopted also by Supomo,[14] de Casparis[15] and Santoso.[16]

A view somewhat closer to Pigeaud's "parallelism" was elaborated by Ensink,[17] who analysed Śivaism and Buddhism in Majapahit Java as a dual system based on the concept of bipolarity that is found in Javanese wayang puppetry as well as in the Indian tradition. Ensink also took account of the more recent Balinese tradition — and especially the aforementioned tale of Bubhukṣa and Gagaṅ Akiṅ first analysed by Rassers — to show how the local people perceived the two religions: Śivaism was regarded to be the older system, while Buddhism the younger, yet the most perfect (or effective) one.

More than a decade later, Nihom[18] challenged the assumption that the Śiva-Buddha coalition of Majapahit Java was a local distinguishing characteristic and — to an even greater extent than Kern and Gonda — emphasized data from the Indian Subcontinent. He argued that the admixture of Śaiva and Bauddha elements found in East Java has to be seen as a common feature of a significant part of Tantric Bauddha literature from the Subcontinent as well as Tibet, where it is virtually impossible to distinguish the Bauddha and Śaiva elements as separated and opposed.

In a recent groundbreaking article, Hunter[19] has challenged the idea that the Lord Śiva-Buddha (*bhaṭāra śivabuddha*) often mentioned in Majapahit sources was part of an established syncretic religious system, arguing that such a situation was due to the politico-religious hegemony introduced by the ruler Kṛtanagara (r. 1265–92 CE), who was deified as a form of both Śiva and Buddha. Hunter has further defined the "syncretism" documented in literary works and artistic remains of the Singhasari period of East Javanese history as a "series of initiatives undertaken by Kṛtanagara with the ultimate aim of forcing a fusion of elements that represented the metaphysical reflection of his pragmatic political policies".[20]

RECENT APPROACHES TO ŚAIVA-BAUDDHA DIALECTICS IN THE INDIAN SUBCONTINENT

Considerable advancements in the understanding of Śivaism and Buddhism and their mutual relationship in the medieval Indian Subcontinent and

Tibet have been achieved in the last two decades or so, mostly thanks to the editing, translating and studying of various scriptures belonging to the vast corpus of nearly coeval Sanskrit and Tibetan textual materials related to the category of Tantra.[21] What are now called Tantric Śivaism and Tantric Buddhism by scholars have turned out to share significant common elements, such as an interdependence of discourse in such disparate domains as philosophy, soteric practices, ritual and iconography. This complex phenomenon of mutual dialectic influence, interchange and interdependence has triggered a wide range of etic interpretations, but three main hermeneutical models have come to dominate the scholarly debate.

The first position, called "substratum model" by its main advocate David Seyfort Ruegg,[22] posits an early "pan-Indian religious substratum" or common cultic stock — mainly constituted by "folk" religion — that would *ex hypothesi* form the common source from which both Śaiva and Bauddha traditions derived, and to which they ultimately owe their shared common elements. Seyfort Ruegg questions that the two religions make sense as discrete and opposed entities "requiring to be kept neatly apart at all levels of analysis".[23] He further detects in the original textual sources the existence of the emic opposition between the categories of *lokottara* and *laukika*, respectively "supra-mundane" and "mundane". This contrastive structure distinguishes two superordinate dimensions within any manifestation of belief, ritual or conduct, where the lower one (*laukika*) is opposed in the sense of relative, inferior and subordinate to the higher one (*lokottara*), or ultimate.[24]

The "substratum model" has been criticized by Alexis Sanderson,[25] mainly on account of its being an abstract and unverifiable, i.e. inferred but never perceived, concept or entity. Sanderson himself has elaborated a paradigm that has been later labelled by his readers, and in particular by his main criticizer Seyfort Ruegg, "borrowing model". Sanderson's research on Sanskrit primary sources of the Śaiva Mantramārga and the Bauddha Yogatantra has highlighted the divide existing between the two traditions, and justified the common elements on the grounds of a great deal of mutual influences, or even manifest plagiarism, occurring between both systems — especially the incorporation of materials of the former, and arguably earlier, textual corpus into the latter. Sanderson has found strong evidence for incorporation of scriptures of the Śaiva canon into the Bauddha Yoganiruttaratantras, and has defined the origin of the dependence of Bauddha Yoginītantras on Śaiva scriptural sources as a "pious plagiarism" of the latter religion on the former.[26] Furthermore, he has stressed the somewhat syncretic attitude of lay devotionalism, characterized by an "inclusivist" attitude that was equally followed in the Subcontinent as in the periphery, e.g., in Java and Cambodia.[27] Rather than a simple opposition between *laukika* and *lokottara*, Sanderson distinguishes in Śaiva texts an emic strategy of polemicizing with different religious and philosophical systems by placing them on a hierarchical scale as "lower level" truths.

In addition to the "substratum model" and the "borrowing model", we can distinguish a third popular paradigm, which Seyfort Ruegg[28] has called "agonistic view", namely "a more or less secular and historicist interpretation of the schema as representing the agonistic or hostile relation 'Buddhism' vs. 'Hinduism' in the world, i.e. in history". According to this view, hostility or (ant)agonism between the two religions is reflected in either actual historical events, such as various forms of competition for royal support, devotees and resources, occasional interreligious violence, or iconographic representations, such as Hindu gods being trampled upon or subdued by Buddhist deities, and vice versa.

The textual evidence presented and analysed in a persuasive manner by Sanderson makes the "borrowing model" an entirely plausible and effective hermeneutical tool. Whereas this standpoint seamlessly espouses the "agonistic model" insofar as it assumes the existence of a divide between the borrower and the source tradition, it may also be used alongside the "substratum model". Notwithstanding his criticism of the model proposed by Sanderson, Seyfort Ruegg himself[29] seems to have adopted a somewhat conciliating position when acknowledging that the two models are not necessarily exclusive of each other, for they can be applied to particular cases and, in any event, in order that the borrowing could take place meaningfully one has to suppose a shared ground represented by his postulated "common substratum". This position is consonant with the attempt by Sferra[30] to integrate the two models, pointing out that they both retain validity insofar as Śivaism and Buddhism share a

> "common way of interpreting reality and of relating to it, which is expressed in a common soteriological strategy". This common "substratum of beliefs and soteric practices" is the presupposition that allowed Buddhist authors to include passages or verses from non-dualist Hindu Tantras in their scriptures, and that permitted Hindu redactors to act in a similar way. Seen from such a perspective, this "substratum", unlike the supposed substratum of the folk religion, is neither radically inaccessible nor hidden.[31]

THE THREE MODELS APPLIED TO ANCIENT JAVANESE ŚIVAISM AND BUDDHISM

The most popular hermeneutical paradigm applied to the study of Śivaism and Buddhism in ancient Java appears to be the "secular-historicist view", which lays emphasis on political, social and historical realities. With respect to pre tenth-century Central Java, one theory has regarded Śivaism as standing in opposition to Buddhism and assumed that the former succeeded the latter. Advocates of this theory were Coedès,[32] Krom[33] and de Casparis,[34] who opposed the Bauddha dynasty of the (non-Javanese) Śailendras, which sponsored the building of Borobudur, to the Śaiva Sañjaya "dynasty" of Javanese pedigree. The latter line of kings would have erected the temple complex of Prambanan in order to celebrate the victory of Śivaism over Buddhism and the expulsion of the Śailendras from Java.

Following the criticism expressed earlier by Damais,[35] Jordaan[36] has challenged this view, arguing that Central Javanese rulers freely patronized both religions, which peacefully co-existed on the island. Pointing at the fact that the Śivagṛha inscription of 856 CE describes several important parts of what seems to be the complex of Prambanan, which may have been built before the expulsion of the Śailendras in 855, and furthermore at the stylistic resemblance and physical proximity of Bauddha and Śaiva temples at the complex, he maintains that the two religions closely and harmoniously coexisted.[37] Relying upon previous works by Bosch[38] and Sarkar,[39] Jordaan concluded that emphasis should be laid on the input by India, where "no sharp distinction existed between the followers of various Hindu and Buddhists creeds", and "existing differences were [...] obliterated even more in the course of the ongoing development of Mahāyāna in a tantristic direction".[40] Jordaan and Wessing are further "inclined to question the validity of some current designations [such] as 'Hinduism' and 'Buddhism' and to wonder whether these terms do full justice to the ideas of the Javanese of the times [...] Both early Hinduism and Buddhism were flexible enough to accommodate and utilize each other's icons".[41]

This view closely accords with that elaborated by Nihom with respect to East Javanese Tantric Śivaism and Buddhism. Nihom, who relied upon the "substratum model" elaborated by Seyfort Ruegg, maintained that

> the academic distinction of "Buddhist" and "Hindu" texts may obscure rather than reveal. Upon reflection, this is not so strange, for the notion that esoteric Buddhism and Hinduism were separate in the sense of being incarnate as "churches" around the middle of the first millennium

> in the Subcontinent may indeed prove to be a false superimposition of European religious history not only upon the history of the texts, but more generally in terms of social history.[42]

In criticizing the view, advanced by Teeuw and Robson,[43] that the Kakawin *Kuñjarakarṇa* was uniquely the product of the syncretistic Śiva-Buddha system of the Majapahit period, Nihom[44] perceived that text and similar ones as thoroughly Tantric Buddhist products, which could be properly understood only in the light of a South Asian religious substratum mingling Hindu and Bauddha elements. Arguing against "the accepted notion that the admixture of Hindu and Buddhist tantric or tantristic elements is both a peculiar and pervasive characteristic of the religious culture of the islands and mainland of Southeast Asia", Nihom remarked that

> the "syncretism" of "Hindu" and "Buddhist" divinities in these *maṇḍala*s is ultimately of Indian origin. Hence, in future, a perception of the co-existence of "Hindu" and "Buddhist" elements in the Archipelago may not be taken *sui generis* as evidence for Indonesian syncretism.[45]

A position that seems to be middling between the "agonistic model" and the "substratum model" is that elaborated by Miksic.[46] While emphasizing the existence of an actual divide and antagonism between Hinduism and Buddhism in ancient Java, as documented by the alleged existence of unambiguously divided architectural and iconographical motifs and the occurrence of a "healthy competition" in order to gain royal support, Miksic passingly conceded that "adherents of both religions used the same substratum of artistic vocabulary to convey their philosophies".[47]

Hunter's study on the Śiva-Buddha syncretism of Singhasari, while apparently conforming to the "agonistic model", attempts at integrating socio-political aspects with theological ones. According to Hunter,

> Krtanagara's greatest achievement may be that in some sense he succeeded in making his own person the locus of unity between the two main streams of East Javanese religion, thereby affecting a religious union aimed at compelling the unseen forces of the cosmos to fall in behind his scheme of internal and external political unification.[48]

Hence the fusion of Śaiva and Bauddha themes in Majapahit Java is to be attributed to the political and metaphysical agenda of Kṛtanagara, who pursued both goals of political hegemony and religious salvation.

A position that entirely conforms to the "borrowing model" is the one advanced by Soebadio[49] when analysing the inter-textual and doctrinal relationships between Śivaism and Buddhism in Sanskrit-Old Javanese religious scriptures of the Tutur class. Substitution of Bauddha deities with Śaiva ones and vice versa is especially common in Tuturs of both religious orientations. Passages of the Śaiva *Jñānasiddhānta* run parallel with others found in the Bauddha *Saṅ Hyaṅ Kamahāyānikan* and the *Kalpabuddha*, but the latter texts substitute relevant terms used in the *Jñānasiddhānta* (e.g. the knowledge of non-duality personified into Vāgīśvarī or Praṇava Tridevī, chapter 3, pp. 80–83) into their Bauddha counterparts (e.g. Prajñāpāramitā). An analogous instance of "translation" of Śaiva ideas into Bauddha terms occurs in the *Sutasoma* Kakawin,[50] whose canto 41 contains speculations on the Bauddha *advayajñāna* or *advayayoga* and the Śaiva "way of dying" (*parātramārga*), both linked with the mantra *aṃ-aḥ*. The supreme goal, called *paraṃbrahma* in the *Jñānasiddhānta*, is changed into *advayajñāna* in the *Saṅ Hyaṅ Kamahāyānikan* and the *Sutasoma*.

In his brief study on Javano-Balinese Śivaism, Sanderson[51] has drawn the attention on the fact that in the Balinese ritual of *Sūrya Sevana*[52] we find Prajñādevī and Parimitādevī as the last two of the eight goddesses of the eight fingers that are counted in the preliminary ritual of the cleansing of the hands. According to Sanderson, these two goddesses were evidently created out of the Bauddha Prajñāpāramitā. Therefore, referring to the ritual "contaminations" which have occurred in Bali, Cambodia and Kashmir, Sanderson expressed the view that "the needs and expectations of the clients have lead to thoroughly syncretistic developments in three independent cultural contexts".[53] This attitude towards eclecticism is found in India as well, especially in the South Indian *paddhati*s, which were intended primarily as manuals whose aim is to guide the priest through the vast forest of Śaiva ritual.

REASSESSING THE SOURCES

On the basis of my reading of Old Javanese texts I have come to realize that any claim made in secondary literature that Śivaism and Buddhism were in Java and Bali syncretically united needs to be checked on the basis of a careful and impartial assessment of the extant textual evidence. Several important textual passages indeed appear to have been either incorrectly grasped or tendentiously (or perhaps subconsciously) misinterpreted, sometimes in order to attune them to modern political or religious agendas.[54]

As noted by Miksic[55] and Santiko,[56] even in the Singhasari-Majapahit period Śivaism and Buddhism did not constitute a merger or synthesis of religious doctrine or praxis but maintained their independence as two discrete systems, having separate types of religious structures for their respective priesthoods. My investigation into the corpus of premodern Old Javanese-cum-Sanskrit scriptures of Śaiva, and more rarely Bauddha, persuasion popularly known as Tuturs or Tattvas[57] has confirmed this view. In what may be identified as the earliest scriptures belonging to that corpus,[58] which stand closer, with respect to doctrine, to Sanskrit prototypical sources from South Asia, I have found no claim of equality between Śaiva and Bauddha elements. In fact no trace whatsoever of Buddhism as a system or of elements directly traceable to Buddhism is found in those sources. It is only in later sources, in all likelihood compiled during the Singhasari and Majapahit period (*c*.thirteenth–sixteenth century CE), or even later on Bali, that Tuturs invariably acknowledge the existence of three different "sects" called *tripakṣa*, namely Śaivas, Ṛṣis and Bauddhas or Saugatas, and to refer to the "Lord Śiva-Buddha".

This state of affairs is mirrored in Kakawins written by Bauddha authors in East Java from the thirteenth to the fifteenth century, as well as in contemporary related pseudo-historical works, such as the *Deśawarṇana*, *Raṅga Lawe*, *Pararaton* and *Kiduṅ Sunda*. These sources are also ready to acknowledge the equality of the Bauddha and Śaiva ultimate goals — yet not their soteric, yogic or ritual paths, which are clearly kept distinct. Correspondences between certain series of popular deities belonging to both traditions are also common. For instance, the Kakawin *Arjunawijaya*[59] of Mpu Tantular (stanzas 26.4–31.1), while maintaining that there is no distinction between Buddha and Śiva, states that they are distinct chosen objects of worship (*iṣṭidharma*) of the respective sects of the *tripakṣa*. It may thus be inferred that these religious streams maintained their integrity and peculiarity in the doctrinal, ritual and priestly domain, and therefore this unification is to be taken only in the ultimate sense. Similarly, *Sutasoma* 42.2 describes the yoga path of the Bauddhas and Śaivas not only as distinct, being respectively *advayajñāna* and *ṣaḍaṅgayoga*, but also leading to different goals; what it is claimed is that the followers of either path, in order to be successful, should know about the other as well. Mpu Tantular in stanzas 40.6 and 41.5 claims that the Bauddha path is more advanced and effective than the Śaiva one, which could become a pitfall to the true seeker of the ultimate Buddhist liberation insofar as it bestows supernatural powers that may lead the yogin astray. Furthermore, as already noted by Aoyama,[60] a marked critical attitude is evidently lying behind the whole *Sutasoma*, conceived as a Bauddha denunciation of the aberrant practices of certain Śaiva currents, embodied by the figure of the man-eater demon Poruṣāda. The pacification and "conversion" of protégées of Śiva by prince Sutasoma thus reveals a Bauddha attempt to "convert" Śaiva followers to Buddhism.

With respect to the alleged syncretistic stance of the poem, we may here reiterate the point already made by Santoso, namely that

> it is clear that the view that Śiva (or any other Hindu deity) may be regarded as Buddha is not held by the adherents of Hinduism. And in so far as Kern has claimed that Śiva is identified with Buddha, it can only be said that at times Śiva, like Brahmā, has appeared as a Bodhisattva. It is self-evident then, that had there been any attempt to bring about a unification of the two deities (which we do not concede) the initiative would come from the Buddhist and not from the Hindu.[61]

As is persuasively argued by Sanderson,[62] the famous passage of the *Sutasoma* equating the realities (*dhātu*) of the Buddha (*jinatva*) and Śiva (*śivatattva*) (139.5) actually says that "the Lord Buddha is both the Buddha and Śiva" rather than espousing "a doctrine of absolute equality between the two religions within a reality beyond both". Thus, to say that the two realities are but two manifestations of the ultimate reality of Buddha amounts to a thoroughly Bauddha perspective, similar to that exposed by Mpu Dusun in the *Kuñjarakarṇa* when stating that "I, Vairocana, am embodied both as the Buddha and as Śiva" (23.4bcd).[63] Several other passages of the *Sutasoma* that have been seen as evidence of either syncretism or coalition, namely 40.1–42.5 and 138.1–7 — to which we may add verses 22.1–23.4 of the *Kuñjarakarṇa*[64] — rather represent attempts from the Bauddhas to appropriate elements of the Śaivas and accommodate them within their own system, perhaps in order to draw support from the followers of the latter tradition. Similar considerations may apply to the Bauddha appropriation of elements of Śaiva iconography.

Now, this kind of attitude conforms quite well to Paul Hacker's famous definition of "inclusivism" (*inklusivismus*):

> Inclusivism is a concept I use to describe data from the area which we term Indian religion and, in particular, Indian religious philosophy. Inclusivism means declaring that a central conception of an alien religious or weltanschaulich group is identical with this or that central conception of the group to which one belongs oneself. To inclusivism there mostly belongs, explicitly or implicitly, the assertion that the alien declared to be identical with one's own is in some way subordinate or inferior to the latter. In addition, no proof is generally furnished for the identity of the alien with one's own.[65]

Thus, even though inclusivism admits that alien religious systems may contain some truth it also regards the home religion as superior in that it teaches (more effectively) a higher level, or greater number, of religious truths. This viewpoint may be compared to the hierarchical distinction between levels of truth that amounts to the emic distinction between *lokottara* and *laukika*. However, from several statements of the *Sutasoma*, such as the famous statement *bhinneka tuṅggal ika* ("they are different; they are one") of canto 139.5d, it is actually possible to understand the author's standpoint to stand closer to Griffiths'[66] definition of "pluralism", according to which (coexisting) separate but equal systems are all effective in bringing salvation about. This is different from the inclusivist perspective, which tends to favour one primary system while absorbing into it certain elements belonging to an alien tradition. Be this as it may, all claims of equivalence of realities made by Old Javanese Bauddha sources must be reconsidered in the light of the fact that for both inclusivistic and pluralistic thought equality does not imply identity. The same holds true with respect to Hunter's claim that

> the shift in emphasis within *kakawin* towards a "principle of equivalence" among the "three major sects" [...] must be linked to the career of Krtanagara, and his attempt to ensure political unity (and hegemony) through a symbolic amalgamation of the major religious currents of his time.[67]

On the basis of the available evidence, it is perhaps too early to claim that "amalgamation" (which reminds us of Kern's *vermenging*) is inherent to the "principle of equivalence", which could otherwise be interpreted as a manifestation of the zealous activity of Bauddha authors and their courtly sponsors seeking to justify the appropriation of Śaiva elements into their pantheons. Even though we may concede that Kṛtanagara's policy implied a genuine attempt on his side to syncretistically merge the two religions, we must remember that "there was never a figure prior to Kṛtanagara, nor one following him, who is described again and again in the inscriptional and literary records as *Bhatara Siwa-Buddha*".[68] This fact suggests that his peculiar view was not endorsed by the majority of the contemporary religious clergies.[69]

It may also be pointed out, as noted by Sferra with respect to South Asian Sanskrit texts,[70] that claims of equivalence between Śaiva and Bauddha supreme realities are a prominent feature of non-dualist Tantric literature. It may thus be argued that monism makes it easier to justify every aspect of existence as relative manifestations of one and the same absolute. It is entirely plausible that Kṛtanagara's milieu, as suggested by the textual references and iconographical elements that are traceable to it,[71] partook of the non-dualist and antinomian currents centred on the cult of Kāla-Bhairava, a deity that in the Subcontinent is worshiped in both Śaiva and Bauddha circles.

Features that are comparable to those attested in non-dualist Tantric sources are also detectable in certain Old Javanese and Old Sundanese Tuturs which, judging from their colophons and palaeographic features, were in all probability composed in the late Majapahit period (sixteenth century) in circumscribed mountainous enclaves where Kabuyutans (i.e. "scriptoria") were located.[72] Showing a marked predilection for mystical, moralistic and didactic purposes, these texts[73] are the expression of a kind of "popular" religiosity characterized by an embedded approach to religious experience, where Śaiva and Bauddha elements are reconfigured along markedly "localized" lines, and where the divide between the two religious schools seems to have become less important and virtually imperceptible. Although the paucity of historical information on the social contexts in which these texts were composed and used does not allow us to draw any firm conclusion, it may be argued that this type of syncretistic approach to religious experience was confined to certain isolated milieus rather than constituting the mainstream.

Shifting our attention to Bali, it may be noted, if only fleetingly, that several Tuturs among those composed in the period following the fall of Majapahit in the sixteenth century share similar characteristics with Tuturs stemming from the Sundanese enclaves described above. These texts, composed in Old Javanese but featuring many Balinisms, bear witness to a status quo where Śaiva and Bauddha elements lose their distinct character and coalesce into a mystical synthesis — witness the frequent references to Bhaṭāra Śiva-Buddha, and claims that the doctrines and yogic techniques they describe are the preserve of the Brahmans of the *tripakṣa* indistinctively.[74] It is to this unwieldy and virtually unstudied corpus of texts that modern *Agama Hindu Bali* owes, in many respects, its textual foundation.

Yet, in spite of the apparent lack of divide between Śaivas and Bauddhas propounded by these predominantly mystical Balinese sources, one hardly notes a syncretistic amalgamation between the two streams. Rather, the relationship between Buddhism and Śivaism on Bali since the Majapahit period seems to have assumed the contours of a symbiosis or Śaiva-Bauddha coalition — not so much in the domain of doctrine as in that of ritual. As the inferior status of the Pedanda Buddha and its subsidiary — albeit indispensable — role in ritual with respect to Pedanda Śiva suggests, Buddhism has traditionally been regarded by the Balinese as inferior to Śivaism. As testified to by the illuminating remarks of such a reliable observer as Crawfurd, there is no doubt that on Bali, even as late as the early nineteenth century, Śivaism was predominant over Buddhism:

> It is of the Hinduism of the sect of Śiva only, that I can furnish any detailed information. The Buddhists are few in number. [...] The followers of Siva spoke of these of Buddha more with contempt than hatred or rancor — the last, indeed, are feelings not likely to be entertained by any people for a fallen sect; in which light the Buddhists were evidently looked upon. The Brahmans in their conversation often let fall expressions, which showed that they entertained no respect whatever for the followers of the opposite worship. The sect of Siva may indeed be denominated the national religion. It is the religion of nine-tenths of the people, of every sovereign on the island, and of every man in power.[75]

Crawfurd's statement suggests that there existed a clear divide between the two religions, and that the Balinese status quo may be comparable to the *laukika/lokottara* contrastive distinction. The situation that developed on the island might be regarded as the result of a dialectic relationship thanks to which the two religions have finally come to terms — one (Śivaism) recognizing the (partial and relative) validity and inferior status of the other.

CONCLUDING REMARKS

Having surveyed the previous literature touching upon the relationship of Śivaism and Buddhism in Java and Bali, as well as in the Indian Subcontinent, I have critically assessed the view that a syncretistic, and unitary, Śiva-Buddha religion characterized the mainstream religiosity of the Singhasari-Majapahit period. Having found the three main hermeneutical models employed by scholars of Śivaism and Buddhism in the Subcontinent to be applicable also to the analysis of the dialectic between the two religions in the Archipelago, I have argued that the equivalence of Śaiva and Bauddha supreme goals and/or deities claimed by certain Old Javanese sources may be regarded as attempts by one system (mostly Buddhism) to appropriate familiar elements of the other. This phenomenon of appropriation would appear to have been driven by an "inclusivist" or, at times, "pluralist" attitude. Going against past claims regarding such a phenomenon as a typically or uniquely local feature that would reflect a supposed "openness" and eclecticism of the people of the Indonesian Archipelago with regard to religious matters, I stressed the need to analyse it against a local, context-specific background on the one hand, and a larger, pan-Asian context of exchange and dialectic between the two religions on the other.

My argument is that in investigating such complex and multifarious phenomenon as the relationship between Śivaism and Buddhism in premodern Indonesia, one cannot follow an approach that is narrowly theoretical (e.g. "structuralist", like Rassers') without running the risk of producing an ahistorical picture. Since this relationship entailed variation according to genres and media of expression, milieu of production and geographical location; underwent considerable development over time; and was context-specific, it follows that a historicist and multidisciplinary approach must be adopted — accompanied by a more careful and philologically sound assessment of original textual sources.

Let me conclude by trying to answer, if only in a very preliminary manner, the question as to what would have triggered Bauddha appropriations of Śaiva elements. Being persuaded by the arguments elaborated by Hunter, which conform to a "secular and historicist interpretation", I am of the opinion that Kṛtanagara's religio-ritual agenda, dominated by antinomian practices associated with Kāla-Bhairava, exerted a significant impact on the formation of a coalition between Śivaism and Buddhism, and between the respective religious clergies — their unease notwithstanding. Kṛtanagara's endeavour would have served the purpose of forming an analogous, and all-powerful, coalition against his external (as well as internal) political enemies in the real world.

Yet, this historical fact alone is not sufficient to fully explain the *status quo* depicted by the (Old Javanese, Middle Javanese and Old Sundanese) written sources. Phenomena of appropriation that reflect what I have deemed to be an "inclusivist" or "pluralist" attitude cannot be uniquely the result of historical-political circumstances but are likely to have been shaped by different cultural dynamics. For example, we may locate these in a Javanese (as well as Balinese) context where Śivaism has been for several centuries the dominant religion and Buddhism, albeit widespread on the territory, represented a minority. In such milieus, where Old Javanese belles-lettres had traditionally been the prerogative of Śaiva poets sponsored by Śaiva Kings, the efflorescence of literary specimens of Bauddha inspiration claiming the identity of Bauddha and Śaiva elements would constitute attempts by pious authors at proselytizing among their readership and, at the same time, gain royal support. The inclusion and appropriation of

Śaiva elements by the Bauddhas through operations of textual bricolage so paradigmatically exemplified by the *Saṅ Hyaṅ Kamahāyānikan*, one recension of which embeds an originally Śaiva treatise on yoga,[76] would constitute attempts at marketing the former system's religious truths in a more effective way, following an approach that is in every respect analogous to the one documented by Sanderson with respect to South Asian Sanskrit sources.

On the other hand, the pronounced Śaiva and Bauddha coalitions — if not actual "syncretisms" — of soteric means and doctrinal items documented in Tuturs stemming from late-Majapahit popular milieus may be regarded as hybrid cultural expressions of peripheral cosmopolitan areas, where original sectarian boundaries ceased to play a relevant role in framing the everyday religious experience. What caused a progressive hybridization of Śivaism and Buddhism, as well as their convergence towards a higher "mystic synthesis" — much like the one that eventually developed in Javanese milieus after the contact with Islam since the fifteenth century — might have been the progressive departure from the point of origin, and zenith, of the Indic religious and cultural values carried by the Sanskrit Cosmopolis; their ensuing transformation and "localization"; and the decadence of traditional forms of clergy, along with the development of new cultic embedded orthopraxies.

Notes

1. According to the Chinese pilgrim Fa-Hsien, on Java (Ye-Po-Ti) around 414 CE the followers of Buddhism were much fewer than the "Brahmans and infidels". A few years later, other Chinese sources speak of a widespread diffusion of Buddhism over the island (cf. Ensink, "Śiva-Buddhism in Java and Bali", pp. 178–79). Yi-Jing visited Sumatra in 689–692 CE, noting a significant Buddhist presence. Although many contemporary expressions of "Balinese Buddhism" may be the result of modern revivalism, it should be noted that enclaves of "Bauddha Brahmans" are extant on Bali, especially in the eastern region of Karangasem; it is these communities that have preserved the rare Old Javanese texts of Bauddha persuasion (cf. Hooykaas, *Balinese Bauddha Brahmans*).
2. See, for instance, Snellgrove's article eloquently titled "Syncretism as a main feature of Indonesian culture".
3. Kern, "Over de vermenging van Çiwaisme en Buddhisme op Java".
4. Krom, *Inleiding tot de Hindoe-Javaansche Kunst*.
5. Rassers, *Pañji, the culture hero*; "Śiva en Boeddha in den Indischen Archipel".
6. The two brothers Bubhukṣa and Gagaṅ Akiṅ have been regarded to represent, respectively, the Śaiva and Bauddha ascetic way (cf. Ensink, "Sutasoma's

Teaching to Gajavaktra," pp. 201–201; "Śiva-Buddhism in Java and Bali", pp. 186–87). Gagaṅ Akiṅ is the quintessentially Śaiva ascetic, practising severe austerities and dietary restrictions, while his brother enjoys eating all sorts of food including meat and indulges in drinking alcohol. After having been put to trial by God who had descended on earth in the form of a tigress, both obtain liberation and ascend to heaven, although Bubhukṣa's method is perceived as superior to the one of his older brother.

7. Krom, *Inleiding tot de Hindoe-Javaansche Kunst,* pp. 118–19.
8. Rassers, *Pañji, the culture hero,* pp. 65–66.
9. Zoetmuder, "Die Hochreligionen Indonesiens", pp. 301–304.
10. Pigeaud, *Java in the Fourteenth Century,* pp. 3–4.
11. Gonda, "Śiva in Indonesien", p. 28.
12. Ibid., pp. 27–30.
13. Soebadio, *Jñānasiddhānta,* pp. 55ff.
14. Supomo, "'Lord of the Mountains' in the Fourteenth Century *kakawin*".
15. de Casparis and I.W. Mabbett, "Religion and Popular Beliefs of Southeast Asia before c. 1500", pp. 328–29.
16. Santoso, *Sutasoma.*
17. Ensink, "Śiva-Buddhism in Java and Bali", pp. 192–93.
18. Nihom, *Studies in Indian and Indo-Indonesian Tantrism.*
19. Hunter, "The Body of the King".
20. Ibid., p. 52.
21. The earliest scriptures belonging to this corpus might have already been in existence by the fifth century CE, however it is only from the seventh century that evidence for the circulation of fully-fledged Tantric texts begins to appear in South Asia. The upper limit for most of the revealed scriptures (Tantras, Āgamas, Sūtras) of both Śaiva and Bauddha persuasion may be drawn to the *c.*tenth–eleventh century CE.
22. Seyfort Ruegg, "Sur les rapports entre le bouddhisme et le 'substrat religieux' indien et tibétain"; "A note on the Relationship between Buddhist and 'Hindu' Divinities in Buddhist Literature and Iconology"; *The symbiosis of Buddhism with Brahmanism/Hinduism in South Asia and of Buddhism with 'local cults' in Tibet and the Himalayan region.*
23. Seyfort Ruegg, *The symbiosis of Buddhism* ..., p. vi.
24. Ibid., pp. 11 and 134, notes that the opposition between *laukika* and *lokottara* recalls the distinction between the etic categories of "Little Tradition" and "Great Tradition".
25. Sanderson, "Vajrayāna: Origin and Function".
26. See Sanderson, "Vajrayāna: Origin and Function"; "History through Textual Criticism in the Study of Śaivism, the Pañcarātra and the Buddhist Yoginītantras", "Śaivism among the Khmers", "The Śaiva Age"; Bühnemann, "Buddhist Deities and Mantras in the Hindu Tantras I", p. 303; and Seyfort Ruegg, "A note on the Relationship between Buddhist and 'Hindu' Divinities in Buddhist Literature and Iconology", p. 737.

27. Sanderson, "Śaivism among the Khmers", pp. 436, 440.
28. Seyfort Ruegg, *The symbiosis of Buddhism …*, p. viii.
29. Ibid., p. 109.
30. Sferra, "Some Considerations on the Relationship Between Hindu and Buddhist Tantras".
31. Ibid., p. 61.
32. Coedès, *Les états hindouisés d'Indochine et d'Indonésie*, pp. 90, 107.
33. Krom, *Hindoe-Javaansche geschiedenis*, pp. 172–73.
34. de Casparis, *Prasasti Indonesia II*, p. 300.
35. Damais, "Bibliographie Indonesienne".
36. Jordaan, *In praise of Prambanan*; "Co-existence of religions in ancient Central Java".
37. Ibid., pp. 122–23.
38. Bosch, *Het vraagstuk van de Hindoe-kolonisatie van den archipel.*
39. Sarkar, "The evolution of the Siva-Buddha cult in Java".
40. Bosch, *Het vraagstuk van de Hindoe-kolonisatie van den archipel,* quoted in Jordaan, "Co-existence of religions in ancient Central Java", pp. 124–25.
41. Jordaan and Wessing, "Human sacrifice of Prambanan", p. 65.
42. Nihom, *Studies in Indian and Indo-Indonesian Tantrism*, p. 15.
43. Teeuw and Robson, *Kuñjarakarṇa Dharmakathana*, p. 9.
44. Nihom, *Studies in Indian and Indo-Indonesian Tantrism*, pp. 20–21.
45. Ibid., p. 114.
46. Miksic, "The Buddhist-Hindu Divide in Premodern Southeast Asia".
47. Ibid., p. 5.
48. Hunter, "The Body of the King", p. 41.
49. Soebadio, *Jñānasiddhānta*, pp. 12–15.
50. Santoso, *Sutasoma.*
51. Sanderson, "Śaivism among the Khmers", p. 377.
52. See Hooykaas, *Sūryasevana*, p. 50.
53. Sanderson, "Śaivism among the Khmers", p. 377.
54. This holds especially true in the case of certain secondary literature in Indonesian, either of scholarly or popular nature that, in the light of the dictum *bhinneka tunggal ika* ("unity in diversity") of the *Sutasoma* that has become the official motto of the Indonesian Republic, likes to see in the religious eclecticism of the Majapahit period the origin of the principle of religious pluralism laying at the basis of the modern Indonesian state, or a manifestation of the "openness" and accommodating attitude of many Indonesians with respect to religious matters.
55. Miksic, "The Buddhist-Hindu Divide in Premodern Southeast Asia", pp. 5–6.
56. Santiko, "Early Research on Sivaitic Hinduism during the Majapahit Era", p. 62.
57. These texts, preserved by the hundreds on Balinese palm-leaf manuscripts, and on just a handful of rare palm-leaf manuscripts from Java, form the textual basis of Śaivism in the Indonesian Archipelago. A salient feature

of the Tutur/Tattva literature is the translation and reconfiguration of Indic elements pertaining to linguistic, soteriological and theological domains into a local context of doctrine and practice. A survey of this corpus of texts may be found in Acri, "The Sanskrit-Old Javanese Tutur Literature from Bali".

58. Namely the *Vṛhaspatitattva*, *Tattvajñāna*, *Mahājñāna*, *Tutur Kamokṣan*, *Bhuvanakośa*, *Bhuvanasaṅkṣepa* and *Dharma Pātañjala*. Although some of these scriptures are compilations of materials of different provenance, they are likely to have reached their definitive forms already by the tenth or eleventh century CE.
59. Supomo, *Arjunawijaya*.
60. Aoyama, "Prince and Priest", pp. 10ff.
61. Santoso, *Sutasoma,* p. 42.
62. Sanderson, "The Śaiva Age", fn. 287, pp. 124–25.
63. Ibid., p. 124.
64. See Teeuw and Robson, *Kuñjarakarṇa Dharmakathana*, pp. 122–25.
65. Quoted and translated from the German by Seyfort Ruegg, *The symbiosis of Buddhism…*, p. 97.
66. Griffiths, *Problems of Religious Diversity*, p. 15.
67. Hunter, "The Body of the King", p. 38.
68. Ibid., p. 34.
69. Ibid., p. 41, refers to a passage of the *Deśawarṇana* (56.2–57.4) mentioning the disappearance of the image of Akṣobhya from Caṇḍi Jawi, which might have been due to the intervention of the Śaiva abbot out of his negative judgment of Kṛtanagara's syncretistic attitude, and which was taken by Prapañca as the cause of the sanctuary being struck by lightning in 1331 CE.
70. Sferra, "Some Considerations on the Relationship Between Hindu and Buddhist Tantras", pp. 68–69, has noted that texts belonging to Bauddha and Śaiva non-dualist traditions tend to show no fundamental difference between the descriptions of the paramount goals of their respective soteriological paths, for instance emptiness (*śūnyatā*) or oneness with Śiva (*śivātmaka*).
71. Witness, for instance, the Sukāmṛta inscription of 1259 CE, which suggests the existence of a link between Kṛtanagara's East Javanese milieu and Bhairavika Śivaism (cf. Santiko, "Early Research on Sivaitic Hinduism during the Majapahit Era", p. 58; Hunter, "The Body of the King", pp. 35–36); and the King's allegiance, as suggested by canto 43 of the *Deśavarṇana*, to Tantric Bauddha rituals connected with the Kālacakra system and such texts as the *Guhyasamājatantra* and *Hevajratantra* — seemingly in response to the consecration of his rival, the Mongol emperor Kublai Khan, into an analogous ritual path (cf. Hunter, "The Body of the King", pp. 35–36; Moens, "Het Boeddhisme op Java en Sumatra in zijn laatste bloeiperiode", especially pp. 527–30).
72. That such Kabuyutans represented what had survived of the hermitages (*patapan*) of the Śaiva ascetics of the Ṛṣi group is suggested by Old Sundanese

accounts such as the Bhujanga Manik (cf. Noorduyn, "Bujangga Manik's journeys through Java", pp. 416–18; Acri, *Dharma Pātañjala*, pp. 44–48; Noorduyn and Teeuw, *Three Old Sundanese Poems*, p. 281). Note further that in the Ciburuy scriptorium, along with a collection of palm-leaf manuscripts, may be found a few Śaiva and Bauddha implements, namely a trident and a *vajra*-bell (I have witnessed this myself on occasion of my visits there).

73. Including the *Saṅ Hyaṅ Siksa Kandaṅ Karĕsian* (Old Sundanese), *Saṅ Hyaṅ Hayu* (Old Javanese) and the many versions thereof, *Siksa Guru* (Old Javanese), *Bhimasorga* (Old Javanese-cum-Old Sundanese), etc. A survey of these texts, a handful of which have been translated into Indonesian, may be found in Noorduyn and Teeuw, *Three Old Sundanese Poems*, pp. 2–6; cf. also *Dharma Pātañjala*, pp. 3–8.
74. See *Gaṇapatitattva* (ed. Sudarshana Devi), Old Javanese prose appendix to *ślokas* 51–53 paragraph 13, referring to the *saṅ brāhmana bhujaṅga* (i.e. Ṛsis) *śaiva sogata* (i.e. Bauddhas); *Jñānasiddhānta* chapter 5 (pp. 86–87, 106–107), mentioning *śaiva* and *bauddha*, both qualified by the expression *saṅ bhujaṅga* — which would thus appear to have lost its usual connotation of "member of the Ṛṣi group" to indicate a Brahman or person of religious rank.
75. Crawfurd, "On the Existence of the Hindu Religion in the Island of Bali", pp. 129–30.
76. See Lokesh Chandra, "Śaiva Version of Saṅ Hyaṅ Kamahāyānikan", p. 7.

Bibliography

Acri, Andrea. "The Sanskrit-Old Javanese Tutur Literature from Bali. The Textual Basis of Śaivism in Ancient Indonesia". *Rivista di Studi Sudasiatici*, no. 1 (2006): 107–37.

——. *Dharma Pātañjala; A Śaiva Scripture from Ancient Java Studied in the Light of Related Old Javanese and Sanskrit Texts*. Groningen: Egbert Forsten, 2011.

Aoyama, Toru. "Prince and Priest: Mpu Tantular's Two Works in the Fourteenth Century Majapahit". Seminar Paper for the International Workshop on Southeast Asian Studies, no. 13. Leiden: KITLV, 1998.

Bosch, Frederik D.K. *Het vraagstuk van de Hindoe-kolonisatie van den archipel*. Leiden: Stenfert Kroese, 1946 (Inaugural address).

Bühnemann, Gudrun. "Buddhist Deities and Mantras in the Hindu Tantras I: The *Tantrasārasaṃgraha* and the *Īśānaśivagurudevapaddhati*". *Indo-Iranian Journal*, no. 42 (1999): 303–34.

Casparis, Johannes G. de. *Prasasti Indonesia II; Selected inscriptions from the 7th to the 9th century AD*. Bandung: Masa Baru, 1956.

Casparis, J.G. de and I.W. Mabbett. "Religion and Popular Beliefs of Southeast Asia before c. 1500". In *The Cambridge History of Southeast Asia, Vol. I: From early times to c. 1500*, edited by Nicholas Tarling, pp. 276–339. Cambridge: Cambridge University Press, 1999.

Coedès, George. *Les états hindouisés d'Indochine et d'Indonésie*. Paris: E. De Boccard, 1964.

Crawfurd, John. "On the Existence of the Hindu Religion in the Island of Bali". *Asiatick Researches,* no. 13 (1820): 128–70.

Damais, Louis-Charles "Bibliographie Indonesienne". *Bulletin de l'École Française d'Extrême-Orient*, no. 54 (1968): 295–522.

Ensink, Jacob. "Sutasoma's Teaching to Gajavaktra, the Snake and the Tigress (Tantular, Sutasoma Kakavin 38.1-42.4)". *Bijdragen tot de Taal-, Land- en Volkenkunde*, no. 130 (1974): 195–226.

——. "Śiva-Buddhism in Java and Bali". In *Buddhism in Ceylon and Studies on Religious Syncretism in Buddhist Countries. Report on a Symposium in Göttingen*, edited by Heinz Bechert, pp. 178–98. Göttingen: Vandenhoeck & Ruprecht, 1978.

Gonda, Jan. "Śiva in Indonesien". *Wiener Zeitschrift für die Kunde Südasiens*, no. 14 (1970): 1–31.

Griffiths, Paul J. *Problems of Religious Diversity*. Malden: Blackwell Publishers, 2001.

Hooykaas, Christiaan. *Sūryasevana; The way to God of a Balinese Śiva Priest*. Amsterdam-London: North Holland Publishing Company, 1966.

——. *Balinese Bauddha Brahmans*. Amsterdam: North Holland Publishing Company, 1973.

Hunter, Thomas M. "The Aridharma Reliefs of Caṇḍi Jago". In *Society and Culture of Southeast Asia: Continuities and Changes*, edited by Lokesh Chandra, pp. 69–100. New Delhi: International Academy of Indian Culture, 2000.

——. "The Body of the King: Reappraising Singhasari Period Syncretism". *Journal of Southeast Asian Studies,* no. 38/1 (2007): 27–53.

Jordaan, Roy E. *In praise of Prambanan: Dutch essays on the Loro Jonggrang temple complex*. Leiden: KITLV Press, 1996.

——. "Co-existence of religions in ancient Central Java". In *Society and Culture of Southeast Asia: Continuities and Changes*, edited by Lokesh Chandra, pp. 121–26. New Delhi: International Academy of Indian Culture, 2000.

Jordaan, Roy E. and R. Wessing. "Human sacrifice of Prambanan". *Bijdragen tot de Taal-, Land- en Volkenkunde,* no. 152 (1996): 45–73.

Kern, Henrik. "Over de vermenging van Çiwaisme en Buddhisme op Java, naar aanleiding van het Oud-Javaansch gedicht Sutasoma". *Verspreide geschriften* 4 (1916): 149–77.

Krom, Nicolaas J. *Inleiding tot de Hindoe-Javaansche Kunst. Tweede herzene druk. Deel I*. s'Gravenhage: Nijhoff, 1923.

——. *Hindoe-Javaansche geschiedenis*. s'Gravenhage: Nijhoff, 1931.

Lokesh Chandra. "Śaiva Version of Saṅ Hyaṅ Kamahāyānikan". In *Cultural Horizons of India V*, edited by Lokesh Chandra, pp. 7–101. New Delhi: International Academy of Indian Culture and Aditya Prakashan, 1997.

Miksic, John. "The Buddhist-Hindu Divide in Premodern Southeast Asia". Working paper no. 1, Nalanda-Sriwijaya Centre 2010. <http://www.iseas.edu.sg/nsc/publications_working_paper_series.htm>. 1 February 2011.

Moens, J.L. "Het Boeddhisme op Java en Sumatra in zijn laatste bloeiperiode". *Tijdschrift van het Bataviaasch Genootschap van Kunsten en Wetenschappen*, no. 64 (1924): 521–79.

Nihom, Max. *Studies in Indian and Indo-Indonesian Tantrism. The Kuñjarakarṇadharma-kathana and the Yogatantra*. Wien: Sammlung de Nobili, Institut für Südasien-, Tibet- und Buddhismuskunde der Universität Wien, 1994.

Noorduyn, Jacobus. "Bujangga Manik's journeys through Java: Topographical data from an Old Sundanese source". *Bijdragen tot de Taal-, Land- en Volkenkunde*, no. 138 (1982): 413–42.

Noorduyn, Jacobus and Andries Teeuw. *Three Old Sundanese poems*. Leiden: KITLV Press, 2006.

Pigeaud, Theodor G. *Java in the Fourteenth Century. A Study in Cultural History, Vol. IV*. s'Gravenhage: Nijhoff, 1962.

Rassers, Willem H. "Śiva en Boeddha in den Indischen Archipel". In *Gedenkschrift 75-jarig bestaan van het Koninklijk Instituut voor Taal-, Land- en Volkenkunde*, pp. 222–53. s'Gravenhage: Nijhoff, 1926.

———. *Pañji, the culture hero: A structural study of religion in Java*. The Hague: Nijhoff, 1959.

Robson, Stuart O. *Deśawarṇana (Nāgarakṛtāgama) by Mpu Prapañca*. Leiden: KITLV Press, 1995.

Sanderson, Alexis G.J.S. "Vajrayāna: Origin and Function". In *Buddhism into the Year 2000. International conference proceedings*, pp. 87–102. Bangkok/Los-Angeles: Dhammakaya Foundation, 1994.

———. "History through Textual Criticism in the Study of Śaivism, the Pañcarātra and the Buddhist Yoginītantras". In *Les sources et le temps. A colloquium. Pondicherry, 11–13 January 1997*, edited by F. Grimal, pp. 1–47. Pondicherry: IFP/EFEO, 2001.

———. "Śaivism among the Khmers. Part I". *Bulletin de l'École Française d'Extrême-Orient*, no. 90/91 (2003–04): 349–462.

———. "The Śaiva Age — The Rise and Dominance of Śaivism during the Early Medieval Period". In *Genesis and Development of Tantrism*, edited by Shingo Einoo, pp. 41–350. Tokyo: Institute of Oriental Culture, University of Tokyo, 2009.

Santiko, Hariani. "Early Research on Sivaitic Hinduism during the Majapahit Era". In *The Legacy of Majapahit*, edited by J. Miksic and E. Soekatno, pp. 55–69. Singapore: National Heritage Board, 1995.

Santoso, Soewito. *Sutasoma: A Study in Javanese Wajrayana*. New Delhi: International Academy of Indian Culture, 1975.

Sarkar, Himansu Bhusan. "The evolution of the Siva-Buddha cult in Java". *Journal of Indian History*, no. 45/3 (1969): 637–46.

Seyfort Ruegg, David "Sur les rapports entre le bouddhisme et le 'substrat religieux' indien et tibétain". *Journal Asiatique*, no. 252 (1964): 77–95.

———. "A note on the Relationship between Buddhist and 'Hindu' Divinities in Buddhist Literature and Iconology: The *laukika/lokottara* Contrast and the Notion of an Indian 'Religious Substratum'". In *Le parole e i marmi. Studi in onore di Raniero Gnoli nel suo 70° compleanno*, edited by R. Torella, pp. 735–41. Roma: Istituto Italiano per l'Africa e l'Oriente, 2001.

———. *The symbiosis of Buddhism with Brahmanism/Hinduism in South Asia and of Buddhism with 'local cults' in Tibet and the Himalayan region*. Wien: Verlag der Österreichischen Akademie der Wissenschaften, 2008.

Sferra, Francesco. "Some Considerations on the Relationship Between Hindu and Buddhist Tantras". In *Buddhist Asia 1: Papers from the First Conference of Buddhist Studies Held in Naples in May 2001,* edited by G. Verardi and S. Vita, pp. 57–84. Kyoto: Italian School of East Asian Studies, 2003.

Snellgrove, David. "Syncretism as a main feature of Indonesian culture, as seen by one more used to another kind of civilization". *Indonesia Circle*, no. 56 (November 1991): 25–48.

Soebadio, Haryati. *Jñānasiddhānta. Secret Lore of the Balinese Śaiva Priest*. The Hague: Nijhoff, 1971.

Sudarshana Devi. *Gaṇapati-tattwa*. New Delhi: International Academy of Indian Culture, 1958.

Supomo, Suryo. " 'Lord of the Mountains' in the Fourteenth Century *kakawin*". *Bijdragen tot de Taal-, Land- en Volkenkunde*, no. 128 (1972): 281–97.

———. *Arjunawijaya: A kakawin of Mpu Tantular* (2 vols.). The Hague: Nijhoff, 1977.

Teeuw, Andries and Stuart O. Robson. *Kuñjarakarṇa Dharmakathana*. The Hague: Nijhoff, 1981.

Zoetmuder, Josephus P. "Die Hochreligionen Indonesiens". In *Die Religionen Indonesiens*, edited by W. Stöhr and P.J. Zoetmulder, pp. 262–314. Stuttgart: Kohlhammer, 1965.

9

BUILDING A BUDDHIST MONARCHY IN ĐẠI VIỆT: Temples and Texts under Lý Nhân-tông (r. 1072–1127)[1]

John K. Whitmore

The lowland territories of Southeast Asia are composed of a variety of localities, each with its own physical and spiritual characteristics. As various realms formed across the region, growing political forces had to bring these scattered localities together under their central umbrellas in order to gain access to the resources, human and material, of these localities. In the process, emerging rulers had to deal with a great variety of local spiritual forces as the kings developed their central ideologies and royal cults. Here we examine the role of Buddhist monarchies in this process, focusing on Đại Việt and the reign of Lý Nhân-tông (r. 1072–1127) in Thăng-long (Hà Nội). Against the background of other Buddhist monarchies across Southeast Asia, we perceive Vietnamese kingship through its texts (chronicles, biographies, cult tales, inscriptions) and the variety of Buddhist temples that existed there.

MANDALAS AND LOCAL CULTS

I approach this study with the belief that localities varied in their characteristics and spiritual beliefs and need to be treated as scattered singular units interacting to greater or lesser degrees with each other.[2]

Dominance fluctuated among them depending on the contingencies of the time, human and material. Constructing hierarchies required the human ability to apply power and belief to these scattered localities, to link the localities to greater concentrations of resources and spiritually to the cosmos at large, to join them to the world of the royal court. Gradually, through the first millennium CE, out of these scattered localities there formed mandalas, cultural and political self-identifying groupings, that saw themselves opposed to other mandalas. We see this in terms, *inter alia,* of groupings called Việt, Champa, Kambujadesa, Rmannadesa, and Mranma across the mainland.

This pattern may be seen in the Khmer territory (as defined by inscriptions) through the middle of the first millennium. Michael Vickery has described the situation of localities there with their leaders, the *pon* and the *mratan,* and their spirits called *kpon* and *kamratan*.[3] While, by the time these inscriptions appeared, there was already the beginning of an admixture of Indic elements in the local societies, the inscriptions do seem to reflect elements of the society that was receiving and accepting the new elements. The *pon* were linked to the ponds, wetlands, rice fields of the localities, in Vickery's terms, "in control of the agricultural base of the economy"; "in origin *pon* was the chief of a small community living around its natural or artificial pond in the lowlands ..." who played political, economic, and ritual roles there. *Mratan* then were *pon* who appear to have gained stature across the Khmer landscape, perhaps by associating with emerging lords.

Linked to these local leaders were the spirit forces of their localities. As described from the inscriptions by Vickery,[4] the world of these spirits ("gods") initially consisted of *kpon*, to all appearances female, the supernaturally enhanced form of *pon*, and tied to local communities. In Vickery's analysis, this transitional period of the mid-first millennium saw a gradual shift to the *vrah*, male and place specific, as well as to the absorption of varied Indic forms. *Kpon* and *pon* were seen as linked in terms of local power, with a matrilineal relationship. Eventually, in the eighth century, this dyadic pattern was replaced by one of *vrah kamratan an* and the *mratan*, emphasizing the male, patrilineal relationship, with the two terms blending as a reflection of divine/human closeness.

We may take the *kpon/pon* pattern of local spiritual/political relationship as a viable model for the localities of early Southeast Asia (though the matrilineal/bilateral aspect requires further study). Through the first millennium, the shrines of local spirit cults similar to those of the *kpon* increasingly absorbed and mixed with a scattered variety of Hindu-Buddhist terms and temples. In what became Kambujadesa, the inscriptions show what we generally define as Hindu and Buddhist institutions with Sanskrit terminology, many presumably integrated with local spirit cults (as *kpon* became *vrah*). Scattered across the Khmer countryside were myriad variations of indigenous and Indic mixtures, created by idiosyncratic local prescriptions, according to place, time, and contingency. Hence a multiplicity of shrines and temples existed among the many localities, each following its own taste.[5]

How did localities in the Việt territories form their spiritual mix? We do not have the inscriptional evidence of Kambujadesa for this region that is now northern Vietnam. Rather it is to Chinese records that we turn, since this Việt area through the first millennium formed part of the Chinese empires, especially that of the Tang (618–907). In a fourteenth century collection of tales of local spirit cults, *Departed Spirits of the Viet Realm* (*Việt Điện U Linh Tập*), the author Lý Tế Xuyên included six tales taken from non-extant Tang dynasty works of the ninth century.[6] Five of these six tales describe spirit cults existing at the time, as witnessed by Tang governors in the province of Annan, what would become Đại Việt. The two Tang authors, Zhao Cheng writing at the beginning of the ninth century and Zeng Gun, towards its end, looked to examine indigenous practices and beliefs. The two provide a narrow, but vivid, view of contemporary local spirit cults and how the populace visualized these spirits. In four of the tales, a Chinese official directly engaged (in a dream) the spirit of his locality. The spirits, very striking figures, saluted and honoured these officials who worked with the local people. The officials in turn built or rebuilt shrines to the spirits. Thus did spiritual and temporal power merge in the locality and bring protection and prosperity to the area. In the process, these local spirit cults were also absorbing Sinic elements and terminology.

Also scattered among these Việt localities were a variety of Buddhist temples that had grown up since the second century CE.[7] Monks arriving from the north and the south, from China proper, island Southeast Asia, India, and Central Asia, sojourned or settled in these temples. Locally oriented, they and their occupants followed a mixture of beliefs. While three temples, those of Pháp Vân, Kiến Sơ (in Phù Đổng village, home of a famous local spirit), and Khai Quốc, stood out, they were only three of a large number of such local temples. By the end of the first millennium, there lay across the Việt lands many localities with their chiefs, their spirit shrines, and their Buddhist temples. As the Tang dynasty crumbled in the north, a number of these localities contested power. This may be seen in the "Twelve Lords" of the mid-tenth century and the strongman who defeated them and began the process of forming Đại Việt within the Việt mandala. The local powers represented by the "lords" were scattered through the mid and upper regions of the Red River valley (the lower delta remained under-populated).[8] As in the Kambujadesa mandala, the task of potential rulers in the Việt mandala was to gather these localities under the protective umbrella the king offered and the spirit cults and Buddhist temples within the supernatural power attached to such a claimant.

In this study, I am utilizing four types of texts: two literati chronicles (*Đại Việt Sử Ký*, *Việt Sử Lược*), a compilation of spirit tales (*Việt Điện U Linh Tập*), and a collection of biographies of Buddhist monks (*Thiền Uyển Tập Anh*), all originally from the thirteenth and fourteenth centuries. These are supplemented by eight inscriptions from the years 1099 to 1126, marking the second half of the long reign of Lý Nhân-tông (1072–1127).[9]

ĐẠI VIỆT, LOCALITIES, AND BELIEFS

For half a century, from the 960s to the 1010s, three strongmen in succession defeated their local rivals and took the throne of the emerging Đại Việt, Đinh Bộ Lĩnh (r. 968–979), Lê Hoan (r. 980–1005), and Lý Công Uẩn (r. 1009–28). They fought off challenges from the north (the new Song dynasty), the south (Champa), and the west (Dali, formerly Nanzhao) and worked to build their strength, utilizing spirit and Buddhist powers. Only the family of Lý Công Uẩn was successfully able to establish its succession on the throne. Lý Công Uẩn (Lý Thái-tổ) moved his capital from the limited location of Hoa-lư in the hills south of the Red River delta to the former Chinese provincial seat of Đại La (Great Walled City) in the middle of the delta. Renaming it Thăng-long (Ascending Dragon, now Hà Nội), the new king engaged the Buddhist community that had raised him and drew on the spirit cults of the localities to enforce his rule, calling them forth to support him.[10]

The establishment of the Lý as a Sinic patrilineal "dynasty", unusual in bilateral Southeast Asia, through the first three quarters of the eleventh century provided Đại Việt a firm foundation of political power. Father (Lý Thái-tổ), son (Lý Thái-tông, r. 1028–54), and grandson (Lý Thánh-tông, r. 1054–72) took the throne successively as mature, experienced adults. In the process, these three rulers engaged the spiritual as well as the political forces of their increasingly integrated realm. Lý Thái-tổ received support from monks at the famed Kiến-sơ Temple in Phù-đổng village and in his home village of Cổ-pháp (Ancient Dharma, now Đình-bằng), both north of the new capital in the middle of the Red River delta. Through his rule, the Lý founder established a number of temples inside his new capital city and out, though there is no apparent hierarchical arrangement among them and Thái-tổ is not known to have advocated any particular school of thought. Initially, the new king built eight temples in the Tiên-du area north of the capital and the centre of Vietnamese Buddhism at the time and three others around the capital region itself. Later he added more temples within Thăng-long. In addition, he too engaged a powerful local spirit, also named Lý and once again a striking figure, in a dream. The two joined to protect the lowlands from the threatening highlands as well as to guard the realm as a whole.[11]

Lý Thái-tổ's son and successor, Lý Thái-tông, engaged with the thriving Buddhist community more directly than did his father. Interacting with a variety of monks, he sought and honoured their varied opinions, including those emanating from both the south and the north, from India and from China. At one point, the king held a vegetarian feast and stated, according to the fourteenth century *Eminent Monks of the Thiền Community*,

> I have noticed that scholars have disputed the mind-source of the Buddhas and patriarchs. I wish that each of you here, men of eminent virtue from various districts, would express his point of view to me so that I could see how to apply mind.

Huệ Sinh, a monk of distinguished local family whom the king had brought from a mountain abode into the capital, made this reply in verse,

> Dharma is originally like non-Dharma,
> Neither existent nor non-existent.
> If one knows the truth,
> Then sentient beings and Buddha are one.
> How great the moon over Lanka!
> Empty, empty, the boat that crosses the ocean.
> If one knows emptiness, by means of
> that emptiness one realizes being,
> Free to go everywhere in *samadhi*.

Thái-tông followed the monk's views, and Huệ Sinh became the court teacher, a position he carried into the following reign. In the process, this monk composed inscriptions for a number of major temples in the Tiên-du and Vũ-ninh areas north of the capital (none unfortunately extant). Thái-tông actively worked to expand the Buddhist community and to encourage its practices. The area of Tiên-du remained significant, but the king continued to engage the spirit world.[12]

Where his father had traveled out to the spirit's locality, Thái-tông brought the spirit cults into the capital. Thái-tông was particularly close to the cult of the spirit of the Mountain of the Bronze Drum from the southern territory of the Việt mandala. In front of this spirit, the king had his courtiers swear their yearly blood oath of allegiance. This king too engaged the spirits in his dreams. As literati (classical scholars) advised the throne on administration, Thái-tông called for spiritual aid on the problems of rule as well. In reply, the spirit of a prior respected official of good family arrived to guide the throne. In another instance, Thái-tông joined the Buddhist and spirit worlds by building the Diên-hựu temple (now the Chùa Một Cột, Single Pillar Temple). Again in a dream, the king beheld the Bodhisattva Guanyin and constructed the pavilion into which she had invited him on the top of a pillar, thus taking the form of a spirit house.[13]

Thái-tông's son, Lý Thánh-tông, seems not to have been as engaged with either the Buddhist or the spirit worlds. He carried on his father's institutions, as with the monk Huệ Sinh and the Tiên-du area and bringing spirit cults into the capital, and built more temples, particularly the renowned Báo-thiên Tower (*Tháp*) in the capital. Late in his reign he embraced the teachings of a Chinese monk brought from Champa, Thảo Đường. Yet, in general, he appears not to have engaged the monks directly, nor to be as involved with the spirit world. Thánh-tông's focus was on the majesty of the throne of Đại Việt vis-à-vis both the north (the Song) and the south (Champa). He incorporated Sinic and Indic elements in his court, constructing a royal cult linked to the Hindu-Buddhist king of the gods Indra as well as Brahma and pushing Lý power out into the countryside.[14]

Yet Thánh-tông was not able to pass his throne on to a mature heir. His first son was born only in 1066 and, with the threat of Song power growing to the north, the king began to construct a scenario to preserve the Lý throne of Đại Việt. Turning to the Chinese Classics, Thánh-tông relied on his chief minister Lý Đạo Thành to guide his young son. At this point we begin to see Sinic literati institutions appear in Thăng-long, both before and after Thánh-tông's death. First came the Temple of Literature (*Văn-miếu*), centered on the Duke of Zhou, the classic model for such a transition to a child king. Accompanying the Duke were Confucius and his disciples. Later there were classical examinations, the Royal Academy (*Quốc-tử-giám*), and the Hán-lâm (Hanlin) Academy to bolster the literati stance in the royal court and the capital. One product of this effort was Lê Văn Thịnh who became tutor to the new young king Lý Nhân-tông

(r. 1072–1127) and who succeeded Lý Đạo Thành as chief minister on the latter's death.[15]

The spirit world remained part of this new approach to governance. Lý Đạo Thành sacrificed at Mt. Tản-viên, home to the Mountain Spirit upriver from the capital. When the Song forces attacked in 1076, the Vietnamese relied on the spirits of two famous warriors, the Trương brothers, from the mountain regions to create a bulwark against the northern invaders and to protect the southern land (Đại Việt). Buddhist activities continued, including bathing an image of the Buddha and bringing such an image into the capital to pray for good weather. At the height of the Song crisis, the royal court called Buddhist priests together to chant the *Benevolent Kings sutra* to ward off the threat, presumably in the then Vietnamese pronunciation of the characters.[16]

During these years, the 1070s and 1080s, as Nhân-tông was growing up and the activist government of the Song threatened Đại Việt, the court felt the need to compile a work on the royal tradition established by the Lý. This was *Tales of the Extreme Reach of Karmic Reward* (*Báo Cực Truyền*), Buddhist miracle tales which combined acts from previous lives and explications of the strange (as Liam Kelley has recently translated the title).[17] Six of the tales survive, mainly in *Departed Spirits of the Việt Realm* from 1329. In *Tales of the Extreme Reach of Karmic Reward*, encompassed within the broader Buddhist context, was recorded a tradition linking the Lý monarchy to both the time and the space of Đại Việt. The tales integrated spirits of the localities with the monarchy and showed a spiritual genealogy from the local powers of northern control (Shi Xie of the second and third centuries C.E. and Gao Pian of the ninth century) through the first three Lý rulers in the capital of Thăng-long. In this tradition, we see Lý Thái-tổ journey to localities where spirit cults and Buddhist worship joined, both Lý Thái-tông and Lý Thánh-tông bring powerful local spirits into the capital, and the two of them apply spiritual power in campaigns against Champa to the south. Buddhism formed an important part, but only a part, of this integrated royal tradition. It followed Lý Thánh-tông's emphasis on the monarchy.[18]

As this work was being compiled in the royal court, the young Nhân-tông and the Queen Mother were pursuing their personal Buddhist interests within the royal palace. Young members of established families had been brought into the palace to accompany the child prince, then king. One of these, though more than a decade older than Nhân-tông, became close to him. Later this young man became a Buddhist monk, and the king and his mother invited this monk (to be known as Mãn Giác) into the palace to teach them. The two, mother and son, also had contact with senior distinguished monks, absorbing the message of the Thiền (Ch. Chan) meditation school that these monks were developing. The *sutra* mainly mentioned with these monks was the *Lotus*, though there was that of Complete Enlightenment as well. Nhân-tông and his mother themselves became active with a number of temples in the capital and out. In particular, the young king favoured the Diên-hựu and Mt. Lam temples. The first, in the capital, was the Single Pillar temple in the shape of a spirit house, dedicated to Guanyin, and the second was a new temple and tower on a hill northeast of the capital.[19]

A BUDDHIST MONARCHY IN ĐẠI VIỆT

In 1096, at the age of thirty, Lý Nhân-tông appears to have taken charge of his court and, with his mother, to have moved their Buddhist beliefs from the palace into the court itself. His grandfather Thái-tông had, over a half century earlier, gathered monks from local temples and attempted to emphasize a doctrine, selecting Huệ Sinh and the monk's advocacy of emptiness.[20] Though Huệ Sinh continued into Thánh-tông's reign, the latter seems to have had little interest in unifying the Buddhist thought of Đại Việt. This remained the case for over four decades.

At the end of the eleventh century, the Buddhism of Đại Việt existed in the numerous local temples, each with its own community of monks. These monks then travelled among the many temples seeking a master and instruction. Our evidence for this comes mainly from the fourteenth-century work, *Eminent Monks of the Thiền Community,* and has been viewed through the prism of Thiền belief. It is therefore difficult to know the detail of the thought and practice in this local variety. Nguyen Tu Cương has described this Buddhism as a diffuse and varied mix of beliefs across the countryside with a growing interest among monks for the new Chan (V. Thiền) thought in Song China. In Nguyen Tu Cương's words, the former included

> meditation, asceticism, magic, wonderworking, and ritualism ... a mixture of some Buddhist elements from India and China and the beliefs and practices characteristic of the indigenous people's religious sensibilities and popular cults. This Buddhism emphasized magic, ritual, and thaumatology.

The new brand of Chinese Buddhist thought brought new works into Đại Việt, especially the imperially supported *Record of the Transmission of the Lamp* (*Chuan Deng Lu*) of 1009 and other transmission histories. The emphasis therein on the mind-seal and passing the realization from master to disciple led to spiritual genealogies going back to India and the Buddha. Through the eleventh century, as Chan Buddhism developed strongly in Song China, there also emerged in and around Thăng-long a new, more focused Buddhism, Patriarchal Chan, that was becoming the Thiền of Đại Việt. Despite Thái-tông's prior effort, as Nguyen Tu Cương concluded, there was yet no "sustained, active, lasting scriptural school" in the realm.[21]

In 1096, at another royal vegetarian feast, the Queen Mother (and undoubtedly Nhân-tông) again sought consistency in Vietnamese Buddhist thought and posed a series of questions on the nature of Buddhism and its existence in Đại Việt. They adopted the presentation of the monk they came to call Thông Biện (Clear Communicator). In this monk's long formulation of Đại Việt's Buddhism, we see the first Vietnamese systematic discussion, royally sponsored, of local Buddhist beliefs and how they fit together. In the process Thông Biện provided a scheme that incorporated scattered and varied beliefs from local monks and temples as he fused these beliefs into two lineages of transmission: the senior one of Vinītaruci linked to India, the junior one of Vô Ngôn Thông linked to China. This scheme gained its authority both from the throne of Đại Việt and from transmitted links back through the famed sixth patriarch Huineng of China all the way to Śākyamuni. Adopting the contemporary Chan transmission history, Thông Biện brought a conceptual unity to Vietnamese Buddhism focused on the court and establishing the Thiền school over the multiplicity of monks and temples. The five Chan lineages of the Song were not distinguished by doctrine or procedure, but by personal authority gained from being in the descent of each, and the two Thiền lineages of Đại Việt appear to have followed this pattern. They were non-competitive, and the king accepted them both. Local monks, whether affiliated with one or the other (or both) lineages, however loosely, benefitted from the two. India was "the center of the world"; China was where "the gist of the teaching became clear". Thông Biện explicitly pointed out that, *c*.600 CE, the Buddhist community in this Việt region had "long been in communication with India", predating the Buddhist establishment in China.[22] Indeed, where contemporary Song China was de-emphasizing the Indian connection, the Vietnamese court was directly laying claim to it. Nhân-tông appears to have ignored a third lineage, that of Thảo Đường, the Chinese monk brought back from Champa and established in the Khai Quốc temple in Thăng-long by his father Thánh-tông. This too may have been part of the Vietnamese court's both adopting the Song model of the day and simultaneously separating itself therefrom, a distinctive Vietnamese trait.[23]

The ports of Đại Việt had long been in contact with the island world of Southeast Asia and via the sea routes with India. In the twelfth century, there was explicit mention of contacts with Java and Sriwijaya. (What role Champa played in Vietnamese religious links is difficult to say.) Sitting at an intersection of communication between India and China, Đại Việt's Buddhist thought was distinctive and unique in its formulation. Huệ Sinh, Thái-tông's favorite, and Chân Không represented the Indian Vinītaruci lineage, and Thông Biện's teacher Viên Chiếu and Quảng Trí that of China and Vô Ngôn Thông. The latter three senior monks had all influenced Lý Nhân-tông and the Queen Mother. In the process, Thông Biện acknowledged Pháp-vân temple east of the capital as the senior Việt Buddhist temple and Kiến-sơ temple of Phù-đổng village in Tiên-du as junior to it. The Khai-quốc temple just north of the capital gained a new significance as the site of Thông Biện's discourse. To borrow Thomas Hunter's words (for thirteenth-fourteenth century east Java), this "represented the metaphysical reflection of [the king's] political policies."[24]

Lý Nhân-tông and the Queen Mother proceeded to establish this discourse in the court, brushing aside literati opposition. Honouring Thông Biện with the purple robe (similar to Song custom), they adopted his formulation of Buddhism, past and present, in their land and subordinated the royal tradition of *Tales of the Extreme Reach of Karmic Reward*. The emphasis shifted away from a monarchy founded on the amalgam of localized Sinic power, indigenous spirits, and the mixed Buddhist thought and practices existing across the countryside. Now the throne stressed its focused Buddhist existence linked to both India and China, going back through the spiritual genealogy of the mind-seal to Huineng and the Buddha. Rather than the gradual study of scripture, this meditation stance emphasized personal connection and sudden enlightenment. Practices counted more than a set of beliefs; finding the original pure mind within oneself was fundamental to realization.[25]

The royal pair proceeded with their Buddhist activities following the acceptance into the royal court of this Thiền approach. While there does not appear to have been any major effort to unify and standardize Vietnamese Buddhist thought among the scattered local temples, the court gathered in the multiplicity of beliefs and practices under its overarching royal umbrella as assembled in Thông Biện's non-extant work *Collated Biographies* (*Chiếu Đối Lục*).[26] In general, later ages would remember Lý Nhân-tông's reign, mainly its second half, as a time of magical monks, with specific reference to India. These monks, especially, Không Lộ/Minh Không, Giác Hải, and Đạo Hạnh, performed miraculous acts under the king's auspices. (The monks seem to have superseded the spirits in their miraculous powers.) One such magical instance involved succession to the throne and aided in the resolution of the problem for the childless Nhân-tông.[27]

In more realistic terms, the king and his mother continued the Buddhist practices they had begun in earlier decades. They requested a set of the Tripitaka from the Song court and replaced the classical examinations for literati with Buddhist examinations focused on the *Lotus* and the *Perfection of Wisdom sutras*. One successful monk was Viên Thông whom Nhân-tông brought into the palace to teach as a Dharma Master. According to *Eminent Monks of the Thiền Community*,

> Viên Thông expounded the doctrine according to circumstances, enlightening people by guiding them to the meaning (of Buddhism). He dispelled their delusion and reproached their ignorance until there was none at all.

The royal activities also included supporting temples, again especially those of Diên-hựu and Mt. Lam. Nhân-tông built towers (*tháp*) at each of them. Another temple of interest was that on Mt. Chương, where he had another tower built. In 1115, they finished a temple in the elderly Queen Mother's home area, north of the capital near Mt. Tiên-du. After she died two years later, Nhân-tông waited a year before beginning to construct his own temple on Mt. Long-đội (Dragon Guard) southeast of the capital.[28]

From this second half of Lý Nhân-tông's reign came eight inscriptions (1099–1126), the first surviving from the dynasty. They are all Buddhist (with numerous classical Chinese references) and demonstrate how the king came to employ Buddhism to bring localities within the royal purview. Four of the inscriptions are from the crucial southern territory of Thanh-hóa, protecting against the realm of Champa to the south. One comes from a territory in the northern mountains guarding against disturbances there. Three come from the capital region, including that of the Great Bell just to the west and the royal inscription on Mt. Long-đội to the southeast. The eighth and earliest was a small fragment on the base of an Amitābha statue also west of the capital.[29]

In these inscriptions, there is little direct reference to the varied Buddhas and Bodhisattvas, mainly the Buddha Śākyamuni, his teaching, and the origins of the religion. Being Thiền, they saw the Buddha as the originator of their lineages and hence felt linked directly to him through the series of personal mind seals. Triads of Buddhas generally do not appear in either the inscriptions or the texts, though a study of contemporary temples and sculptures might prove differently. This seems to have been a Chan/ Thiền pattern, as evidenced in work on eleventh century Song China.[30] The 1109 bell inscription identified its location as that of Mt. Potala of Avalokiteśvara, while the second of the Thanh-hóa inscriptions (1118) noted statues of Śākyamuni, Kāśyapa, and Maitreya, the last of the Thanh-hóa inscriptions (1126) involved the Vajradhātu mandala with its Buddhas of the Five Directions (Vairocana at the centre, Akṣobhya to the east, Ratnasambhava to the south, Amitābha to the west, and Amoghasiddhi to the north), and the royal inscription of 1121 referred to the magical monk Amoghavajra. I suspect that each temple had its own pantheon, with no dominant pattern imposed from the capital. This most likely depended on the local monkish community. Only the *Lotus sutra*, of all the writings, appears (once) in the inscriptions.[31]

India (Tianzhu) was, for all these inscriptions, the source and root of the Buddhism they espoused. The 1107 inscription stated, "(The local lord) floats on the source and branches of India", and the royal inscription of 1121 declared, "In India was manifested the divine." The authors of the inscriptions linked their own locations to the origins of Buddhism, to places like Kapilavastu and Rajagrha (Magadha), to the sites of the kings Udayana and Asoka (including Lanka), and to Mt. Potala. Where the Song Chan Buddhists were increasingly focused on their own land as the center of their religion, the Vietnamese were consciously and explicitly recognizing and reaching back to their Indian roots. Yet, even as they differentiated themselves from their northern brethren, the Vietnamese did follow the Song Buddhists in linking their religion to King Mu of Zhou over two millennia earlier.[32]

The inscriptions were all oriented towards the royal court and the capital. In 1100, Lý Thường Kiệt was finishing his eighteen year tenure as lord of Thanh-hóa and the south. This inscription for the temple built in Kiệt's territory showed the reach of the throne into this southern border region. Kiệt was assisting and supporting his ruler there, protecting and maintaining this territory. Therein lay prosperity and abundance. The Buddhism for Kiệt was active and public, not restricted to the monastery. Looking back to the kings Udayana and Asoka in India, the inscription called for royal service and preserving the dharma. Yet to be tied to worldly detail was not the way to realize this dharma. Man, with the Buddha nature inside him, had to overcome this world to see clearly. The temple, with its magnificent stone chimes, locally made, would bring this realisation to the people, their sound flowing across the land.[33]

To the north, in the year 1107, the local Hà chiefs of territory in the mountains between Đại Việt and the Song, set up a stele recording their service to the Lý court and to Nhân-tông. Deserving of being subject to their king, the sun, this family protected their territory, the distant wilds, for Thăng-long and played privileged roles in the royal court. Consequently, this territory was populated and prosperous. Taking refuge in the Buddha, the dharma, and the sangha, this family led their people to the Way, fulfilling their destiny and building temples. Their bells and stone chimes sounded through the ravines. Abandoning the burning house (the world), they looked to India as the origin of their beliefs. Emptiness and clarity in realisation marked their Buddhist existence. At the same time, the inscription also linked this hill family and its Buddhism to Chinese antiquity with its Zhou dynasty, following Song Chan developments, and contained numerous classical citations, particularly to the Book of Poetry.[34]

Two years later, on the western outskirts of Thăng-long atop Mt. Phật-tích (Imprint of the Buddha), there was consecrated a great bell, organized by Đạo Hạnh, one of the magical monks mentioned earlier. The inscription noted its attachment to the royal throne and the Queen Mother's devotion. The entire populace, nobles and commoners, came to worship there. The temple's blessings were said to have brought prosperity to the land and support for the monarchy, reinforcing Nhân-tông's rule. It too had a connection to India, being dubbed the temple of Mt. Potala of Avalokiteśvara. Explicitly Thiền, the inscription spoke of "transforming the destiny of the country of Đại Việt", and the great bell represented its truth. Its exterior showed the complexity of the world and its surface; its interior the world's full emptiness. This was the Buddha's message. Awareness and realization of the three worlds of desire, form, and formlessness thus emerged, and the Vietnamese role was to transmit this message. Blessings, joy, and purity followed therefrom. The bell and its peal carried these blessings across the countryside, awakening all those who heard.[35]

The three other inscriptions from Thanh-hóa in the south (1118–1126) continued the legacy of Lý Thường Kiệt and the Buddhism in that southern border region. All were apparently composed by the same person, the monk Pháp Bảo (Hải Chiếu). The occasion for the first of these inscriptions was king Nhân-tông's royal progression south to the area two years earlier, and the temple was named "Venerating Buddhism and Prolonging the Dynasty". To bring order out of disorder was the role of both the king and Buddhism. The king's local lord acted to carry this out for his ruler. The people of this territory thereby achieved both peace and prosperity and the way out of *samsara*. Awareness and realization showed the way. This inscription too both harked back to the origins of Buddhism in India and made reference to the Zhou dynasty in China (which happened to be the name of the local lord, in Vietnamese Chu). The following two inscriptions, seven and eight years later, continued the connection between local lord and royal family. Monks from this local family constructed and repaired temples in the region. The final inscription of 1126 noted that worshippers came from the southern lands of Champa and Cambodia to its temple. Generally, these three inscriptions show the extension of royal Lý power and of the Buddhism that reinforced this power. India remained the emphasized point of origin for this thought. These inscriptions noted the strong religious involvement of both Nhân-tông and the Queen Mother in this southern region.[36]

The inscriptions saw their fullest expression in Lý Nhân-tông's own inscription of 1121 on Mt. Long-đội southeast of the capital. It is the longest of the eight inscriptions and requires more detailed study. Here is a general outline. The title on the stele has calligraphy in Nhân-tông's own hand. It is well decorated with Lý-style dragons (and indeed the text refers to Nhân-tông as "ruler of men, king of dragons"), two embracing the title at the top and nine elsewhere on the stele. The king began construction of the temple the year after his mother's death in 1117 and inspected the site personally. The temple was completed three years later in 1121. In the midst of the Buddhist mysteries, Nhân-tông, "of profound stillness and spiritual brilliance", sought the inside, what lay beneath form and manifestation and gained clarity. Order prevailed as a result, both natural and social as the Celestial Script proceeded. The Buddha and India formed the source and brought awareness. Such beautiful teaching illumined ignorance and developed the heart's natural goodness. The great temple and tower represented all this, from time immemorial to the present, passing it on undiminished and flourishing. This the king, in his fiftieth year on the throne, brought to his populace and to all sentient beings.[37]

Lý Nhân-tông was pictured in his inscription as a perfect monarch with all the proper qualities for the throne. This temple marked the apogee of his reign (and, as it turned out, of his dynasty). Mastering government as well as the religious, the king ruled well and brought both material and spiritual benefits to his realm, the inscription declared. His grand court in Thăng-long put on great spectacles. His great victories against the Song on the north, the Ma Sa in the mountains, and Champa to the south protected the Việt mandala. Good signs (strange animals and rare plants) reflected his success. All this the inscription described and the temple on the hilltop marked. This work was meant to protect and prolong Buddhism and the Lý dynasty in Đại Việt.[38]

In this temple on Mt. Long-đội we see the culmination of Lý Nhân-tông's effort to construct a Buddhist monarchy in Đại Việt. Within six years, at the end of 1127, he would be dead at the age of sixty-one, the longest reigning monarch in Vietnamese history. His last years saw the establishment of what would be a government of dominant court ministers and queen mothers for the rest of the twelfth century. The accomplishments of Nhân-tông and his three royal predecessors, the patrilinial dynasty of the Lý, established Đại Việt and its monarchy. The Buddhist rule of Nhân-tông brought the focus of the Việt mandala to the capital and its glories, binding the localities, their spirit cults, and local temples more tightly to the throne as the bells and the stone chimes sent their sound through the lowlands and into the mountains. What had begun with the young king and the Queen Mother as personal religious reflection became in time a means to integrate the realm better.[39]

Yet, for the last century of Lý rule, to 1225, we need to know if this model of Buddhist monarchy continued. The royal court changed, as did the realm. The great growth and prosperity of Đại Việt in the mid-river segment of the Red River valley drew in international commerce and Chinese immigration, developing the under-populated coastal zone and ultimately leading to the Trần dynasty (1225–1400) conquest of the Lý.[40] The general impression of these times in Đại Việt is of a move in a more Sinic direction. Later twelfth-century funeral inscriptions of court lords and ladies were classically Sinic with no mention of Buddhism (1159, 1161, 1174). There was also a swing towards Lý Thánh-tông's Chinese-connected Thảo Đường lineage, which had been ignored by his son Nhân-tông. This lineage skipped over Nhân-tông and his successor Thần-tông (r. 1128–38), a renowned Buddhist ruler. Instead the transmission passed from Thánh-tông to Anh-tông (r. 1138–75) and Cao-tông (r. 1176–1210) and included the chief minister Đỗ Anh Vũ, subject of the 1159 funerary inscription above. Another inscription of 1157, for Đỗ Anh Vũ's mother, noted how she had established a Buddhist temple to maintain the local landholdings of her family. While the Buddhist biographies mention the post-Nhân-tông rulers (Thần-tông, Anh-tông, Cao-tông) frequently, reflecting these kings' continued personal engagement with Buddhism, the *sutras* recorded were those of *Complete Enlightenment* and of *Diamond*. The *Lotus sutra* appeared only once with that of *Benevolent Kings*. The spirits reappeared, as Anh-tông was mentioned twice in *Departed Spirits of the Việt Realm* as directly involved (via his dreams) with the spirit world (the Trưng Sisters and the Lady God of the Earth), in both cases involving rain.[41] It may have been that Nhân-tông's Thiền scheme was unique and not supported by the later Lý monarchs. This requires further examination.

BUDDHIST MONARCHIES IN EARLY SOUTHEAST ASIA

During the classical age of Southeast Asia, a number of Buddhist monarchies developed in the effort to absorb the political and spiritual powers of the localities. These monarchies began along the coasts and developed successively in Sriwijaya, Mataram, and Đồng-dương (Sumatra, Java, and Champa) in the seventh to tenth centuries before appearing elsewhere on the mainland at Pagan, Thăng-long, and Angkor in the following two centuries.

The papers included in this volume show, through the second half of the first millennium CE, an expansive penetration of Buddhist thought and items across the maritime regions and up the river valleys of the Southeast Asia mainland. This spread of varied Buddhist influences, offering blessing and protection, localized in numerous places, moved from the Malay Peninsula, to Sumatra, Java, around the coasts of Kalimantan, and into the present southern Philippines, as well as into present day Myanmar, Thailand, Cambodia, and the central coast of Vietnam. It formed a broad open field of numerous Buddhist locations lying between India and China, with little meaning attached to individual schools of thought. China, in turn, had by the end of this period begun to see itself as a Buddhist field in its own right, separate from India, and it was Chan that made it so.[42]

In the seventh century, Sriwijaya rose in southeast Sumatra as the first of the great Southeast Asian coastal entrepots. Dominating the Straits of Melaka, it channelled both the international trade flowing between east and west, China, India, and the Mediterranean, and the religious beliefs following this communications route. Buddhism, in various guises, formed the main ideology of the age, maintaining a position in various parts of the Indian subcontinent as well as in Tang China. Indeed, Sriwijaya, with its connection to Nalanda, became a major stopping point on this international Buddhist circuit that included India, Central Asia, and China, a point where the classical sacred language Sanskrit could be studied. Inscriptional evidence shows Buddhism as an element in the relation of the Sriwijaya capital to its localities, both in the mountain hinterlands and along the coasts. Ceremonies and pageantry helped consolidate this relationship in a mixture of spirit cult and Buddhist worship. Overall, Buddhism allowed the Sriwijaya rulers to bring the local chiefs and their beliefs into the new and more expansive cosmic world of the royal court. With these rulers seen as Buddhist religious figures, Sriwijaya stood at the nexus of the local and the international, forming the system in both material and spiritual ways. The shift to Vajrayana would have encouraged this further.[43]

By the mid-eighth century, Buddhism was penetrating inland Java, and the rise of Mataram saw another Buddhist monarchy appear. On the Kedu Plain, the Sailendras superseded the Saivite rulers of the Dieng Plateau and took the position of maharaja over the local lords. Their court too became a centre for international scholarship and in the great Borobudur built their cosmic mountain (amidst the surrounding volcanoes). This monument both embodied the human ascent to the ultimate realisation and the Sailendra monarchy's centrality over the localities and their temples and cults of whatever sort. Later Sailendra rulers moved into the Sriwijayan system as Buddhist rulers of the coasts (and still later, in east Java, the Majapahit monarchy blended Hindu and Buddhist concepts in the royal Tantric Siva-Buddha cult).[44] The broad international Buddhist field doubtless aided the relationship of these two realms in central Java and southern Sumatra.

Outside the island world, though still in the coastal domain, the northern region of Champa (now central Vietnam) introduced Buddhist elements focused on Avalokiteśvara, Vairocana and Vajrapāṇi into its monarchy at Đồng-dương in the Thu-bồn river valley during the ninth century and extended its Buddhist temples farther north almost to the Việt mandala. Behind its own international port (now Hội-an), this court with its new Buddhist aspects, displaying the triad of Śākyamuni, Lokeśvara, and Prajñāpāramitā, too succeeded earlier Saivite ones. The shift perhaps stemmed from the strong international Buddhist influence and had more to do with the trade route than with control over the much looser mandala of Champa and its scattered localities. These Buddhist elements marked the rise of a new family to power in the region, and Buddhism encompassed the older royal Saivite pattern, reinforced by the Buddhist field of the islands. There are references to a link to Java and hence to international Buddhism. Later, in warfare with the Vietnamese to the north in the eleventh century, this capital of Champa was called by the invaders Phật-thệ, Oath of the Buddha, as the 1126 inscription noted.[45]

Elsewhere on the mainland, but upriver, in the eleventh century Buddhist monarchies developed at Pagan in the Irrawaddy River valley and, as we have seen, at Thăng-long in the Red River valley. Each of these two regimes worked to create an ideological system that encompassed and overarched the local powers, absorbing them into their particular cosmic whole. In Mranma, a complex network of Buddhist practices, texts, and ideas had spread across the landscape. Here the Pali scriptures, rather than

Sanskrit or Chinese, held sway. Like the first Lý kings of Đại Việt, the rulers of Pagan encouraged the development of the Buddhist community and the construction of myriad temples. From a Mahayana sect focused on Avalokiteśvara and Prajñāpāramitā as well as Maitreya, there too developed Tantric beliefs involving the Vajrayāna pantheon. An inscription of 1081 sought benefit for the monarchy, and the older contemporary of Lý Nhân-tông, King Kalancacsa (r. 1084–1113), by constructing temples and providing statues, wished to rescue his people from suffering and *samsara,* seeing himself as prophesied to be a bodhisattva and future Buddha. Indeed this king portrayed himself living in India at the time of the Buddha Kassapa, being linked to Śākyamuni as well as to Asoka, and various other significant times in the series of his lives. Kalancacsa completed the Shwezigon temple begun by Aniruddha (r. 1044–1077) and sent a mission to Bodhgaya. It would appear that, like Nhân-tông, this Burmese ruler linked himself and his realm directly to India and the Buddha as he tied the localities and his throne more tightly together; secured by the Buddha's prophecy, he worked strongly and creatively to form a field of social integration in an innovative and unprecedented manner. He did this verbally and visually, as he provided refuge and protection for those localities under his umbrella. His genealogy, like the transmission history of Đại Việt, provided direct and personal contact between himself and the origins of Buddhism.[46]

Later in the twelfth century, after a devastating break in the tradition of its monarchy, Angkor too turned towards a Buddhist monarchy under Jayavarman VII with its triad of Śākyamuni, Avalokiteśvara, and Prajñāpāramitā, like that at the earlier Đồng-dương. This king applied his Buddhism as a way to bring Kambujadesa back together under his rule. Returning from living in central Champa, Jayavarman established his Tantric Mahayana beliefs in the capital and rapidly built the Bayon with its four-faced (himself as Avalokiteśvara) towers showing omniscience and omnipotence. Constructing roads and rest houses through the realm, he reintegrated the kingdom under his overarching cosmic view and brought local cults into the centre. Out of the disorder, the king thereby brought material and spiritual well-being to his populace. The shade of his umbrella provided relief from the fierce sun for the localities of the mandala, just as the great *naga* sheltered the Buddha. By joining compassion and knowledge, Jayavarman led his realm to realization and salvation. He distributed images of himself as a Buddhist figure throughout the realm, proclaiming the central dominance of his beliefs over the many varied local manifestations of indigenous and Hindu beliefs.[47]

Where, then, did Lý Nhân-tông's Buddhist monarchy in Đại Việt stand in comparison with the other Buddhist monarchies of early Southeast Asia? They all grew out of the vibrant Buddhist world of the seventh to tenth centuries. Mranma and Đại Việt both saw the emergence of Buddhist kingships out of the broad existing mix of local beliefs and Buddhist temples and created direct links between their realms and the Buddha. Sriwijaya may too have been this way, whereas the monarchies of Mataram, Đồng-dương, and Angkor marked changes from earlier Hindu (Saivite/Vishnuite) royal cults and shifts in local and familial power. The Mataram royal cult developed over the centuries and a regional shift into the Siva-Buddha cult of the Majapahit monarchy. The Sriwijaya, Đồng-dương, and Angkor monarchies all suffered and changed as shifting political, economic, and religious configurations took place across the region.

In Đại Việt, Lý Nhân-tông established a Buddhist system that, to all appearances, resembled Jayavarman VII's at Angkor in his effort to spread his beliefs across the countryside and bind the localities to his capital, though without such a strong central monument. Nhân-tông's system of belief too was glorious, but seemingly without lasting impact on later reigns, which in Đại Việt became increasingly more Sinic classical. The realm of Đại Việt, like that of Angkor, changed greatly in the surge of international commerce during the twelfth and thirteenth centuries. Eventually, under the succeeding Trần dynasty, the monarchy of Đại Việt attempted to build on what Lý Nhân-tông had established in its early fourteenth century effort to create an integrated Thiền orthodoxy. Like Jayavarman's effort at Angkor, this orthodoxy, the Bamboo Grove (Trúc-lâm) school, was meant to hold together a realm undergoing increasing internal and external stresses. Both efforts ultimately failed, but in the case of Đại Việt it produced the source materials on early Vietnamese religion, *Departed Spirits of the Việt Realm* (1329) and *Eminent Monks of the Thiền Community* (1337).[48]

Notes

1. My great thanks to D. Christian Lammerts for his cogent comments, to the conference participants for their excellent contributions, and to Victor Lieberman for his close reading of the paper.
2. Wolters, *History, Culture, and Region*, pp. 27–31, 107–108, 112–18, 122–29, 151–56.
3. Vickery, *Society, Economics, and Politics*, pp. 190–204 (quotation, p. 200), 251, 269–70, 306–10, 324.
4. Ibid., pp. 140–56, 170, 207–209, 374–76; Aeusrivongse, "Devaraja Cult and Khmer Kingship", pp. 114–17.

5. Vickery, *Society, Economics, and Politics*, pp. 41–42, 140–43, 147, 149–51, 170; Woodward, "Bronze Sculptures of Ancient Cambodia", pp. 34–46.
6. Taylor, *Birth of Vietnam*, pp. 222–26, 254–56, 330–33, 353–54; Lý Tế Xuyên, *Departed Spirits*, pp. 33, 38, 57–58, 82.
7. Nguyen, *Zen in Medieval Vietnam*. pp. 105–11, 164–74; Võ Văn Tường, *Những Ngôi Chùa*, pp. 26–51.
8. Taylor, *Birth of Vietnam*, 80-86, 139-40, 155–58, 174, 181–83, 212–15, 217, 229–30; Whitmore, "The Rise of the Coast", pp. 104–107. Interestingly, similar to contemporary Cambodia (Woodward in this volume), there was a Vietnamese mention of Avalokitesvara and her benevolent water attributed to the tenth century in the fourteenth century text *Eminent Monks of the Thiền Community* (Nguyen, *Zen in Medieval Vietnam*, p. 172).
9. Whitmore, "Why Did Lê Văn Thịnh Revolt?", pp. 108–109, 117–18, 123.
10. Taylor, *Birth of Vietnam*, pp. 267–96.
11. Nguyen, *Zen in Medieval Vietnam*, pp. 113–14, 174–76; Taylor, "Rise of Đại Việt", p. 174; Taylor, "Authority and Legitimacy", p. 165; *Đại Việt Sử Ký Toàn Thư/Việt Sử Lược* (in both these works I give the range of years covered, here) 1010–1028 C.E.
12. Nguyen, *Zen in Medieval Vietnam*, pp. 124, 126, 165, 184 (quotation)–85, 387–88, n. 186; *Đại Việt Sử Ký Toàn Thư/Việt Sử Lược*, 1028–44; Taylor, "Rise of Đại Việt", pp. 175–78; Taylor, "Authority and Legitimacy", pp. 145, 148, 166.
13. Lý Tế Xuyên, *Departed Spirits*, pp. 40–46, 64–65; *Đại Việt Sử Ký Toàn Thư/Việt Sử Lược*, 1045–1053.
14. Nguyen, *Zen in Medieval Vietnam*, pp. 51–54, 124, 184, 204, 440–41, n. 644; Taylor, "Rise of Đại Việt", pp. 179–80; *Đại Việt Sử Ký Toàn Thư/Việt Sử Lược*, 1054–1072.
15. Taylor, "Authority and Legitimacy", pp. 153–55; for a summary of the reign of Lý Nhân-tông, see K.W. Taylor, *A History of the Vietnamese*, pp. 73–93.
16. Taylor, "Authority and Legitimacy", pp. 154–55; Lý Tế Xuyên, *Departed Spirits*, pp. 49–51, 75–77; *Đại Việt Sử Ký Toàn Thư/Việt Sử Lược*, 1072–1096; Nguyen, *Zen in* Medieval Vietnam, p. 399, n. 274.
17. Liam Kelley, personal communication (October 2011).
18. Taylor, "Authority and Legitimacy", pp. 143–45, 156–62; Lý Tế Xuyên, *Departed Spirits*, pp. 9, 37–39, 61–65, 71–74.
19. Whitmore, "Why Did Lê Văn Thịnh Revolt?", pp. 112, 115–16; Nguyen, *Zen in Medieval Vietnam*, pp. 92, 116, 123, 126, 130–33, 174, 194–95; *Đại Việt Sử Ký Toàn Thư/Việt Sử Lược*, 1080–1096.
20. Nguyen, *Zen in Medieval Vietnam*, p. 184.
21. Ibid., pp. 7 (quotation), 19–20, 27–28 (quotation, p. 28), 43; Schlutter, *How Zen Became Zen*, pp. 8–10, 13–16, 22–25, 32–33, 49, 51, 60, 66–67.
22. Nguyen, *Zen in Medieval Vietnam*, pp. 12, 28, 30, 35–36, 55, 66, 68, 81,

127–30 (quotations, pp. 128, 129), 225–27; Schlutter, *How Zen Became Zen*, pp. 17–21, 25–26, 39, 48, 55–62.

23. Sen, *Buddhism, Diplomacy, and Trade*, pp. 134, 137–41; Nguyen, *Zen in Medieval Vietnam*, pp. 204–205.
24. Nguyen, *Zen in Medieval Vietnam*, p. 130; *Đại Việt Sử Ký Toàn Thư*, 1149, 1184; Whitmore, "Rise of the Coast", p. 110; Hunter, "The Body of the King", p. 52.
25. Whitmore, "Why Did Lê Văn Thịnh Revolt?", pp. 113, 115–17; Nguyen, *Zen in Medieval Vietnam*, pp. 90–91, 98–99; Schlutter, *How Zen Became Zen*, p. 32; Sen, *Buddhism, Diplomacy, and Trade,* p. 122.
26. Nguyen, *Zen in Medieval Vietnam*, pp. 217–19.
27. Ibid., pp. 136–37, 152–53, 177–81, 186–87, 233–54.
28. *Đại Việt Sử Ký Toàn Thư/Việt Sử Lược*, 1096–1117; Nguyen, *Zen in Medieval Vietnam*, pp. 185, 200–201 (quotation); Sen, *Buddhism, Diplomacy, and Trade*, p. 117.
29. *Épigraphie*, #s 10-17.
30. Schlutter, *How Zen Became Zen*.
31. *Épigraphie*, #s 13-15, 17; Nguyen, *Zen in Medieval Vietnam*, pp. 354–55, n. 61.
32. *Épigraphie*, #s 11-17 (quotations #s 12, 15); Sen, *Buddhism, Diplomacy, and Trade*, p. 137.
33. *Épigraphie*, #11; Lý Tế Xuyên, *Departed Spirits*, pp. 34–35.
34. *Épigraphie*, #12; Sen, *Buddhism, Diplomacy, and Trade*, pp. 134, 136.
35. *Épigraphie*, #13; Võ Văn Tường, *Những Ngôn Chùa*, pp. 112–17.
36. *Épigraphie*, #s 14, 16, 17; Nguyen, *Zen in Medieval Vietnam*, pp. 182, 192, 427, n. 523, 433–34, nn. 572–80; Võ Văn Tường, *Những Ngôn Chùa*, pp. 124–27.
37. *Épigraphie*, #15; Võ Văn Tường, *Những Ngôn Chùa*, pp. 128–31; *Đại Việt Sử Ký Toàn* Thư/*Việt Sử Lược*, 1122.
38. *Épigraphie*, #15.
39. Whitmore, "Why Did Lê Văn Thịnh Revolt?", pp. 120–21.
40. Whitmore, "Rise of the Coast," pp. 107–14; for a discussion of this last century of Lý rule, see Taylor, *A History of the Vietnamese*, pp. 91–107.
41. *Épigraphie*, #s 18-20, 22; Taylor, "Voices Within and Without", pp. 59–70; Nguyen, *Zen in Medieval Vietnam*, pp. 134–56, 162, 181–205 passim; Lý Tế Xuyên, *Departed Spirits*, pp. 23, 62.
42. Conference on Buddhist Dynamics in Premodern Southeast Asia, Singapore, March 2011; Sen, *Buddhism, Diplomacy, and Trade*; Schlutter, *How Zen Became Zen*.
43. Hall, *History of Early Southeast Asia*, pp. 109, 114–19; Sen, *Buddhism, Diplomacy, and Trade*, p. 107; Griffiths, "New and Old, Published and Unpublished Epigraphical Discoveries Relevant to the History of Buddhism in Sumatra".

44. Hall, *History of Early Southeast Asia*, pp. 122–26, 279; Acri in this volume.
45. Woodward, "The Temple of Đồng Dương and the Karandavyuha Sutra", and in this volume; Hall, *History of Early Southeast Asia*, pp. 68–71, 101; Coedes, *Indianized States of Southeast Asia*, pp. 122–24; *Đại Việt Sử Ký Toàn Thư/Việt Sử Lược*, 1044, 1069; *Épigraphie*, #17; Vickery, "Short History of Champa", pp. 50–51; Schweyer, "Buddhism in Campā", pp. 309–37.
46. Aung-Thwin, *Pagan*, pp. 36–38, 43–44, 47–49, 58, 60, 63–64; Handlin, "The King and His Bhagavā: The Meanings of Pagan's Early Theravādas", pp. 165–236.
47. Hall, *History of Early Southeast Asia*, pp. 192–99; Woodward, "Bronze Sculptures", pp. 54–70, and in this volume; Aeusrivongse, "Devaraja Cult", pp. 135–36.
48. Whitmore, "Rise of the Coast", pp. 108–20; Whitmore, "Why Did Lê Văn Thịnh Revolt?", pp. 123–24; Sen, *Buddhism, Diplomacy, and Trade*, p. 118.

References

Aeusrivongse, Nidhi. "Devaraja Cult and Khmer Kingship at Angkor". In *Explorations in Early Southeast Asian History,* edited by K. R. Hall and J.K. Whitmore, pp. 107–48. Ann Arbor: Center for South and Southeast Asian Studies, University of Michigan, 1976.

Aung-Thwin, Michael. *Pagan: The Origins of Modern Burma*. Honolulu: University of Hawai'i Press, 1985.

Coedes, George. *The Indianized States of Southeast Asia*, trans. Honolulu: University of Hawai'i Press, 1968.

Đại Việt Sử Ký Toàn Thư [Complete Book of the Chronicle of Đại Việt], 4 vols. Hà Nội: NXB Khoa Học Xã Hội, 1998.

Épigraphie en chinoise du Việt Nam, vol. 1. "De l'occupation chinoise à la dynastie des Lý", edited by Phan Văn Các and C. Salmon. Paris: École francaise d'Êxtrême Orient; Hà Nội: Viện Nghiên Cứu Hán Nôm, 1998.

Griffiths, Arlo. "New and Old, Published and Unpublished Epigraphical Discoveries Relevant to the History of Buddhism in Sumatra". Conference on Buddhist Dynamics in Premodern Southeast Asia, Singapore, March 2011.

Hall, Kenneth R. *A History of Early Southeast Asia: Maritime Trade and Societal Development, 100–1500*. Lanham: Rowman & Littlefield, 2011.

Handlin, Lillian. "The King and His Bhagavā: The Meanings of Pagan's Early Theravādas". In Peter Skilling et al. eds., pp. 165–236. *How Theravāda is Theravāda?*, Explaining Buddhist Identities (Chiang Mai: Silkworm Books, 2012).

Hunter, Thomas. "The Body of the King: Reappraising Singhasari Period Synchretism". *Journal of Southeast Asian Studies* 38, no. 1 (2007): 27–53.

Lý Tế Xuyên. *Departed Spirits of the Việt Realm (Việt Điện U Linh Tập)*, translated by B.E. Ostrowski and B.A. Zottoli; edited by K.W. Taylor. Ithaca: Southeast Asia Program, Cornell University, 1999.

Nguyen, Cuong Tu. *Zen in Medieval Vietnam: A Study and Translation of the Thiền Uyển Tập Anh (Eminent Monks of the Thiền Community)*. Honolulu: University of Hawai'i Press, 1997.

Schlutter, Morten. *How Zen Became Zen: The Dispute over Enlightenment and the Formation of Chan Buddhism in Song-Dynasty China*. Honolulu: University of Hawai'i Press, 2008.

Schweyer, Anne-Valérie. "Buddhism in Campā", *Moussons* 13–14 (2009), pp. 313–24.

Sen, Tansen. *Buddhism, Diplomacy, and Trade: The Realignment of Sino-Indian Relations, 600–1400*. Honolulu: University of Hawai'i Press, 2003.

Taylor, Keith W. "The Rise of Đại Việt and the Establishment of Thăng-Long". In *Explorations in Early Southeast Asian History*, edited by K.R. Hall and J.K. Whitmore, pp. 149–91. Ann Arbor: Center for South and Southeast Asian Studies, University of Michigan, 1976.

———. *The Birth of Vietnam*. Berkeley: University of California Press, 1983.

———. "Authority and Legitimacy in 11th Century Vietnam". In *Southeast Asia in the 9th to 14th Centuries,* edited by D.G. Marr and A.C. Milner, pp. 139–76. Singapore: Institute of Southeast Asian Studies, 1986.

———. "Voices Within and Without: Tales From Stone and Paper about Đỗ Anh Vũ (1114–1159)". In *Explorations into Vietnamese Pasts,* edited by K.W. Taylor and J.K. Whitmore, pp. 59–80. Ithaca: Southeast Asia Program, Cornell University, 1995.

———. *The History of the Vietnamese* (Cambridge: Cambridge University Press, 2013).

Vickery, Michael. *Society, Economics, and Politics in Pre-Angkorian Cambodia: The 7th–8th Centuries*. Tokyo: The Centre for East Asian Cultural Studies for Unesco, The Toyo Bunko, 1997.

———. "A Short History of Champa". In *Champa and the Archaeology of Mỹ Sơn (Vietnam),* edited by A. Hardy, M. Cucarzi and P. Zolese, pp. 45–60. Singapore: National University of Singapore Press, 2009.

Việt Sử Lược [Short Chronicle of Việt], translated and edited by Trần Quốc Vượng. Huế: NXB Thuận Hóa, 2005 [1960].

Võ Văn Tường. *Những Ngôi Chùa Nổi Tiếng Việt Nam* [Vietnam's Famous Temples]. Hà Nội: NXB Văn Hóa-Thông Tin, 1994.

Whitmore, John K. "The Rise of the Coast: Trade, State, and Culture in Early Đại Việt". *Journal of Southeast Asian Studies* 37, no. 1 (2006): 103–22.

———. "Why Did Lê Văn Thịnh Revolt? Buddhism and Political Integration in Early 12th Century Đại Việt". In *The Growth of Non-Western Cities: Primary and Secondary Urban Networking*, edited by K.R. Hall, pp. 107–26. London: Routledge, 2011.

Wolters, O.W. *History, Culture, and Region in Southeast Asian Perspectives*, rev. ed. Ithaca: Southeast Asian Program, Cornell University, 1999.

Woodward, H.W., Jr. "Bronze Sculptures of Ancient Cambodia". In *Gods of Angkor: Bronzes from the National Museum of Cambodia*, edited by L.A. Cort and P. Jett, pp. 34–46. Washington, D.C.: Arthur M. Sackler Gallery, Smithsonian Institution, 2010.

——. "The Temple of Đồng Dương and the Karandavyuha Sutra". In *From Beyond the Eastern Horizon*, edited by M. Gupta. New Delhi: Aditya Prakashan, 2012.

10

SĪHAḶA SAṄGHA AND LAṄKĀ IN LATER PREMODERN SOUTHEAST ASIA[1]

Anne M. Blackburn

INTRODUCTION

It is a commonplace within much scholarly writing (including textbooks)[2] on Buddhism in southern Asia[3] that the second millennium CE witnessed an intensification of ties between Laṅkā (now Sri Lanka) and parts of mainland Southeast Asia now referred to as Burma (Myanmar) and Thailand. Buddhist monks said to be Lankan, or participants in monastic ordination lineages and educational practices rooted in Laṅkā, are described as altering the character of the mainland Southeast Asian Buddhist world by dispersing Lankan Buddhist monastic forms of practice, as well as linguistic and textual preferences, through kingdoms like Pagan, Sukhothai, Chiang Mai, and Pegu.

Our understanding of the history of southern Asian Buddhism during the second millennium remains very limited. The careful research required in order to understand movements of people, ideas, linguistic preferences, and textual forms, as well as social relations and institutional arrangements relating to the *Buddha-sāsana* (the world of Buddhist texts, persons, and practices) has barely begun. The reasons for this are many. They include a preference for the study of "early Buddhism" and doctrinal texts (understood narrowly) among early generations of Buddhist studies scholars, research programmes oriented by the boundaries of contemporary nation-states and national languages that have sometimes deflected or hindered the examination of regional and transregional histories, the daunting multilingual competences required for research, and a relatively weak intellectual interface between the disciplines of Buddhist studies, Asian history, art history, and epigraphy. This chapter draws on a new research project examining texts related to Lān Nā's Buddhist history during the late second millennium. Reading these texts raises valuable questions for historians of Buddhism, questions that carry us beyond the particular context of Lān Nā's Buddhist history. These texts invite us to consider how we can — creatively but with empirical rigour — use Buddhist textual sources from the later history of southern Asia as evidence to reconstruct histories of monastic mobility, including the sorts of travel that are understood to have linked Laṅkā and other parts of southern Asia more closely as the second millennium wore on. In this chapter, I explore some of the possibilities and limits of these texts as sources for the reconstruction of second-millennium Buddhist monastic networks. I hope that a fresh look at these texts from Lān Nā — texts of the type long understood as the primary evidence from which to write histories of mobile monks and transregional Buddhist institution-building — will suggest ways of gaining a better purchase on the histories of Buddhist monks and institutions in Lān Nā, as well as other political-cultural centers of second-millennium mainland Southeast Asia, such as Sukhothai, Ayutthaya, Pegu, and Pagan. I also indicate areas in which further research is desirable. I wish to emphasize that this chapter represents a still-early phase in my research and reflection on the way that the idea of Laṅkā and connections to Lankan Buddhism figured in second-millennium southern Asian Buddhist histories. I hope that this essay will encourage scholarly rejoinder and consultation. This conceptually and empirically challenging set of problems will only be resolved through collaborative research.

LAṄKĀ & LĀN NĀ

On the basis of *Jinakālamālī*, as well as the *Tamnān (Mūlasāsanā) Wat Pa Däng* [Chiang Tung], important early work by Swearer[4] and Swearer and Sommai[5] identified "two streams of Sinhalese [Lankan] Buddhism … the first mediated through Burma and the second brought directly from Sri Lanka by Thai and Sihala monks."[6] The first lineage became associated with Wat Suon Dòk of Chiang Mai, while the second was established in Chiang Mai's Wat Pa Däng. Here, I look closely at *Jinakālamālī* as well as two versions of the *Tamnān (Mūlasāsanā) Wat Pa Däng,* focusing on the sections of these texts that discuss the fifteenth-century ordination of monastic visitors to Laṅkā and their subsequent return to Lān Nā, where they formed the "second stream" that became the Wat Pa Däng lineage in Lān Nā. Looking at these texts, I attempt to read them in several different ways. In the first place, *Jinakālamālī* and the *Tamnān (Mūlasāsanā) Wat Pa Däng* invite consideration of the textual work accomplished by persons, places, and institutions from Laṅkā within these Lān Nā narratives. What is the narrative structure and apparent function of such invocations of Laṅkā in these Lān Nā texts? Does the narration of Lān Nā-Laṅkā connections vary in relation to the language of text, or in relation to the apparent context for composition?

Secondly, these texts are suggestive for our understanding of how mid-second-millennium Buddhists in Lān Nā conceived of forms of monastic collective belonging that linked Lān Nā (or locations within it) and Laṅkā (or her privileged Buddhist sites). Reading such works, it is beneficial to investigate the affiliative terms used to describe monks brought into contact and connection through the travel of monks who visited Laṅkā and then returned to Lān Nā. Are they said to become participants in something "theravādin", "mahāvihārin", a "Sīhaḷa Saṅgha", or some other collective(s)? Why is Laṅkā seen as a desirable focus for their pilgrimage and ordination? Finally, these texts — while obviously not transparent windows onto the social realities of mid-millennium Lān Nā and Laṅkā for reasons I acknowledge further below — depict intra-monastic and monastic-courtly interactions in the context of transregional Buddhist movement. These depictions are sometimes at odds with conventional scholarly understandings of the causality and patronage that characterized travelling monks and importations of monastic lineage across the borders of polity. As such, they deserve further consideration by historians.

Jinakālamālī

I turn first to *Jinakālamālī*, as we know the text through the Pali Text Society (PTS) edition prepared by Buddhadatta. Composed in some form probably in the 1510s or 1520s, or perhaps extended in the 1520s from a version completed in 1517,[7] *Jinakālamālī* is an ambitious account of the *Buddha-sāsana*, moving from Buddha biographies to the Laṅkā of Buddhaghosa's era, and on to the unfolding of Buddhist history in the region we now know as central and northern Thailand, Laos, and the Shan States of Burma. We cannot be confident that the sources from which the PTS edition and translation were made (they do not rely entirely on the same source base, and the sources are relatively late manuscripts and/or printed texts) carry forward with stability or integrity the contents of the original work, or even an early version of Ratanapañña's composition.[8] Further work on manuscripts of this text is an urgent desideratum. However, since the events narrated by *Jinakālamālī* conclude in the early sixteenth century, and because the work is fairly lean in its treatment of Lān Nā-based events without an accretive narrative style, it is not altogether implausible at this stage of research to suggest that the PTS edition brings us close to an early sixteenth-century version of the text.

According to the PTS edition of *Jinakālamālī*, *mahātheras* from Chiang Mai, as well as "kambojaraṭṭha" further south,[9] decided to bring *upasampadā* from Laṅkādīpa to instantiate it in their own land (*satthusāsanopasampadaṃ āharitvā amhākaṃ dese ropessāma*).[10] They are said to have met Mahāsāmi Vanaratana (apparently in southern Laṅkā), have studied Lankan writing and recitation practice, and to have received higher ordination at "Yāpāpaṭṭana in Kalyāṇi".[11] The text indicates carefully the astrological conjuncture for this ordination, and that the monk Vanaratana served as *kammavācācariya* while Dhammacārī was their *upajjhāya*. Their stay in Laṅkā was very brief (only four months), and they are said to have requested that two Lankan *theras* return with them as *upajjhāyas* for subsequent ordinations. The seniority of these *theras* is carefully noted in the text (93), which goes on to detail the group's places of *vassa* residence upon return to the mainland, prior to the return of the Chiang Mai monks to Chiang Mai. This is perhaps to show that by the time they began to conduct *upasampadā* in Lān Nā they possessed the required seniority to do so as *upajjhāyas*. Their first *upasampadā* in the region is specified as occurring in or shortly after the year in which they had attained ten *vassa*. A string of ordinations is then reported, identifying key monks by name (e.g. tattha laddhūpasampadā Dhammarakkhita-Dhammaratana-Ñāṇabodhimahātherā veditabbā). All this resulted in a growing number of "Sīhaḷa *bhikkhus*" in the region (tadā bahū Sīhaḷabhikkhū ahesuṃ) even before King Tilakarāja (r. 1441/2–87) ascended the throne.[12] The king is said to have supported an *upasampadā* ritual (perhaps of 500 men) only five months after accession, with the ritual acts performed by a *saṅgha* led by Medhaṅkara, Ñāṇamaṅgala, and Sīlavaṃsa.[13] These were all monks who had made the ordination journey to Laṅkā. Interestingly, neither the reciter of *kammavācā* nor the *upajjhāya* for any ordinands is specified, perhaps because the text focuses on royal patronage rather than lineage details. Monks and the king go on to do various acts in favour of the *sāsana*, including in lands outside *müang* Chiang Mai that are seemingly subjected to the king's military ambitions, perhaps partly in relation to the king's fraught relationship to his deposed father. After the death of both royal parents, King Tilakarāja dedicates a new *sīmā* for *upasampadā*, and conducts an *upasampadā* in which a Mahānārada is singled out twice for special mention. Perhaps because his lineage is of concern to the author, Mahānārada's *upajjhāya* and the recitor of *kammavācā* are both mentioned by name.[14] The text goes on to state that, since then, all the "Sīhaḷa *bhikkhus*" in the areas under the control of the king of Chiang Mai (Nabbisindassa vijite sabbe Sīhaḷabhikkhū) bring potential ordinands to that *sīmā*.[15] In *Jinakālamālī*, *monastic-technical* references dominate the story of travel to Laṅkā and return, although no reason for their wish to obtain higher ordination from Laṅkā is expressed. Since the text discusses studies related to recitation and pronunciation (relevant to the key rituals of *upasampadā* and *pātimokkha*, and to divisions among monastic lineages including the manner of their ordination[16]), this suggests that concerns for the integrity or durability of existing Chiang Mai ritual practice helped catalyse the journey. Certainly the Chiang Mai sections of the text favour the Wat Pa Däng line from within which Ratanapañña wrote.[17]

Tamnān (Mūlasāsanā) Wat Pa Däng

Without reading skill in Thai and Thai Yüan, I am dependent on others' translations when working with *Tamnān (Mūlasāsanā) Wat Pā Däng*, a monastic history written in celebration of the Wat Pa Däng line, though of uncertain authorship. Fortunately, translations exist for two versions of the text. Each translation is based on a different manuscript, though both manuscripts show signs of composition in Chiang Tung (also Jengtung and Kengtung) rather than in Chiang Mai.[18] The manuscript of the *Tamnān Mūlasāsanā Wat Pā Däng* translated by Swearer and Sommai is of uncertain date.[19] Because it closes with a narrative of monastic disputes in Chiang Tung, and a list of royal supporters of the Pa Däng lineage in Chiang Tung prior to 1521, Swearer and Sommai reasonably suggest that the work was composed, or copied from an earlier text and expanded through Chiang Tung details, not long after 1521.[20] The manuscript from which their translation was made is, however, almost certainly much later. After the death of Ñāṇagambhīra, portrayed as the leader of the monastic voyagers to Laṅkā, the text takes up the story again, focusing not on Ñāṇagambhīra's own activities but on disputes arising in Chiang Tung between monks of his ordination line and a rival group. This narrative of dispute closes the *tamnān*, along with a list of kings who supported Ñāṇagambhīra's Wat Pa Däng lineage in Chiang Tung. In this work, the trigger event for the fifteenth-century journey of monks to Laṅkā from Chiang Mai and kingdoms further south is a report brought back to Chiang Mai by a Wat Suon Dòk *thera* (a *thera* associated with the first Laṅkā-oriented monastic "stream") who went to Anurādhapura (in Laṅkā) and there suffered criticisms of his mode of conducting *kammavācā* and *pātimokkha*. Therefore, he and his fellow travellers had been excluded from *saṅghakamma*s in Laṅkā on grounds that their improper pronunciation would pollute the ritual.

> The Sangha in Lankā accused us saying, "Then none of you is a monk. Our language has 41 consonants, but yours has only 32; you make the *am* sound into *ām*. You are not following the method set forth for us by Buddhaghosa in Lankā. ... Your ordination is fruitless."[21]

Following this monk's return to Chiang Mai and the report of his limited welcome at Anurādhapura, Ñāṇagambhīra, star pupil of Rājaguru Dhammakitti in Chiang Mai, is sent by his teacher to garner support from King Sam Fang Kaeng and, later, from the head of the *saṅgha* in Ayutthaya, in order to make a trip to "Wat Thūpārāma in Laṅkā to study the dhamma in the language[22] they use in Laṅkā."[23] Once the possibility of the journey has been broached by Dhammakitti via Ñāṇagambhīra, the king of Chiang Mai is portrayed as keen to clear the name of Chiang Mai's monks: "bring back what you have learned, so that the monks of Laṅkā will not doubt that the monks of Chiang Mai are properly qualified." The Rājaguru of Ayutthaya, Dhammagambhīra, is portrayed as giving something close to grudging assent: "Our teachers have handed down the teaching in this manner. If you have doubts about it, you should go to ask the Mahā Thera who is *our teacher at Anurādhapura in Laṅkā*."[24]

Upon arrival in Anurādhapura, Ñāṇagambhīra and his fellows meet the Lankan monk from "Wat Thūpārāma" whose criticism of their Wat Suon Dòk brother precipitated their journey. The text describes this monk, Surinda Thera, as criticizing the instability and impurity of Lankan Buddhism in various places "because Burmese, Mon [meng], and Kulāphāsī[25] monks have mixed in with us." He recommends that Ñāṇagambhīra and his fellow travellers go to Rohana,[26] the only place where "proper adherence to the *dhamma-vinaya* and the [tradition of] the commentaries is found", guarded by the *devatā* on the Buddha's orders. The *devatā* screen the foreigners who, eventually, are allowed to reach the royal court. There the king agrees to organize a massive monastic assembly through which the visiting monks will learn the proper *sāsanā*.[27] Here, "*sāsanā*" seems to mean, centrally, instruction on monastic practice. The new arrivals tell of monastic practice in their lands and are immediately criticized, after which Ñāṇagambhīra and a representative of the Ayutthayan court are ordained by way of corrective.[28] They are ordered to study and ordain according to the grammar of Kaccāyana, in order to protect the heavens, the monarch, the *dhamma*, and the *saṅgha*. Rohana's monastic chief instructs them:

> Take the *sāsanā*, the *dhamma-piṭaka* in the Pāli language of Laṅkā which consists of 41 letters according to the text based on the *Saddasandhi, Nikhādanasaddā, Cintāmaṇī* and *Vuttisaddā*. This text of Kaccāyana Thera follows the teaching of Buddhaghosa as he propounded it for the monks in Jumbudvīpa.[29]

The new ordinands study in Laṅkā for five years,[30] mastering the *dhamma*. In preparation for departure they are given a Buddha image, a *bodhi* tree, and a *tipiṭaka*, with instructions to use the Lankan mode of recitation in order to preserve the *saṅgha* in their own lands and to garner favor from the *yakkhas* and *devatā*. This text emphasizes that failure to recite correctly will produce cataclysmic effects: monks will abandon discipline, political order will decline and "that country will be destroyed because the religion of the guardians of the four quarters and the *devatā* of the world is ill-founded".[31]

Interestingly, it is not said that they brought more senior monks with them from Laṅkā to serve as *upajjhāyas*, perhaps because they had remained five years in Laṅkā. Upon their return to Ayutthaya, the Rājaguru there is said to have asked the king "to abandon the old *sāsanā*" and to support reordination and study according to the teachings brought from Laṅkā. At Sukhothai they are described as bringing "the true *sāsanā*" with them, to the delight of the king and *saṅgha*.[32] Upon arrival in Chiang Mai, Ñāṇagambhīra receives the support of his preceptor, Rājaguru Dhammakitti, to reordain Chiang Mai monks. As numbers grow, a new monastery becomes necessary, and Wat Pā Däng is constructed with royal support. And, as the text reports, the new ordination line "has been called the Siṅhala Order (*pakkha*) from that time to this".[33] Much of the remainder of the text concerns events in Chiang Tung, now in the Shan States to the north of Chiang Mai. The monastic lineage there, rooted in the previous Laṅkā-oriented lineage of Sumana brought from Sukhothai in the "first stream", is said to have merged with that brought by Ñāṇagambhīra, yet a dispute later arises emphasizing differences between the Sumana lineage housed at Wat Suon Dòk (Chiang Tung) and Wat Pā Däng (Chiang Tung). Other monastic difficulties are also mentioned, along with praise for Wat Pā Däng and its royal supporter during the era of Ñāṇagambhīra. In Chiang Tung events the *devatā* play a key role at various moments, harkening back to their place of guardians of the *sāsana* in Rohana.

A comparison of the *Tamnān Wat Pa Däng* manuscript translated by Saimong with that translated by Swearer and Sommai underscores the fluidity of the *tamnān* genre. Saimong's manuscript has no copy date, though a middle portion of the text is dated to 1870 by a scribe. The work is effectively a compendium text, containing several monastic and *sāsana* histories, as well as sections describing local monastic practice and *saṅgha* regulation that are in some ways comparable to the *katikāvaṭa* texts of Lanka.[34] The first twenty-six printed pages appear to function as a narrative unit. Prior to that point there is no explicit chapter break, but there the text states a preliminary conclusion.[35] Prior to this chapter break, the text dates some events, the latest being C.S. 810 (1448). This suggests, though certainly does not prove, that this section as it appears in Saimong's manuscript is close to a late fifteenth- or early sixteenth-century version of the *tamnān*.[36] Considerable overlap with the text translated by Swearer and Sommai strengthens this possibility, though concordance between texts might be the result of later scribal practice. This manifestation of *Tamnān Wat Pa Däng* offers a richer and more complex account of the state of the Lān Nā *saṅgha* prior to Ñāṇagambhīra's trip to Laṅkā and the inauguration of what becomes the Wat Padäng lineage. Here, Ñāṇagambhīra is an independent-minded close reader of the Pāli *dhamma* and *vinaya* alert to inconsistencies and improprieties within monastic recitation texts. After studying *dhamma* and *vinaya* for five *vassa*, he is convinced that Sumana's ordination line (associated with Wat Suon Dòk) does not perform *upasampadā* correctly, owing to faulty recitation pronunciation. These concerns take him to his teacher, then to Ayutthaya, and on to Anurādhapura. Again, he is directed to Rohana, in order to access untainted and stable monastic practice. In Rohana he is explicitly informed by the head of the Rohana *saṅgha* that Sumana — source of the Wat Suon Dòk Lankan lineage in Chiang Mai — had been to Laṅkā (not only to Martaban as *Jinakālamālī* reports) but violated both the form and the word of *saṅghakamma*s upon his departure, failing to adhere to the grammatical tradition of Kaccāyana.

> He took the Sāsanā from Laṅkā and established [it] in Möng Sukhodaiy first, spreading the Sāsanā to Möng Nabbaburī Jenghmai, adding made-up words creating perversity not in accord with good grammar thus, and it would be immoral frivolity to the Sāsanā everywhere.[37]

The leader of the Rohana *saṅgha*, here referred to as Sudassana, Rājaguru of Koṭṭē (one of Laṅkā's several, sometimes rival, kingdoms during this period), recriminates Sumana and his line through examples of Pāli spelling and pronunciation, used to discuss the incorrect pronunciation and grammatical frailty of Sumana's lineage.[38]

Upon return to Chiang Mai, Ñāṇagambhīra's teacher orders a reordination on grammatical grounds.

> All of us ordained under ordination procedures brought by Lord Mahā Sumana of Sukhodaiy with Lord Ānanda Bhikkhu, and later by Lord Mahā Sujāto of Jaleng ... have been ordained incorrectly, not in accord with the true Grammar. All of you will leave the Order and go for ordination at the residence of Mahā Ñāṇagambhīra.[39]

When the action moves to Chiang Tung, Ñāṇagambhīra's Wat Pa Däng monks overcome natural and supernatural disaster through perfect *dhamma* recitation, implicitly justified as congruent with proper grammar. The spread of the Wat Pa Däng line in the region is described partly in terms of grammar studies. As for the monks of Sumana's line associated with Wat Suon Dòk, according to the *tamnān*,

> their doctrine was not consistent. Their recitation... was not consistent... They followed the dictates of their hearts... That was why the *sasana* of the monasteries of the Garden [Suon Dòk] sect was not consistent, tending to be frivolous.[40]

READING MONASTIC HISTORIES

Genealogy and Performance

What we think we know of Lankan monastic influence in mainland Southeast Asia after the eleventh century is indebted significantly to Buddhist monastic lineage histories like the ones I have just discussed. Although scholars have not always indicated the evidence on which they base their accounts of second millennium monastic mobility in the southern Asian region, it often appears as though *Jinakālamālī*, versions of the *Kalyāṇī Inscriptions* and/or *Sāsanavaṃsa* lie at the root of historical reconstructions. All three of these texts (or text-clusters) must be handled with care. I have already noted the seemingly late source base for the standard edition of *Jinakālamālī*. As Lammerts has noted, editions of the Pāli and Mon texts of the *Kalyāṇī Inscriptions* rely on *manuscripts* of the *Kalyāṇī Inscriptions* in order to compensate for illegible faces of the rock *inscriptions*. It is not certain that such manuscripts were prepared as faithful copies of original stone engravings. Moreover, manuscripts of the inscriptions may have circulated and been reproduced independently (without recourse to the stone inscriptions), transmitting a somewhat fluid memory about the ordination mission sponsored by King Dhammaceti in the fifteenth century.[41] Therefore, much of the *Kalyāṇī Inscriptions* now extant cannot be treated as inscriptional evidence. In some cases it may be more valuable as evidence of the place of monastic histories in Buddhist institution-building and the monastic work of memory after the fifteenth century. *Sāsanavaṃsa* is a nineteenth-century text, composed at least in part to satisfy the request of Lankan monks involved in Lankan lineage experiments and disputes. It is a heavily layered text that draws on several centuries of Burmese and Pāli language *vaṃsa* (lineage) text production and discourse in what is now Burma. As such, it cannot be used straightforwardly to reconstruct early second-millennium monastic movements on the central Southeast Asian mainland or even as evidence of a nineteenth-century Mandalay *saṅgha*'s historiography.[42]

Such monastic histories, along with other *saṅgha* histories and lineage texts like the *Tamnān (Mūlasāsanā) Wat Pa Däng* explored earlier in this chapter, cannot be used as transparent evidence of regional monastic mobility and shifting forms of connection between Laṅkā and the central Southeast Asian mainland.[43] These works were sometimes written long after the events they purport to describe, and then transmitted through unstable scribal practices that did not necessarily privilege verbatim copying. Even when possibly composed in closer temporal proximity to the monastic activities they discuss, as may be the case for the Lān Nā texts introduced earlier in this essay, they were composed not as neutral accounts of the *sāsana*'s unfolding, but in the explicit or implicit service of a particular monastic group, generally in the context of a competitive local and/or regional monastic conversation (or debate) about the purity and authenticity of various lineages and their practices. These are partial and argumentative expressions of local memory. What Collins and Walters have persuasively suggested for earlier Pāli *vaṃsa* texts from Laṅkā[44] is likely true for these later lineage narratives as well. They are tendentious texts.

I am not the first to note this feature of monastic lineage texts from the region we now know as Southeast Asia. Years ago, Tambiah proposed that Tai Buddhist textual celebrations of connections to Laṅkā be seen as strategic and connected to new trends in the self-identification of Buddhist literati — and, implicitly, their patrons — at least in the Tai states from the era of Sukhothai onwards.

> Whatever the circumstantial facts and influences, what we must accept as of prime importance for the ideological inflection of Sukhodaya, and its setting the precedent for later Thai understandings of their history, is that it enthusiastically championed Lankavangsa [Lanka-lineage] or Sinhalese Theravada Buddhism.... The conspicuous fact is that the Thai chronicles and inscriptions of the thirteenth to fifteenth centuries turn the spotlight on their affiliation with Sinhalese Pali Buddhism and the transformation it wrought on their way of life.[45]

A recognition of the "ideological" or "genealogical" character of monastic lineage narratives might be seen as deeply discouraging in our attempts to understand the connected histories of Laṅkā and Southeast Asian *saṅgha*s and polities. To the contrary, I would argue that recognition of the rhetorical, performative, and locally argumentative character of monastic lineage texts opens important avenues for our historical research. Elsewhere, I have stated that Lankan Buddhist monks used a repertoire of terms

> to claim or report monastic inheritance, belonging, and affiliation. Looking closely at monastic accounts of lineage and ordination histories, with an eye to differences in genre and contexts of composition, further suggests that claims to collective belonging or difference within the monastic world are context sensitive. Depending on the circumstances in which such claims are narrated, including the identity of the patrons and interlocutors addressed, some terms and historical claims are more suitable for use than others.[46]

Language and genre, the context of composition, and the degree of technical monastic understanding expected of the reader, could all affect the choices made to draw on the monastic repertoire in order to discuss monastic affiliation, difference, and belonging in some terms rather than others. This means that close readings of lineage texts, attentive not only to *what* arguments are made but *how* they are made, provides valuable indications of the contexts within which a particular text was composed and the work it was intended to accomplish.

It may be fruitful to consider references to non-local monasticism generally, and Lankan monasticism in particular, as an element within the textual repertoire of monastic literati from the second-millennium Buddhist central Southeast Asian mainland. Regardless of what was, empirically, the history of monastic mobility and connection within the southern Asian region during this period — a separate research problem to which I shall shortly return — there is already enough evidence to suggest that references to Laṅkā, and to Laṅkā-oriented or Laṅkā-originated monastic lineages, are an important feature of central Southeast Asian texts composed to affirm the authority, purity, and vitality of some monastic lines and royal-monastic patronage arrangements (typically at the expense of others). It would be illuminating, in all likelihood, to investigate more broadly and deeply how this Lankan element worked in lineage texts and other monastic histories produced within the historical kingdoms of central mainland Southeast Asia. The few published texts we possess deserve more careful scrutiny than they have received, in addition to manuscripts composed and/or copied in Pāli and/or local literary languages. Reading a larger number of monastic histories from a wider range of locales, with an eye to the textual and argumentative "work" performed by references to Laṅkā/Sīhaḷa/Sīhaḷa Saṅgha, etc. should allow us to identify more historical moments in the history of the southern Asian Pāli-using region during which something important was held to be at stake between monastic groups, and to develop more refined hypotheses about the place of specific lineage text compositions within monastic and lay-monastic relations.

Here I presume, at least for the time being, that references to Laṅkā and a constellation of related terms (such as Sīhaḷa/Sīhaḷa Saṅgha) function (at least often) in monastic lineage texts and histories composed outside Laṅkā in ways similar to the place of *araññavāsin* references in Sinhala and Pāli Buddhist texts from Laṅkā (Blackburn 2001).[47] That is, whatever their empirical value for the reconstruction of the events they narrate, these texts use Laṅkā to add value in some way. In other words, where Laṅkā (and her related terms) are present in texts composed outside the island, we have a textual indication that something of significance was at stake outside Laṅkā where the work was composed (or, perhaps, redacted). To put it another way, I am suggesting that references to Laṅkā and Lankan monasticism are "symptomatic". They are literary indications that invite us to probe more deeply into the local history of Buddhist institutional life near the time of the text's composition (and/or redaction). Probing that history would involve the close reading of other lineage texts near in time and location, but also an inter-textual leap to the world of epigraphy where possible, as well as consideration of other material remains such as those increasingly available thanks to the painstaking work of art historians and archaeologists.

Language and Context of Composition

The preceding preliminary investigation of *Jinakālamālī* and manifestations of *Tamnān (Mūlasāsanā) Wat Pa Däng* also suggests that it may be fruitful to develop a more sustained examination of regional monastic lineage texts, comparing the form and content of lineage texts composed in Pāli with those composed in regional literary vernaculars. The admittedly small textual sample from Lān Nā discussed earlier in this chapter includes one Pāli-language text — *Jinakālamālī*. Its narration of the fifteenth-century origins of the Wat Pa Däng lineage is quite spare, without a textually rich depiction of catalysts for the journey to Lanka, monastic personalities, dialogue, and monastic disputes. (It also includes fewer magical-supernatural elements than both manuscripts of *Tamnān (Mūlasāsanā) Wat Pa Däng*.) This suggests that *Jinakālamālī* was not intended primarily as a contribution to small-scale (e.g. urban, sub-regional) wars of monastic position within the Lān Nā *saṅgha*. *Jinakālamālī* does affirm the authority and prestige of the Wat Pa Däng lineage, but at slightly greater narrative remove, perhaps oriented ultimately to a royal audience (as the concluding chapters on King Tilakarāja and his successors suggest). The local language *tamnān* that recount the history of the Wat Pa Däng lineage do so through more detailed references to monastic education and ritual practice and passages of emphatic dialogue, along with a larger cast of characters and more supernatural elements. A closer look at monastic histories composed in Pāli, Burmese, Mon, central Thai, and Thai Yüan would indicate whether the differences initially apparent in this small sample from Lān Nā hold more widely across the central Southeast Asian mainland. Do lineage texts in Pāli (without substantial debt to those in local literary vernacular)[48] typically unfold with less richness of scene-setting, character development, dialogue, and supra-human action than their counterparts composed in local literary languages? Do local language monastic histories function more often as accretive compendia texts than do their counterparts composed in Pāli? Moreover, are there evident patterns in the relationship between patronage of a monastic history's composition and the language used in the composition? That is, are Pāli-language texts recounting monastic lineage histories more often associated with royal patrons and/or more likely to focus on royal rather than monastic protagonists? While Pāli is often, rightly, considered a language distinguished by its capacity to speak widely in the Buddhist world, across a southern Asian region otherwise divided by diverse mother tongues, it has also functioned as a locally engaged praśāstic language within royal courts.[49]

Monastic Affiliation

I suggested earlier that monastic histories such as those discussed here are valuable also for the record they offer of how Buddhist authors expressed textually memories of affiliation, and ways of identifying collective belonging locally and transregionally. How are local and transregional collectives identified in such texts? In what affiliative terms do authors writing from the Southeast Asian mainland link themselves and their brothers to the monastic worlds of Laṅkā and Sīhaḷa? It is striking — given the way these terms have dominated specialist and semi-specialist histories of Lān Nā Buddhism history until recently — that the monastic travellers to Laṅkā portrayed in *Jinakālamālī* are not described as involving themselves with anything *theravādin* or *mahāvihāravāsin*. Indeed, it is interesting how little detail is given about the Lankan lineage through which the Lān Nā monks and their southern fellows became "Sīhaḷa *bhikkhus*." Nothing is said to place Vanaratana, Dhammacārī, or Sudassana within the monastic hierarchy of Laṅkā besides Vanaratana's title of Mahāsāmi. No claims are made to Lān Nā monks' participation in any specific Lankan monastic lineage through their Lankan *upasampadā*. The ritual details intermittently offered by the text appear more concerned with establishing a pedigree for selected Lān Nā monks within the lineage newly imported to Lān Nā.

Both versions of *Tamnān (Mūlasāsanā) Wat Pa Däng* were composed with an obvious narrative interest in enhancing the standing of the Wat Pa Däng lineage, especially at Chiang Tung. In the text translated by Swearer and Sommai, the Lankan *saṅgha* at Anurādhapura is portrayed as possessing enough authority in the minds of Chiang Mai monks to impel Ñāṇagambhīra's journey to Laṅkā when word of Anurādhapura's disapproval reaches the Chiang Mai *saṅgha*. However, understandably, it is only the *saṅgha* in Ayutthaya, associated with Sumana's "first stream" that claims a teacher-student relationship to monks in Anurādhapura. The texts stress Lankan self-criticism of the *saṅgha* in Anurādhapura as corrupt, with the leading local monk himself urging the visitors to travel further south in search of proper practice. This nicely undercuts the earlier portrayal of the Ayutthayan Rājaguru as confident in the Anurādhapura connection. None of the Lankan monks is referred to as a member of *mahāvihāravāsin* lineage. This might have been implied to be the case for monks at Anurādhapura's Thūpārāma yet, even if the Thūpārāma was understood to have been associated with a *mahāvihāravāsin* line, Ñāṇagambhīra and his fellows were not re-ordained there but sent off to Rohana. No specifics are offered regarding the monastic lineage so well protected by Rohana and her *devatā*. Since one monastic line in Lān Nā (associated with Wat Suon Dòk, as well as with the royal court of Ayutthaya) was understood by the text to be at least indirectly rooted in Anurādhapura, it was natural for the authors of *Tamnān (Mūlsāsanā) Wat Pa Däng* to emphasize that their ordination originated from a different and better lineage. The *tamnān* is both provocative and imaginative when it has a leading monk at "Wat Thūpārāma" in Anurādhapura blame the corruption of the Lankan *saṅgha* on the arrival of monks from what is now Burma and Thailand, implying that Wat Suon Dòk monks in Chiang Mai are mistaken in thinking that they participate in a pure Lankan lineage and that they have perhaps contributed to its further decay. Yet even as the authority, purity, and ritual efficacy of the Wat Suon Dòk lineage is called into question by the *tamnān* in ingenious ways throughout the work, the narrative does not complement these destructive moves by developing a robust account of the Rohana monastic line into which Ñāṇagambhīra and his fellows enter through ordination and instruction. What is brought back from Laṅkā by Ñāṇagambhīra and his fellows is described as the/a *sāsana* rather than a specific monastic lineage. Even the very general term "Sīhaḷa pakkha" (the "Sihala side/camp/company") seems to be used only once, when monastic action again reaches Chiang Mai. Nowhere is there any mention of *theravādin* affiliation. As with the *tamnān* translated by Swearer and Sommai, the manuscript *Tamnān Wat Pa Däng* translated by Saimong does not claim for Ñāṇagambhīra and his fellows any *theravādin* or *mahāvihāravāsin* connection. Nor is any lineage history of the Lankan monks whom they joined through ordination provided. What is emphasized is the Rohana *saṅgha*'s role as the source of grammatical — and therefore ritual — purity and efficacy. Rather than emphasizing that Wat Pa Däng monks are good monks *because they have become participants in Lankan lineage*, *Tamnān Wat Pa Däng* argues that its lineage is accomplished and authoritative because sharing Lankan lineage *gave them access to powerful ritual tools*.

Is the absence of detailed Lankan lineage claims and information related to Laṅkā a clue that Ñāṇagambhīra and his fellows did not actually reach Laṅkā for ordination? At this stage of research, this possibility should not be altogether discounted, since the account presented by the Lān Nā monastic histories is not corroborated by *Mahāvaṃsa*, a serial royal-monastic history composed in Laṅkā. However, *Mahāvaṃsa* also fails to mention Dhammacetī's fifteenth-century embassy from Pegu to Koṭṭē. The eighteenth-century Lankan author who composed the section of *Mahāvaṃsa* in which both of these monastic missions would have figured may not have had access to monastic histories of the *saṅgha* of southwestern Lanka, or interest in them. To the best of my knowledge at present, there is no mention of Ñāṇagambhīra and his mainland monastic colleagues in works composed in Pāli or Sinhala from Laṅkā during the Koṭṭē period or thereafter prior to the Kandyan period. However, much work remains to be done in such literary materials, which have not been read historically with questions of monastic mobility centrally in view.[50] It is clear that there was a robust *saṅgha* in southwestern Lanka oriented towards the royal court of Koṭṭē (1412–1580). A leading monastic luminary of that time was Mahāthera Vanaratana, discussed in *Haṃsa Sandeśaya* composed in the mid-fifteenth century. Vanaratana was the abbot of Padmavati Piriveṇa at Kāragala in the area near what is now Colombo, and referred to as Saṅgharāja in *Haṃsa Sandeśaya*.[51] This information accords well with the account given in *Jinakālamālī*. Available volumes of *Epigraphia Zeylanica* contain no references to monastic visitors in the Koṭṭē court, but most of the inscriptions collected there are considerably earlier, from the early courtly centers of Anurādhapura and Pollonāruva.[52]

If Ñāṇagambhīra and his fellow monks did visit Laṅkā, and ordain within a Lankan monastic lineage there, one might expect that they would have learned something about the way such a lineage was referred to, as well as its history. In that case, silence on these matters suggests that references to Lankan monastic lineage (the "kinship charts" of the *saṅgha*) were not considered relevant status indicators when articulating monastic pedigree in Lān Nā. This is consonant with Skilling's suggestion that

> the Southeast Asian *saṅgha*s that renewed their ordination lineage in Sri Lanka were, as soon as they returned to their own lands, autonomous or rather independent entities. They invoked their Lankan credentials as a claim to ritual purity, but they did not maintain binding institutional links with Lanka.[53]

On the other hand, it is also possible that offering *upasampadā* to non-local monks was not (or not always) a matter of robust significance to local *saṅgha*s although it was celebrated by foreign monks upon their return home. If providing ordinations was (at least on some occasions) more a diplomatic gesture (at the behest of monastic and/or court leadership) rather than a substantial act of incorporation deemed central to the life-history of the Lankan *saṅgha*, it might not have been accompanied by instruction in the lineage histories of officiating Lankan monks. Of course, it would have been possible, presumably, for Lān Nā monks well educated in Pāli to make *mahāvihāravāsin* or *theravādin* lineage claims in their texts if they wished, simply on the basis of the information included within *Mahāvaṃsa*, some version of which likely circulated in Lān Nā, whether or not their fellows reached Laṅkā in person, and whether or not they received instruction in Lankan lineage history upon arrival. The absence of such claims therefore underscores that, at least in the Wat Pa Däng lines of Lān Nā as best we understand them now, desirable Lankan monasticism was not made more desirable if identified as *mahāvihāravāsin* or *theravādin*, and that student-teacher connections to eminent Lankan monks were not much celebrated, even if these ties existed.

Mobile Monks, Royal Patrons?

Much scholarship on monastic movement between Laṅkā and the regions we know now as Burma and Thailand has claimed or hinted at causal links between monastic mobility, the spread of Lankan monastic ordination lines and education, and the development of royal courts in the central Southeast Asian mainland during both the so-called "classical" and "early modern" periods.[54] This is due partly to the strong presence of royal characters in the Buddhist monastic histories that have dominated the reconstruction of this transregional monastic history. Moreover, royal inscriptions are a significant presence in the epigraphic record that has been used sometimes to augment and corroborate textual narratives of monastic mobility and royal patronage. In addition, scholarly emphasis on royal patronage of Buddhist monks, and the role of kings in the geographic dispersal of the *Buddha-sāsana*, likely stems from the naturalization of a certain Buddhist textual model of the Indic King Asoka within academic descriptions and analyses of Buddhism. Scholars of Buddhism have tended to write *saṅgha* histories of the post-Asokan era within the confines of an "Asokan discourse",[55] thus helping to naturalize in scholarly writing a common literary framework found within our sources.

There is ample evidence that royal patronage did matter, and matter greatly, to Buddhist monks, their institutions, and their mobility. Those hypotheses and arguments should not be discounted. However, the monastic histories from Lān Nā discussed earlier suggest that historians of Buddhism should remain alert to a wider range of persons, motivations, and catalysts within the second-millennium history of southern Asian Buddhist monastic travel. It is striking that in all three of the Lān Nā works explored earlier in this chapter (composed both in Thai Yüan and Pāli), monks are portrayed as initiating the process that eventually results in the advent of a new Lankan lineage in Chiang Mai (and elsewhere in the northern region). Even in

Jinakālamālī, which seems distinguished by a more royal and prāśastic spirit (at least in the Chiang Mai sections) than do versions of *Tamnān (Mūlasāsana) Wat Pā Däng*, Chiang Mai *thera*s are portrayed as taking the initiative. It is, of course, not unnatural that in narratives composed by monks they would be portrayed as crucial agents of positive change. Yet we have other examples, especially in Laṅkā's Pali *vaṃsa* literature, of monastic narratives about the intersection of monks and kings that place much more emphasis on kings than monks. Much surely depends on authorial intention (which we cannot recover, except via the text itself in Skinnerian fashion) as well as period-specific understandings of the genre and the historical context of composition. At this point all I wish to suggest is that these Lān Nā narratives, with their accounts of monks as the catalysts for royally supported interventions in existing monastic lineage arrangements, remind us that even royally sponsored ordination embassies may have originated in monastic rather than royal impulses. Further, monastic travel (including transregional travel involving imported textual and ritual practice) may have occurred with a certain independence from courtly patrons, even if royal patronage was eventually sought in order to help stabilize new lineages once they arrived.

I have read these Lān Nā narratives with the question of the relationship between royal and monastic leadership and agency in mind partly as the result of recent research on much later (nineteenth-century) Lankan monastic contact with the *saṅgha*s of Burma and Siam.[56] That study revealed many aggressive and creative attempts by Lankan monks to galvanize royal and monastic support from the central Southeast Asia mainland for lineage interventions on the island. The evidence from nineteenth-century Laṅkā reminds us that monks as well as kings may broach changes in patronage relations, ritual practice, and institutional organization. Moreover, monks may have had a very local, or a wider regional/transregional — rather than a proto-national — conception of both the *sāsana*'s destiny and its potential patrons.[57] Although one might be tempted to assert that nineteenth-century Lankan Buddhist overtures to the central Southeast Asian mainland were as plural and multi-sited as they were because there was no controlling Buddhist royal presence on the island to prevent it, that assertion may be misguided, overestimating the determinative power of Buddhist kingship in any period. It is instructive to recall that for much of the second millennium the royal courts of central Southeast Asia were many and unstable, characterized by shifting borders and changeable tributary relations. They were not always in a position to take the lead in *saṅgha* activities, and they often had far more pressing concerns in view.

Comparative histories from western Asia and archipelagic Southeast Asia during the second millennium are also suggestive in this regard. The histories of Persian scholars looking for patronage further and further to the east, seeking to draw South Asia's rulers into a deepening engagement with Persian literary culture may have something to teach historians of Pali-using Buddhism.[58] So, too, do the networks of Arab and western Indian Muslim intellectuals who appear to have triggered reconfigurations of both polity and Islam through their presence.[59]

MOVING BEYOND MONASTIC HISTORIES

Monastic histories have much to offer us in reconstructing the history of Laṅkā-oriented and Laṅkā-originated monastic lines in central Southeast Asia, and I hope to have suggested here some ways of working with such texts. However, for reasons already noted they are not sufficient sources for such historical investigation. Although some scholars including Kanai Lal Hazra and W.M. Sirisena, in their ambitious and valuable studies,[60] have drawn on inscriptions to a degree in the study of monastic lineage networks, many epigraphic sources remain unexamined. This is partly due to formidable linguistic challenges. Scholars with transregional interests rarely have all the languages required for such research. Moreover, the publication and digitization of extant inscriptions have proceeded slowly. If we wish to investigate more deeply, and to refine, the suggestive picture of monastic mobility provided by lineage texts and other monastic histories composed in Pāli and local literary languages, one obvious move is to read such texts in much closer conversation with epigraphic evidence. A corpus of Lān Nā inscriptions is available, for instance, that must be examined in relation to the claims made by the lineage texts discussed earlier in this chapter. Working with epigraphy may help us see whether and how signs of connection to or identification with Laṅkā and her *saṅgha*s appeared within inscriptional records of lay-monastic patronage and other inscribed instances of Buddhist memorializing. Collaborative work on inscriptions and monastic histories is of the essence, since only by working within and across the multi-lingual environment of southern Asian Buddhism will we be able to reconstruct the movement of Buddhist monks, their texts and ideas, trends in self-representation, and their forms of practice across and within this Buddhist world. Archaeological and art historical evidence will also be of significant value as we attempt to write more thorough and more careful histories of transregional monastic mobility. Making historical arguments from the visual materials of art history is a delicate matter, given uncertain dating, the possibility of shared provenance for certain styles, and the difficulty of relating visual and verbal content across written texts and images. However, archaeological and art historical studies may, for instance, help to confirm or call into question arguments for the relationship between two geographic locations. They may also point to changes in ritual practice that may relate to monastic travel and exchange.

In addition to making better use of epigraphy, archaeology, and art history, I urge at least some of us trained to work with Buddhist texts to attempt to integrate critically what we can learn about monastic networks from the sources already mentioned with other evidence of commercial, diplomatic and military activities in the southern Asian region. Lankan kingdoms, and many on the central Southeast Asian mainland, were bound together through a combination of maritime and riverine networks. One way of testing the empirical plausibility of the narratives of monastic connection that appear in monastic histories (the itineraries, patronage arrangements, etc.) is to examine more closely the evidence we have for non-monastic links between the same locations. Monks, texts, and relics travelled along the same waters and roads as other persons and objects.[61] Where we have strong or strongly suggestive evidence of trade and diplomacy between nodal points of the Buddhist world in approximately the periods evoked by Buddhist monastic histories, it is at least more likely that the *saṅgha* did move within that connected space as the texts relate. Where monastic histories do not clarify whether a lineage said to be Lankan/Sīhaḷa is brought to a new location from Laṅkā or from elsewhere in the Southeast Asian region where a Lankan connection already existed, patterns in trade, diplomacy, and warfare suggest which avenues for monastic movement would have been open or closed, from city to city, at any point in time. Where there is no such evidence of extra-monastic connection between Laṅkā and some part of the mainland, or it is very weak, we should consider more seriously the possibility that claims to the heritage and practice of Laṅkān Buddhism and Sīhaḷa monasticism were made within Buddhist monastic communities even when Lankan and Laṅkā-originated monastic lineages were inaccessible.

Notes

1. I would like to thank Christian Lammerts for several years of valuable conversation on the topic explored here, as well as his intellectually rigorous editorial work on this volume. A small portion of what follows draws on work presented at the University of Pennsylvania in 2010, for a workshop on "Histories and Religious Change Beyond Sri Lankan Centers". I am grateful

to Daud Ali and Alan Strathern for their comments and questions on that occasion. *This chapter was submitted for publication in 2012.*

2. Aung-Thwin, *Pagan*, pp. 138–40; Harvey, *Introduction*, esp. pp. 143–44, Lieberman, *Strange Parallels*, p. 242; Reynolds and Hallisey, "Buddhism and Asian History", esp. pp. 16–19; Reid, *Southeast Asia* 2, pp. 193–95; Robinson, Johnson et al., *The Buddhist Religion,* esp. pp. 140–56; Swearer, "Buddhism in Southeast Asia", pp. 107–15; Swearer, *Buddhist World*, pp. ix–x, Veidlinger, *Spreading the Dharma,* p. 3.
3. I use the term "southern Asia" to refer to the regions usually referred to in post-WWII discourse as South Asia and Southeast Asia.
4. Swearer, "Buddhism in Southeast Asia".
5. Swearer and Sommai, "Relationship".
6. Ibid., p. 22.
7. See Buddhadatta, *Jinakālamālī*, p. vii; Saeng, "Some Observations", p. xxxiii; and Penth, "Buddhist Literature", p. 59.
8. Buddhadatta's Pāli edition was prepared on the basis of a "book" (seemingly printed, apparently in Thai script) that he received with the assistance of a monastic colleague in Bangkok. See Buddhadhatta, *Jinakālamālī*, p. ix. See also Jayawickrema, *Epochs*, pp. vii–viii.
9. *Thera*s resident in "rāmañña" are also mentioned in the group (93), but it is not clear whether these are identical with those earlier referred to as residing in kamboja-raṭṭha.
10. Buddhadatta, *Jinakālamālī*, pp. 92–93.
11. Laṅkādīpe pavattitaṃ akkharapaveṇiñ ca tadanurūpaṃ padabhāṇañ ca sarabhaññañ ca uggahetvā uttamatthaṃ patthayamānā upasampadaṃ yāciṃsu (93). On the term Yāpāpaṭṭana, see Hazra, *History*, pp. 156–58.
12. Buddhadatta, *Jinakālamālī*, pp. 93–94.
13. Ibid., p. 94; cf. Jayawickrema, *Epochs*, p. 134.
14. Buddhadatta, *Jinakālamālī*, p. 97. niṭṭhite pana sīmāsammutikamme Dhammarājā sattadivasāni mahāmahaṃ akāsi. Tato pubbe mahātherā Biṅganadiyā udakukkhepasīmāya upasampadakammam akaṃsu. Sammatāya pana Siridhammacakkavatti-Bilakasīmāya tasmiṃ yeva vassamhi Mahānāradappamukhe bahū kulaputte upasampādesi. Tesu hi bhikkhusaṅgho Atulasaktyādhikaraṇa-mahāsāminā upajjhāyena āyasmatā Mahāmeghiyattherena kammavācācariyena Mahānāradattheraṃ upasampādesi. When the agreement on the *sīmā* had been accomplished, the Dhammarāja conducted a great festival for seven days. (Formerly, *mahāthera*s performed the act of *upasampadā* within the Biṅga River *udakukkhepasīmā*.) Further, when the Siridhammacakkavatt-Bilaka [Tilaka]sīmā had been confirmed, in that very year many respectable young men received *upasampadā,* led by Mahānārada. Indeed, among these [young men], the *bhikkhusaṅgha* conferred *upasampadā* on Mahānāradathera with Mahāsāmi Atulasaktyādhikaraṇa as *uppajjhāya* and Venerable Mahāmeghiyathera as *kammavācācariya*.)
15. Buddhadatta, *Jinakālamālī*, p. 98.

16. For example, Buddhadatta, *Jinakālamālī*, p. 93. bandhāpitaṃ nāvāsaṅghāṭam āruyha ... upasampannā ahesuṃ.
17. See also McDaniel, "Transformative History" and Blackburn, "Writing".
18. See also Swearer and Sommai, *Translation*, p. 73, n.1.
19. Their translation followed the text of Volume IX of the Transliteration Series, Department of Sociology and Anthropology, Chiang Mai University, using the transcription prepared by Sommai Premchit. No manuscript copy date is given in the transliteration or translation. The translators mention (p. 74, n. 2) that they consulted two other manuscripts for which copy date information is also not given. I thank François Lagirarde for information about Sommai's transliteration as well as data concerning additional manuscripts of the *Tamnān Mūlasāsanā*.
20. Swearer and Sommai , *Translation*, pp. 109–10.
21. Ibid., p. 87.
22. It is not clear to me what word is here translated by "language". The context here, and in the manuscript translated by Saimong, reveals a concern for ritually correct pronunciation. The manuscript translated by Saimong (for which plates of the manuscript leaves are available) does not contain this passage.
23. Swearer and Sommai, *Translation*, p. 87.
24. Ibid., pp. 88–89. It is not clear whether "our teacher" is Lankan or Thai or originated in some other location.
25. Here "Kulāphāsī" is likely to be kulā-phāsī, to be translated as "foreigners and Muslims". See Saimong, *Chronicle*, p. 108 for a similar passage translated as "foreigners, Muslims, Burmese, Môns intermingling" in which the compound "gulā-phāsī" refers to the first two of this quartet. I am grateful to Christian Lammerts, Peter Skilling, François Lagirarde, and Justin McDaniel for checking Thai and Northern Thai sources related to this question.
26. "Rohana" in Lankan texts typically refers to the southeastern region. There was no mid-second millenium royal capital in that region. The closest seat of royal power in the south at this time was the kingdom of Koṭṭē, located near Colombo, on the southwestern coast. A famous Lankan monk named Vanaratana (the name mentioned in *Jinakālamālī*) was active at Koṭṭē during the mid-fifteenth century. See further below.
27. Swearer and Sommai, *Translation*, p. 89.
28. Ibid., p. 90.
29. Ibid., p. 90.
30. This contrasts with the account in *Jinakālamālī*, and provides a stronger record of training for the monastic travellers.
31. Swearer and Sommai, *Translation*, p. 91.
32. Ibid., pp. 92–93.
33. Ibid., p. 94.
34. The manuscript seems to have functioned as an ongoing record of some kind. It contains discussion of temple boundaries, proper and improper action,

offerings made by specified donors, a narrative of the construction of Wat Pa Däng in Chiang Tung, and so on.

35. "The narration of the chronicle of the past events of the two sects [Pa Däng and Suon Dòk], from the beginning, is here ended as a chapter". Saimong, *Chronicle*, p. 125.
36. See also Saimong, *Chronicle*, p. 40, where ethnic references suggest but certainly do not prove that the text was composed or amended after intensifying Burmese control of Lān Nā in the late sixteenth century.
37. Saimong, *Chronicle,* p. 110.
38. Ibid., pp. 109–10. Cf. this reference to Sudassana with *Jinakālamālī*'s reference to leading monk Vanaratana, on whom see further below. Taw Sein Ko's edition of the *Kalyāṇī Inscriptions* also refers to Vanaratana. Taw, *Kalyāṇī Inscriptions*, p. 79.
39 Sāimöng's Cheng Tung manuscript follows the same narrative formula with reference to the spread of Ñāṇagambhīra's line in Shan States: their protective recitation practice succeeds where that of other monks does not, winning the confidence of local residents in several locations. The narrative is more expansive as the story moves north, with increasingly detailed scene-setting and more dialogue.
40. Saimong, *Chronicle*, p. 125.
41. Lammerts, *Dhammavilāsa*, pp. 18–19. See also Taw Sein Ko, *Kalyāṇī Inscriptions*, p. v.
42. Lieberman, "A New Look".
43. Here, for instance, despite years of respectful indebtedness to his research, I am at odds with Hazra, who combines such *vaṃsa*-style sources and epigraphy without hesitating as to the rhetorical-contextual context for either form of evidence.
44. Collins, "Pali Canon" and Walters, "Buddhist History".
45. Tambiah, *World Conqueror*, p. 80.
46. Blackburn, "Lineage", pp. 1–2.
47. I recognize that *araññavāsin* references appear also in some Buddhist texts of Southeast Asia, where their textual significance awaits a fuller investigation.
48. *Sāsanavaṃsa* is a Pāli work with considerable dialogue and local colour, obviously composed with heavy debts to a variety of lineage narratives. However, it may be an exceptional case, at least partly on account of its heavy debt to earlier works in literary Burmese.
49. Relatedly, see Blackburn, "Textual After-lives".
50. Though see some valuable references for a slightly earlier period in Sirisena, *Sri Lanka*.
51. Sannasgala, *Siṃhala*, pp. 246, 278, 289. Sannasgala does assume that monks from "Kamboja" and "Siyam" came to Laṅkā during the reign of Parākramabāhu VI (r. 1412–67). See Sannasgala, *Siṃhala*, p. 244. However, his source for this is the *Kalyāṇī Inscription*, on which see further above.

I have not yet worked independently with *Haṃsa Sandeśaya*, so my remarks here derive from Sannasgala, *Siṃhala* and Hazra, *History*.
52. There are no inscriptions from the Koṭṭē period in *EZ* Volumes 1–4, Part 1 of Volume 6, or Volume 7. Despite efforts, I have not obtained copies of Volume 5 or Part 2 of Volume 6. However, published reviews of these volumes suggest that they contain nothing from the relevant period and location. Further work remains to investigate unpublished inscriptions from the post-Pollonāruva period (including the era of the kings of Koṭṭē) collected by the Sri Lanka Department of Archaeology.
53. Skilling, "Ubiquitous and Elusive", p. 4. This was the case also in the other direction, at least some of the time, as the eighteenth-century imported ordination from Ayutthaya to Kandy indicates. See Blackburn, *Buddhist Learning*. Nineteenth-century Lankan importations from Burma included more ongoing institutional contact with Burmese *saṅgha*s. See Malalgoda, *Sinhalese Buddhism*; Blackburn, *Locations*; and Kirichenko, "New Spaces".
54. See, for instance, Aung-Thwin, *Pagan*; Lieberman, *Parallels*; Prapod, *Ascendancy*; Reid, *Southeast Asia*; Swearer, "Buddhism in Southeast Asia"; Tambiah, *World Conqueror*.
55. Duncan, *City as Text*.
56. Blackburn, *Locations*.
57. In this regard, for nineteenth-century Burma, see usefully Kirichenko, "New Spaces".
58. Hodgson, *Venture*; Alam, *Languages*.
59. Feener, "Southeast Asian Localisations"; Ho, *Graves*.
60. Hazra, *History* and Sirisena, *Sri Lanka*.
61. In this regard, see Blackburn, "Buddhhist Connections in the Indian Ocean: Changes in Monastic Mobility 1000–1500", *Journal of the Social and Economic History of the Orient* 58, no. 3 (2015).

References

Alam, Muzaffar. *The Languages of Political Islam*. Chicago: University of Chicago Press, 2004.

Aung-Thwin, Michael. *Pagan*. Honolulu: University of Hawai'i Press, 1985.

Blackburn, Anne M. "Lineage, Inheritance, and Belonging: Expressions of Monastic Affiliation from Lanka". In *How Theravāda is the Theravāda?*, edited by Peter Skilling, Jason Carbine, and Claudio Ciuzza, pp. 1–20. Chiang Mai: Silkworm Publications, 2012.

———. *Locations of Buddhism: Colonialism and Modernity in Sri Lanka*. Chicago: University of Chicago Press, 2010.

———. "Writing Buddhist History From Landscape and Architecture: Sukhothai and Chiang Mai". *Buddhist Studies Review* 24, no. 2 (2007): 192–225.

———. *Buddhist Learning and Textual Practice in the Monastic Culture of 18th-century Sri Lanka*. Princeton: Princeton University Press, 2001.

——. "Textual After-Lives of Scholar Monks in Later Medieval Pali-land". I.B. Horner Memorial Lecture, September 2011.

——. "Buddhist Connections in the Indian Ocean: Changes in Monastic Mobility 1000–1500". *Journal of the Social and Economic History of the Orient* 58, no. 3 (2015).

Buddhadatta, A.P. *Jinakālamālī*. London: Pali Text Society, 1962.

Collins, Steven. "On the Very Idea of the Pali Canon". *Journal of the Pali Text Society* 15 (1990): 89–126.

Duncan, James S. *The City as Text: The Politics of Landscape Interpretation in the Kandyan Kingdom*. Cambridge: Cambridge University Press, 1990.

Epigraphia Zeylanica, Being Lithic and Other Inscriptions of Ceylon. 7 vols. Colombo: Ceylon Government Printer, 1904–1984.

Feener, R. Michael. "South-East Asian localisations of Islam and participation within a global umma, c. 1500–1800". In *The New Cambridge History of Islam*, Vol. 3, edited by David O. Morgan and Anthony Reid, pp. 470–503. Cambridge: Cambridge University Press, 2010.

Harvey, Peter. *Introduction to Buddhism*. Cambridge: Cambridge University Press, 1990.

Hazra, Kanai Lal. *History of Theravada Buddhism in South-East Asia*. Delhi: Munshiram Manoharlal, 1982.

Ho, Engseng. *The Graves of Tarim*. Berkeley: University of California Press, 2006.

Hodgson, Marshall. *The Venture of Islam: Conscience and History in a World Civilization*. 3 vols. Chicago: University of Chicago Press, 1974.

Jayawickrema, N.A. *The Sheaf of Garlands of the Epochs of the Conqueror*. London: Pali Text Society, 1968.

Kirichenko, Alexey. "New Spaces for Interaction: Contacts between Burmese and Sinhalese Monks in the Late Nineteenth and Early Twentieth Centuries". Forthcoming.

Lammerts, Dietrich Christian. "Buddhism and Written Law". Ph.D. dissertation, Asian Religions Field, Cornell University, 2010.

——. "The *Dhammavilāsa Dhammathat*: A Critical Historiography, Analysis, and Translation of the Text". M.A. Thesis, Asian Studies Field, Cornell University, 2005.

Lieberman, Victor. B. *Strange Parallels*. Vol. 1. Cambridge: Cambridge University Press, 2003.

——. "A New Look at the Sāsanavaṃsa". *Bulletin of the School of Oriental and African Studies* 39, no. 1 (1976): 137–49.

Malalgoda, Kitsiri. *Buddhism and Sinhalese Society, 1750–1900, A Study of Revival and Change*. Berkeley: University of California, 1976.

McDaniel, Justin Thomas. "Transformative History: Nihon Ryōiki and Jinakālamālīpakaraṇam". *Journal of the International Association of Buddhist Studies* 25, no. 1-2 (2002): 151–207.

Penth, Hans. "Buddhist Literature of Lan Na on the History of Lan Na's Buddhism". *Journal of the Pali Text Society* 23 (1997): 43–81.

Prapod Assavavirulhakarn. *The Ascendancy of Theravāda Buddhism in Southeast Asia*. Chiang Mai: Silkworm Books, 2010.

Reid, Anthony. *Southeast Asia in the Age of Commerce 1450–1680*. Vol. 2. New Haven: Yale University Press, 1993.

Reynolds, Frank and Charles Hallisey. "Buddhism and Asian History". In *Buddhism and Asian History*, edited by Joseph M. Kitagawa and Mark D. Cummings, pp. 3–28. New York: Macmillan, 1989.

Robinson, Richard H., Willard L. Johnson, et al. *The Buddhist Religion*. 5th ed. Belmont: Wadsworth Publishing, 2005.

Saimong Mangrāi, Sao. *The Pā Daeng Chronicle and the Jengtung State Chronicle*. Ann Arbor: University of Michigan Press, 1981.

Saeng Manavidura. "Some Observations on the Jinakālamālīpakaraṇa". In *The Sheaf of Garlands of the Epochs of the Conqueror,* edited by Jayawickrema, N.A., pp. xxxii–xlvi. London: Pali Text Society, 1968.

Sannasgala, P.B. *Siṃhala Sahitya Vaṃśaya*. Colombo: Lake House, 1964.

Sirisena, W.M. *Sri Lanka and South-East Asia: Political, Religious and Cultural Relations from A.D. c. 1000 to c. 1500*. Leiden: Brill, 1978.

Skilling, Peter. "Ubiquitous and Elusive: Theravāda in History". *Pacific World*, Third Series, 11 (2009): 61–93.

———. "The Advent of Theravāda Buddhism to Mainland South-east Asia". *Journal of the International Association of Buddhist Studies* 20, no. 1 (1997): 93–107.

———. "The Place of South-east Asia in Buddhist Studies". *Buddhist Studies (Bukkyō Kenkyū)* 30, no. 1 (2001): 1–17.

Swearer, Donald K. *The Buddhist World of Southeast Asia*. 2nd ed. Chiang Mai: Silkworm Books, 2010.

———. "Buddhism in Southeast Asia". In *Buddhism and Asian History*, edited by Joseph M. Kitagawa and Mark D. Cummings, pp. 107–29. New York: Macmillan, 1989.

Swearer, Donald K. and Sommai Premchit. "A Translation of Tamnān Mūlasāsanā Wat Pā Daeng: The Chronicle of the Founding of Buddhism of the Pā Daeng Tradition". *Journal of the Siam Society* 65, no. 2 (1977): 73–110.

———. "The Relationship Between the Religious and Political Orders in Northern Thailand (14th–16th Centuries)". In *Religion and the Legitimation of Power in Thailand, Laos, and Burma*, edited by Bardwell L. Smith, pp. 20–33. Chambersburg: Anima Books, 1978.

Tambiah, Stanley J. *World Conqueror, World Renouncer.* Cambridge: Cambridge University Press, 1976.

Taw Sein Ko. *The Kalyāṇī Inscriptions Erected by King Dhammaceti at Pegu in 1476*. Rangoon: Government Printer, 1892.

Veidlinger, Daniel M. *Spreading the Dharma*. Honolulu: University of Hawai'i Press, 2006.

Walters, Jonathan. "Buddhist History: The Sri Lankan Pali Vamsas and Their Commentary". In *Querying the Medieval,* ed. Ronald Inden, Jonathan Walters, and Daud Ali. Oxford: Oxford University Press, pp. 99–164.

11

DYNAMICS OF MONASTIC MOBILITY AND NETWORKING IN THE SEVENTEENTH- AND EIGHTEENTH-CENTURY UPPER BURMA[1]

Alexey Kirichenko

The present paper is an attempt to describe key monastic structures in Upper Burma of the seventeenth and eighteenth century, analyse the way they worked and what kind of processes were instrumental in their development. This documentation effort is based on fragmentary factual evidence mined from diverse sources, such as monastic biographies, religious chronicles, colophons of Buddhist texts, etc. As the sources of information are quite limited, the results of investigation are intrinsically provisional and open to reinterpretation. However, as so far there was no attempt to describe how Burmese monasticism functioned as a system during the period in question, the paper seeks to fill in this lacuna and provide a frame of reference for further discussion. The paper also integrates this description with arguments made in existing scholarship and suggests a number of revisions that position Burmese monasticism as a highly dynamic social reality.

The paper has the following structure. As surviving evidence limits the discussion to elite monasticism, I present a summary description of the court saṅgha in the seventeenth and eighteenth centuries, showing that it paradoxically combined exclusivity (limited access, specific mechanisms of reproduction, etc.) with openness and so was in a number of ways connected with monastic communities beyond the court. Then I outline the rise of extensive "non-central" monastic networks that at least since the early eighteenth century functioned as a viable and thriving alternative to court monasticism and developed a number of competencies that allowed them to successfully compete with older, established court communities. Finally, I try to analyse the factors that contributed to the development of such communities, discuss why they constitute a unique phenomenon, and compare Burmese monastic networks that I have identified with contemporary monasticism in other areas where textual Buddhism was mostly based on Pāli sources.

BURMESE COURT MONASTICISM IN THE SEVENTEENTH AND EIGHTEENTH CENTURIES

The period from the seventeenth century onwards is the time when more detailed evidence on Burmese monasticism becomes available. While prior to that period the research is based mostly on archaeological and inscriptional data that are either too general or too fragmentary, the burst of literary activity in Burma since the seventeenth century provided new types of sources that allow tracing the life and activities of particular persons and communities in a more consistent manner and within longer time-frames. It is from that time one can document the functioning of what I call Burmese court saṅgha.

First of all, a terminological explanation is necessary. I use the term "court saṅgha" to describe monastic establishments patronized by members of Burmese royalty and royal court. The term has no direct equivalent in old Burmese and, most likely, monastic communities that I include in the court saṅgha did not have a common self-consciousness. In reality, the court saṅgha was an aggregate of individual monastic units, monastery complexes, and networks based on ordination lineages, traditions of scriptural training, and transfers of monastic property. Though there were no specific ecclesiastical structures that could integrate all these elements into a single functional entity, the fact that the patronage derived from a single source lent the court saṅgha a degree of cohesion. As the members of the court saṅgha depended on the court and were deeply involved in its various activities (such as court rituals, merit-making, and even power struggles) it makes sense to approach them collectively for research purposes.

Key figures in the court saṅgha were monks patronized by overlords and principal members of the royal family (senior queens, king's brothers and sisters, king's children by senior queens, etc.).[2] Such monks were known as royal teachers (*hsayadaw*), and in contrast to contemporary usage where this term applies indiscriminately to almost any abbot, in the seventeenth and eighteenth centuries it was exclusive and applied only to incumbents of monasteries donated by royalty.[3] Monks patronized by ministers, leaders of crown service units, etc., were known as teachers (*hsaya*) of respective donors. Though they had lower status as compared to royal teachers, such abbots and their disciples represented an important stratum of court monasticism as they often acted as subordinates to royal teachers and comprised a pool of candidates for promotion to higher positions.

Major division among the royal teachers was related to holding of monastic titles conferred by the crown and to possession of iron seals carrying such titles. Conferral of title/seal (both were denoted by the word *dazeit*) was a principal form of royal recognition of individual monk in addition to construction or donation of a monastery. All key royally supported monastic leaders held such seals and were known as "royal teachers holding royal titles/seals" (*dazeit-taw-ya-hsayadaw*). Junior leaders did not receive such distinctions and thus were known as royal teachers "without titles/seals" (*dazeit-taw-ma-ya*).[4]

Further status segmentation derived from the length of time a particular monk or monastic lineage enjoyed royal recognition and support. Being a status-conscious system, Nyaungyan court prized high-profile monastic pedigrees as much as it cherished royal and ministerial genealogies. As a result, many important saṅgha leaders had shared family background — monastic succession often went from uncle to nephew or from elder to junior brother — and access into the system was basically reserved for disciples of established court monks.[5] Though perhaps never achieving the degree of concentration of key monastic positions in the hands of few aristocratic families characteristic of seventeenth- and eighteenth-century Kandyan court of Laṅkā, Nyaungyan court in Upper Burma still seems to have granted the highest privileges to monks who were *ekarāja* kings' teachers for several generations.[6]

Besides such established monastic leaders and their disciples, other segments of the court saṅgha seem to be comprised of "vocationally specialized" monks engaged either in learning/tutorship or in forest-dwelling practices. In Nyaungyan period (and perhaps earlier) these categories of "learner/tutor" monks (*sathin*) and "forest-dwellers" (*taw-ne* or *ekacāra*) seem to have had separate identities, unrelated to basic stages of monastic career such as discipleship and scriptural training in one's youth or retirement for meditation at advanced age. Both *sathin* and *taw-ne* clearly had lower status than "royal teachers holding royal titles/ seals" and perhaps could not claim celebrated genealogy.[7] However, as few documents mentioning these categories are available, it is not fully clear to what extent they were mutually exclusive and if there were channels for migration from one category into another.

Functionally, monks patronized by the court were regarded as the highest authority in the matters of Buddhist teaching and practice (*sāsana*) and partnered with the crown in ensuring the latter's symbolical and ritual pre-eminence. Historically Burmese court monasticism placed a marked emphasis on the preservation of the *sāsana* as a means to perpetuate the conditions allowing accumulating merit and improving one's status in present and subsequent births. The members of elite monastic establishment were supposed to maintain manuscripts (royal copies) of Buddhist texts, supervise over their copying, transmit scriptural learning, train new generations of monks to reproduce saṅgha physically, officiate at the ceremonies, and provide the expertise necessary to lay supporters of the *sāsana*.

To handle these tasks, specific functional ranks have been instituted in the court saṅgha, namely, the editors of royal copies of *pitakat* texts,[8] monks conducting scriptural examinations (*same-hsayadaw*), and ecclesiastical judges settling disputes involving monks and novices (*vinayadhara*). It seems that the establishment of at least some of these ranks was a Nyaungyan period innovation as no references to them appear in the earlier sources. Appointments to these functional ranks were made by the overlord among the titled hsayadaws and their disciples with all appointees receiving donations of food products and monastic requisites as remuneration for fulfilling their duties.[9]

Editors were divided into several grades (*sa-ma*, *sa-ti*, and *sa-kyi hsayadaws*) and had to check the copies of manuscripts to ensure that no mistakes were made. Manuscript copies made under their supervision were placed in royal libraries (*pitakat-taik-taw*) and occasionally distributed among influential monks. Though the copying of religious texts at the court was a long-established activity, it seems that Nyaungyan period saw a movement towards its routinization. The references to editors in the sources become common from the 1630s onwards.[10] The copying of royal manuscripts became a part of the coronation ritual and since the mid-seventeenth century every Burmese overlord ordered to copy the *pitakat* at least once he had ascended the throne.[11] Royal copies of Buddhist texts were also used in palace and royal city construction rituals.[12]

The establishment of annual exams for schoolboys and novices in Ava is credited to King Thalun-min (1629–48).[13] Though the actual date when these exams became a regular enterprise is debated, it is clear that they were in existence at least since the 1660s.[14] Curriculum (at least, in the early eighteenth century) included Kaccāyana's grammar, *Abhidhammattha-saṅgaha* and *Dīgha-nikāya* with the emphasis being made on Pāli grammar as a prerequisite for correct understanding of texts.[15] Candidates who passed the exams successfully were ordained as novices or monks with courtiers assuming the roles of their donors. The highest honour was given to three novices who showed the best results. Called afterwards the "first royal monks" (*pahtama-pazin-daw*), they were almost guaranteed to reach the highest positions in monastic hierarchy in the future.

Participation in the exams was limited, as the number of those ordained as a result did not exceed 100 persons a year (more often it varied from thirty to seventy).[16] It also seems that only disciples of royal teachers could sit at the exams. So, aspiring applicants coming from the villages first had to get admission to the monasteries of royal abbots and receive training under them. Thus, the examination system functioned mainly as a mechanism of recruitment into and reproduction of the court saṅgha, while the abbots who supervised the exams controlled one of the key channels of vertical mobility available to Burmese boys.[17]

As members of the saṅgha were excluded from the jurisdiction of civil officials, experts in the Vinaya (*vinayadhara*) were appointed to try all types of disputes involving monastic population.[18] In addition, they had to ensure that monastic communities at the court were worthy to receive elite support and that the flow of merit to donors was unobstructed. Formally their task was to guarantee that there were no monks guilty of the *pārājika* offences and to settle disciplinary disputes when such arose. In cases when a conflict of interests was expected, supervisors of religious exams or monks responsible for the editing of texts and taking care of royal library could be called in to try the case as specially appointed *vinayadhara*s.[19]

Besides the tasks related to Buddhist texts, training, and discipline, the court saṅgha functioned as an expert body advising the court on all matters it may inquire into. As a result, royal teachers would occasionally render assistance in such issues as banishing of ghosts, bringing on the rain, choosing the location of temporary palaces, arranging military campaigns, calculation of time for various ceremonies and determination of their procedure, prediction of the future, etc.[20] Such activities were also justified by means of rhetoric of preservation of the *sāsana*. The underlying rationale was the following: the overlord was the chief patron of the teaching which existed perpetuated by his teachers and relying (*ahmi-pyu*) on him. The well-being of the people depended on the overlord for if the latter faced difficulties, the affairs of his realm spiralled into chaos and all the population suffered. Such situation inevitably led to the decline of the *sāsana* as the overlord was unable to patronize it and the people could not observe the precepts and make donations. Alternatively, a successful reign resulted in the prosperity of royal city, a location where the *sāsana* was believed to repose (*thathanadaw-ti-ya*).[21]

An important development in the functioning of court monasticism during the period in question was the concentration of royal support almost exclusively in the capital area. In the fourteenth and fifteenth centuries the overlords of Ava built monasteries, stupas, and temples not only in the royal city, but in other places as well, for they strived to establish their superiority as the patrons of Buddhism over subordinate rulers. In the second half of the sixteenth century the court of Hanthawadi Hsinbyumyashin (1551–81) patronized monasteries in the secondary centres of his polity, such as Taungngu, Pyi, Ava, Bagan, Mottama, and Chiang Mai. Early rulers of Nyaungyan dynasty, such as Anaukhpetlun-min (1606–28) and Thalun-min, emulated Hsinbyumyashin's example and patronized not only monks of diverse origin who moved to Ava and Sagaing, but also those who continued to reside in Hanthawadi, Taungngu, Pyi, etc. This situation seems to have changed after mid-seventeenth century and later overlords stopped giving support to monasteries in Lower Burma.[22] As far as the available evidence is concerned, the only city outside the capital area where several key clusters of monasteries continued to enjoy occasional royal support after the 1660s was Bagan.[23]

Accordingly, for the most of Nyaungyan period the court saṅgha was concentrated in the capital area of Ava, Pinya, Sagaing, and their immediate environs (Tada-U, Taywinche, Kyetyet, and Kaunghmudaw). Monastic population of the elite complexes in the capital area was recruited mostly from the core areas of Burmese culture, i.e. from cities and villages of Upper Burma. Though the seventeenth-century saṅgha of Ava and Sagaing continued to be polyethnic (just like monastic communities of Hanthawadi, Taungngu, Pyi or Mottama in the sixteenth century) and there were Mon, Northern and Central Thai, Tai, Tenasserim, and Manipuri monks in the capital area,[24] very few of them received honours from the crown. Since the mid-seventeenth century onwards the majority of royal teachers were predominantly Burman.

In terms of material infrastructure, the landscape of elite monasticism consisted of a number of "shared" and "proprietary" spaces. As shared spaces I understand ritual sites such as stupas and temple complexes, meeting halls, royal libraries, buildings for copying and checking of manuscripts, etc. Collective undertakings of the court saṅgha such as convening of exams, copying of manuscripts, holding of important ceremonies and meetings of royal teachers with the king, trying of Vinaya disputes, etc. were held in these shared spaces. Such sites served as a forum were the court saṅgha appeared as a collective social agent.

"Proprietary" were individual monastery complexes that were usually associated with specific lineages. Movement from one such complex to another might require reordination unless both complexes belonged to one or affiliated lineages.[25] As far as my understanding goes, in the seventeenth and eighteenth centuries Burmese monasticism did not have a large-scale integrated ecclesiastical organization, even at the court. The presence of a certain formal structure (such as functional ranks and particular divisions of court monks) did not affect the nature of Burmese saṅgha as a loose aggregate of different groupings, communities, and lineages in the state of constant flux.[26]

Accordingly, a basic unit of court monasticism was a monastery complex (*kyaung-taik*) comprised of several residential buildings, with the main one (called *kyaung-ma* or *kyaung-gyi*) occupied by the presiding abbot and a number of smaller structures (called 'the retinue' (*kyaung-yan*) of the main monastery) housing his disciples. Complexes usually were walled compounds, also housing a library, *sīmā*, meeting hall, water reservoir, well, open sheds for taking rest, utility buildings, etc.[27] As a rule, monasteries were built of wood and often rebuilt (to compensate for damage made by rain and frequent fires), thus a life-cycle of leading monastery complexes was not particularly lengthy. In the period under study it varied from twenty to seventy years after which the monastery was either rebuilt or disappeared.

Reproduction of monastic communities in this context required an ability to secure donations of new and rebuilt monastery complexes. A career of a successful court monk usually consisted of studying at some elite complex(es) as a schoolboy or a novice, passing of exams, continuation of studies, incumbency at *kyaung-yan*, receiving a donation of a monastery built by a junior courtier or member of royalty, and, finally, the upgrade to a monastery built by a senior courtier or member of royalty. Throughout his lifetime, a successful court monk could receive several monasteries that he usually transferred to his disciples. Participation in functional activities of the court saṅgha also allowed him to secure the appointment of his disciples to various ranks in the elite establishment and thus boost their chances of getting donations themselves.

This system was essentially competitive and generational changes of patrons, as well as the influx of new aspiring candidates from other cities and villages contributed to that competition. Fluidity and flexibility of patronage structures ensured the rotation of beneficiaries, so the long-term survival required being one step ahead of competitors rather than simply maximizing the flow of donations to a current leader of community.[28]

As the court did little to patronize the monks in the countryside, the court communities as such did not spread beyond the capital area. However, there existed active movement of personnel between elite monasteries in the capital and monasteries in the provinces. First, elite establishments consistently attracted novices and young monks from other places. Next, many monks from peripheral locations who came to Ava/Sagaing and spent some time at the court often returned to their native or neighbouring areas, apparently to enjoy greater respect and more enthusiastic patronage locally. The shifts to the countryside could be temporary and after successful incumbency in provincial monasteries the most mobile monks returned to the court again.[29]

Accordingly, as far as I understand the way Burmese court saṅgha interacted with other monastic communities, there existed a steadily growing group of core lineages that were present only in the capital area. Their monasteries were accessible to outsiders who managed to move to the capital and be admitted. The movement in reverse direction (back to the countryside) was also possible, but did not create offshoots of court communities linked with parent monasteries elsewhere. Instead, the returnees joined or established local lineages supported by local or provincial patrons, such as headmen, officials, bankers, etc. The movements between the court and the "periphery" could be repeated throughout the course of monastic career.

Such understanding may be impressionistic and arise from the fact that the evidence that is available to a student of Burmese monastic history is severely limited. However, imagining that Nyaungyan court patronized monasteries in multiple locations outside of the capital area or that leaders of court monastic communities actively moved around the country and maintained links with monastic communities in the villages (though for some reasons these activities were either not documented in the sources or such sources were not recopied) is much more problematic.

If put forward, such claims would be based on even less grounded assumptions that relatively compact size of core areas of Upper Burma would favour frequent movement of senior monastic personnel, that Nyaungyan court should have been interested in supporting monastic communities in secondary cities by definition, and that Nyaungyan court monks (who emulated the common elite pattern of maintaining status distinctions and visually stressed them by using different types of monastic hats, fans, and other insignia) would forego their privileges and strive to bring town- and village-based communities in closer relationship and conformity with themselves.

Social divisions and status-based boundaries could be a serious obstacle to integration and unification even if other factors might favour it. As Nyaungyan court invested a lot of effort in maintaining status differentiation at least in principle, I feel it more appropriate to follow a reductionist approach and assume that the absence of data on the spread of court monastic networks to the countryside even in a small sample of sources is the evidence in itself. As the sources that I use have diverse origins and belong to different types of texts (royal and monastic chronicles, inscriptions, royal orders, monks' replies to queries, colophons of *pitakat* texts, polemical literature, etc.), it is quite safe to assume that this absence could not be explained by an aberration in a particular type of sources.

Also, saying that Nyaungyan court did little to patronize the monks in the countryside, I imply direct patronage and direct interactions only. I do not discount the possibilities and influence of "distributed" patronage or interactions between different monastic segments that could have occurred through the mediation of regional governors, local hereditary officials, traders and bankers, all of whom were more or less integrated with Nyaungyan court and could be interested in promoting locally the types of monasticism favored by the court or in helping local monks to interact with court communities. However, such "distributed" patronage is almost impossible to trace due to the limitations of the source base and so I prefer to bracket it out of the discussion, though acknowledging its likely existence and contribution to the development of monastic communities beyond the court.

As a result, my evaluation of influence of court monastic communities at their counterparts in the countryside between the 1660s and the 1750s is a departure from the scholarship that assumes that Burmese saṅgha was frequently dominated by the crown, integrated by means of monastic reform, and followed the court-prescribed models of monasticism. For example, Michael Aung-Thwin argued that royal interventions into saṅgha affairs were a constant factor in Burmese history as the crown needed to stem the flow of wealth to non-taxable sector.[30] Juliane Schober assumed that Burmese kings periodically initiated monastic reforms that led to unification of the saṅgha and purification of ordination lineages in order to boost their image and establish themselves as *dhammarājas*.[31] Khammai Dhammasami credited Thalun-min with a quite radical attempt at purging and reforming Burmese saṅgha in the 1630s and 1640s.[32] Victor Lieberman wrote that

> following the return of the capital to Upper Burma in the early seventeenth century, Restored Toungoo and then Konbaung kings pursued a ... policy of cultural and especially religious integration. They established a reasonably elaborate hierarchy and examination system to supervise the monkhood in leading provincial centers. ... To bring texts and monastic rituals in line with capital practices, they also dispatched missionary monks to outlying areas.[33]

On the contrary, in my analysis there is a conspicuous lack of evidence on Nyaungyan court's or court monks' direct engagement with provincial or local saṅgha between the 1660s and 1750s.[34]

If true, this means that the situation in Upper Burmese saṅgha was quite different from contemporary Sinhalese monasticism. A top-down control over Sinhalese saṅgha by royally appointed hierarchs existed at least in principle since the mid-thirteenth century. Through these mechanisms, the admission to the saṅgha as a fully ordained monk, the obtaining of independent monastic status in the saṅgha, and the abbot's ability to accumulate monastic following were all subject to approval from royally appointed leadership.[35] In the late eighteenth century individual monks were required to channel their petitions to lay authorities through the heads and vice-heads of Malwatta and Asgiriya Vihāras, two principal monasteries of the island.[36] The nominal monopoly of "official" hierarchy on control over the saṅgha was broken only in the nineteenth century with the establishment of Amarapura Nikāya in British-controlled areas.[37]

Furthermore, key pilgrimage sites located in different parts of the island were placed under the custodianship of monks centrally appointed from the ranks of court aristocracy at least as early as the seventeenth century. That alone resulted in the establishment of a territorially distributed network aligned with Sinhalese court monasticism.

As for comparing Burma with other so called "Theravāda" locations, the state of research on Thai, Lao, and Cambodian monastic Buddhisms during the period in question precludes judgement on the possible spread of royally supported monastic networks from the capital to countryside.

For example, Yoneo Ishii claims that Ayutthayan saṅgha had hierarchical structure and that kings "built numerous royal monasteries in their capitals and in the provinces", but fails to provide any detailed evidence or discuss how this system worked.[38] Khammai Dhammasami presents evidence which suggests that monastic ordination in the late seventeenth century Ayutthaya might have required obtaining permission from lay authorities or be free, but in this case monks were subjected to examinations after which many of them were disrobed. He also mentions that in the late seventeenth century the right to confer ordinations was given only to four *saṅgharājas*.[39] At the same time, Justin McDaniel argues that even in modern period effective central control over Northern Thai and Laotian saṅghas and their ritual and curricular canons was never achieved.[40] This throws some doubt on the possibility of monastic unification in the seventeenth century as the efficiency of central control in Siam of that period was apparently lesser than in the twentieth century.

Nevertheless, even if in terms of nominal extension of centralized control over the saṅgha the Thai, Lao, and Cambodian cases might theoretically have been different from the conditions in Laṅkā, that still did not bring them closer to the situation in Upper Burma. The examination of Burmese monasticism at the other side of the equation, i.e. from the perspective of communities based outside of the capital area, shows that Burmese case was somewhat unique.

THE RISE OF "NON-CENTRAL" COMMUNITIES AND COMPETITION OF MONASTIC NETWORKS

The situation when court and non-court monasticism were not aligned and when resources used to support Buddhism were distributed quite unevenly reflects the privileged status of elite sites and practices in Upper Burma. The evidence on elite communities is also more easily available which hinders documentation of premodern forms of non-elite Buddhism and the extent to which they were common. However, from the late seventeenth and early eighteenth centuries onwards there is enough evidence to demonstrate that by that time Burmese regional and local monastic communities could successfully develop supralocal networks without direct involvement and support of the court and challenge the privileged access of court-based monastic communities to patronage with increasing efficiency.

In this paper I would limit myself to two points that testify to the development of monastic networks in the countryside operating, to a certain degree, as an alternative to the court saṅgha. The first is the development of *pitakat*-type textual production outside of the capital area and the second is the growth of specialized scriptural education beyond the court. In both cases that brought non-court monasticism to a comparable level of expertise with court-based communities and allowed to supplant the lineages of Nyaungyan period with newer ones originating in the countryside in the 1750s.

Textual Production beyond the Court

One of the peculiarities of surviving *pitakat* texts that once circulated in Upper Burma is that prior to the seventeenth century such texts and translations seem to be compiled in large, well-established centres of monasticism such as Bagan, Ava, Pinya, Sagaing, Pyi, Taungngu, Hanthawadi, Mottama, and Chiang Mai, all of which have been royal cities. There is no clear surviving evidence of production of *pitakat* texts such as Pāli subcommentaries, handbooks, etc. and Burmese *nissaya*s in lesser cities and villages, though at least from the fifteenth century onwards there was a rich tradition of vernacular Buddhist poetry and other types of works compiled by monks over broader geographical space.[41]

This situation seems to have changed in the seventeenth century. As much as my search for the evidence progressed, the first place to appear on a new, more "detailed" map of sites contributing to the production of new *pitakat*-type texts was Pakhangyi (Pakhan). About 1638–43, Shin Jambudhaja residing in Shweumin monastery near Pakhan compiled *nissaya*s on canonical Vinaya and *Samantapāsādikā* commentary which subsequently enjoyed wide acceptance.[42] Jambudhaja was also recognized by Thalun-min who conferred on him the title/seal of *rājaguru*.[43] Accordingly, the case of Jambudhaja could not be really isolated from the workings of court monasticism but it is an indication of broadening geography of textual production sponsored not so much by the crown as by local elites (Shweumin monastery was supported by the *min*s of Pakhan). Another quite early text produced in a secondary city is a *nissaya* of *Kaccāyana* written by Ācārathera from Yethanot-taik in Madaya in 1656.[44]

The earliest specimens of *pitakat* works produced in the villages that I have managed to identify so far are *nissaya*s of some of the Vinaya texts compiled by Shin Paramakhema from Tamakha, a subordinate village (*myo-kye*) of Ngathayauk (city close to Bagan) about 1674–75.[45] Since the early eighteenth century, subordinate villages of Pakhan and Bagan became the locations of translation projects lasting for several years or even dozens of years. The most conspicuous case is that of Shin Ariyālaṅkāra from Neyin village (Pakhan *myo-kye*). From roughly 1718 to 1753 that prolific author translated into Burmese almost every text from what seems an advanced monastic curriculum of that period.[46] Ariyālaṅkāra's activities were continued by his disciple Shin Sāradassī.[47]

Slightly later (1730s) is the work of Shin Guṇaraṃsālaṅkāra who compiled *nissayas* of ten major *jātakas* and sections of Taungbila Hsayadaw's *Vinayālaṅkāra-ṭīkā* while residing in Myaing village (Pakhan *myo-kye*).[48] Kyawaungsanhta Hsayadaw Shin Ñāṇavara (1705–53) compiled several texts while staying in the Mataungta monastery in Pakhan in the 1730s. His disciple and successor as the abbot of the Mataungta monastery Shin Jotayanta continued this work in the mid-eighteenth century.[49] The *nissaya*s of Vaṃsābhilaṅkāra who worked in Ngatayaw (east of Pakhan) belong to the same time-frame.[50]

Bagan area in the mid-eighteenth century is represented by the work of Shin Dhammanandī from Kinbuntaung (who later resided in a monastery built by Min Sithu in Bagan and in the 1740s moved to Ava) and his disciples.[51] In the 1730s the geography of *pitakat*-related textual production was broadened with addition of Lower Chindwin area (Bagyitaik and Badon *myo-kye*).[52] In the later part of the eighteenth century this trend continued with more and more works produced in places like Minbu, Salin, Hsinbyukyun, Kyaunggauk, Ngwetha, Padu, Alegyun, Monywe, Nyaunggan, etc.

The production of the *pitakat*-type texts (and their manuscripts) beyond the court meant that at least some villages and secondary cities formed networks circulating highly specialized and standardized texts belonging to what was locally understood as the Buddhist canon. *Nissaya*s of *pitakat* texts mentioned above covered complete Pāli works and were recopied by more or less professional monastic and lay scribes (moreover, a possibility of commercialized production of palm-leaf manuscripts should not be completely ruled out, for at least in the late nineteenth century such production clearly existed). The scale of variations in recopied manuscripts was quite low and besides incidental scribal errors the only notable difference in the resultant copies was the degree of abbreviation of vernacular text (Burmese glosses to Pāli expressions could have been reproduced in full or reduced to final grammatical markers in the syntagms; abbreviated versions thus focused more on grammar and syntax of original Pāli texts taking the meaning of many Pāli words and expressions as self-evident[53]). Accordingly, as far as I could find, the earliest available *nissaya* manuscripts copied in the seventeenth century contain essentially the same text as modern printed editions of these *nissaya*s published on the basis of nineteenth and twentieth century manuscripts.[54] Thus, the production and circulation of *pitakat nissaya*s in the villages reflected not so much personal textual or pedagogical interests of village monks (such were likely reflected in *parabaik* and palm-leaf manuscripts that those monks made for their personal use), but rather their collaborative engagement in creation and dissemination of current versions of Buddhist canon.

The specialized nature of these textual activities testifies to the development of other prerequisites of textual production in the countryside. It meant that non-royal cities and villages possessed cadre of competent monks, manuscript collections, readership or users of such texts (the majority of whom apparently were teacher-monks and their students as well as local elites who now get mentioned as initiators of compilation of certain works), qualified scribes, etc. They also apparently formed networks through which these texts were circulating with copies of newly compiled texts reaching other locations quite fast.[55] The availability of this infrastructure also means that from that time on villages could furnish prospective editors of royal *pitakat* manuscripts.

Another important point becomes apparent if one compares this work with textual production in the capital area. Though it might be misleading to judge by surviving and catalogued manuscript collections as the majority of manuscripts in these collections were copied some fifty to 150 years later than the period in question and so might reflect copying preferences of a later time, still one cannot avoid noting that there exists no record for comparable *pitakat*-type translation activity in Ava in the first half of the eighteenth century. Few surviving texts compiled by court monks of that time belong to non-*pitakat* types,[56] while several monks who are known to compile surviving *nissaya*s in the mid-eighteenth century Ava (Taungbalu Hsayadaw Shin Uttamasāra (? after 1660–733), Kyawaungsanhta Hsayadaw Shin Ñāṇavara, and Kinbuntaung Shin Dhammanandī) have just been mentioned as non-court-based *nissaya* authors or would be mentioned below as monks with strong regional affiliation. Thus, their *nissaya* production at the court looks like a continuation of work that they began elsewhere or as a function of their regional connections.

Accordingly, it seems that *nissaya*s of *pitakat* texts that were produced in the capital area roughly from 1710 to 1752 by representatives of older court-based communities (if any) did not influence subsequent development of monastic education and textual activities in Upper Burma.[57] Only after the change of dynasty in the 1750s and transformation of court monasticism (which is discussed below) *pitakat* texts produced by monks patronized by the court become available again in surviving manuscripts. Thus, the survival of *nissaya*s of Uttamasāra, Ñāṇavara, and Dhammanandī perhaps means either that by the 1750s regions became primary locations for *nissaya* production or that only *nissaya*s of regionally-connected monks enjoyed subsequent use. Whatever the case, it means that in the first half of the eighteenth century production of *nissaya*s in the villages and secondary cities was a viable alternative to textual activities of older court-based communities.

Educational and Career Opportunities beyond the Capital Area

The strongest evidence on the existence of well-developed monastic networks connecting secondary cities and their surrounding villages and operating basically without reliance on the court comes from available works on monastic biographies and the emergence of sectarian divisions in the saṅgha. Here I'd like to compare the data on the careers of five monks dating from the mid-seventeenth to mid-eighteenth centuries. The monks I'm referring to are Nyaungzin-shwekyaung Hsayadaw Shin Uttamasikkhā (? – ? after 1714), Ton Hpongyi Shin Guṇābhilaṅkāra (1639 — ? about 1720), Taungbalu Hsayadaw Shin Uttamasāra, Kyawaungsanhta Hsayadaw Shin Ñāṇavara, and the First Monywe Zetawun Hsayadaw Shin Vicittālaṅkāra (1715–801). The first and the last of them have left personal accounts of their educational careers, the training of Guṇābhilaṅkāra and Uttamasāra is traced on the basis of eighteenth-century historiographic works, and Ñāṇavara's career is traced with the help of colophons of his writings and details about him in *Nyaunggan-thathanawin*.

Our earliest case is Uttamasikkhā, an influential court monk of the late seventeenth to early eighteenth centuries who participated in a number of religious projects of Nyaungyan court, such as the fixing of contents of royal collection of the *pitakat* texts in 1681–83, the construction of Mahaaungyadana stupa in 1699–1700, and translation of Pāli and Sanskrit texts for the royal library at this stupa in 1700–06.[58] Structurally, Uttamasikkhā's education (which occurred in the 1640–60s) consisted of training as a novice in a village, transfer to a monastery in the capital area (which was eased by his kinship relationship to a number of court monks) and subsequent studies at two other monasteries there.[59] At one of these monasteries he stayed in *kyaung-yan*, then received a monastery donated by a minister, and finally moved to a monastery built by a member of royalty. If my understanding of court monasticism of the seventeenth century is correct, Uttamasikkhā represents what might be called a "classical" type of a court monk firmly rooted in the capital area.

Cases of Uttamasāra, Ñāṇavara, and Vicittālaṅkāra contrast the career of Uttamasikkhā. Uttamasāra had an excellent monastic pedigree. As a novice he studied at two monasteries in Sagaing (Lehtat in Sagaing

Minwun and Pinlegyi in Sagaing Kinmaw), the former being one of the first royal monasteries built by the kings of Nyaungyan dynasty in the early seventeenth century, and the latter being one of the top educational institutions of the mid-seventeenth century.[60] Uttamasāra became a laureate of exam for novices and was ordained as the "first royal monk" (*pahtama-pazin-daw*). After the reconstruction of Lehtat-kyaungdaw in Sagaing Minwun in 1701 he was installed in one of *kyaung-yan*s there.[61] Later Uttamasāra decided to move from Sagaing to Hsalingyi and Amyint in order to continue his studies and spent several years there.[62] Upon his return to the capital area he received golden royal monastery at Taungbalu (north of Sagaing) and a title reflecting his affiliation with the Minwun Lehtat lineage.[63] His monastery at Taungbalu remained one of the key court complexes until the 1790s. Several of his disciples became the laureates at royal exams and occupied prominent positions in the court saṅgha.[64]

Uttamasāra's departure from Ava apparently was not a downshifting as he achieved greater prominence on his return. Uttamasāra was actively engaged in teaching and made a lasting impact on Abhidhammic studies and literature in Burma, and his studies in Hsalingyi and Amyint were most likely motivated by this orientation. According to available data, monks under whom he studied had a reputation of Abhidhamma scholars. No such information is available on the abbots of Minwun Lehtat and Pinlegyi.

Ñāṇavara's career had a comparable trajectory. He was born in a village in Pakhan area and became a novice there.[65] After the demise of his teacher in 1723, he moved to Ava where he was admitted to a monastery complex of one of the top royal teachers who was a supervisor of religious exams.[66] A year later he became a laureate at the exams and was ordained as a royal monk. Five years later Ñāṇavara moved out of Ava and returned to Pakhan receiving a considerably large monastery (Mataungta) built by a member of local elite. Until 1731, he supposedly stayed there and then moved to another place I was not able to identify so far. After 1735 he again resurfaced in Ava where he became a royal teacher and a head of 50 *kyaung-yan* comprising a half of the Kyawaungsanhta monastery complex constructed by King Mahādhammarājādhipati (1733–52).[67] In 1748 he left Ava again and moved to Nyaunggan village (Badon *myo-kye*) where he died five years later.[68] Similarly to Uttamasāra, Ñāṇavara's quick return to Pakhan apparently made sense. It allowed Ñāṇavara to achieve the position of the abbot faster and to do that in a location hosting important monastic communities and ritual complexes, having its own traditions of textual production, education, etc. This move seemingly allowed him to make a further career step and land as an abbot of royally supported monastic complex.

Finally, Vicittālaṅkāra's educational career which occurred in the 1730–40s furnishes the most convincing evidence on educational infrastructure outside of the capital area. In one of his works Vicittālaṅkāra provided a detailed account of his teachers and texts he studied under them. This account (if it reflects reality) draws a fascinating picture of a novice affiliating himself with a court-originating lineage in a village in Talot-myo, then moving to Ava to study and be ordained in one of the major monastery complexes there, and then moving from Ava and back to it in order to study in different villages in Hsalingyi, Wetlet, Pakhan, and Talot areas.[69] Given that Vicittālaṅkāra's curriculum is logically organized (being, at the same time, more or less in agreement with what one may call a basic monastic curriculum in Upper Burma of that time), that his choice of teachers was apparently based on their specialization, and that his educational career cut across all known sectarian divisions in contemporary saṅgha of Upper Burma, it could be argued that Vicittālaṅkāra's wanderings were perhaps dictated by his desire to get the best possible monastic education and that required not only staying at the capital but travelling extensively to various villages.[70]

The Rise of Regional Monastic Network: The Case of the *Tisiwareit* (Ton) Lineage

Why villages and secondary cities in the eighteenth century could provide educational facilities successfully competing with those at the capital becomes clear when we briefly survey the career of Guṇābhilaṅkāra. Guṇābhilaṅkāra was born in Ton village close to Amyint and Hsalingyi. To be ordained as a monk by his grandfather, he moved from Ton to Pazwa, another village located at roughly equal distance between Amyint and Pakhan. After one rainy season he relocated to Amyint to a monastery complex headed by his maternal uncle and stayed there at least for several years. After that he studied under two more teachers from Amyint and then relocated briefly to Pakhan. From Pakhan he moved to Ava to study *Kātantra* and *Vidagdhamukha maṇḍana* under the already mentioned Uttamasikkhā.[71] After that he moved to Pinya to the Aungtat-kyaung monastery (likely building on his connection with Uttamasikkhā here, as Aungtat was Uttamasikkhā's earlier monastery) and studied *Netti* there.

That completed his scriptural training and he began travelling to study practical aspects and (also possibly) teaching techniques. In this capacity he spent some time in Hsalingyi area, then in one of the key monasteries in Bagan, then returned to Sagaing and Ava where he practised under three different Mon abbots (he was also reordained) and in the Taungbila monastery, and then moved to Ywathitkyi. Finally he returned to Amyint to the complex of his uncle but soon requested a permission to retreat to the forest in Chaung-U area where he started his own community (the *tisiwareit* or Ton lineage) based on distinct disciplinary code, reformist programme, and approach to scriptural studies focused on Abhidhamma.[72]

It seems that as a leader of community Guṇābhilaṅkāra continued active travels, staying for certain periods of time in the areas of Chaung-U, Talot-myo (across the river from Ywathitkyi), Yezagyo, Hsalingyi, in the city of Talot itself, and in several key villages of Pakhan area. All these locations are situated close to the banks of Chindwin and Ayeyarwaddy and were important transportation and trading hubs. Guṇābhilaṅkāra also made a pilgrimage to Shwedagon in Lower Burma attracting a number of new disciples on the way.

In the early eighteenth century, when he already was an influential monastic leader, he managed to establish a hold in the capital area where, as it seems, he received two monasteries built by ministers. His appearance at the court was not entirely unproblematic due to reformist nature of his community and his criticism of established monastic lineages at the court for non-observing Vinaya. Accordingly, in 1711 he had to move from Ava to a nearby village as his former teacher Uttamasikkhā initiated a campaign of physical intimidation against roughly fifty monks who were residing in Guṇābhilaṅkāra's monastery in Ava.

Though Guṇābhilaṅkāra himself never became a royal teacher and his relationship with the court saṅgha was quite ambiguous, he still managed to achieve formidable results in terms of regional-based community building. The list of his disciples who were abbots of individual monasteries or heads of several monasteries I have compiled based on various sources runs to more than seventy persons. Geographically they were concentrated mostly in Bagyi (present Hsalingyi, Pale, and Yinmabin townships), Badon, and Amyint (present Chaung-U and Monywa townships), with offshoots in Sagaing/Ava, Dipeyin, Halin, Talot, Pakhan, and Pyi areas. In the first half of the eighteenth century the efforts of the first and second generations of Guṇābhilaṅkāra's disciples led to a proliferation of a network of monks associating themselves with Guṇābhilaṅkāra and his lineage in various locations in present Dipeyin, Ayadaw, Ye-U, Wetlet, Shwebo, Khin-U, Sagaing, Myinmu, Chaung-U, Monywa, Budalin, Hsalingyi, Yezagyo, Myaing, and Myingyan townships. In more general terms, during the first fifty to sixty years of its history Guṇābhilaṅkāra's network covered roughly 25 to 35 per cent of Burmese areas in Upper Burma. Numerically the strength of Guṇābhilaṅkāra's community is testified by his ability to convene at least two large monastic assemblies in Amyint and near Hsalingyi with 1,000 monks supposedly attending each of them. No surprise, that already the first generation of Guṇābhilaṅkāra's disciples (such as the already mentioned Uttamasāra) became royal teachers. Members of his lineage remained a key component of the court saṅgha roughly until the late 1780s.

However, in my analysis the rise of the Ton lineage could not be explained by royal support alone. Moreover, I think that the Ton community would not be able to establish itself at the court had it not commanded the support of local monastic communities and their donors outside of the royal city. According to the sources, the majority in the first generation of Guṇābhilaṅkāra's disciples was elder than he was and passed reordination to join the community. They would not be doing that if Guṇābhilaṅkāra's offer was not strong enough. My impression is that local monastic leaders were jumping on the bandwagon of a rapidly spreading monastic network which offered efficient tools of attracting lay support. Moreover, many leaders of local communities who cooperated with Guṇābhilaṅkāra at one point in time soon switched sides and withdrew to join other competing lineages such as the *thingan-yon*. This testifies that the Ton community operated in an area with multiple local agents able to form various tactical alliances and easily switching sides as soon as any existing alliance became less promising or rewarding.

To summarize, the career of Guṇābhilaṅkāra shows that by the late seventeenth century "peripheral" locations of Burmese Buddhism already had material and social infrastructure necessary for large-scale networking. To initiate it, a capable leadership was needed and monks such as Guṇābhilaṅkāra provided it.

SECONDARY CENTRES, SOCIAL INTEGRATION, AND THE DYNAMICS OF REGIONAL MONASTIC NETWORKING

The prominence of the royal city as a location of Buddhism, however, made a conflict between large regional networks such as the *tisiwareit*s and the court monastic establishment almost inevitable.[73] Royal patronage did not extend beyond the capital area and in terms of size court monastic establishment could not be stretched indefinitely. Given the fact that local elites who supported regional communities in Upper Burma (especially in the areas we deal with) were closely integrated with the court and that the access to the court system was limited but possible, the next logical step in the development of such large-scale community was to try landing its representatives as royal teachers and gaining control of elite monastic infrastructure.

Members of the Ton lineage have achieved that by the 1730s or 1740s but that did not eliminate competition with communities with earlier genealogies of royal support and with other aspiring regional groupings (such as the *thingan-yon* lineages or the Zawti-gaing) that followed the example of Guṇābhilaṅkāra and offered alternative reformist agendas. As a result, for most of the eighteenth century Burmese saṅgha was shattered by constant debates and squabbles between monks (with active involvement of the laity). That made a thorough monastic reform ultimately aimed at achieving better alignment between court monasticism and regional communities desirable or perhaps necessary. Such reform proceeded with varying pace during the early Konbaung period culminating in religious policies of Badon-min's reign (1782–1819).[74] One of the ultimate outcomes of this reform was achieving a degree of cooperation between court and local monastic hierarchies and the extension of selection mechanisms of the court saṅgha to the countryside.[75]

The discussion of monastic reform in Burma as such deserves a separate study and could not be made within the scope of this paper. Here I prefer to limit myself to such issues as what conditioned the pluralization of locations of monastic learning and activity in the seventeenth century Upper Burma, what favoured the development of monastic networking in villages and regional towns, and led to formation of specific translocal communities in "peripheral" areas. In this context it is also necessary to relate my findings with the recent work of Michael Charney who has pioneered the notion of regional monastic community in Burma studies.[76]

Charney argues that by the reign of Badon-min Upper Burma saw the emergence of a regional monastic community based in the area he calls Lower Chindwin. According to him, this community possessed a particular knowledge of Buddhist and non-Buddhist texts that supposedly was facilitated by community's location on a border with Manipur which allowed the members of community an access to Sanskrit texts through Manipur and particularly through Manipuri brahmins.[77] This presumed access to unnamed Sanskrit texts apparently formed the basis of what Charney calls "Lower Chindwin literary culture", a phenomenon he defines in very general terms by claiming that Lower Chindwin literati composed all major royal and religious chronicles of Konbaung Burma, had a huge impact on legal, religious, and court ritual texts, and effectively created the knowledge that defined what was "old Burma" both for Burmese and Europeans. The position of literati from this community was strengthened by particular importance of Lower Chindwin for the Konbaung polity as major military units were settled in this area and also because the natives of Lower Chindwin played special role in the rise of Badon-min to power.

The spread of literacy and greater demand for knowledge caused by the bureaucratization of Konbaung polity created a situation in which Lower Chindwin monks could demonstrate their superior knowledge of Pāli and Sanskrit texts.[78] As claimed by Charney, the opponents of Lower Chindwin monks relied on oral teachings transmitted from teacher to student while Lower Chindwin monks relied on texts.[79] The winning of royal support allowed Lower Chindwin monks to launch a reformation that resulted in their establishment as the only official monastic tradition until the end of Burmese monarchy. Moreover, from the 1780s Lower Chindwin lay and monastic literati became the dominating social force and interpreters of knowledge at the Burmese court.

This narrative differs radically from the perspective suggested in this paper. In fact, Charney arrives to his conclusions because he combines arbitrary manipulation of data with selective treatment of sources where the priority is given to materials available in English and to secondary literature. Defining the region under investigation, Charney first claims that Lower Chindwin was comprised of Badon, Kanni, Bagyi, and Amyint areas.[80] However, later through the course of the book he broadens Lower Chindwin to include Dipeyin (an area closer to Mu than to Lower Chindwin) and a number of places in Pakhan.[81] As a result, at least half of sites located on the right bank of the Ayeyarwaddy in the core part of Upper Burma were lumped into a greater "Lower Chindwin" than claimed initially. With "Lower Chindwin" extending from Maungdaung in the northwest, Dipeyin in the north, and Ngayan-o, Neyin and Pakhan in the east and southeast (on the confluence of Ayeyarwaddy and Chindwin), the area that Charney defines as Burma — Manipur frontier stretches down to the major waterway of Burma and deep into Upper Burmese hinterland. Extremely vague definition and free manipulation of the region in question allows Charney to ignore the existence of different and competing communities within such large area.

In making a point about the rise of regional networks, Charney does not consider the evidence dating to or dealing with Nyaungyan period and thus dates this rise several decades later than the present author. Such communities as the *tisiwareit* are completely overlooked and no mention is made that they originated from the same Lower Chindwin area. In fact, any recognition of the *tisiwareit*s' existence would dismantle Charney's argument that the literati responsible for monastic reform under Badon-min were trying to win the support of the crown for the natives of Lower Chindwin by means of particular regional knowledge. If so, these literati were vying with the natives of the same region presumably sharing the same knowledge and thus their proximity to Manipur gave them no strategic advantage over their opponents.

The transmission of texts in the eighteenth century Burma went not in the eastward direction as Charney implies (from Manipur to Lower Chindwin and then to Central Burma), but from the centre to the west. Instead of spreading their *nissaya*s to monks outside of Lower Chindwin (if we stick to the definition of Lower Chindwin as comprised of Badon, Bagyi, Kanni, and Amyint), the monks from Maungdaung, Nyaunggan, and neighbouring villages of Badon area (who were among the key figures in the reforms described by Charney) relied on *nissaya*s produced in Pakhan and Bagan areas. The same *nissaya*s formed the basis of monastic instruction in the nineteenth century Burma (hence the broad availability of their copies noted above).

In geographical terms, the base of the *thingan-yon* network that promoted the reform under Badon-min was also broader than Lower Chindwin: Pakhan and Bagan areas were not less important for its functioning. At the same time, the *tisiwareit* network that historically has been the key opponent of the *thingan-yon* was much more concentrated in Lower Chindwin area and so the displacement of the *tisiwareit*s in the 1780s resulted rather in broadening of regional connections of court monks, than in the rise of Lower Chindwin literati to power.

Finally, as the careers of Guṇābhilaṅkāra and Uttamasāra analysed above show, the *tisiwareit*s did not rely on "oral transmission" vs. the "textual knowledge" of Lower Chindwin literati. Textual excellence was equally important to both networks (the *thingan-yon* and the *tisiwareit*), however, their approaches to textual exegesis and understanding of the sources of authority in interpreting the texts were different.

Instead of presumed connections with Manipur and ability to tap into Sanskrit texts, I believe that important contributing factor to the emergence of regionally-based monastic networks in Upper Burma outside of the court control was the long-term evolution of power structures and its implications for religious activities. The polycentrism of the fourteenth to sixteenth centuries made overlords of Pinya, Sagaing, and Ava broaden their patronage arrangements beyond the primary royal city in order to maintain ritual superiority vis-à-vis numerous other rulers nominally subordinate to them. That created a more diversified religious landscape as compared to the Bagan period (when the polity was more compact and power structures outside of Bagan were less sophisticated). After the fourteenth century Bagan remained a key centre of ritual, educational, and literary activities but that was due to a momentum it gained earlier. If we switch our attention to emergent locations, such centres as Pinya, Ava, Myinzaing, Metkhaya, Sagaing, Amyint, Pakhan, and Salin operated in a more synchronized way and their outlook and orientation was comparable with contemporary institutions at Bagan.

Political integration of the seventeenth century has eliminated the reality of parallel courts in Upper Burma and allowed for centralization of ritual and symbolical arrangements. If in the fifteenth century the patronage of monks in the secondary cities such as Pakhan, Bagan, Amyint, Yamethin, or Taungdwin was an important tool allowing the overlords of Ava to demonstrate their political and ritual superiority over their relatives who ruled as almost independent sovereigns in such secondary cities, since the mid-seventeenth century independent sub-rulers were almost non-existent and so it was possible to demonstrate ritual superiority by contracting the patronage to the capital area and transforming it to a kind of exclusive field of merit.

At the same time, such places as Pakhan, Bagan, Amyint, Talot, and other secondary centres of Nyaungyan polity remained critically important. Though they did not claim their own dynasties anymore, they were distributed among the members of royalty as appanages and also had their own hereditary local officials. In these ways, the natives of these cities could maintain links with the court and exploit the avenues of access to court officialdom and court monasticism.

Moreover, relative stability enjoyed by Upper Burma during the seventeenth century ensured better integration of secondary cities with their surrounding villages, created wealth that could be redistributed there, and allowed local elites to start imitating their overlords in many aspects of merit-making at local level. Different regions were also closely integrated with each other which served an important condition for increased movement of lay and monastic personnel. Eventually, that created the infrastructure and networks I have tried to describe above.

Throughout the paper I have consistently emphasized the influence of patronage arrangements on the structure of monasticism. As mentioned above, regional monastic networks relied mostly on local elites so the integration of such elites should have been an important condition for their emergence. In this regard it is relevant to mention the evidence provided by *The History of Hngetpittaung* on what might be considered as such integration.

The History of Hngetpittaung, a late eighteenth century text documenting the succession of abbots of an important monastery in Bagan, gives a detailed account of whereabouts of some of its monks during the dynastic crisis of the 1740s and 1750s. The text makes it quite clear that in some cases monks sought refuge from plunder and devastation by following their donors who went to places where their relatives resided. In other cases monks went to their own relatives. In yet some other cases the way the monks moved is not discussed, but it is clear that they did not simply flee but went to places where they could stay for prolonged periods of time and that their whereabouts were known to their colleagues as they continued to communicate with each other. It seems logical to assume that in these cases monks probably moved to places from which they originated, where they had relatives or, perhaps, donors. If this interpretation is correct, it means that the support base or at least the zone of social contacts of a monastery in Bagan stretched over a vast area from Aneint village in Amyint area in the north to villages across the river from Bagan, to Taywindaing to the east of Bagan, and to Yenangyaung and Pin to the south of Bagan.[82] Given the prominence of Hngetpittaung in Bagan and the fact that its abbots occasionally enjoyed royal recognition, the connections of this monastery could not be extrapolated to an average monastery in a secondary city or village, but even as unique case it shows that personal networks of monks, local officials, and members of crown-service units in secondary cities were not really "local", but covered a significant part of Upper Burma.

At the same time, the emergence of regional monastic networks was not a function of social integration alone. They did not develop simply because of the spread of literacy and greater demand for knowledge due to the bureaucratization of the polity. Also, they did not emerge because certain regions were particularly important for Burmese polity and thus could achieve a degree of control over court hierarchy (as argued by Charney).

Monastic networks were regional and distinct from court monasticism because integrative and centralizing processes characteristic of the mid-seventeenth to mid-eighteenth centuries were coupled with the court's attempt to distance the royal city (with all its unique features, such as court monasticism) symbolically from the subordinate countryside.[83] Integration fostered networking, but the exclusivity of royal patronage made resultant networks only indirectly related to court monasticism. As a result, instead of a large-scale ecclesiastical organization Upper Burma during the period in question was characterized by plurality of monastic systems and quite different types of monasticism (many of which are beyond the scope of this paper).

Burmese monastic regionalism was also dependent on the unique status of core Burman areas of Upper Burma with their greater degree of cultural integration as compared to other areas of Burmese polity (Lower Burma, Shan states, etc.) in the Nyaungyan and early Konbaung periods. That explains why geographically the spread of monastic networks in question did not go beyond the recruitment base of the court saṅgha.

Accordingly, the situation described above was unique and did not exist for long. Political integration, rise of literacy, demand for professional education, all these factors continued well into the nineteenth and twentieth centuries. However, already since the early nineteenth century large monastic networks in Upper Burma were not purely "regional" anymore (i.e. more or less direct linkage with the court or court monasticism became an integral part of their functioning), villages no longer served as a base for ambitious and historically successful *nissaya* projects (i.e. one finds no parallels to Ariyālaṅkāra from Neyin village in the nineteenth or twentieth centuries), and monastic mobility of a type demonstrated by Vicittālaṅkāra became irrelevant (i.e. Burmese villages no longer offered education avenues that could compete with the key urban locations).

As soon as monastic reforms of the second half of the eighteenth century established direct links between monastic hierarchy at the court and regional monastic leaders, expanded court monasticism,[84] and made it more inclusive and open to infiltration from the villages, as well as decreased the importance of kinship relationships for the succession in royal monasteries, the ability of local centres to offer stimuli for alternative scholarship and *nissaya* production also decreased. Socio-economic transformations of the nineteenth century related to commercialization of economy, integration of Burma into global market, foreign expansion, etc. made many Upper Burmese villages and secondary cities much less able to retain the best monastic talent. In terms of functioning of monastic system in general, by the early twentieth century the role of villages contracted to being, first, a recruiting ground of personnel for urban monastic centres and, second, locations for guest appearances of key monastic leaders. That has obviously diminished the capacity of villages and small towns to serve as a basis for important regional networks.

The analysis presented above further highlights the differences between Burmese monastic networks in the eighteenth century and their Sinhalese counterparts. In both Burma and Laṅkā in the eighteenth century we find reform movements promoting the centralization of the saṅgha. Similarities are great in terms of rhetoric, mechanisms of mobilization, marketing tools used to present the community and its agenda to the public, as well as in mechanisms of ensuring the superior educational and practical experiences. However, in terms of sociology these movements were quite different. For example, if we compare monks from the Ton community (that emerged in the early eighteenth century) and the *thingan-yon* lineages (who supplanted the members of the Ton lineage in the capacity of monastic elite in the late eighteenth century) with Silvat Samāgama and Siyam Nikāya in Laṅkā several differences are clear.

It seems that from their inception the Silvat Samāgama and the Siyam Nikāya were elite communities drawing mainly members of aristocracy and high-caste individuals. Next, in the course of their institutionalization they did not rely on any parallel monastic networks that were alternative to court hierarchy. Furthermore, the establishment of the Siam Nikāya led to restoration of durable large-scale ecclesiastical structures that were characteristic of Sinhalese monasticism in the Anurādhapura, Poḷonnaruva, and Dambadeṇi periods.[85] Finally, before the British annexation of Kandy in 1815 the structure of the Siyam Nikāya did not evolve into a system perpetuating reformism and favouring vertical mobility, but remained within the paradigm of royally-centred monasticism. The significance of villages as the social base for saṅgha in Laṅkā becomes apparent only in the nineteenth century with the emergence of Amarapura and Rāmañña Nikāyas.

On the contrary, the members of the *tisiwareit*s, *thingan-yon*, and Zawti gaings, three major reform-oriented monastic movements in the eighteenth-century Upper Burma had distinctly local roots, relied on regional networks independent of the court system, tended to manipulate the crown and local elites (instead of allowing the latter to push their own agendas), and created conditions for greater vertical mobility in Burmese monasticism.[86] In this way, natives of Burmese villages and secondary cities first conquered the court monastic establishment and reformed it in the later half of the eighteenth and early nineteenth centuries. Only after achieving that, they gave way to new forms of monastic mobility and networking.

Notes

1. I would like to thank D. Christian Lammerts for his extensive comments on this paper and Ko Kyaw Hswe Myint, Ko Kyaw Win, Ko Min Ye Lat, Ko Than Zaw, and Ko Thein Naing, the members of my research team, for their

dedication during the fieldwork. The generous help of the late Taungpaw-kyaung Hsayadaw U Ādiccavaṃsa from Hsalingyi, Hpaungdaw-U-kyaung Hsayadaw U Paññinda from Padu village, Hsayadaw U Kesara and the saṅgha of Kanbya-kyaung in Okshitkyi village, as well as of the officials and staff of the Universities' Central Library, research library of the Ministry of Religious Affairs, National Library, Research Centre for Ancient Myanmar Manuscripts (Yangon), Bagan Archaeological Museum, and the library of Shwedagon stupa was essential for this project.

2. The capital area hosted numerous other communities that were not patronized by the court but such communities never belonged to the court saṅgha operationally.
3. As a rule, overlords personally donated both the monasteries built by them and those that were constructed by their relatives and key courtiers. They also conducted merit-sharing ceremonies after such donations.
4. In a certain way, this arrangement mirrored the division of courtiers into two major categories of those who had fixed seats at royal audiences (*ne-ya-ya*) and those who did not enjoy such privilege (*ne-ya-ma-ya*) and formed a crowd at the back.
5. A glimpse on the importance of kinship and familial relationships for Nyaungyan court monks is provided by account on the disciples of Tisāsanadhaja, a sixteenth-century monk from Sagaing, compiled by Nyaungzin-shwekyaung Hsayadaw Shin Uttamasikkhā at some date between 1706 and 1720 (palm-leaf ms. no. Kin 85 in the National Library (NL), Yangon). This work (identified in manuscripts either as *Shin Tithathanadaza ahse-anwe-sadan* or as *Thamanawuntha*) is the earliest and most detailed available source on lineage links of Upper Burmese court monks in the sixteenth and seventeenth centuries.

   For semi-closed nature of Nyaungyan court monasticism, see below.
6. A telling example is provided by royal order issued by King Minye Kyawhtin (1673–98) on 30 October 1679. The order allowed a minister to construct a monastery with architectural elements reserved for royalty, thus breaking established sumptuary rights and acknowledging that the status of recipient monk was more important than the status of the donor (though theoretically the design of the monastery was supposed to reflect the latter). The justification for that was that the incumbent monk belonged to a monastic succession that held royally conferred titles for a long time and was venerated by the king's grandmother. The document in question specifically contrasted the incumbent's status as a person with celebrated monastic pedigree to other categories of court monks that could not claim a record of highest recognition. Than Tun, ed. *The Royal Orders*, vol. II, p. 234.
7. A clear distinction between *sathin*, *taw-ne*, and *dazeit-taw-ya* monks is, for example, drawn in the above-mentioned royal order dated 30 October 1679.
8. The term *pitakat* referred to the three canonical piṭakas together with

commentaries, sub-commentaries, handbooks, works on Pāli grammar, translations of such texts, etc. Generally speaking, the *pitakat* corpus included almost all types of Pāli-related or Pāli-derived texts transmitted in Burma. For more details on the notion of the *pitakat*, see Kirichenko, "Classification of Buddhist Literature" and Lammerts, "Narratives of Buddhist Legislation", p. 120.

9. She-haung-sape-thutethi-ta-u, *Nyaung-yan-hkit amein-daw-mya*, vol. 2, p. 64.
10. Palm-leaf ms. no. Kin 58 in NL, folio *kā* r; She-haung-sape-thutethi-ta-u, *Nyaung-yan-hkit amein-daw-mya*, vol. 2, pp. 59–61, 64; Kala, *Mahayazawin-gyi*, vol. 3, p. 238.
11. Thiyiuzana, *Lawkabyuha-kyan*, pp. 160–61; Kala, *Mahayazawin-gyi*, vol. 3, pp. 242, 286, 304, 351.
12. Than Tun, ed. *The Royal Orders*, vol. I, pp. 175–76, 214–16.
13. Sandawarabiwuntha, "Pahtamabyan-thamaing", p. 287.
14. The holding of yearly exams since the reign of Thalun-min was questioned by Khammai Dhammasami. Dhammasami, *Between Idealism and Pragmatism*, pp. 70–78. It should be noted, however, that his arguments about monastic examinations in Nyaungyan period are highly problematic due to misinterpretation and misquotations of supporting evidence. At the same time, official Burmese chronicle dating to the early eighteenth century indeed records the regular holding of exams only after 1662. Kala, *Mahayazawin-gyi*, vol. 3, pp. 292, 286ff.
15. Thiyiuzana, *Lawkabyuha*, p. 301.
16. Kala, *Mahayazawin-gyi*, vol. 3; Thiyiuzana, *Lawkabyuha*, pp. 300–302.
17. In addition to career opportunities for a laureate, the successful passing of exams was often rewarded with transfer of laureates' relatives from lower- to higher-status social groups, such as cavalry units. See, for example, Than Tun, ed. *The Royal Orders*, vol. II, p. 348.
18. For the examples of cases tried by *vinayadhara*s, see Than Tun, ed. *The Royal Orders*, vol. II, pp. 350–51 and palm-leaf ms. no. 544 in the Resource Centre for Ancient Myanmar Manuscripts (RCAMM), Yangon, folios *pā* v – *pi* v. For additional data on the latter case, see Kala, *Mahayazawin-gyi*, vol. 3, p. 357. For a discussion of Nyaungyan monastic jurists in the context of laws and jurisdictions applicable to the inheritance of monastic property, see Lammerts, "Genres and Jurisdictions". It might be noted that the latter paper argues for a less clear separation of monastic and lay legal systems in the Nyaungyan period than my description given above presupposes.
19. For example, in 1729 the dispute on the proper dress for novices going to collect alms-food was tried by the supervisors of exams as the current *vinayadhara* (Hpyaukhseit-min Hpongyi Shin Varamedhā) was the initiator of the case. *Tisiwarika-thathanawin* by Sāsanālaṅkāradhaja Hsayadaw, palm-leaf ms. from the Taungpaw-kyaung monastery, Hsalingyi, Hsalingyi township, folio *kaw* r.

20. See, for example, palm-leaf ms. no. 11953 in the Universities Central Library (UCL), Yangon, and palm-leaf ms. no. 610 in RCAMM that contain collections of replies given by court monks to various queries of overlords. A small, but very interesting collection of monastic advice on the banishment of ghosts from the royal palace and proper geomantic arrangements in Ava is available in She-haung-sape thutethi-ta-u, ed., "Lawka-zeya-sadan". For further evidence of monastic involvement in similar rituals, see Kala, *Mahayazawin-gyi*, vol. 3, pp. 302, 303, 304, 305. For assistance in military campaigns, see Than Tun, ed. *The Royal Orders*, vol. I, pp. 196, 200. For predictions and numerological calculations of Nyaungyan court monks, see palm-leaf mss. nos. 704 and 1452 in RCAMM.
21. For more details on this concept, see Kirichenko, "Living with the Future".
22. This trend is perhaps related to a general withdrawal of Upper Burmese royalty from Lower Burma in the seventeenth century. The changes in administrative practices and royal politics led to discontinuation of royal court in Hanthawadi in 1635, decrease in a number of appanages being granted in Lower Burma, absence of overlord's relatives appointed to the region as semi-independent rulers (*bayin-khan*) after the 1660s, and gradual decline in the number of officials of Mon descent in Ava. For a more detailed discussion of these developments see Lieberman, "Provincial Reforms" and Lieberman, "The Transfer of Burmese Capital".
23. Thanbawdi, *Maha-hngetpittaung*, pp. 48–49, palm-leaf ms. no. 544 in RCAMM, folios *hpay* r – *hpaw* v.
24. Than Tun, ed. *The Royal Orders*, vol. I, pp. 427–28, 440.
25. I assume this on the basis of few references in the sources that mention such reordinations (for example, palm-leaf ms. no. Kin 58 in NL, folios *hke* v, *hkaw* r, *Tisiwarika-thathanawin* by Sāsanālaṅkāradhaja Hsayadaw, palm-leaf ms. from the Taungpaw-kyaung monastery, Hsalingyi, folio *kā* r) or claim that practice in particular monastery was based on specific ordination tradition (Bur. *theitkha*, Pāli *sikkhā*).
26. For more arguments on the fluidity of Burmese monastic structures during the period in question, see Kirichenko, "Change, Fluidity".
27. For a description of royal monasteries, see Than Tun, ed. *The Royal Orders*, vol. I, pp. 173–74; *Inscriptions of Pagan*, p. 376.
28. This description is based on the evidence on monastic careers provided in palm-leaf ms. no. Kin 85 in NL as well as on the data on the construction and rebuilding of royal monasteries found in Kala, *Mahayazawin-gyi*, vol. 3. A fuller discussion of this evidence is given in Kirichenko, "Organizatsiya patronazha".
29. Such mobility is evident in some monastic biographies of the eighteenth century. The movement between the capital and provinces was likely facilitated by channels and patronage opportunities created by persons who combined

presence at the court with links to peripheral locations (e.g., appanage holders, court merchants and bankers, etc.).

30. Aung-Thwin, "The Role of Sasana Reform", especially p. 685.
31. Schober, "The Theravada Buddhist Engagement", p. 311.
32. Dhammasami, *Between Idealism and Pragmatism*, pp. 63–64.
33. Lieberman, "Was the Seventeenth Century", pp. 24–43. It should be noted that in his main work on Nyaungyan period Lieberman was quite cautious in crediting the capital with a vast control over religious landscape in the provinces. In *Burmese Administrative Cycles*, his first major work, Lieberman mentioned the appointment of lay and monastic officials responsible for enforcing Vinaya observance, the registration of monks, and an inquest into monastic landholdings, and admitted that policing the Order could not be effectively achieved (pp. 109–12).

    However, in later works dealing with broader chronological periods and wider regional perspectives Lieberman apparently started taking the elements of monastic reform under Badon-min (1782–1819) as a key reference point. As a result, in the paper quoted above and in Lieberman, *Strange Parallels* (pp. 62 and 64) the situation characteristic of the late eighteenth century came to be projected back into Nyaungyan period.
34. A mention of registration of monks made in *Burmese Administrative Cycles* (p. 110) is based on an early twentieth century monastic chronicle; in fact, there is no evidence that Nyaungyan kings ever tried to register religious personnel, except for temple/stupa and monastery serfs and laymen residing in monasteries.
35. For example, Daṁbadeṇi Katikāvata promulgated by Parākramabāhu II (1236–70), the earliest of surviving *katikāvata*s issued by Sinhalese kings between the thirteenth and eighteenth centuries, subjected monastic ordination to approval from at least three *sthavira*s and the Nāyaka (a head of the saṅgha). It also required an approval from the Nāyaka when a monk was released from the dependence on a teacher, or promoted to sthavirahood and obtained the right to develop a group of monastic (?) dependents. Appointments of the head of the saṅgha, heads of the village- and forest-dwelling branches of the saṅgha, and heads of important ecclesiastical units (Mūḷa, Ayatän, great Pariveṇas) located in different parts of the island required an approval by the saṅgha and the king. Ratnapala, *The Katikāvatas*, pp. 141, 144, 145, 147. These provisions were later incorporated in Kīrti-Śrī Rājasiṃha's (1747–82) Katikāvata I. Ratnapala, *The Katikāvatas*, p. 169. In the 1780s the control of key monastic leaders over the conferral of monastic ordination was strengthened by requirement to perform such ordinations only in the *sīmā*s of Malwatta and Asgiriya Vihāras.
36. Ratnapala, *The Katikāvatas*, p. 180.
37. Even if we admit that these requirements were theoretical and in reality the system could have worked quite differently, the dissimilarities between Burma

and Laṅkā still remain. Before the 1780s there is no evidence that Burmese court tried to prescribe any uniform model of monasticism for all the monks in the realm or created any arrangements to monitor the conformity with such model. The earliest document in which a key royal teacher addressed the heads of local monastic communities that I have managed to find dates to the 1750s and provides a brief exposition on basic Vinaya rules (see a work of Atula Hsayadaw titled *Vinaya-pakinnaka-kyan* in palm-leaf mss. nos. 6303 and 6520 in UCL and no. 656 in the library of the Shwedagon stupa, Yangon). It does not envisage any structured control of the court saṅgha over the activities of local monks. Thus, both in terms of content and application this document is very different from Sinhalese *katikāvata*s.

38. Ishii, *Sangha, State, and Society*, pp. 61, 63.
39. Dhammasami, "The Impact of Political Instability", pp. 192, 181.
40. McDaniel, *Gathering Leaves*, esp. pp. 99–116; McDaniel, *The Lovelorn Ghost*.
41. I am ready to admit that secondary cities and villages could have been the sites for production of manual and "notebook" types of texts transmitted on *parabaiks* but the survival of such texts from the early period is almost unimaginable and thus no study of that type of literary activity might be possible.
42. Palm-leaf ms. dated 1852 (1214) from Pazwa village, Myaing township, folio *ḷaw* v; palm-leaf ms. dated 1895 (1257) from Hpaungdaw-U monastery in Padu village, Hsalingyi township, folio *yi* v.
43. I am quite sure that this text was far not the earliest specimen of *pitakat*-type composition done outside of royal cities. Moreover, a number of seemingly early works are undated or their place of compilation is unknown. However, it is quite logical to find a relatively early text originating from Pakhan as this city was an important religious and administrative centre at least from the thirteenth to the late nineteenth centuries.
44. Maung Maung Nyunt, *She-khit myanma*, p. 50. This text is known only through references as no manuscript was found so far.
45. Maung Maung Nyunt, *Myanma-naingngan*, p. 179.
46. In 1718 he compiled *nissaya* of *Khuddasikkhā* (palm-leaf ms. dated 1766 (1127) from Hsula-kyaung monastery in Padu village, Hsalingyi township, folio *ḍe* v), in 1723 *nissaya*s of *Tika-gyaw* (palm-leaf ms. dated 1863 (1225) from Hpaungdaw-U monastery, Padu village, Hsalingyi township) and *Kaṅkhāvitaraṇī aṭṭhakathā* (palm-leaf ms. dated 1910 (1272) from Hpaungdaw-U monastery, Padu village), in 1726 *nissaya* of *Saṅkhepavaṇṇanā* (BM I no. 91), in 1727 *nissaya* of *Aṭṭhasālinī aṭṭhakathā* (palm-leaf ms. dated 1783 (1145) from Kanbya-kyaung monastery, Okshitkyi village, Ayadaw township, folio *kye* v), in 1736 *nissaya* of *Suttasīlakkhandha aṭṭhakathā* (not dated palm-leaf ms. from Hpaungdaw-U monastery, Padu village), and in 1753 *nissaya* of *Kaccāyana vaṇṇanā* (Maung Maung Nyunt, *She-khit myanma*, p. 48).

47. Shin Sāradassī compiled a *nissaya* of *Netti* in 1760. Kelatha, *Pakhokku thathanawin*, p. 170; Maung Maung Nyunt, *Myanma-naingngan*, p. 126.
48. Palm-leaf ms. dated 1774 (1136) from Beikman-tha monastery, Ton village, Hsalingyi township, folio *dhu* v; not dated palm-leaf ms. from Kanbya-kyaung monastery, Okshitkyi village.
49. Even when a dynastic crisis caused him to move to Pauk village in 1749 to order to escape from "thieves and rebels" he wrote a *nissaya* on *Kaṅkhāvitaraṇī aṭṭhakathā* (palm-leaf ms. dated 1929 (1289) from Shwebontha-kyaungtaik monastery, Thitkyo village, Ayadaw township, folios *la:* r – *wa* v; Maung Maung Nyunt, *Myanma-naingngan*, p. 163). In 1762 he also compiled *nissaya* of *Vinayavinicchaya* (Maung Maung Nyunt, *Myanma-naingngan*, p. 178).
50. Maung Maung Nyunt, *Myanma-naingngan*, p. 125.
51. Palm-leaf ms. no. AS 68.1 from the Archaeological Museum, Bagan; palm-leaf mss. nos. 6714 and 7672 in UCL.
52. In 1748 anonymous abbot of a forest monastery in Maungdaung village (Badon *myo-kye*) compiled a Vinaya decision on staying in forest monasteries (palm-leaf ms. no. 271 in the library of Shwedagon stupa, Yangon, folios *khay* – *gā*). Also in the mid-eighteenth century Shin Puññārambha who resided in the Myauk-taik monastery in Hsalingyi made an adaptation of *Dhātukathā* for student monks (palm-leaf ms. no. 1081 in the library of Shwedagon stupa, Yangon, folio *pī* v).
53. It is not clear to what extent the degree of abbreviation of vernacular depended on the choice of individual scribes, manuscript donors or owners or was a result of parallel circulation of several versions of a *nissaya* differing in completeness of vernacular glosses.
54. Cf., for example, palm-leaf ms. of the second bundle of Shweumin's *nissaya* of *Pārājika-kaṇḍa* (*Samantapāsādikā*) dated 1679 from the Hsula-kyaung monastery, Padu, and Zambudipadaza, *Parazikan at-hta-kahta neitthaya*, vol. 3, pp. 123ff and vol. 4.
55. The shortest time-frame I have so far for the period under study is less than one year. In late 1776 or early 1777 Hsonda Hsayadaw Shin Nandāmāla (1718–? *c*.1784) compiled *nissaya* of *Jinālaṅkāra* while staying in Hsinbyukyun village (Hsinbyukyun township, Magwe division). A copy dated late 1777 is now kept in Hpaungdaw-U monastery, Padu village (Hsalingyi township, Sagaing division). As there are no indications of owner, monastery or donor in the manuscript and the monastery that holds the manuscript now dates to the nineteenth century, it could not be said with certainty that the copy was made in or travelled directly to Padu. It might have come from Yemein, a neighbouring village from which few of the early manuscripts in Hpaungdaw-U collection originate. It might have come from elsewhere. In case the manuscript was initially intended for Padu or Yemein, the transmission of the *nissaya* was most likely based on a personal or lineage connection, as Hsonda Hsayadaw lived for some time near these two villages and some monks there belonged

to the same faction in the saṅgha as him. In this case it might be said that in several months from its compilation a text could easily travel for about one hundred miles (that is the approximate distance between Hsinbyukyun and Padu). However, even if the manuscript came to Padu from elsewhere its mere existence indicates that texts written in the villages in the eighteenth century were recopied and travelled almost instantly after being compiled.

56. For example, in 1720 the first abbot of the Yadanathahte-kyaung Shin Abhiseka who occupied the position of *pitakat sa-ma* compiled *Kappavaṇṇanā*, a cosmological text in vernacular (palm-leaf ms. dated 1774 from the Taungpaw-kyaung monastery, Hsalingyi).
57. A seemingly large set of *nissaya*s was produced by royal teachers in 1700–06 with the sponsorship of King Sane-min (1698–1714) and placed in the *pitakat-taik* of Manaungyadana stupa (Kala, *Mahayazawin-gyi*, vol. 3, pp. 359, 380) but I did not manage to find any texts belonging to it among surveyed manuscripts.
58. On the projects see Kala, *Mahayazawin-gyi*, vol. 3, pp. 351–58, 359, 380.
59. First, his uncle taught him Jātakas of *Mahānipāta*, *Kaccāyana*, and "secular literature" (*lawka-wut-sa*) such as texts on astrology, calendar calculations, mathematics and various other calculations in a village close to the capital area. After that, he was sent to the Pithsimawun monastery in Sagaing and continued studying *Kaccāyana* there. He also started studying *Mukhamattadīpanī*, *Vuttodaya*, and *Tikapaṭṭhāna* at Pithsimawun. Then he moved to the Aungtat-shwekyaung monastery in Pinya where continued studying *Tikapaṭṭhāna*, started *Dukapaṭṭhāna* and continued until he mastered the complete text of *Paṭṭhāna*. Also at this monastery he studied *Vinaya*, *Samantapāsādikā,* and *Vimativinodanī*. In parallel to his stay in Aungtat (which lasted until 1675) he studied *Sutta-piṭaka* in the Kongyang monastery in Sagaing under Shin Ñānindadhaja. The choice of that teacher was motivated by the fact that Ñānindadhaja supervised the editing of royal copies of *Sutta-piṭaka* texts. Palm-leaf ms. no. Kin 85 in NL, folios *khi* v – *khu* r, *khaw* v, *gaw* r.

    As in the cases of Vicittālaṅkāra and Guṇābhilaṅkāra analysed below, the source does not detail the method how the above mentioned texts were studied. The training could include both the study of a *nissaya* and memorization of original text.
60. Palm-leaf ms no. 123369 in UCL, folio *khan* v.
61. A survey of biographies of distinguished *thera*s of Sagaing by unknown author, palm-leaf ms. no. 1447 in the library of the Department of Historical Research (DHR), folio *nga* r.
62. Ibid.
63. Palm-leaf ms no. 123369 in UCL, folio *khan* v, dates the donation to the reign of Sane-min and gives no timeline for bestowing of title. According to palm-leaf ms. no. 1447 in the library of DHR, folio *nga* r, the title was bestowed by Taninganwe-min (1714–33).

64. Palm-leaf ms. no. 123369 in UCL, folio *khan* v, also Kirichenko, "Atula Hsayadaw", pp. 9, 11.
65. A survey of monastic biographies compiled by Minhla Thiri Thihathu in 1851, handwritten copy of a ms. no. 2030 in UCL, p. 3.
66. Palm-leaf ms. no. Kin 58 in NL, folios *kū* v, *ke* v.
67. Than Tun, ed. *The Royal Orders*, vol. VI, p. 389.
68. Thudathana, *Nyaunggan thamaing*, p. 53.
69. Initially he studied in a village in Talot-myo under a monk who belonged to a lineage originating in Sagaing. There he mastered alphabet and spelling, *Paritta*, *Temiya*, *Janaka* and *Suvaṇṇasāma-jātaka*s, as well as *suttas* (*thot-sin*) from *Kaccāyana*. Next he moved to a well-known complex (Gabanni-taik) in Ava which was quite influential in the late Nyaungyan. There he studied *Sandhī* and *Nāma* from *Kaccāyana* as well as *Mahāsamaya-sutta*. Then he was ordained and as a monk studied *Mūlasikkhā*, *Khuddasikkhā*, *Vinayasaṅgaha*, and a text that I believe signifies *Brahmajāla-sutta*. This was done under a monk from a different monastery in the same complex. Then the teacher changed again (yet another monk from the same complex) and curriculum expanded to cover *Vācakopadesa*, *Kaccāyanabheda*, and *Vinaya Cūlavagga*. After that Vicittālaṅkāra apparently left Ava and went to a village in Hsalingyi area. There he studied the full text of *Kaccāyana* and *Kaṅkhāvitaraṇī*. Describing his next teacher, Vicittālaṅkāra identifies him by a complex where that monk resided later so it is not easy to understand where Vicittālaṅkāra went to from Hsalingyi area. My working supposition is that it might have been a native area of the monk in question. If that is true, Vicittālaṅkāra must have moved to a village in Wetlet area to study *Kaccāyana* again. The next stage apparently implied a return to Ava and studying *Abhidhammatthasaṅgaha*, *Mātikā, Dhātukathā,* and *Yamaka*. After that he seems to move to Pakhan area to study under three teachers in different villages there. The first taught him *Pārājika-kaṇḍa* from *Samantapāsādikā*, the second instructed in *Vinaya Cūlavagga*, and the third in *Bhikkhunīpātimokkha*. After that Vicittālaṅkāra returned to Gabanni-taik in Ava and studied *Vinayasaṅgaha* again. Then he moved to a fourth village in Pakhan area to complete the study of the commentary on *Ubhatovibhaṅga* (*Samantapāsādikā*) and master what seems to be *Kappālaṅkāra*. The last village he apparently went to to study *Vuttodaya* allows several identifications but it seems more plausible to me to chose the one located in Talot-myo (as the village thus identified is close both to the native village of a teacher and the village Vicittālaṅkāra stayed afterwards). In a separate sequence Vicittālaṅkāra identifies three monks in Ava under whom he studied astrological/calendar texts and the art of *yantrā*. *Monywe Zetawun-kyaung thamaing*, palm-leaf ms. from the Monywe Zetawun monastery, Monywe village, Monywa township.
70. The educational sequence progressed from introductory texts and basics of grammar to Vinaya handbooks, then to a more thorough study of grammar

and Vinaya, then to study of Abhidhamma on both basic and advanced levels, then to advanced study of Vinaya and finally to Pāli metre. As for the choice of venues, Vicittālaṅkāra studied Abhidhamma exclusively under the teachers of the Ton lineage, basic Vinaya under the teachers of the *gāmavāsī* lineages from Ava, advanced Vinaya mostly under the teachers of the *thingan-yon* lineages and also under one teacher of the Ton lineage, grammar under teachers of all lineages, and astrology with *gāmavāsī* and *pwekyaung* monks from Ava.

71. It is equally possible that he studied these works on grammar and lexicology in Sanskrit or in Pāli translation.
72. Guṇābhilaṅkāra's reformist programme focused on ensuring eventual kammatic progress of monks and laity by means of promoting proper behaviour and avoidance of unwholesome activities leading to rebirth in woeful states. On the lay side of the equation, that implied observance of basic moral precepts, abstinence from intoxicants, animal sacrifices and other forms of improper placation of spirits, and from supporting immoral monks as that caused the decline of the *sāsana*. For monks, that meant a promotion of strict conformity to the Vinaya which ranged from purging those who committed *pārājika* offences to eradicating improper monastic utensils. The point about monastic utensils was particularly important for Guṇābhilaṅkāra who stressed the necessity to discontinue using various hats, fans, and other regalia which were commonly used to differentiate monks of specific communities and lineages. He also argued against smoking pipes. Disciplinary measures promoted by Guṇābhilaṅkāra were coordinated and integrated into a campaign for revival of forest-dwelling monasticism (which supposedly has almost disappeared) as an epitome of ideal monastic practice. Disciples of Guṇābhilaṅkāra symbolically identified themselves as those who follow an ascetic practice of using a single set of monastic robes (*tecīvarika dhutaṅga*), as this *dhutaṅga* was considered particularly important for the forest-dwelling monks. Hence they were known as the *tisiwareit* (Burmese form of *tecīvarika*).

    Despite this broad programme, Guṇābhilaṅkāra and the *tisiwareit*s are much better known as the champions of a particular dressing mode they required of novices when going on alms-round. One of the most common practices of novices of the late Nyaungyan period, to which the *tisiwareit*s also subscribed, was wearing the upper robe in a manner that leaves the right shoulder bare and the left hand completely wrapped. The right shoulder was then covered with undersized robe called *dukot* (or *dukot-nge* to differentiate it from *saṃgāṭi*). *Dukot*, in its turn, was secured in place by binding the chest. However, contrary to the claims of later opponents of the Ton community, this dressing manner was neither an innovation of Guṇābhilaṅkāra nor a point of particular importance for the *tisiwareit*s. In my analysis, the issue of novices' dress became important for the Ton community only because it was chosen as a rallying point by a competing reformist faction which challenged both the court monks and Guṇābhilaṅkāra and his disciples with accusations of contradicting the Vinaya (this faction became known as the *thingan-yon* lineage or monks favouring the "covering [of two shoulders] with the upper robe").

As a result, the monks of the Ton community were embroiled in a protracted debate on the correct dressing mode for novices from the 1720s to the 1780s and finally lost it. For more details on Guṇābhilaṅkāra and the "one-shoulder" vs. the "two-shoulder" debate, see Kirichenko, "Atula Hsayadaw". The debate is also addressed in Leider, "Text, Lineage", and Pranke, "The Treatise on the Lineage".

73. In addition to structural factors there have been many conceptual reasons for such conflicts which were related to ideological evolution of Burmese saṅgha. The scope of the paper does not allow exploring that important dimension of the problem as well.
74. So far there has been no consistent study of monastic reform during the early Konbaung period. A brief comment on the reform during the reign of Alaungmintaya (1752–60) is provided in Kirichenko, "Atula Hsayadaw", pp. 14–19. The same paper also notes some of the developments under Nga Singu-min (1775–82). Kirichenko, "Atula Hsayadaw", p. 20. Reforms of Badon-min's reign received a more comprehensive and nuanced discussion in a number of works, though little consensus in interpreting these events was achieved. The most recent studies include Pranke, "The "Treatise on the Lineage"; Leider, "Text, Lineage and Tradition"; Charney, *Powerful Learning*; Kirichenko, "Changes and Continuity"; Kirichenko, "Atula Hsayadaw", pp. 22–34; Kirichenko, "Appendix to 'Atula Hsayadaw'."
75. Kirichenko, "Changes and Continuity".
76. Charney, *Powerful Learning*; Charney, "Literary Culture".
77. Charney, *Powerful Learning*, p. 49; Charney, "Literary Culture".
78. Charney, *Powerful Learning,* chapters 1–2, especially pp. 54–58; Charney, "Literary Culture", p. 172.
79. Charney, "Literary Culture", p. 175.
80. Charney, *Powerful Learning*, p. 15.
81. See further locations defined as "Lower Chindwin" in Charney, *Powerful Learning*, pp. 23, 64, 96, 103, and 213.
82. Thanbawdi, *Maha-hngetpittaung*, pp. 51–91. Though I quote *The History of Hngetpittaung* from a twentieth-century edition that incorporates this chronicle as a separate chapter, I also have a handwritten copy of a palm-leaf ms. (dated 1909) containing the text that seems to date to about 1778.
83. The process of political and cultural integration of Upper Burma has been described by Lieberman, see, in particular, Lieberman, "Was the Seventeenth Century", pp. 236–49, and Lieberman, *Strange Parallels*, pp. 158–202. Lieberman also addressed the issue of divisions created by status differentiation

of various categories of elites and the populace; see, for example, *Strange Parallels*, p. 194.

In the context of this paper I find particularly useful Lieberman's discussion of the spread of popular literacy that he sees as a process only indirectly encouraged by the state (Lieberman, "Was the Seventeenth Century", pp. 245–46, and Lieberman, *Strange Parallels*, pp. 188–89) that thus resembles the decentralized spread of monastic networks outlined above. Equally relevant in this context is the latest research by art-historians Cristophe Munier-Gaillard and Alexandra Green. The former has traced particular scenes and iconographic features in Nyaungyan-style mural paintings that have distinctly regional character (Munier-Gaillard, "Édifier, surprendre et faire rire") while the latter argued that the production of paintings in provincial temples was fairly autonomous from the influence of the court and the elite saṅgha (Green, "From Gold Leaf", pp. 308–309).

84. For example, from the 1780s to 1880s the number of monks in the capital grew roughly from 3,000 to 10,000. Quite soon after its construction Mandalay had more than two hundred monastic complexes established and patronized by the court (in addition to older monasteries in Sagaing, Amarapura, and Ava) while the number of known court-patronized monasteries in the capital area in the 1770s seems not to exceed one hundred and fifty.
85. Gunawardana, *Robe and Plough*; Malalgoda, *Buddhism in Sinhalese Society*; Blackburn, *Buddhist Learning*.
86. In this regard I agree with Charney who interprets Burmese monastic communities as independent agents capable of pushing their agenda and making the crown implement it, and not as the tools of royalty/aristocracy.

References

Aung-Thwin, M. "The Role of Sasana Reform in Burmese History: Economic Dimensions of a Religious Purification". *Journal of Asian Studies* 38, no. 4 (1978): 671–88.

Blackburn, Anne. *Buddhist Learning and Textual Practice in Eighteenth-Century Lankan Monastic Culture*. Princeton, NJ: Princeton University Press, 2001.

Charney, Michael. *Powerful Learning: Buddhist Literati and the Throne in Burma's Last Dynasty*. Ann Arbor: Center for South and Southeast Asian Studies, University of Michigan, 2006.

Charney, M. "Literary Culture on the Burma—Manipur Frontier in the Eighteenth and Nineteenth Centuries". *The Medieval History Journal* 14, no. 2 (2011): 159–81.

Dhammasami, Khammai. "Between Idealism and Pragmatism: A Study of Monastic Education in Burma and Thailand from the Seventeenth Century to the Present". PhD dissertation, Oxford University, 2004.

———. "The Impact of Political Instability on the Education of the *Saṅgha* in the 17th Century Siam". *Journal of the International Association of Buddhist Universities (IABU)* 1 (2008): 171–202.

Green, A. "From Gold Leaf to Buddhist Hagiographies: Contact with Regions to the East Seen in Late Burmese Murals". *Journal of Burma Studies* 15, no. 2 (2011): 305–58.

Gunawardana, R.A.L.H. *Robe and Plough: Monasticism and Economic Interest in Early Medieval Sri Lanka*. Tucson: University of Arizona Press, 1979.

Inscriptions of Pagan, Pinya, and Ava Deciphered from the Ink Impressions Found among the Papers of the Late Dr. E. Forchhammer, Government Archaeologist, Burma. Rangoon: Govt. Printing, 1892.

Ishii, Yoneo. *Sangha, State, and Society: Thai Buddhism in History*. Honolulu: University of Hawai'i Press, 1986.

Kala, U. *Mahayazawin-gyi* [The extensive great chronicle], in 3 vols. Yangon: Myanma thutethana-athin, 1960–61.

Kelatha, Ashin. *Pakhokkhu-thathanawin* [The history of the sāsana in Pakokku]. Yangon: Thathana-ye uzihtana, 1967.

Kirichenko, Alexey. "Living with the Future: Succession of Royal Cities Preserving Sasana and Its Influence on the History of Myanmar and Myanmar Historical Writing". In *Myanmar Historical Commission Conference Proceedings*, pt. 2, pp. 1–37. Yangon: Myanmar Historical Commission, 2005.

——. "Changes and Continuity in Burmese Buddhism". Paper read at the 2nd Conference of the South and Southeast Asian Association for the Study of Culture and Religion "Syncretism In South And Southeast Asia: Adoption And Adaptation". Mahidol University, Bangkok, 24–27 May 2007.

——. "Classification of Buddhist Literature in Burmese Inscriptions and 'Histories of Pitakat'." Paper read at the Eighth International Burma Studies Conference, Northern Illinois University, DeKalb, 3–5 October 2008.

——. "Organizatsiya patronazha i pridvornoe monashestvo kak osobaya kategoriya v buddhiskoi sanghe Myanmy v 17 i 18 vekah [The organization of patronage and court monks as a specific entity in Burmese Buddhist saṅgha of the seventeenth and eighteenth centuries]". *Vestnik Moskovskogo Universiteta. Seriya 13: Vostokovedenie*, no. 4 (2008): 3–24.

——. "Change, Fluidity, and Unidentified Actors: Understanding the Organization and History of Upper Burmese Saṃgha from the Seventeenth to Nineteenth Centuries". Paper read at the AAS/ICAS joint meeting in Honolulu, 31 March–3 April 2011.

——. "Appendix to Atula Hsayadaw Shin Yasa: a Critical Biography of an Eighteenth-Century Burmese Monk: Documents related to Atula's trial in 1784 (version 1.1)". <http://www.niu.edu/burma/publications/jbs/vol15.2/Kirichenko Atula biography Appendix.pdf> (accessed 7 May 2012).

——. "Atula Hsayadaw Shin Yasa: a Critical Biography of an Eighteenth-Century Burmese Monk. Version 1.1 (2 April 2012)". <http://www.niu.edu/burma/publications/jbs/vol15.2/Kirichenko Atula biography online.pdf>. (accessed 7 May 2012).

Lammerts, D. Christian. "Genres and Jurisdictions: Laws Governing Monastic Inheritance in 17th Century Burma". In *Buddhism and Law: An Introduction*, edited by R. French and M. Nathan. New York: Cambridge University Press, forthcoming.

———. "Narratives of Buddhist Legislation: Textual Authority and Legal Heterodoxy in Seventeenth through Nineteenth Century Burma". *Journal of Southeast Asian Studies* 44, no. 1 (2013): 118–44.

Leider, J. "Text, Lineage and Tradition: The Struggle for Norms and Religious Legitimacy under King Bodawphaya (1782–1819)". *Journal of Burma Studies* 9 (2004): 82–129.

Lieberman, Victor. *Burmese Administrative Cycles: Anarchy and Conquest, c. 1580–1760*. Princeton, NJ: Princeton University Press, 1984.

———. "Provincial Reforms in Taung-ngu Burma". *Bulletin of the School of Oriental and African Studies, University of London* 43, no. 3 (1980): 548–69.

———. "The Transfer of Burmese Capital from Pegu to Ava". *Journal of the Royal Asiatic Society* 112, no. 1 (1980): 64–83.

———. *Strange Parallels: Southeast Asia in Global Context, c. 800–1830. Volume 1: Integration on the Mainland.* Cambridge: Cambridge University Press, 2003.

———. "Was the Seventeenth Century a Watershed in Burmese History?". In *Southeast Asia in the Early Modern Era: Trade, Power, and Belief*, edited by A. Reid, pp. 214–49. Ithaca: Cornell University Press, 1993.

Malalgoda, Kitsiri. *Buddhism in Sinhalese Society 1750–1900: A Study of Religious Revival and Change*. Berkeley: University of California Press, 1976.

Maung Maung Nyunt, U. *Myanma-naingngan pali-hnin pitakat-sape thamaing-thit* [New history of Pāli and *Pitakat* literature of Burma]. Yangon: Sape-beikman, 2003.

———. *She-khit myanma-sape-hsaing-ya kyan-mya lelahmu* [The study of texts related to old Burmese literature]. Yangon: Sape-beikman, 2008.

McDaniel, Justin. *Gathering Leaves and Lifting Words: Histories of Buddhist Monastic Education in Laos and Thailand*. Seattle: University of Washington Press, 2008.

———. *The Lovelorn Ghost and the Magical Monk: Practicing Buddhism in Modern Thailand*. New York: Columbia University Press, 2011.

Munier-Gaillard, C. "Édifier, surprendre et faire rire: La société bouddhique birmane dans les sermons visuels de la Chindwin". *Moussons* 16 (2010): 103–32.

Pranke, Patrick. "The "Treatise on the Lineage of the Elders" (Vaṃsadīpanī): Monastic Reform and the Writing of Buddhist History in Eighteenth-Century Burma". PhD dissertation, University of Michigan, 2004.

Ratnapala, Nandasena. *The Katikāvatas: Laws of the Buddhist Order of Ceylon from the 12th Century to the 18th Century (Critically Edited, Translated and Annotated)*. München: Kitzinger, 1971.

Sandawarabiwuntha, A. "Pahtamabyan-thamaing [History of *pahtama-byan* examinations]". In *Thirikhittaya Pyi-myo Zawtikayon Pali-tetkado Shwe-*

yadu-Metgazin [Golden jubilee magazine of Zawtikayon Pāli university of Pyi], pp. 287–92. S.l., 1989.

She-haung-sape-thutethi-ta-u [Researcher of ancient literature]. *Nyaung-yan-hkit amein-daw-mya* [Royal orders of Nyaungyan period]. Vol. 2. Yangon: Myanma-hmu-beiman sape-ban, n.d.

——, ed. "Lawka-zeya-sadan [Treatise on worldly success]". In *She-haung-hmat-sa-padetha* [Collection of old records]. Vol. 7. Yangon: Myanma-hmu-beiman sape-ban, n.d.

Schober, J. "The Theravada Buddhist Engagement with Modernity in Southeast Asia: Whither the Social Paradigm of the Galactic Polity?". *Journal of Southeast Asian Studies* 26, no. 2 (1995): 307–25.

Than Tun, ed. *The Royal Orders of Burma, A.D. 1598–1885*. Vols. I, II & VI. Kyoto: The Center for Southeast Asian Studies, Kyoto University, 1984–87.

Thanbawdi, Hsayadaw U. *Maha-hngetpittaung yazawin-thamaing-kyan* [The history of Mahahngetpittaung]. Mandalay: Thukhawati, 1955.

Thiyiuzana, Wungyi. *Lawkabyuha-kyan* [The arrangement of the world]. Yangon: Aso-ya, 1962.

Thudathana, U. *Nyaunggan thamaing hpyit-sin thathanawin* [History and sāsanavaṃsa of Nyaunggan village]. Yangon: Sidaw, 2002.

Zambudipadaza. *Parazikan at-hta-kahta neitthaya* [Pārājika-kaṇḍa aṭṭhakathā nissaya]. Vols. 3 & 4. Yangon: It-hsa-thaya, 1970–73.

12

BUDDHIST DIPLOMACY
Confrontation and Political Rhetoric in the Exchange of Letters between King Alaungmintaya and King Banya Dala of Pegu (1755–56)

Jacques P. Leider[1]

ABSTRACT

The pervasive use of Buddhist terms and notions in the political field is a well-known example of Buddhism's dominance as a cultural force throughout premodern Southeast Asia. While scholars have duly recognized the key concepts pertaining to Buddhist kingship, the tendency to generalize the meaning of common concepts such as *dhammarājā* may have obscured the fact that expression of such concepts is always local and meanings may have varied over time and place. This paper offers a case study and may contribute to comparative approaches. As he was relentlessly waging war against the Mon king Banya Dala, the Burmese king Alaungmintaya sent letters to Pegu to demonstrate his political claims, letters that were countered by similar claims on behalf of Banya Dala. Read against the background of the political record as drawn out in Burmese historiography, an examination of the letters offers an exceptional insight into diplomatic practice carved out of the ethical and cosmological stuff of Burma's Buddhist environment. The paper presented here offers an example of the practical and complex use of Buddhist rhetoric at a critical moment of Burma's eighteenth century history.

Alaungmintaya (r. 1752–60, *aka* Alaungphaya) was the founder of the third Burmese dynasty (1752–1885). Banya Dala (r. 1747–57) was the ruler of the predominantly Mon kingdom of Pegu (Hamsawadi). The years 1755–56 were the key years of Alaungmintaya's war efforts to gain supremacy over the whole of the territory traditionally understood to have been the realm of Burmese kings.

INTRODUCTION

Addressing the plural dynamics of Buddhist culture across geography and time, this paper offers a study of Buddhist diplomacy with its rhetorical modes as they are revealed in the letters that a Burmese and a Mon king exchanged while they were waging war against each other.[2] Both kings were Buddhists sharing in the same *Weltanschauung* and religious background. They were also new men without proven links to preceding dynasties.

From the early seventeenth century onwards, a single kingdom had existed in the Irrawaddy valley. Its unity was broken when in 1740, a new, predominantly Mon kingdom was refounded in the old and prestigious city of Pegu. From that moment onwards, war ensued between the southern Mon and the northern Burmese kingdom. It dragged on for twelve years until the fall of the northern capital of Ava. Banya Dala, the king of Pegu, reigned since 1747. His opponent, Alaungmintaya started his political career after the fall of Ava in 1752.[3] Being one of a few local strongmen who had decided to resist the Mon supremacy, he soon built up a local power network, entrenched his authority, fought back the Mon detachments sent against him and, starting late 1754, led his armies down south to conquer the Pegu kingdom. In 1757 Pegu fell. The key years of military and political events that led to the end of the Mon kingdom were 1755 and 1756, the final chapter of military confrontation being played out in the early months of 1757.

As both Banya Dala and Alaungmintaya, as we have said, were new men whose link to former dynasties was uncertified, they were craving recognition beyond their triumphs on the battlefield. In their quest for legitimacy within the social/cosmological order, they were moreover keen to establish their Buddhist credentials by linking their rise to supernatural causes. Reading the letters that these two kings sent each other while they were at war may lift the veil on a hitherto poorly investigated subject —

precolonial Southeast Asian diplomacy — and, more generally, the forms of communication between Southeast Asian élites.

The first part will focus on the representation of royal status and the command of language codes which were key tools of diplomacy. The second part is an attempt to contextualize the letters by linking them to the chronology of events, giving a view on Buddhist diplomacy in practice.[4] No attempt is made to reconstruct diplomatic history as such by unfolding political agendas linked to the record of events on the battlefield, but an understanding of diplomatic interaction is not possible without a reasonable awareness of the political chronology. Extracting modes of language from the syntax of these letters and interpreting their meaning by associating them with the process of decision making should thus contribute to a better understanding of the historical process itself.

It should be understood that historical analysis will intuitively restrict research on matters of style to questions that pertain to the core domain of historical research, i.e. the understanding and reconstruction of past events. Within a historical framework, two overlapping questions particularly stand out when studying the language used by the two Buddhist kings who were so violently opposed to each other. First, how could Buddhist beliefs and concepts be instrumentalized in diplomatic language so as to morph into a specifically Buddhist, or say Buddhicized, political rhetoric? Second, how did the kings, in a context of war and clashing political ambitions, deal in their letters with the issue of violence which is contrary to Buddhist scriptures. Due to constraints of space, the paper will only briefly sketch the second question.

STATUS AND LANGUAGE: TOOLS OF DIPLOMACY

It is remarkable that King Alaungmintaya has been recognized as a great military leader, but not as an inspired diplomat.[5] It is not an exaggeration to say that he was a believer in communication and diplomatic engagement. To quote two major examples, he took the initiative to write to his main foe, Banya Dala, the king of Pegu, but had to patiently wait a full year to get a reply. He also took the initiative to get into contact with the East India Company on which he put many hopes that were later disappointed. As he wanted to make himself and his political aims known, reaching out to foes and potential allies looks like a self-serving business at first hand. But there was obviously more to the pursuit of diplomatic ways than self-promotion. In historiography as well, it looks sometimes as if diplomacy came as a distant second after battles had already been fought.

Chronicle records, the most common historical source, lack immediacy. They describe the political history mainly as a succession of confrontations including battle preparations and clashes and their focus on deeds rather than their genesis. Causal links are often dressed up in supernatural garb and great care is taken to provide the reader with ceremonial minutiae. Occasionally consultations at the court are reported in the form of verbal statements put into the mouth of individual historical actors, but the way such verbal expression is woven into the streamlined historical narrative does barely allow a critical feedback on political discontent or complexity.

The set of original letters used in this study offers a chance to appreciate a context that stretches beyond the lining of troops. It provides an insight into the cultural, properly Buddhist dimension pertaining to the down-to-earth context of ongoing warfare and rivalry between two powerful kings. It opens thus a venue to reconsider historical narratives and should pave the way for alternate interpretations of the early Konbaung period of Myanmar history.[6]

We may assume that in the case of Alaungmintaya, the messages contained in the letters were generally drafted by the king himself together with his closest advisors. Common orders were most probably formulated, written, checked and copied by scribes of the royal chancellery under the authority of a select number of royally appointed officers. But the writing of important letters where matters of style and protocol counted highly, were entrusted to men like Letwè Nawrahta, a minister, poet and close advisor of the king.[7] But empathy and individualized expressions in Alaungmintaya's letters — and notable differences with the letters of his sons and generals, for example — provide sufficient evidence to postulate that Alaungmintaya's letters were not merely products of advisors, ministers or scribes, but reflected the king's own voice.[8]

Besides Alaungmintaya's letters to the king of Pegu, letters to the king of Ayutthaya, the king of Great Britain, the *sawbwa* of Hsenwi, the English East India Company, the French East India Company, the king's chief queen and the people of the country have come down to us.[9] They were part of collections that included as well edicts of the king and were probably formed already since the lifetime of the king himself. Henry Burney, the British resident at the court of Ava in the 1830s, owned such a collection preserved in a palm leaf manuscript.[10] The edition of Alaungmintaya's edicts by the Burma Historical Commission in 1964 was based on two such collections.[11] At the current level of research, their genealogy cannot be reconstituted. Than Tun held the opinion that surviving royal orders were copies kept by the recipients while the archival versions had entirely disappeared.[12] But this hypothesis can only imperfectly account for the way that particular orders and letters have come down to us in form of collections.

The study of Alaungmintaya's and Banya Dala's letters is particularly interesting to gain an insight into elite communication in a Buddhist environment. Royal letters have also been referred to in the chronicles and are known at least since the seventeenth century. Even a superficial glance at letters that have come down to us in the original version with their adaptation in the chronicles shows that the chroniclers paraphrased and shortened the letters to make them more readable. Obviously such changes could impart slightly changed meanings. A thorough record of such parallels and a stylistic comparison would be of great interest for the sake of historiographical research.

Most letters start with an elaborate list of royal titles. These lists were neither pedantic nor vain, they were important political expressions. As both kings were, politically and dynastically speaking, new men, they were keen to stress and constantly reiterate their royal identity and their supranatural legitimacy. The self-representation reflected in their titles was not only a prominent formal aspect in the text of the letters, but also a corner stone of political rhetoric.

Calling oneself "*dhammarājā*" or "*mintaya*" (the vernacular equivalent) established a link with well-established royal deportment and it expressed a shared understanding of ideal kingship, but in the confrontational environment of war, it was first of all a statement of detaining legitimate and exclusive power. As a tool of diplomatic interaction, the definition of status was a key issue. Both kings defined themselves as sovereign kings (*min ekarāj*) and they stressed their Buddhist credentials and adherence to a set of ethical concepts. Both stated and mutually recognized that they were kings due to the religious merits acquired in their former lives — having performed "good deeds and reached *pāramī* virtues in the times of former buddhas", as Alaungmintaya wrote in his letter of 10 June 1755.[13]

Both stated in their letters, like many other kings over hundreds of years in Burma and in its neighbouring countries, that they wanted to obtain the "Buddha-prize", defined in one letter forwarded by a group of monks as "the triple prize of becoming a *savaka[buddha]*, a *paccekabuddha* and a *sammasambuddha*".[14] Banya Dala also expressed a wish for obtaining the omniscience of an enlightened one (*sabbaññuta-ñāṇa*).[15] Alaungmintaya insisted on his superiority over other kings, legitimized by his claim of being a predestined lord. But so did, in slightly varying turns of expression, his colleague of Pegu. Actualizing by repetition in public and potentially hostile minds the supernatural link was a device that matched political necessity. Banya Dala's letters exist only in Burmese translations and may thus have been altered, while Alaungmintaya's letters are a primary Burmese source to observe the king's never-ending diligence to adjust the series of his titles to his political needs and the relative position of his letters' addressees.

The issue of defining one's status in one's own perception was more important at the beginning of diplomatic exchanges than at a later stage of the confrontation. As the power relation between Alaungmintaya and Banya Dala tremendously changed over one and a half years — as the Mon king was about to lose the war — news of events on the battlefield made statements on Alaungmintaya's self-ascribed status somewhat redundant. In a word: When the bloody record of the battlefield sufficiently underscored the political agenda, the need for status-building rhetoric in diplomatic interaction was slightly reduced.

Alaungmintaya stated that his rise to power had been "foretold by the *yathe* flying in the skies who know the preordained events announced by the omniscient Buddha".[16] Banya Dala's first letter to Alaungmintaya (13 June 1756) also established the Mon king's credentials by invoking a prediction of the Buddha. According to the prediction, Banya Dala would "honour the *sāsana* in the middle of the *sāsana's* life". Then he goes on stating his accession to the throne repeating the reference to the prediction ("when the year *2290 of the sāsana was* over [1746], I established and spread the sāsana in the royal place of Haṃsāvatī thanks to my former merits and *pārami* virtues as had been predicted by the omniscient Buddha who is the lord over many *ekarāj* kings in the world...etc."),[17] introduces himself as somebody who has already been diligently spreading the Buddhist teaching, and exhorts people to lead a virtuous life. The Mon king mimics a predominantly religious discourse and dwells on the religious ideal of kings dedicated to a pursuit of moral purity so as to "gain the approval of men, *brahmās* and gods". To fit such a letter into a narrative of warfare looks difficult as it does not even hint at the fact that at the moment of its writing, Syriam, the Mon kingdom's main port of trade and important economic asset was about to fall into the hands of the enemy. The political message of the letter that can be retrieved from the Buddhist slang of somewhat pompous self-representation could be freely interpreted as "mark my words and take note who you are talking to".

The invocation of royal best practice with reference to the *dhammarājā* ideal is not a highly explicit feature of the letters discussed here, but it implicitly puts into evidence its principles. Expressing their best intentions, both kings were keen to repeat that they wanted to work for the welfare of the people and the prosperity of the religion. This aspiration to ensure the prosperity of the Buddhist *sāsana* was indeed part and parcel of royal speech at all times. But as we will show in the second part, the letters of both kings, while being exposés of royal ideology, were embedded in a tangible context of ongoing warfare. This should explain why standard assertions as this one were only exceptionally more elaborate. Peter Skilling has referred to royal titles of Siamese kings of Ayutthaya as "potent condensations" and this characterisation fits our case well.[18] An accumulation of such potent condensations is found in Alaungmintaya's first letter to Banya Dala of 10 June 1755 which associates several of the rhetoric devices mentioned above and offers an intricate display of his acclaimed status.

> a donor of the *sāsana,* fulfilling all the duties of the kings such as the ten *rājadhamma,* the seven principles of worldly kings, the four precepts of *saṅgaha*, the five commitments (*paṭiññāñ*), the four good courses of being impartial like Yama, being a lord endowed with the wisdom and the strength to rule with justice and crush the cunning enemies according to his own wish just as if they were destroyed by the four weapons of Sakrā,[19] Vessavaṇṇa,[20] Yamaka[21] and Āḷavaka.[22]

We find in this short paragraph the titles of what Collins called the "recipes for a good king" next to a statement of powerfulness and physical strength.[23] The tenfold *rājadhamma*, included in U Kala's early eighteenth century chronicle connected this ethical code to the primordial elected king Mahāsammata. It became one of the most important sets of principles to define righteous kingship in eighteenth and nineteenth century Burma. Translations of the ten seminal virtues vary among authors. This is not surprising. Aurore Candier who investigated successive interpretations during the Konbaung period sees the tenfold *rājadhamma* as "the first argument of a discourse on kingship, constantly redefined by successive normative texts throughout the middle and late Konbaung periods".[24] The ten are alms-giving (or charity), morality (or observance of the precepts of law), liberality (also indicated as self-sacrifice), honesty (or integrity), mildness, religious practice (or practice of austerity), non-anger, non-violence, patience and non-offensiveness (or harmony).[25]

The seven principles of worldly kings, *aparihāniya*, are commonly known as the conditions conducive to prosperity or factors of non-decline. They are derived from injunctions the Buddha made to the monks in the *Mahāparinibbāna-sutta*.[26] The following presentation expressive of the political duties implied, is derived from Than Tun and U Pho Lat: (1) The king should hold regular meetings with his ministers to discuss political affairs, (2) the meetings are attended punctually and when everyone leaves, common decisions should be implemented as agreed, (3) decisions taken at the meeting should not be contrary to ancients laws and customs, (4) the advice of elders and wise men should be respected, (5) women should not be molested or taken by force, (6) customary offerings should be made to the protective spirits, (7) monks who are present or due to arrive should be protected and taken care of.[27] The four precepts of *saṅgaha* (*saṅgahavatthū*), originally derived from the Vedic great sacrifices (*assamedha, purisamedha, sammāpāsa,vācāpeyya*) were redefined by Buddhist commentators as the grounds of royal popularity of the king, such as the fair assessment of taxes, the protection by the ruler's men, the providing of opportunities, notably the provision of interest-free loans, to farmers and merchants, and pleasant talk.[28] The originally monastic context of the five commitments (*paṭiññāñ*) was the teaching of the Buddha on the way that a bhikkhu can admonish another bhikkhu for a disciplinary transgression.[29] As a duty of kings, it was adapted as the five modes of speech, (1) speaking when it is timely to speak, (2) speaking about fact, (3) speaking when it is advantageous to speak, (4) speaking gently, (5) speaking with loving kindness.[30] The four good courses (*gati*) of being impartial like Yama, the king of death, are also derived from scriptural formulations. One should avoid being biased by desire, anger, fear or ignorance when taking a decision.[31]

How can we interpret the display of these ethical toolboxes in this first introductory letter of Alaungmintaya? Three points can be made. First, it is clear that they did not serve to legitimize a specific political course of action as they do not form part of an argument and their practical relevance is not made explicit. Second, their place within the list of royal attributes and titles identifies them as markers of royal status building. It is important to note that this letter was written in a transitional phase when people beyond the core area that he controlled in Upper Myanmar, were increasingly recognizing Alaungmintaya as the Burmese king. Captain Baker, an East India Company officer, makes this point clear in his observations on the situation in Pathein in early 1755, referring to the "new king of Momchabue [Shwebo]" "whom I now call the Bûraghmah King".[32] Alaungmintaya, a simple village chief who had raised himself to local leadership, when setting out to conquer the whole country, had to show that he knew the principles of a rightful king. Thirdly, despite the formulaic character of the list of titles, it would be careless to assume that a scribe had simply inserted them to bolster his master's credentials.

Given the fact how much these lists represent contemporary Myanmar ethical and political thinking, they actually show that Alaungmintaya was embraced by a milieu of educated men who joined him after the fall of Ava, men who were the bearers of Myanmar legal culture and institutional routine and procedure.

The letters are occasionally peppered with Pali citations from the scriptures that spell authority. Their insertion stressed the moralizing tone that impregnated the political messages. At the same time they worked as doctrinal markers which rhetorically transpose the real-world between the two kings into a friendly rivalry for moral excellence. Banya Dala aiming for negotiations under the increasing pressure of the Burmese siege of Syriam, concluded his letter of 28 June 1756 with the following sentence:

> Me and my younger royal brother should [have our minds] filled with *lokatta-cariyam*, *ñātatta-cariyam* and *buddhatta-cariyam* for the future and should venerate at this time in close relationship to each other the three jewels so as to obtain the wisdom of the omniscient Buddha.[33]

It is important to understand that such turns of phrases were not merely stylish exercises to impress and display erudition. Translated into terms of diplomatic efficiency, Banya Dala wanted to save his face as a sovereign king as much as he needed to soften his opponent's aggressive stance. In his reply, Alaungmintaya, after stressing both his great military power and his wish to see an end to hostilities, concludes his answer with an appeal to practice insightful meditation:

> (The Buddha) has told the people to practice energetically as much as they can for example concentration with mindfulness.[34]

This sentence was the discombobulated way of introducing, one line further on in the letter, Alaungmintaya's key demand to the Mon king, namely to surrender. Drawing attention to the need of meditation may thus not have been so much a call to reflect on doctrinal truths than an injunction to ponder seriously the fact that Syriam was about to fall.

A corollary of Alaungmintaya's claim to superior kingship was his attempt to delegitimize his adversary. He told King Banya Dala that though he had become the lord of a golden palace due to his merits in former lives and effectively ruled over the country, his present capital of merit would not last much longer. He had rebelled against his true lord, the former king of Ava, and should consider that the people whom he was trying to subjugate at the present moment would be his enemies in future lives.[35] Alaungmintaya thus rejected Banya Dala's royal claims on moral grounds. In a more ordinary and direct way, Alaungmintaya continuously derided the Mon king's selfish attitude (*attanomati ayū kui yū*), arrogance (*mān māna*) and stubbornness (*khak than so sabho*) that prevented him, said the Burmese king, from accepting his political inferiority.[36]

Alaungmintaya's argument highlights the fact that kingship as much as the claim for political power were not the objects of a legal debate. The question who was the right king at the moment was not a matter of newly established or formerly acquired rights.[37] Neither was it only a matter of exerting sheer physical superiority.

Generally, the letters between Alaungmintaya and Banya Dala were written in a polite and polished language. Independently from events on the battlefield, a constant level of mutual consideration was maintained while addressing each other.[38] Contemporary English sources show that Alaungmintaya was imbued with a feeling of invincibility and had a tendency for boasting in direct verbal exchanges.[39] But in his official letters such instances are somewhat rare to find. We rather find occurrences of irony and sarcasm.[40] But there was no rude language and physical superiority was only referred to symbolically. With the exception of his letters to the East India Company, victories on the battlefield were never explicitly mentioned. Threats came generally in an understated form. Take the following example from Alaungmintaya's letter to Banya Dala of 19 December 1756: "I kindly send this letter telling you that I will not send it one or two more times."[41]

Sources do not allow us to make elaborate comments on Banya Dala's character in the light of or in contrast with the style of his letters. As much as we can judge, his style remained very polite while his political position steadily declined. More even than Alaungmintaya, Banya Dala introduced himself primarily as a devout Buddhist king and he defined kingship as a privileged condition that he shared with his opponent; both were brothers in a spiritual quest, so to say. On the other hand, the degree of measured restriction in arguing with Alaungmintaya borders on humility which could at least be partly due to the way his letters were translated from Mon to Burmese.

Communication can only flow if those who communicate share a common language. But when the language is permeated by symbols, references and indirect meanings, it is not necessarily transparent to outsiders. So it is important to pay attention to the formal and stylistic aspects of diplomatic exchange and, more obviously, the meaning and the eventual connotations of the shared code. The ideal vision of the

"Buddha prize", as mentioned above, is one striking example. Expressed as the ardent wish of kings, it is not unusual and can be traced back to Pagan inscriptions.[42] Was it mostly brought up as a mark of style and distinction? Did obtaining the "Buddha prize" truly mean in the minds of those kings liberation from suffering and detachment from the world or rather omniscience (*sabbaññuta-ñāṇa*) as only a Buddha would possess it?

One example of Buddhist code is Alaungmintaya's reference to the "Bhūridatta jātaka", an indication that had to be interpreted as a call to surrender. During the siege of Syriam where the besieged found themselves in an increasingly difficult situation, Alaungmintaya told Banya Dala to take inspiration from the Bhūridatta jātaka.[43] At the end of December 1756, when his military situation was hopeless, Banya Dala signalled that he was ready to surrender, and he declared that he wanted to "take refuge under the power of his younger brother" considering, as he humbly put it, what friendship meant in the Bhūridatta jātaka. The lesson to be taken from the Bhūridatta jātaka was to understand one's inferiority and submit in due time. The traditional way to signify surrender and submission was to send presents, foremost among which were female relatives of the defeated king. Like Brahmadatta Kumara, the king of Benares, who had to send his daughter Samudajja to Dhatarattha, the king of the nāgas after being defeated, so should Banya Dala send a princess to Alaungmintaya to put an end to the war.

A common set of Buddhist values was embedded in the language used by both kings. Peace was desirable, violence and conflict were not. Wishing to become an enlightened Buddha in the future implied not to destroy the prosperity of the people, not to kill and not to lower the status of lords who wilfully surrendered as most Shan *sawbwas* had already done.[44]

While the issue of necessary or actual violence is often dealt with ambiguously, the advantage of peace is constantly stressed. War is ruinous and threatens the welfare of the people. It prevents monks to study and follow their precepts. Kings have a duty to protect the Buddhist teaching and ensure the welfare of the people. Appeals to leniency built on the conviction that one should not be cruel and try to forgive one's enemy. Belligerence was nowhere celebrated in the letters. There was nothing such as a glorious death to be found in a battle and physical prowess was not linked to a myth of warrior heroism. Such may have existed among those who were fighting, but it was not part of the Buddhist language shared in the diplomatic exchanges of kings. The dominant cord that vibrated in the rhetoric of diplomacy sounded philosophical and consensual: we are all bound by the cycle of rebirth and the laws of retribution.[45] Even enemies who have been plotting each others' death can become friends, stated Alaungmintaya.[46] It was this set of shared values and ideals that were constantly reiterated in the letters and lay the groundwork for diplomatic initiatives.

Diplomacy in Burma at an elite level was thus inherently Buddhist in the way that it constantly referred to Buddhist values and norms. Using a language of popular symbols and literary references rooted in the Buddhist *imaginaire*, drawing on the tales of the Buddha's former lives as much as on the basic philosophical concepts of the Buddhist scriptures, the diplomatic discourse carried the idea of a Buddhist commonwealth not as a commonly agreed-upon and concrete political project, but as a projected ideal. The realization of this ideal was open for interpretation. It is all too obvious that for Alaungmintaya, peace and coexistence could only refer to a *pax birmanica*. As he told the *sawbwa* of Hsenwi in June 1755, all the local rulers who had taken an oath of loyalty enjoyed henceforth "happiness of body and mind" (*kāyasukkha cittasukkha*).[47]

A state of good relations between countries was described as friendship between kings. *Sakha* presented as one of the seven marks of a royal capital, implied friendly talk or negotiations with a view on eventual positive or negative outcomes (*sukkha-dukkha*), or say, advantages and disadvantages.[48] *Rājamahāmit*, friendship between kings, combined with *sahāya*, friendship, was referred to as a condition of peace and happiness. It was mutually beneficial.[49] Politically it implied a way of moving on with non-violent means, but it did not necessarily imply a compromise or arrangement between equals. For Alaungmintaya, the right understanding of friendship meant an understanding and acceptance of the balance of power relations. "Concerning enduring friendship, take the Bhūridatta Jātaka to heart (i.e. surrender)", he told Banya Dala.[50]

The study of the letters shows that political messages were rarely conveyed in explicit arguments, but dressed up in symbolic or quasi-symbolic figurations that occasionally appear, at least to modern eyes, less ideal than surreal. Take the example of Alaungmintaya's presentation of his 1755 southern campaign as being both a pilgrimage to the Shwedagon and a tour to give information on his political claims. The king was really referring to what in military terms was the sweeping campaign he led down south from late 1754 to June 1755 giving him the full control of the Irrawaddy valley including the western part of the delta.[51]

Unabashedly denying the face of reality was Alaungmintaya's disclaimer made during the most intense phase of the siege of Syriam (June-July 1756) that he was not an aggressor:

> I am not making war because I want to eat the flesh and the blood of the people. I do only fight because I have been attacked by an enemy. I do not wish to see hostility last during my next lives.[52]

Such hyperbole was infrequent and came in stark contrast with the king's usual quest for self-elevation and aloofness. The scary imagery is rather typical of the letters of the king's sons and generals who used a stronger language when talking to the enemy. In the letters under review here — unlike a few written by Alaungmintaya's sons or generals — death as a daily factor of military confrontation is not presented through its gruelling aspects of bloodshed, misery and despair. Death and destruction take their place in a Buddhist reading of our world's reality where they were signified by the "ignorance" and the "darkness" that are said to ultimately cause people to go to hell and preclude a more promising future. They are thus not seen narrowly *hic et nunc* as the fatal effects of warfare hurting the socio-political and economic situation of a country in *this* world, but in their individually negative implications for the *future* life-cycles of all those who perished.

Understood in terms of his own political correctness, Alaungmintaya would not have wavered to consider aggression as the second best way to obtain the sovereign power. But why kings who declared that they wanted to obtain the "Buddha-prize" nonetheless sent their troops to fight each other ruthlessly, this issue is actually nowhere addressed in clear terms. Actually the question of war ethics was sidelined in a practical way, or one may say, overtaken by a rhetoric of realpolitik. Alaungmintaya argued that he was fighting a defensive war, a statement which was true in 1752, but could not reasonably be upheld after 1754 when the Burmese entirely held the initiative on the battlefield. He said that it was Banya Dala's stubbornness, read his unwillingness to surrender, that was the main impediment to stop fighting. As Banya Dala's power was receding continuously, he appealed to Alaungmintaya to negotiate, compromise, and ultimately to show mercy, all of which figured rhetorically as demonstrations of *pāramī* virtue in his letters. Alaungmintaya for his part, was absolutely not ready to renounce aggression before he had obtained due recognition as the sole overlord.

But the rhetoric cloak thrown over the bare realities cannot, in the eyes of the observer, disguise the ideological implications, or rather complications, that underpin royal action. A discussion of Alaungmintaya's political rhetoric as much as his warfare ties with the broader social and civilizational issue of the relationship between religion and violence. Within the academic forum, the relationship between Buddhism and violence had for a long time been a marginal topic when compared with the vast literature on, say the crusades in the Mediterranean or the sixteenth century wars of religion in the northwest of Europe.[53] But the global post-11/09 context that engendered a greater awareness of the nexus of religion and violence, on the one hand, and the excesses of the Sinhala/Tamil conflict in Sri Lanka on the other, provoked a heightened interest in the ambiguities of Buddhism and within Buddhist societies towards violence. As an antidote to misconceptions about the founding figure, it may not be useless to recall Bareau's statement at the end of his comprehensive review of the Buddha's relations with kings, namely that the Buddha never told any king face to face not to enter a war or not to commit a crime. He treaded carefully with kings and mostly expounded to them, just as to commoners, the tenets of his teaching.[54] In the introduction to *Buddhist Warfare* co-edited with Mark Juergensmeyer, Michael Jerryson states as the "chief" motivation of their volume, "the goal of disrupting the social imagery that holds Buddhist traditions to be exclusively pacifistic and exotic".[55] But while this fine selection of papers pioneers a necessary task of further deorientalizing Western writing on Buddhism, lumping together studies of historically and socially complex issues essentially as an investigation of "the dark underbelly of Buddhisms" pre-empts the correlation of Buddhism and violence within an ethical framework.[56] It thus looks as if, at least within the scope of Western readership, Buddhism has fallen from grace and *should* actually be the peaceful religion we expect it to be. Kent's engaging paper on Buddhist preaching to Sri Lankan soldiers precisely challenges such a narrow moralistic approach. Kent's interviews with both soldiers and preachers in a contemporary twenty-first century context closely echo Alaungmintaya's words. Violence is deplorable as it undeniably produces negative consequences for its individual perpetrators. The issue raised a problem and was/is rhetorically side-lined. Preacher monks would rather try to instil confidence into the soldiers, but not *directly* encourage them to kill. On the other hand, war as a duty to protect the Buddhist faith is perceived for better or worse as an overruling justification, just as it was for a Buddhist king 250 years ago.

Early Western scholarly work on Buddhist warfare has, unsurprisingly, focused on East Asian and Tibetan Buddhism, but recent publications have usefully underscored historical complexity within Asia's other Buddhisms as well. The discussion of violence in Buddhist political and cultural settings has mostly been dominated by the question of the justification of war.[57] Bernard Faure argues that in all the countries where Buddhism took roots, its followers were often eager to sustain war efforts as one of the reasons of Buddhism's success in the first place was its instrumental role to defend the state.[58] If this assessment is correct, violence should be paid much greater attention as a social phenomenon in itself in the discussion. Structural violence is built into the constitution of human societies and the cultural input of Buddhism is clearly playing out one but not the only constitutive role of what are phenomena of violence in varying East and Southeast Asian contexts. Jerryson calls violence "a slippery term to define" and Faure apparently dismisses the term for its diffuseness as by now, he writes, it has become "a conceptual tool supposed to understand all the religions".[59] This is unhelpful.

Recent scholarship on religion and violence in the early modern Western world goes beyond the description of violence and its ritualization, emphasizes attention to social perceptions of violence, and stresses the need for a greater qualification of violent phenomena and their interpretation. In this context, the distinction between legitimate and illegitimate violence (*violentia* vs. *potestas;* just punishment *vs* wanton cruelty) is seen as an important analytical differentiation and it is relevant for our own investigation, too.[60] Violence in Buddhist societies may also not be so much of a scandal when we broaden the historical investigation and reconsider our mental filters. Steven McFarlane's sophisticated discussion of Buddhism and the martial arts of China and Japan, for example, addresses the ambiguous relationship between Buddhism and warfare in literature, popular representations and in history, and demonstrates the ethical dimension that Buddhism brought to violent practices.[61] It is true, on the other hand, that it is precisely narratives about the allegedly pacifying power of Buddhism that have come recently under fire.[62] Baudler's introduction to his work on violence in world religions takes the discussion further back in time as he states the common roots of violence and religion. Recalling research on prehistoric mankind and primeval symbolism, he shows that violence was built, so to say, into the genetic code of religion itself.[63]

Given that one of the doctrinal foundations of Buddhism, the law of karma, states that bad consequences flow out of bad acts, violence was irrevocably detrimental to one's progress on the road of enlightenment. The question how this rigorous position was advanced, represented, or negotiated within the Pali textual tradition has been investigated by Steven Collins in his chapter on "kingship and its discontents" where he explores the projections of paradise on earth of the Pali *imaginaire*.[64]

His discussion of the contentious relationship between Buddhist ethics and political leadership (and/or ideologies that condoned violence) starts with two key questions. The first one is "How exactly did Buddhist ideology coexist with kingship, given the realities of such a world?" — the Southeast Asian world alluded to being a place where "war was a fact of political life, and the character of kingship was moulded by preparations for armed conflict".[65] The other question is "How could Buddhist ideology attempt to justify king(s)?". With regard to the second question, the distinction between two modes of *dhamma*, mode 1 being "an ethics of reciprocity in which the assessment of violence is context-dependent and negotiable" and mode 2 being "an ethic of absolute values, in which the assessment of violence is ... non-negotiable", is a useful analytical tool to differentiate heterogeneous messages in the scriptures. Collins' evaluation of the performance of Pali Buddhist literature is illustrated with a large choice of significant textual references pertaining to the exercise of sovereign power and amply demonstrates that the scriptures cater for both *dhamma* modes besides the display of an anti-kingship stance in several jātaka stories. As Collins suggests "some strategies of interpretation which ... might help to show how Buddhist clerics could draw on this fund of narrative and aphoristic exempla in complex and subtle ways, at different times and for different reasons, both to contest and to justify military and political power", he undermines the perception of Buddhism as a dogmatically pacifist religion.[66]

Though violence was a problem for people bound by the Buddhist teaching, a man like Alaungmintaya did not have a split vision of the world, Buddhist principles on the one hand, and hard-to-live political imperatives on the other. Alaungmintaya's symbiotic conciliation of a view of social harmony with the necessity of going to war was grounded in his conviction that a predestined king like himself stood on the moral high-ground and exercised legitimate violence. Once he had earned recognition of being the one he purported to be, it was understood that as a king he had to maintain social order eventually by force; he had to know his enemies and destroying them was a kingly virtue.[67] A striking aspect of the letters is, as we have suggested earlier, the rhetoric reduction of war and conquest to an intimately personal opposition of conflicting ambitions and cosmological legitimacy to rule the whole of Burma. It is not irrelevant to mention that Alaungmintaya did not brandish his opponent as a Buddhist heretic or discriminate against his ethnic belonging. Nor did he, in any of his letters, collectively address the Mon majority of Lower Burma as his enemies. True, the situation on the ground may have felt and indeed been different, but the verbal absence of the horrifying aspects of violence in the letters reflects a rhetorical strategy of displacement which left the self-construed image of the predestined coming ruler unscathed.[68]

Kingship and its constituents have a place in the Buddhist perception of the world and the political language was dependent on Buddhist terminologies, narratives and concepts. What we see in the letters of King Alaungmintaya and Banya Dala is how moral and metaphysical concepts and beliefs underpinned diplomatic language and buttressed similar, but disjointed political agendas. Tactics of communication dictate per se a quest of face-saving flexibility and politics require a pragmatic use of apparently rigid notions, but this does not disqualify ethical standards and values and entail any relativism. It points rather to the malleability of such concepts, the fact that key words adopted a particular meaning in various discursive contexts. Banya Dala's defensive stance during the siege of Pegu was interpreted by Alaungmintaya as a show of stubbornness. The political contestation included a moral condemnation. As we will see below, loving kindness (*metta*) could be understood at one point as a sign of tactical weakness unbefitting a self-conscious king like Alaungmintaya. It is important to note that the references to ethical standards that were re-contextualized according to political needs and circumstances did not make them into empty shells.

To state that we have to pay attention to the applied meaning of key terms in their context has an important implication for our historical appreciation of Burmese kingship and of Burmese Buddhist culture in general. The very notion of human culture implies both continuity *and* change, but pre-colonial Burmese Buddhist culture was definitely not, as has been stated, a static monolith.[69] It was dynamic and subject to change. Doctrines and beliefs may not have been tremendously altered over the centuries in the sense that they continued to impregnate social values and structures in similar ways, but it is safe to assume that, as elsewhere in the world, varying political and economic conditions had an impact on the expression and the interpretation of norms and on the social forms of religious practice.

But the sphere of the Buddhist language, however dynamic it was, was self-contained and culturally bounded. While the adaptability of the Buddhist language in a political context may be justifiably stressed, it did not extend to cultural outsiders. To convey to the king of Pegu the idea that Alaungmintaya had of himself was not a problem of communication, as both shared the same cultural code. But Alaungmintaya did not refer to himself as a *sāsana-dāyaka* when he wrote letters to the East India Company, because the Burmese court must have rightly considered that the term had no meaning for the Western merchants. When he wrote his famous letter on a gold plate to King George II, Alaungmintaya considered the employees of the East India Company as servants of the English king executing the will of their monarch.[70] He did not understand, and possibly did not know, that the East India Company was a largely autonomous body of merchants that decided and ruled in its own name, independently from the British sovereign.

LETTERS IN CONTEXT: BUDDHIST DIPLOMACY IN PRACTICE

The letters themselves did not refer to battles, victories, defeats or losses, and they did not mirror the daily military situation on the ground. They were, as we have seen, essentially political statements formulated in a sophisticated language code drawing on Buddhist vocabulary. But the messages they contained were neither cryptic nor detached from the reality of warfare. In this second part, we will try to contextualize the letters within the chronology of events to gain a better understanding and point to their relevance for a critical study of Alaungmintaya's reign. Though they have been quite easily accessible to historians since their first edition in 1964, it is surprising that no historian of early modern Burma has seriously paid attention to them.

Alaungmintaya's rise to power unfolded between the two key dates of March 1752, the fall of Ava and the end of the Nyaung-yan dynasty that kicked off his career, and May 1757, the fall of Pegu, his ultimate moment of triumph. From being a rebel in 1752, he established himself in a period of five years as the undisputed, all-powerful king of the country. The war to conquer Pegu took place between late 1754 and late 1756. Alaungmintaya had already full control over the Irrawaddy valley and a large part of the delta when he wrote his first letter to Banya Dala in early June 1755. At all times Alaungmintaya made his demands from a position of military superiority, backed by his successes on the battlefields. Until early 1757, his letters to Banya Dala were variations of his call to Banya Dala to submit unconditionally. Banya Dala, on the other hand, confronted the Burmese first defiantly and drifted then from a position of political insecurity in early 1755 (when Burmese troops entrenched themselves at the opposite bank of Syriam) to a situation of blatant inferiority when any further resistance to Alaungmintaya became utterly hopeless.

This general outline of the political events can be structured from an analytical point of view in various modes of diplomatic action depending on the shifting power balance. Alaungmintaya's mode of diplomatic action can be described as a constantly result-driven, generally aggressive mode where superior power backed the exercise of pressure to enforce a claim and obtain recognition and acceptance of particular demands. Banya Dala's diplomatic stances had to change over the months. In 1755, he displayed a defiant mode, rejecting diplomatic interaction, refusing to negotiate and simply ignoring the challenge. In early 1756, he switched to a mode where he tried to maintain his status quo. His diplomatic efforts were invested in keeping relations at a level that could satisfy both parties. This conservative mode recalls to historians the quasi ritualization of central and local political hierarchies typical of sixteenth century Burma. With the advantage of looking back at the past, we can say that with the rise of the Konbaung dynasty, the option for a local power to preserve its political autonomy was outdated and politically excluded. In the last quarter of 1756, Banya Dala had to downgrade his diplomatic and political aims and switch to a defensive mode, realizing his inferiority, backtracking and ready to make concessions with the hope to achieve face-saving compromises.

It is not irrelevant at this point to highlight a few simple, but important contextual elements that may be easily overlooked. A letter does not only exist by its written contents bearing a message, but the materiality of the letter is a constitutive part of its meaning. The inherent communicative "weight" of the material support of the letter, its aesthetic quality, material value and the nature of its packaging may have varied, but in our context of diplomatic exchange, it was highly relevant. Unfortunately, we rarely know any details unless mention is made of them at the end of the letters themselves.[71] There is close to no such information available for the particular set of letters investigated in this paper. There is some information at hand though on the material support and the packaging used for a few other letters of Alaungmintaya. Royal orders were generally written on long palm leaves that were rolled up (*borassus flabellifer* leaves rather than the flattened, cut and polished *corypha umbriculifera* leaves used for long texts). We know of letters written on gold sheets sent by the late Ava kings to the Emperor of China, but only a single letter of that type, Alaungmintaya's letter to George II adorned with twenty-four rubies and the king's seal, has materially survived.[72] Messages were sent in sealed packages that could consist of lacquer boxes, ivory casks and red colour tissue bags.[73]

Of equal contextual substance was the status of those envoys who acted as messengers. We might think of them as men who merely acted as postmen, but should rather imagine delegations headed by ambassadors surrounded with guards and beefed up with clerical staff and interpreters. By choosing particular men to convey their letters, both kings underscored their intentions or mood by the profile of their messengers. Choosing a prisoner of war or a servant doing menial works (such as collecting grass for the elephants), a king visibly demonstrated his lack of consideration, his anger or his impatience. In June 1755, Alaungmintaya had a young monk called Panyadipa picked up by his grass-cutters to forward his first letter to King Banya Dala.[74] Note that the king expressly mentions this fact in the letter. We can thus interpret both context and intention. The fact that it was a monk who was sent (and not a servant) denoted a fair measure of respect, but he was a casual choice, not a senior monk of some distinction. It is not difficult to spot the mark of dissatisfaction expressed by the king as, we may guess, he felt that the first step of entering into talks should have been taken by his opponent who was in a weakening military position. By choosing a monk, and preferably a monk of high consideration, such as his own religious teacher, a king could mark his consideration for an opponent or stress his good intentions. But it remains an open question if monks were a standard choice of kings to act as messengers or negotiators. Diplomacy was a job for professionals who were well informed, preferably trusted members of the inner royal clan, and familiar with procedure. Diplomats had to serve above all the interests of their lord. We may wonder if monks could generally fill positions where they needed familiarity with political issues, if they were qualified to act as intermediaries and if the kings had particular interests to choose monks besides their advantageous status-linked authority. Monks were teachers and instrumental as exponents of royal ideologies, but it does not appear that they ever enjoyed fixed functions in the alleys of royal bureaucracy. Still the presence of educated monks at the court and their role as advisors of kings is often postulated in a historically somewhat diffuse way. In the wider context, our letters illustrate how scriptural knowledge and moral advice taken from the scriptures could be used in the political sphere, though it did not instantly translate into straightforward political recommendations. It would indeed be difficult not to see well-informed monks behind such formulations. Nonetheless, in practical terms their role as diplomats may have been the exception rather than the rule. Underscoring "the dissimilarity and hierarchy" between monks and kings, Collins has warned of a historically naive perception of the "symbiosis of clerics and kings".[75] There are actually no simple answers to the many questions which a discussion of this issue raises. Monks could play a specific role rather in ad hoc situations or at critical moments when they would be recognized as neutral intermediaries. The historical record leaves space for various interpretations, but would not necessarily warrant extrapolations. Lingat's punctilious examination of intense king-saṃgha interaction recorded in Sri Lanka's *Mahavamsa* chronicle does not only demonstrate the political leverage of the monkhood in early Sri Lankan history, but also its continuous presence at the court.[76] What we see in Burmese history is that monks were occasionally entrusted with particular missions to gain intelligence, convey political messages and lead peace initiatives. But resorting to monks was only an advantage in spaces where their immunity or inviolability and authority *qua* religious status were recognized and respected. Burmese kings never sent monks to discuss with the representatives of the East India Company. Nor were monks as diplomats a safe bet for successful missions. In October 1756, when the military situation was getting hopeless, Banya Dala appealed to three monks, one Burmese, one Mon and one Yuan (northern Thai) to intercede on his behalf. The mission failed. When the Mon king sent a Burmese monk from Ava (together with a local Burmese lord) to declare his intention to surrender rather than sending one of his Mon lords, Alaungmintaya was unimpressed and considered the move as a sign of Banya Dala's crookedness.[77]

Phase 1 — The Conquest of the Irrawaddy Valley: Alaungmintaya Introduces Himself as the Rightful King

Alaungmintaya sent his first letter to Banya Dala on 10 June 1755 after the foundation of Yangon situated on the opposite bank of Syriam, Pegu's major port. At that moment, his power was already firmly established in the centre of the country and he entirely controlled the Irrawaddy valley and large parts of the western delta. In the letter, Alaungmintaya introduced himself in a very elaborate way as the rightful king due to reign and explained to Banya Dala that lords in the upper and central part of the country who used to be unruly under the preceding dynasty had peacefully submitted.

The implication was obvious: Banya Dala should submit as well, peacefully putting down his arms. In Alaungmintaya's speech, the political question if the Mon king would go on fighting or surrender was shaped as a religious issue where the option of surrendering was presented as the morally correct way to follow. Alaungmintaya told the Mon king:

> I stay here to admonish you according to the law contained in the three parts of the *pitakat* that were taught by the omniscient Buddha who [practised] 528 kinds of compassion towards all living beings.[78]

Going on fighting would entail a bad karma. The Burmese king explained:

> Having already subjected people, don't you consider that they will be [your] enemies in the course of the cycle of retribution [in future

> lives] just as in the case of Buddha and Devadatta, as [Buddha] did not reach *nibbāna* because of the grudge and the enmity [existing] throughout the course of his former lives.[79]

But neither was the military-cum-political core of the issue left out of sight. Alaungmintaya told Banya Dala not to be overconfident with regard to his capital of merit that had ensured his rise to kingship. The king concluded:

> Though you have come to wage war with all your troops, horses and elephants I do not want to retaliate and I will exert patience like the big earth that is 240,000 [*yujana*] deep.[80]

The intriguing association of barely veiled threats and moral urge was a typical mark of Alaungmintaya's sermonizing style. The invocation of the law of retribution softens, as we see, in no way the political message. The letter perfectly illustrates the ambiguous way in which the diplomatic language bypasses the fact that Alaungmintaya daily sent troops to fight and kill so as to reach his political aims. The onus of inevitably exerting violence was thus subtly displaced. Waging war became a matter of conscience for the enemy, but not for the king who saw himself as rightful by the interpretation of his own destiny. More than that, he even saw himself in the role of a religious teacher.

> I want to let the kings of all the countries get to know that I am a lord of destiny [endowed with] power due to his merits. (...) I want to receive the obeisance of all the kings and give guidance about the way to *nibbāna* and about the life beyond death following the teaching of the omniscient Buddha to all living beings.[81]

Banya Dala did not care to reply to Alaungmintaya's letter. This denial of verbal interaction was a clear rejection of diplomacy to be categorized as a mode of defiance.

Phase 2 — The Final Battle for Syriam (June 1756)

In May 1755 Alaungmintaya founded Rangoon/modern Yangon, opposite the old port of Syriam/modern Thanlyin, vowing to raze Syriam to the ground. The siege dragged on for over a year. In June 1756, during the final phase of the siege by the Burmese, Banya Dala wrote for the first time to Alaungmintaya and signalled his readiness for negotiations. The promptness to talk came at a critical moment of the siege when the Mon resistance was giving way. It is only apparent in the final passage of the letter where Banya Dala states that he was going to send his *sayadaw* (a senior monk) to meet Alaungmintaya. The major part of the letter was a self-appraisal of Banya Dala's works of religious merit and an invitation to Alaungmintaya to "perfect his *pāramī* virtues by helping to save all living beings".[82] Interpreted in its context, the letter was, rather obviously, a Buddhist way to call for an armistice.

Three days later, on 16 June 1756, Alaungmintaya replied sarcastically that Banya Dala behaved like an old man, who shaken from his sleep, was groping around, having lost orientation. After another bout of verbal abuse, notably scolding the Mon king for "being stubborn in his pride like an old man who does not hear the noise around",[83] Alaungmintaya displayed a more conciliatory mood. Closeness between countries is desirable and it implies friendly talk. Considering the prosperity of the people is a mark of a wise and integer man. Even enemies who plot the death of other people can become friends again. But this feel-good rhetoric cannot distract from our ruler's unwavering core position that was masterfully woven into the text: the sole and exclusive control over the rival kingdom.

> Even when the world is destroyed, our proclamation of friendship will not be destroyed, for the people of our two countries will form but one country [like] two leaves of gold that become one [or] like when you draw a line in the water, you cannot think of any separation....[84]

Only knowledge of the political context and more precisely the military state of affairs in mid-June 1756 allows for a correct interpretation of these lines handed over to Banya Dala by two monks. The metaphors of a country-wide union subtly veils Alaungmintaya's request that Pegu would surrender unconditionally and preferably in an orderly fashion.

No surprise that Banya Dala had a different understanding of future relations. Under the veil of their Buddhist rhetoric, the two kings were poles apart on the question of the exercise of power. Banya Dala warmly welcomed the Burmese king's message, but his interpretation of the "friendship" constantly alluded to in the letters postulated the coexistence of both kings on the same hierarchical level. With the resolution of their conflict, he wrote, friendship would increase and both "Haṃsāvatī (the Mon kingdom) *and* the golden city of Rātanasiṅgha (Shwebo, Alaungmintaya's capital, metonym of the Myanmar realm) would flourish and be prosperous...".

Visibly Banya Dala did not think about giving up to Alaungmintaya yet. In a letter that lacks much formality, Alaungmintaya immediately made clear that he did not appreciate his opponent's conception of good relations.

> Though you have been making a lot of words on making friendship (*poṅ: phak*) and that there should be friendship (*sahāya*), among these many words, some are useful and some are not. Considering enduring friendship between kings… you should take inspiration from the Bhūridatta Jātaka…[85]

In a word, Banya Dala should send a princess as a sign of wilful submission. Two weeks later, in the middle of July 1756, Syriam fell and the front shifted towards the east, hailing the siege of Haṃsāvatī's capital Pegu. During the months of August and September, operations came apparently to a standstill due to the rains. It was probably around that time that the Mon court made peace overtures in a letter sent to Shwebo in which Banya Dala restated his position that there would be "happiness and prosperity like in the Tāvatiṃsa heaven of the gods" if "Sri Haṃsāvatī and Rātanāsiṅgha Konbaung" advanced "on a golden road".[86] The Mon king suggested a meeting of the two monarchs at the Shwedagon pagoda to negotiate an end to the hostilities. Incidentally, the Mon king complained about Alaungmintaya's lowly messengers whom he called "strange captives". "To know exactly what your demands are", he sent two senior Mon ministers and called for the appointment of experienced Burmese ambassadors able to negotiate.[87]

Phase 3 — The Burmese Siege of Pegu (September–October 1756)

In late September and October, the Mon endured further setbacks and were no more able to lead an offensive warfare. Pegu's leading commander, Daw-zway switched sides and the hastily built fortress of Kamapi fell in late September. Banya Dala sent a delegation of monks to negotiate, but was not yet willing to concede defeat. So on 28 September Alaungmintaya dispatched a prisoner of war with a provocative letter poking fun at the fear and cowardice of the Mon officers. Outlying fortresses had to fend off the danger from the capital, but when the fortress of Nyaungbin came under increasing pressure, the Mon court prevailed on their king to send a delegation of monks to negotiate peace.

The letters that were sent back and forth during the second half of October 1756 are highly interesting pieces of Buddhist diplomacy and a multifaceted rhetoric practice, but only their political messages can be abstracted here. Three *sayadaws*, a Burmese monk, a Mon monk and a Northern Thai (Yuan) monk, were sent to Alaungmintaya to convey a conciliatory message invoking historical and scriptural examples of royal graciousness and readiness to compromise. The letter presents itself as an invitation of goodwill sent to both kings on behalf of the Mon, Burmese and Northern Thai saṅgha.[88] Indeed, the principle that was given emphasis by the monks was that Alaungmintaya and Banya Dala were two rightful legitimate Buddhist kings. For Alaungmintaya such an assumption was totally unacceptable. In one more well-articulated reply given to the monks, Alaungmintaya rejected the idea that he would ever look at the Mon king as a sovereign equal to himself. Having enjoyed a successful rise to near absolute power in the realm for several years and praying to reach enlightenment in the future, Alaungmintaya implicitly compared his political choice with the best practice of what a *bodhisatta* would opt for. He wrote:

> For *bodhisattas*, it depends on the conditions of time and place if anger comes first and loving-kindness next, or loving-kindness first and anger next.[89]

With the argument that loving-kindness was not a one-fits-all political recipe, he abruptly discarded the appeal of the monks to be compassionate toward his Mon foes.

Imitating the rhetoric of the monks who cited historical precedents of royal mercy, Alaungmintaya also brought to mind a purportedly historical precedent that he considered as a better example to compare with the current political situation. Referring to King Kyaukpyumin of Pagan, he argued that a new king who enjoyed the support of the gods would be welcomed by the people and bring peace. But, says Alaungmintaya, the "people of Haṃsāvatī only know that their king has been making war again and again".[90] As all the other lords of the country had submitted and enjoyed by now "bodily and mental happiness", Alaungmintaya told the religious mediators:

> There is no question of not submitting to me now. I kindly let you know that I have nothing special to say about what the person who acts as king of Pegu and others should know.[91]

This reply was such a provocation and expressed such disdain in the eyes of the court of Pegu that it reignited a sense of determination among the Mon leadership. Mon general Talaban's appeal to stay united and get ready to cross swords with the Burmese, a harangue which made it into the chronicle record, is a powerful illustration of this newly found sense of purpose.[92]

Surprisingly, just a week later, Alaungmintaya sent a letter to Banya Dala that sounded a bit more lenient. As in his first letter written a year before, he told the Mon king that he had not come to wage war, but that he was merely touring the provinces for the benefit of the Buddhist religion. The start of hostilities was only due to the Mon king's stubbornness and arrogance. *Lokadhamma*, the political principles of this world, could only be applied if "there was an expression of loyalty". The letter ended with another soft stance.

> As any lord who rules a country will cherish the life and the welfare (*asak sañ:cim*) of the people, I kindly write you this letter to tell you that you do not need to worry about the life and the welfare of the people.[93]

Later events suggest that the Mon leadership was much afraid that it would be entirely wiped out following a Burmese victory. It is likely that with this letter, Alaungmintaya wanted to momentarily calm the passions and send a message of reassurance to the Mon elite. One may wonder if at this stage of ongoing warfare, with the Burmese troops exhausted and forces strained, Alaungmintaya might eventually have preferred a negotiated solution to more fighting as long as he could gain what he aimed for.

Phase 4 — Banya Dala's Surrender and the Fall of Pegu

There is no doubt that towards the end of the year 1756, the military situation of the Mon was ultimately hopeless. Pegu was fully encircled, the outlying fortresses had been raided by the Burmese and the population suffered under the pressure of the siege. Banya Dala finally decided to surrender. On 13 December 1756, he sent Alaungmintaya a letter which was formulated as a call for mercy:

> When you arrived I had the plan to oppose you and I was there day and night making all kind of preparations such as [building] defence-works for the city, moats and canals. Thanks to your karma in the past, your meritorious power has been growing day by day and it is huge. However hard I have been trying to prepare myself to face you, I have been unable [to do so]. As you want to obtain the prize of buddhaship, fulfil your *pāramī* virtues by having mercy on me.[94]

As the letter of the Mon king was handed over by a Burmese officer together with a Burmese monk, Alaungmintaya made a scathing remark to his entourage about the identity of the messengers, considering that it showed Banya Dala's crooked nature to send Burmese emissaries while there were enough Mon ministers to be entrusted with such a task.[95]

In his letter Banya Dala told Alaungmintaya also that he would heed the lesson of the Bhūridatta Jātaka, but by then Alaungmintaya had distrusted the Mon king. In his response sent a week later, the Burmese king first pondered upon the fleeting nature of human life and the world as such ("At one moment of time, even Mount Meru and Cakravāḷa will perish."). Once more he presented himself as a man imbued with Buddhist wisdom ("I do not hold the view to obtain prosperity for myself. I only think about *nibbāna* which is established forever."). Then he abruptly restated his own interpretation of their recent relations: "If one person is lenient and the other person is arrogant, it's like there can be no issue."[96] After so many attempts of Banya Dala to get out of the loop and put off his final defeat, Alaungmintaya was not yet sure about the king of Pegu's intentions. But he would not tolerate any further hum and haw.

> It is difficult to know if you are true. The voice of a king who observes the law is like thunder. I kindly send this letter telling you that I will not send it one or two more times.[97]

In a quite different formulation of Alaungmintaya's response to Banya Dala of December 1756 given in the *Alaungmintayagyi Ayedawpon,* Alaungmintaya explicitly stated that Banya Dala, like other local lords, should send a daughter to show that he would submit to the Burmese king. The example of the scriptures that is referred to here was the wedding of Pañcālacaṇḍi, the daughter of king Cūḷanī-Brahmadatta, to King Videha, the king of Mithilā, as told in the *Mahā-ummagga Jātaka.*[98]

With due respect to protocol and ceremonial requirements, Banya Dala sent a daughter and numerous high ranking hostages to the Burmese camp.[99] Preparations for doing so were elaborate and ceremonious and took weeks. The surrender was not a matter of a few days and we may consider, as suggested above, that the Burmese troops were worn out and unable to simply walk into the city of Pegu and take over. Banya Dala's dithering that Alaungmintaya earlier hinted at was largely due to the pressure of a diehard faction at the court that wanted to resist and preferred to die rather than fall into the hands of the enemy. While the capitulation procedures went on, members of this faction locked up the king. It seems though that a line of communication still existed as the *Alaungmintayagyi Ayedawpon* and the *Konbaungzet* quote letters that were exchanged between the two kings in early 1757.[100] As Banya Dala reiterated his honest will to surrender and enumerated the presents he had already sent, Alaungmintaya lost patience and scolded him.[101] While skirmishes took place around the city in April, the Burmese led their final attack in early May and took the city by storm on 12 May 1757. It brought an end to the Mon kingdom of Haṃsāvatī.

CONCLUSION

Alaungmintaya's guerrilla warfare against the Mon invaders and his Burmese competitors in Upper Burma started in 1752. But no official letter of Alaungmintaya datable before early 1755 is known. It would be easy to discard the relevance of diplomatic interaction deeming it mere polite talk or arguing that it took place after the dust had settled on the battlefield. But while they may have started late, the exchanges at the top level were intense during the year 1756 and not just a sideshow. Because both kings took so much care to formulate and forward these letters, we should recognize that diplomacy mattered both tactically and strategically.

Sounding diplomacy's overall importance, we first have to bear in mind that diplomacy meant the existence of a line of official communication and information. Across the divide, the political bottom lines were still clearly recognizable despite the much formalized type of communication replete with moralizing allusions that worked as a rhetoric demonstration of power and authority. Matters of principle were thus reiterated. Alaungmintaya's unwavering claim on sovereign power runs like a red thread through his correspondence as much as Banya Dala's inherently defensive stance that the two kingdoms could co-exist.

The second contribution of diplomacy was the assertion of status and political standing. While confirming one's status was always part of the rhetoric strategy and may thus be qualified as a way of grandstanding, the definition of status was in fact a substantial political input. Its performative value was an ongoing and updated process of identity building (the great forthcoming king!) which extended beyond the narrow circle of the elite and replicated the political dynamics in the popular minds as well. The messages of the letters were also part of a wider public sphere of communication and may eventually be interpreted within royal efforts to gain support among the ranks of the opponent. Admittedly this is a point which is rather difficult to prove, but Alaungmintaya's relatively patient, if not to say laid-back approach towards the confrontation with Banya Dala between June and October 1756 does not just reflect a sense of superiority. Causing greater havoc could have taken his troops to a faster, but politically cheap victory. Increasing the pressure so as to push enemy soldiers to abandon the fight, making promises to set free local people who were in debt slavery, and bringing top Mon officers to switch sides, these were in terms of tactical investments more economic choices than shedding blood and they tie rather well with the general sound of Alaungmintaya's letters.

Set within the theme of Buddhist plural dynamics, we have suggested that our investigation could contribute to comparative approaches within the larger Southeast Asian context. Within the geographical boundaries sketched in this study, we have to recognize that we know as yet much too little about the court of Haṃsāvatī during the period when it flourished, i.e. from 1740 to 1757, to perceive and understand its distinctive court culture. Very basic questions such as what were the conditions of the kingdom's rise and success, what was the basis of its military expansion, on what ancient traditions did the "new" Mon kings built their kingship etc. have never or only imperfectly been addressed by scholars.[102]

One lesson to be drawn from the study of the letters is a sense of the common historical and civilizational background of both Mon and Burmese. Their fighting was not a confrontation of strangers; it was rather a culturally inbound affair or, seen along a time-line, the new edition of an old north-south conflict. As they shared the same conceptual and moral ground, the kings — both new men who for many years had to tread carefully with their entourage as their claims were not yet solidified by hard facts — were testing their ideological and cosmological claims against each other in their letters. As they told each other that they were both meritorious lords who had done well in former lives, they also measured their strength rhetorically. Alaungmintaya may have constantly claimed that he was a much superior lord than the Mon king; but he never contested his opponent's royal authority as such, though he considered it *stricto sensu* as temporary.

The letters that were exchanged show us that the violent clashes were not the only framework that defined the encounters and relations between the court of Alaungmintaya and the court of Banya Dala. Diplomatic exchange well existed, and it was Buddhist in form and content. Its rhetoric exploited the wealth of commonly held popular beliefs, doctrines and moral certainties. Educated members of the élite were able to interpret without any hesitation the bits of Pali citations and the hints at Buddhist tenets constantly spotted in the letters. Quoting, repeating and emphasizing what everybody believed and adhered to in a shared Buddhist cultural environment was the

ABC of this Buddhist rhetoric at the service of diplomatic interaction and public relations. To be socially accepted as a holder of royal power, a king or a king-to-be had to win battles, but he was lent moral authority only by establishing credible claims that he enjoyed a supernatural mandate. War was not legitimized by historical claims, dynastic rights or the right of the conqueror, but constantly presented as a campaign to spread or restore the Buddhist *sāsana*. In a leaflet of pro-Burmese propaganda presented as a letter of Sakka (Indra), the king of the gods, we read:

> The *sāsana* came to an end at Rātanāpura Ava and its line of kings ended.... The king from the north is not just an ordinary king.... he will take care to make the *sāsana* shine. He will bear the name of *sāsanadāyaka*. The brightness of the *sāsana* will increase and shine like the sun.[103]

While it would be naïve to ignore the ethnic dimension of the conflict with Pegu/Haṃsāvatī being a predominantly Mon kingdom and Alaungmintaya becoming the champion of a Burmese/Myanmar resurgence, the letters do not reflect any ethnic bias. Nowhere the argument of ethnicity is raised as a political argument. No one will put into doubt ethnic diversity and the contemporary mid-eighteenth century awareness of such diversity. But if a modern historian wants to read back into time a potential of ethnic bias, he cannot draw it from the key primary source studied here. One should incidentally take note of Alaungmintaya's proclamation of early 1755 which is unmistakably ethnically inclusive. In this proclamation, he welcomes the Mon if they will submit to his authority stating: "I will not make a difference between the Myanma ethnicity and the Talaing who have been rebels."[104] Ben Kiernan puts the king's war of conquest in the south in a row with the little and big genocides of world history as he defines them and denounces the king's assumed "ethnic chauvinism" and "systematic ethnic discrimination". But such a thesis does not stand up to a fair interpretation of all the available sources.[105] While Kiernan's sharpening of the ethnic argument borders on an anachronism, Michael Charney's characterization of Alaungmintaya as "possessed of great animosity toward the Mons generally" is unhelpful to any critical discussion of the ethnic dimension of the conflict.[106]

Alaungmintaya fits the image and the proportions of a national hero, but one searches the letters in vain for modern notions of a "nation" bound to an "inherited territory" that had to be urgently unified within frontiers defined by history. In the mid-eighteenth century, members of the elite definitely had a perception of what was meant by place names such as

"Sunaparanta" and "Tambadipa" that were the core lands of the kingdom. But from the precolonial Burmese understanding of political geography we cannot derive any kind of territorialism linked to ethnic categories. National unity was not a concept of eighteenth century minds in Upper Burma, and it is an anachronism to call Alaungmintaya a "unifier" of the country. The term *mranmā prañ*, referring to the realm of the Burmans, may already have been a geographical concept in the minds of eighteenth-century Burmese writers, but it is found in none of Alaungmintaya's letters as a definition of his realm. Alaungmintaya did nowhere state that he wanted to unify the country and set up border controls. As he said early on, he wanted to restore peace, or say just as well, put an end to anarchy, and obtain the submission of local lords. His political programme was all in his name, to be seen as the forthcoming king. He wanted recognition as a predestined *dhammarājā*, an as yet human condition that he felt was a natural step forward to the highest stage of spiritual maturity.

The overall important notion of kingship which dominates specifically in Alaungmintaya's letters was linked to the political exclusiveness of the king's cosmic status and his absolute claim on power. This claim was theoretically limitless. Its geographical centre-focusedness as demonstrated in the emphasis on the golden palace with its multi-tiered roofs in the capital totally eclipsed the need to demarcate any frontiers. The extension of royal power and, as such a drive to expansionism, was built into this very conception of the kingdom and the surrounding world. Alaungmintaya set lose these forces and his sons, successfully fighting invading Chinese armies in the 1760s, razing to the ground Ayutthaya, the capital of Siam, in 1767, and finally putting an end to the kingdom of Arakan in 1785, were engulfed by the dynamics of their father's reign.

Western textbooks on Southeast Asian history have amalgamated evidence from various sources and countries to reconstruct a supposedly commonly shared notion of Southeast Asian Buddhist kingship. As I have repeatedly noted, such an idea deserves a critical review. The abstract notions and ceremonial forms of Indian heritage were inculturated and emphasized in different ways in the Southeast Asian lands. Suffice to say here that the concept of the *cakkavatti* king, often presented as conterminous with the perception of kingship in Burma, is nowhere used or explicitly referred to by either Alaungmintaya or Banya Dala. After his death, Alaungmintaya was compared in an inscription authored by Sinbyushin, one of his sons, to Mahāsammata and to Asoka, but he himself never used these similes to represent himself or his political action.[107] These "names" stood for ideals and were part of a political vocabulary derived from the

Buddhist textual heritage that was shared in Pali-land as much as it was open for interpretations, adaptations and reformulations. The concept of *cakkavatti* was attractive at some places in time: Swearer and Premchit have stressed its "pervasive significance" for fifteenth century Lanna and it has been a standard epithet of Siamese monarchs.[108] But while later texts in Pali used the *Cakkavatti-sīhanāda sutta* (as well as the *Aggaññasutta*) as a legitimization of kingship, the opinion of modern scholars such as Gombrich and Collins would suggest that elements of hyperbole, irony, satire and comedy made the text an unlikely blueprint for ideal kingship.[109] Gombrich called the *Cakkavatti* world ruler an "institutionalized fantasy" while Yashpal commented that "the thirty-two marks of a superman ... must have made him look like a monster".[110] Collins states: "CSS [*Cakkavatti-sīhanāda sutta*] does not express a Buddhist social theory."[111] Earlier John Strong showed how the ideal was accommodated as a "compromise of the mythic ideal" in texts like the *Ashokavadāna* because "the *cakravartin* myth presented Buddhists with the problem of a rather inflexible ideal of kingship [and] the figure of the *cakkavatti* was, as Melford Spiro has pointed out, too ideal, too "mythical" for actual historical Buddhist kings to be identified with it".[112] This lack of attractiveness may eventually contribute to an explanation why the *cakkavatti* ideal, though part of the political vocabulary in Burma, did not gain a prominent place in the self-representation of early Konbaung kings.

In sum, we should take an investigation of the body of letters of Alaungmintaya and Banya Dala as the starting point to enrich our discourse on Burmese/Mon kingship and eventually question the smooth textbook extrapolations we are used to. As moral exhortations take so much more space in the letters than purely political or matter-of-fact arguments, we may confidently conclude that Alaungmintaya and Banya Dala were not only warrior chiefs driven by their political agendas, but also diplomats whose hearts and minds were ruled by Buddhist beliefs and values.

Notes

1. Head, *Ecole française d'Extrême-Orient*, Chiang Mai and Yangon. I sincerely thank D. Christian Lammerts for his insightful comments, criticism and suggestions.
2. All the letters of King Alaungmintaya (1752–60) and King Banya Dala (1747–57) referred to in this paper are quoted following the text and with the dates as they appear in volume 3 of *The Royal Orders of Burma (1598–1885)*, edited by Than Tun. Alternately one may consult the annotated edition of

Alaungmintaya's edicts and letters in the volume edited by Khin Khin Sein, *Alaungmintaya Ameindaw-mya*.

3. Western authors have consistently used the abbreviated form "Alaungphaya" (spelt "Alompra" in pre-1900 texts) to refer to the founder of the Konbaung dynasty. This usage, probably derived from a contemporary oral usage in Lower Myanmar, gave undue importance to the discussion if the king considered himself as a "future Buddha". In line with Burmese/Myanmar historiography, both traditional and modern, the author of this paper prefers "Alaungmintaya".
4. The term Buddhist in "Buddhist diplomacy" qualifies the diplomatic practice of kings who were Buddhists and whose political discourse and rhetoric was drawing on Buddhist textual heritage and Buddhist concepts. It does not describe the nature of political relations or essentialize such diplomatic practice as Buddhist per se. Buddhist facets of Alaungmintaya's kingship are explored in Leider, "The Rise of Alaungmintaya" and Leider, "Kingship by Merit". An account of Alaungmintaya's political and military career is found in Leider, *King Alaungmintaya's Golden Letter*, pp. 10–21.
5. See Leider, *King Alaungmintaya's Golden Letter*, pp. 43–68 for an appreciation of the record of Alaungmintaya's negotiations with the East India Company between 1755 and 1757.
6. A study of over 200 years of Western interpretations of the reign of King Alaungmintaya shows that the representation of the King himself has turned from overall positive to entirely negative. See my critical remarks on Kiernan later in this paper and Leider, "Alaungmintaya, König von Birma".
7. A biographical account with a list of his works in found in Thaw Kaung, "Letwè Nawratha (1723–1791)".
8. Various orders from the second part of the year 1757 underscore the great care taken by Alaungmintaya to check the routine procedures of his chancellery. See Leider, *King Alaungmintaya's Golden Letter*, pp. 91–93. I deal with stylistic issues and expression in Leider, "Kingship by Merit", and Leider, *King Alaungmintaya's Golden Letter,* pp. 95–97.
9. Than Tun, *Royal Order*, vol. 3. The text of Alaungmintaya's letter to King George II appears in Maung Maung Tin, *Konbaungzet*, pp. 145–46. The *Konbaungzet* is a compilation of nineteenth century public and personal records published in 1905 by a former courtier, Maung Maung Tin. It covers the reigns of the last Burmese dynasty, the Konbaung (1752–1886).
10. "Doctor Bayfield's Historical Review", p. 20.
11. Than Tun merely reproduced the texts of the 1964 edition in the third volume of his *Royal Orders*. The preface of that volume (*Royal Orders*, vol. 3, p. VII) gives details on the two palm leaf manuscript collections.
12. Than Tun, personal communication, May 2003.
13. Alaungmintaya's letter to Banya Dala of 10 June 1755 ((Than Tun, *Royal Orders*, vol. 3, pp. 98–99).

14. The group of monks alluded to here were called up by the Mon king to negotiate an end to the ongoing hostilities in October 1756. On the role of monks as messengers, see below part 2.
15. See the concluding passage of Banya Dala's letter to Alaungmintaya of 28 June 1756 (Than Tun, *Royal Orders*, vol. 3, p. 161).
16. Alaungmintaya's letter to Banya Dala of 10 June 1755 ((Than Tun, *Royal Orders*, vol. 3, pp. 98–99). The term *yathe* is derived from *ṛṣi*, the ancient wise men of Brahmanism who "heard" the Veda. See also the king's letter to the *sawbwa* of Hsenwi of 20 June 1755 (Than Tun, *Royal Orders*, vol. 3, pp. 100–101).
17. Banya Dala's letter to Alaungmintaya of 13 June 1756 (Than Tun, *Royal Orders*, vol. 3, p. 158).
18. Skilling, "King, *Sangha* and…".
19. The weapon of Thagya (Sakka/Indra), the king of the *devas* in Tāvatiṃsa heaven, is the thunderbolt.
20. Vessavaṇṇa (or Kubera), one of the four great kings, rules over the *yakkhas* and his weapon is the Gadāvudha, a club that would fall on the head of many thousands of *yakkhas* and return to Vessavaṇṇa's hand (Malalasekera, *Dictionary*, vol. 1, p. 743; vol. 2, p. 949).
21. This should be Yama, the god of death, who has the reputation of being a good king. His weapon, the Nayanāyudha, is "mentioned among the most destructive of weapons" (Malalasekera, *Dictionary*, vol. 2, p. 681).
22. Before his conversion by the Buddha, Āḷavaka was a *yakkha* to whom human sacrifices had to be made. His special weapon was the *dussāvudha*. If he threw it up into the sky, no rain would fall for twelve years. If he let it fall on the earth, all plants and trees would die and nothing would grow for twelve years. If he threw it into the seas, the sea would completely dry up. (Malalasekera, *Dictionary*, vol. 1, p. 291 and p. 1100).
23. Collins, *Nirvana*, p. 460.
24. Candier, "A norm of…", p. 5.
25. The *rājadhamma* have been listed by many authors. See Collins, *Nirvana*, pp. 460–61 from whom I adopt the list. For a nuanced translation with Burmese equivalents, see Huxley/Okudaira, "A Burmese tract", p. 250. A standard Burmese list is U Kala, *Mahayazawingyi*, pp. 66–67; an early mention in Western literature is Bigandet, *The Life or Legend of Gaudama*, p. 20.
26. They are extensively discussed by Collins, *Nirvana*, pp. 437–45.
27. Than Tun, *Royal Orders*, vol. 10, 30–31; U Pho Lat, *Sutesana*, 33. See also Bhaddanta Vicittasarabhivamsa, *Great Chronicle, vol. 5*, pp. 135–49.
28. See Lammerts, *Buddhism and Written Law,* p. 117 (n. 284) and p. 176 (n. 438). U Tin, *The Royal Administration*, pp. 32–34; Burmese text in U Tin, *Myanma Min*, pp. 63–66.
29. Scriptural sources are the *Kakacūpama Sutta* in the *Majjhima Nikāya* (Ñāṇamoli and Bodhi, *The Middle Length Discourses of the Buddha*, Wisdom,

1995, p. 221), the Vinaya Cūḷavagga and the Codanākaṇḍa of the Vinaya-parivāra (I.B. Horner, *The Book of the Discipline*, vol. V, pp. 347–48, and vol. VI, p. 260.)

30. U Tin, *The Royal Administration*, p. 52; Burmese text in U Tin, *Myanma Min*, p. 100.
31. A list of the four *agati,* bad courses appears in U Tin, *The Royal Administration*, pp. 43–46; U Tin, *Myanma Min*, pp. 83–88.
32. Baker, *Observations*, p. 102.
33. Banya Dala's letter to Alaungmintaya of 28 June 1756 (Than Tun, *Royal Orders*, vol. 3, p. 161). Read *lokatthacariyaṃ, ñātatthacariyaṃ*, and *buddhatthacariyaṃ,* translated by Masefield as "conduct beneficial to the world, conduct beneficial to relatives, and conduct beneficial to Buddhas" (Masefield, *The Commentary on the Itivuttaka*, pp. 603–604). A discussion with Peter Skilling (oral communication 19 October 2011) confirms me in the idea that the last expression could be plausibly translated as "conduct in order to [achieve] buddhahood". Christian Lammerts comments that this conduct is said of the Buddha and described throughout Pali commentarial literature, thus underscoring in our context the royal wish of becoming a Buddha.
34. The letter has *dvattisākāya satipaṭṭhāna;* read *dvattiṃsākāra satipaṭṭhāna*, establishing mindfulness of the 32 parts of the body. Alaungmintaya's letter to Banya Dala of 28 June 1756 (Than Tun, *Royal Orders*, vol. 3, p. 162). The king's letter is dated the same day as the one of Banya Dala. As the exchange of letters took place during the decisive phase of the siege of Syriam with Alaungmintaya directing operations from Yangon, the contestants faced each other at a very short distance and there would be no problem to receive a letter and send a reply the same day. But it is unlikely that Banya Dala himself was at Syriam during the siege. His brother, the *uparāja* was and could have issued the letter in the king's name. There are several letters in the East India Company archives which show that the *uparāja* handled commercial and foreign affairs in the name of the king. See, for example, letter of the "wopparajah" (*uparāja*) to the governor of Madras of 20 January 1754 in *Records... 1754*, p. 61. Another hypothesis is that the Burmese simply recorded the date when the Mon king's letter arrived.
35. Alaungmintaya's letter to Banya Dala of 10 June 1755 (Than Tun, *Royal Orders*, vol. 3, pp. 98–99).
36. Alaungmintaya's letters to Banya Dala of 16 June 1756, 28 September 1756 and 25 October 1756 (Than Tun, *Royal Orders*, vol. 3, pp. 159, 165 and 173).
37. Even in a purely Upper Myanmar context, Alaungmintaya could confidently make his claim to be a forthcoming king only after the execution in October 1754 of King Mahadhammayazadhipati, the ruler of Ava, who had been deported by the Mon invaders to Pegu in 1752.

38. The generally prevailing form and politeness of the diplomatic exchanges with Banya Dala is particularly striking when compared with Alaungmintaya's later letters to the king of Ayutthaya which are noteworthy for their rudeness. See in particular the letter of 25 March 1760 (Than Tun, *Royal Orders*, vol. 3, pp. 263–64).
39. See Baker, "Observations", p. 13, and Lester, "Proceedings", p. 10.
40. As Banya Dala did not feel a need to get in touch with the Burmese troops during their advance in 1755, Alaungmintaya ironically noted in his first letter: "It looks as if there are no good teachers, good officers or wise men in the cities and villages of Lower Burma, as I did not get any news from you". Letter of 10 June 1755 (Than Tun, *Royal Orders*, vol. 3, p. 99). An example of Alaungmintaya's sarcasm is found in his reply to Banya Dala's first letter a year later. Given the fact that the Mon king took over a year to send a reply, Alaungmintaya comments: "Right now I notice that you come to talk to me like someone asleep who suddenly wakes up, (but) is not yet fully awake, talks in his sleep, absent-minded and groping about." Letter of 16 June 1756 (Than Tun, *Royal Orders*, vol. 3, p. 159). For more textual references, see Leider, "Kingship".
41. Alaungmintaya's letter to Banya Dala of 19 December 1756 (Than Tun, *Royal Orders*, vol. 3, p. 176).
42. I thank Christian Lammerts for providing me references to several Pagan inscriptions of the twelfth and thirteenth centuries. The expression, he says, is also found in scribal colophons.
43. Brahmadatta Kumara, the king of Benares, refused to give his daughter Samuddaja, though she herself was born from a Naga mother, to the king of the Nagas, Dhatarattha. Dhatarattha threatened the city of Benares and its king (Brahmadatta Kumara) had to submit and give up his daughter. Samuddaja's second son, Bhūridatta, was the future Buddha in one of his previous lives.
44. Alaungmintaya's letter to Banya Dala of 28 September 1756 (Than Tun, *Royal Orders*, vol. 3, p. 166).
45. In what must have been one of his last letters to the king of Pegu, Alaungmintaya mused about the transitoriness of all things while admonishing Banya Dala (19 December 1756; Than Tun, *Royal Orders*, vol. 3, p. 176).
46. Alaungmintaya's letter to Banya Dala, 16 June 1756 (Than Tun, *Royal Orders*, vol. 3, p. 159).
47. I translate *kāyasukkha cittasukkha* as happiness, meaning a state of physical safety and mental bliss. The expression is variously found, for example in Alaungmintaya's letters of 16 and 28 June 1756 (Than Tun, *Royal Orders*, vol. 3, pp. 159, 161) and the letter of the peace entreating monks of 19 October 1756 (Than Tun, *Royal Orders*, vol. 3, pp. 167–68). Alaungmintaya's letter to the *sawbwa* of Hsenwi, 20 June 1755 (Than Tun, *Royal Orders*, vol. 3, p. 100). For the same expression, see also Alaungmintaya's proclamation

of January 1755 (Than Tun, *Royal Orders*, vol. 3, pp. 90–91) and the reply given to the monk delegation on 19 October 1756 (Than Tun, *Royal Orders*, vol. 3, p. 168).

48. *Sakha* (Pali), derived from *sakhi*, a friend or companion. The other marks are a ruler (*sāmin*), a minister, a friend, a storehouse, a fortress, a dominion, an army. The letter refers the list to an unnamed Pali subcommentary. Thanks to Christian Lammerts for mending the garbled list of Pali words. He draws attention to parallel lists in the *Rājanīti* and the *Sīlakkhandhavaggaṭīkā*, a subcommentary on the *Kūṭadanta-sutta*.

    The seven marks of a royal city are first referred to in Alaungmintaya's letter to Banya Dala of 10 June 1755 (Than Tun, *Royal Orders*, vol. 3, pp. 98–99). They are listed in his letter of 16 June 1756 (Than Tun, *Royal Orders*, vol. 3, p. 159) and are referred to in his letter of 28 June 1756 as praised by the wise (Than Tun, *Royal Orders*, vol. 3, p. 162). For Banya Dala, spelling the seven marks was nothing less than preaching the *dhamma* (letter of 28 June 1756; Than Tun, *Royal Orders*, vol. 3, p. 161). Another instance is Alaungmintaya's first letter to the East India Company (Than Tun, *Royal Orders*, vol. 3, pp. 92–93).

49. This idea is not found in the letters exchanged between Alaungmintaya and Banya Dala, but emphasized in a concluding phrase in the four letters dated 8 May 1756 sent by Alaungmintaya to George II, the Court of directors of the East India Company, the governor of the East India Company in Madras and the chief of the Negrais settlement. A comparison of the variations of that phrase (denoting "friendship between kings") is found in Leider, *King Alaungmintaya's Golden Letter*, p. 93.
50. Alaungmintaya's letter to Banya Dala, 28 June 1756 (Than Tun, *Royal Orders*, vol. 3, p. 162).
51. Alaungmintaya's letter to Banya Dala, 10 June 1755 (Than Tun, *Royal Orders*, vol. 3, pp. 98–99).
52. Alaungmintaya's letter to Banya Dala, 28 June 1756 (Than Tun, *Royal Orders*, vol. 3, p. 162).
53. See, for example, Baudler, *Gewalt in den Weltreligionen*, pp. 105–18.
54. Bareau, *Le bouddha et les rois*, pp. 37–38.
55. Jerryson/Juergensmeyer, *Buddhist Warfare*, p. 3.
56. I do not fail to see that the Western imagery was duly sustained by the discourse of Buddhists themselves, portraying Buddhism as a religion of tolerance at all times. See, for example, the quotations of Walpola Rahula by Faure, *Bouddhisme et violence*, p. 9.
57. Faure, *Bouddhisme et violence*, pp. 25–42.
58. Ibid., p. 44. See also Lingat, *Royautés bouddhiques*, pp. 140–46 and Jerryson/Juergensmeyer, *Buddhist Warfare*, p. 9: "in regions where Buddhism is part of the ideology of statecraft, there is a pervasive tendency for Buddhists to sanction state violence"; and p. 13: "history confirms a widespread propensity

among state to adopt Buddhisms as the official religion and for Buddhisms to provide the rationalization for the state's sanctioned use of violence".

59. Faure, *Bouddhisme et violence*, p. 11 and Jerryson/Juergensmeyer, *Buddhist Warfare*, p. 6.
60. Greyerz/Siebenhüner, *Gewalt in den Religionen*, pp. 11–12.
61. McFarlane, "Fighting Bodhisattvas", pp. 186–90.
62. See Maher, "Sacralized Warfare", p. 78.
63. Baudler, *Gewalt*, pp. 16–34.
64. Collins, *Nirvana*, pp. 414–96. To fully appreciate the deepness of Collins' work within the chapter alluded to here, it is important to understand the situatedness of the texts (which he quotes plentifully) within the "stable ideological force" that was the Pali imaginaire, the Pali imaginaire being the incarnation of a powerful connection between religion and ideology over an extended period of time. One of his introductory chapters, "The Pali-imaginaire in real world history" (*Nirvana*, pp. 40–59), details the trans-locality of Pali and the necessity of understanding Buddhism as "culturally instantiated", and is a warning against philologically intricate, but essentialist readings of texts, notably those which display the "always-ambiguous ideals of kingship" (*Nirvana*, p. 448).
65. Collins, *Nirvana*, p. 414, quoting Mabbett and Chandler, *The Khmers* and p. 415.
66. Collins, *Nirvana*, p. 419.
67. See Harris, *Violence and Disruption*, p. 25 and Collins, *Nirvana*, p. 455, for a reference to the Rājanīti, and p. 467 for his comparison of Buddhism and Brahmanical Hinduism. Alaungmintaya was particularly proud to have re-established order and peace in Central Burma, having inherited, as he wrote to the *sawbwa* of Hsenwi on 20 June 1755 (Than Tun, *Royal Orders*, vol. 3, p. 100), the "country that was like the stem (of a flower) dropping, and no one to pick it up and take care...".
68. It echoes the fifth Dalai Lama's downplay of intrareligious warfare (Maher, "Sacralized Warfare", p. 83) and the majority of Sri Lankan monk preachers who refrained from specifically encouraging soldiers to kill during the civil war (Kent, "Onward Buddhist soldiers", p. 168).
69. Michael Aung Thwin thinks that "the entire pre-colonial monarchical era should be viewed as one entity in which classical forms, rituals, structures, and beliefs were created, elaborated upon, refined, embellished and preserved" an opinion which leads him to the peremptory conclusion: "More precisely, were 11th century conceptions of the state and king, of legitimacy and authority, of man, of order and disorder, and of salvation vastly or profoundly different from 19th century ones? My answer [...] is 'no'." (Michael Aung Thwin "Jambudipa", pp. 39–40).
70. Regarding the letters the king sent to the East India Company, see Leider, *King Alaungmintaya's Golden Letter*, pp. 37–70.

71. A detailed description of the gold leaf used for Alaungmintaya's letter to George II is provided at the end of the letter sent in parallel to the East India Company chief in Negrais. A description is also given of the packaging and seals attached. The ivory box that contained the letter is still kept together with the golden letter at the Gottfried Wilhelm Leibniz Bibliothek in Hanover, Germany.
72. Thaw Kaung, *Palm leaf record*, p. 4.
73. In the *Alaungmintaya Ayedawpon*, it is said that Banya Dala's letter of surrender that was brought by the Mon minister Maṇiratanā Brahmā to Alaungmintaya, was packed in a red bag put in a big chest. *Alaungmintayagyi Ayedawpon*, p. 202.
74. Alaungmintaya's letter to Banya Dala of 10 June 1755 (Than Tun, *Royal Orders*, vol. 3, pp. 98–99).
75. Collins, Nirvana, p. 474.
76. Lingat, *Royautés bouddhiques*, pp. 175–230.
77. Letwè Nawrahta, *Alaungmintaya Ayedawpon*, p. 156.
78. Alaungmintaya's letter to Banya Dala of 10 June 1755 (Than Tun, *Royal Orders*, vol. 3, p. 99). I thank Christian Lammerts for drawing my attention to the *Paṭisambhidāmagga* where the 528 forms of *mettā* or loving-kindness are enumerated. For an English translation, see Ñāṇamoli, *The Path of Discrimination*, pp. 317–23.
79. Alaungmintaya's letter to Banya Dala of 10 June 1755 (Than Tun, *Royal Orders*, vol. 3, p. 99).
80. Ibid.
81. Ibid.
82. Banya Dala's letter to Alaungmintaya of 13 June 1756 (Than Tun, *Royal Orders*, vol. 3, p. 158).
83. Alaungmintaya's letter to Banya Dala of 16 June 1756 (Than Tun, *Royal Orders*, vol. 3, p. 159).
84. Ibid.
85. Alaungmintaya's letter to Banya Dala, 28 June 1756 (Than Tun, *Royal Orders*, vol. 3, p. 162).
86. Banya Dala's letter to Alaungmintaya, 25 October 1756 (Than Tun, *Royal Orders*, vol. 3, p. 171).
87. The exact dating of the letter is problematic. It arrived in Shwebo on 25 October 1756. Given the time that it took to forward a letter from Lower Burma to Upper Burma during the monsoon season, it is likely that it was dispatched after the fall of Syriam or eventually just before Syriam fell. It is unlikely that Alaungmintaya received the letter in Shwebo as he was directing the siege of Pegu in late October. This makes it unlikely that he received the letter in due time as the progress of the Burmese towards Pegu was so fast that a suggestion to meet at the Shwedagon towards the end of the year sounds highly improbable.

88. The elaborate style of the original letter was paraphrased in a simplified way in Letwè Nawratha's *Alaungmintayagyi Ayedawpon*.
89. Alaungmintaya's letter to a group of monks of 19 October 1756 (Than Tun, *Royal Orders*, vol. 3, p. 167).
90. Ibid., p. 168).
91. Ibid.
92. Maung Maung Tin, *Konbaungzet*, vol. 1, p. 170 and Letwè Nawrahta, *Alaungmintayagyi Ayedawpon*, p. 191.
93. Alaungmintaya's letter to Banya Dala of 25 October 1756 (Than Tun, *Royal Orders*, vol. 3, p. 173).
94. Banya Dala's letter to Alaungmintaya of 13 December 1756 (Than Tun, *Royal Orders*, vol. 3, p. 175). The letter is paraphrased in Letwè Nawrahta, *Alaungmintayagyi Ayedawpon*, p. 197.
95. Letwè Nawrahta, *Alaungmintayagyi Ayedawpon*, p. 197.
96. The three quotations in this paragraph are taken from Alaungmintaya's letter to Banya Dala of 19 December 1756 (Than Tun, *Royal Orders*, vol. 3, p. 176).
97. Alaungmintaya's letter to Banya Dala of 19 December 1756 (Than Tun, *Royal Orders*, vol. 3, p. 176).
98. Letwè Nawrahta, *Alaungmintayagyi Ayedawpon*, p. 197.
99. Twinthin-taikwun U Htun Nyo, "Alaungmintayagyi Ayedawpon", pp. 589–90; Letwè Nawrahta, *Alaungmintayagyi Ayedawpon*, pp. 198–99.
100. See Maung Maung Tin, *Konbaungzet*, vol. 1, p. 151 and Letwè Nawrahta, *Alaungmintayagyi Ayedawpon*, pp. 201–202. The *Alaungmintayagyi Ayedawpon* is a record of Alaungmintaya's political rise largely focusing on military events. Probably written around 1766 by Letwè Nawrahta, a close advisor, poet and minister of the king, it has come down to us in several versions. The *Konbaungzet chronicle* is a compilation of records published in 1905 by Maung Maung Tin, a former courtier. It covers the reigns of the last Burmese dynasty, the Konbaung (1752–1886).
101. Letwè Nawrahta, *Alaungmintayagyi Ayedawpon*, pp. 201–202.
102. The context to broach such questions is set in Tun Aung Chain, *Pegu*.
103. Than Tun, *Royal Orders*, vol. 3, pp. 144–46. For references to the letter in the chronicles, see *Alaungmintaya Ameindaw-mya*, p. 29.
104. Lit. "those who are of our Myanma kind" (*jāt tū*); Than Tun, *Royal Orders*, vol. 3, p. 91.
105. Kiernan, *Blood and soil*, pp. 152 and 154. Kiernan derives his thesis from what I see as a tendentious reading of various established scholars, namely Victor Lieberman. But Lieberman's statement on Alaungmintaya's "systematic policy of ethnic appeals" was accompanied by a caveat to his readers not to overemphasize the ethnic dimension of the ongoing warfare between the south and the north. See Lieberman, *Ethnic Politics*.
106. Charney, *Powerful Learning*, p. 137.
107. Inscription of King Sinbyushin at the Nibban-hseit-oo Pagoda in Shwebo,

1765 (Courtesy of Archaeology department, Shwebo). I thank Kyaw Minn Htin for drawing my attention to this inscription and providing me with a transcription.

108. Swearer/ Sommai, "The relation between ...", Chutintaranond, "Cakravartin Ideology".

109. Collins, *Nirvana*, p. 496. To understand the power of attraction of the *cakkavatti* ideal, one may have to take a look beyond the *Cakkavatti-sīhanāda sutta*. Analysing the attributes of the Buddha in the Mahāparinirvāṇasūtra of the Dharmaguptaka, Bareau has shown the strong connection between the Buddha's personality — notably his image of conqueror and hero — and the "myth ... of universal royalty", "serving to define Buddha's social position, to acknowledge his absolute supremacy in the world of men". Bareau, *The Superhuman Personality*, p. 20. Lammerts draws attention to the importance of "the theory of the *cakkavatti*" being "as much a regional and Sanskritic phenomenon as it is a Pali one". Lammerts, *Buddhism and Written Law*, p. 117.

110. Gombrich, *Theravada Buddhism,* p. 82; Yashpal, *A Cultural Study*, p. 154. I adapt here an earlier comment regarding Arakanese kingship. See Leider, *Relics*, p. 359. Gombrich, *Theravada Buddhism*, p. 82; Yashpal, *A Cultural Study*, p. 154.

111. Collins, *Nirvana*, p. 495.

112. Strong, *The Legend of King Ashoka*, p. 49.

References

Aung Thwin, Michael A. "Jambudipa: Classical Burma's Camelot". In *Contributions to Asian Studies, vol. 16, Essays on Burma*, edited by John P. Ferguson, pp. 38–61. Leiden: Brill, 1988.

Baker, Georges. "Observations at Persaim and in the Journey to Ava and Back in 1755". *SOAS Bulletin of Burma Research* 3, no. 1 (2005): 99–118.

Bareau, André. "The Superhuman Personality of Buddha and its Symbolism in the Mahāparinirvāṇasūtra of the Dharmaguptaka". In *Myths and Symbols Essays in Honor of Mircea Eliade*, edited by Joseph M. Kitigawa et al., pp. 9–22. Chicago: The University of Chicago Press, 1969.

——. "Le Bouddha et les rois". *Bulletin de l'Ecole française d'Extrême-Orient* 80, no. 1 (1993): 3–39.

Baudler, Georg. *Gewalt in den Weltreligionen*. Darmstadt: Wissenschaftliche Buchgesellschaft, 2005.

Bhaddanta Vicittasarabhivamsa. *The Great Chronicle of Buddhas*. Yangon: Ti-ni Press, 1999.

Bigandet, Paul Rev. *The Life or Legend of Gaudama The Budha of the Burmese with annotations The Ways to Neibban and Notice on the Phongyies or Burmese Monks*. Rangoon: American Mission Press, 1866.

Candier, Aurore. "A Norm of Burmese Kingship? The Concept of *Raza-dhamma* through Five Konbaung Period Texts". *Journal of Burma Studies* 11 (2007): 5–47.

Charney, Michael Walter. *Powerful Learning Buddhist Literati and the Throne in Burma's Last Dynasty, 1752–1885*. Ann Arbor: University of Michigan, 2006.

Chutintaranond, Sunait. "Cakravartin Ideology, Reason and Manifestation of Siamese and Burmese Kings in Traditional Warfare". In *On both sides of the Tenasserim Range – History of Siamese-Burmese Relations,* edited by S. Chutintaranond and Than Tun, pp. 55–66. Bangkok: Institute of Asian Studies, 1995.

Collins, Steven. *Nirvana and Other Buddhist Felicities Utopias of the Pali Imaginaire*. 2 vols. Cambridge: Cambridge University Press, 1998.

Dalrymple, Alexander. *Oriental Repertory published at the charge of the East India Company*. London: George Bigg, 1791.

"Doctor Bayfield's Historical Review of our Political Relations with the State of Ava". London: British Library, IOC F4/1582, 20.

Faure, Bernard. *Bouddhisme et violence*. Paris: Le Cavalier Bleu, 2008.

Gokhale, Balkrishna. G. "Dhammiko Dhammaraja: A Study in Buddhist Constitutional Concepts". In *Indica, the Indian Historical Research Institute Silver Jubilee commemoration volume*. Bombay: St Xavier's College, 1953.

Gombrich, Richard F. *Theravada Buddhism: A Social History from Ancient Benares to Modern Colombo*. London and New York: Routledge and Kegan Paul, 1988.

Greyerz, Kaspar von and Kim Siebenhüner. *Religion und Gewalt. Konflikte, Rituale, Deutungen (1500–1800)*. Göttingen: Vandenhoeck & Ruprecht, 2006.

Harris, Elizabeth J. *Violence and Disruption in Society A Study of the Early Buddhist Texts*. Kandy: Buddhist Publication Society, 1994.

Huxley, Andrew and Ryuji Okudaira. "A Burmese tract on kingship: political theory in the 1782 manuscript of Manugye". *Bulletin of SOAS* 64, no. 2 (2001): 248–59.

Jerryson, Michael and Mark Juergensmeyer, ed. *Buddhist Warfare*. New York: Oxford University Press, 2010.

Kent, Daniel W. "Onward Buddhist Soldiers: Preaching to the Sri Lankan Army". In *Buddhist Warfare*, edited by Michael Jerryson and Mark Juergensmeyer, pp. 157–78. New York: Oxford University Press, 2010.

Khin Khin Sein, ed. *Alaungmintaya Ameindaw-mya (Royal edicts of Alaungmintaya)*. Yangon: Myanmar Historical Commission, 1964.

Kiernan, Ben. *Blood and soil: A world history of genocide and extermination from Sparta to Darfur.* New Haven: Yale University Press, 2007.

Lammerts, Dietrich Christian. "Buddhism and Written Law: Dhammasattha Manuscripts and Texts in Premodern Burma". PhD Dissertation. Cornell University, 2010.

Leider, Jacques P. "Relics, Statues and Predictions: Interpreting an Apocryphal Sermon of Lord Buddha in Arakan". *Asian Ethnology* 68, no. 2 (2009): 333–64.

——. *King Alaungmintaya's Golden Letter to King George II (7 May 1756): The story of an exceptional manuscript and the failure of a diplomatic overture*. Hannover: Gottfried Wilhelm Leibniz Bibliothek, 2009.

——."Kingship by Merit and Cosmic Investiture: An Investigation into King Alaungmintaya's Self-representation". *Journal of Burma Studies* 15, no. 1 (2011): 165–88.

——."Alaungmintaya, König von Birma (1752–60) Darstellung und Interpretationen in der westlichen Geschichtsschreibung". In *Du Luxembourg à l'Europe Mélanges offerts à Gilbert Trausch*, edited by Jacques P. Leider, Jean-Marie Majerus, Marc Schoentgen and Michel Polfer, pp. 609–30. Luxembourg: Imprimerie St Paul, 2011.

——."The Rise of Alaungmintaya, King of Myanmar (1752–60): Buddhist Constituents of a Political Metamorphosis". In *Buddhist Narrative in Asia and Beyond,* edited by Justin McDaniel and Peter Skilling. Bangkok: Institute of Thai Studies, 2012.

Lester, Robert. "Proceedings of an Embassy to the King of Ava, Pegu, etc. in 1757". *SOAS Bulletin of Burma Studies* 3, no. 1 (2005): 127–42.

Letwè Nawrahta. *Alaungmintayagyi Ayedawpon (Royal Deeds of the Great Alaungmintaya)*. Typewritten copy of a palm-leaf manuscript. Mandalay: Mandalay University Library. Ms. 327.

——. *Alaungmintayagyi Ayedawpon (Royal Deeds of the Great Alaungmintaya)*, edited by Daw Ohn Kyi. Yangon: Historical Research Department, 2011.

Lieberman, Victor B. "Ethnic Politics in Eighteenth Century Burma". *Modern Asian Studies* 12 (1978): 455–82.

Lingat, Robert. *Royautés bouddhiques: Aśoka et La fonction royale à Ceylan*. Paris: Editions de l'Ecole des Hautes Etudes en Sciences Sociales, 1989.

Maher, Derek F. "Sacralized Warfare: The Fifth Dalai Lama and the Discourse of Religious Violence". In *Buddhist Warfare,* edited by Michael Jerryson and Mark Juergensmeyer, pp. 77–90. New York: Oxford University Press, 2010.

Malalasekera G.P. *Dictionary of Pali Proper Names,* 2 vols. London: Luzac and company, 1937. (Reprint 1960)

Masefield, Peter. *The Commentary on the Itivuttaka*. Oxford: Pali Text Society, 2009.

Maung Maung Tin. *Konbaungzet Mahayazawintawgyi (The Great Royal Chronicle of the Konbaung),* vol. 1, 5th ed. Yangon: Yapye, 2005.

McFarlane, Stewart 1995. "Fighting Bodhisattvas and Inner Warriors: Buddhism and the Martial Traditions of China and Japan". In *The Buddhist Forum*, vol. 3, edited by Tadeusz Skorupski and Ulrich Pagel, pp. 185–210. New Delhi: Heritage Publishers, 1991–93.

Ñāṇamoli. *The Path of Discrimination*. Oxford: Pali Text Society, 2002.
Records of Fort St. George Country Correspondence Military Department 1754. Madras: Government Press, 1912.
Skilling, Peter. "King, Sangha and Brahmans Ideology, ritual and power in pre-modern Siam". In *Buddhism, Power and Political Order*, edited by Ian Harris, pp. 182–215. London/New York: Routledge, 2007.
Strong, John. *The Legend of King Asoka. A Study and Translation of the Asokavadana*. Princeton: Princeton University Press, 1983.
Swearer, Donald K., and Sommai Premchit. "The relation between the religious and political orders in northern Thailand (14th–16th Centuries)". In *Religion and Legitimation of Power in Thailand, Laos, and Burma*, edited by Bardwell Smith, pp. 20–33. Chambersburg: Anima Books, 1978.
Than Tun, ed. *The Royal Orders of Burma (1598–1885)* 10 vols. Kyoto: Centre for Southeast Asian Studies, 1983–90.
Thaw Kaung. "Letwè Nawratha (1723–1791), Recorder of Myanmar History". Unpublished paper, 2008.
——. "Palm-leaf Manuscript Record of a Mission Sent by the Myanmar King to the Chinese Emperor in the Mid-Eighteenth Century". *SOAS Bulletin of Burma Research* 6, nos. 1&2 (2008): 3–18.
Tun Aung Chain. "Pegu in Politics and Trade, Ninth to Seventeenth Centuries". In *Recalling Local Pasts Autonomous History in Southeast Asia*, edited by Chris Baker and Sunait Chutintaranond, pp. 25–52. Chiang Mai: Silkworm Books, 2002.
Twinthin-taikwun U Htun Nyo. "Alaungmintayagyi Ayedawpon". In *Myanma-min Ayedawpon*, pp. 547–603. Yangon: Yapye Books, 2005.
U Kala. *Mahayazawingyi (Great Chronicle)*, vol. 1. Yangon: Yapye, 2006.
U Pho Lat. *Sutesana-sarup-pra abhidhān*. Rangoon: Pinyananda Press, 1955.
U Tin. *Myanma Min Okchokpon Sadan (The Administration of the Kings of Burma)*. Yangon: Department of Archaeology and Culture, 1963–1970.
——. *The Royal Administration of Burma*. Bangkok: Ava House, 2001.
Yashpal, Dr. *A Cultural Study of Early Pali Tipitakas*. Delhi: Kalinga Publications, 1999.

13

COURT BUDDHISM IN THAI-KHMER RELATIONS DURING THE REIGN OF KING RAMA IV (KING MONGKUT)

Santi Pakdeekham

ABSTRACT

This paper studies Khmer Buddhism from the perspective of the relations between the Thai and Khmer courts during the reign of King Rama IV of Siam (contemporary Thailand). After a period of civil war and war with Cambodia's neighbours Thailand and Vietnam, many Buddhist temples had been destroyed. Therefore, when King Ang Duong came to the throne, he undertook to restore Khmer Buddhism, drawing on Thai court Buddhism.

In the field of Khmer Buddhist literature, he had Thai Buddhist literature translated into Khmer, for example the *Paṭhamasambodhikathā* (the Pali-Thai account of the life of the Buddha) and the *Trailokavinicchayakathā* (Buddhist cosmology). King Ang Duong also requested King Rama IV to send Dhammayutika Nikāya monks to ordain Khmer monks and to disseminate Buddhism in Cambodia.

INTRODUCTION

Thailand and Cambodia have a long-standing relationship. Particularly language, literature and Buddhism have extensive connections, both in terms of cultural borrowing and of cultural exchange. This relationship has been there especially since the founding of Sukhothai in the eighteenth century of the Buddhist Era (BE), and the founding of Ayutthaya in the nineteenth century BE, and has continued through the Thonburi and Rattanakosin eras to the present day, without interruption, only changing according to the circumstances in each era.

Buddhism in Siam had a particularly close relationship with Cambodia in the early Rattanakosin period and Oudong period in Cambodia, and especially so when King Mongkut (Rama IV) reigned in Siam and King Ang Duong ruled Cambodia.[1]

Since the reigns of King Ang Chan II and King Ang Mey, Cambodia endured civil war due to Vietnamese interference. At this time, Vietnam destroyed temples and burned numerous Buddhist scriptures in Cambodia,[2] as evidenced by inscriptions at the Phnom Penh temple Wat Preah Putkosa about temple restoration by Chao Phraya Bodindecha (Sing Singhaseni), which states that

> when Chao Phraya Bodindecha conducted warfare in Phnom Penh, many districts were devastated. A desire arose to donate funds for the salaries of soldiers who were hired to help restore monasteries, images of the Buddha, stupas and chedis to perpetuate Buddhism[3]

After King Ang Duong ascended the Cambodian throne in Oudong in 1854, he issued a royal letter to request a copy of the Pali *Tripiṭaka* and other Buddhist scriptures, as well as for Dhammayutika Nikāya monks to spread the religion and convene a council for compiling a version of the Tripiṭaka in the city of Oudong.

This paper addresses the relationship between Thai and Cambodian Buddhism, especially in the period of King Mongkut's reign in Siam and King Ang Duong's in Cambodia, elaborating the areas where there were connections, and how this has affected Cambodian Buddhism.

RELATIONS THROUGH THE DHAMMAYUTIKA NIKĀYA SECT

After King Mongkut had established the Dhammayutika ("adhere to the law" or "Thommayut" in Khmer) Nikāya, King Ang Duong requested that the sect disseminate Buddhism in Cambodia. King Mongkut sent Phra Amarābhirakkhitta (Koet) and Phra Mahā Pān (who was to become Somdec Phra Sugandhādhipati the supreme patriarch of the Dhammayutika Nikāya sect in Cambodia) to build the sect in Cambodia.[4]

Somdec Phra Sugandhādhipati (1824–94), who previously had the monastic name "Pān" was a Cambodian monk who had come to study in Bangkok under the tutelage of Phra Vajirañāṇa (King Mongkut) while staying at Wat Baromniwat, Bangkok and later, after successfully completing his monastic exams, became "Phra Mahā Pān".

Around 1855, Phra Mahā Pān returned to Cambodia to build the Dhammayutika Nikāya sect there as King Ang Duong had requested and King Mongkut had granted.

Phra Mahā Pān, after becoming Somdec Phra Sugandhādhipati (Pān), stayed at Wat Botum Vaddey (Padumavati) of Phnom Penh. He was an important scholar in the courts of both King Ang Duong and King Norodom. Many of his works have been preserved and remain important today, such as the *Robaksat* (Cambodian royal chronicles) and *Lboek Angkor Wat baeb Chas*, compiled together with Okña Santhorwohar (Muk).[5]

Somdec Phra Sugandhādhipati (Pān) died in 2437 BE (1894 CE).[6] This was during King Chulalongkorn's reign in Siam and King Norodom's in Cambodia. Besides that Phra Amarābhirakkhitta (Koet) and Phra Mahā Pān were sent to disseminate Dhammayutika Nikāya Buddhism in Cambodia. There is also evidence that King Mongkut arranged the ordination of Prince Norodom and Prince Sisowath, two sons of King Ang Duong, at Wat Phra Kaew (Wat Phra Sri Rattana Satsadaram) in Bangkok. After ordination, Prince Norodom and Prince Sisowath stayed at Wat Bowonranives. This means that Prince Norodom and Prince Sisowath were ordained in the Dhammayutika Nikāya sect.[7]

For this reason, the Dhammayutika Nikāya was under royal patronage in Cambodia, and it became a tradition for members of the Cambodian royal family to be ordained in this sect, which thus spread from Siam to Cambodia and became popular there, which it still is today.

RELATIONS THROUGH BUDDHIST LITERATURE

In nineteenth century CE, Cambodia had many civil wars and many Buddhist temples and Khmer manuscripts were destroyed. Therefore, when King Ang Duong acceded to the throne, he had Khmer literature developed in many fields, especially those with Thai influence on literary form. In the field of Buddhist literature, Thai Buddhist literature was translated into Khmer. In the field of Khmer narrative literature, Khmer had borrowed some plots from Thai narrative literature like "the story of Kaki". In the field of drama, two Khmer plays: *Rieamker* (Ramayana in Khmer version) and *Inao*, were translated from Thai and they were usually performed in the Khmer royal court.[8]

Due to the relations described above, Khmer Buddhist literature of the Oudong era is closely related to early Rattanakosin Thai Buddhist literature, which is particularly clear in the case of *Paṭhamasambodhikathā* and a Khmer translation of the *Traibhūmi* (Buddhist cosmology).

Paṭhamasambodhikathā

The *Paṭhamasambodhikathā* is an account of the Buddha's final incarnations, from being a Bodhisattva from Tusita (abode of gods, one of the heavens described in Buddhist cosmology) to being born as the son of King Suddhodana and Queen Māyādevī of Kapilavastu, his awakening and eventual passing away.[9]

Manuscripts of the Pāli version of the *Paṭhamasambodhikathā* have been found in Cambodia, comprising twenty-one *phūk*, divided into thirty chapters. This text is the same as the Pali source text of the Thai version, composed by Krommaphra Paramanuchinorot.[10] However, there are three different Khmer translations of the text, as outlined below.

Paṭhamasambodhi saṃkhepa, also known as *Paṭhama-tras'*, comprises five or six *phūk*.[11] It relates the Buddha's life from being a Bodhisattva from Tusita to being born as the son of King Suddhodana and Queen Māyādevī, his ordination and awakening, but no further. It is not known who composed this version and when, but the language used is not particularly archaic; in any case it does not predate the Oudong era. This scripture is often used as a sermon in *bon abhiseka preah put* merit making ceremonies.[12]

Paṭhamasambodhi vitthāra comprises thirty chapters. Somdec Phra Mahā Sumedhādhipati (Chuon Nath) explains that this version was translated by Mahā Nāk, Mahā Phu, Achār Son and others in Battambang from the *Paṭhamasambodhikathā* in Thai version of Krommaphra Paramanuchinorot in the era when Phraya Khathathonthoranin (Chum Abhaivong) was the governor of Battambang. This version is widespread in Cambodia.[13]

Paṭhamasambodhikathā by Phra Inthamuni (Baen) of Wat Botum Vaddey, Phnom Penh, was translated from the Thai version of Somdet Phra Sangkharat (Sa) (the Supreme Patriarch of Siam) in the reign of King Sisowath (1904–27). It contains thirty chapters like the original. This version has been used for Visākha pūjā[14] sermons in many Cambodian Dhammayutika Nikāya temples.[15]

It can thus be said that the Khmer versions of *Paṭhamasambodhikathā* found in Cambodia can be divided into two types — those based on the original Pali version predating the extended version of Krommaphra

Paramanuchinorot, and those translated from Thai to Khmer from the version composed by Krommaphra Paramanuchinorot and by Somdet Phra Sangkharat (Sa), which is closely associated with the Dhammayutika Nikāya sect.

Cambodian Buddhist Cosmology

The Cambodian Buddhist cosmology composed in the Oudong-era is an important piece of evidence that demonstrates connections in Buddhist literature between Rattanakosin-era Siam and Oudong-era Cambodia. There are two Cambodian Buddhist cosmology versions that survive today,[16] and both are related to the Thai version.

However, the nature of the relationship is different in each case, as one is a translation of *Traibhūmi Phra Ruang* or *Traiphūmikathā* (Thai Buddhist cosmology composed by King Luethai in the Sukhothai era)[17] and the other is related to *Trailokavinicchayakathā* (a Rattanakosin era version of Thai Buddhist cosmology composed by Phraya Thamma Pricha (Kaew)). The version which illustrates Thai-Cambodian Buddhist connections is the version of King Ang Duong.

Traibhūmi, King Ang Duong Version, was the second Khmer version of Buddhist cosmology found in Cambodia. It comprises ten *phūk*, thus differing from the Khmer version translated from *Traibhūmi Phra Ruang*, which has thirteen *phūk*. King Ang Duong had his version translated by monks and his royal scholars from the Thai version in 2396 BE (1853 CE) and it is thus known as *Traibhūmi, King Ang Duong Version*.[18]

Three complete copies of the *Traibhūmi, King Ang Duong Version* survive today, namely copies given serial numbers 822 and 825, kept at the French National Library in Paris, and the copy held by FEMC, given the code number 170/1 B.01.163. 01. V.1 by EFEO-FEMC from Wat Srey Phum Thmey, Kampong Cham, Cambodia.[19]

The introduction of *Traibhūmi, King Ang Duong Version* explains that the work was translated from a Thai version donated to Cambodia by King Mongkut.[20] However, some changes seem to have been made during the translation, as the Khmer version has some differences in both content and order of presentation from the Thai version.

RELATIONS THROUGH BUDDHIST CEREMONIES

Besides the evidence that shows that the *Tripiṭaka*, Commentaries and other Buddhist scriptures were brought from Bangkok to Cambodia, important Cambodian royal ceremonies (such as the royal Visākha pūjā ceremonies in which the *Paṭhamasambodhikathā* is the sermon text)[21] were also introduced to Cambodia in this era, as described in 'Ceremonies Royales des Douze Mois' or 'Phra Rājabidhī Dvādasamās' by Okñā Debbidū (Krasem):

> in Cambodia, Visākha pūjā ceremonies, as many elders of various positions have recounted, were begun in the era of King Ang Duong and first conducted in the city of Oudong, because in 2397 B.E. (1854 C.E.), this King made a written request to King Mongkut (Rama IV) for Phra Mahā Pān, that is, Somdec Phra Sugandhādhipati, being a monk of the Dhammayutika Nikāya sect in Bangkok. One year after this, that is, in 2398 B.E., Phra Mahā Pān arrived from Bangkok to the great pleasure of King Ang Duong, and was made the abbot of Wat Sālā Khū ... in the city of Oudong. And since this senior monk had previously resided in Bangkok and performed the Visākha pūjā ceremonies there before, and then come to stay in Cambodia and also risen to a high position in the Dhammayutika Nikāya, he started performing the ceremonies as he had done before. But in which year this first took place – that has not been recorded by anyone. It has merely been asserted by people in various positions that it was done while he was still in the city of Oudong. He came to stay at Wat Botum Vaddey in 2408 B.E. and stayed there until he passed away. And when the Dhammayutika Nikāya temples were established, the Visākha pūjā ceremonies spread to all of them, and they perform them today.
>
> Mahā Nikāya temples, however, only began performing the ceremonies in the Phnom Penh era, during King Sisowath's reign, as Somdec Phra Maha Sumedhādhipati (Chuon Nath) recounts that Preah Vanaratta (Can) at Wat Onnalom went to Bangkok and saw both Dhammayutika Nikāya and Mahā Nikāya monks conduct Visākha pūjā ceremonies and gained faith in them. Having returned they made a request to the supreme patriarch, using the monastic name Tieng to also conduct Visākha pūjā ceremonies, which he granted. And so these ceremonies have been conducted to day, but not in all temples, only those in the capital city — in other provinces, only big temples have them. There are still many small temples that don't perform them, as in Siam, but in the future, they surely will.
>
> As for the King of the country, from the reign of King Ang Duong to the current one, they also had faith in them. Here, the characteristics of King Ang Duong should be addressed, as he was the initiator of the first Visākha pūjā ceremonies. This king had previously been to Bangkok and ordained as a monk there as well, studied Dhamma, had a deep understanding of the *Tripiṭaka*, and when he ascended the throne he had Visākha pūjā ceremonies in the way he had learnt and seen the process while still in Bangkok in the company of Somdec

> Phra Sugandhādhipati, which then became a tradition that continues to day. But in summary, Cambodia begun performing the Visākha pūjā ceremonies in a style copied from Thailand, which already had been performing them earlier; the *Pathamasambodhi* scripture used for sermons in this ceremony was also copied and translated from Thai, as explained above, and so were the prayers, crafted by King Mongkut himself, and popular in both Thailand and Cambodia to day..."[22]

THAI-KHMER POLITICAL RELATIONS

Besides directly Buddhist connections, Buddhism in the era of King Mongkut was also involved in Thai-Khmer political relations. In the beginning of the twenty-fifth century Buddhist Era, France increasingly intervened in the internal politics of Cambodia. King Mongkut was concerned about this state of affairs, but it proved too late, also for the following Cambodian monarch, King Norodom, to solve these problems in the internal politics of Cambodia after the death of King Ang Duong.[23]

In 2406 BE (1863 CE), during the reign of the French Emperor Napoleon III, King Norodom of Cambodia agreed to make a treaty with France, turning Cambodia into a French protectorate.[24] While King Mongkut first tried to make use of various kinds of relationships to keep Cambodia under Thai domination to the greatest extent possible, when this could not be accomplished, he turned to another type of relationship building with Cambodia, which was now a French protectorate.[25]

The ruling elite in Thailand had an interest in the Cambodian question in Thai-French politics. Thus, in 2409 BE (1866 CE) Phra Amarābhirakkhitta (Koet) of Wat Baromniwat sent a letter to Somdec Phra Sugandhādhipati (Pān), the Supreme Patriarch of the Cambodian Dhammayutika Nikāya, requesting news from Cambodia since it had fallen under French control. This letter cites Buddhist scriptures to make an allegorical reference to politics.

The letter from Phra Amarābhirakkhitta (Koet) to Somdec Phra Sugandhādhipati (Pan) states that it was sent

> on Sunday 14th day of the waxing moon, of the 10th lunar month, being the 3rd month of the rainy season, in the year of the tiger, 2409 years since the nirvana of Lord Buddha[26]

The letter from Phra Amarābhirakkhitta (Koet) demonstrates that this was an important period for Cambodian–Thai–French relations, because it was after the coronation of King Norodom, and Thailand agreed to make a border treaty with Cambodia and France, but the treaty itself had not been made, and the exact border had not been established by surveying by representatives of the involved parties.[27]

Phra Amarābhirakkhitta (Koet) cited the *Tripiṭaka* to conceal the political question he in fact wanted to ask Somdec Phra Sugandhādhipati (Pān). The sutta to which he referred was the *Cūḷadhammasamādāna-sutta majjhimanikāya mulapaṇṇāsa*, in essence containing the following account.[28]

The Buddha told his monks that in the last month of the hot season, long creeper would bear fruit, and its seeds would be spread under a Sāla tree. The spirits inhabiting the Sāla tree thus became anxious.

At that time, Ārāma-devatā, Vana-devatā and Rukkha-devatā (Grove-, Forest- and Tree-spirits), all friendly to the Devatā of the Sāla tree, hurried to console the Sāla tree devatā not to be afraid, since peacocks surely would come to eat the seeds of the creeper tree, or deer would eat them, or a forest fire would destroy them, or the foresters would pull the saplings out, or termites would invade the tree, or maybe the fruits would have no seeds.

But it turned out that peacocks would not eat the seeds of creeper; neither would the deer; there were no fires in the forest, and the fruit had seeds that became saplings after the rains had come. The Sāla tree spirits were very concerned. But the other spirits consoled them that this danger had not reached them yet. In the end the creeper grew and destroyed the Sāla tree, and the mansion of the Sāla tree spirits thus was lost.

In the end of this *sutta*, the Buddha concludes that indeed, some Brahmins think that sensual pleasures (*kāma*) are not harmful and thus fully indulge in them, which leads them to the lower planes (*apāyabhūmi*) upon death, because while still alive they think those dangers have not reached them yet. The Buddha then spoke of the renunciation of sensual pleasures and suffering caused by sensual pleasures.[29]

There is no evidence whether Somdec Phra Sugandhādhipati (Pān) replied to the inquiry or explained the situation in Cambodia to Phra Amarābhirakkhitta (Koet) or not, but the letter itself is probably not as important as the attitudes of Thai intelligentsia toward the situation in Cambodia at the time, demonstrated in the letter but otherwise difficult to study.

The message contained in the letter demonstrates that the Thai intelligentsia were beginning to perceive the attempts of France to dominate Cambodia, and attempting to communicate this view to their Cambodian counterparts. However, this probably had little impact on Cambodian politics since France finally succeded in turning Cambodia into a French protectorate.

CONCLUSION

The above accounts show that the era of King Mongkut and King Ang Duong saw close Buddhist connections between Siam and Cambodia, whether through the Dhammayutika Nikāya sect, through the transmission of Buddhist literature and ceremonies from Siam to Cambodia, or through political relations.

The connections through the Dhammayutika Nikāya sect were established after King Ang Duong had requested the sect to disseminate its faith in Cambodia, and King Mongkut sent Phra Amarābhirakkhitta (Koet) and Phra Mahā Pān to Cambodia in order to do so.

The connections through Buddhist literature emerged at a time when Cambodia had long suffered from warfare and many scriptures had been destroyed. In this situation, King Ang Duong requested King Mongkut's aid, and the latter provided Cambodia a copy of the *Tripiṭaka*. In this era, Khmer translations of the *Traibhūmi* and *Paṭhamasambodhikathā* were also made.

The connections in terms of Buddhist ceremonies comprised using Thai ceremonies as a model for arranging similar ones in Cambodia, such as Visakhabucha.

Besides this, there were also political connections through a monastic letter inquiring into the political situation in Cambodia, which demonstrates a close relationship between Thailand and Cambodia in the period, especially through Buddhism.

Notes

1. Ian Harris, *Cambodia Buddhism: History and Practice*, p. 105.
2. Ibid., p. 44.
3. Santi Pakdeekham, "Sila Caruek Chao Phraya Bodindecha (Sing singhaseni) Na Wat Putthakosacan krung Phnom Penh (K.1213)", p. 178.
4. See Ian Harris, *Cambodia Buddhism: History and Practice*, pp. 105–106.
5. Santi Pakdeekham, "Political Letter of Phra Amaraphirakkhit: Relations among Siam-Cambodia-France", pp. 62–81.
6. Ian Harris, *Cambodia Buddhism: History and Practice*, p. 105.
7. Santi Pakdeekham, "King Mongkut arranged the ordination of Prince Norodom and Prince Sisowath of Cambodia: Buddhism Relationship Siam–Cambodia", pp. 382–83.

8. Santi Pakdeekham, "The Relationship between Thai and Khmer literature during 2325–2403 B.E.", p. 17.
9. See Henry Alabaster, *The Wheel of the law. Buddhism illustrated Siamese Sources by the Modern Buddhist, A Life of the Buddha and Account of the Phrabat*, pp. 75–241.
10. See Peter Skilling and Santi Pakdeekham, *Pāli Literature Transmitted in Central Siam*, pp. 101–103. On the Pali version of the *Paṭhamasambodhi*, see also Petra Kieffer-Pülz, "Die *Paṭhamasambodhi*".
11. Okñā Debbidū Krasem, *Braḥ Rāja Bidhī Dvādasamāsa bhāg 2*, p. 73.
12. Ibid.
13. Ibid.
14 Visākha pūjā had first been instituted in Siam around 1817 under King Rama II. See Ian Harris 2006, p. 107.
15. Okñā Debbidū Krasem, *Braḥ Rāja Bidhī Dvādasamāsa bhāg 2*, p. 74.
16. Olivier de Bernon, "Le Trai Bhūmi khmer du roi Ang Duong: Une introduction", (unpublished). The author is grateful to Olivier de Bernon for granting permission to cite his paper in this article.
17. See English translation in Frank E. Reynolds and Mani B. Reynolds, *Three Worlds According to King Ruang: A Thai Buddhist Cosmology*. On the Date of the Traibhūmikathā, see Michael Vickery, "Note on the Date of the Traibhūmikathā", *JSS* 62 (1974): 275–84; Michael Vickery, "On Traibhūmikathā", *JSS* 79 (1991): 24–33.
18. Olivier de Bernon, Le Trai Bhūmi khmer du roi Ang Duong: Une introduction", (unpublished).
19. See Olivier de Bernon, Kun Sopeap and Leng Kok-An, *Inventaire provisoire des manuscripts du Cambodge Première partie*, p. 105.
20. Olivier de Bernon, "Le Trai Bhūmi khmer du roi Ang Duong: Une introduction", (unpublished).
21. See Ian Harris, *Cambodia Buddhism: History and Practice*, p. 107.
22. Okñā Debbidū Krasem, *Braḥ Rāja Bidhī Dvādasamāsa bhāg 2*, pp. 75–77.
23. The internal political situation in Cambodia after the death of King Ang Duong was rather unstable due to the rebellion led by Ang Wattha, which could only be suppressed with Thai military involvement, after which France began its interference in the internal politics of Cambodia.
24. Milton E. Osborne, *The French Presence in Cochinchina and Cambodia*, p. 183.
25. David Chandler, *A History of Cambodia*, p. 141.
26. *Prachum Phra Ratchaniphon nai Ratchakan thi* 4, p. 190.
27. Chao Phraya Thipphakornwong, *Phra Ratchaphongsawadan Krung Ratanakosin ratchakan thi si*, p. 367.
28. *Prachum Phra Ratchaniphon nai Ratchakan thi* 4, pp. 175–94.
29. Ibid.

Bibliography

Alabaster, Henry. *The Wheel of the law. Buddhism illustrated Siamese Sources by the Modern Buddhist, A Life of the Buddha and Account of the Phrabat.* London: Trübner & Co., 1871.

Chandler, David. *A History of Cambodia.* 2nd ed. Chiang Mai: Silkworm Books, 1998.

de Bernon, Olivier. "Le trai Bhūmi khmer du roi Ang Duong: Une introduction".

——, Kun Sopeap and Leng Kok-An. *Inventaire provisoire des manuscripts du Cambodge Première partie.* Paris: École française d'Extrême-Orient (Materials for the Study of the Tripiṭaka, Volume 3), 2004.

Debbidū (Krasem), Okñā. *Braḥ Rāja Bidhī Dvādasamāsa bhāg 2.* Phnom Penh: Institut Buddhique 2494/1952. (In Khmer).

Harris, Ian. *Cambodia Buddhism: History and Practice.* Chiang Mai: Silkworm Books, 2006.

Kieffer-Pülz, Petra. "Die *Paṭhamasambodhi:* Eine 'indochinesische' Buddhabiographie". *Zeitschrift der Deutschen Morgenländischen Gesellschaft* 160, no. 2 (2010): 415–30.

Osborne, Milton E. *The French Presence in Cochinchina and Cambodia.* Bangkok: White Lotus, 1997.

Prachum Phra Ratchaniphon nai Ratchakan thi 4 lae niphon khong Phra Amarābhirakkhita (Koet). Bangkok: Phutthauppatham Karnphim, 2516/1973. (In Thai).

Reynolds, Frank E. and Mani B. Reynolds. *Three Worlds According to King Ruang: A Thai Buddhist Cosmology.* Berkeley: Asian Humanities Press, 1982.

Santi Pakdeekham. *Nakhornwat Thatsana Khmer.* Bangkok: Matichon, 2545/2002. (In Thai).

——. "Sila Caruek Chao Phraya Bodindecha (Sing singhaseni) Na Wat Putthakosacan krung Phnom Penh (K.1213)". *Damrong Wichakarn* 5, no. 2 (2549/2006): 172–86. (In Thai).

——. *Khwam Samphan Wannakhadi Thai–Khmer.* Bangkok: Amarin, 2550/2007. (In Thai).

——. "Political Letter of Phra Amaraphirakkhit: Relations among Siam-Cambodia-France". *Najua* 7 (2553/2010): 62–81. (In Thai).

——. "King Mongkut arranged the ordination of Prince Norodom and Prince Sisowath of Cambodia: Buddhism Relationship Siam–Cambodia". *Najua* 8 (2554/2011): 378–89. (In Thai).

Skilling, Peter. *Buddhism and Buddhist Literature of South-East Asia: Selected Papers.* Bangkok: Fragile Palm Leaves Foundation/ Lumbini International Research Institute (Materials for the Study of the Tripiṭaka, Volume 5), 2009.

—— and Santi Pakdeekham. *Pāli Literature Transmitted in Central Siam.* Bangkok: Fragile Palm Leaves Foundation/Lumbini International Research Institute (Materials for the Study of the Tripiṭaka, Volume 1), 2002.

Thipphakonwong, Chao Phraya. *Phra Ratcha Phongsawadan Krung Rattanakosin ratchakan thi si*. Bangkok: Khuru Sapha, 2521/1978.

Tully, John. *A Short History of Cambodia: From Empire to Survival*. Chiang Mai: Silkworm Books, 2006.

Vickery, Michael. "Note on the Date of the Traibhūmikathā". *JSS* 62 (1974): 275–84.

——. "On Traibhūmikathā". *JSS* 79 (1991): 24–33.

INDEX

Note: Page numbers followed by "n" refer to notes.

A

Abhidhamma, 348, 350, 367
Agama Hindu Bali, 272
ajñānāc cīyate verse, 26, 47
  distribution of, 44–47
  school affiliation of, 47–56
  status of, 47
Ālasantan inscription, 129, 131–33
Alaungmintaya, 373, 374
  letters of, 376–82
Alaungmintayagyi Ayedawpon, 399
Amarābhirakkhitta, Phra, 418, 419, 423–24
Amoghavajra, 226, 234
Ānanda temple
  khakkhara, 189, 191
  Janaka holding ringed finial staff, 197, 199
Ang Duong, 417–19, 421, 422
Angkor National Museum, 227
  caitya in, 229
aparihāniya, 379–80
Ārāma-devatā, 424
arga ritual, 187
Ariyālaṅkāra, Shin, 344–45
Asiatic Society of Bengal, 20, 24
Aśoka/Asoka, 25, 323
Aṣṭamahāsthāna-caitya-vandanā-stava, 124
Astawa, A.A., 127
Aung-Thwin, Michael, 341–42
Avalokiteśvara, 149–50, 192 , 221–26, 228, 230, 231, 236, 237, 240, 246, 247

B

Baan Chiang Hian, 91, 95
Baan Fai, 88
  bronze bodhisattva, 90
  bronze Buddha, 89
Baan Korn Sawan, 109
Baan Kum Ngoen, 111
Baan Kut Ngong, 109
Baan Nohn Muang, 95
Baan Nong Hang, 109
Baan Nong Kluem, 109–10
Baan Pailom, 109
Baan Talad, 112
Baan Tanot, 88
Bailey, Greg, 84
Bajang Ratu, 120
Bali, stone relief of stūpa, 54, 55
Ban Chiang Museum, 86
Bandar Seri Begawan, 38–39
  inscription, 68n79
Bangkok National Museum, 46
  stele in, 223–25
  stone tablet in, 182
Bangkok Vajrapāṇi, 244
Banya Dala, 373–74, 381, 394

letters of, 377–78, 382
surrender and fall of Pegu, 398–400
Bat Chum inscriptions, 232–36
Batu Jaya artefacts, 20
Batu Pahat inscription, 35, 47
Batujaya, 27–31
Bauddha dynasty of Śailendras, 266
Bauddha Prajñāpāramitā, 268
Bauddha Yogatantra, 264
Bayard, Donn, 81
Beng Vien inscription, 226–28
Bentor, Yael, 187
Bhatara Siwa-Buddha, 271
Bhūridattajātaka, 383, 384, 399
Boisselier, Jean, 172, 180, 184
Borneo, island of, 139, 140
Borobudur
khakkharas finials in, 195–96
scripts from, 131, 132
sealings, 130
Brahmans, 220
Bronkhorst, Johannes, 220
Bronze Age settlement, 92
bronze bodhisattva, 90
bronze Buddha, 89
bronze mirrors, Central Java, 184, 185
bronze rosette, 178, 179, 182
bronze stūpa, 52, 53
Brunei, 44–45
inscribed stone stūpa, 38–39
Buang Abai stūpas, 39, 43
buat phra, 187
Buddha
accepting alms statue, 190, 191
final demise, 189, 190
Kuta Bangun Buddha, 143–45
from Manyargading near Jepara in Central Java, 145
miscellaneous scrap items, 158–59
representation of, 127–28
Sanggata Buddha, 166
Si Kendeng Buddha, 140–43
silver repoussé plaque with, 178
tantra attributes, 245
triad of, 236, 237
Buddha-Avalokiteśvara-Prajñāpāramitā triad, 230, 231
Buddhagupta inscription, 46
Buddha Mothers, 231, 240
Buddha-prize, 377, 383, 385
Buddha Śākyamuni, 293
Buddha's prophecy, 300
Bunnag, Jane, 85
Burma (Myanmar), 115n53, 197, 199, 202, 205n21, 208n65, 210n106, 284, 298, 299, 301, 307, 308, 309, 316, 321, 323, 324, 330n53, 333–58, 373, 377, 379, 384, 388, 390, 391, 400, 403, 404, 408n40, 410n67, 411n87,
Burmese monasticism, 333–34, 339, 343

C

caitya, 228, 229, 240–48
Vajradhara/Vajrasattva/Vajrin on, 243
cakkavatti, 403–4
Cambodia
civil war, 419
internal politics of, 423
Paṭhamasambodhikathā in, 420
relations through Buddhist ceremonies, 421–23
Thailand and, 417–18
Candi Brahu, 120, 122
Candi Gedong, 120
Candi Gentong. *See also* Candi Gentong I; Candi Gentong II
existence of, 120
miniature stūpas and Buddhist sealings, 123–29, 131
rediscovery of, 121

scripts from, 131, 132
structure of, 120
Candi Gentong I
shape of, 121–22
Trowulan, Mojokerto, East Java, 121
Candi Gentong II, 121–22
Candi Muteran, 120
Candi Tengah, 120
candis, characteristics of, 122
de Casparis, J.G., 24, 31, 32, 34, 35, 44, 49
Central Asia, *khakkhara* in, 192–95
Central Java
bronze mirrors, 184, 185
khakkhara finials, 184, 186, 196, 197
Central Thailand, Dvāravatī moated sites in, 93
Cha-em Kaeokhlai, 86
Chaiyaphum province, 86, 99, 101
Cham inscription, 222
Champa, 291, 292, 296, 299
Champa heritage, 221–26
Chan Buddhism, 291
Chan lineages of Song, 291
Chantaratiyakarn, 91
Chan/Thiền pattern, 294
Chao Phraya Basin, 83
Chao Phraya Bodindecha, 418
Charney, Michael, 402
chedi, 179
Chedi Chula Prathon
brick depicting human face from, 180, 181
bronze rosette, 178, 179, 182
cross sectional view, 174
excavated bricks with motifs from, 180, 181
function, date and terminology, 176–87
golden lotus flower, 178, 179, 182
jātaka, 172, 175
mirror fragments, 176, 177
reconstitution of ground plan, 174
silver repoussé plaque, 178
Chhabra, Bahadur Chand, 21, 24, 35, 37, 38
Chi river system, 91, 99–102, 111
Chulalongkorn, King, 419
Cœdès, George, 232–33
Collins, Steven, 379, 387, 388, 392, 404
Colonial Exhibition in Paris in 1931, 139, 145
consecration deposits, 179–83
Crawfurd, John, 273
Cūḷadhammasamādānasutta, 424
Cudamani, 86
cymbals, 176

D

Đại Việt, 286–90
Buddhist monarchy in, 290–97
daṇḍas, 190
Dangrek Mountains, 83
Dazu caves, monks holding *khakkhara*, 193, 195
deconsecration, 186–87
von Dewall, H., 147
dhammarāja, 373, 377–79, 403
Dhammasami, Khammai, 342, 343, 360n14
Dhammayutika Nikāya, 419, 422, 423
in Cambodia, 10, 419
monks, 418
relations through, 418–19
Dharmaguptaka Vinaya lineage, 200
diplomacy
Buddhist diplomacy, 374, 375. *See also* Buddhist diplomacy
contribution of, 400–401
Dong Mae Nang Muang, 94, 115n44
Dunhuang caves, silk banners, 192, 194

Dupont, Pierre, 172, 173, 178, 179, 184, 203n2, 204n11, 205n25
Dvāravatī period, 80, 97, 98, 172, 184
- Buddhism in, 81, 82, 86
- demographic understanding of Buddhism during, 111–12
- and geographical extent, 82–83
- Khorat Plateau during, 102, 112
- monks in, 85
- population levels in, 88–95

E

East Java, relocation of, 129–30
East Mebon inscription, 226
Eminent Monks of the Thiền Community, 287, 290, 293
Epigraphia Zeylanica, 322

G

Gabaude, Louis, 85, 87
Gapura Jati Pasar, 120
garbhanyāsa ritual, 180
gold Buddha, 178, 184
gold foil plate, 27–31
gold plates, from National Museum, Jakarta, 31–35
gold seated Buddha from Long Lalang, 164–65
gold tortoise, 165
golden lotus flower, 178, 179, 182
Gombrich, Richard F., 404
Grabowsky, Volker, 87
Guimet, Musée, 240, 243
- Central Java, *khakkhara* finials, 196, 197

Guṇābhilaṅkāra, 349–51, 367n72
Guṇaraṃsālaṅkāra, Shin, 345
Guhyasamāja Tantra, 244, 245, 248

H

Hacker, Paul, 270
Hanthawadi Hsinbyumyashin court, 338
Haripunchaiya, 82
Haṃsa Sandeśaya, 322
Hassan, Fekri A., 80
Higham, Charles, 91, 92, 113
Hin Khon inscription, 86
Hinduism
- Hindu-Buddhist settlement, 45
- Hindu institution, 285

Hodge, Stephen, 225
Huệ Sinh, 287, 290, 292
Hunter, Thomas, 292

I

Inao, 420
Indian Museum, 23, 24
- Mahānāvika Buddhagupta inscription in, 23

Indian Subcontinent
- Buddhism in, 262
- Saiva-Bauddha dialectics in, 263–65

Indianization, 80
Indonesia
- Buddhist-related materials in, 139
- inscribed rock from Batu Pahat, 35–38
- Sanskrit inscriptions in, 140, 146
- terracotta tablet and gold foil plate, 27–31

Indonesian archipelago, 140, 146
Inthamuni, Phra, 420
Iron Age/early Dvāravatī period, 92
Iron Age site of Non Chai, 91
Irrawaddy River valley, 299
- conquest of, 393–94

Ishii, Yoneo, 343

J

Jambudhaja, Shin, 344
Jātaka, 98, 99, 172, 175
Javanese syncretism, 262

Jayavarman V, 238–40
Jayavarman VII, 6, 300, 301
Jinakālamālī, 309–11, 315, 319–20, 322–24
Jñānasiddhānta, 268
Joko Dolok statue, 121

K

Kaccāyana, 313, 314
Kalibukbuk, Buddhist sealing from, 127, 128
Kalimantan inscription, 47, 140, 141, 143
Kalyāṇī Inscriptions, 315–16
Kambujadesa, 285, 300
kammavācā, 310, 311
Kampung Buang Abai stone stūpa, 39–44
Kampung Sungai Mas inscription, 25–26, 44, 61n26
kamratan, 284
Kandyan court of Laṅkā, 335
Karaṇḍavyūha Sūtra, 221–26, 237, 240, 247
Karama River valley, 142
Kāśyapaśilpa, 180, 205n22
kattaradaṇḍa, 192
kattarayaṭṭhi, 192
Kavīndrārimathana, 232
Kawi script, 131
  with Buddhist formula, 130
  in Buddhist sealing, 131
  in miniature stūpas, 124, 126, 131
Kbal Sre Yeai Yin, 240–46
Kedah, 25–26, 45
Kedaton, 121
Kent, Daniel W., 386
khakkhara, 175–77, 184, 186, 187
  in Borobudur, 195–96
  in Central and East Asia, 192–95
  from Central Java, 196, 197
  in East Asia, 192–95
  four-pronged, 197, 198
  fragment, 166–68
  origins and functions, 188–89
  short-handled, 194, 197
  in South Asia, 189–92
  in Southeast Asia, 195–201
  with vajra, 197, 198
  in Vietnam, 192
Khandhaparitta, 34
Khathathonthoranin, Phraya, 420
Khmer Buddhist literature, 417
  of Oudong era, 420
Khorat Plateau, 81, 83, 86, 91, 94
  distribution of moated sites in, 96
  distribution of *sema* locations throughout, 100
  during Dvāravatī period, 102, 112
  map of, 84
  sema clusters in, 103–7
  sema stones and distribution of Buddhism in, 95–98
    distribution and groups, 99–102
    narrative art and its distribution, 109–11
    sema amounts and quantitative analysis of Buddhist monasticism, 102–9
Kinney, Ann R., 122
Kīrtipaṇḍita, 225, 238, 239, 247
Kizil caves, mural paintings in, 192, 193
Knapper, S.C., 147
Kongkaew Weeraprajak, 38, 68n79
kpon, 284, 285
Kṣitigarbha, 192
Kṛtanagara, 272
Kuṣāṇa Brāhmī script, 33
Kuta Bangun Buddha, 143–45
Kutei
  earlier finds from, 159–65
  Museum, 145

L

Laidlay, J.W., 24, 57n1

Lān Nā, 308–9, 321
inscriptions, 325
in *Jinakālamālī,* 309–11
narratives, 324
in *Tamnān (Mūlasāsanā) Wat Pa Däng,* 311–15
Laṅkā, 308–26
in *Jinakalamālī,* 309–11
Laṅkā-originated monastic lines, 325
monastic affiliation, 320, 322
in *Tamnān (Mūlasāsanā) Wat Pa Däng,* 311–15
Lankan Buddhist monks, 317, 320–22, 324
Lê Văn Thịnh, 288
van Leur, J.C., 220
Lieberman, Victor, 342, 362n33, 368n83, 369n83
Ligor inscription, 222
lime container, 159, 160
Long Lalang Buddha, 164–65
Lotus sūtra, 293, 294, 297
Lý Công Uẩn, 286
Lý Đạo Thành, 289
Lý Nhân-tông, 288, 296

M

Mahā Pān, Phra, 418, 419, 422
Mabbett, Ian, 84
Mahānikāya temples, 422
Mahakam River of eastern Kalimantan, 139, 142, 143, 145
Mahākāśyapa with *khakkhara,* 189, 190
Mahāmantrānusāriṇī, 34
Mahāmāyūrī, 49
Mahānāvika Buddhagupta inscription, 21–25
Mahānirvāṇa Tantra, 148, 165
Mahāpratisarā, 56
Mahāsāṃghika-Lokottaravādins, 33
Mahāsāṃghikas, 49
Maha-vairocana-abhisaṃbodhi Tantra, 221–26
Mahāvairocana Sūtra, 222, 225, 226, 231, 236, 239, 240, 244, 246
Mahāvaṃsa, 321
mahāvihāravāsin, 320, 322, 323
Majapahit
archeological remains of, 120
Mojopahit period influence, 165
monarchy, 299, 301
Makam Dagang, 38–39, 43
Malayo-Polinesian tribe, 262
Malaysia, 19
inscribed stone stūpa, 39–44
Mahānāvika Buddhagupta inscription, 21–25
stone inscription, 25–26
stone slab, 20–21
Mãn Giác, 289
Mataram royal cult, 301
Matussin Bin Omar, Haji, 43
McDaniel, Justin, 343
McFarlane, Steven, 387
McNeil, Judith, 92
Menak Jinggo, 121
Middle Mekong river system, 99–101
miniature *stūpa*
and Buddhist sealings, 123–29
in Candi Gentong, 131
in Kawi script, 124, 126
Kawi script in, 131
with *oṃ ye te svāhā* inscription, 124, 126
scripts, 122
shape of, 124
Mohammad Bakri Udin, Haji, 138
Mon kingdom, 374, 378
Mongkut (Rama IV), Thai-Khmer relations during, 417–25
Mountain of the Bronze Drum, 288
Mranma. *See* Burma (Myanmar)
mratan, 284

Muang Fa Daed, 94, 95, 98, 99, 102, 109
Muang Sema, 93, 94, 112
Muara Kaman, 140, 145–49
  earlier finds from, 159–65
  gold tortoise, 165
  Kuta Bangun Buddha, 143–45
Mūlasarvāstivādins, 33, 175, 192
  Sarvāstivādins and, 203n6
Mūlawarman, 139
  yūpa inscriptions of, 146
Mun river system, 99–101, 112
mural paintings in Kizil caves, 192, 193
mūrdheṣṭakā ritual, 180
Myanmar. *See* Burma (Myanmar)

N
Ñāṇagambhīra, 320–22
nāga-protected Buddha, 223, 226, 228, 240, 246
Nakhon Pathom, 94
  archaeological sites in, 173
  stone tablet in, 182
Nam Ngum River, 101
Ñāṇagambhīra, 311–12, 314, 315
Ñāṇavara, Kyawaungsanhta Hsayadaw Shin, 345–47
National Museum of Bangkok, 89, 90
National Museum of Cambodia, 227, 240, 241, 246
National Museum of Jakarta
  gold plates, 31–35, 44, 47, 48, 49, 54
Newar Buddhism, in Nepal, 194
Nguyen Tu Cương, 290, 291
Nhân-tông, 290
  Buddhist rule of, 297
Nidānasaṃyukta, 64n41
Niṣpannayogāvalī, 244
nissaya manuscripts, 345–46
Norodom, King, 419, 423
Northeast Thailand, 83
  Dvāravatī moated sites in, 93
Nyaungyan court, 335, 340–42, 347
Nyaungyan period, 335, 336, 338, 344, 353, 360n14, 362n33, 367n72

O
Okñā Debbidū, 422
Okña Santhorwohar, 419
oṃ ye te svāhā inscription, 124, 126
Oudong era
  Cambodia, 421
  Khmer Buddhist literature of, 420

P
Pagan mural paintings, short-handled *khakkhara,* 194, 197
Paṭhamasambodhikathā, 417, 420
Paṭhamasambodhi saṃkhepa, 420
Paṭhamasambodhi vitthāra, 420
paraṃbrahma, 268
Paramakhema, Shin, 344
Paramanuchinorot, Krommaphra, 420, 421
Pegu
  Burmese siege of, 396–98
  fall of, 398–400
Perfection of Wisdom sūtra, 293
Phật-thệ, 299
Phetchabun, 83
Phimai Phase, 92
Phnom kulen river system, 100
Phnom Trap, 236–38
Phu Phra Angkhan, 111
Pichard, Pierre, 116n53
Pigeaud Th., 263
Piriya Krairiksh, 172, 175, 184, 200
pon, 284
post-Pallava script, 86
Prajñāpāramitā, 225–26, 228, 231–32, 235, 236, 240, 244–48
Prasat Phase, 92

prastāra, 233–35
prathameṣṭakā ritual, 180
Prātimokṣa-sūtras, 38
pratītyasamutpāda, 31, 32, 48
Preah Vanaratta, 422
Prinsep, James, 24

R
rājabhikṣu, 86
rājadhamma, 379, 406n25
Rājamahāmit, 384
Rajendravarman, 226–32
Raktamṛttikā, 25
Rattanakosin-era Siam, 418, 421
Red River valley, 286, 297, 299
relics, 179–83, 186–87
Renfrew, Colin, 91
Rieamker, 419–20
Roth, Gustav, 65n60
Ruegg, David Seyfort, 264, 265
Rukkha-devatā, 424

S
Sāgaramati-paripṛcchā verses, 45
Saṅgharāja, 322, 343
Sailendra monarchy, 299
Saimong Mangrāi, Sao, 314, 321
Saiva-Bauddha dialectics in Indian Subcontinent, 263–65
Śaiva Mantramārga, 264
Sāla tree spirits, 424
Sambas Buddha, 140, 156, 159
Sāmmitīya saṃgha, 49
Sanderson, Alexis, 264, 265, 268, 270, 275
Sanggata Buddha, 165–68
Sarvabuddhasamāyogaḍākinījālasaṃvara, 234–35
Sarvāstivādin, 32, 33, 49
  and Mūlasarvāstivādins, 203n6
Sarvatathāgatattvasaṃgraha, 239, 244, 245
Sāsanavaṃsa, 316, 329n48
Schober, Juliane, 342
Schopen, Gregory, 86
Scott, James George, 199
Segaran Pool, 121
Segaran V temple, 27
sema amounts and quantitative analysis of Buddhist monasticism, 102–109
sema clusters, 101–102
  in Khorat Plateau, 103–107
sema per site, distribution of amount, 108
sema stones and distribution of Buddhism in Khorat Plateau. *See* Buddhism, in Khorat Plateau, *sema* stones and distribution of
Sénart, Émile, 218
shakujō, 194
Shin Dhammanandī, 345
Si Ariya, Phra, 200, 201
Si Kendeng Buddha, 139–43
siddhayātrā, 25
Sīhaḷa pakkha, 321
Sīhaḷa *bhikkhus,* 310, 311, 320
Silvat Samāgama, 358
Siṇḍok, 129, 133
Singhasari-Majapahit period, 262, 268, 269
Sircar, Dinesh Chandra, 24
Sisowath, 420, 422
Siti Hinggil, 121
Śivagṛha inscription of 856 CE, 266
Siyam Nikāya, 358
Skilling, Peter, 200, 203n1, 379, 407n33
Ślączka, Anna, 180, 183
Somdec Phra Mahā Sumedhādhipati, 419, 420, 422–24
Somdet Phra Sangkharat, 420, 421
Sonobudoyo, Museum
  khakkhara finial with *vajra,* 197, 198
Sri Lankan Anuradhapura style, 141–42, 149

Sri Lankan *Maitreya* images in Pallava style, 150
Sri Saket province, 101
Sri Thep, 94
Sriwijaya, 292, 298, 299, 301
standing Buddha
  fragmentary, 154
  image of, 148–49
  from Kutei, 161–64
  from Muara Kaman, 159–60
  National Museum, Bangkok, 230
  Si Kendeng Buddha, 140–43
stūpa-*kumbha* motif, 97
sukhinaḥ sarvve satvā hi verse, 49
Sutasoma, 262, 269–71
syncretism, 262, 263, 267, 270, 275
Syriam
  Burmese siege of, 381
  final battle for, 394–96

T
Tales of the Extreme Reach of Karmic Reward, 289, 292
Tamnān (Mūlasāsanā) Wat Pa Däng, 309, 311–15, 319, 321
Tang dynasty, 285
Tantric Buddhist products, 267
Tantric Śivaism, 264
Tārī, 231
Tattvas, 269
Thai-Khmer relations during King Mongkut (Rama IV), 417–25
Thái-tông, 287–88, 292
Thalun-min, 337
Thăng-long, 286
theravādin, 320–23
Thonburi, 418
Thông Biện, 291, 292
Thosarat, Rachanie, 91, 92
Tibet, Buddhism in, 262
tisiwareit (Ton) lineage, 349–51, 354, 358
Ton community, 351, 358, 367n72
Traibhūmi Phra Ruang, 421
Trailokavinicchayakathā, 417, 421
Traiphūmikathā, 421
Trần dynasty, 297, 301
tripakṣa, 269
Tripiṭaka, 418, 424
Tuturs, 268, 269, 272, 275

U
Ubon Ratchathani province, 101
ubosot, 97
Udānavarga, 33
Udon Thani Province, 101
upajjhāya, 310, 311
upasampadā, 320, 322
Upasena-sūtra, 34
upāya, 231–32
Uttamasāra, 347–48

V
Vaiśalīpraveśa-mahāsūtra, 34
Vajirañāṇa, Phra, 419
Vajradhara, 245
Vajrapāṇi, 236–38, 244
Vajrasattva, 245
Vajrin, 245
Vana-devatā, 424
Vanaratana, Mahāthera, 322
Vat Sithor inscription, 218, 219, 231, 238
Verbeek, R.D.M., 120
Vicittālaṅkāra, Monywe Zetawun Hsayadaw, 347–49
Vickery, Michael, 284
Vīṇāśikhatantra, 234
vinaya, 314, 339, 344, 350, 362n33, 363n37, 364n52, 366n70, 367n72
Vinītaruci lineage, 291, 292
Visākha pūjā ceremonies, 422
vrah kamratan, 284

W
Wales, H.G. Quaritch, 44, 69n89, 70n102

Wardenaar, J.W.B., 120, 122
Wat Kaeo, 222
Wat luang, 85
Wat Pa Däng, 319
Wat Preah Putkosa, 418
Wat raad, 85
Wat Suon Dòk monks, 321
Welch, David, 92
West Java, 28
Woodward, Hiram, 184, 186

X
Xuanzang, 25

Y
yamabushi, 194
Yasothon province, 101
  stūpa-*kumbha* motif from, 97
Yaśovarman, 219
ye dharmāh verse, 48
Yijing, 47–49, 189, 190, 207n58
Yoga of the Secret Assembly, 226
yūpa inscriptions of Mūlawarman, 146

Z
Zeng Gun, 285
Zhao Cheng, 285
Zhou dynasty in China, 295

NALANDA-SRIWIJAYA SERIES

1. *Nagapattinam to Suvarnadwipa: Reflections on the Chola Naval Expeditions to Southeast Asia*, edited by Hermann Kulke, K. Kesavapany and Vijay Sakhuja
2. *Early Interactions between South and Southeast Asia: Reflections on Cross-Cultural Exchange*, edited by Pierre-Yves Manguin, A. Mani and Geoff Wade
3. *Hardships and Downfall of Buddhism in India*, by Giovanni Verardi
4. *Anthony Reid and the Study of the Southeast Asian Past*, edited by Geoff Wade and Li Tana
5. *Portuguese and Luso-Asian Legacies in Southeast Asia, 1511–2011, Vol. 1: The Making of the Luso-Asian World: Intricacies of Engagement*, edited by Laura Jarnagin
6. *Portuguese and Luso-Asian Legacies in Southeast Asia, 1511–2011, Vol. 2: Culture and Identity in the Luso-Asian World: Tenacities & Plasticities*, edited by Laura Jarnagin
7. *Sino-Malay Trade and Diplomacy from the Tenth through the Fourteenth Century*, by Derek Heng
8. *Tradition and Archaeology: Early Maritime Contacts in the Indian Ocean*, edited by Himanshu Prabha Ray and Jean-François Salles
9. *The Sea, Identity and History: From the Bay of Bengal to the South China Sea*, edited by Satish Chandra and Himanshu Prabha Ray
10. *Early Southeast Asia Viewed from India: An Anthology of Articles from the Journal of the Greater India Society*, edited by Kwa Chong-Guan
11. *The Royal Hunt in Eurasian History*, by Thomas T. Allsen
12. *Ethnic Identity in Tang China*, by Marc S. Abramson
13. *Buddhism and Islam on the Silk Road*, by Johan Elverskog
14. *The Tongking Gulf Through History*, edited by Nola Cooke, Li Tana and James A. Anderson
15. *Asia Redux: Conceptualizing a Region for Our Times*, edited by Prasenjit Duara

16. *Eurasian Influences on Yuan China*, edited by Morris Rossabi
17. *Of Palm Wine, Women and War: The Mongolian Naval Expedition to Java in the 13th Century*, by David Bade
18. *Offshore Asia: Maritime Interactions in Eastern Asia before Steamships*, edited by Fujita Kayoko, Momoki Shiro and Anthony Reid
19. *Literary Migrations: Traditional Chinese Fiction in Asia (17th–20th Centuries)*, edited by Claudine Salmon
20. *Trails of Bronze Drums Across Early Southeast Asia: Exchange Routes and Connected Cultural Spheres*, by Ambra Calo
21. *Buddhism Across Asia: Networks of Material, Intellectual and Cultural Exchange, volume 1*, edited by Tansen Sen
22. *A 14th Century Malay Code of Laws: The Nītisārasamuccaya*, by Uli Kozok
23. *China and Beyond in the Medieaval Period: Cultural Crossings and Inter-Regional Connections*, edited by Dorothy C. Wong and Gustav Heldt
24. *Buddhist Dynamics in Premodern and Early Modern Southeast Asia*, edited by D. Christian Lammerts

www.ingramcontent.com/pod-product-compliance
Lightning Source LLC
Chambersburg PA
CBHW052049290426
44111CB00011B/1676